Introduc
Human Resource
Management

Introducing
Human Resource
Management

Seventh Edition

Margaret Foot
Caroline Hook
Andrew Jenkins

PEARSON

Harlow, England • London • New York • Boston • San Francisco • Toronto • Sydney
Auckland • Singapore • Hong Kong • Tokyo • Seoul • Taipei • New Delhi
Cape Town • São Paulo • Mexico City • Madrid • Amsterdam • Munich • Paris • Milan

PEARSON EDUCATION LIMITED
Edinburgh Gate
Harlow CM20 2JE
United Kingdom
Tel: +44 (0)1279 623623
Web: www.pearson.com/uk

First published under the Longman Group Limited imprint 1996 (print)
Second edition published under the Addison Wesley Longman imprint 1999 (print)
Third edition published 2002 (print)
Fourth edition published 2005 (print)
Fifth edition published 2008 (print)
Sixth edition published 2011 (print and electronic)
Seventh edition published 2016 (print and electronic)

The Financial Times. With a worldwide network of highly respected journalists, *The Financial Times* provides global business news, insightful opinion and expert analysis of business, finance and politics. With over 500 journalists reporting from 50 countries world-wide, our in-depth coverage of international news is objectively reported and analysed from an independent, global perspective. To find out more, visit www.ft.com/pearsonoffer.

ISBN: 978-1-292-06396-6 (print)
978-1-292-06399-7 (PDF)
978-1-292-06397-3 (eText)
978-1-292-12565-7 (ePub)

British Library Cataloguing-in-Publication Data
A catalogue record for the print edition is available from the British Library

Library of Congress Cataloging-in-Publication Data
A catalog record for the print edition is available from the Library of Congress

10 9 8 7 6 5 4 3 2
20 19 18 17

Front cover image: © Getty Images

Print edition typeset in 9.75/13 ITC Giovanni Std Book by 76
Printed and bound by CPI Group (UK) Ltd, Croydon

NOTE THAT ANY PAGE CROSS REFERENCES REFER TO THE PRINT EDITION

Brief contents

Contents

Lecturer Resources

For password-protected online resources tailored to support the use of this textbook in teaching, please visit **www.pearsoned.co.uk/foothook**

Preface

What's in this book?

Managing people is a vital part of all managers' jobs whether they are line managers or human resource (HR) specialists, and successful management and leadership make a huge difference both to the performance of teams and individuals and to the achievement of the organisation's strategic objectives. Increasingly HR takes a lead in informing and driving the strategic direction of the organisation itself and frequently this is in an international context. This book emphasises both the role of HR in forming and achieving the organisation's strategic objectives and the increasingly globalised context in which this happens. Technology is also changing the way in which HR managers operate and this book will discuss this and its effects on different aspects of human resource management (HRM).

The chapters

The content of this book represents an introduction to the philosophical and legal framework of people management strategies aimed at achieving a high-performance workplace. The book further examines the basic operational areas and good practice associated with HRM. Chapter 1 provides an introduction to the subject of HRM and the role that both HR professionals and line managers play in dealing with people issues in the workplace. It provides a background and history of the HR role and gives an overview of current issues in HRM which are then examined in more detail in other chapters.

Chapters 2–5 discuss issues of central importance to HR today. This includes an exploration of employment relationship issues such as the psychological contract, employee engagement, high-performance working, strategic HRM and human resource planning. Together with an in-depth coverage of diversity and equality the discussion of these issues provides a background to the areas dealt with in the next chapters.

In Chapters 6–10, we focus on the functional areas that, if executed well, can add value for both employers and employees. We examine strategic and good practice issues in recruitment and selection, performance management and performance appraisal, learning, training and talent development, pay and reward systems, and health, safety and wellbeing.

More HR managers are working in multinational organisations dealing with international assignments and global staffing issues, so Chapter 11 is a new chapter covering international HRM. The final two chapters consider how to deal with situations where problems develop in the employer–employee relationship, with an examination of discipline and grievance and then dismissal, redundancy and outplacement.

Who the book is for

This textbook is targeted at business and management students on degrees and diplomas around the world. It is intended primarily as an introductory text for those students who, as a part of their career strategy, are studying and working towards management positions whether in HRM or another area of management. Some students will aim to be a specialist in HRM by studying on a degree such as a BA in Human Resource Management or a course linked to a professional body such as the Chartered Institute of Personnel and Development (CIPD). However, managing people today is so important that it is not only a job for the HR specialists but now forms an important and integral part of all managers' jobs. This book is also intended for these students whose degree is in other subject areas but where HRM plays an important part such as business administration and business management, business studies, events management, hospitality management, tourism management, marketing or logistics management.

This book will also be of use as an introductory text to students on some master's degree programmes such as an MBA, particularly where the students do not have much prior knowledge of this subject area. The 'What Next?' exercises in particular are designed to encourage students to take their studies to a higher level.

The CIPD has developed an HR profession map designed to be relevant to all HR professionals, whether they are specialists or generalists in large or small organisations, and which is intended to help individuals plan their professional development and careers. The map consists of four bands ranging from Band 1 which is applicable to those just starting their careers through to Band 4 for the most senior leaders. The map comprises 10 professional areas and eight behaviours and at the heart of the profession map are the first two professional areas, which are the need for HR to provide *insight, strategy and solutions* and *to lead HR*. The other eight professional areas are: *resourcing and talent planning, learning and development, performance and reward, employee engagement, employee relations, services delivery and information, organisation design* and *organisational development*. The map is continually updated and the need to develop *a global outlook* in these areas is also important. The eight behaviours are: curiosity, decisive thinking, being a skilled influencer, personal credibility, collaborativeness, being driven to deliver, having the courage to challenge and acting as a role model. Most of the professional topics the CIPD list are included in this book and should help you develop along these lines.

Those at or near the start of their careers who are perhaps studying at the intermediate level of the CIPD's qualifications will find this book useful and we map chapters of the book against the CIPD's intermediate level standards below. It will also be of use for foundation level students and as introductory reading for those on more advanced courses as they plan their professional development or plot their careers against the CIPD profession map.

Chapter in *Introducing HRM* **Seventh edition**	CIPD intermediate level module
1. Introducing human resource management	Developing Professional Practice Business Issues and the Context of Human Resources Using Information in Human Resources Managing and Co-ordinating the Human Resources Function
2. High-performance working: employee engagement through involvement and participation	Employee Engagement Improving Organisational Performance Employment Law
3. The employment relationship	Contemporary Development in Employment Relations Employment Law
4. Diversity and equality	Developing Professional Practice Employment Law
5. Human resource strategy and planning	Resourcing and Talent Planning Organisation Design
6. Recruitment and selection	Managing and Co-ordinating the Human Resources Function
7. Performance management and performance appraisal	Human Resources Service Delivery
8. Learning, training and talent development	Contemporary Developments in Human Resources Development Meeting Organisational Development Needs Developing Coaching and Mentoring within Organisations Knowledge Management
9. Pay and reward systems	Reward Management Employment Law
10. Health, safety and wellbeing	Contemporary Developments in Human Resources Employment Law
11. International human resource management	Contemporary Developments in Human Resources Managing and Coordinating the Human Resources Function
12. Discipline and grievance	Contemporary Developments in Human Resources Employment Law
13. Dismissal, redundancy and outplacement	Contemporary Developments in Human Resources Employment Law

Skill building

Nowadays there is an increasing emphasis on developing skills to ensure employability of graduates so in this edition there will also be a focus on skills in terms of both generic employability skills and HR skills. There is a great deal of debate about what constitutes employability skills. The Confederation of British Industry (CBI) and the National Union of Students (NUS) in their 2011 publication *Working towards Your Future: Making the Most of Your Time in Higher Education* say employability skills comprise 'a set of attributes, skills and knowledge that all labour market participants should possess to ensure they have the capability of being effective in the workplace – to the benefit of themselves, their employer and the economy'. The main attributes necessary are to have a positive attitude and to be open to new experiences, new ideas, to be willing to participate in new activities and also to have a desire to achieve results. We hope you will have enthusiasm and openness to new ideas as you study HRM and read this book. However, they go on to say that the other key capabilities are: self-management, team working, business and customer awareness, problem solving skills, communication skills, application of numeracy and application of information technology. We have included in each chapter exercises called Improving your employability which are designed to provide opportunities for you to start to develop some of these generic employability skills. The table below shows the chapters in which these exercises are mainly found. Your university or college and other modules that you are studying should also help provide opportunities to develop your employability skills further.

Skills to improve your employability	The chapters in which exercises to improve these skills are mainly found
Self-management	Chapter 1 – Analysis of extent of own employability skills
	Chapter 2 – Analysis of extent of own commitment or engagement and examples of this in various situations so these could be used in an interview for employment
	The *Financial Times* (FT) article about volunteering
	Chapter 3 – Preparing for a presentation
	Chapter 6 – Writing a curriculum vitae (CV)
	Chapter 7 – SWOT analysis of own strengths, weaknesses, opportunities and threats available
	Chapter 8 – Keeping a learning log and analysing own preferred learning styles
	Chapter 11 – Review of own competencies
Team working	Chapter 2 – Engagement and commitment in team working
	Chapter 10 – Research and team debate about health and safety
Business and customer awareness	Chapter 2 – Motivating employees in difficult times such as in a redundancy situation
	Chapter 3 – Research about flexible working
	Chapter 10 – Research and team debate about health and safety issues
	Chapter 12 – Research and report writing about grievance procedures
	Chapter 13 – Redundancy pay calculation
	All the *Financial Times* (FT) articles
Problem solving	Chapter 2 – Motivating employees in difficult times such as in a redundancy situation
	Chapter 10 – Research into health and safety
	Chapter 12 – Research and report writing about grievance procedures

Skills to improve your employability	The chapters in which exercises to improve these skills are mainly found
Communications	Chapter 2 – Motivating employees in difficult times such as in a redundancy situation
	Chapter 3 – Presentation using PowerPoint
	Chapter 4 – Noting the effects of 'banter' and potential for unfair discrimination
	Chapter 5 – Presentation using PowerPoint
	Chapter 6 – Writing a CV
	Chapter 9 – Presentation and report writing about wages and salary figures
	Chapter 10 – Debate about health and safety
	Chapter 12 – Writing a business report about grievance procedures
Application of numeracy	Chapter 3 – Presentation using PowerPoint about flexible working
	Chapter 5 – Presentation using PowerPoint about labour turnover figures
	Chapter 9 – Presentation and report about wages and salary figures
	Chapter 13 – Redundancy pay calculation
Application of information technology	Chapter 3 – Presentation using PowerPoint about flexible working
	Chapter 5 – Presentation using PowerPoint about labour turnover figures
	Chapter 9 – Presentation using PowerPoint and report about wages and salaries
	Use of all web links at end of each chapter

Your involvement

We intend that you become actively involved in your own learning as you progress through this book, and to this end, as well as the chance to improve your employability skills, there are other HR-related activities for you to undertake and opportunities to pause and think about issues raised in each chapter. We recommend that you have a pen and paper beside you as you read the book, so that you can complete the activities. Reflection is important so resist any temptation to skip these exercises.

At the end of each chapter there are review questions and activities designed to help you examine key learning points in-depth. There are articles from the *Financial Times* to provide some real-life scenarios and promote business awareness together with questions to stimulate discussion. The What next? exercises aim to provide opportunities to take things to a higher level for those wanting to study aspects of the topic in more depth. As mentioned earlier there are also exercises at the end of each chapter designed to focus on improving aspects of your employability.

Discussion about specific points raised in the activities is often an integral part of the text, but suggested answers to review questions are included later in the book where this is appropriate. You should try to answer the questions and think things through on your own first before turning to the answers. Your tutor should also have a further set of activities and exercises to help with the main learning points in each chapter.

Some of the organisations discussed in the case studies or activities, such as AirgardXL or the Sheffley Company, are fictitious. Though they are based on scenarios from real-life situations the people or organisations named in them do not actually exist and details have been drawn from a number of events to create totally fictitious, although realistic, situations. Real organisations are, however, mentioned in the text, particularly where they serve as examples of good practice, and the *Financial Times* articles obviously describe real-life people, events and organisations.

Margaret Foot, Caroline Hook and Andrew Jenkins
March 2015

Acknowledgements

Publisher's acknowledgements

We are grateful to the following for permission to reproduce copyright material:

Logos

Delicious logo on page 265 from Yahoo! Inc., reproduced with permission of Yahoo! Inc. © 2011 Yahoo! Inc. DELICIOUS and the DELICIOUS logo are registered trademarks of Yahoo! Inc.; Facebook logo on page 265 from Facebook, Inc.

Tables

Table 1.2 adapted from *Working towards your future: making the most of your time in higher education*, CBI/NUS (2011) p. 13, Copyright © CBI 2011; Table 10.1 adapted from *How to tackle work-related stress: A guide for employers on making the Management Standards work*, Health and Safety Executive (2009) pp. 7–9, © Crown copyright. Contains public sector information licensed under the Open Government Licence (OGL) v3.0. http://www.nationalarchives.gov.uk/doc/open-government-licence/version/3/

Text

Article on pages 31–2 from The Connected Business – Human touch gets a helping hand, FT.com (Taylor, P.), 6th November 2013, © The Financial Times Limited 2013. All Rights Reserved; Article on pages 62–3 from The volunteer spirit that binds a team more than cash, FT.com (Hill, A), 13th January 2015, © The Financial Times Limited 2015. All Rights Reserved; Article on pages 93–4 from VIRGIN - Branson tells staff to take as much holiday as they want, *Financial Times* (Barrett, C.), 26th September 2014, © The Financial Times Limited 2014. All Rights Reserved; Article on page 118 from Career Counsel: How do I increase diversity without alienating people?, FT.com (Conboye, J.), 6th November 2014, © The Financial Times Limited 2014. All Rights Reserved; Article on pages 145–6 from Shortage of engineers threaten UK growth, employers warn, *Financial Times* (Groom, B.), 30th July 2014, © The Financial Times Limited 2014. All Rights Reserved; Article on pages 202–3 from Smart questions root out CV liars, FT.com (Conboye, J.), 19th March 2014, © The Financial Times Limited 2014. All Rights Reserved; Article on pages 241–3 from Unpaid workers need deft handling, *Financial Times* (Marsh, V.), 8th May 2014, © The Financial Times Limited 2014. All Rights Reserved; Article on pages 288–90 from Nations fight global war for talent, FT.com (Boesrma, M.), 12th June 2014, © The Financial Times Limited 2014. All Rights Reserved; Article on page 332 from Network rail face equal pay claim from women, *Financial Times* (Plimmer, G.), 17th July 2014, © The Financial Times Limited 2014. All Rights Reserved; Article on pages 375–6 from Workforce health on a par with profits and dividends, FT.com (Betts, P.), 19th February 2010, © The Financial Times Limited 2010. All Rights Reserved; Article on pages 396–8 from Expat life sets challenge for families with special needs, FT.com (Clegg, A), 2nd December 2013, © The Financial Times Limited 2013. All Rights Reserved; Article on pages 430–1 from Executive appointments – Your questions answered - 'How can we control misuse of group email system?', *Financial Times* (Plimmer, G.), 13th February 2014, © The Financial Times Limited 2014. All Rights Reserved; Article on pages 458–9 from The 'hello there memo' that meant goodbye staff, *Financial Times* (Kellaway, L), 28th July 2014, © The Financial Times Limited 2014. All Rights Reserved.

Articles sourced from the Financial Times have been referenced with the FT logo. These articles remain the Copyright of the Financial Times Limited and were originally published between 2010 and 2015. All Rights Reserved. FT and 'Financial Times' are trademarks of The Financial Times Limited.

In some instances we have been unable to trace the owners of copyright material, and we would appreciate any information that would enable us to do so.

1

Introducing human resource management

Objectives

By the end of this chapter you will be able to:

- define what is meant by the term 'human resource management'
- understand the roles of line managers and human resource managers in managing people
- outline the range of activities with which practitioners of human resource management are likely to be involved
- demonstrate how human resource management can make a difference by adding value to an organisation
- outline some of the current issues facing HR managers
- start to review and develop your employability skills.

Introduction

This book is designed as an introductory text for students studying human resource management (HRM) either with a view to becoming HR specialists themselves, or starting or hoping to start a career in management. As you will discover, people management forms a large part of every manager's job, whether they work in a large multinational organisation, a not-for-profit organisation or a small charity. Organisations also increasingly aim for all employees to be motivated and involved, so an understanding of the subject is important for everyone.

As stated in the preface, we intend that you should become actively involved in your own learning as you progress through the book. Learning how to learn is a vital skill not just so that you achieve a qualification, though of course that is also important, but also so that you can continue to learn and so update skills and knowledge throughout life.

HRM skills

According to the Chartered Institute of Personnel and Development (CIPD) (2014a), as well as achieving qualifications and gaining work experience there are some personal qualities needed to be a success in HR, which include being

- balanced and objective, since there is a need to sometimes represent both employees and the employer
- trustworthy and discreet
- a strong communicator
- aware of and interested in the ways that businesses work
- able to work as a part of a team
- curious with a questioning mind
- flexible, adaptable and patient.

Being a strong communicator, being curious and continuing to learn, an ability to work in a team and being aware of and interested in the ways businesses work are also skills that employers say that they want in anyone starting a job with them. The 'HRM activities', 'Review questions', 'Pause for thought', 'Did you know?' and 'HR in the news' topics included in each chapter aim to enhance your knowledge as well as help you to develop some of these HRM skills. Studying HRM will also enable you to see things from the perspective of an HR practitioner, which may also be useful in increasing your business awareness and enable you to gain better insights in planning your own career and in job applications in particular.

Employability skills

We have also focused on some specific generic skills in a section called 'Improving your employability' at the end of each chapter. While there are many things which could contribute to improving employability the Confederation of British Industry (CBI) and the National Union of Students (NUS) (2011) say that students need to be proactive about using their time at university or college to gain experience by volunteering or getting involved in clubs and societies and trying to gain work experience in their chosen topic or topics. They go on to say that a positive attitude and willingness to participate in new things or try out new ideas is important as is a desire to get things done. The knowledge and qualifications gained on your course, which in this instance is knowledge about HRM, are also important but other generic capabilities are also often required by employers. These include the following:

- Self-management – this could include skills such as time management, management of your own learning, flexibility and a willingness to learn from feedback and reflecting on your learning.
- Problem solving – learning to be more analytical to identify causes of problems or situations and then selecting solutions that would be appropriate in the circumstances.
- Working with others – working in teams, pairs or small groups and contributing to discussion as well as using skills of cooperation, persuasion or negotiation.
- Communication – the ability to communicate clearly in various forms, both written, such as business reports, and spoken, such as making a presentation.

- Business awareness – understanding more about what drives a business to achieve success and also about building customer satisfaction and loyalty.
- Application of numeracy – being able to work with numbers to use them in an appropriate business context.
- Application of information technology – IT skills and familiarity with commonly used programs.

While we cannot hope to perfect your skills in all these areas in an introductory textbook on HRM, we nevertheless hope to help you to start to develop some of these while you learn more about the subject of human resource management.

HRM? What's it all about?

Even though you are just beginning this subject, you may already have ideas about some of the topics that you are about to study and you may even have a general idea of the role and functions of the human resource management or personnel department in an organisation. Your ideas may not all be right but, after all, that is why you are studying the subject. Many students talk of studying HRM because they would 'like to work with people', and they seem to think of human resource management as a cosy job that involves being nice to people at all times. While this view is not entirely accurate, it is certainly a career which provides a wealth of variety and a great deal of job satisfaction. HRM is also a career which is constantly changing as the role evolves in response to changing social, political, economic and demographic issues, and we shall examine some of the ways the profession is changing in response to these later in this chapter.

According to the CIPD (2014a) a career in HR offers endless possibilities with a huge variety of roles. This is one of the main reasons people give for enjoying their HR careers as they say they provide variety, challenge and interest, in organisations where HR is at the heart of the business and can make a difference. A survey by XpertHR in 2014 found that 58.7 per cent of those surveyed would choose to pursue a career in HR again in spite of the fact that almost half of them (48.5 per cent) had actually started work in other areas prior to HR and said they had entered the HR profession by chance. Of those surveyed 36.8 per cent had made a deliberate choice to pursue a career in HR because they wished to work with people (Murphy, 2014a).

We shall discuss in this book the variety of roles and tasks that modern HR professionals cover but it is important to note that it is not just the HR professionals who work in these areas: line managers are also involved. Therefore, this book is also written as an introduction to HRM for them too.

Let us start with an activity to help you focus on your ideas about human resource management and the respective roles of HR managers and line managers. You can compare your answers with the answer that we give at the end of the chapter. Later in the chapter we shall also look at what researchers and HR practitioners say HR is about.

Did you know?

The Chartered Institute of Personnel and Development (CIPD) is the professional body that represents over 135,000 people worldwide who are involved in the management and development of people.

(*Source*: CIPD, 2015a)

Activity 1.1

What do you think are the main areas in which a human resource manager is likely to be involved? Make a list of these areas. For each of the areas on the list, indicate the type of involvement of the human resource practitioner and whether other managers are also likely to have a role in handling this activity (use Table 1.1). We have completed the first row of Table 1.1 to start you off. Our suggestions for this activity are given at the end of the chapter in Table 1.3.

Table 1.1 The main activities of human resource practitioners

Main areas of activity of human resource/people management specialist	Type of involvement of the human resource/people management specialists	Type of involvement of line manager
Recruitment and selection	Design of policies and procedure for fair recruitment and selection in order to contribute to the fulfilment of the organisation's corporate strategy Commission online recruitment activities Carry out interviews or monitor and give advice on interview technique or on terms and conditions of employment	Prepare and carry out interviews and other selection tests Participate in selecting the successful candidate(s)
Learning, training and talent development		

The main activities of human resource management

The areas that we would list are as follows:

- recruitment and selection
- learning, training and talent development
- human resource planning
- provision of contracts
- provision of fair treatment
- provision of equal opportunities
- managing diversity
- motivating workers to achieve improved performance
- employee counselling
- talent management
- employee wellbeing

- payment and reward of employees
- health and safety
- disciplining individuals
- dealing with grievances
- dismissal
- redundancy
- negotiation
- encouraging involvement and engagement
- adding value
- ethics and corporate responsibility
- knowledge management
- change management
- managing cross-cultural issues or international HRM.

You may have included some slightly different activities since human resource managers, as you can see from this list, do become involved in a wide range of issues and it is difficult to predict the exact nature of the job in any particular enterprise. We have selected the main topics with which we feel most human resource managers are likely to be involved, but this will vary from organisation to organisation and may also depend on the way the function itself is organised. The type of involvement of the HR specialists will also vary. Some HR specialists operating at a high level in the organisation will be concerned with the provision of clear strategic direction for HR and linking this to the strategic objectives of the organisation. Others will be concerned to provide specialist advice, while still others will focus on the provision of administration and support. All will be concerned in some way to ensure that HRM activities add value by helping the organisation achieve its strategic objectives. They will focus on ensuring that the overall HR policies and procedures support the strategic objectives and that there is consistency in approach and implementation across the organisation.

However, for each activity it is likely that other managers will also be involved to some extent. Line managers will be concerned with the actual implementation of the policies and procedures in so far as they affect their team, whereas the HR specialists will also be involved in the bigger picture, although the extent of the differences in role will vary between organisations.

The fact that aspects of managing the human resource are an element of every manager's or supervisor's job is an important point for you to keep in mind. Many of you will find that your career may take you from line management to human resource management and then back to line management, or vice versa.

Pause for thought 1.1	A line manager is a person who has direct responsibility for employees and their work. Since line managers seem to have such a large part to play in people management, to what extent do you think they need human resource managers at all?

Obviously, we consider that line managers do need to call on the services and expertise of human resource specialists. If you look at our discussion of Activity 1.1 in Table 1.3 at the end of this chapter, you will see that although a great deal of what was once regarded as HR work is now done by line managers, there is also a role for a person skilled in human resource management to establish policies, standards and procedures, to integrate these with the organisation's objectives to ensure that they contribute to the organisation's strategic objectives, to provide expert advice and consistency and to coordinate and provide training and development. Human resource practitioners will also often be involved in initiating company-wide programmes such as promoting employee engagement, communication and consultation. The exact nature of their involvement will vary from one organisation to another, as will the range of activities they cover. The human resource department may carry out some administrative work and maintain central records on people and may also provide advice and expertise for other managers to draw on. In some organisations the human resource department may carry out all the activities listed above, while in others many or most of these functions may be an important part of the jobs of other managers. Increasingly more and more aspects of the HR function are being carried out by line managers and you will find as you work through the book that we emphasise the roles of line managers in HR activities.

Even among human resource managers there will be differences in the scope of their job, so it is also important to consider the ways in which HR jobs are organised as specialist or generalist roles. Does an organisation employ its own HR practitioners in-house, or is the HR department outsourced and provided by a form of shared services for other divisions of the same organisation or with other organisations? Are the individuals themselves consultants or business partners or do they have some other job title? Is their role dealing with issues just in one country or multinational? We shall deal with some of these issues about the variety of roles in HRM and the ways in which HRM can be organised later in this chapter.

Cross-cultural issues will provide another dimension to be considered in relation to each of these tasks. Multinational organisations have to consider both expatriates and host-country nationals employed by them around the world as well as their home-country-based employees. Recently several of our students who have graduated from the University of Huddersfield have taken up first jobs in HR which have involved them working at least for some of their time in other countries and this has meant that they needed an awareness of cultural issues in human resource management quite early in their careers. The expansion of the European Union (EU) with the entry of several Eastern European countries such as Poland has also meant an increase in workers from these countries coming to the UK to seek employment, so an awareness of cross-cultural issues is also of value to HR managers, even if they work exclusively in the UK.

Given the changes to the way organisations are operating in terms of their recruitment, you may find yourself working with migrant workers in this country, recruiting internationally or working in another country yourself in an international organisation. We shall therefore consider some of these cross-cultural or international issues in HRM in Chapter 11.

As you have already discovered human resource management can include a diverse range of activities and it is constantly changing. The variety is in part a result of the history of HRM and the way it has developed. Theories of HRM have also been influential in shaping the role as have changes to the economic, social, demographic and technological contexts in which human resource managers operate. People also adapt their roles, and the context in which they operate shifts in response to these varying demands. We shall explore these varying influences on the changing HR function in the rest of this chapter.

Did you know?

According to Gerwyn Davies, the CIPD's labour market advisor, there is now a great deal of competition for entry level and low-skilled jobs and some employers are using overqualified migrant labour to help their businesses grow where they find it hard to attract UK-born candidates to unskilled or semiskilled jobs. However, many of these employers are also trying to help young people entering the labour market by offering work experience, internships and apprenticeships.

(*Source*: Davies, 2014)

The main factors that have made HRM what it is today

The history of human resource management

The role of an HR manager has changed in response to social, economic and political conditions and to changes in technology, and it is still developing dynamically. The relative importance of many of the activities has changed as external circumstances have affected the needs of organisations and it is still a dynamic area where the roles and ways of organising the HR function continue to change and develop.

It may help you to understand the diversity of roles that are sometimes adopted by human resource managers if we look briefly at the development of the profession. A variety of names have been used to describe those who specialise in managing people. In this book we have chosen to use the terms 'human resource manager' or 'people manager' as these are increasingly the main terms used but you will also find other terms such as 'personnel manager' still being used and some other job titles such as reward manager or learning and talent development manager for those who have specialised in specific areas of HRM. However, while it is important to have some idea of the background of HRM it is of even greater importance to examine current roles and issues and to consider possible developments in HR of the future in the world in which most of you will find yourself working. We shall discuss recent and possible future developments in more detail later in this chapter.

Industrial welfare

The earliest activity with which the HR practitioner was involved was welfare work. During the nineteenth century the conditions of work for men, women and children in the factories were generally appalling compared to today's accepted standards. There were some enlightened employers who wanted to try to improve working conditions for their employees and adopted schemes to improve the lot of their workforce as part of their company policy. Among these were several Quaker organisations, and it is generally held that the first personnel officer, referred to at that time as an industrial welfare officer, was Miss Mary Wood who was appointed by Rowntree's in York in 1896. She was appointed to be a type of social worker for the factory, with responsibility for ensuring the wellbeing of women and children in the workforce and watching over their health and behaviour.

Although Mary's first day at work over 100 years ago is very different from the type of work that we associate with human resource managers of today, welfare and the wellbeing of the workforce is still an area in which many HR practitioners will be involved. Levels of absenteeism are expensive, so modern organisations which are proactive in encouraging a healthy workforce have also shown benefits in reduced levels of absence with consequent saving for the organisation.

Did you know?

Mary Wood's first day at work at Rowntree's was rather different from the type of activity you would associate with human resource managers today.

Her first morning was spent placing flowers in work-rooms – perhaps not so ineffectual a beginning as might be thought when the drabness of factories and homes at the time is remembered – and in the afternoon she went to visit girls who were sick, ordering groceries for the most necessitous cases and seeing such slums that she had never dreamt existed. Her first opportunity for making headway came during the dinner hours, when the fact that there was no supervision meant that pandemonium broke out. By degrees she brought order and discipline and before long was arranging an occasional concert or talk during the last half hour of the break. She then turned to organising games as an outlet for the high spirits of the younger girls and as a means of strengthening their physique.

(*Source:* Niven, 1978)

● Recruitment and selection

The early industrial welfare workers met with great success, and Mary Wood and others were soon asked to start recruiting girls, which was the beginning of the development of the role of recruitment and selection. (Remember this was well before equal opportunities had been thought of!) During the First World War there was rapid development in many fields of personnel management, largely as a result of government initiatives to encourage the best possible use of people, and also because of legislation.

● Acquisition of other people management activities

In 1921 the National Institute of Industrial Psychologists was established, and its members published results of studies on selection tests, interviewing techniques and training methods so providing an academic rationale for some aspects of people management.

During the Second World War the work spread from welfare, recruitment and selection to training, improving morale and motivation, discipline, health and safety, joint consultation and often wages policies. This expansion of duties required the establishment of an adequate personnel department with trained staff.

● Employee relations

Joint consultation between management and workforce spread during the Second World War, and personnel departments became responsible for its organisation and administration. There was an increased emphasis on health and safety and a need for specialists to deal with employee relations, so that gradually the personnel manager became the usual spokesperson for the organisation in discussion with trade unions and shop stewards. This aspect of their role gained further impetus in the 1970s, where in many organisations the personnel manager had executive authority to negotiate deals about pay or other collective issues.

● Legislation

During the 1970s the growth in the amount of employment legislation resulted in the personnel function often adopting the role of specialist adviser, ensuring that managers did not fall foul of the law and that cases did not end up at industrial tribunals, as they were then called.

● Flexibility and diversity

In the 1990s there was a major trend for employers to seek increasingly flexible arrangements in the hours worked by employees, with a growth in the number of employees who worked part-time or on temporary contracts, and an increase in distance working and working from home. This trend has continued in the early years of the twenty-first century. The workforce and patterns of work are becoming increasingly diverse and this presents its own challenges to HR managers.

Thinking strategically, adding value and talent management

As well as increasing diversity there has been a continuing focus on the need to build a skilled workforce and to develop and retain talent. While the economic recession has led to many job losses it has also resulted in an increased focus on the need for those in HR to clearly link all HR initiatives with the organisation's strategic objectives to ensure that they not only achieve value for money but that they go further and add value to the organisation. While there are still redundancies being made there are also skills shortages in some sectors, meaning that it is even more important to recruit, develop and keep talent. The development of what is known as the human resource management approach discusses some of the theory related to these changes.

The development of the human resource management approach

The concept of human resource management first appeared in the 1980s and the use of the term grew in the 1990s. Initially, writers in the field focused on trying to distinguish between personnel management and HRM, but according to Boxall and Purcell (2008) HRM has, in spite of the lack of clarity over definition, become the most popular term to refer to the activities of managers in relation to people management.

The major characteristics of the HRM approach to people management have been identified as follows:

- The importance of adopting a strategic approach is emphasised.
- Line managers play an important role.
- Organisational policies must be integrated and cohesive in order to better project and support the central organisational values and objectives. Along with this, communication plays a vital role.
- An underlying philosophy is adopted that emphasises the achievement of competitive advantage through the efforts of people. This can variously be interpreted into actions that are known as hard HRM or those that are known as soft HRM.
- A unitarist rather than a pluralist approach prevails in the relationship between managers and employees.
- All people who work in an organisation are important whether they are part-time or full-time employees or not employees of that organisation at all. In this way agency staff and consultants, or volunteers in a charity, are all perceived to be important to the organisation.

Focus on strategy

Throughout the 1980s and 1990s business leaders came to accept more and more that competitive advantage could be achieved only through the efforts and creativity of the people employed by them. In companies that follow through with the logical conclusions to this statement rather than simply paying lip service to the rhetoric, developing strategies for their human resources will inevitably play a prominent role when they are formulating the corporate strategy, and senior managers will want to call on the expertise of a specialist to get the best input possible. Thus strategic activity becomes a major focus for specialists in HRM, but probably only those acting at the higher levels will be involved in board-level meetings where strategic alternatives are discussed. It should also be noted that in order to have effective input into the corporate strategy, the HRM specialist will require a high level of business acumen in addition to knowledge of people strategies and programmes. It is this recognition that people are a resource to be managed as efficiently and effectively as any other resource that has led to the term 'human resource management'.

Role of the line manager

We have defined strategic involvement as being a key characteristic of HRM and noted that this means a focus on strategic activity for high-level HRM practitioners. However, the HRM approach recognises the centrality of the human resource for all business activities, and therefore consideration of the people management aspects would be expected in the strategic planning input from managers in all business functions (e.g. production, marketing). Likewise, the importance of active management of people matters becomes more clearly an integral part of every line manager's job. Line managers must combine their commitment to the technical aspects of task completion with attention to people aspects and recognise the symbiotic nature of these two elements of the managerial role.

This means that some activities that might traditionally have been undertaken by specialist HR management staff are now undertaken by line managers. Increased line involvement in training and recruitment and performance management can be cited as areas where this has occurred. There is still, however, a substantial role for human resource specialists, as you discovered when you completed Activity 1.1, in designing strategic HR solutions, in leading, advising and disseminating information about evolving people management programmes to line managers, in ensuring consistency in the treatment of employees company-wide and, in general, in being supportive partners to managers in their efforts to achieve company goals.

The pivotal role of the line manager is one of the most often cited characteristics of human resource management. According to the CIPD (2014b) there have been a number of changes in the relationship between HR and line managers, and line managers in many instances have responsibility for much of what were previously main HR activities such as recruitment and selection, training and development or the setting of objectives. In some organisations the line managers now have responsibility for record keeping, inputting data about their staff, planning and booking training and dealing with wage queries. This is particularly true in organisations where much of the HR function has been outsourced to other organisations.

This places additional responsibilities on line managers. Finding ways of training, supporting and encouraging line managers to take responsibility for the people management aspects of their job and to develop sufficient confidence in their ability to do this is still one of the key challenges that face HR specialists and training and support for line managers is essential to enable them to fulfil these new tasks.

Integrated policies and effective communication

Proponents of HRM emphasise that policies across the whole HR spectrum (recruitment, selection, reward, employee relations) must be fully integrated and consistent with the organisation's culture. This is logically consistent with the strategic, forward planning nature of HRM. Effective communications are a pivotal aspect of this as they constitute a means of conveying senior management's values and commitment to their goals (Legge, 1995, p. 75). It is also an important aspect of knowledge management.

Competitive advantage through people

The balanced scorecard

At this point it is appropriate to introduce the concept of the balanced scorecard (BSC). This concept emanates from work done on business strategy by Kaplan and Norton (1992, 1996) in the Harvard Business School which emphasises the role of the human resource in the achievement of business strategy. The BSC has become a well-established technique used extensively not only in the USA, but also worldwide, including some UK companies, for instance Tesco (see Industrial Relations Services, 2000).

The essential idea behind the balanced scorecard is the notion that businesses must measure the success of their plans in order to validate their actions, identify and evaluate their successes, and build on them for the future. Traditionally businesses have focused mainly, if not exclusively, on financial results to evaluate the success of their strategy, but Kaplan and Norton propose that measuring success in only one area is inadequate for a number of reasons. One argument is that financial results are always a retrospective measure of past success and do not necessarily indicate that similar actions in the future will meet with similar achievements. Also, although financial gains may be the ultimate desired outcome, it is imperative to know exactly what factors contributed to this outcome and in what way they contributed.

A more satisfactory approach to formulating strategic initiatives, and subsequently evaluating their success, is to take a more balanced approach, which is represented by the balanced scorecard. The scorecard is a flexible tool, which can be adapted according to the nature of the business adopting it, but the original model proposes four elements that should be evaluated in order to achieve a balanced overview of what contributes to a company's success:

- financial results
- customer relations
- internal processes
- learning and development.

The examination of financial results is, of course, still a necessary part of evaluating business success but, according to Kaplan and Norton, this focus needs to be balanced out by taking the other criteria into consideration. Each of the three other criteria contributes to financial success, and purposively focusing on them helps to shift managerial awareness to the role each plays. Typically, the formulation of a corporate strategy would start with a goal to increase shareholder value, and a strategy that focuses on the customer's perspective is most likely to succeed in achieving this aim (Kaplan and Norton, 2000). A company must then examine its internal processes with regard to their fitness to achieve this customer strategy and adapt them where necessary. This in turn goes hand in hand with the development of the human resource that will deliver the strategy. An organisation's capacity for learning and development is regarded as being one of the key factors contributing to success in today's competitive environment.

Just as the balanced scorecard is used to formulate the overall corporate strategy and measure its success, it can also be used to plan for the component parts and measure their contribution to the achievement of company strategy. Thus, while the examination of internal processes must be carried out throughout the organisation and constitutes one component of the balanced scorecard used to measure the whole company's performance, the BSC can also be used to guide and evaluate each individual's performance. That is, the development of individuals becomes explicitly tied in to the key issues addressed in the BSC at corporate strategy level, and in appraising each individual the question is asked to what extent the individual contributed to the financial success of the company, to customer relations, to the improvement of internal processes and to learning and growth. The Halifax is one company in the UK that has used a balanced scorecard to evaluate its employees' performance.

The adoption of the balanced scorecard by Tesco also served to strengthen and redefine the role of the stores' HR managers. The scorecard highlighted the importance of employee contribution to the success of the company, and therefore the importance of people management issues. To complement this, personnel managers in Tesco stores are also expected to be fully involved in the day-to-day running of the stores, thus enhancing their business awareness and their credibility (IRS, 2000).

Hard and soft HRM

The basic requirement of HRM to serve the corporate strategy and achieve corporate aims by means of a high-performance workforce can be read in two ways:

- The primacy of business needs means that human resources will be acquired, deployed and dispensed with as corporate plans demand. Little regard is paid to the needs of those human resources and the emphasis is on quantitative aspects. This is known as hard HRM.
- In order to gain a competitive advantage through the workforce, regardless of whether they are full-time or part-time, temporary or contract staff, all potential must be nurtured and developed, and programmes that pay due notice to knowledge about the behavioural aspects of people at work are developed. This is characterised as soft HRM.

In hard HRM, the duty of managers is to make money for the owners and a focus on any other issues, such as employee rights, is simply a distraction. In contrast, in soft HRM the emphasis is on employees as a valuable asset and a source of competitive advantage (Collings and Wood, 2009). The emphasis in our text lies mainly with soft HRM, but as Legge (1995, pp. 66–67) argues, the two are not mutually exclusive, and you will detect elements of hard HRM in the discussion of human resource planning.

Unitarist and pluralist approaches to management–employee relations

Human resource management is identified as being a unitarist rather than a pluralist approach (Legge, 1995, pp. 72–73). Briefly, the unitarist stance is characterised as a senior management assumption that all members of the organisation are dedicated to the achievement of a common goal with no conflict from personal interests. Pluralism, on the other hand, recognises that within a large group of people there are inevitably a variety of interests and that these have to be managed. The adoption of one or other of these two philosophies obviously has a major impact on the way that managers treat the workforce.

We explore the concepts of unitarism and pluralism in greater depth in Chapter 2, where we come to the conclusion from observing current rhetoric that we may now be witnessing a merging of the two stances in the development of the partnership theme. This promotes the idea that managers and employees can pursue common goals while still recognising that diverging interests exist. The common purpose of the unitarists is pursued in a pluralist framework.

We refer throughout the text to the key characteristics described here and their links with specific activities. In particular, we emphasise the role of the line manager in all of the activities we discuss, but in addition we focus on the theme of strategy in Chapter 5, where we examine the human resource planning activity, and the topics of employee involvement/engagement and communication as a part of high-performance working in Chapter 2.

The context in which HRM operates

The political and economic environment

The state of the national and global economy has a direct impact on all types of organisation and will inevitably influence their people practices and strategies. In the simplest of terms, consumer spending power dictates what goods and services need to be produced, which has an impact on employers' employment decisions and intentions. The CIPD (2013) emphasises the need for HR practitioners to understand the economy and its impact on the labour market. The economy is affected by the interplay of a wide variety of factors including rates of unemployment, the demand for goods and services as reflected by consumer decisions on spending and saving, the costs of importing and exporting goods and the policies of the political party in power on issues such as inflation. HR managers need to keep an eye on official statistics such as those published for the Office for National Statistics (ONS) or from surveys by organisations such as the Confederation of British Industry or the

Chartered Institute of Personnel and Development. The ability of the government to influence employment decisions and consumer spending as strategies to improve the economic outlook has been a matter of debate in recent years.

Pause for thought 1.2 Statistics on factors such as consumer spending choices and employment rates are also open to interpretation, and therefore cannot be taken as direct indicators of the health of the economy. Take unemployment rates as an example! Lower levels of unemployment would normally indicate a healthier economy. But are the figures artificially lowered because numbers of people who would normally be counted as available for work but unemployed have opted for further study instead and are therefore not counted as unemployed?

The global economy has been a major focus of everyday news reports and financial analysis for many years. Following a period of growth that had persisted for a number of years, many countries, including the UK, went into a recession in 2008. Reporting in the final quarter of 2014 the CIPD *Labour market outlook* report showed that employment prospects had risen to a seven-year high with more employers planning to recruit new staff than were planning to make staff redundant. There are, however, fewer jobs for those with low skills compared to previous years (CIPD, 2014c). West (2015) goes further and says that Britain is facing its biggest skills shortage for a generation and that some sectors such as engineering and the construction industry are facing huge problems resulting in one in three construction companies in London turning work away due to a shortage of skilled labour. This has also meant that firms in the capital have to bring in Portuguese bricklayers on wages of £1,000 per week, double the normal rate.

Improvements in employment rates are cited as a positive indicator, but some commentators sound a note of caution, pointing out, for example, that public authorities are still expected to reduce their numbers of employees during 2015–2016. According to the CIPD (2014d) the key economic challenge to face the government from 2015 onwards is to create conditions for productive growth as a means to economic growth. However, labour productivity as measured by the output per hour worked remains weak and at the time of writing (2015) is still below its pre-recession level. This is one reason why wages have not kept pace with inflation and according to the CIPD (2014d) there is no guarantee that real earnings will rise. There is an apparent contradiction here as there are skills shortages in some areas of work but at the same time many people still face problems in finding jobs and those with low skill levels face particular problems because of a lack of jobs and training opportunities. Although unemployment levels are improving there are many working on zero hours contracts or short-term contracts and more than a million people are unemployed: many of these are young people and more needs to be done to improve their employment prospects.

Did you know?

The Chartered Institute of Personnel and Development has celebrated 100 years in business. It started life as the Welfare Workers Association in 1913 with a membership of only 34 people.

(*Source*: CIPD, 2015a)

There are many mixed messages in the analyses of the current and expected economic situation, so this is a difficult but crucial area for employers to factor in to their decision making. Business leaders who think strategically must also strive to focus on future needs as well as the demands of current circumstances. This means, for example, that while recessionary effects may have required the contraction of business and reduction in the numbers of employees in the short term, an organisation also has to be ready for potential future growth as the economy recovers, and be in a position to seize the opportunities this may bring. This is indeed a difficult balancing act.

Social and demographic trends

Though understandably the economic situation has taken precedence recently there are other social and demographic factors that also have an effect on the HR department and the HR techniques it uses. Most advanced capitalist economies have an ageing workforce. In the UK those aged over 50 accounted for slightly less than 25 per cent of the total workforce in 2002 but accounted for 29 per cent of it by 2012. During the same period the percentage of younger workers in the 15–24 age range fell from 15 per cent to 13 per cent (CIPD, 2014e).

There are now several different generations of workers who it is claimed have different attitudes to work and who will consequently be motivated by different things. Writers have used various terms to describe these groups. Penna and CIPD (2008) identify five groups.

Veterans are those born between 1939 and 1947. Though the numbers of this group have reduced as many have already retired, there are still people in this age group who have chosen to continue to work since there is now no compulsory retirement and people are actively encouraged or may need to work longer to obtain pensions. It is claimed that this group likes to feel valued and consider working beyond traditional retirement ages particularly if they can work flexibly and achieve a reasonable work/life balance.

Penna and CIPD (2008) describe those who were born between 1948 and 1963 as baby boomers. This group has traditionally been prepared to work long hours and, according to Penna and CIPD (2008), they are more individualistic than some other groups and less inclined to favour team working. They want to feel engaged with the organisation but also seek work/life balance particularly if they want to work longer than the state pension age. They do tend to value social responsibility and tend to feel more engaged working for an employer who demonstrates a sense of social/environmental values. They have respect for authority and want to have careers.

Generation X consists of those born between 1964 and 1978. They are supposed to be used to uncertainty as they moved into the workforce at the worst time for jobs since the Depression. It is claimed that they are very focused on achieving results. They are used to flatter organisational structures and dispersed working environments but also demand flexibility. Many in generation X regard the workplace as a place to also socialise, enjoy team working and may feel more loyalty to people in the organisation rather than the organisation itself. They also want access to personal development opportunities (Penna and CIPD, 2008).

Generation Y were born between 1979 and 1991. According to Allen (2010) this is the most technologically aware generation so far and they are highly desirable to employers. Penna and CIPD (2008) also found that as well as being more technologically aware this group is more ethnically diverse than previous generations and they are also multitaskers who like to work collaboratively. They also need rapid two-way communication, fairness and flexibility and are concerned about the organisation having a meaningful policy for corporate and social responsibility.

However, while Generation Y should be desirable to employers they are also the group that has suffered most from the recent recession, which impacted disproportionately on employment for the under 25s. While it is understandable that those in this generation who have experienced periods of unemployment or have been unable to find a job at all are likely to be highly dissatisfied, it also appears that those working are a particularly unhappy group who experience low levels of job satisfaction (CIPD, 2010). This dissatisfaction appears to be the result of a contribution of factors: this generation has not experienced economic problems before as they grew up in times of relative affluence; they are also unhappy with the provision of opportunities to learn new skills and lack of progress at work but a stagnant job market also limits opportunities for progression (CIPD, 2010).

Generation Z are, according to Penna and CIPD (2008), those born between 1992 and 2008, so some of this group have already entered the workforce too. It is claimed that this group is even more technologically savvy and is more socially networked than earlier groups. According to Churchard (2014) this group often has less respect for authority and may not be so concerned with career development. At interview they are less concerned to ask questions about salaries or company cars but are more focused on wanting to know how many women are working in senior positions and the organisation's policies on sustainability.

Pause for thought 1.3	Which generation are you?
	Do you recognise these descriptions as accurate?
	Are there any dangers in using such stereotypes?

While these are all stereotypes of different generations of workers, if there is any truth at all in them, it does mean that HR and managers will need to be very flexible in their approaches if they are to lead, motivate and retain these differing groups with their differing aspirations and will need to adapt their HR processes accordingly. (The dangers of stereotyping are discussed in more detail in Chapter 6.) As older workers stay in the workforce longer some have claimed that this could result in resentment towards older generations as more baby boomers and those from generation X retire later with some younger workers feeling that this stops or limits their career progression. Churchard (2013) says that the number of over 65s in work in the UK is already more than one million. However, although employers will need to adopt different policies to attract, retain and motivate the different age groups, it does not mean that the younger age group will necessarily miss out. Employers do need to manage their skills base and ensure flexibility and career progression. All generations of workers can also learn from each other and the baby boomer generation could adopt the role of mentor to those entering the workforce (Churchard, 2013). This can also work in reverse and already some organisations such as Estee Lauder have younger techno-savvy workers acting as coaches or mentors to older workers (Churchard, 2014).

Information technology

Information technology (IT) has had a huge impact on all aspects of our lives, including human resource management. If you glance through any journal relating to human resource management nowadays, you will find countless articles relating to the various ways that information technology can assist both HR mangers and line managers to do their jobs. These include: systems for e-recruitment, on-line shortlisting of applicants, online performance management and appraisals, e-learning, online psychometric testing, as well as IT systems to help with payroll, employment data, recruitment administration, references and pre-employment checks. There are also some large organisations which use HR shared service centres where they bring many of the HR services together and use technology such as email, a company intranet or telephones to provide HR information in order to deal with HR queries and provide expert advice for people working at various sites, sometimes in different countries.

Developments in social networking have meant more involvement is possible from employees and this too is having an effect in some organisations on approaches to recruitment and selection and learning and talent development with organisations using Facebook, LinkedIn or Second Life as a part of their HR approach. As well as being a means for controlling or reducing costs through using IT there is also the potential to get better quality information, better decision making and, with the latest developments, increased involvement and engagement of the workforce which may also prove attractive to generation Y or Z workers.

Pause for thought 1.4   How do you think the increased use of information technology will affect the job of the HR manager and line manager? Will it enable them to get rid of the routine jobs by delegating them to IT systems or by outsourcing them to specialist organisations, or will it mean that more people end up in routine jobs working with computers? What effect do blogs or social networking sites have?

The increasing use of information technology is already having all of these effects, at least to some extent. For many HR managers, using IT for routine tasks frees them from more mundane tasks, so they have more time to think strategically, and increasingly line managers are also using IT to maintain records for their own staff. Increasing use of IT has also ensured a much greater amount of information is available on which to base decisions and to plan for the future.

Teleconferencing, teleworking, Skype and FaceTime mean that people no longer have to be in the same place to hold a meeting or to work in the same building. E-learning and m-learning (mobile) means people are often able to learn at their desks, in their cars or at home via their tablet or smartphone. All such developments raise issues and pose different problems about the ways staff should be managed and these will be of concern to both the HR manager and the line manager.

Some people will be in high-value jobs, using their expertise to design these labour-saving IT systems. Others may find that, perhaps for part of their career, they are dealing with completion of basic tasks using computers; or, on the other hand, they may use their knowledge and expertise in people management to deal with HR queries from around the world, via computers or telephones in shared service centres.

> **Pause for thought 1.5** In Japan the biggest bank, Mitsubishi UFJ Financial Group, has already started trials with a humanoid robot called Nao to help its customers find the appropriate services for them. Nao analyses customer emotions from their facial expressions and tone of their voice and is programmed to speak 19 languages.
>
> Nestlé Japan has also announced plans to use an 'emotional robot' called Pepper to sell its coffee machines and to explain Nescafé products to customers.
>
> What do you think the role of robots will be?
>
> In your view which jobs are most likely to be done by robots?
>
> How do you think the use of robots will affect the jobs of the HR manager and line manager?
>
> (*Source*: McCurry and Gibbs, 2015)

Current issues in HRM

Added value

The concept of added value is of great importance in HRM and is concerned with making a difference, and in the recent difficult economic times this has been particularly important. This concept aims to show how the HRM function or other related functions make a difference to the organisation and how they can help to shape the organisation's business strategy. Once again one of the concerns is for measurement of the difference the people initiatives have made. According to Harrison (2002), in order to add value, HRM or human resource development (HRD) must

> achieve outcomes that significantly increase the organisation's capability to differentiate itself from other similar organisations, and thereby enhance its progress. It must also achieve these outcomes in ways that ensure, through time, that their value will more than offset the costs that they incurred.

So, they have to make a difference to the organisation but do so in a way that is also cost-effective.

Green (1999) had criticised HR professionals for not having sufficient awareness of the effects that new HR interventions would have on the organisation, and maintained that in order to provide added value, people professionals needed to provide three things:

- *alignment* – pointing people in the right direction
- *engagement* – developing belief and commitment to the organisation's purpose and direction
- *measurement* – providing the data that demonstrate the improved results achieved (Green, 1999).

Knowledge workers

In the UK there has been a decline in traditional manufacturing industry and a growth in areas of work such as the service sector or knowledge economy, where the workers are sometimes referred to as knowledge workers. The management guru Peter Drucker (1999) predicted that the growth and management of knowledge workers would be one of the key issues for the twenty-first century. According to the Industrial Relations Services (IRS) (2006) knowledge workers are able to be very selective about who they want to work for. Before joining any organisation they will want to establish whether it will be suitable for them and whether their work will be valued and they, like applicants from generation Y, will be concerned to know whether or not the organisation's ethos and values are similar to their own. The way organisations share and manage knowledge and motivate their knowledge workers may be a critical factor in attracting and retaining this group and will also be crucial in determining the success of organisations in the twenty-first century. This is likely to be an issue for many involved in managing people, and according to Birkinshaw and Cohen (2013) as much as 41 per cent of knowledge workers' time is spent on activities that do not offer them this type of personal satisfaction and which could be delegated. The authors do point out, however, that the nature of their work makes the knowledge workers hard to manage as so much of what they do is unseen as it is about ideas and is in their heads. Moreover, in the recent recession as organisations have been forced to cut costs many people have also had to take on more routine administrative jobs. However, as we said earlier, all workers are vital for an organisation if it is to be successful and all workers should be managed in ways that will motivate them and help them to contribute to the achievement of their organisation's objectives. According to Birkinshaw and Cohen (2013) this could mean that some low-value tasks need to be stopped or redesigned or delegated perhaps to give experience to more junior staff.

There are varying views about the importance of knowledge workers and how they should be managed. Suff (2006) says that 'knowledge workers can be highly challenging to manage effectively'. She says that the defining feature for knowledge workers is their attitude to work and the value their employer attributes to them. They are primarily motivated by career and personal development and need full involvement in issues that affect them and their work or they may become alienated and leave to join an organisation that appreciates them more.

Talent management

XpertHR (2015) say that the term 'talent management' is used to described ways in which employers 'attract, develop, engage and retain individuals of particular value to their organization'. This definition shows that talent management is a process that uses many different HR techniques and as such it will be discussed in more detail in several chapters of this book, in particular recruitment, selection, performance management, reward and learning and talent development.

The definition also seems to imply a fairly exclusive approach to talent management as being just for those who have been identified as being of particular value to the organisation and when there are tough financial constraints it is easy to see the attraction of this rather limited approach. However, a broader interpretation of talent management can be and is used in many organisations as all employees should be making a contribution to the organisation and should have talents: if the employee wants to develop in ways that will contribute to the organisation, there should be opportunities for that development. Stewart and Rigg (2011) indicate that the way in which talent management is defined depends on the perceived scarcity or abundance of the talent needed and also whether the organisation tends to be more individual or organisation focused. For example, if the talent which the organisation requires appears to be in short supply and the organisation adopts an individual focus, then they will pay attention to a limited number of people who are seen to be high flyers or stars and will try to attract and retain these for future high potential. However, if talent is scarce but the organisation is focused more on the whole organisation there will tend to be an emphasis on HR processes such as succession planning.

On the other hand, if talent is perceived to be plentiful then organisations with an individual focus will try to ensure opportunities for learning and development for each individual, while if there is more of an organisation focus they will instead tend to try to develop the talent pool across the whole organisation to improve the overall capacity of the organisation (Stewart and Rigg, 2011). Whichever approach is chosen needs to suit the organisation and fit with their strategic objectives and according to the CIPD (2014f) the business case for taking a strategic approach to talent management is very strong.

While the term 'talent management' does nowadays seem to have a variety of interpretations, according to Clake and Winkler (2006) there is broad agreement that

> talent management is not just about upward career moves. Horizontal career moves that broaden an individual's experience are also an integral part of many processes. For many, detailing a talent management strategy has seen a deliberate increase in the 'sharing' of talent within an organisation and opportunities to gain experience in other departments or to work shadow are comparatively cheap ways of giving people opportunities to develop.

According to the CIPD's learning and development survey (2014g) over 50 per cent of those surveyed use some form of talent management and their talent management programmes include a variety of HR practices such as coaching for leadership, networking events, as well as the provision for opportunities for exposure to board-level members and clients.

The term 'talent management' is now widely used, and even where there is currently a high level of unemployment many organisations still complain of being unable to fill their vacancies, so the idea of attracting and keeping talented workers as a way of achieving the organisation's strategic objectives is becoming increasingly important. In this sort of economic environment it is important not only to attract but to develop and retain talented workers and the war for talent and talent management affects all aspects of HR from recruitment and selection to reward and motivation and learning and development. Generation Y workers, in particular, may feel that the opportunity to develop their talent is vital if they are to be attracted to an organisation and to stay with it, but it is also important to ensure fairness and consistency and that relevant stakeholders are asked to contribute to designing the process.

Knowledge management

Another related area of concern nowadays is in knowledge management. All workers possess a great deal of knowledge which can be easily lost to the organisation when systems change or when there is a reorganisation and of course when people leave an organisation. HR specialists today also therefore have a role to play in trying to ensure that knowledge is shared and retained since this knowledge is a great source of competitive advantage. This presents issues about the best ways of communicating and sharing knowledge but also raises other issues about retention of workers.

Corporate responsibility

This is an area that is becoming of increasing interest and importance to organisations and to the people in them. Frequently the interest has been generated by public scandals and mismanagement such as in the world of finance, or by the great disparity in salaries of directors in some organisations who get hefty rewards even though their organisation has not done well under their leadership. It also includes issues about fairness and ethics as well as environmental concerns about the threat of global warming and about ways organisations can help to minimise their carbon footprint. According to the CIPD (2014h), the term is frequently used interchangeably with the term 'Corporate Social Responsibility' (CSR) or 'sustainability' or 'sustainable business'. Corporate responsibility (CR) includes issues about the following:

- The environment – this could include topics such as the organisation's carbon footprint, pollution or recycling.
- The marketplace – this could include issues such as fair trading practices or the organisation's tax affairs.
- Workplace issues – these could include workers' rights or issues about wellbeing.
- Community issues – this could be about financial support for local community projects or encouraging volunteering.

In effect CR covers all aspects of company governance. It is about how companies conduct their business in an ethical way, taking account of their impact economically, socially, environmentally and in terms of human rights.

As such it affects everyone and not just those who are the core stakeholders in the business: the shareholders, the workforce, suppliers and customers. There are other stakeholders such as local communities which may be affected by the action or inaction of businesses and their impact on the community or its environment. If some of its goods are produced in another country the organisation may have global responsibilities towards the workforce in terms of their fair treatment as well as to its suppliers and the local communities. An organisation's actions can even affect future generations.

There are a great many areas in CR in which HR can become involved, although clearly others will also need to be involved in any form of organisational culture change such as this. HR can play an important part in initiating and coordinating ideas or by providing a forum for discussion as many of the best ideas will come from the workforce. HR can also contribute through training, communication and support and by setting objectives for change. For CR ideas to be acted upon, they also need to make business sense and many simple ideas (for example switching off lights in offices or installing time controls on water coolers to switch them off at night) help the environment and also save organisations' money.

CR is increasingly of importance to people when choosing which organisation they want to work for and for some of you this may be a strong guiding factor in your choice. According to the CIPD (2014h) CR helps organisations to rebuild trust in their business practices and is necessary as it also helps them to provide data and evidence when needed about their standards of business practice. It can help significantly with recruitment, engagement and retention of employees and can be a very important part of the organisation's brand and image too. People, especially generation X and younger, don't want to work where there is a clash with their personal values and are placing increasing value on the credibility of an organisation's brand. Employers are using the positive aspects of their brand in recruiting, motivating and retaining highly skilled people. However, it is not sufficient just to have policies about the environment and corporate social responsibility if they are not implemented. According to Emmott (2005):

> Companies that want to build or protect their brand also need to think about their employer brand, and there is evidence that more and more people want to work for organisations that they respect. No company competing in the 'war for talent' can afford to ignore this advice.

Other approaches to HRM

Research into the organisation of HR departments and the roles of HR specialists

Another way to try to establish what HRM is about and the roles HR managers and line managers take in managing people-related issues is to look at research into the way HR departments are organised and the roles that HR practitioners and line managers have.

The people and performance model

John Purcell and a team of researchers from the University of Bath carried out studies sponsored by the CIPD over a three-year period to try to ascertain what aspects of HRM actually make a difference to performance within organisations (Purcell *et al.*, 2003).

They found that, on their own, good HR policies were not sufficient to create an effective organisation but excellent policies about recruiting, developing and retaining the people in the organisation were important. Purcell *et al.*

(2003) referred to this as the 'human capital advantage'. Much of this book will address ways to achieve this type of human capital advantage. However, the other key factor that distinguished effective organisations from those that were less effective was the way they 'worked together to be productive and flexible enough to meet new challenges'. We also emphasise this approach throughout this book.

The researchers identified two vital ingredients in effective organisations. According to Purcell *et al.* (2003) these are:

- First, they had strong values and an inclusive culture.
- Second, they had enough line managers who were able to bring HR policies and practices to life.

Strong values and an inclusive culture

Purcell and his team of researchers (Purcell *et al.*, 2003) found that organisations that developed a strong and inclusive culture usually had what they called a 'big idea'. This was always something that was clearly communicated to everyone in the workforce and that could be easily understood.

The big ideas the researchers identified were ideas such as the 'pursuit of quality' at Jaguar cars, 'living the values' at Tesco and the 'principles of mutuality' at Nationwide Building Society. Everyone shared and understood these ideas and they became the foundation for all the HR policies and procedures, enabling everyone to see why they were necessary.

Line managers who could bring the policies to life

We have already mentioned the importance of line managers in the HRM approach to the management of people and here we have recent evidence that substantiates this view. In the research by Purcell and his team (Purcell *et al.*, 2003) the line managers were found to be the other vital ingredient in making an effective organisation. The line managers had to see not only the relevance of the HR policies and procedures to themselves, but also how they could use them to contribute to an effective organisation.

Pause for thought 1.6	The researchers from Bath University said, 'It's better to ensure that HR policies are properly implemented than to try to develop new policies' (Purcell *et al.*, 2003). As you work through this book and learn more about HR policies and procedures, remember that the way they are introduced into an organisation is also very important and worker involvement and excellent communication are also crucial to the effectiveness of the organisation.

Research by Ulrich

Dave Ulrich has been very influential in trying to clarify what makes an effective HR specialist and has continued to research and develop his ideas. Some large organisations have restructured along the lines of the Ulrich model of HRM. This has sometimes been referred to as the 'three legged stool model of HRM' though the term was not used by Ulrich himself. This consisted of three main elements:

1. the HR business partner
2. centres of excellence
3. shared services (CIPD, 2014i).

This three-way division in HR was most suited to large organisations.

The HR business partner

The role of HR business partner proved extremely popular with many job advertisements carrying this job title. This is a very senior role that is supposed to work closely with business leaders with a key role to influence and steer the strategic direction of the organisation.

Centres of excellence

These would be groups of HR managers with expertise in particular areas of HR, such as reward, learning, engagement or talent management, who would provide competitive business solutions through delivering HR innovations in these areas.

Shared services

This would probably be a large unit that handles all the transactional services across the business such as recruitment administration, payroll, absence monitoring as well as the provision of advice on simple HR issues. This could be within one large organisation or operate across several organisations. The aim is normally to reduce costs, avoid duplication of effort and at the same time improve the quality of the service provided to the customers. Improvements in technology have enabled people to input information more easily and to access more information for themselves (CIPD, 2014j).

Although it has been influential there have also been criticisms of Ulrich's model as each segment may be seen in some organisations to work in isolation from the other parts and so weaken the role of HR. Line managers may not be willing or able to take on some of the more routine areas of HR work so it might be impossible for the HR managers to become more strategic and act as business partners (Stephens, 2015). Ulrich himself says that his model was not that of a three-legged stool but rather that the HR structure chosen by an organisation should match the business structure of that organisation. So if 'the business is centralized and functional then the HR function also needs to be centralized and functional' (Ulrich in Stephens, 2015).

Ulrich *et al.* (2013) conducted research with 20,000 respondents to review the competencies which are needed by effective HR professionals. They asked HR professionals to rate themselves against this set of competencies and then compared their ratings with those of others, some of whom were in HR and some who were not. They then compared this to data on business performance. Six areas of HR skills and knowledge emerged from the 20,000 survey of participants, though not everyone would have all these skills. They were:

1. Strategic positioner – who considered business context, customer needs and used HR knowledge and skills to co-create business strategy.
2. Credible activist – who was trusted as an HR professional because of their influencing skills and by clear communication.
3. Capability builder – who conducted audits of capability and improved the capacity of the organisation.
4. Change champion – who developed the rationale for change and implemented change.
5. Human resource innovator and integrator – who provided integrated solutions for the organisation based on the latest ideas and insights in HR practice.
6. Technology proponent – who used technology to good effect in improving both efficiency and effectiveness in the organisation.

When Ulrich *et al.* (2013) analysed the scores of the HR professionals in these areas they found that most performed best in the role of credible activists but were weakest as technological proponents. The competency domains which had the most impact on business performance were also different to those competency domains in which most HR professionals were strongest. The competency domains of HR professionals said to have the greatest impact on the business are those of capability builder, HR innovator and integrator and technology proponent, so there is a need for more HR professionals to develop further competencies in these areas.

Ulrich went on to say that the HR profession had grown and developed from what was a purely administrative role to a more functional role and then to a more strategic role, but as it continues to grow and develop the role should now focus more on the external market in which their organisation is operating. This means that HR departments should focus on the customers of the organisation, rather than focusing just on the employees, and let them define the culture. They should work closely with the marketing department and other service departments to ask customers what they want. HR professionals should then provide leadership to bring details on people, skills, workforce planning, talent and organisation culture together (Ulrich, 2015 in Lewis, 2015).

Pause for thought 1.7   What do you think the role of the HR professional should be?
Should they, as Ulrich says, become more focused on the organisation's customers?

The changing HR function

Reality does not always match the theories. In a survey comprising 1,152 HR professionals the CIPD (2014k) found that the most popular structure adopted by HR departments was that of a single team with a mix of expertise within it. Larger organisations and the public sector tended to favour Ulrich's three-legged model comprising HR business partners, centres of HR excellence and shared services. Just over half of the HR departments outsource some of their services.

According to this CIPD survey (2014k) four out of five (79 per cent) HR professionals described themselves as generalists whose work covers many HR areas, while just 21 per cent regarded themselves as specialists in particular areas of HR. Three quarters of the respondents reported that they had started their careers working in areas other than HR and this is in line with the findings from an XpertHR survey quoted earlier in the chapter (Murphy, 2014a).

Most HR professionals see their focus as being on specific HR issues rather than organisation-wide issues, with less than 47 per cent of HR professionals indicating that they prioritise business issues and only 36 per cent of HR professionals in this survey indicating that they look for opportunities to improve revenue. The main priority for all is managing performance, though in the public sector the management of change is also an issue and there is a focus on staff engagement, workforce planning, staff retention and talent management (CIPD, 2014k).

There is agreement among 66 per cent in the survey that HR data is an important basis for decision making and also strong agreement among 65 per cent of the sample that measures should also be used to improve HR. There is also general agreement among 63 per cent of those surveyed that HR uses people measures that are aligned with strategic priority areas (CIPD, 2014k).

A smaller survey of 338 respondents conducted by XpertHR (Murphy, 2014b) shows differences between public and private sector HR managers in their priorities for 2015 and beyond. In the private sector the focus is on reviewing salaries and benefits packages, while in the public sector there continues to be restructuring and redundancies, and reviews of costs and terms and conditions of employment are seen as important.

As we have said it is not just HR managers but also line managers who nowadays have an important role in managing people in their teams or departments. Purcell *et al.* (2003), as discussed earlier in this chapter, researched the roles of line managers and indicated that they had a very important role both in bringing HR policies to life and in improving the discretionary behaviour of their workers. A CIPD (2015b) online survey conducted by YouGov examined line manager behaviours in several important HR areas to find out what contribution they made. They asked 2,153 working adults their views of their managers across the following dimensions:

- the behaviour of line managers in supporting employee engagement and well-being
- the amount of time spent with each of their team in one-to-one reviews
- performance management
- levels of empowerment and employee voice
- fairness and trust in the organisation.

The behaviours analysed here were all things which could support high-performance working and indicate the important role of the line managers and supervisors in achieving this. They found that 67 per cent of those polled were satisfied or very satisfied with their managers or supervisors and that almost 70 per cent meet with their managers for one-to-one discussions of their performance at least once a month. Those who were dissatisfied with their line manager, however, did experience a lack of motivation and this became worse the more time they spent with that manager or supervisor.

Among those workers who had annual performance reviews, 63 per cent agreed or strongly agreed that they understood how their particular objectives fitted into the organisation's overall strategy, though this dropped to just 44 per cent of those who had less frequent performance reviews. Rather worryingly 25 per cent of employees did not feel that HR acted in their best interests, while only 12 per cent felt this about their supervisors or managers!

What are the best places to work?

Many of the principles identified by Purcell *et al.* (2003) as of importance in achieving high performance are also to be found in organisations that have been judged as some of the best workplaces in which to work and these may also provide insights into how good HR and line managers work. According to Will Hutton (2010), former Executive Vice-Chair of the Work Foundation, the work of researchers means that we now know much about

what makes for good work and good workplaces. It is in the mix of performance, engagement and fairness: a steely commitment to excellence and quality; a sense of integrity and high trust in working relationships; and developing the practices, structures and (whisper it) terms and conditions of employment that help people feel valued and well-treated and facilitate their participation in the life and objectives of organisations.

It should not be surprising that organisations that have been judged by their employees to be excellent places to work have also been among some of the most successful organisations to survive or even expand during the recent recession (Paton, 2010).

In the following chapters we examine many of the key HR policies, practices and procedures that can contribute towards making an effective workplace that will hopefully also be one of the best places to work, and we have tried to emphasise the roles of both the specialists in HR and the line managers in implementing these in ways which will benefit the organisation. We have already shown how the role of HR practitioners and the importance of the role of line managers in HRM have evolved, and both continue to develop and alter in response to social, technological and economic factors and to suit the changing needs of the organisations themselves.

Did you know?

In 2014 in the *Sunday Times* 'Best Company to Work For' poll, the UKRD Group, a commercial radio group, was voted by its employees as the best medium-sized organisation in which to work for the fourth consecutive year. Here, leadership, excellent communication and team spirit are vital and help create an engaged, reliable, committed team. The organisation was also committed to improving terms and conditions for workers and this led to longer holidays for new staff, a pension scheme and improved reward programme.

According to William Rogers, its chief executive, 'tens of thousands of pounds are spent each year on a "cuddle budget" for treats for staff, such as a night out, a bottle of champagne, chocolates, flowers or a trip to an international sporting event'. This helps reinforce and recognise success and all staff feel that they are contributing to the organisation's success.

In 2014 Iceland Foods was voted first in the category of the best big company to work for. Staff feel that managers and their chief executive Malcolm Walker motivate them to work harder and give their best every day. They take employee engagement very seriously and staff feel motivated and encouraged so that everyone wants the organisation to be successful.

(*Source*: Leonard 2014)

Conclusion

In this chapter we have briefly discussed the background to HRM, introduced some of the areas in which HR managers are currently working, and introduced you to some of the discussions and debates about the ever-changing roles of HR specialists. We have chosen to focus on current thinking and research about HRM and the extent to which various HRM strategies contribute to the organisation being effective. We have also emphasised the fact that line managers nowadays play important roles in many aspects of managing people.

In reality, HR roles are very diverse and no one model explains them completely. In small or medium-sized organisations there will be HR practitioners who will deal with all aspects of HRM and who will regard themselves as generalists. In larger organisations there may be a much greater degree of specialisation and some will use business partners and may adopt a shared services approach alongside this. Therefore not all HR managers will be involved in all aspects of HR, and we have chosen to focus in this book on the topics most likely to be of importance to those starting to study HR with the intention of either becoming HR managers or managers in other functions who will have an increasing level of responsibility for HR.

HR departments continue to adapt to meet new demands and continue to search for ways to add value to their organisations and contribute to their strategic objectives. This will carry on as organisations find and adapt different HR strategies to help them to achieve success in response to the varying economic, social, demographic and technological changes which occur and as ways of leading and motivating their own often diverse workforces in situation-specific ways.

In the next chapter we focus on some of the issues relating to the achievement of high-performance working since this is a key area for both HR managers and line managers. Since each organisation will have different strategic objectives, it is actually not surprising that they do not just adopt one approach to the way they organise and provide leadership in their HR departments, and rather than looking to one model of 'best practice' we should be considering different approaches to 'good practice' depending on what works for specific organisations in the context in which they operate. We shall continue in the next chapters to explain the key aspects of areas of HRM and will take into account when doing so other important issues in the way these topics are handled, such as economic circumstances, social and demographic trends, cross-cultural issues and issues relating to ethics and corporate social responsibility.

Review questions

You will find brief answers to these review questions on page 462.

1. We include here a pictorial representation of this chapter in the form of a mind map (Figure 1.1). Use the key words we have included to refresh your memory of what we have covered in this chapter. Add your own key words or drawings to this mind map to reinforce your learning.

2. Identify at least three issues that currently engage the attention of people managers. Explain why each of these is important.
3. Examine three job advertisements for HR specialists. To what extent do the job advertisements compare or contrast with our descriptions of HR professionals' roles provided in this chapter?
4. Interview a human resource specialist about his or her job and main duties. Does this person think of himself or herself as a business partner to the organisation? How do the results from your interview compare with the roles and main duties we described in this chapter?

Figure 1.1   Mind map of Chapter 1

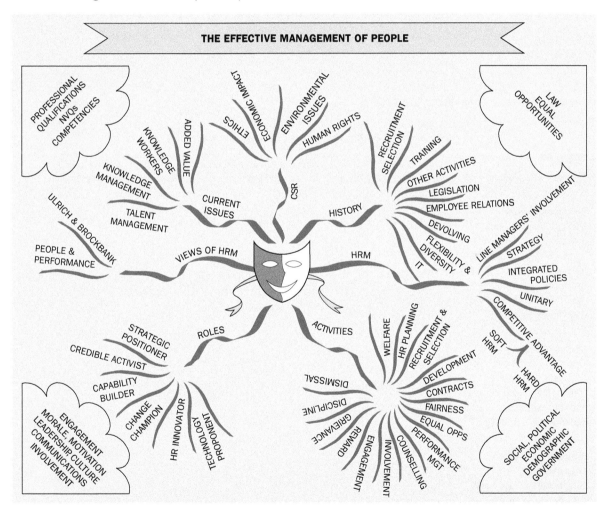

Improving your employability

The CBI and NUS (2011) say that the most important employability skill is to have a positive attitude but also that there are seven generic employability skills needed by everyone in the workplace which also help to contribute to that positive attitude. Use Table 1.2 to rate yourself on your current level of skills in each of these areas as you start this course. For each employability skill area where you feel that you need to improve your skills indicate what action you plan to take to make the required improvement and give yourself a target date for achieving this.

You may find that you already have many of these employability skills but by analysing your own skills' levels and making decisions about the need to develop others you are starting to take responsibility for your own learning and for your self-management, the first of the skills listed by the CBI and NUS.

Your university or college will provide many opportunities for you to develop and reflect on your employability skills but you could return to this exercise at a later date to see for yourself the extent to which your skills have changed.

Table 1.2   Assess your employability skills

Employability skills	Rate yourself on a scale of 1–5 with 1 being poor and 5 being excellent	What efforts will you make to improve your skills in areas which you feel appear to be weak?	By what date do you hope to achieve this improvement?
Self-management This includes: readiness to accept responsibility, resilience, self-starting, appropriate assertiveness, readiness to improve your own performance based on feedback and reflective learning			
Team working This includes: respecting others, cooperating, persuading, contributing to discussions and your awareness of interdependence with others			
Business and customer awareness This includes: Your basic understanding of the key drivers for business success and the importance of the provision of customer satisfaction and of building customer loyalty			

Employability skills	Rate yourself on a scale of 1–5 with 1 being poor and 5 being excellent	What efforts will you make to improve your skills in areas which you feel appear to be weak?	By what date do you hope to achieve this improvement?
Problem solving skills Analysing facts and circumstances to determine the cause of a problem and identifying and selecting appropriate solutions			
Communication skills Your application of literacy, ability to produce clear, structured written work and oral literacy, including listening and questioning skills			
Application of numeracy Manipulation of numbers, general mathematical awareness and its application in practical contexts (e.g. estimating, applying formulae and spotting likely rogue figures)			
Application of information technology Basic IT skills, including familiarity with commonly used programs			

(*Source*: Adapted from CBI/NUS (2011) *Working towards your future: making the most of your time in higher education*, p. 13, Copyright © CBI 2011

HR in the news

Human touch gets a helping hand

By Paul Taylor

Cloud-based software and services, social networks and big data are transforming how companies' human resources (HR) departments operate, reshaping such activities as recruitment, employee engagement, training and career development.

Underscoring the growing importance of technology to HR – or human capital management (HCM) as it is more fashionably called – the leaders in the enterprise software market have spent billions of dollars over the past 18 months acquiring cloud-based talent management start-ups. SAP bought SuccessFactors, Oracle snapped up Taleo and IBM purchased Kenexa.

"Over the past five years, and accelerating in the past three, the industry has changed markedly," says Andrea Bertone, executive vice-president for sales in Europe and North America at Monster, the jobs website.

Mr Bertone identifies four main ways in which technology is changing HR: the increasing use of social networks, the growth of mobile (smartphones and tablets), the expanding use of mixed content – particularly video – for training and other functions, and the use of big data analytics to discover unexpected patterns in employee data.

But perhaps the most obvious way in which IT has changed HR is in the use of online recruitment services such as Monster and social networks such as LinkedIn to augment traditional recruitment methods.

That does not mean that companies – even cloud-based companies such as Box.com – are abandoning traditional recruitment methods altogether. "We use both new and traditional methods," says Aaron Levie, Box.com's chief executive. Those traditional methods include recruitment agencies, referrals and college recruitment drives.

But Box.com, along with a growing number of companies, also uses online services and talent management software to help recruit, train and retain employees. The consultancy Capgemini, for example, processes about 1m job applications and hires some 30,000 employees every year.

Its HR system helps the talent team manage employees, from the recruiting process to their performance, compensation and also as they move around the world.

Jeremy Roffe-Vidal, Capgemini's HR director, says: "Right now, we are embarking on deploying SAP HR globally, which will enable a much more seamless, comprehensive HR process worldwide. In addition to bringing together our two current resourcing systems, it will also help us manage mobility."

Capgemini has also introduced an element of "self-service" to its HR systems. The company's 125,000 employees maintain their own CVs in a database that can be searched by skills, sector and client experience.

Sarah Sandbrook, HR director at Deutsche Telekom's T-Systems unit, says her company faces similar challenges. "We need to know what skills and experience employees have and what skills they need or want to develop," she says. "We use an internally developed system called "skill shift" ... that allows us to know all about our employees and identify the best place to deploy them, both for T-Systems' purposes and to enable the employee to progress."

More generally, "new digital HCM functions are giving line managers more control over relationships with employees", says Michael George, a senior director at Appirio, a cloud services provider. "We're seeing organisations use HCM data to put together elite teams with specific skill sets that are built for the long term, as well as improve their ability to react to changing business priorities by putting the right talent in the right place at the right time."

HR professionals are relying on these and other specialised IT tools to help prepare them for the developments they expect in coming years. Those challenges, identified in a recent survey undertaken by the Washington-based Society for Human Resources Management, include retaining and rewarding the best employees, developing the next generation of corporate leaders and creating a corporate culture that attracts the best recruits.

"Paying more doesn't keep valuable employees, but not paying enough is a sure way to lose them," says Ms Sandbrook. "Once you have such basic "hygiene factors" in place, the challenge for HR professionals looking to keep their best employees is to give them a sense of purpose and provide opportunities for development.

"In a very large multinational employer, the trick is to know where the development opportunities lie. This is a constant challenge and is where software tools really come into their own."

Questions

1. In what ways is information technology being used by HR professionals?
2. In what ways is information technology being used by line managers?
3. What are the main benefits of using more information technology?
4. Are there any disadvantages?
5. When managing the workforce of the future what future uses of IT are envisaged?

What next?

Now that you have read the first chapter and completed the exercises, you may want to go further and test your understanding.

1. Listen to the following podcasts at **www.cipd.co.uk** to gain a further understanding of the social, political and ethical issues that face HR managers as they try to build capacity and competence in a global economy.
   a. Podcast 36: Next Generation HR and Podcast 45: Building HR capability. Each of these involves HR managers discussing the changing role of HR.
   b. Podcast 63: Business Savvy HR. According to this podcast what knowledge and skills do HR practitioners need to develop?
2. Go to **www.greatplacetowork.co.uk** and read about the organisations that have been judged to be great places to work in their 2014 survey. How do the findings about what makes the 100 best places to work in the UK compare with the work of Purcell *et al.* (2003)?

Table 1.3   The main activities of human resource practitioners (Activity 1.1 answer)

Main areas of activity human resource/people management specialist	Type of involvement of the human resource/people management specialist	Type of involvement of line manager
Recruitment and selection	Design policies and procedure for fair recruitment and selection in order to contribute to the fulfilment of the organisation's corporate strategy. Commission online recruitment activities. Carry out interviews or monitor and give advice on interview technique or on terms and conditions of employment	Prepare and carry out interviews and other selection tests Participate in selecting the successful candidate(s)
Learning, training and talent development	Plan learning and talent development opportunities for the whole organisation, to meet the needs of the organisation as expressed in its strategic plan and to meet the needs of individuals. These could be formal training courses, online materials or less formal approaches such as coaching or mentoring Design and organise training courses for groups and sometimes run them Keep training records centrally and request information from line managers as part of planning exercise or to monitor success of training and development	Plan and provide learning, training and talent development opportunities to meet the needs of individuals and their departmental needs linked to the organisation's strategic plan, primarily for employees in their own department Provide training and keep records of training and provide information to central HRM department

Table 1.3   (*continued*)

Main areas of activity human resource/people management specialist	Type of involvement of the human resource/people management specialist	Type of involvement of line manager
Human resource planning	Depending on the level of appointment, involvement to various degrees in contributing to the strategic plan Collect and analyse data, monitor targets for the whole organisation. Provide information to managers. Conduct exit interviews and analyse reasons for leaving	Collect information on leavers and provide information on anticipated requirements for employees for their own department
Provision of contracts	Provide written statement of particulars for new employees and issue them to these employees having checked that the detail is correct. Keep copies of all documentation relating to the employee and advise on any alterations to the contract	Issue documents and obtain signature of new employee
Provision of fair treatment	Design policies and procedures for the whole organisation to encourage fair treatment at work. Inform and train people in these policies and procedures. Monitor the success of these policies	Ensure fair treatment of people in their own department. Listen and respond to grievances at initial stage in the formal grievance procedure or informally before someone starts the formal grievance procedure. May contribute suggestions about design of policies
Equal opportunities	Design of policies to encourage equal opportunities. Train and inform managers and all employees throughout the organisation in these policies. Monitor the effectiveness of the equal opportunities policies by collecting and analysing information	Possible involvement in, and contribution to, the design of policies. Responsible for ensuring that all employees for whom they are responsible do not suffer from any form of unfair discrimination while at work
Managing diversity	Develop policies about diversity and promote and ensure a diverse workforce so that the organisation can benefit from ideas generated by individuals from a range of different backgrounds	Active encouragement of valuing diversity in their own team or department
Motivating workers to achieve improved performance	Design and implement techniques to effectively assess performance of employees in a way that links clearly with the organisation's strategic plan. Review all HR policies to ensure strategic integration with the strategic plan. Train, inform and involve people in performance management techniques and encourage line managers to work towards a high-performance workplace. Monitor the effectiveness of the procedures. Maintain central records about performance of individual employees	Contribute to achievement of a high-performance workplace by taking an active role in people management and performance management of their own department. Assess performance of those in own department. Involve teams and individuals in setting and agreeing to targets and monitoring performance. Monitor their success and give feedback

Main areas of activity human resource/people management specialist	Type of involvement of the human resource/people management specialist	Type of involvement of line manager
Employee counselling	Establish appropriate system, either in-house or by external consultants, for employee counselling or for employee assistance programmes. Counsel employees with problems or refer them to specialised counselling service	Be involved in the initial counselling of employees in their own sections. Suggest alternative sources of counselling if they do not feel qualified to deal with the situation
Employee wellbeing	Establish appropriate systems for employee wellbeing in accordance with the objectives of the organisation. Monitor the cost and effectiveness of this provision	Ensure the wellbeing of employees in their own department and draw their attention to, and encourage use of, any provisions designed by the organisation to improve their wellbeing
Payment and reward	Establish appropriate payment and reward systems for all employees in order to support achievement of aspects of the organisation's strategic plan. Monitor the success of these systems. Collect comparative data for other organisations in area or nationally. Deal with individual problems about pay. Negotiate payment or reward systems. Tell individuals of their level of pay when they join the organisation or change jobs. Deal with individual problems or complaints about pay	Contribute ideas about appropriate systems of payment or reward to be used in the organisation. Possible involvement in negotiation over issues relating to own department. Deal with problems concerning pay raised by employees in their own department in the first instance
Health and safety	Design and implement the organisation's health and safety policy in order to contribute to the organisation's strategic plan and ensure policies are integrated with other HR policies. Monitor the effectiveness of this policy. Possible involvement with safety committee or line manage the safety officer or organisation's nurse. Promote health and safety awareness activities and encourage involvement of others throughout the organisation	Be responsible for health and safety of employees working in their own department. Encourage the involvement of individuals and teams in health or safety awareness activities. Monitor activities of own staff. Carry out regular safety inspections in own department. Take initial disciplinary action against those who infringe health and safety rules
Disciplining individuals	Design disciplinary procedure. Monitor the effectiveness of the procedure. Give advice to line managers on disciplinary problems. Organise training for line managers and employees about disciplinary issues to ensure they comply with organisation's policy and with the law. In some organisations they may still issue warnings in later stages of disciplinary procedure. Maintain central records of disciplinary action taken	Conduct informal disciplinary interviews with own staff if necessary. Issue formal warnings as outlined in disciplinary procedure. Maintain records of warnings issued. Ensure compliance both with the organisation's policy and with the statutory discipline, dismissal and grievance procedures

→

Table 1.3   (*continued*)

Main areas of activity human resource/people management specialist	Type of involvement of the human resource/people management specialist	Type of involvement of line manager
Dealing with grievances	Participate in the design of grievance procedure and encourage the involvement of others in this design process. Inform and train people in grievance handling and in the requirements of the statutory procedure. Monitor the effectiveness of the grievance procedure. Deal with some stages in the grievance procedure or with appeals	Deal initially with grievances raised by employees in their own department, handle informally at first or later as part of the formal grievance procedure. Deal with grievances within specified time limits and ensure that these are dealt with in accordance with the organisation's policy and the statutory procedures
Dismissal	Review procedures for dismissal to ensure that they comply with legislation. Provide advice and guidance on fair dismissal procedure. Provide training for all who may be involved in the dismissal process. Possibly dismiss employee	Managers in many organisations will be fully trained to take full responsibility for dismissing an employee in their section in a fair way. In other organisations they may require a higher level of management or the HR department to take this action
Redundancy	Consult with appropriate people with regard to redundancy. Involved in selection of those to be made redundant. Inform employees of redundancy and amount of pay and rights. Organise provision of more generous redundancy payment if this is in line with organisation's policy. Possibly also provide outplacement facilities either in-house or by consultants	Be involved in selection of those to be made redundant from their own department. Tell them of the decision to make them redundant and the reasons
Negotiation	Negotiate on a wide range of organisation-wide issues	Negotiate on a wide range of issues that affect employees in their own department
Encouraging involvement and engagement	Have an extremely important role in creating a culture within the organisation in which employees are encouraged to be involved in decision making and engaged in working towards the organisation's objectives. Design policies and procedures to encourage employee involvement in line with strategic plan. Provide training to encourage employee involvement	Contribute to the organisation's policies and encourage involvement and engagement of employees in their own department
Adding value	Ensure that all HR activities help to add value to the organisation by helping it achieve its objectives and become a high-performance workplace	Ensure that all HR activities help to add value to their department or section by ensuring they contribute to its objectives

Main areas of activity human resource/people management specialist	Type of involvement of the human resource/people management specialist	Type of involvement of line manager
Ethics and corporate responsibility	HR managers are concerned with all issues relating to fairness whether or not this is covered by legislation. Increasingly they are becoming involved in design of policies and procedures which take account of the impact of their business economically, socially, environmentally and in terms of human rights. They may challenge the way things have been done to draw attention to the corporate and social responsibility issues. They are likely to play an important role in support of environmental issues	Ensure that all activities in their own section comply with the organisation's policies on corporate responsibility and that they always act in a way consistent with these policies
Knowledge management and talent management	Devise polices and strategies to encourage the sharing of knowledge within the organisation. Try to ensure that the organisation keeps its knowledge workers and that it has communications systems that facilitate the sharing of knowledge so it is not lost to the organisation if someone leaves	Manage knowledge workers in sensitive ways to ensure they stay with the organisation. Encourage the sharing of knowledge within their team
	Play a key role in identifying talent and nurturing it within their team	Play a key role in identifying talent and nurturing it within their team
Change management	Deal with the people aspects of change, and design policies and procedures to support change. Ensure that there is clear communication, consultation, involvement and engagement with the workforce with any changes that are planned. Design learning and talent development initiatives to support the changes	Implement the changes but also play an important part in communicating issues relating to the changes to their team and in communicating concerns about the changes upwards to senior management. Run learning and development activities to support the changes
Managing cross-cultural issues or international HRM	Recruit in other countries or manage cross-cultural issues within home country as workers from many differing ethnic origins are employed. Design policies and procedures which take account of cross-cultural issues and if working in a multinational organisation make decisions made about the way HR policies are implemented within each country. Design and implement involvement in learning and talent development initiatives to support the management of cross-cultural issues	Manage the day-to-day cross-cultural issues that arise in the workplace, whether a worker is working in their home country or working in another country with host-country nationals and expatriate workers

References

Allen, A. (2010) Generational divide, *UK's Best Workplaces: Special Report*, May, Great Place to Work Institute UK, 28–29.

Birkinshaw, J. and J. Cohen (2013) Make time for work that matters, *Harvard Business Review*, Vol. 91, No.9, September, 115–118.

Boxall, P. and J. Purcell (2008) *Strategy and Human Resource Management*, 2nd edition, Palgrave McMillan, Basingstoke.

Chartered Institute of Personnel and Development (2005) *Survey report 2005. HR: Where Is Your Career Heading?* CIPD (www.cipd.co.uk; accessed 03.02.15).

Chartered Institute of Personnel and Development (2010) *Gen Y or Gen Lost? The Effect of the Recession on Our Future Workforce*, CIPD (www.cipd.co.uk; accessed 21.8.10).

Chartered Institute of Personnel and Development (2013) *Understanding the Economy and Labour Market*, CIPD (www.cipd.co.uk; accessed 02.02.15).

Chartered Institute of Personnel and Development (2014a) *Endless Possibilities... A Career in HR Takes You Further*, CIPD (www.cipd.co.uk/careers; accessed 03.02.15).

Chartered Institute of Personnel and Development (2014b) *The Role of Line Managers in HR*, CIPD (www.cipd.co.uk; accessed 03.02.15).

Chartered Institute of Personnel and Development (2014c) *Labour Market Outlook, Autumn 2014*, CIPD (www.cipd.co.uk; accessed 03.02.15).

Chartered Institute of Personnel and Development (2014d) *CIPD Manifesto for Work: A Policy Programme to Champion Better Work and Working Lives*, CIPD (www.cipd.co.uk; accessed 03.02.15).

Chartered Institute of Personnel and Development (2014e) *Survey Report: Managing an Age-Diverse Workforce – Employer and Employee Views*, CIPD (www.cipd.co.uk; accessed 04.02.15).

Chartered Institute of Personnel and Development (2014f) *Talent Management: An Overview*, CIPD (www.cipd.co.uk; accessed 09.02.15).

Chartered Institute of Personnel and Development (2014g) *Learning and Development Survey*, CIPD (www.cipd.co.uk; accessed 09.02.15).

Chartered Institute of Personnel and Development (2014h) *Factsheet: Corporate Responsibility*, CIPD (www.cipd.co.uk; accessed 09.02.15).

Chartered Institute of Personnel and Development (2014i) *Factsheet: HR Business Partnering*, CIPD (www.cipd.co.uk; accessed 11.02.15).

Chartered Institute of Personnel and Development (2014j) *Factsheet: HR Shared Services*, CIPD (www.cipd.co.uk; accessed 11.02.15).

Chartered Institute of Personnel and Development (2014k) *HR Outlook: Views of Our Profession, Winter 2012–13*, CIPD (www.cipd.co.uk; accessed 11.02.15).

Chartered Institute of Personnel and Development (2015a) *Factsheet: History of HR and the CIPD*, CIPD (www.cipd.co.uk; accessed 02.02.15).

Chartered Institute of Personnel and Development (2015b) *Employee Outlook: Focus on Managers, Winter 2014–15*, CIPD (www.cipd.co.uk; accessed 11.02.15).

Churchard, C. (2013) 'Age warfare', the new threat to workforce productivity, *People Management Magazine*, July (www.peoplemanagement.co.uk; accessed 03.02.15).

Churchard, C. (2014) Five things we learned at *The Economist* talent conference, *People Management*, 10 July (www.peoplemanagement.co.uk; accessed 05.02.15).

Clake, R. and V. Winkler (2006) *The Change Agenda: On Talent Management*, CIPD (www.cipd.co.uk; accessed 09.04.07).

Collings, D. and G. Wood (2009) *Human Resource Management: A Critical Approach*. Routledge, Abingdon.

Confederation of British Industry and the National Union of Students (2011) *Working towards Your Future: Making the Most of Your Time in Higher Education*, CBI/NUS (http://www.nus.org.uk/ Global/CBI_NUS_Employability%20report_May%202011.pdf; accessed 03.04.15).

Davies, G. (2014) quoted in Immigration is good for business, *People Management*, November, 6.

Drucker, P. (1999) *Management Challenges for the Twenty-first Century*, Harper Business, New York.

Emmott, M. (2005) CSR laid bare, *People Management*, Vol. 11, No. 16, 11 August, 38–40.

Green, K. (1999) Offensive thinking, *People Management*, Vol. 5, No. 8, 27.

Harrison, R. (2002) *Learning and Development*, CIPD, London.

Hutton, W. (2010) Foreword, *UK's Best Workplaces: Special Report*, May, Great Place to Work Institute UK, 4.

Industrial Relations Services (2000) In-store personnel managers balance Tesco's scorecard, *IRS Employment Trends*, May, 13–16.

Industrial Relations Services (2006) Recruiting knowledge workers, *IRS Employment Review*, No. 859, 17 November, IRS.

Kaplan, R.S. and D.P. Norton (1992) The balanced scorecard – measures that drive performance, *Harvard Business Review*, January–February, 71–79.

Kaplan, R.S. and D.P. Norton (1996) *The Balanced Scorecard: Translating Strategy into Action*, Harvard Business School Press, Harvard.

Kaplan, R.S. and D.P. Norton (2000) Having trouble with your strategy? Then map it, *Harvard Business Review*, September–October, 167–176.

Legge, K. (1995) *Human Resource Management: Rhetorics and Realities*, Macmillan Business, London.

Leonard, S. (2014) Tuned in to the people who matter, *The Sunday Times,* 25 February.

Lewis, G. (2015) Dave Ulrich: Let your customers define your culture and values, *People Management*, February. (www.peoplemanagement.co.uk; accessed 09.02.15).

McCurry, J. and S. Gibbs (2015) Meet Japan's modern bank manager: cheery, polite and speaks 19 languages, *The Guardian*, 5 February, 3.

Murphy, N. (2014a) *HR Careers: 2014 XpertHR Survey*, XpertHR (www.xperthr.co.uk; accessed 13.02.15).

Murphy, N. (2014b) *HR Roles and Responsibilities: 2014 XpertHR Survey*, XpertHR (www.xperthr .co.uk; accessed 13.02.15).

Niven, M. (1978) *Personnel Management 1913–63*, IPM, London.

Paton, N. (2010) Preparing for the upturn, *UK's Best Workplaces: Special Report,* May, Great Place to Work Institute UK, 6–7.

Penna and the Chartered Institute of Personnel and Development (2008) *Gen Up: How the Four Generations Work Together*, Joint survey report, September, Penna and CIPD (www.cipd.co.uk; accessed 03.02.15).

Purcell, J., N. Rinnie and S. Hutchinson (2003) Open minded, *People Management*, Vol. 9, No. 10, 31–33.

Stephens, C. (2015) Are HR business partners a dying breed? *People Management*, February, 36–37.

Stewart, J. and C. Rigg (2011) *Learning and Talent Development*, CIPD, London.

Suff, R. (2006) Managing knowledge workers, *IRS Employment Review*, No. 861. 15 December, IRS (www.xperthr.co.uk; accessed 22.08.10).

Ulrich, D., J. Younger and W. Brockbank (2013) The state of the HR profession, *Human Resource Management*, Vol. 52, No.3, May/June, 457–471.

West, K. (2015) Good pay, lots of work – so why aren't more of us plotting a course for skills black hole? *The Guardian*, 11 February, 23.

XpertHR (2015) Develop a talent management programme, *Reed Business Information Services* (www.xperthr.co.uk; accessed 09.02.15).

Further study

Books

Armstrong, M. and A. Baron (2008) *Human Capital Management; Achieving Added Value Through People*, Kogan Page, London.
This is a useful book for those interested in finding out more about human capital and added value and it describes how human capital management provides a bridge between human resource management and strategy.

Robinson, S. and P. Dowson (2012) *Business Ethics in Practice*, CIPD, London.
An interesting book designed to help you think ethically and learn how to make ethical decisions.

Routledge, C. and J. Carmichael (2007) *Personal Development and Management Skills*, CIPD, London.
This book is good for students who are starting to develop their personal, professional or management skills.

Journals and reports

Chartered Institute of Personnel and Development (2015) *Employee Outlook: Focus on Managers, Winter 2014–15*, CIPD (www.cipd.co.uk; accessed 11.02.15). The CIPD publish the results of regular surveys in their *Employee Outlook* series. In this instance they examine the role of managers in achieving a high-performance workplace and the HR practices that they adopt.

Confederation of British Industry and the National Union of Students (2011) *Working Towards Your Future: Making the Most of Your Time in Higher Education*, CBI/NUS (http://www.nus.org .uk/Global/CBI_NUS_Employability%20report_May%202011.pdf; accessed 03.04.15). This gives excellent general guidance about steps for those starting in further or higher education to help develop your employability skills.

People Management. Monthly journal produced on behalf of the CIPD with topical articles relating to personnel management issues. The online version of the journal contains additional articles not always included in the paper version. www.peoplemanagement.co.uk

Personnel Today. This is a free-access online journal which contains topical articles on personnel management and is produced by the team at XpertHR. www.personneltoday.com

Internet

There are numerous useful sources of information relating to human resource management and also to both careers in general and careers in HRM. We have found the following to be particularly useful:

The Advisory, Conciliation and Arbitration Service　**www.acas.org.uk**
Useful articles, news and online resources.

Chartered Institute of Personnel and Development　**www.cipd.co.uk**
This is the website of the professional body that represents most personnel and development professionals in the UK. It includes a wide range of information, including podcasts, but some of the information is accessible only to CIPD members.

Chartered Institute of Personnel and Development　**www.cipd.co.uk/careers**
This provides guidance about careers and qualifications in HRM.

Chartered Institute of Personnel and Development　**www.cipd.co.uk/binaries/employment-top-tips-and-guidance-from-the-people-who-recruit_2013.pdf**
This provides general guidance about careers and applying for jobs.

GOV.UK　**www.gov.uk**
Useful information site covering a wide range of employment-related topics such as holiday entitlements and disability issues.

Great Places to Work UK　**www.greatplacestowork.co.uk**
This organisation has a set of criteria that it feels makes for a great place to work. It reviews UK and European organisations against these criteria and makes annual awards to organisations.

Plotr　**www.Plotr.co.uk**
This provides guidance about careers, including those in HRM, in the form of an online game and aims to provide career guidance for students aged 11 to 24.

Trades Union Congress　**www.tuc.org.uk**
This gives the TUC's views on many current HRM issues and new legislation in Britain.

XpertHR　**www.xperthr.co.uk**
This is an extensive database of HR resources and includes some publications that are now only available online such as the *IRS Employment Review* and *Personnel Today*.

High-performance working: employee engagement through involvement and participation

Objectives

When you have studied this chapter you will be able to:

● explain what is meant by the terms 'unitarism' and 'pluralism'

● understand the key employment relations concepts of partnership, participation, employee involvement, commitment, engagement and high-performance working

● describe European Union initiatives relating to employee rights to information and consultation

● appreciate the importance of communication and consultation in the employment relations arena

● identify and describe the techniques that can be used to enhance employee involvement

● describe the concepts of commitment and employee engagement, and explain how they are related to employee involvement and high-performance working.

Chapter 1 established that the HRM approach to managing employees requires the development of strategies and the use of techniques that result in employees reaching their full potential and giving their best efforts in order for the organisation to succeed. This approach to management recognises the critical contribution of an organisation's people to the creation of competitive advantage. Employers recognise that their organisation will succeed if they can engage their employees, meaning that their workers will be fully committed. In order to develop a motivated workforce a strategy of employee engagement can be introduced, thereby creating a high-performance workforce that will give the organisation a competitive edge. Sisson (2007, p. 21) goes so far as to say that 'employee engagement can make or break a business', and ACAS (2009a) reviews research that indicates the continuing importance of engagement to firms in recessionary times, so that employees provide the high level of performance necessary for an organisation to survive, and also that effective workers are retained and are ready to help the organisation compete when the economy starts growing again.

Other chapters examine specific HR functions that can be performed in such a way as to acquire such employees (strategy and planning; recruitment and selection), retain them (pay and reward systems) and develop them (performance management and appraisal; learning, training and talent development). These HR practices, if carried out strategically, should result in the desired high-performance workplace (EEF/CIPD, 2003; CIPD, 2014a). However, the willingness of employees to contribute their best efforts to the organisation can be affected by the way they are treated on a daily basis, by their relationships with management and by the attitude they perceive management in general has towards them. All of these factors are greatly influenced by the organisation's culture which develops over time and is, in part, moulded from the philosophical stance of the founders and senior managers as to the role they expect employees to play in the life of the organisation.

This chapter reviews major concepts from the field of high-performance working (HPW) that have developed over several decades, including a review of the current discussion of employee engagement. We examine the basic approaches that managers can adopt towards the workforce, assessing the concepts of unitarism and pluralism, which provide a framework for an examination of partnership, participation and employee involvement. The techniques of participation and employee involvement are believed to increase employee engagement and enhance the willingness and ability of employees to contribute to the achievement of their organisation's goals. The levels of commitment and engagement that are expected to arise from these approaches are fundamental to the creation of a high-performance workplace.

Pause for thought 2.1   Given that the aim of human resource management is to use employees to their full potential, how would you expect this to be achieved in relation to management attitudes towards employees and the role of employees in organisational decision making?

In keeping with basic concepts of motivation theory, you have probably stated that employees are more likely to provide greater effort if they are responsible for their work and get a feeling of achievement from their work. According to Herzberg *et al.* (1959) and later work by Hackman and Oldham (1980), one of the ways to achieve this is by job enrichment. One method of job enrichment is to move responsibility for some decision making from managers and supervisors to more junior employees. This is known as a vertical job loading factor and is designed to improve motivation. Employee empowerment became popular in the 1990s and this too involves devolving the responsibility for decision making through all levels in the organisation.

The fact that we can talk about decision making being devolved implies that decision making lay elsewhere before it was devolved. Traditionally, owners and managers have regarded the right to make decisions as solely theirs, an attitude reflected in the ideas and work of Frederick Winslow Taylor (1911). In Taylor's concept of 'scientific management', managers were responsible for planning and controlling the work and giving orders, while other employees were meant simply to carry out these orders. Taylor's ideas were underpinned by the notion that workmen (at the time Taylor's work was conducted, men predominated in most workplaces) were motivated only by money and the possibility of getting more money for producing more work.

Later theories of motivation, such as those of Herzberg, have moved away from the concept of money as being the only motivating factor for employees, with a growing acceptance of the fact that people look for responsibility, achievement and a sense of autonomy at work. The ability or willingness of managers to share decision making with employees below them in the organisation's hierarchical structure would be very much influenced by those managers' general attitudes towards the management–employee relationship. The two major philosophical stances, unitarism and pluralism, and another important concept, partnership, have become the focus of debate since the late 1990s. Recent and ongoing legal developments emanating from the European Union have also meant that there is a heightened need to address employees' rights.

The unitary and pluralist perspectives

The type of relationship that will develop between the employer, as represented by managers, and the employee, and the techniques that are used to regulate this relationship, are influenced by the beliefs of the employer. Therefore, a unitary stance is likely to result in a workplace culture that is very different from an organisation that follows a pluralist stance. These concepts were developed in the work of Fox (1974).

The unitary perspective

Unitarists believe that all members of an organisation share the same interests, accept the organisation's goals and direct all their efforts towards the achievement of these goals. This implies that there is no conflict in such organisations and, if conflict were to arise, it would be because of some misunderstanding concerning the organisation's goals or deliberate troublemaking on the part of an individual. The unitarist stance also implies that the leadership of the organisation has decided what the goals are, and there is an expectation that everyone in the organisation will accept and seek to achieve these goals. Unitarist organisations, therefore, depend on strong, top-down leadership and are likely to purposefully recruit like-minded people. The cornerstone of this philosophical stance is the belief that there is a common goal and that everyone will direct their efforts towards the achievement of this goal.

The pluralist perspective

Pluralists, on the other hand, believe that in any organisation there will be a range of interests among the members. One example of this concerns pay versus profit. Employees are likely to be interested in increasing the pay they receive for work they do, whereas owners and managers will likely be concerned with increasing profits. This is a clear example of different objectives or a plurality of interests between different groups of people in the workplace, and this means that conflicts are likely to arise as the various parties pursue their interests. Pluralists accept that this is natural and needs to be managed. These conflicts should be managed in such a way that they do not disrupt the effective running of the organisation, or even so that they potentially contribute to its success.

Pause for thought 2.2   Having read about unitary and pluralist approaches to employment relations, which approach would you consider more likely to accept trade union representation in the workforce and which approach is more likely to resist it? Give reasons for your choice.

From the above, you should have concluded that unitary employers are more likely to resist unionisation whereas pluralist employers are more likely to accept trade union representation. Unionisation implies the existence of different sets of interests and mechanisms for resolving these differences. Pluralists accept the existence of these differences and the need to work towards their resolution, whereas unitarists expect everyone to share the same goals. Unitarists believe that there should be no conflict in the organisation, and therefore there is no need to have mechanisms for representing differing perspectives or for resolving conflict. On the other hand, pluralists recognise that differing interests in the workplace will have an impact on the achievement of organisational goals, and therefore need to be incorporated into the decision-making process. This is an important point to consider when you read about the methods employers can use for involving employees in decision making.

Partnership, participation and employee involvement

In addition to the effects that involvement in decision making has on employee motivation, as discussed earlier, there is also a broader philosophical debate about the role of owners, managers and employees in employment relations. There are a number of pertinent questions regarding this debate: Are owners and managers the only participants in the workplace with the right to make decisions? Are the shareholders the only party with a vested interest in the success of an organisation? The concept of stakeholders, defined by Johnson *et al.* (2014, p. 107) as 'those individuals or groups that depend on an organisation to fulfil their own goals and on whom, in turn, the organisation depends', suggests that the success of an organisation is affected not only by those who have a financial stake in it, but also by other people who have a direct interest in the success of the organisation. Everyone who is affected in any way by the decisions and actions of an enterprise is a stakeholder, including:

- employees, who depend on their organisation for their livelihood and for the contentment of their working life;
- customers, who depend on an organisation to supply products and services to meet their needs and wants;
- suppliers, who depend for their own livelihood on the success of client organisations;
- the community, which depends on organisations to be good neighbours;

- the government, which depends on organisations to make a financial contribution through taxation;
- the planet, which has finite resources and needs to be protected for future generations.

Based on the above, it is evident that an organisation has many stakeholders and organisations cannot operate in isolation without having regard to the effects of their actions on the different stakeholder groups. This raises the question of managerial prerogative in deciding what should happen in the workplace versus the right, for example, of employees to have their interests represented. Arguments for maximising employees' input in organisational decision making include their democratic right to have a say in any decisions that will affect them directly, their vested interest in the success of the organisation and the fact that it makes business sense to use the expertise that is available throughout the organisation.

The preceding discussion deals with major political and ethical considerations to which there are no easy answers, and certainly no one answer that everyone will readily accept. In any discussion about the role that employees should play in an organisation there is often perceived to be a tension between economic and social imperatives (McGlynn, 1995). Improvements in employee consultation, especially if they arise through legislation and are therefore compulsory, are frequently seen as essentially social measures that impose unnecessary costs on businesses. Adopting an HR approach would mean that these improvements are viewed as measures leading to economic success. That is, an organisation can attain a competitive edge by maximising the contribution of its employees. The contribution of employees is greater the more they are consulted, and therefore involved and engaged in what is happening in the organisation. These arguments lead us into a discussion of the principal ways in which employees' input can be obtained: partnership, involvement and participation.

Partnership

As is the case with HRM itself, partnership is an evolving concept and several commentators in the late 1990s observed that there was, at that time, no accepted definition of what partnership was and what it encompassed (Beardwell, 1998; Marchington, 1998). Indeed, the IRS (2004) comments that companies tend to adopt their own definition of partnership. More recently, Townsend *et al.* (2014) have stated that there is no universally accepted definition of partnership. We have gathered a number of descriptions of partnership from a number of publications and presented them here, followed by a comment on the similarities that emerge.

Employers and employees working together jointly to solve problems.

ACAS (1997, p. 13)

Key components (of partnership) might include high degrees of communication, personal development, employment security and an emphasis on ethical people management.

Beardwell (1998, p. 36)

Individual representation; consultation and communication; values; and understanding and promoting the business.

> Allen (1998, p. 41), describing the partnership deal
> agreed between Tesco and Usdaw.

- Employment security and new working practices.
- Giving employees a voice in how the company is run.
- Fair financial rewards.
- Investment in training.

> Monks (1998, p. 176)

1. A commitment to working together to make a business more successful.
2. Understanding the employee security conundrum and trying to do something about it.
3. Building relationships at the workplace which maximise employee influence through total communication and a robust and effective employee voice.

> Coupar and Stevens (1998, p. 157)

- Commitment to the success of the enterprise.
- Recognizing the existence of different interests.
- Employment security.
- Quality of working life.
- Genuine sharing of information and consultation.
- Added value from both partners.

> Gennard and Judge (2005, pp. 224–225)

Relations … conducted on the basis of a common interest in the success of the organisation.

> ACAS (2009b, p. 20)

The core principles are: mutuality, dignity and respect, fairness, competitiveness, flexibility and joint and direct communication and consultation.

> Rittau and Dundon (2010, p. 11)

Partnership is about 'good' industrial relations with competent managers.

> Townsend et al. (2014, p. 917)

The common themes that emerge from these definitions are the importance of security, the common aim of business success and the concept of employee voice. Of these three themes, the one which is probably the most contentious is security as it seems to imply that employees are promised that their jobs will be safe no matter what happens. The large number of redundancies in the first decade of this century is an indicator of how difficult it has been for many organisations to keep such a promise, and the threat of redundancy continues at least for some workers. The CIPD (2014f) *Labour Market Outlook Survey (Autumn)* reported a positive outlook for employment prospects with the net employment balance – the difference between the proportion of employers who expect to increase staffing level and those employers that expect to decrease staffing levels – increased to

+30, an increase of 7 on figures from the *Labour Market Outlook Survey (Summer)* (CIPD, 2014g) report. These figures demonstrate that fewer employers intend to make redundancies whilst a greater proportion of employers are planning on recruiting staff. However, these figures represent employment as a whole and mask key differences between the private and public sector. Whilst private sector firms are optimistic about job growth, the opposite is true for public sector employers (CIPD, 2014e).

There is a symbiotic relationship between security and partnership. As John Monks points out: 'Security in exchange for positive work flexibility is at the heart of the partnership approach' (1998, p. 176). You will note, however, that Monks and Beardwell, as cited above, both refer to *employment* security rather than *job* security. This distinction is important to the concept of partnership and the modern psychological contract. Employment security implies that employees will be developed so that should an employer ultimately have to make redundancies the employees affected will be highly skilled and their chances of employment elsewhere will be increased. Despite this, redundancies can still pose a problem for the effectiveness of the partnership approach, a fact that we shall return to in our concluding comments on partnership.

In their review of the literature on partnership up to 2008, Johnstone *et al.* (2009) also identify employee voice as a common, and indeed central, theme in definitions of partnership. Given our previous discussion of unitarism and pluralism, the combination of a 'common aim of business success' and the concept of 'employee voice' is interesting. Working in partnership calls for the recognition of a mutually desirable goal for business success but seems to imply at the same time that employees may have different opinions from management. Therefore, a mechanism is needed to facilitate 'employee voice'. We shall return to this point after our initial overview of participation and involvement.

Some further interesting points to note about partnership before investigating ways in which it can be achieved are as follows:

- The Labour Government of 1997–2010 emphasised the development of a satisfactory work–life balance for employees as being another key feature of effective partnership. This has, to a large extent, been continued by the Conservative and Liberal Coalition Government of 2010–2015 and is likely to be continued by the new Conservative government.
- Partnership can be achieved in both a unionised and non-unionised workplace. There is nothing to stop a non-unionised organisation from making arrangements with its employees to consult with elected representatives on a wide range of issues. This is described in more detail later in this chapter.

There is a definitive link between partnership and employee participation, which can be the channel for employee voice, and between partnership and employee involvement initiatives in that these can represent the way to achieve partnership. Coupar and Stevens (1998) comment that partnership can be viewed as a unique combination of employee involvement processes which can potentially maximise the benefits to the company and to employees. They also comment that 'companies typically use many different partnership activities to gain staff commitment and achieve business success'.

The next section will provide an overview of the difference in approach implied by the terms 'employee involvement' and 'participation', sometimes referred to together as EIP (Marchington and Cox, 2007), although some writers make a distinction between the two. We shall also comment again on the concept of partnership in that context before continuing with a more detailed exploration of EIP.

Pause for thought 2.3	Government policy affects employment relations and will, at least, seek to provide a direction with the ultimate goal of increasing economic growth. In May 2015 the Conservative party won a majority of seats in the UK parliamentary elections. Investigate the developments and changes in relation to employment relations. The website for the Department for Business, Innovation & Skills (**www.bis.gov.uk**) and the UK Government's website (**www.gov.uk**) are good places to start.

Employee involvement and participation

The main purpose of employee involvement and participation (EIP) is to make workers feel like they are active participants in workplace decision making. There are many practices aiming to achieve this, and these have been categorised as *representative* methods and *direct* methods. Representative methods mean that workers are not directly involved in communications and decision making individually, but through elected representatives who will put forward their views. This type of representation is often referred to as workers having a *voice*, and practices involving employee representatives are typically categorised as *participation*. Often, such participation is supported by legal structures as in the case of European Works Councils which are discussed later in this chapter.

Direct methods are those typically described as constituting *employee involvement*, and they include communications targeted straight at employees (i.e. not communicated by representatives) and other techniques that involve individuals or groups of workers. Employee involvement practices focus on the agenda set by management and attempt to get employees to understand the importance of organisational goals and commit to them.

Pause for thought 2.4	Given the descriptions of employee involvement and participation, what methods is a unitary employer likely to adopt and what methods is a pluralist employer likely to adopt?

Employee participation recognises that different groups within an organisation will have different points of view and will allow for the input of these differences. This will give employees a voice during the decision-making process at higher levels. In accepting the validity of the differing interests, employee participation is pluralist in nature. Employee involvement requires a commitment to decisions managers have made and the organisational goals they have set, so it is essentially unitary in nature.

A number of commentators on employment relations in the UK state that a combination of direct and representative approaches is likely to work best (Sisson, 2007; Earls, 2007; Coupar, 2007), although they also indicate that direct practices are likely to predominate (Coupar, 2007; Marchington and Cox, 2007). It is certainly true that a partnership approach, as we have described it, comprises both employee involvement and participation. It can be said, then, that partnership exemplifies a mixture of some aspects of unitarism with some aspects of pluralism. Appealing as this may be, some critics question the viability of partnership agreements pointing to the imbalance of power between management and worker representatives so that the management agenda is likely to prevail (Smith, 2006; IRS, 2006b).

We shall now review in more detail the concept of worker participation, developments with regard to regulatory information and consultation rights, especially in relation to European initiatives such as European Works Councils, and a variety of employee involvement practices that have been identified in a number of companies.

EU rights to information and consultation

European Works Councils

The UK was obliged to establish European Works Councils (EWCs) following the implementation of the Transnational Information and Consultation of Employees Regulations 1999, updated in the Transnational Information and Consultation of Employees (Amendment) Regulations of 2010 (Keith, 2014). These regulations implement the European Works Council Directive (2009/38/EC), an updated version of the 1994 European Works Council Directive (94/45EC).

The key issues in the Directive are that employees should be properly informed and consulted about major issues that will affect them. The Directive refers to a transnational 'undertaking', defined as a public or private entity undertaking economic activities for economic gain or not, or a transnational 'group of undertakings', defined as an entity employing at least 1,000 persons throughout the European Economic Area (EEA), with at least 150 people in each of two separate EEA states (Keith, 2014).

EWCs bring together employee representatives from different European countries in which the firm operates and, during EWC meetings, the representatives are informed by management about transnational issues of concern to the company's employees (**www.worker-participation.eu**). According to the Department of Business, Innovation & Skills (2012), the European Works Council Directive establishes a legal procedure for the establishment of European Works Councils in Europe, and employees of large transnational companies based in the UK with a presence elsewhere in Europe have the right to ask for a European Works Council to be set up.

The EWC, once established, has the right to meet central management every year and to be informed and consulted on the organisation's prospects. It also has the right, in exceptional circumstances, to be informed and consulted on significant measures likely to affect employees' interests. The firm's management must ensure that the EWC has the necessary financial and material support for it to be able to undertake its duties. It therefore has a duty to pay for the cost of organising meetings and the cost of travel and subsidence.

An example of a UK-based firm that has established an EWC (reported in *Personnel Today*, 2005) is the supply chain solutions firm Wincanton PLC, a company with more than 15,500 employees. In 2004 the firm started creating an EWC for white- and blue-collar workers across 12 European countries where it had a presence. In November 2004, the company set up a negotiating body with the job of outlining the Works Council's parameters, as well as the election process for its councillors. The formation of the Works Council was overseen by a specialist information and consultation team from Eversheds, the international law firm. The establishment of the EWC at Wincanton was welcomed by employees and unions.

The Transnational Information and Consultation of Employees (Amendment) Regulations 2010, known as TICE 2010, was implemented on 5 June 2011. To add to the complexity these regulations affect companies differently depending on whether the company adopted a voluntary EWC prior to the implementation of the 1999 regulations or set one up under the terms of these regulations. Thus, an exceedingly complicated picture has emerged. The Transnational Information and Consultation of Employees (Amendment) Regulations 2010 can be found on the UK Government's legislation website (**www.legislation.gov.uk**).

The CIPD (2009) identifies some of the new aspects of the amended regulations, including:

- The requirement to set up a Special Negotiating Body (SNB) to organise the establishment of an EWC. The SNB will include employee representatives whose task is to negotiate with management on what issues the EWC will cover.
- A broader scope of issues is identified in the new regulations, including a new right for training for the EWC employee representatives to enable them to carry out their role and the need to amend EWC agreements following any corporate restructuring.

Information and Consultation of Employees: works councils and employee forums

The EU Directive on Information and Consultation of Employees came into force on 23 March 2002 after many years of discussion about its content. The Department of Trade and Industry, as it was called at that time, engaged in extensive consultation to establish the context of communication and consultation that already existed in the UK in order to provide a suitable framework for the national regulations. These came into force on 6 April 2005 as the Information and Consultation of Employees Regulations 2004 (often abbreviated as the ICE Regs) and apply to businesses with 50 or more employees (ACAS, 2014a).

The ICE Regulations give employees certain rights in terms of being informed and consulted about issues in the organisation. This requirement does not, however, operate automatically. It occurs either by a formal employee request or by employers opting to start the process. If a pre-existing agreement exists, in order to be valid it needs to be in writing, cover all the employees in the undertaking, state how the employer will inform and consult employees and be approved by the employees (ACAS, 2014b). In order to comply with ICE Regulations, the Advisory, Conciliation and Arbitration Service (ACAS, 2014b) states that arrangements must

Did you know?

The Bank of Ireland provides a good example of an organisation which has an employee forum that drives the engagement agenda in the organisation. Their employee forum, called 'Partners' Council', focuses on eliciting information from all workers on key aspects of employee engagement. Feedback is synthesised to provide a 'Barometer' of engagement levels to senior management. The Barometer is a tool designed to solicit information about employee engagement and identify issues that might affect employee wellbeing and performance. In order for the Barometer to be kept easy to use and interpret, it was agreed that there should be a maximum of five feedback areas, these being: Involvement, Resources, Communication, Employment and Wellbeing. Each area of the business has its own Barometer. This is updated every month. Where issues are identified as needing action in the Barometer, an action plan is agreed upon. The Barometer includes a traffic light system: green (positive feedback or no issues), amber (areas of potential concern) or red (issues are likely to have an impact on the business if left unchecked). In addition, gold is used to indicate wholly positive feedback where there is a general feeling that best practice is undertaken in this area.

(*Source*: Involvement and Participation Association (2010) Bank of Ireland employee forum drives engagement agenda, *IPA Bulletin*, No. 88, January, available at **www.ipa-involve** .com; accessed 16.01.15)

cover all employees and employees can be kept informed of issues in the organisation in one-to-one meetings, company handbooks, newsletters, emails, the intranet or via an employee forum such as a Works Council or Joint Consultative Committee (JCC).

A report by Hall *et al.* (2008) for the Department for Business, Enterprise and Regulatory Reform (BERR) presented the findings of research into the implementation of the ICE Regulations 2004 based on eight case study organisations with 100–150 employees. The research found considerable similarities between the case study organisations' information and consultation bodies and those of larger organisations with some differences in practice reflecting the greater informality in employment relations and more limited HR capacity in smaller organisations. Hall *et al.*'s (2008) research pointed to senior managers becoming seriously engaged with information and consultation bodies, with some significant issues being discussed. However, there was little evidence to suggest that information and consultation bodies were able to influence management decisions.

The IRS (2006a) reports that only 19 per cent of employers surveyed stated that they had made changes to their information and consultation processes as a direct result of the ICE Regulations, but 31 per cent had introduced changes since their implementation anyway. Later IRS research by Wolff (2008) indicates some progress in the development of formal information and consultation arrangements, with 69 per cent of surveyed organisations reporting the establishment of a works council.

Employee involvement and high-performance working

As described previously, direct methods of employee involvement (EI) are widely used to achieve employee commitment and engagement. This leads to the high-performance workplace which is necessary to maintain and improve levels of productivity. Our focus for the rest of this chapter is first on a detailed overview of employee involvement practices, followed by an exploration and discussion of commitment and engagement.

Pause for thought 2.5 Identify three techniques that could be used by an organisation to promote the involvement of employees in decisions relating directly to their work, or in general to make them feel like they are an equal partner in the workplace whose contribution is sought and valued. As you read the next section you can check your list against the practices that are discussed.

In 1994, the Department of Employment (DoE), as it was then called, used six categories to describe employee involvement and these are still useful as a basis for an examination of EI practices. They are summarised in Table 2.1 but extended and updated to include more recent developments, such as the focus on employee wellbeing, and discussed in more detail below. The practices listed by the DoE remain representative of the bundles of HRM practices described by later researchers and commentators such as MacLeod and Clarke (2009), reporting to the government, and Alfes *et al.* (2010) for the CIPD. Different combinations of practices will be suitable for different types of businesses, and Edwards (2007) states that it may be difficult, for example, to adapt HPW practices for small businesses which are so important to the UK economy. Marchington and Cox (2007) also conclude that EI practices work well in combination with each other, depending on the circumstances, and that often one practice will support the effectiveness of another.

It must be stressed again that various combinations of these measures are taken up by organisations at different times (MacLeod and Clarke 2009; Alfes *et al.* 2010) and individual managers may adopt their preferred measures, which might be subsequently dropped. This is an unfortunate aspect of the voluntary

Table 2.1 Employee involvement categories and practices

Category	EI practices
Sharing information	Team briefing Employer and employee publications Company videos Company website, intranet and email Roadshows
Consultation	Employee suggestion schemes Employee opinion surveys Works committees Health and safety committees
Financial participation	Profit-related pay Employee share schemes Share incentive plans
Commitment to quality	Continuous improvement Teamwork Total quality management Quality circles Self-managed project groups Employee award schemes
Developing the individual	Performance management Appraisal schemes Employee development programmes Investors in People A qualified workforce
Health and wellbeing	Line manager relationship Wellbeing programmes
Beyond the workplace	The community The environment

and flexible nature of involvement arrangements. As you will see in the discussion of the initiatives, a longer-term commitment on the part of managers is needed if the techniques are to work effectively. Formal partnership deals agreed between managers and employees may introduce an element of continuity into this scenario.

Sharing information

Keeping people informed is one of the cornerstones of employee involvement and in fact provides the foundation on which many of the individual techniques can be built. Without information it is impossible for people to become involved in the organisation's decision making. A commitment to sharing information is an essential part of involvement and engagement. The methods that can be used to share information with employees include face-to-face meetings, team briefings, emails, the company's intranet (company and staff newsletters, notices, posters), social media channels and videos. Careful consideration should be given to choosing the form of communication most appropriate to the type of message.

The CIPD (2014b) states that effective communication is an essential part of employee engagement and is important in building trust between leaders and workers. This fact is reiterated by Mishra *et al.* (2014, p. 183) who state that 'communication is important for building a culture of transparency between management and employees, and it can engage employees in the organization's priorities'. The CIPD (2014e) goes on to warn about the danger of top-down communication. Instead, two-way or multi-directional dialogue is needed so that employees can share their views with colleagues and managers. Especially during reorganisation and redundancies effective communication is essential in minimising any negative effects (IRS, 2009).

Marchington and Cox (2007) report on research that shows that team briefings and mass meetings with the workforce are by far the most popular methods chosen by organisations to involve their employees, with 91 per cent of organisations surveyed using this method. An IRS survey into internal communications, as reported by Wolff (2010), confirms that face-to-face meetings with line managers (99 per cent of employers), departmental meetings (99 per cent of employers), management meetings (98 per cent of employers) and team meetings (96 per cent of employers) are the most popular methods to communicate with employees, in spite of technological developments. With more legal pressures to inform and consult employees, for instance because of the ICE Regulations, we can expect to see even more attention being paid to this area of employment relations.

Consultation

Along with sharing of information, consultation is a key concept in the development of good employee relations. Much of the ongoing debate about the development of mechanisms to improve the employer–employee relationship centres on the employee's right to information and consultation. Of the information-sharing techniques discussed in the previous section, with the exception of briefing sessions which allow for some immediate feedback from employees, the other methods encourage only one-way communication. According to ACAS (2014), whilst the terms 'communication' and 'consultation' are often used interchangeably, communication refers to 'the interchange of information and ideas within an organisation' whereas consultation concerns managers 'actively seeking and then taking account views of employees before making a decision'.

The consultation mechanisms named in this section essentially provide a means for employees to feed ideas back to their employers. These methods only represent true consultation, however, if there is an honest willingness to consider the ideas offered and to incorporate reasonable suggestions into the decision-making process. As the regulations on information and consultation continue to develop, the use of voluntary consultation mechanisms described here will be further supported by regulatory measures.

Most staff suggestion schemes contain a reward for successful suggestions, especially those where there is a cost saving for the organisation or other improvements in productivity. The reward does not, however, have to be financial in order for people to feel encouraged to put forward a suggestion. Often people merely wish to see their ideas recognised, gaining a sense of value and achievement from this, and they need only to be encouraged by the introduction of a recognised scheme. The reward for successful suggestions could be linked to information from other methods such as the company or staff newsletter.

Macdonald (2014), in proposing a model staff suggestion scheme, suggests that the organisation needs to state why a staff suggestion scheme is being used (e.g. to improve operational practices, to reduce waste, to cut costs, to improve service), how the staff suggestion scheme will operate (e.g. in writing), the timescale for suggestions (e.g. one month from a given date), the reward (financial or non-financial), people exempt from the scheme (e.g. company directors) and what happens if the scheme is misused (e.g. malicious or vexatious suggestions).

Employee opinion surveys are an excellent method of collecting feedback from employees about what they perceive to be important issues, and what aspects of the workplace positively and negatively affect their levels of commitment and engagement. These surveys need to be constructed with care and attention, addressing appropriate issues. Also, employees need to be sure that their feedback is taken seriously and the results of the survey lead to action being taken, otherwise the system of obtaining employee feedback will cease to be taken seriously by the employees. Another important aspect of employee opinion surveys is to ascertain what motivates employees as not everyone is motivated by the same things (Gratton, 2007). Thus, employee feedback can enable management to tailor their EI practices to the needs of different groups of employees.

Works committees to promote information and consultation involve meetings of management and employee representatives who may be elected directly or nominated through the trade unions. Their terms of reference can be tailored to the requirements of the organisation concerned, and may vary widely from one organisation to another. The Advisory, Conciliation and Arbitration Service, in its work with companies, very often establishes joint working committees to solve a variety of problems. In some organisations, works councils have been established on a voluntary basis, but the Information and Consultation of Employees (ICE) Regulations now also provides a framework for the constitution and remit of such councils. You will find information about health and safety committees in Chapter 10.

All of the methods in this category of EI practices involve upward communication, an opportunity for employees to put forward their point of view and ideas and for these to be heard. We have already noted that this relates to *employee voice*, an important concept in modern employment relations. Several commentators emphasise the crucial nature of employee voice in achieving successful employee involvement, leading to engagement (Purcell, 2006; Incomes Data Services, 2007; MacLeod and Clarke, 2009). The CIPD (2010b), in a research report concerning employee engagement, concluded that employee voice, concerning opportunities for employees to input into decisions affecting themselves and the organisation and to be properly consulted and communicated over workplace issues that affect them, is a key driver of engagement.

Financial participation

A number of share schemes exist to provide employees with financial participation in their organisations, often with tax relief approved by HM Revenue and Customs. The schemes include group or individual bonuses (which are subject to income tax) linked to the company's performance, and ownership of shares.

Various schemes exist in relation to share ownership. In some schemes, shares may be bought by a trust for employees, usually at no direct cost to them, and are later distributed to them. In other schemes employees are given the opportunity to buy shares directly. A variety of arrangements exist regarding the percentage of shares that employees can hold, what happens to the shares when an employee leaves the company and whether the shares are voting or non-voting shares. If ownership of the shares gives employees the right to attend shareholders' meetings and to vote on certain proposals, this is essentially a form of employee participation as it has been defined in this chapter.

The rules, regulations and legislation concerning employee share schemes are complex and constantly changing. Approved share schemes are regulated by HM Revenue and Customs and are subject to restrictions and limitations as contained in the Income Tax (Earnings and Pensions) Act 2003 and the Finance Act 2013. Ashall (2014) lists a number of tax-advantaged employee share schemes. These include Share Incentive Plans (SIPs), Save As You Earn (SAYE) and Company Share Option Plans (CSOPs).

As indicated above, financial participation is certainly recognised as an EI practice but evidence suggests that it is not used as frequently as other methods and its use is declining. The 2004 *Workplace Employment Relations Survey*

Did you know?

People Management (2014) reported on how thousands of staff at BT benefited from participation in the firm's share ownership scheme. Almost 23,000 BT employees received an average of £49,000 each as the five-year scheme matured. Staff who joined the Save As You Earn (SAYE) scheme in 2009 received discounted shares in the firm for 61 pence per share. As the scheme matured each share in BT had risen to 388.5 pence per share. Under the scheme, employees saved between £5 and £225 every month until July 2014. This amounted to almost a third of all BT staff investing £177 million over 5 years, who witnessed the return increase to £1.1 billion.

(*Source*: Lewis, Grace (2014) Thousands of BT staff profit from £1.1 billion share plan, *People Management*, 5 August)

(Kersley *et al.*, 2005) reported that only 21 per cent of workplaces had at least one Employee Share Ownership Scheme (ESOS). The most common scheme was SAYE (operated by 13 per cent of workplaces), followed by SIP (8 per cent of workplaces), CSOP (6 per cent of workplaces) and 'other' (4 per cent of workplaces). As reported in *The 2011 Workplace Employment Relations Study* (van Wanrooy *et al.*, 2013), the percentage of private sector workplaces using share schemes had halved since the 2004 *Workplace Employment Relations Survey*.

Commitment to quality

The human resource management approach and contemporary ideas about employee motivation go hand in hand with an emphasis on the social aspects of work. On the whole, human beings work better in groups, they respond to feedback on their achievements and there are synergies, in terms of improved ideas and methods of working, to be gained from having people work in teams rather than isolated as individuals. All these factors are reflected in the techniques listed above.

The idea that benefits can be gained from the formation of teams and self-managed groups is addressed in the work of Trist and Murray (1993) at the Tavistock Institute. Basically this theory says that organisations must pay attention to the social systems in the workplace as well as the technical systems when designing jobs. ACAS (2005) also addresses the value of teamwork as a means to improve productivity, quality, innovation, motivation and commitment.

Total quality management (TQM) has been defined as 'the mutual co-operation of everyone in an organization and associated business processes to produce value-for-money products and services which meet and hopefully exceed the needs and expectations of customers' (Dale *et al.*, 2013, p. 30). TQM emphasises the responsibility of each individual for ensuring the quality of their work and de-emphasises the role of supervisors or managers in inspection. This places responsibility firmly with each individual employee. If this is combined with employee award schemes it increases an individual's awareness of the contribution they make to the organisation and of the extent to which this is valued.

The term 'quality circles' is linked with an approach to quality adopted by Japanese companies but the method itself stems from the work and thinking of Dr W. Edwards Deming. Essentially, quality circles involve a group of people, usually from one work area, meeting to solve problems using a systematic method and application of a standard set of tools (Li and Doolen, 2014). The group analyses data and sets up proposals which are presented to senior managers who consider the new ideas and report back to the quality circle, either accepting the proposal or providing explanations for why it is rejected. As this requires a higher level of analytical skill than the employees may need for their jobs, quality circles often have a facilitator who provides assistance in the presentational aspects but does not usually contribute ideas as far as content is concerned.

'Continuous improvement' is an umbrella term for any programme focusing on identifying and solving problems or exploring opportunities to improve organisational performance. These programmes often focus on an improved response to customer needs or reducing the number of errors, which can be targeted by a combination of initiatives such as teamwork, total quality management and problem-solving groups. Continuous improvement can be both incremental, involving relatively small changes, or breakthrough, involving large and rapid improvement (Bhat, 2010).

Providing an employee with an award through a recognition scheme, such as a non-cash gift or an accolade, such as employee of the month, can play an important role in employee motivation and engagement (CIPD, 2010a). Daniels (2014) comments that an employee-of-the-month scheme should be reviewed by HR annually, making alterations to ensure that it continues to be an effective motivational tool for employees.

Developing the individual

All the employee involvement techniques that we have discussed contribute to the development of employees. Better communication means that people are well informed; encouragement to share ideas through consultation means that employees are more likely to develop ideas rather than accept the status quo; and financial participation increases awareness and knowledge of the firm's economic performance. Employee development further extends the boundaries of knowledge, interest and understanding and enables each employee to feel more involved and more able to participate in decisions. Chapters 8 and 9 explore in detail all the practices mentioned above and the contribution that these practices make to the organisation.

Health and wellbeing

Silcox (2014) states that there is a strong business case for investing in employee wellbeing as poor employee wellbeing leads to increased absence, higher costs and reduced job performance.

The CIPD (2013) factsheet on health and wellbeing at work states that employers who invest in the health and wellbeing of their staff will benefit from enhanced employee engagement, resulting in lower levels of absenteeism and lower turnover rates. ACAS (2012) states that there are six indicators of a healthy workplace:

1. Line managers are confident are and trained in people skills.
2. Employees feel valued and involved in the organisation.
3. Managers use appropriate health services to deal with absence and get employees back on track.
4. Managers promote an attendance culture by having return-to-work discussions with employees.
5. Jobs are well-designed and flexible.
6. Managers know how to manage common health problems.

Chapter 10 provides a more in-depth discussion of health and wellbeing issues.

Beyond the workplace

Attempts to make employees feel more committed to the organisation should not be limited to activities at work. We have stated in other chapters, for instance with regard to human resource planning, that employers need to be aware of the

Did you know?

HSBC has, since the 1980s, supported the charity 'Young Enterprise'. The bank provides volunteers (who mentor students, offering advice, skills and experience), training for teachers and volunteers involved and business advisors who help young people successfully run a business. The programme is aimed at people aged 15–19. In addition to benefiting younger people by developing their business acumen, it also helps HSBC employees develop their personal skills including communication, negotiation, mentoring and influencing.

(*Source*: www.young-enterprise.org.uk; accessed 18.01.15)

community within which they operate, and this could mean the global community as well as the local community. A number of employers have empowered their staff to become involved in community initiatives, such as working with schools, environmental organisations or underprivileged groups. This has the effect of increasing the loyalty of employees and strengthening the organisation's public image.

These initiatives can be part of an organisation's strategy regarding corporate social responsibility (CSR), defined by Johnson *et al.* (2014, p. 127) as the 'commitment of organisations to behave ethically and contribute to economic development while improving the quality of life of the workforce and their families as well as the local community and society at large'. An example of a firm with a well-respected CSR strategy is Deutsche Post DHL, the global supply chain firm, which has a number of initiatives. These include 'Go Green' (protecting the environment), 'Go help' (delivering help), 'Go Teach' (championing education) and the 'Global Volunteer Day' (encouraging employees to volunteer). The key objectives, key performance indicators (KPIs) and results of responsibility initiatives are outlined in the firm's annual Corporate Responsibility Report (**www.dpdhl.com**).

Additional influences

In addition to the practices described above, the CIPD (2014c) comments on the importance of providing flexible work patterns for employees, and state that employees who are able to access flexible work arrangements have a positive attitude towards the psychological contract. Richman *et al.* (2008) also provide research evidence that flexible working practices can contribute to enhanced engagement and retention. The CIPD (2010a) takes a broader look at the impact of reward systems on the employer brand and how this can affect employee commitment and engagement. The concept of total reward addresses issues such as pay, incentives, bonuses and benefits in addition to the forms of recognition, development and financial participation we have discussed in this chapter. Flexible working arrangements and work–life balance are addressed in more detail in the next chapter, and you can read more about total reward in Chapter 9.

Commitment

As discussed previously, the reason for pursuing a programme of employee involvement is the expectation that there will be improvements in productivity levels leading to a high-performance workplace. By informing and consulting with employees and using other techniques to make them feel more involved in the workplace, workers will feel empowered to add more value to their organisations. An important concept in terms of the expected motivational improvements of EI is employee commitment. The direct effect of involvement in the organisation is expected to be an increase in the individual employee's commitment to colleagues, the workplace or the job, resulting in increased productivity, lower labour turnover and reduced absenteeism.

The human resource management approach aims to maximise the contribution of employees to the organisation and increasing employee commitment through involvement is seen as a way of doing this. There is, however, some debate about whether involvement arrangements result in increased commitment. Commitment is an attitude, and the relationship between attitudes and behaviour is not a straightforward one. Behaviour depends on a variety of influencing factors. These include values and beliefs and what each individual sees as motivating factors, so attitudes are not always reflected in behaviour. For example, if a person has a positive emotional reaction to a management initiative, we could say that that person may feel greater commitment to the job or the organisation. If, however, that employee is influenced by colleagues who do not share these opinions, and the person values his or her relationship with those colleagues, then the positive attitude may not be reflected in subsequent behaviour. EI practices could therefore engender a positive attitude in some people but not in others. Even where it does result in positive attitudes, it is only one feature of the workplace and other influences could result in this positive attitude not being reflected in the behaviour managers seek to influence.

In recent years there has been considerable interest in commitment among academic researchers, including Wright and Kehoe (2008), Elias (2009), Conway and Monks (2009) and Juhdi *et al.* (2013). Wright and Kehoe provide a good overview of recent research examining types of commitment and their links with HR practices and productivity whilst Elias examines the interplay between change and organisational commitment. Conway and Monks focus on the point we have made that an individual employee may react in different ways to particular HR practices. Juhdi *et al.* examine the mediating effects of organisational commitment and organisational engagement on the relationship between human resource practices (career management, performance appraisal, compensation, person–job fit and job control) and turnover intention, focusing on a selected region of Malaysia.

In general the introduction of EI initiatives is welcomed by the workforce and results in a positive response. However, increases in commitment and productivity are not a foregone conclusion. Some reactions will depend on the culture of the organisation and relations that have traditionally existed either in the organisation or in a particular industry. If employees do not trust management, they will react to management initiatives with scepticism. If employers wish to encourage change in these circumstances, they will have to build trust, which can only be achieved in the long term.

Engagement

Employee engagement is recognised as being the stage beyond commitment. The CIPD (2014d) comments that employee engagement is a combination of commitment to the organisation and to the organisation's values, and a willingness to help colleagues. Anitha (2014, p. 308) defines employee engagement as 'the level of commitment and involvement an employee has towards their organisation and its values', whereas Purcell (2014, p. 241) states that work engagement relates to 'an individual's psychological state of mind whilst at work'. Employees may feel committed to their workplace and yet may not expend the sought after effort expressed in the well-known HRM phrase 'going the extra mile'. It is when employees go the extra mile that they can be said to be engaged (Coupar, 2007). The Incomes Data Services (2007) uses phrases such as 'passionate about their job' (p. 2) and a firm's 'ability to ignite enthusiasm' (p. 3) as indicators of engagement. All of the practices we have discussed in relation to participation and involvement can contribute to the creation of commitment. As Woodruffe (2006, p. 9) states: 'Engagement has become something of a vogue word, eclipsing commitment and motivation in the management literature.'

In spite of the long-established pedigree of EI practices and the much talked-about importance of engagement to business, surveys of the level of engagement in the UK report poor results. In recent research by Gallup, as reported by Kirton (2014) in *People Management*, only 17 per cent of employees in the UK described themselves as 'engaged'. The research, based on a survey of 600,000 employees over five years, and an additional study of 32 companies with very high levels of employee engagement, identified seven key issues that lead to disengaged staff: the leaders were not involved or curious; the basics were not in place; the state of the economy was used as an excuse; managers were not trusted or made accountable; the approach to performance management was unclear; there was no clear sense of what enhanced engagement was used for; and the HR department was ineffective.

In the CIPD's (2014h) *Employee Outlook (Autumn)* survey, an Engagement Index was used to measure levels of engagement. The Index comprised seven factors: going the extra mile; alignment to organisation purpose; work–life balance; relationship with colleagues; satisfaction with the job role; attitude to senior managers; and satisfaction with the line manager/advocacy. The Autumn 2014 survey reported an Engagement Index of 38 per cent, a growth of 3 per cent since the Spring 2014 (CIPD, 2014e) survey.

The fact that, depending on which survey results we analyse, more that 50 per cent of employees are not engaged (the figure could be considerably higher) leads to the question: why are EI practices not more effective? The current focus of debate revolves around the question about what the crucial elements are that drive employees from commitment to engagement. Observers of employment relations repeatedly emphasise the prime importance of communication and leadership, and the CIPD (2014d) confirms this view by identifying effective communication by leadership as important in keeping employees well informed and reinforcing the organisation's purpose. We have already established that various forms of communication, and in particular employee voice, are essential components of EI. Beyond actually communicating, organisations need to demonstrate that they are fully committed to the processes involved and provide evidence that employee voice is being taken seriously.

Managers may make choices about the extent to which they wish to subscribe to and encourage EI practices and this will have an impact on the effectiveness of EI programmes within an organisation. Among a number of writers on EI, Marchington and Cox (2007) emphasise the importance of line managers in creating engagement. They also allude to 'informal EIP' (p. 189) and link this with management style. Other commentators also draw attention to the importance of adopting an appropriate management style to encourage involvement, commitment and engagement (Earls, 2007), and to the need to ensure that managers have the appropriate skills to be able to provide leadership in this area (Gratton, 2007). Alfes *et al.* (2010) conclude that close attention must therefore be paid to the recruitment, selection, development and performance management of line managers to ensure that they maximise their potential to become engaging leaders. Leadership is a key antecedent of employee engagement (Xu and Thomas, 2011). Without effective leadership, employee engagement is likely to suffer.

Conclusion

We have discussed a range of management approaches to the workforce in this chapter and the implications that different philosophies have for employee participation in decision making. The development of employee involvement initiatives, partnership deals and a focus on engagement are likely to be found in organisations that embrace the tenets of human resource management. Through the use of involvement and partnership practices, these organisations will attempt to maximise their employees' contribution to the achievement of organisational goals whilst adding value through high-performance working.

Review questions

You will find brief answers to these review questions on page 462–3.

1. Describe the two main philosophical approaches underlying management–employee relations and comment on how these approaches affect employee involvement initiatives.
2. Explain the relationship between employee involvement, employee commitment, engagement and high-performance working.
3. Describe the principal employee involvement categories and practices.
4. What can an organisation do to ensure that its workers are fully engaged?

Improving your employability

Based on your work or study experience, identify and assess situations where you were fully engaged and committed and situations where you were not engaged or committed. If, in a job interview, you were asked to give examples of how commitment has affected your work or study, how would you respond? In addition, think about how you might answer the question 'How would you motivate employees in difficult times, for example when a lot of redundancies are taking place?' Another question to ponder is 'How would you motivate a team?' Recently, you were part of a team for an assignment and it really didn't work out. Some people did a lot of work whilst others did very little. Being engaged and committed yourself is one thing but how would you ensure that your team is engaged and committed?

HR in the news

The volunteer spirit that binds a team more than cash

By Andrew Hill

If you have room left in your 2015 diary, then volunteer. If you feel overwhelmed by work – the main reason UK citizens claim they cannot devote time to a good cause – then volunteer. It will teach you something you can use to improve as a manager and as an employee.

It sounds counter-intuitive. Some groups run by volunteers are, frankly, a mess. Everyone knows of an amateur sports team held back by disorganised amateur coaches; a choral society torn apart by discord over what to sing and who should sing it; or a local charity bogged down by endless debate about its terms of reference.

Poor stewardship hurts the people non-profit organisations help. It is also bound to depress their many supporters. In the US, Canada and New Zealand, more than 40 per cent of people devote time to volunteering every month. Those are the highest ranking developed countries in the latest World Giving Index. In the UK nearly one in three volunteer regularly, still an impressive commitment.

Improving how charities and voluntary groups are managed is therefore critical. Peter Drucker was, as often, ahead of his time in spotting why. He wrote in a 1990 handbook for the sector that non-profits, from Girl Scouts to Bible circles, "know they need management so they can concentrate on their mission". Rick Wartzman, of the Drucker Institute, says the management writer realised "non-profits are as important for their volunteers, in giving them a sense of purpose

and citizenship, as for the people they serve". As a result of such insights, most big charities are now run more like businesses, drawing on the advice of corporate donors and board members.

At the same time, companies themselves now know, and often crow about, how their staff contribute to the community. They are finding ways in which staff can reap benefits from involvement in corporate giving campaigns. Ever since I heard a junior banker complain that his boss had threatened his team that their bonuses would be in danger if they did not take part in a charity "fun run", I have worried about the coercion implicit in such initiatives. But no matter, they are usually well-intentioned.

But as Justin Davis Smith of the UK's National Council for Voluntary Organisations wrote last year, charities "hear very little about reciprocal learning – what we in the sector can teach businesses". My own experience helping a school, a university and a charity suggests managers could benefit just by trying to work out why unpaid helpers keep turning up.

Shared purpose is one answer. Purpose is already a perilously overused buzzword in modern business, but it is built into the way every voluntary organisation operates. Peter Tihanyi, a consultant who had a long career in the area, asked volunteers in the 1990s why they came and stayed. The reply: "Because they enjoy the work, because they feel valued, and because they want to serve the [beneficiary] population."

Of course, unlike volunteers, many people work because they have to, and have little choice about what they do. But managers should still strive to achieve Mr Tihanyi's treble: merely by trying, they would increase the chance of developing a happy team. Their staff would, in turn – as good volunteers do – almost certainly attract similarly dedicated new recruits. Volunteers tend to melt away if they are fed up or bored; paid workers are contractually obliged not to play truant. But a business leader whose team is physically present but mentally elsewhere is in a worse position than a charity head who can fill a gap with other well-motivated volunteers.

As for the main difference between employees and volunteers – pay – many companies already rely on staff goodwill at critical moments. Monetary incentives, beyond the requirement to offer a fair salary, are of limited use in keeping staff keen. Bonuses may even reduce the quality of work done. Softer motivational tools are underused.

The NCVO's Mr Davis Smith called on companies to commission voluntary groups to teach them how to develop "a psychological contract in place of the 'cash nexus'" and nurture engagement.

It is a great idea. But as a manager, you could simply start by asking yourself this: what would you do to persuade your staff to come to work if you could no longer pay them? If you know the answer, why are you not already doing it? If you do not, then volunteer. You may well find out.

Questions

1. How might volunteering help the employer and the employee?
2. Why do people volunteer for non-profit-making organisations and what can these organisations do to ensure their volunteers are engaged?
3. Imagine that, as an employer, you were no longer able to pay your staff. How would you motivate them?
4. What volunteering have you done and why did you volunteer? If you haven't volunteered for anything, why haven't you?

What next?

Much has been written about high-performance working systems, what these systems may include (for example job security, employee involvement, performance-related pay, performance appraisals, recruitment, training and development) and how management incorporates such systems into their HR practices, but what do employees think of such systems? This is an issue addressed by Hyde *et al.* (2013) in their study of National Health Service (NHS) employee perspectives on how high-performance HR practices contribute to their performance. In total, 11 high-performance HR practices and four reactions to a range of HR practices (personal gain, organisational gain, both gain and no one gains) were identified. The authors found that employees react differently to HR practices. Some practices were viewed as being beneficial to employees, the organisation or both, whilst other practices were considered meaningless and contributed little to employee performance. The authors further established that employees bundle groups of HR practices into three 'mental models' (for understanding how performance is organised and delivered): professional development, high-quality team work and personal expectations. As the NHS undergoes further structural change, understanding what employees think of high-performance HR practices is important in moving this huge and important organisation forward.

References

Advisory, Conciliation and Arbitration Service (1997) *Annual Report*, ACAS, London.

Advisory, Conciliation and Arbitration Service (2005) *Teamwork: Success through People*, ACAS (available at www.acas.org.uk; accessed 16.01.15).

Advisory, Conciliation and Arbitration Service (2009a) Employee engagement: is it still relevant in a recession? *Employment Relations Matters*, Vol. 13, Winter, 5–7 (www.acas.org.uk accessed 24.03.10).

Advisory, Conciliation and Arbitration Service (2009b) *Representation at Work*, ACAS (available at www.acas.org.uk; accessed 30.07.10).

Advisory, Conciliation and Arbitration Service (2012) *Health, Work and Wellbeing*, ACAS (available at www.acas.org.uk; accessed 18.01.15).

Advisory, Conciliation and Arbitration Service (2014a) *Employee Communications and Consultation Booklet*, ACAS (available at www.acas.org.uk; accessed 16.01.15).

Advisory, Conciliation and Arbitration Service (2014b) *Information and Consultation of Employees: ICE*, ACAS (available at www.acas.org.uk; accessed 14.01.15).

Alfes, K., C. Truss, E. Soane, C. Rees and M. Gatenby (2010) *Creating an Engaged Workforce: Research Report*, CIPD, London.

Allen, M. (1998) All-inclusive, *People Management*, 11 June, 36–42.

Anitha, J. (2014) Determinants of employee engagement and their impact on employee performance, *The International Journal of Productivity and Performance Management*, Vol. 63, No. 3, 308–323.

Ashall, V. (2014) *Basic Pay and Benefits* (available at www.xperthr.co.uk; accessed 16.01.16).

Beardwell, I. (1998) Voices on, *People Management*, 28 May, 32–36.

Bhat, K. (2010) *Total Quality Management*, Himalaya Publishing House, Mumbai.

Chartered Institute of Personnel and Development (2009) *European Works Councils*, CIPD (factsheet available at www.cipd.co.uk; accessed 06.07.10).

Chartered Institute of Personnel and Development (2010a) *Employer Branding and Total Reward. Research Report March 2010*, CIPD, London.

Chartered Institute of Personnel and Development (2010b) *Creating an Engaged Workforce. Research Report*, January, CIPD.

Chartered Institute of Personnel and Development (2013) *Health and Well-being at Work*, CIPD (factsheet available at www.cipd.co.uk; accessed 18.01.15).

Chartered Institute of Personnel and Development (2014a) *Sustainable Organisation Performance*, CIPD (factsheet available at www.cipd.co.uk; accessed 11.01.15).

Chartered Institute of Personnel and Development (2014b) *Employee Communication*, CIPD (factsheet available at www.cipd.co.uk; accessed 16.01.15).

Chartered Institute of Personnel and Development (2014c) *Flexible Working*, CIPD (factsheet available at www.cipd.co.uk; accessed 18.01.15).

Chartered Institute of Personnel and Development (2014d) *Employee Engagement*, CIPD (factsheet available at www.cipd.co.uk; accessed 18.01.15).

Chartered Institute of Personnel and Development (2014e) *Labour Market Outlook. Quarterly Survey Report*, Spring 2014, CIPD, London.

Chartered Institute of Personnel and Development (2014f) *Labour Market Outlook. Quarterly Survey Report*, Autumn 2014, CIPD, London.

Chartered Institute of Personnel and Development (2014g) *Labour Market Outlook. Quarterly Survey Report*, Summer 2014, CIPD, London.

Chartered Institute of Personnel and Development (2014h) *Employee Outlook. Quarterly Survey Report*, Autumn 2014, CIPD (available at www.cipd.co.uk; accessed 18.01.15).

Conway, E. and K. Monks (2009) Unravelling the complexities of high commitment: an employee-level analysis, *Human Resource Management Journal*, Vol. 19, No. 2, 140–158.

Coupar, W. (2007) Employee involvement and high performance, in *High Performance Working*, Involvement and Participation Association, London.

Coupar, W. and B. Stevens (1998) Towards a new model of industrial partnership: beyond the 'HRM versus industrial relations' argument, in P. Sparrow and M. Marchington (eds), *Human Resource Management: The New Agenda*, Financial Times Pitman, London.

Dale, B., van der Wiele, T. and van Iwaarden, J. (2013) *Managing Quality*. Wiley-Blackwell, Hoboken.

Daniels, K. (2014) *Employee of the Month Policy* (available at www.xperthr.co.uk; accessed 18.01.15).

Department for Business, Innovation and Skills (2012) *The European Works Council Directive – Guidance* (available at www.gov.uk, accessed 14.01.15).

Department of Employment (1994) *The Competitive Edge: Employee Involvement in Britain*, Department of Employment, London.

Earls, J. (2007) Good work: an agenda for trade unions and employers, in *High Performance Working*, Involvement and Participation Association, London.

Edwards, P. (2007) The high performance work system and the small firm, in *High Performance Working*, Involvement and Participation Association, London.

EEF/CIPD (2003) *Maximising Employee Potential and Business Performance: The Role of High Performance Working*, EEF/CIPD, London.

Elias, S.M. (2009) Employee commitment in times of change: assessing the importance of attitudes toward organizational change, *Journal of Management*, Vol. 35, No. 1, February, 37–55.

Fox, A. (1974) *Beyond Contract: Work Power and Trust Relations*, Faber and Faber, London.

Gennard, J. and G. Judge (2005) *Employee Relations*, 4th edition, CIPD, London.

Gratton, L. (2007) *Why Some Companies Buzz with Energy and Others Don't* (MBA podcast available at www.timesonline.co.uk; accessed 13.07.07).

Hackman, J.R. and G.R. Oldham (1980) *Work Redesign*, Addison Wesley, Harlow.

Hall, M., S. Hutchinson, J. Parker, J. Purcell and M. Terry (2008) *Implementing Information and Consultation: Early Experience under the ICE Regulations – Interim Update Report. Employment Relations Occasional Paper*, Department for Business, Enterprise & Regulatory Reform, London.

Herzberg, F., B. Mausner and B. Snyderman (1959) *The Motivation to Work*, Wiley, Hoboken.

Incomes Data Services (2007) Employee engagement, *IDS HR Studies Update 846*, May.

Hyde, P., P. Sparrow, R. Boaden and C. Harris, C. (2013). High performance HRM: NHS employee perspectives, *Journal of Health Organization and Management*, Vol. 27, No. 3, 296–311.

Industrial Relations Services (2004) We're all in this together – partnership at work, *IRS Employment Review 801*, 4 June, 15–17.

Industrial Relations Services (2006a) A two-way process: informing and consulting employees, *IRS Employment Review 859* (available at www.xperthr.co.uk; accessed 20.07.10).

Industrial Relations Services (2006b) Unions in search of a new role in employee engagement, *IRS Employment Review 860* (available at www.xperthr.co.uk; accessed 20.07.10).

Industrial Relations Services (2009) Communicating during reorganisation and redundancy, *IRS Employment Review 922* (available at www.xperthr.co.uk; accessed 16.01.16).

Johnson, G., R. Whittington, D. Angwin, P. Regner, and K. Scholes (2014) *Exploring Strategy: Text and Cases*, Pearson Education Limited, Harlow.

Johnstone, S., P. Ackers and A. Wilkinson (2009) The British partnership phenomenon: a ten year review, *Human Resource Management Journal*, Vol. 19, No. 3, 260–279.

Juhdi, N., F. Pa'wan, and R.M.K. Hansaram (2013). HR practices and turnover intention: the mediating roles of organizational commitment and organizational engagement in a selected region in Malaysia. *The International Journal of Human Resource Manag*ement, Vol. 24, No. 15, 3002–3019.

Keith, P. (2014) *European Works Councils* (available at www.xperthr.co.uk; accessed 14.01.15).

Kersley, B., C. Alpin, J. Forth, A. Bryson, H. Bewley, G. Dix and S. Oxenbridge (2005*) Inside the Workplace: Findings from the 2004 Workplace Employment Relations Survey*, DTI, London.

Kirton, H. (2014) Seven reasons your employees are not engaged, *People Management*, 16 April (available at www.cipd.co.uk; accessed 18.01.15).

Li, J. and T. Doolen (2014) A study of Chinese quality circle effectiveness. *International Journal of Quality and Reliability Management*, Vol. 31, No. 1, 14–31.

Macdonald, L. (2014) *Staff Suggestion Scheme Policy* (available at www.xperthr.co.uk; accessed 16.01.15).

MacLeod, D. and N. Clarke (2009) *Engaging for Success: Enhancing Performance through Employee Engagement: A Report to Government*, Crown Copyright, London.

Marchington, M. (1998) Partnership in context: towards a European model? In P. Sparrow and M. Marchington (eds), *Human Resource Management: The New Agenda*, Financial Times Pitman, Harlow.

Marchington, M. and A. Cox (2007) Employee involvement and participation: structures, processes and outcomes, in J. Storey, *Human Resource Management: A Critical Text*, 3rd edition, Thomson, London.

McGlynn, C. (1995) European Works Councils: towards industrial democracy? *Industrial Law Journal*, Vol. 24, No. 1, March, 78–84.

Mishra, K., L. Boynton, and A. Mishra (2014) Driving employee engagement: the expanded role of internal communications. *International Journal of Business Communication*, Vol. 51, No. 2, 183–202.

Monks, J. (1998) Trade unions, enterprise and the future, in P. Sparrow and M. Marchington (eds), *Human Resource Management: The New Agenda*, Financial Times Pitman, Harlow.

Personnel Today (2005) *Why the Works Council Works* (available at www.personneltoday.com; accessed 14.01.15).

Purcell, J. (2006) Building better organisations, in CIPD, *Change Agenda: Reflections on Employee Engagement*, CIPD, London.

Purcell, J. (2014). Disengaging from engagement, *Human Resource Management Journal*, Vol. 24, No. 3, 241–254.

Richman, A.L., J.T. Civian, L.L. Shannona, E.J. Hill, and R.T. Brennanc (2008) The relationship of perceived flexibility, supportive work-life policies, and use of formal flexible arrangements and occasional flexibility to employee engagement and expected retention, *Community, Work and Family*, Vol. 11, No. 2, May, 183–197.

Rittau, Y. and T. Dundon (2010), the role and functions of shop stewards in workplace partnerships: evidence from the Republic of Ireland, *Employee Relations*, Vol. 32, No. 1, 10–27.

Silcox, S. (2014) *Employee Wellbeing Policy* (available at www.xperthr.co.uk; accessed 18.01.15).

Sisson, K. (2007) Right challenge – wrong conclusion, in *High Performance Working*, Involvement and Participation Association, London.

Smith, A. (2006) 'Partnership' at work? *Work, Employment and Society*, Vol. 20, No. 4, 811–817.

Taylor, F.W. (1911) *The Principles of Scientific Management*, Harper, New York.

Townsend, K., A. Wilkinson and J. Burgess (2014) Routes to partial success: collaborative employment relations and employee engagement, *The International Journal of Human Resource Management*, Vol. 25, No. 6, 915–930.

Trist, E. and H. Murray (eds) (1993) *The Social Engagement of Social Science: A Tavistock Anthology*, Vol. II: The Socio-Technical Perspective, University of Pennsylvania Press, Philadelphia.

Van Wanrooy, B., H. Bewley, A. Bryson, J. Forth, S. Freeth, L. Stokes and S. Wood, S. (2013) *The 2011 Workplace Employment Relations Study. First findings*. ESRC/ACAS/NIESR (available at www.gov.uk; accessed 16.01.15).

Wolff, C. (2008) Survey: employee communications, *IRS Employment Review 903* (available at www.xperthr.co.uk; accessed 19.07.10).

Wolff, C. (2010) Employee communications: the 2010 IRS survey, *IRS Employment Review* (available at www.xperthr.co.uk; accessed 16.01.15).

Woodruffe, C. (2006) From 'Whatever' to 'My pleasure': how can employers increase engagement? in CIPD, *Change Agenda: Reflections on Employee Engagement*, CIPD, London.

Wright, P.M. and R.R. Kehoe (2008) Human resource practices and organizational commitment: a deeper understanding, *Asia Pacific Journal of Human Resources*, Vol. 46, No. 1, 6–20.

www.dpdhl.com. *Communicating Sustainably*; accessed 18.01.15.

www.worker-participation.eu. *European Works Councils*; accessed 14.01.15.

Xu, J. and H. Thomas (2011) How can leaders achieve high employee engagement? *Leadership & Organization Development Journal*, Vol. 32, No. 4, 399–416.

Further study

Books and reports

Advisory, Conciliation and Arbitration Service (2014) *The People Factor - Engage Your Employees for Business Success*, ACAS (available at www.acas.org.uk; accessed 21.01.15).
A practical guide for improving employee engagement in organisations, which is useful to employers, managers, employees and employee representatives.

Bridger, E. (2014) *Employee Engagement*, Kogan Page, London.
A textbook grounded in engagement theory and providing an understanding of psychology combined with practical tools, techniques and diagnostics. The book also contains case studies on British Gas, Capital One, ASDA, Ministry of Justice, Mace and RSA.

Pritchard, K. (2014) *Employee Engagement Surveys. Good Practice Manual*, XpertHR (available at www.xperthr.co.uk; accessed 21.01.15).
This good practice manual will help you construct, implement and interpret an employee engagement survey.

Truss, C., R. Delbridge, K. Alfes, A. Shantz and E. Soane (2014) *Employee Engagement in Theory and Practice*, Routledge, London.
This book provides in-depth psychological and critical HRM perspectives on engagement as well as their practical application.

Articles

Johnstone, S., P. Ackers and A. Wilkinson (2009) The British partnership phenomenon: a ten year review, *Human Resource Management Journal*, Vol. 19, No. 3, 260–279.
Summarises the major points made in the literature on partnership from 1998 to 2008.

Markey, R. and K. Townsend (2013). Contemporary trends in employee involvement and participation, *Journal of Industrial Relations*, Vol. 55, No. 4, 475–487.
Provides a useful overview of the key concepts (involvement, participation, voice) discussed in this chapter.

Nohria, N., B. Groysberg and L.-E. Lee (2008) Employee motivation: a powerful new model, *Harvard Business Review*, July–August, 78–84.
A very readable article which presents an overview of motivation in terms of four drives (to acquire, bond, comprehend and defend), and links these to outcomes such as engagement, commitment and retention. The article offers advice on practical ways to achieve these outcomes, but stresses both that all drives must be addressed simultaneously and that senior and line managers contribute greatly to the potential success of any initiatives.

Park, R., E. Appelbaum and D. Kruse (2010) Employee involvement and group incentives in manufacturing companies: a multi-level analysis, *Human Resource Management Journal*, Vol. 20, No. 3, 227–243.
Park *et al.* examine group incentives and other employee involvement practices separately to discover differences in the effect of these techniques on commitment and turnover intentions. They find that employee involvement is more effective in capital-intensive companies whereas group incentives are more effective in labour-intensive companies.

Internet

Advisory, Conciliation and Arbitration Service   www.acas.org.uk
Provides good practice advice on how to implement the ICE Regulations. Also has a downloadable advisory booklet on employee engagement, communications in the workplace and an e-learning course on informing and consulting.

Chartered Institute of Personnel and Development   www.cipd.co.uk
The CIPD provides information on consultation and information, employee voice and high-performance working. The website also has a number of resources on employee engagement, including factsheets, survey reports, research reports and blogs.

Involvement and Participation Association   www.ipa-involve.com
A good source of information on partnership, employee involvement, high-performance working, information and consultation. Follow IPA on Twitter and you can keep informed about a wide range of employment relations issues.

3

The employment relationship

Objectives

When you have read this chapter you will be able to:

- understand and describe the rights and obligations of the employer and employee to the employment relationship

- understand the basis of the contract of employment and know what should be in a contract of employment

- describe the main employment rights as stated in the law

- examine a variety of flexible working arrangements and assess their usefulness and impact for employers and employees

- understand the issues to be considered when an employee leaves an organisation.

There are many ways of describing the relationship between employers and their employees. To get a picture of what this might entail, think about the relationships that exist between people. These might include personal relationships between friends, partners and relatives as well as the context of employee, for example the relationship between a manager and a subordinate. Any relationship between two parties is formed within a context of rights, expectations and obligations. These rights, expectations and obligations may be individualised for each pair of individuals, as in a marriage or civil partnership, or it may be that a group of people see themselves as one party to a relationship with shared interests that they wish to see represented on a collective basis. Some of these rights, expectations and obligations are unspoken and there is a 'cultural' understanding of the norms relating to these rights, expectations and obligations. Sometimes, negotiation is needed to reach an agreement: for example, in spite of the much heralded concept of the equality of the sexes, the division of labour in the household can still be a contentious area. Beyond what individuals agree among themselves, both implicitly and explicitly, there is a legal framework that imposes obligations and guarantees rights. In addition to cultural norms, customs and practices, relationships are also affected by power: who has more power, who has less power and how power is changing. These influences may be relatively stable for long periods of time, but the twentieth century has witnessed great and rapid change, a phenomenon which will no doubt continue in the twenty-first century.

Pause for thought 3.1	For an organisation with which you are familiar, identify who has more power and who has less power. Why does such a difference in power exist? What are the determinants of power in relationships within this organisation? What changes to power in relationships have occurred in this organisation?

The employment relationship is governed by a complex arrangement of individual and collective agreements, implicit and explicit understandings, and rights and obligations enshrined in legal statutes. It is also affected by other influences such as culture and the balance of power. This chapter will give you an overview of the many threads that weave together to create the canvas of the employment relationship, and will also examine how trends within it can be monitored. In particular, we will examine the legal aspects of the employment relationship, together with some cultural and psychological factors and the concept of flexibility in working arrangements. We will also examine what happens when an employment relationship is terminated.

Rights and obligations of the two parties

Balance of power

The extent to which one party in a relationship has rights and obligations depends, in some measure, on the balance of power between the two parties.

Pause for thought 3.2	Is it possible to create a workforce that shares a common purpose? Where all parties work harmoniously together for the common good of the organisation? Where conflicts do not arise? Where power is shared between its members?

In spite of legislation protecting a range of employee rights, the general feeling in the industrial relations arena in the 1990s was that the balance of power lay with the employer rather than the employee. These sentiments had been reinforced by legislation throughout the 1980s and early 1990s which progressively limited the powers of the trade unions, and by high levels of unemployment and frequent job redundancies which undermined many employees' sense of job security. There were also a large number of redundancies in the early years of the twenty-first century, partly attributed to the global effects of the slowdown in the American economy at that time, and the recession in 2008–2009, which brought further fears of potential redundancies and job losses.

The relationship between employees and managers is affected by trust, openness, willingness to cooperate and amenability to different points of view. Where an imbalance of power exists, these areas of a relationship can suffer or at least they can be difficult to maintain. In an organisational setting, this means that managers will have to find ways of reassuring employees that they will be treated as equal partners in the employment relationship. If managers believe that an employee relationship based on partnership is in fact a contributory factor to the success of their organisation, then managers will attempt to do this of their own volition. We have already explored this belief more fully in our examination of employee involvement and engagement in Chapter 2.

Between 1997 and 2010, the Labour Government produced a programme of employment measures emphasising the development of fairness at work and a partnership approach to the relationship between employer and employee. Some of its original proposals have subsequently been enshrined in the Employment Relations Act 1999 (and other regulations) and include improved regulations on union recognition, enhanced rights to time off work and rights to request serious consideration of flexible working arrangements to support people in combining their family life commitments with work. The Employment Relations Act 1999 is widely seen as one of the most important and wide-ranging pieces of employment legislation for many years.

In May 2010, the Coalition Conservative and Liberal Democrat Government produced a document entitled *The Coalition: Our Programme for Government*. In Section 12 of the document, 'Equalities', there were specific policies relating to the employment relationship. These included: promoting equal pay, ending discrimination in the workplace and extending the right to request flexible working to all employees (Cabinet Office, 2010). It is too early to determine how the new Conservative government will deal with issues concerning the employment relationship but it is likely to continue policies followed by the previous coalition government.

The implementation of EU legislation on consultation and information is also shifting the focus more firmly towards employees' rights. We have discussed some of these issues in Chapter 2 in our detailed discussion of partnership, participation and employee involvement. These developments all strengthened workers' rights. This chapter attempts to construct a fuller picture by addressing more of the elements that combine to create our employment relations climate.

Expectations of the two parties: the psychological contract

The psychological contract has been defined as 'the set of expectations held by the individual employee that specify what the individual and the organisation expect to give to and receive from each other in the course of their work relationship' (Sims, 1994, p. 375). The concept of the psychological contract was introduced in the 1960s but became more popular following the economic downturn in the 1990s (CIPD, 2014a). The concept was attributed initially to Argyris (1960) and further developed by Schein (1978), among others. It concerns the perceptions of the obligations that employees and employer have towards each other.

The psychological contract is different to a legal contract in that much of it will be assumed and unspoken. It represents the reality of work as perceived by both parties and may be more influential than the formal written contract in influencing how people behave in the workplace. The psychological contract includes factors that result in feelings such as loyalty and perceptions of fair treatment, and many intrinsic factors that affect motivation. Much of the debate in the 1990s was about expectations of job security as an element of the psychological contract and the extent to which organisations could or could not continue to offer this. Guest and Conway (1997) refer to the new psychological contract where the focus has changed to employment security or employability rather than job security. This means that employees can no longer expect their employer to guarantee them a job for life but they might instead expect their employer to support their development, making them more employable.

The nature of the psychological contract and the motivation of the individual can be influenced by the organisational culture and its predominant management style, and can be seen as coercive, calculative or cooperative (Handy, 1985). Coercion is where people are motivated to expend effort in order to avoid punishment and is generally regarded as unproductive and inappropriate in today's working environment. A calculative style means that the connection between effort and reward is made explicit, and each employee can calculate the value to themselves of expending extra energy on the organisation's behalf. The cooperative style leads to individuals who identify with the organisation's goals. This type of psychological contract can be found in organisations that espouse the human resource management approach towards maximising the contribution of its employees through the use of practices that involve and engage them.

The cooperative contract implies a more participative style of management and greater employee involvement in decision making. However, people differ in what they perceive as motivating. Managers may also be sometimes disappointed at a lack of response when they try to change from, say, a calculative contract to a cooperative contract but if an organisation is run on participative lines it is likely to engender positive attitudes in new employees, and perseverance with new techniques may help to alter attitudes among existing staff. The emphasis in the late 1990s on fairness at work and partnership between employers and employees tied in well with the concept of a cooperative contract, and the work by Guest and Conway (1997) also highlights the link between a climate of employee involvement and a positive psychological contract.

More recently, the CIPD (2014a) strongly emphasised the importance of trust in the psychological contract. This means clarifying what the employer has to offer, ensuring that commitments are met, explaining what has gone wrong, where necessary, and monitoring employee attitudes on a regular basis. In undertaking these activities managers need to become more effective negotiators and communicators. Whilst a positive psychological contract will support a high level of employee engagement, a negative psychological contract, where expectations are not effectively managed, can cause serious damage to the employment relationship.

Woodruffe (2005) points out that different employees may be motivated by different things, commenting, for example, that graduates are 'the talent pool from which the future senior management of an organisation will be drawn' (p. 8), suggesting that their need for independence will require careful management in order to retain them. The CIPD (2014a) state that while employees in general may be concerned with security, 'many younger people are not interested in the concept of a job for life, being more likely to move between jobs and change careers'.

This brings us to the issues of flexible working practices and work–life balance. Later sections in this chapter examine flexible working arrangements as a contractual matter and the rights of certain groups to request flexible working. There is, however, much managerial judgement involved in deciding whether or not to adopt various patterns of work flexibility and how to manage these patterns. This means that access to flexible working patterns and, therefore, the related outcomes in terms of the work–life balance vary and are part of what constitutes the psychological contract.

The legal framework

Employment law

Employment law is complex and it is beyond the scope of this text to provide a comprehensive discussion of this aspect of law. To help employers understand and keep up to date with legislation on employment issues, a number of professional journals, such as *People Management*, publish regular briefings which help employers to interpret the law, especially in the light of new decisions on tribunal or court cases. XpertHR also produces law reports, legal guidance and legal timetables. Government websites, such as **www.gov.uk**, also provide guidance on various aspects of the law as they relate to employment. Web pages showing FAQs are also often particularly useful and several of these sites are listed at the end of this chapter. We shall be looking at various aspects of employment law in greater detail, but remember that if you are in any doubt about an employee's or worker's rights, it is best to consult a solicitor.

You should also be mindful of the fact that the law usually states the minimum entitlement of an employee, and in most circumstances employers can decide to enhance the legal entitlement with a more generous contractual provision. Enhancing an employee's entitlements may be a way of attracting and retaining 'better' employees, and so may be a consideration in pursuing the corporate strategy, particularly one of innovation or quality enhancement. All employees and workers should familiarise themselves with their contractual provisions, but as a line manager or HR practitioner you are likely to be asked to explain such provisions.

In the UK, employment law is derived from common law and statute and codes and practices of EU law (Scott and Phillips, 2013). Common law is established by judges' decisions rather than by statute and is an important component of the legal framework that delineates the employment relationship. EU law provides employees, workers and certain self-employed workers with employment rights enforceable in the UK courts (Cabrelli, 2012). In particular, membership of the EU has been significant in terms of employment protection in the UK, related to such things as discrimination in employment, paternal leave, paternity and adoption leave (Turner, 2013).

The first question that arises is whether or not a person is regarded in the eyes of the law as being an employee as this has implications for a person's ability to claim the right to the protections provided by statutory employment law. It is not always clear whether a person is an employee although it is certainly a person who works (Nairns, 2008). An employee and a worker are not necessarily the same thing as, in the UK, the latter has a wider meaning (Sargeant and Lewis, 2012). According to GOV.UK, a 'worker' has a contract or other arrangement to work, the reward is money or benefit in kind, they only have a limited right to subcontract the work, they have to turn up for work, even if they don't want to, the employer has to supply work for the duration of the contract and they are not doing the work as part of their own limited company. The same government website defines an 'employee' simply as a person who works under an employment contract.

In a website table (member access only) showing the entitlements of employees and workers, the CIPD (**www.cipd.co.uk**) indicates that both workers and employees are covered by certain pieces of legislation (for example the Working Time Regulations and the National Minimum Wage Act), but that workers would not have all of the statutory rights that can be claimed by those classed as employees (such as unfair dismissal rights, the right to request flexible working arrangements and a right to statutory redundancy pay). People working for an organisation on a temporary basis tend to be those classed as workers unless they are, in fact, self-employed. However, the distinction between 'worker' and 'employee' status can be difficult to identify and ultimately only an employment tribunal can pass a definitive judgement on the status of the person concerned.

Due to the changing world of work, with employers demanding more labour-market flexibility, organisations are increasingly looking to hire people where there is demand, and reduce the size of the workforce where there is less demand. This has led to the use of 'atypical' workers such as casual workers (for example, working on a zero hours contract), agency workers, fixed-term workers, part-time workers and homeworkers (Cabrelli, 2012). It is unlikely that the courts and tribunals will view these workers as employees since there is an absence of any mutuality of obligation or control (Cabrelli, 2012).

As with many legal questions, there are instances where there is no straightforward answer to who is an employee (or worker) and who is an employer, and it is up to the courts to interpret the law and make a decision. There is also a distinction between an employee and a person who is self-employed or an independent contractor. In deciding whether the person is an employee or a self-employed person/independent contractor, the courts and tribunals apply a 'multiple' test addressing, amongst other factors, the following:

- Is the person an integral part of the business or organisation?
- Is the person working for his/her own account?
- Is there an obligation on the part of the enterprise to provide a reasonable amount of work and pay?
- Does the person have control over the work to be done, how it is done, where it is done and how it is done? (Cabrelli, 2012).

HM Revenue and Customs (**www.hmrc.gov.uk**) states that there is no legal definition of employment or self-employment and whether a person is employed or self-employed depends on the terms and conditions of work. In fact, it is possible to be employed and self-employed at the same time! (For example, working for an employer during the day and running your own business in the evening.) According to HM Revenue and Customs (**www.hmrc.gov.uk**, 2014), a self-employed person:

- runs his/her own business and is responsible for the business' success or failure;
- has several customers at the same time;
- can decide when, where and how to do the work;
- is free to hire people to do the work;
- provides the main equipment to do the work.

The European Union (EU) and UK employment law

Member states of the EU are affected by primary and secondary EU legislation. Primary sources of EU law relate to the various treaties creating the EU, the most important being the Treaty on the Functioning of the European Union (TFEU) and the Treaty on European Union (TEU), whilst secondary sources include regulations, directives, recommendations and opinions (Davies, 2013). In relation to employment law, probably the two most important sources of EU legislation are regulations and directives. Regulations ensure uniformity on a point of law throughout the EU, they have general application and they are binding (Kaczorowska, 2013). On the other hand, directives, unless applicable to all EU states, have no general application, are binding but the method of achieving the directive is left to the member state to decide (Kaczorowska, 2013).

Some directives, for example those relating to health and safety or working conditions, can be adopted by qualified majority voting (QMV), which means that they must be enacted by all member states including the minority that voted against them. In relation to Article 153 of the TFEU, which concerns employment and industrial relations, QMV applies to the following matters:

- improvement to the working environment to protect workers' health and safety and consulting with workers
- integration of persons excluded from the labour market
- equality between women and men in relation to labour market opportunities and treatment at work
- combating social exclusion
- modernising social protection systems (**www.eurofound.europa.eu**).

The key EU directives that have affected employment and employment relations in the EU concern discrimination in the workplace (2000/78/EC and 2000/43/EC), the equal treatment of men and women in the workplace (75/117/EC, 76/207/EC and 86/378/EC), fixed and part-time work, including employment contracts (2003/88/EC, 93/104/EC, 2000/34/EC, 1999/70/EC, 97/81/EC, 91/533/EC), maternity rights (92/85/EEC and 89/391/EEC), parental leave (96/34/EEC), social security and pension rights (86/378/EEC, 96/97/EC and 98/49/EC), personal data (95/46/EC), transfer of undertakings (TUPE) (2001/23/EC) and informing and consulting employees (2002/14/EC, 94/45/EC and 98/59/EC). It is not within the scope of this book to discuss these directives but more information regarding EU legislation can be found on the EU's legislation website (europa.eu).

> **Pause for thought 3.3**   How might the further development of 'family friendly' EU employment legislation affect businesses in the EU?

The contract of employment

A contract of employment is a legally binding contract between an employer and an employee. According to the Employment Rights Act (1996), employers are required to give each employee a written statement setting out certain particulars of the employee's terms of service (Sargeant and Lewis, 2012). The employment contract forms the basis of the relationship between the employer and employee and is based on the ordinary law of contract (Nairns, 2008). With some exceptions (such as apprentice-ships and fixed-term contracts), contracts of employment can also be made orally, or may be implied from parties dealing with each other over a period of time (Turner, 2013). In order to avoid any disputes between employer's and employee's reading of responsibilities and duties, it is good practice to set out as many terms as possible in writing. Contracts of employment include implied and expressed terms.

Implied and express terms

As the phrases indicate, an express term is something that is regarded as important enough to be dealt with specifically and agreed on. Some terms may be assumed and are therefore not stated explicitly. For example, it may be stated how much notice an employee is required to give if they wish to terminate the contract of employment, but if it is not explicitly stated the implied term would be whatever is customary in that particular sector, industry or line of work. As far as the amount of notice that an employer should give is concerned, there is a statutory minimum, so if there is no explicit mention of this in the contract, the statutory minimum will be the implied term.

According to the CIPD (2013), examples of implied terms of contract include a duty of mutual trust between employer and employee, the employer's duty to pay wages and provide a safe working environment, the right to receive a national minimum wage, the right to a minimum period of notice and the right to equality of pay. In addition, other aspects of the employment contract may be implied because they are incorporated into collective agreements, part of workforce agree-ments, incorporated into statute, incorporated into contracts by custom over a period of time, needed for business efficacy reasons or because they are so obvious that they do not require stating.

It is usually best for employers to be explicit about any terms they require, for example with regard to travelling. If the job entails an employee working at various geographically dispersed locations, it is advisable to include this requirement as an explicit term in the contract. Even then the enforcement of such contract terms is not without difficulties as you have to be able to demonstrate that the term is justified and it has to be applied in a reasonable manner.

In a case involving a British Council requirement of its employees to work anywhere in the UK on promotion to a certain grade, *Meade-Hill and National Union of Civil and Public Servants* v. *British Council* (7 April 1995), it was held that this could amount to indirect sex discrimination unless the broadly stated requirement could be justified. Such a clause could be seen as indirect discrimination because a higher proportion of women are secondary earners who would find it impossible to move their workplace which involved a change of home (XpertHR, 1995).

Variation of the terms of a contract

An employer is required to give the employee written notification of changes to the terms of an employment contract at the earliest opportunity and no later than one month after the change (Lewis and Sargeant, 2010). An employer needs to treat any changes to the employment contract with care as some changes constitute a funda-mental breach of contract and could be challenged in an employment tribunal.

According to the CIPD (2013), there are three main options for employers who wish to change the terms of an employment contract:

- after consultation with the employee, agree the changes
- make the changes unilaterally
- terminate the employee's contract by notice and offer to re-employ the person on a new contract.

The first option is preferable and a small incentive may be offered to encourage the employee to accept the change. The second option is risky, even where it appears that the employee has accepted the change and continues working. The last option is also risky as the employee may be able to claim unfair dismissal.

A final point to consider in relation to changes to the employment contract relates to redundancies. Many employers have attempted to avoid redundancies by altering the working pattern of employees to cut costs and, thereby, save jobs. Reducing an employee's working hours would constitute a variation of the contract and would normally be to the detriment of employees if they had not requested this change. Both Adams and Stakim (2008) and Doran (2010) point out, however, that such a variation is more likely to be accepted by employees if they are properly consulted and accept that it is an alternative to redundancy.

Some businesses are affected by the Transfer of Undertakings (Protection of Employment) Regulations 2006 (TUPE, 2006). The regulations protect the terms and conditions of employees in cases of a transfer of ownership of a trade or business, and state that dismissal because of the transfer is unfair. The regulations were further amended in 2014. For more details on TUPE see the government's legislation website (**www.legislation.gov.uk**).

We have dealt with certain employee rights in other chapters, so we shall not repeat that information here. You will find a discussion of the equality legislation in Chapter 4, certain aspects of the right to consultation and information in Chapter 2, dismissal and redundancy rights in Chapter 13 and health and safety regulations in Chapter 10. Our discussion here will focus on:

- the statement of particulars of employment;
- notice of termination of employment;
- employee rights to time off work;
- guaranteed payments;
- the written statement of reasons for dismissal;
- maternity and other parental rights;
- the rights of part-time staff;
- working hours;
- protection of employee data.

Written statement of particulars of employment

Employers must provide an employee who has a contract of work for at least one month a written statement of the terms and conditions of employment. This needs to be provided within two months of the commencement of employment. Certain key information needs to be contained in a single document or principal statement with additional information being provided either in the principal statement or in further instalments. The details to be made explicit in the principal document are:

- the names of the parties involved in the contract (i.e. the employer and employee);
- date of commencement of employment;
- date of commencement of period of continuous employment;
- details about remuneration – rate of pay or how it is calculated; frequency of payments (weekly, monthly, etc.);
- hours of work, including information about normal working hours, if these exist;
- location of the workplace, including the employer's address, and an indication if there could be a requirement to work elsewhere;
- job title or a brief job description.

Terms that may be included in instalments include:

- holiday entitlements;
- arrangements about sick pay and sick leave;
- details about any company pension plan;
- entitlement to receive notice of termination of employment and obligation to give notice;
- expected length of temporary employment where there is a fixed-term contract;
- any terms of a collective agreement that affect working conditions;
- where an employee is required to work overseas for more than a month, details regarding period of work, remuneration and benefits;
- information concerning rules, disciplinary decisions, dismissals and grievances.

Did you know?

The Department for Business, Innovation & Skills (BIS) has produced an interactive template to help employers produce a written statement of employment particulars. This meets the current requirements of employment legislation in the UK. The template is available at: www .gov.uk/government/uploads/system/uploads/ attachment_data/file/183185/13–768-written-statement-of-employment-particulars.pdf

(*Source*: Department for Business, Innovation & Skills (2012), accessed 01.09.14)

As was stated previously, employees must be notified in writing of any changes made to the contract of employment. Employment policies and procedures may be contained in a works' handbook. This may be a written document or consist of electronic information made available via the staff intranet. The handbook may identify those elements subject to change and, therefore, may represent a more convenient method of informing employees of changes to work rather than trying to amend written contracts (Marson, 2014).

Termination of employment and notice of termination

There are a number of ways in which a contract of employment is terminated. These include: events outside the control of the parties (called 'frustration' in common law), death of the employer or employee, voluntary resignation, termination by agreement and termination by dismissal (Sargeant and Lewis, 2012). An employment contract should include the period of notice required so that it is clear how much notice each party is required to give to terminate the contract. Employers may have their own schedule of the minimum notice period required of both parties, but the statutory rights of employees as stated in Section 86 of the Employment Rights Act (1996) are shown in Table 3.1.

Table 3.1   The statutory rights of employees regarding period of employment and notice required

Period of employment	Notice required
Less than one month	None
More than one month but less than two years	One week
More than two years but less than twelve years	Maximum of twelve weeks (one week for every year in employment)
More than twelve years	Twelve weeks

(*Source*: Marson, 2014).

Employee rights to time off work

Part VI of the Employment Rights Act (1996) provides for employees to have a right to time off work in various circumstances. This may be unpaid or paid, depending on the circumstances, and includes time off for:

- trade union representative and learning representative duties and training (paid);
- health and safety representative duties and training (paid);
- members of a recognised union to participate in certain activities (unpaid);
- public duties such as acting as a magistrate (unpaid);
- pension scheme trustee duties and training (paid);
- study or training (in organisations employing 250 or more) (unpaid);
- mobilisation for a volunteer reserve (unpaid);
- employees selected for redundancy to look for work or make arrangements for training (paid);
- antenatal care where attendance is recommended by a medical practitioner (paid);
- parental leave for a parent whose child is under 18 years of age (unpaid);
- dependants (unpaid);
- employee representative duties, including EWC (European Works Council) duties (paid);
- companion at disciplinary or grievance hearing (paid).

Did you know?

Many employees have caring responsibilities. But what information does the employer need in order to make a decision regarding time off work for the employee? The employee should inform the employer of the reason for the absence and the duration of leave. The employer needs to establish if the amount of time requested (or actually taken) is reasonable in the circumstances but it is important that employers are not overly demanding in the information they require before granting time-off.

(*Source*: CIPD Employment law FAQ, available at **www.cipd.co.uk**; accessed 01.09.14)

A phrase that is often applied to the entitlement to time off is that it should not be unreasonably refused, and in some circumstances, for example those related to the performance of a public duty, employers are entitled to give consideration to business needs in assessing what a reasonable amount of time off work would be.

The Employment Relations Act 1999 introduced rights to time off which had been addressed in the Labour Government's *Fairness at Work* White Paper (Department for Business, Innovation & Skills 1998): revised maternity rights and rights to paternity leave (both discussed in more detail later in this chapter), and entitlement for all to time off for dependants, that is, unpaid leave in cases of emergency to arrange for care for any person who is dependent on the employee to do so. According to the CIPD (2014d), a dependant is a spouse, parent or child of the employee, or a person living in the household as part of the family. It does not include a lodger or a tenant. It also includes a person who reasonably relies on the employee for assistance to take care of arrangements because the dependant is ill, injured or has been assaulted.

Guaranteed pay

If an employer is unable to provide work to an employee on a normal working day (not including, for example, days on which industrial action takes place), then the employee is entitled to be paid for a 'workless day'. In order to receive payment for a 'workless day', the employee has to have worked continuously for a minimum of one month and the employee must be available on stand-by to meet any reasonable requests to undertake work.

Written statement of reasons for dismissal

According to the CIPD (2014e), at the very least the employer should inform the employee, in writing, of the alleged offence, meet with the employee to discuss the issues and the employee should have the right to appeal against a decision made by the employer.

Maternity and other family support rights

An issue that has grown in importance over the years for government, employers and employees is support for family life. The following sections give an overview of parental and other family support rights as they stand at the time of writing (June 2015), but since this is an area of continuing change, any practitioner responsible for interpreting related rules and policies will need to study this area in more depth and check for the latest updates to regulations.

All pregnant women are entitled to 52 weeks' maternity leave: the first 26 weeks 'Ordinary Maternity Leave' (OML) and the second 26 weeks 'Additional Maternity Leave' (AML). A woman cannot start maternity leave earlier than the eleventh week of the Expected Week of Childbirth (EWC), unless the baby is born before the eleventh week, and maternity leave cannot commence after the birth of the baby. As long as these conditions have been met, the woman is free to choose when she wishes to take maternity leave. She may, for example, choose to take 10 weeks' leave before the birth of the baby and the remainder after.

Women who have been on maternity leave are entitled to return to work at the end of this leave period. The Department for Business, Innovation & Skills (2010) booklet *Pregnancy and Work*, written for employees, explains that women have the right to return to the same job after ordinary maternity leave on the same pay and conditions as they would have received if they had been at work during that period. However, if the employer cannot give her the same job for good reasons, then the employee must be given a suitable job at the same level without any detriment with regard to terms and conditions.

Keeping in touch days

Employees can work up to 10 days during maternity, adoption or additional paternity leave. These days are termed 'keeping in touch days'. They are optional and both parties need to agree to them. The type of work needs to be agreed before the employee comes into work and the employee's terms and conditions are protected. The purpose of these days might be for training, attending conferences, attending team meetings or to do a day's work.

Maternity pay and conditions

During maternity leave, both ordinary and additional, an employee continues to benefit from all the terms and conditions of her contract with the exception of remuneration. This means, for example, that she continues to accrue holiday entitlement and the maternity leave period counts as continuous service.

All qualifying pregnant employees are entitled to statutory maternity pay (SMP), although many employers choose to offer contractual maternity pay (CMP) which may override SMP, as long as CMP benefits are more beneficial than the statutory ones. SMP is payable for 39 weeks with the first 6 weeks being paid at 90 per cent of the average weekly earnings and the remainder at £138.18 per week (from 6 April 2014). To obtain SMP, an employee must have worked for their employer for at least 26 weeks in continuous service by the qualifying week (i.e. the 15th week before the week of expected childbirth) and be paid at least the Lower Earnings Limit for National Insurance contributions. From 5 April 2015, shared parental leave (SPL) will be available. Pregnant employees who do not qualify for SMP may be eligible for the maternity allowance paid by Jobcentre Plus.

An XpertHR (2014) survey on maternity pay and leave established that 54.5 per cent of businesses offer enhanced maternity pay (going beyond statutory requirements), including such practices as offering a lump sum to return to work and payment for keeping in touch. The survey also revealed that enhanced maternity pay is almost universal in the public sector but much less common in the private sector (offered by 54.3 per cent of businesses).

Paternity leave and pay

This is available for the father of a child or a person who has the responsibility for raising a child. It is also available for those who are adopting a child. In order to qualify for paternity leave and pay, ACAS (2014a) states that the employee has to satisfy a number of criteria:

- they will be responsible for the child's upbringing
- they are the child's biological father or the mother's husband or partner, including same-sex partners
- they have worked continuously for their employer for 26 weeks
- they give the correct notice.

The period within which ordinary statutory paternity pay must occur for a birth child is 56 days after the child's birth date. For an adopted child, the period within which ordinary statutory paternity pay must occur is 56 days after the child's placement for adoption. Additional statutory paternity pay is available for fathers and partners of mothers who are eligible and who wish to take 2 to 26 weeks' additional paternity leave. In September 2014, the weekly rate of ordinary statutory paternity pay was £138.18 or 90 per cent of the normal weekly earnings where the figure is less than £138.18. In September 2014, the daily rate of additional statutory paternity pay was £19.74.

A number of enhancements in maternity and other parental rights have come into effect in the last 15 years. Major pieces of legislation include the Maternity and Parental Leave etc. Regulations 1999 and the Work and Families Act 2006, which brought in key changes with regard to rights connected with maternity, paternity and some other family relationships. The rights we describe apply to same-sex relationships and to adoptive parents. New arrangements for shared parental leave came into force at the end of 2014 (The Children and Families Act 2014). This act gives greater protection to vulnerable children, provides better support for children whose parents are separating, better help for children with special educational needs and disabilities, more help for parents in balancing work and parental duties and changes to the adoption system.

Parental leave

The UK government's web portal, GOV.UK, sets out conditions for parental leave. The employee can take unpaid leave to look after a child, visit new schools, arrange childcare and spend more time with family. The child must be under 5 years of age (or under 18 in special circumstances) and a parent can claim a maximum of four weeks in a year. In order to qualify for parental leave, the employee must have been an employee with the company or organisation for at least a year, they are named on the child's birth or adoption certificate, they are not self-employed and they are not a foster parent. Employees must give at least 21 days' notice, confirming start and end dates.

Right to request flexible working arrangements

According to the CIPD (2014f), flexible working relates to an organisation's arrangements in terms of working hours, place of work and pattern of work. There are many forms of flexible working practices including part-time work, term-time work, flexitime, job-sharing, compressed hours, annual hours, working from home, mobile working, teleworking, career breaks and zero hours contracts (CIPD, 2014f).

The rights and obligations of employers and employees concerning flexible working were introduced in Section 47 of the Employment Act 2002, supplemented by the Flexible Working (Procedural Requirements) Regulations 2002 and the Flexible Working (Eligibility, Complaints and Remedies) Regulations 2002. More recently, the right to request flexible working has been extended to all employees under the Children and Families Act 2014.

Employers have a legal duty to consider flexible working for employees with at least 26 weeks of service and must deal with such requests in a 'reasonable manner', providing a decision within three months and giving acceptable reasons for refusal. If an employee wishes to request flexible working, they need to do this in writing stating that the request relates to statutory procedure, the specific change of work and when the change comes into effect, the effect of the change on the employer and how this might be dealt with and if a previous application for flexible working has been made by the employee to the employer. The application then needs to be dated and submitted.

ACAS (2014c) has produced a useful guide for handling, in a reasonable manner, requests for flexible working. According to the guide, once a request has been received, a talk should be arranged with the employee as soon as possible, unless the intention is to approve the request, in which case such a talk is not necessary. The employee should be allowed to be accompanied by a work colleague and the request discussed. The employer needs to consider the request, weighing up the pros and cons, but must not discriminate unlawfully against the employee. Decisions should be made in writing and may take one of three forms: accepting the request without changes, accepting the request with modifications or rejecting the request. You may only reject an application because of a reason or reasons set out in the legislation. These include:

- the burden of additional costs on the business;
- an inability to reorganise work amongst existing staff;
- an inability to recruit additional staff;
- a detrimental impact on quality and performance;
- a detrimental effect on the ability to meet customer demand;
- insufficient work for the periods the employee proposes to work;
- a planned structural change to your business.

Activity 3.1

It has come to light that one of your managers is not enthusiastic about flexible working. He has made his opinion clear that only full-time employees provide the necessary level of commitment and requests for flexible working should be turned down. How would you convince the manager that flexible working is a good idea and legislation requires the firm to deal with requests in a 'reasonable manner'?

Part-time employees

Traditionally, the treatment accorded to part-time employees in the UK was inferior to that given to full-time employees. However, as employers came to rely more on employees being flexible, and the benefits of employing people on non-standard contracts, they also had to recognise the necessity of addressing the needs of part-time employees and treating them fairly. The Part-time Workers (Prevention of Less Favourable Treatment) Regulations 2000 states that part-time workers should not be treated less favourably than full-time workers unless the employer can justify the less favourable treatment on objective grounds. The meaning of 'part-time' corresponds to the customs and practices for full-time work in the organisation. Thus, if the norm is for full-time employees to work 40 hours per week, a 24 hour contract would constitute part-time work.

Employers must pay part-time workers the same basic hourly rate as full-time employees, unless the difference in pay can be objectively justified. However, part-time employees do not have the same legal rights to overtime premium payments as full-time employees. For example, if the full-time employee typically works

40 hours per week then the employee who works 24 hours per week would not be eligible for overtime premium payments unless they have worked at least 40 hours per week. Where redundancy is concerned, employers must not select part-time workers ahead of full-time workers unless there is an objective reason for doing so. In relation to pay, both full and part-time employees are covered by the Working Time Regulations 1998 which states that workers have the legal right to 5.6 weeks' annual paid holiday.

The rights of part-time staff in the EU are enshrined in Council Directive 97/81/ EC. EU law protects part-time workers with respect to pay, benefits, pensions and working conditions. Discrimination against part-time workers refers to the unfair treatment of these workers with respect to the treatment of full-time workers, unless the different treatment can be objectively justified. In view of the predominantly female composition of part-time employment in the EU, the EU's agreements on the protection of part-time workers cannot contravene EU legislation on sex discrimination, including treaties, directives and case law.

Working time

The Working Time Regulations (1998) implemented the European Working Time Directive into UK law. The regulations state that a worker's working time, including overtime, shall not exceed an average of 48 hours for each seven days averaged over a period of 17 weeks. Other rights afforded by the Working Time Regulations (CIPD, 2014c) include a right to:

- a limit of an average of 8 hours work in a 24-hour period;
- 11 hours of rest per day;
- a day off each week;
- an in-work rest break where the working day is more than 6 hours;
- 28 days paid leave for full-time workers per year.

There are provisions in the regulations for employers to reach an agreement with employees to work longer hours. These regulations were amended in August 2003 to include workers in the transport sector, such as those working on the roads, railways and waterways. According to Lamont (2014), workers should not be put under pressure to opt out of the Working Time Regulations and those who do not agree to opt out should not be placed at a disadvantage. This opt-out provision has been the subject of much debate, with opposition for the opt-out in the UK stronger amongst trade unions and support stronger amongst the business sector. The Working Time Regulations have been subject to review by the European Commission, with social partners being involved in the negotiation. However, as workers' and employers' organisations were unable to reach an agreement, the Commission itself is currently undertaking a detailed review of the regulations (Hogg, 2014).

Activity 3.2

Consult a number of sources on EU employment law (such as XpertHR, europa.eu and employment law textbooks). What recent developments to the Working Time Regulations have taken place?

Did you know?

If employees are normally required to work on a bank and public holiday, the employer may receive a number requests for time off on those days. These requests may be from employees who want to be off work at the same time as family and friends, or who have children who will be on holiday.

Employers will have to deal with holiday requests in a fair and consistent manner as they could be vulnerable to claims of discrimination or that they have acted unfairly. Therefore, they should determine how they will deal with competing requests for leave and should ensure that their policies and procedures on this matter are clear.

Criteria for dealing with holiday requests should be fair and objective. For example, if four out of ten people are required to work on Christmas Day one year, then an objective criterion would be to give priority for time off to workers who worked on Christmas Day the previous year.

(*Source:* Shaw and Silkin, 2014)

Annual leave

Until the introduction of the Working Time Regulations (WTR), there was no legal obligation for employers to provide paid annual leave for their employees, other than statutory holidays. Of course, the majority of employers did provide paid leave, and annual leave has often been part of collective bargaining agreements between employers and trade unions. Many employers will provide more than the basic entitlement provided by the WTR, but under Regulation 13A of the Working Time (Amendment) Regulations 2007, workers have the legal right to a minimum of 5.6 weeks' paid annual leave.

Derogations and subsequent amendments

There were some groups of workers who were not originally covered by these regulations, including workers involved in transport, junior hospital doctors and people who have autonomous decision-making powers, such as senior managers. These exemptions arose where the nature or location of the work made the regulations unfeasible, such as oil rig workers, or people whose working hours are not usually measured, such as executive directors. The CIPD website law pages (**www.cipd.co.uk**; accessed 24.10.14; available to CIPD members only) point out that excluded groups are progressively being brought under the regulations. For example, there is no daily rest provision for offshore workers and special provisions apply to weekly rest breaks. The NHS is still allowed to require its doctors in training (junior doctors) to work longer hours and it is possible for these workers to opt-out from the regulations, although this cannot be done collectively by a group of doctors, only on an individual basis. However, even where NHS doctors choose to opt out of the regulations, there is a ceiling of 56 working hours per week.

Data protection

Employers obtain and store a wide range of personal information about employees, and employees have a right to expect that this data will be kept safe and confidential. The Data Protection Act 1984 provided for some assurances with regard to computerised information, and since 1 March 2000, when the Data Protection Act 1998 came into effect, manual filing systems which were in existence before 24 October 1998 were required to comply fully with the Data Protection Directive (95/46/EC) of the European Union. The EU General Data Protection Regulation (EC) Number 45/2001 provides a number of updates to the Data Protection Directive (95/46/EC) and will become binding on all EU states as it is a regulation rather than a directive. The regulation will harmonise data protection across the EU and will apply to non-EU companies processing information on EU residents. It will provide for the creation of a single data protection authority for the EU, provide for fines of 100 million euros or 5 per cent of global turnover (whichever is greater), require consent from individuals to have their data processed, provide for notification of breach of regulations to the data protection authority and extend special categories of information.

The Freedom of Information (FOI) Act 2000 provides a statutory right of access to 'recorded' information held by public authorities (unless the organisation can demonstrate that the information requested is exempt from disclosure) and this act came fully into force from 1 January 2005. Under the terms of the FOI Act, any person who makes a request to a public authority, such as the NHS, a school, the police or the Post Office, will be entitled to be informed if the information is held and to have the information communicated to them. The Information Commissioner's Office in the UK is an independent authority established to uphold information rights in the public interest and has responsibilities for providing an integrated role relating to the Freedom of Information Act 2000 and to the Data Protection Act 1998 (and other legislation such as the Privacy and Electronic Communications Regulations 2003, the Environmental Information Regulations 2004 and the INSPIRE Regulations 2009).

The Data Protection Act 1998

The Data Protection Act 1998 controls how personal data is used by organisations, businesses and the government. According to the UK government's gov.uk website, those using data must adhere to the data protection principles, ensuring that data is:

- used fairly and lawfully;
- used for limited, specifically stated purposed;
- adequate, relevant and not excessive;
- accurate;
- kept no longer than is absolutely necessary;
- handled according to people's data protection rights;
- kept safe and secure;
- not transferred outside the UK without adequate protection.

Information that is more sensitive, such as ethnicity, religious beliefs, political opinions, health, sexual health and criminal records, are subject to more stringent controls.

The Information Commissioner's Office (ICO, 2014) has produced a number of resources, including a guide, covering the handling of personal data in the areas noted above. The purpose of the guide is to enable employers to understand better their obligations under the Data Protection Act 1998. The guide gives advice and practical examples to illustrate the principles and is useful for anyone with responsibility for data protection.

The data protection principles apply to personal data held by all managers, not just HR managers, and therefore most organisations need to complete an audit to establish exactly what data is kept and by whom. Many managers and other professionals maintain their own filing systems and they may store inappropriate or out-of-date personal data. A person from within the organisation, possibly from within the HR department, has to take on the role of data controller and ensure that everyone who keeps personal data also complies with the eight data protection principles. Personal data means information that can identify an individual. It is

Did you know?

An employee has the right to request data from his/her employer but is there any personal data that the employee may not see? Under the terms of the Data Protection Act 1998 an employee has no right to obtain information regarding a proposed pay rise, promotion, transfer, training, downgrading, redundancy or the employer's bargaining positions concerning an employee's pay and benefits. Also, there is no legal right for the employee to obtain, via a previous employer, a reference that it has provided.

(*Source*: Is there any information an employee may not see under the terms of the Data Protection Act 1998? Available at **www.xperthr.co.uk**; accessed 23.10.14)

not likely that information which, for instance, reviews salary structures for a whole workforce or for particular groups of staff can be deemed personal information.

People have a right to know what information is kept about them and can ask to see the data by means of a subject access request. In most cases, employers must supply the information within 40 calendar days. The data controller may be liable if there are breaches in the security of information, or if losses occur as a result of such a breach, but the ICO (2014) guide states that even where an individual within an organisation is given this responsibility, the organisation is still the data controller in the terms of the ICO.

Statutory rights: a concluding statement

As well as understanding the rights and obligations of employers and employees already established in law, it is essential to be aware that this is an area where issues develop and change on a regular basis. These changes can arise from formal consideration of statutes in Parliament, following discussions at EU level, or because new understanding of various circumstances arise when judgments are handed down on cases in the courts. One way of staying informed about developments in employment law is to read the legal update articles that appear in publications such as *People Management*, *Personnel Today* and XpertHR.

It is essential to review and update policies and practices to reflect changes to employment law as new requirements come into effect. The willingness of employers to offer employees more than the minimum that is required by the law might also contribute to improved employment relations and so enhance the motivation and commitment of staff to the organisation.

Activity 3.3

The Employment Law Frequently Asked Questions (FAQs) on the CIPD website, a resource for CIPD members, has links to frequently asked questions on a wide range of popular topics such as age discrimination and retirement, fixed-term work, references, trade union recognition and industrial action, whistle-blowing and wrongful dismissal. The CIPD also produces factsheets on employment law such as the October 2014 factsheet concerning employment law developments in 2013 and 2014. Look at some of the FAQs and formulate your own response before reading what the CIPD says. Go to **www.cipd.co.uk** and follow the links to the Employment Law and FAQs pages (accessed 23.10.14).

Flexible working arrangements

The traditional image of working patterns involved employees working about 40 hours per week from nine to five, Monday to Friday with four weeks paid annual leave. There are, however, many new patterns of work that suit both the changing requirements of businesses, some of them due to the need to provide goods and services on a 24/7 basis, and employees' needs to balance their family, personal and working life. Many supermarkets now open 24 hours a day and the once restrictive Sunday opening hours have been relaxed. Some people are working fewer hours to provide flexibility, for themselves and the organisation, and some are working more to cope with the pressures of work. In a period of economic downturn, such as 2008–2009, organisations have also used flexible working patterns as a way of avoiding redundancies.

Suff (2013) reports the results of an XpertHR survey into flexible working policies and practices. Of the 144 employers surveyed, 79.2 per cent had a policy on flexible working and the most popular flexible working practices were part-time hours (47.8 per cent), flexitime (23.5 per cent), variable start/finish times (13.2 per cent), partial homeworking (3.7 per cent) and term-time working (2.9 per cent). Under the Children and Families Act 2014, from 30 June 2014 all employees, whether they have children or not, may request flexible working. In order to make a request, an employee needs to have worked for a 26-week period and employees can make only one request for flexible working in a 12-month period. These requirements are outlined in the Flexible Working Regulations 2014.

Activity 3.4

Bedford Hospital NHS Trust has produced a *Guide to Flexible Working*. The trust has identified a number of flexible working arrangements including staggered working hours, part-time working, temporary reduced working hours, job share, annual hours, phased return to work, employment break, special leave, self-rostering, flexitime and flexible retirement.

What are the advantages and disadvantages of the above flexible working arrangements for the employer (Bedford Hospital NHS Trust) and the employee?

(*Source: Bedford Hospital NHS Trust guide to flexible working*, available at **www.bedfordhospital.nhs.uk/upload_folder/flexible%20working.pdf**; accessed 23.10.14)

Newer forms of working patterns include shift work, part-time employment, contracting-out of work, arrangements for flexitime, and contracts based on annual or zero hours. All this variety and change suggests that for at least some part of your working life you are as likely to be working under flexible conditions as you are a supposedly traditional working arrangement.

The range and mix of working arrangements can mean that employers have the flexibility to call on employees' services only when they need them. The emphasis is therefore on developing arrangements to increase flexibility in the availability of human resources and to ensure that the organisation is able to respond rapidly to changing requirements. Meeting the needs of business can also be synonymous with meeting employee needs if an organisation wishes to use flexibility as a strategy to attract and retain valuable workers. Of the 162 employers surveyed by the IRS in 2010 (Wolff, 2010), all but one of them (161) had flexible working practices of some kind in place. Retention of employees was one of the major benefits reported (73 per cent) along with improved ability to provide cover (65 per cent).

Since the late 1990s there has been growing recognition of the importance of achieving a good balance between work and a person's private commitments.

A good work–life balance can meet the needs of both the employer and employee in terms of stress management, health, productivity and caring responsibilities. These aspects of employee wellbeing are very much a part of a positive psychological contract and are likely to affect the employee's level of engagement. Indeed, 63 per cent of respondents to the 2010 IRS survey (Wolff, 2010) rated employee engagement as a business benefit of flexible working practices.

We shall now review some of the important developments in flexible working, specifically examining annual hours contracts, job-sharing, fixed-term contracts, homeworking and zero hour contracts.

Annualised hours

Under this arrangement, the employer estimates the number of hours he or she will need an employee to work over the period of a year, and contracts the employee to work those hours at the standard rate but according to an agreed, irregular pattern that corresponds better to fluctuating business needs. This means that the employer, subject to agreed arrangements, can call on the services of employees when they are needed, and does not pay employees for their presence at times when they are not needed. Employees are guaranteed payment for the hours that they have been contracted for, with the salary usually being paid in equal amounts spread over the year.

Terms that would have to be established in an annualised hours contract include agreements on things such as the maximum number of hours an employee could be expected to work in a given number of days, entitlement to a consecutive number of days off and notice of a call in to work. The arrangements should be such that employers are able to cover both scheduled and unscheduled requirements. Annualised hours contracts often incorporate rostered and reserve hours with the split between these depending on the nature of the contract and negotiation between the employer, employee and, sometimes, the trade union.

Job share

The concept of having two (or more) people share the tasks designated as constituting one post probably grew out of the recognition that some women did not wish to return to full-time work after maternity leave but would prefer to work a reduced number of hours. Some employers developed job-sharing schemes partly to accommodate this desire, but also because they recognised that this was a way of retaining scarce talent. It has also become increasingly clear that there is an obligation on all employers to at least consider the viability of flexible arrangements such as this.

Job sharing requires additional arrangements to ensure coordination between job-share partners. This has implications for their managers, but there are numerous benefits: it can bring additional flexibility in terms of availability of staff when required for extra work; it shows that the employer is willing to consider arrangements that accommodate the needs of staff; the talents and ideas of two people are applied to one job; and it is good for morale. In fact, it is an arrangement that can clearly bring benefit to both the employer and employee. Also, although we stated earlier that the arrangement probably grew out of the wishes of women returning from maternity leave, job share is, of course, not just of benefit to women. Men can also have responsibilities as the primary care givers in their families and welcome the opportunity to work part-time, and job share is also attractive to people who wish to combine a steady income with freelance consultancy activities.

Job-sharers are classified, for the purposes of employment law, as part-time workers and are protected against discrimination under the Part-time Workers (Prevention of Less Favourable Treatment) Regulations 2000. Job-sharing contracts need to make clear how duties will be organised, the working hours, holiday arrangements, bonuses and handover provisions.

Fixed-term contracts

A fixed-term contract is one that ends on a specific date or related to a specific event, such as the end of funding for a project. Fixed-term contracts obviously offer some flexibility to employers in terms of adjusting the numbers of employees at different times to suit fluctuating business needs. Employees on fixed-term contracts are entitled to equal treatment as employees on permanent contracts under the Fixed-term Employees (Prevention of Less Favourable Treatment) Regulations 2002. A particular type of fixed-term contract is the rolling contract which self-renews on a particular date. For these contracts, it is essential to have a notice of termination clause in order to allow either party to end the contract without breach of contract.

Homeworking

Homeworking is generally used to describe an arrangement where a worker performs some or all of their work at home on a full-time or part-time basis. With the development of information technology systems, including email, the Internet and broadband, people do not need to be in the same building to transmit written documents and reports instantaneously. The worker may be more efficient and productive working at home but some managers equate effectiveness with time spent in the workplace. The manager may also fear loss of control as the worker is 'out of sight'. Such a fear may be understandable as some workers may not be suited to homeworking.

Pause for thought 3.4 Make a list of the qualities needed to be an effective homeworker. To what extent do you have these qualities? If you do, would you prefer to work at home or 'in the office'?

Zero hours contracts

These contracts represent an agreement to employ a person as and when required. There is no commitment to a minimum number of working hours and the person is only paid for the hours that they actually work. The term 'casual work' is often used to describe zero hours contracts. Zero hours contracts are more commonly used in industries that are highly seasonal or where demand fluctuates from day to day or week to week and work is unpredictable, such as agriculture, tourism, retail and health care. The number of workplaces using zero hours contracts has been increasing and, according to statistics from the Office for National Statistics, the number of people on zero hours contracts in the UK has increased from 134,000 in 2006 to 250,000 in 2012 (ONS, 2012). More recent figures from the ONS suggest

Did you know?

The *Telegraph* (Devlin, 2010) reports on an American study of IBM workers which revealed that employees who are allowed to work at least part of the time from home are likely to be able to work for longer before they begin to feel the pressures of work. The pressure point of 38 hours in a week in the office transforms into 57 hours in a week if some working from home is included. Meanwhile, in the UK, the Transport Minister at the time, Norman Baker, is reported to be investigating ways of encouraging homeworking to alleviate pressures on the transport systems in the UK among other benefits to business and individuals (Millward, 2010).

(*Sources*: Devlin, K. (2010) Home working 'allows employees to clock up an extra couple of days of work a week', *Telegraph*, 5 June and Millward, D. (2010) Let staff work from home: employers told, *Telegraph*, 10 July; available at **www.telegraph.co.uk**; accessed 03.08.10)

that the number of employees in the UK on zero hours contracts is 583,000 (ONS, 2014). However, as there are problems in identifying employees on such contracts, the actual figure may be much higher, perhaps more than a million.

There is much controversy and debate over the use of zero hours contracts. Much of the debate has focused on the negative aspects of such contracts. Indeed, in a speech to the Trades Union Congress (TUC) Conference in 2013, Ed Miliband, leader of the Labour Party, stated that zero hours contracts belonged more 'to the Victorian era than they do to the kind of workplace we should have in the 21st century' (**www.labourlist.org**). Whilst there continues to be much criticism of zero hours contracts, the CIPD (2014b) states that such contracts, if used properly, can provide flexibility for both individuals and organisations. CIPD (2014b) suggests that, in order to improve practice in the use of zero hours contracts, a code of practice needs to be developed, a national campaign needs to raise understanding and awareness of such contracts and all workers should be legally entitled to a written copy of the terms and conditions of employment no later than two months into employment.

Activity 3.5

As assistant human resource manager of a retail firm, you have been asked by your boss to give a 10-minute presentation about zero hours contracts. This presentation needs to cover definitions of such contracts, the benefits to the firm and to the employee and legal and ethical issues concerning their use.

Termination of employment

Employees leave their organisations for a variety of reasons and under different circumstances, but the two basic reasons are voluntary and involuntary. Voluntary reasons include taking up another post; retirement or early retirement; and voluntary non-employment, often due to a change in circumstances including parenting or studying. The involuntary reasons may include redundancy or dismissal.

For each of these reasons for exit, there is a range of circumstances that apply, except perhaps for retirement, which is essentially age related. People taking up another post, for example, may be doing so for a number of reasons, such as personal reasons for moving to another geographical area; because they have been offered more pay or better conditions for doing the same or similar work with another employer; opportunities for promotion; to escape from uncongenial managers or colleagues; or related to a change of career.

In the chapter on human resource strategy and planning (Chapter 5), we discuss that it is essential for employers to understand the reasons why people leave their organisations so that appropriate recruitment and retention plans can be devised as part of the talent management strategy. For this reason many employers obtain information from staff who are leaving, especially those leaving for voluntary reasons, by conducting an exit interview with them.

Exit interviews and employee opinion surveys

It is important to gather data on any problems connected with the employment relationship so that employers can take action to remedy any policies and practices that might potentially cause more valuable employees to leave. The areas usually covered in an exit interview include: the reason for leaving; relationships with supervisors and co-workers and working conditions in general and specific ones that might be problematic, such as shift work.

ACAS (2014b) suggests asking the employee why they are leaving the organisation and if it is due to the job itself, line management, pay and other terms and conditions, training, career prospects, working conditions, amenities or equal opportunities. However, employees may not reveal the true reasons for them leaving the organisation. Therefore, in order to increase the likelihood of obtaining useful data, ACAS (2014b) recommends having the exit interview being carried out by someone other than the employee's line manager (usually by someone in the human resource management department), conduct the interview away from the employee's usual place of work, explain the reason for the interview and that it is confidential and explain that the outcome of the interview will not affect any references written about the employee or the employee's chances of working for the organisation again. It should be noted, however, that any references to bullying or harassment do need to be followed up as it would not be acceptable to ignore reports of unlawful harassment. It is good practice, before the exit interview, to ask the employee to complete a form that can be used to structure the interview and clarify details.

Activity 3.6

You have been asked to design an exit interview form. The following aspects need to be incorporated into the form: the employee's details, their employment history in the organisation, their current job and duties, relationship with managers, relationship with colleagues, working conditions and reason(s) for leaving. What other sections might you include and how might you use open questions (where responses are longer), closed questions (where responses are short, for example, yes/no) or scaled questions (e.g. excellent/good/satisfactory/poor)?

Rather than waiting to gather information from employees who have decided to leave the organisation, employee opinion surveys can be used to assess the levels of satisfaction within an existing workforce. It is well recognised that management must demonstrate a willingness to take action on any issues raised, or at least respond to these issues in some way, if they wish to retain the trust of their employees and have employees take any subsequent surveys seriously.

Retirement

Retirement is an important phase in an employee's life and employers can help these workers prepare for retirement through a formal pre-retirement programme. Moving from working life to retirement requires major adjustment, and can be achieved more successfully with careful planning, in terms of coping with a changed financial situation as well as increased leisure time. It is also important that the employer continues to engage with employees as they near retirement as older workers may have considerable knowledge and expertise that can be passed on to younger workers. Unfortunately, there are instances where employers discriminate against older workers, assuming that they are out of touch and not interested in training or promotion. Such negative stereotypes should be challenged.

Employers can further consider programmes for keeping in touch with people who have retired from employment with them. It can be a low-cost benefit to arrange occasional social gatherings for past and present employees and to send the organisation's newsletter to past employees, and the returns in terms of morale and commitment from current employees who witness this evidence of their employer's concern for employee welfare may well repay these costs many times over.

Conclusion

We have seen that the employment relationship consists of rights and obligations for employers and employees, and that these are determined by legislation and various other agreements. Innovations in terms, conditions and working arrangements are constantly developing as organisations attempt to respond to increasing competitive challenges, global economic developments and to social changes such as growing expectations of an acceptable work–life balance. The likelihood of further developments in legislation also guarantees that this will continue to be an area of change in the future, and recent research indicates that work–life balance ideas need to be more holistically embraced as a strategic business approach.

Review questions

You will find brief answers to these review questions on page 463.
1. What does the term 'employment relationship' mean?
2. What are the differences between an 'employee', 'worker' and 'self-employed person'?
3. What should a contract of employment contain?
4. What are the pros and cons for zero hours contracts for employees? Do you agree with certain commentators who believe they should be made illegal?

Improving your employability

You have applied for a traineeship focusing on human resource management with a large retailer and have been shortlisted for an interview. In addition to the interview, you are required to give a 10-minute presentation on 'how the firm might use flexible working arrangements'. You have decided that, in preparing for the presentation, you will consult a wide range of published resources. What sources might you consult? What information and statistics would you choose to use? To differentiate yourself from other candidates you have decided to carry out a focus group (a type of group interview) with fellow students. Ostensibly, the aim of the focus group will be to ascertain students' views on flexible working. You have formulated the following questions: What do you understand by the term? What are the advantages of flexible working to you? What are the disadvantages of flexible working to you? How might flexible working affect your motivation and commitment? You need to think of other questions to ask and how your findings could be incorporated into your presentation.

HR in the news

VIRGIN – Branson tells staff to take as much holiday as they want

By Claer Barrett

Sir Richard Branson, the billionaire founder of Virgin Group, has told 170 staff working for its head office that they can take as much annual leave as they like, providing it will not damage the business. "Flexible working has revolutionised how, where and when we all do our jobs," Sir Richard said on his website. "'So if working nine to five no longer applies, then why should strict annual leave (vacation) policies?" Sir Richard said he was inspired by Netflix, the US based video streaming service that has a similar policy on not tracking staff holidays. The company reported that staff morale, creativity and productivity had all risen since the "non policy" was introduced.

The blurring of the boundaries between work life and home life caused by advances in mobile technology meant that companies were "no longer able to accurately track employees' total time on the job," Sir Richard said, adding that there was no need for his staff to ask for approval before taking time off. "It is left to the employee alone to decide if and when he or she feels like taking a few hours, a day, a week or a month off, the assumption being that they are only going to do it when they feel 100 per cent comfortable that they and their team are up to date on every project and that their absence will not in any way damage the business or, for that matter, their careers," he added. The rules apply to about 170 staff working at the Virgin head offices in the UK and US. The wider Virgin Group, which employs about 50,000 people around the world in transport, aviation, technology and banking, will not adopt the same policy yet.

"Assuming it goes as well as expected, we will encourage all our subsidiaries to follow suit, which will be incredibly exciting to watch," Sir Richard added.

Sir Richard could run into resistance from his partners or indeed outright owners of many of the Virgin-branded companies. In many cases, Sir Richard either has a minority stake or, where he has no stake at all, there is a brand licence in place for the use of the name.

Some employment experts on Twitter criticised the claim as a "publicity stunt" for Sir Richard's forthcoming book. But many other social media users said employees would reward such a level of trust with greater loyalty.

Questions

1. In what ways has flexible working revolutionised employment?

2. What are the benefits and dis-benefits of flexible working to employers and employees?

3. Should employees be able to take as much time off work as they want?

4. To what extent do you agree with some critics who have claimed that Richard Branson's statements on time off work for his employees is a 'publicity stunt'?

What next?

Relax and listen to the CIPD's podcast on flexible working. Podcast 75 from February 2013 addresses a variety of issues raised concerning flexible working by HR professionals. Podcasts are available at **www.cipd.co.uk**. What are the key issues in relation to flexible working? What is meant by flexible working? What different types of flexible working are there?

Read the ACAS (2014) guide 'Homeworking: a guide for employers and employees'. How would the employer decide if homeworking is feasible? Are there jobs where homeworking is not feasible? Would you like to spend at least some of your working time at home? This guide is available at **www.acas.org.uk**; accessed 15.02.15.

References

Adams, B. and C. Stakim (2008) How to use flexible working to avoid redundancies, *Employers' Law* (available at www.xperthr.co.uk; accessed 17.11.08).

Advisory, Conciliation and Arbitration Service (2014a) *Paternity Leave and Pay* (available at www .acas.org.uk; accessed 19.09.14).

Advisory, Conciliation and Arbitration Service (2014b) *Managing Attendance and Employee Turnover* (available at www.acas.org.uk; accessed 06.11.14).

Advisory, Conciliation and Arbitration Service (2014c) *Handling in a Reasonable Manner Requests to Work Flexibly* (available at www.acas.org.uk; accessed 19.09.14).

Argyris, C. (1960) *Understanding Organisational Behaviour*, Dorsey Press, Homewood.

Cabinet Office (2010) *The Coalition: Our Programme for Government*, Crown Copyright, London.

Cabrelli, D. (2012) *Employment Law*, Pearson Education, Harlow.

Chartered Institute of Personnel and Development (2013) *Contracts of Employment*, CIPD (factsheet available from www.cipd.co.uk; accessed 20.08.14).

Chartered Institute of Personnel and Development (2014a) *The Psychological Contract*, CIPD (factsheet available from www.cipd.co.uk; accessed 19.08.14).

Chartered Institute of Personnel and Development (2014b) *Zero-Hours Contract*, CIPD (factsheet available from www.cipd.co.uk; accessed 06.11.14).

Chartered Institute of Personnel and Development (2014c) *Working Hours and Time Off Work*, CIPD (factsheet available from www.cipd.co.uk; accessed 16.10.14).

Chartered Institute of Personnel and Development (2014d) *Employment Law FAQ*, CIPD (available from www.cipd.co.uk; accessed 01.09.14).

Chartered Institute of Personnel and Development (2014e) *Dismissal*, CIPD (factsheet available from www.cipd.co.uk; accessed 01.09.14).

Chartered Institute of Personnel and Development (2014f) *Flexible Working*, CIPD (factsheet available from www.cipd.co.uk; accessed 19.09.14).

Davies, K. (2013) *Understanding European Union Law*, Routledge, London.

Department for Business, Innovation & Skills (1998) *Fairness at Work*, Government White Paper, May (paper available at www.berr.gov.uk; accessed 30.07.10).

Department for Business, Innovation & Skills (2010) *Pregnancy and Work: What You Need to Know as an Employer*, BIS, London.

Doran, N. (2010) *Topic of the Week: Varying Contracts* (available at www.xperthr.co.uk; accessed 02.08.10).

Guest, D. and N. Conway (1997) *Issues in People Management No. 21: Employee Motivation and the Psychological Contract*, IPD, London.

Handy, C. (1985) *Understanding Organizations*, 3rd edition, Penguin, London.

Hogg, S. (2014) *Hours of Work* (available at www.xperthr.co.uk; accessed 23.10.14).

Information Commissioner's Office (2014) *The Guide to Data Protection*, ICO (available at www.ico .org.uk; accessed 23.10.14).

Kaczorowska, A. (2013) *European Union Law*, Routledge, Hoboken.

Lamont, V. (2014) *How to Obtain a Worker's Agreement to Opt Out of the 48-Hour Maximum Working Week* (available at www.xperthr.co.uk; accessed 16.10.14).

Lewis, D. and M. Sargeant (2010). *Employment Law*, Pearson Education, Harlow.

Marson, J. (2014) *Beginning Employment Law*, Routledge, Abingdon.

Nairns, J. (2008) *Employment Law for Business Students*, Longman, Harlow.

Office for National Statistics (2012). *Labour Force Survey: Fourth Quarter* (available at www.ons.gov .uk; accessed 06.11.14).

Office for National Statistics (2014). *Estimate of People in Employment Reporting a Zero Hours Contract* (available at www.ons.gov.uk; accessed 06.11.14).

Sargeant, M. and D. Lewis (2012) *Employment Law*, Pearson Education, Harlow.

Schein, E. (1978*) Career Dynamics: Matching Individual and Organizational Needs*, Addison-Wesley, London.

Scott, K. and G. Phillips (2013) *Employment Law*, College of Law, Guildford.

Shaw, K. and L. Silkin (2014). *How to Manage Bank Holidays* (available at www.xperthr.co.uk; accessed 24.10.14).

Sims, R.R. (1994) Human resource management's role in clarifying the new psychological contract, *Human Resource Management*, Vol. 33, No. 3, 373–382.

Suff, R. (2013) *Flexible Working Policies and Practice: 2013 XpertHR Survey* (available at www .xperthr.co.uk; accessed 23.10.14).

Turner, C. (2013) *Unlocking Employment Law*, Routledge, Hoboken.

Wolff, C. (2010) IRS flexible working survey 2010: benefits, issues and making it work, *IRS Employment Review* (available at www.xperthr.co.uk; accessed 05.08.10).

Woodruffe, C. (2005) Commitment and satisfaction: the true state of the psychological contract, in Chartered Institute of Personnel and Development, *The State of the Employment Relationship. Reflections on Employee Well-Being and the Psychological Contract*, CIPD, London.

XpertHR (1995) *Mobility Clause Challenged. Law Report* (available at www.xperthr.co.uk; accessed 20.08.14).

XpertHR (2014) *Maternity Pay and Leave. Survey* (available at www.xperthr.co.uk; accessed 19.09.14).

www.eurofound.europa.eu. Qualified Majority Voting; accessed 21.08.14.

www.gov.uk. *Employment Status*. accessed 19.08.14.

www.hmrc.gov.uk. *Work Out if You're Employed or Self-Employed*; accessed 20.08.14.

www.labourlist.org. *Ed Miliband's TUC Conference Speech*; accessed 06.11.14.

Further study

Books and reports

Advisory, Conciliation and Arbitration Service (2012) *ACAS Future of Employment Relations Discussion Paper Series*, ACAS (available at www.acas.org.uk).
A series of discussion papers on the future of employment relations. Topics covered include employment relations and outsourcing, health and wellbeing in the workplace, voice and participation, migrant labour, ageing workforce, trade unions and the public sector.

Aylott, E. (2014) *Employee Relations*, Kogan Page, London.
This book is a guide to the fundamental principles of employee relations and offers the reader a complete overview of the field, strongly aligned to the organisational and HR strategy and objectives.

Marson, J. (2014) *Beginning Employment Law*, Routledge, Abingdon.
This is an introductory and accessible textbook on employment law. The book breaks the subject down using practical, everyday examples to make it understandable to everyone, whatever their background.

Rankin, N. (2015) *Flexible Working* (available at www.xperthr.co.uk).
This good practice manual contains a range of information concerning flexible working. It also contains links to reports on team working.

Articles

Druker, J. and G. White (2013) Employment relations on major construction projects: the London 2012 Olympic construction site. *Industrial Relations Journal*, 44(5–6), 566–583.
This research paper examines the employment relations in relation to a mega construction project: the London 2012 Olympic Games. This project provides a model of employee relations that crosses organisational boundaries.

Pedersen, V. and S. Lewis (2012) Flexible friends?: Flexible working time arrangements, blurred work-life boundaries and friendship, *Work, Employment and Society*, Vol. 26, No. 3, 464–480.
The changing nature of work raises concerns about how workers can find time for activities such as friendship and leisure. This article explores how individuals do friendship in a period characterised by time dilemmas, blurred work–life boundaries and increased employer- and employee-led flexible working.

Zagenczyk, T.J., R. Gibney, C. Kiewitz and S.L.D. Restubog (2009) Mentors, supervisors and role models: do they reduce the effects of psychological contract breach? *Human Resource Management Journal*, Vol. 19, No. 3, 237–259.
This research article provides a readable and accessible explanation of the psychological contract and explores the importance of mentors and line managers in maintaining it.

Internet

There are many Internet sites that can give you access to legal information and related employment matters. We have listed only a selection here for you to try. Most of them have numerous linked sites that you can click on to get more specific information.

Advisory, Conciliation and Arbitration Service   **www.acas.org.uk**
In addition to advisory booklets, the website has a helpline where you are able to ask for advice on employment matters.

Chartered Institute of Personnel and Development   **www.cipd.co.uk**
A number of legislation-related factsheets are available to all visitors to the CIPD website as is the employment law podcast which covers a range of issues. The Employment Law Frequently Asked Questions (FAQ), for members of the CIPD, links to many interesting and informative pages.

Equality and Human Rights Commission   **www.equalityhumanrights.com**
The Commission prepared a very interesting document in 2009 presenting guidance for managers with regard to flexible working practices. It outlines the business benefits and presents a number of cases, including IBM, Sainsbury's and National Grid. Look for *Working Better: A Manager's Guide to Flexible Working*.

Government services website   **www.gov.uk**
A government-sponsored website with a lot of employment-related information for employers. Specific employment-related information includes sections dealing with business and self-employment, employing people and working, jobs and pensions.

hrzone   **www.hrzone.co.uk**
This website contains a wide assortment of articles on various aspects of HR, including legal issues. The site also contains a blog dealing with employment and HR issues.

4

Diversity and equality

Objectives

When you have studied this chapter you will be able to:

- explain the concept of workforce diversity and how to manage it successfully
- understand the issues relating to equality of opportunity in the workplace
- describe the legislation that addresses workplace equality
- explain the practical implications of the equality legislation with regard to recruitment and selection.

Diversity and equality in the workplace are strategically important for organisations (Incomes Data Services (IDS), 2010), and there is a perception that diversity can improve organisational performance (Allen *et al.*, 2008). Diversity and equality are rising up the corporate agenda (Stevens, 2012) as more and more organisations identify the benefits of a diverse workforce. Initiatives for improving diversity and equality have a demonstrable impact on productivity and costs, and can help an organisation achieve its strategic goals. This chapter firstly examines workforce diversity, reviewing key concepts of why an organisation adopts diversity initiatives, and the managerial imperatives of how to obtain the advantages envisaged from having a diverse workforce. We then turn our attention to the related topic of workplace equality, examining equality legislation in detail and reviewing the practicalities of equality in the workplace.

Diversity in the workplace

Definitions of diversity

When describing diversity, the CIPD (2014a) comments that each one of us is unique. We are different in visible and non-visible ways. Different characteristics include personality, background, language, age, ethnicity, disability, gender, sexual orientation and marriage. Some of these are covered by law on discrimination in the workplace and represent 'protected characteristics' (described later on in this chapter) while others are not covered by anti-discrimination legislation and are, therefore, not protected. It is through recognising, responding to and managing these differences and realising each individual's unique potential that diversity can thrive and make a contribution to the success of the organisation. Managing diversity is about valuing every person as an individual, whether they are customers, suppliers, employees or managers. Wolff (2007) reinforces some of this terminology when describing how Arriva, the European transport services provider, has approached diversity, stating that the firm has recognised the importance of having a diversity strategy by valuing differences in staff and customers in terms of all aspects of difference. These differences do not only relate to colour, religion, birthplace, gender, sexual orientation and age, 'but also which school people have been to, what they like and do not like, what they believe in and what is important to them'. Although diversity relates to many characteristics, the case studies presented in various publications (e.g. IDS, 2010; Trades Union Congress, 2013) often reflect a tendency to focus on attempts to improve diversity by attracting members of specific under-represented groups, such as people from certain ethnic backgrounds, women and people with disabilities.

Business case arguments for workplace diversity

It is widely accepted that there are good business reasons for attempting to build and maintain a diverse workforce (Allen *et al.*, 2008; IDS, 2010). A CIPD survey (2012) on diversity and inclusion revealed that 83 per cent of employers have an articulated diversity and equality strategy, policies or guidelines with 74 per cent of respondents considering diversity and inclusion as central to its people management strategy. One of the 12 critical human capital trends, as identified by Deloitte Consulting (2014), is how companies can use diversity and inclusion as a business strategy. According to Daft and Marcic (2013), organisations that are more diverse are better placed to use employee talent, have a better understanding of the marketplace, have better leadership, have increased quality of team problem solving and have lower costs because of reduced labour turnover, lower levels of absenteeism and fewer lawsuits. There are four major areas of business advantage to be gained from promoting diversity in the workforce: recruitment and retention; employee satisfaction and productivity; employer brand; customer orientation and product innovation. The following sections will review these business case factors in more detail.

Recruitment and retention

Aiming for a diverse workforce means that organisations can recruit from a wider pool of applicants and are more likely to gain access to the talent they require. Skills shortages, due in part to population change, low unemployment or lack of skills in the labour market, can mean that it is difficult to recruit suitably qualified personnel. Being open to a more diverse pool of candidates can help an organisation overcome, at least in part, recruitment problems. The Trades Union Congress and the Confederation of Business Industry (TUC and CBI, 2008) also identify lower staff turnover with the subsequent reduction in recruitment costs as an outcome of greater diversity in the workplace.

Employee satisfaction and productivity

The reduction in staff turnover, combined with lower recruitment costs mentioned above, can be interpreted as indicators of higher employee satisfaction. Improved diversity can result in fewer disciplinary problems and lower absence rates (TUC and CBI, 2008). This is, perhaps, an outcome of the promotion of teamwork and the improved management skills of line managers, which are key components of successful diversity management. The IDS (2010) link diversity with better employee engagement and improved retention.

Employer brand

Being seen as an employer that believes in and promotes diversity and equality is likely to contribute to the organisation's image, and is a desirable component of any corporate social responsibility (CSR) programme (Singal, 2014). Also, if an organisation promotes diversity and equality it can recruit from a wider pool of talent (Niederle et al., 2013) and is more likely to be recognised as an employer of choice.

Customer orientation and product innovation

There are many business arguments for diversity. One of these is that the organisation is better able to the meet the needs of its customers. A workforce which reflects the diversity of an organisation's customers should be better placed to understand and better respond to its customers' needs and wishes. Combined with this, organisations can expect to achieve greater creativity and access to a wider range of ideas from a diverse workforce. This has been known to result in greater levels of innovation and even gaining access to new markets (TUC and CBI, 2008; IDS, 2010; Derven, 2014; Nathan, 2015).

Management of diversity

As with the other people management issues we address in this book, line managers play a front-line role in the delivery and achievement of objectives. This also relates to diversity management objectives. In order for diversity management to be successful, senior management need to have a commitment to diversity and to develop clear diversity goals. These need to be communicated to line managers.

Line managers need to be trained in understanding what the organisation aims to achieve from diversity, and how people can be managed so that they can achieve their full potential. The organisation may wish to link the achievement of diversity objectives to rewards for its managers (CIPD, 2014a).

Of course line managers are not the only people involved in making diversity work; everyone is. Organisations need to communicate to all employees what is expected of them in terms of diversity and equality. This can be incorporated into an induction programme. In order for diversity management to be effective, training will be needed. However, because of the cost of diversity training, it may be almost impossible to offer training to all employees (Reynolds *et al.*, 2014).

Recruitment is a major source of diversity and a broader approach to recruitment must be adopted to ensure that a full range of people are attracted to the organisation. Initiatives that allow disadvantaged groups to be able to compete during the recruitment process can be used. These include providing application forms in Braille, having information in different languages and adjusting the recruitment process for candidates who have a disability.

Another issue for employers to consider is the need to offer flexible working arrangements to accommodate the differing needs of a diverse workforce. Various employees will require leave at different times of the year for religious observances whilst some employees will need to adapt their working hours to fit in with childcare or care of dependants and others may wish to take extended study leave. Offering such flexibility can itself engender further benefits for employers. An XpertHR survey (2013) reported that flexible working offered the employer a number of distinct advantages. These include improved retention (mentioned by 64.7 per cent of respondents), increased employee commitment (63.2 per cent), flexibility of cover (47.1 per cent), cost savings (36.0 per cent), reduced absence (34.6 per cent) and promotion of equal opportunities (31.6 per cent).

McCartney and Worman (2010) offer advice on how to set about building and strengthening diversity initiatives in the workplace. The approach outlined below is based on their project plan and involves the following steps:

- Get the support of the leadership team by persuading them of the business benefits to be gained from a diversity strategy.
- Integrate diversity goals into plans for recruitment and selection, performance management, development and reward.
- Involve the whole range of stakeholders from the beginning of the initiative: board members, team leaders, employees. This requires clear communication of the goals and objectives of the programme, including how everyone is affected and how everyone can gain from diversity.
- Challenge negative behaviours and encourage people to think the issues through. Offer relevant training and keep the communication lines open.
- Monitor and evaluate progress. Appropriate metrics on recruitment, selection, performance, promotion and retention could provide feedback on the success of diversity initiatives, and employee opinion surveys could be used to measure job satisfaction and to identify any areas needing attention.

The IDS (2010) further suggest that employers could benchmark their programmes against those of other organisations to identify areas of good practice and ideas for improvement. All of these actions will involve a cost, but not always a substantial cost. Organisations which have a track record of successful diversity demonstrate that the rewards in terms of business benefits outweigh the costs of their diversity programmes. In the 'diversity' category of the 2013 CIPD People Management awards, the following organisations were shortlisted: Antrim Borough Council, Birkbeck (University of London), Central Manchester University Hospitals NHS Foundation Trust, Hampshire Constabulary, NHS Employers, Obelisk Support, Sue Ryder and The Random House Group. Sue Ryder was the overall winner.

Equality and diversity

Equality and diversity are major issues that affect everyone in society and everyone in the workplace. All employees, current and potential, have a right not to be discriminated against unfairly and held back in their careers for reasons that have nothing to do with their abilities in relation to their work. Legislation exists to protect the interests of people belonging to groups who may have historically been discriminated against in terms of employment and services, and employers have a duty to ensure that this legislation is upheld in their organisations. Beyond the need to comply with legislation, however, there are also business arguments for equality and diversity as described above and ethical arguments for equality and diversity.

We have discussed business case arguments for workplace diversity but there are also moral or ethical arguments for diversity. Thus, it can be considered that should an organisation promote employment practices that do not allow everyone equality of opportunity, this is immoral and unethical (Daniels and Macdonald, 2005). Clements and Jones (2010) state that ethics is concerned with the frameworks we use to make judgements and an ethical argument for diversity is that it is the right thing to do.

The distinction between equality of opportunity and the management of diversity is described by Kandola and Fullerton (1998) in terms of equal opportunity being driven by legislation and applying to specified groups whereas diversity refers to all differences among people. The distinction between these two terms has become more and more tenuous as the equality legislation has expanded to include ever more segments of society. One way of understanding the two terms is to reflect that, logically, compliance with the equality laws will inevitably lead to a diverse workforce. If we accept that compliance with equality legislation will lead to a diverse workforce, it becomes important to have a good understanding of this area of law, given all the advantages that can accrue to an organisation from having a diverse workforce. In the previous chapter, on the employment relationship, there was an in-depth discussion of employment law and this will provide a good basis for understanding legislation in relation to diversity and equality in the workplace.

There have been many developments in equality legislation over the years and activity in this area continues apace. The many strands of previous discrimination legislation, developed over more than a quarter of a century, have been consolidated into a single equality act, the Equality Act 2010. Part of this process was the establishment of a single equality commission, the Equality and Human Rights Commission, which has oversight of all equality issues. The new Commission took up its full mandate in October 2007, and the separate commissions relating to gender, race and disability were all subsumed under this one body. The aim, as with the formation of the single equality Act, was to create a higher level of simplicity so that organisations and individuals could receive better and more coordinated guidance on an integrated framework of equality legislation.

Activity 4.1

Check the website of the Equality and Human Rights Commission (**www.equalityhumanrights.com**) to get an overview of current issues relating to equality and diversity in the UK.

Discrimination in the workplace

Discrimination is not necessarily a negative term as its literal meaning is to identify differences (Thompson, 2012). All organisations discriminate in that they have to choose between individuals when recruiting, selecting and promoting. If undertaken with care, this would constitute fair discrimination. Unfair discrimination occurs when non-relevant criteria are used, such as the colour of a person's skin, the individual's gender or the person's age (Newell, 1995). Discrimination in employment concerns the inequitable treatment of some employees, irrespective of their skills, knowledge and abilities (Rose, 2001).

Discrimination can be either direct or indirect (Tomei, 2003). Direct discrimination takes place where an employee is treated less favourably on the grounds of age, gender, race and so on than an employee of a different age, gender, race and so on (Daniels, 2004). Indirect discrimination takes place when an employer applies an unjustifiable criterion to different groups which adversely affects one group, resulting in a person from the disadvantaged group being unable to comply with the criterion (Daniels, 2004). It is perhaps unsurprising that direct discrimination is easier to uncover than indirect discrimination (Tomei, 2003).

A similar concept to indirect discrimination is the concept of adverse impact which refers to a 'substantially different rate of selection in hiring, promotion or other employment decision which works to the disadvantage of members of a race, sex or ethnic group' (Biddle, 2006, p. 1). However, unlike direct or indirect discrimination, adverse impact is not a legal term (Biddle, 2006).

Before discussing the Equality Act 2010 in detail, we thought it would be interesting to describe a range of discrimination cases that have appeared in employment tribunals in the last few years. We have tried to be brief, just to give a flavour of the types of discrimination that may be encountered.

Discrimination cases

● Sex discrimination

Furlong v. *BMC Software Ltd* [2009] ET/2701283/09

In 2007, Ms Furlong started work as a senior account manager for BMC Software, a technology company. Soon after joining the company she was informed by a top salesman in the firm that he used lap-dancing clubs to entertain clients. Ms Furlong had a moral objection to lap-dancing clubs. Ms Furlong alleged that the company used lap-dancing clubs and brothels to entertain clients and for non-work social events. There was also an instance of inappropriate sexual conduct (groping of Ms Furlong), which was not appropriately addressed by her managers. The employment tribunal (ET) ruled in Ms Furlong's favour with regard to direct sex discrimination, victimisation and harassment, and awarded her £12,000 for injury to feelings, £20,618 for loss of earnings and £2,000 for personal injury. The tribunal made recommendations that the company review its equal opportunities training for managers and ensure that its managers understand anti-discrimination law.

● Race discrimination

Jurga v. *Lavendale Montessori* [2012–2013] ET/3302379/2012 and ET/3300884/2013

Mrs Jurga, a Polish national, worked as a nursery teacher at a multinational school. There were a number of Polish speakers at the school, including some children and members of staff. Mrs Jurga claimed that another member of staff, Mrs Howes, had criticised her on several occasions for speaking Polish to her colleagues and children and had banned Mrs Jurga from speaking Polish at work, even during breaks. Mrs Jurga complained to the directors, Mr and Mrs Todd, about Mrs Howes but they failed to do anything about her complaints. Mrs Jurga resigned her post and then brought various tribunal claims, including discrimination on the grounds of race. The employment tribunal agreed that Mrs Jurga had been racially harassed and upheld Mrs Jurga's claim of race victimisation. After the judgement the parties agreed that Mrs Jurga would receive £7,000 in compensation.

> **Did you know?**
>
> The number of tribunal cases brought between January and March 2014 in the UK is significantly lower than the same period in 2013, following the introduction of tribunal fees in July 2013. In January–March 2014 there were 5,619 single claims compared to 13,739 for the same period in 2013. The trade union, UNISON, strongly opposed the introduction of fees and is continuing its opposition in the courts. On the 17 December 2014 UNISON was granted permission to appeal the High Court's decision which turned down UNISON's second judicial review over the introduction of fees for employment tribunals. If successful, the government could be forced to change its policy on employment tribunal fees.
>
> (*Sources*: Roberts, H. (2014) Tribunal fees have caused 'perilously low' number of cases, www.hrmagazine.co.uk; accessed 25.01.15 and UNISON (2014) UNISON to appeal high court decision over tribunal fees, available at www.unison.org.uk; accessed 25.01.15)

● Disability discrimination

Horler v. *Chief Constable of South Wales Police* [2012] ET/1600591/2012

Many disability discrimination cases centre on the failure of the employer to make reasonable adjustments to enable a disabled person to either commence or continue employment. Mr Horler, who joined South Wales Police as a police officer when he was 36, began suffering from knee pain following an injury in 2009 and was diagnosed with synovitis, a form of arthritis. It was accepted by South Wales Police that Mr Horler's condition met the definition of disability under the Equality Act 2010. Mr Horler was placed on restricted duties and in October 2010 he was advised by the police force's medical advisor that it was unlikely he would ever return to ordinary front-line duties. A doctor subsequently concluded that Mr Horler was permanently unable to undertake ordinary police duties and he would, therefore, be eligible to retire due to ill health. Mr Horler disagreed with the doctor, believing that operations on his knee had been successful and his condition was under control. Mr Horler was moved temporarily to a camera room operator but his employment with South Wales Police was terminated in December 2011. Mr Horler was to be pensioned off. He disagreed with the decision and brought a tribunal claim against South Wales Police claiming discrimination arising from disability. The employment tribunal found that South Wales Police had not met its duty to make reasonable adjustments for Mr Horler because it had failed to consider alternative posts for him. South Wales Police were ordered to pay £230,215 before tax to Mr Horler.

Age discrimination

Wright and others v. Purple Parking Ltd [2012] ET/3302277/2012

Purple Parking provides shuttle bus and car services at Heathrow airport. It had dismissed 20 drivers over 67 years of age, claiming the reason for the dismissals was that its insurer would not cover a driver over that age because of concerns over the high number of claims involving older drivers. The drivers brought a case of unfair dismissal due to age discrimination and unfair dismissal to the tribunal. Midway through the hearing it came to light that the company had, in fact, requested that the insurance provider change its policy to exclude older drivers. Purple Parking admitted liability for age discrimination and unfair dismissal and was ordered to pay over £700,000 compensation to the drivers, with compensation ranging from £17,094 to £78,080 per driver. Individual compensation included over £10,000 for injury to feelings and £4,000 in aggravated damages.

Williams v. Mistral Telecom Limited t/a Free Upgrades [2009] ET/1806715/09

Mr Williams, who was 17 at the time, had worked for just three and a half hours for his new employer before being dismissed because of his age. He was informed by the employer that the company's policy was to only employ people aged 18 or above. During the tribunal the employer claimed that its policy on the age of its workers was a proportionate means of achieving objectives, including protecting the health and safety of young people, and its actions in dismissing Mr Williams were therefore justified. The tribunal disagreed with the employer, awarding Mr Williams £4,000 for injury to feelings because of age discrimination. The employer was also ordered to pay damages because of unfair dismissal and unlawful deduction of wages.

Sexual orientation discrimination

English v. Thomas Sanderson Blinds Ltd [2009] IRLR 206 CA

Mr English's case was upheld on appeal by the Court of Appeal (CA) after an ET had dismissed his case. The case raised a complex area of the law. Mr English had been harassed through name-calling by a small group of co-workers after they found out, among other things, that he had been educated in a boarding school and he lived in Brighton, facts perceived by his colleagues as characteristics of a homosexual. These co-workers started taunting him with homophobic names. The complexity of the case arose from the fact that they actually knew that Mr. English was not homosexual, and Mr English was aware that his co-workers knew this. Given the fact that Mr English was not homosexual, and this was known to the harassing co-workers, the legal question was whether or not this amounted to harassment on the grounds of sexual orientation. The Court of Appeal, in a majority judgement, decided that the law could be interpreted in that way.

Religion or belief discrimination

Mba v Mayor and Burgesses of the London Borough of Merton [2010] ET/2350743/10

Ms Mba is a practicing Christian and she believes that Sunday is a holy day on which to rest and obey the Ten Commandments. On Sundays she attends church and has a ministering role. In July 2007 she started working as a residential care officer at a registered children's home which provides short residential breaks for children with serious disabilities. Because of the nature of provision, the home offers round-the-clock care. The home operated a shift system for its workers and when Ms Mba was interviewed for the job she said that she would have 'some difficulties' working on Sundays due to her church-related activities. However, she did not say that she would never be able to work on Sundays. In her contract of employment it stated that shift times would be determined by the manager to meet the needs of the service. In September 2008, Mr Deegan, the home manager, gave Ms Mba the choice of working either a morning or night shift when rostered on a Sunday but Ms Mba rejected the offer. Subsequently, Ms Mba was rostered for work on a number of Sundays but did not turn up for work. As a result, a disciplinary was taken out against her and she was given a six month written warning. She resigned on 30 May 2010, claiming indirect discrimination on the grounds of religion or belief. The tribunal held that the employer's business requirements outweighed Ms Mba's desire not to work on Sundays because of her Christian beliefs. The tribunal therefore rejected Ms Mba's discrimination claim.

Equal pay discrimination

Gibson and others v. Sheffield City Council [2010] IRLR 311 CA

A group of women working as carers and in school meals claimed for equal pay with men working for the council as street cleaners and gardeners. The council's case for the difference in pay rates hinged on a bonus scheme which applies to the male worker groups, but the Court of Appeal judged the bonuses to be discriminatory.

Gutridge and others v. *Sodexho and another* [2009] IRLR 752 EAT

A group of female cleaners from a hospital who had been transferred to an external provider of services under a transfer of undertakings brought a claim for equal pay by comparing themselves with a group of male hospital employees, maintenance assistants, who had not transferred. A major question in this case was whether such a comparison was allowable, and the Court of Appeal held that it was.

Brierley and others v. *ASDA Stores Limited* [2014–2015] Current Case

An equal pay claim is being brought against the retailer, ASDA, in an employment tribunal. Hundreds of female ASDA store workers are claiming that they are doing work of equal value to distribution workers in the company, which are predominantly male employees, but are being paid less. The individual cases were brought by female ASDA workers in different locations but have now been consolidated into one case (as reported in 'Cases on appeal', available at **www.xperthr.co.uk**, accessed 28.01.15).

It is noticeable from the two equal pay cases described above that such cases involve groups of women working for public service organisations. Such organisations usually employ people in a wide range of jobs, and it is important that they ensure that pay systems are fair. You can read more about pay systems in Chapter 9.

Equality

As already stated, legislation exists in the UK to protect the interests of groups of people that have historically been discriminated against in terms of employment and services. Discrimination, in general, is about treating certain groups less favourably than others because of a particular characteristic that members of the group share, for example being a woman, being regarded as too old or too young or practicing a religion. Areas of discrimination that are prohibited with regard to work apply to employees and applicants in terms of the arrangements made for deciding to whom to offer work, the terms of work offered and the decision of whether or not to offer work. These types of discrimination typically occur when a person is refused employment, promotion or training opportunities or is unfairly dismissed.

We shall outline the characteristics which are covered by the Equality Act 2010, why discrimination occurs, the issues of combined discrimination and positive action, how an individual can raise a complaint about discrimination and good practice employers can engage in to ensure they are achieving equality goals. Because of historical developments in Northern Ireland, certain legislation applies that is different from the rest of the UK. For example, in Northern Ireland separate legislation related to each of the protected characteristics remains in force and there are also differences in tribunal rules (CIPD, 2014b).

A further group of people who may be prone to discriminatory treatment in employment are those who have prior criminal convictions. The Rehabilitation of Offenders Act 1974, which provides some protection for this group, is also described briefly.

The Equality Act 2010

This act was designed to bring a more uniform approach to equality legislation in the UK and addresses unlawful discrimination in terms of employment and the provision of facilities, goods and services (Sargeant and Lewis, 2014).

Protected characteristics

The characteristics which are protected under the Equality Act 2010 are listed as:

- age;
- disability;
- gender reassignment;
- marriage and civil partnership;
- pregnancy and maternity;
- race;
- religion or belief;
- sex;
- sexual orientation.

Age

The act protects 'older' and 'younger' people against discrimination, although no specific chronological age is stated in the act. Since 2006, when age was added into the previous regulations as a protected characteristic, the equality legislation has emphasised that employers need to focus on competencies when making selection decisions rather than making stereotypical judgements about people's capabilities based on their age. Although these regulations, like any other aspect of equality, affect all aspects of the employment relationship, their immediate impact has been in the area of recruitment and selection. Much guidance has been offered to organisations in terms of redesigning their application forms and other parts of the recruitment and selection processes to comply with the legislation (see, for example, the Employers' Network for Equality and Inclusion information at **www.enei.org.uk** and Age Positive publications on the UK Government's website at **www.gov.uk**).

The Conservative–Liberal Coalition Government further strengthened the age discrimination provisions in 2011 by abolishing the default retirement age (Sargeant and Lewis, 2014).

Disability

Disability is defined under the act as a mental or physical impairment which has a substantial and long-term adverse effect on a person's ability to carry out normal day-to-day activities. This definition is very broad and open to interpretation, and decisions on whether a person is disabled may hinge, for example, on judgements about the meaning and applicability of the terms 'substantial', 'long-term' and 'normal day-to-day activities'. 'Long-term' is defined in the act as having lasted or being likely to last for at least 12 months, including being likely to last for the rest of the person's life. A range of conditions may, depending on the circumstances, contribute to a person being deemed disabled. Examples include individuals with cancer, multiple sclerosis, HIV/AIDS, chronic fatigue syndrome, schizophrenia, rheumatoid arthritis, diabetes, epilepsy, dyslexia, depression and, in some cases, obesity (CIPD, 2014c).

Employers must make reasonable adjustments in any arrangements or to work premises in order that people who are disabled can apply for work and are able to undertake such work. This may include consideration of flexible hours to accommodate the needs of a disabled person and the modification of equipment or installation of equipment to allow for optimal working or easier access. For example, where a staff canteen is accessed via steps it is reasonable that the employer install a ramp so that step-free access can be obtained. Employers are compelled at least to consider these matters seriously and be prepared to justify their decisions with regard to their reasonableness. In order to fulfil this duty it is reasonable for employers to ask at the application stage whether an applicant requires any adjustments to be made to enable them to apply for the position (such as an application form in large script), attend an interview or participate in any scheduled assessments. It is not permissible, however, at this stage to issue a pre-employment health questionnaire or to ask questions about a person's absence record. These issues may be raised once a job offer is being considered, and the emphasis should be on the reasonable adjustments that may be required to enable the person to take up the work on offer.

Gender reassignment

This characteristic refers to persons planning to undergo, in the process of undergoing or who have undergone procedures to change their sex from male to female or vice versa. Such persons are also referred to as transsexuals. However, it is important to note that according to the Equality Act 2010 a person does not have to be under medical supervision to be protected. Also, a person who has started the gender reassignment process but has withdrawn still has the protected characteristic. A person undergoing gender reassignment treatment or surgery should be treated fairly in terms of a request for time off work. At the very least, employers should discuss with transgender staff how much time off they are likely to need and try to accommodate the request.

Marriage and civil partnership

These are protected characteristics. It was the case that same sex couples could obtain a civil partnership but could not marry in the UK. However, in February 2014 the Scottish Parliament voted in favour of introducing marriage for same sex couples under the Marriage and Civil Partnership (Scotland) Bill 2013. Same sex marriage was introduced in England and Wales in March 2014 under the Marriage (Same Sex Couples) Act 2013. Only same sex couples are able to register for civil partnerships although there is discussion about whether all couples should be able to register for a civil partnership.

Pregnancy or maternity

Under the Equality Act 2010, pregnancy and maternity are a separate protected characteristic to sex. The general principle is that women should not be treated unfairly because they are pregnant or because they have maternity responsibilities.

Race

Characteristics protected against discrimination include colour, nationality and ethnic or national origins and membership of a racial group. Other relevant characteristics could include a common language or a sense of being in a minority.

Religion or belief

This characteristic refers to any religion or belief, including lack of religion or belief. The act does not state what constitutes a religion but it does say that the religion must have a clear structure and belief system. Denominations within a religion constitute a religion. Belief relates to how a person lives their life or perceives the world. Examples include humanism and atheism but not followers of a football team.

Sex

Protection applies to both men and women. Issues of equal pay for equal work, with reference to like work, work of equal value and work rated as equivalent, are a matter of sex equality. Sex does not include sexual orientation discrimination which is a separate category of discrimination.

Sexual orientation

Sexual orientation is defined as a person's orientation towards persons of the same sex, of the opposite sex, of both the same sex and the opposite sex. Note that the legislation addresses sexual orientation and not sexual practices.

Types of discrimination

Discrimination can occur in four basic ways:

- direct discrimination
- indirect discrimination
- harassment
- victimisation.

Direct discrimination occurs when someone is treated less favourably for a reason directly to do with their sex, age, race, and so on, and in comparison to how a person without that protected characteristic would be treated. Examples of this would be to refuse a woman a job as a construction worker simply because she is a woman, and to refuse a Kenyan a job in a restaurant simply because all the other employees are white European and the employer fears that a person from a different racial background will not 'fit in'.

With regard to the protected characteristics and discrimination, it does not matter whether or not the person actually has the characteristic that is the focus of the discrimination. So, for example, if an employer refuses to hire a woman because the employer thinks she is lesbian (and that is the reason for the rejection), this is discrimination because of the applicant being considered a lesbian, even if she is not. This is known as perceptive discrimination but it does not apply to the protected characteristics of marriage or civil partnership or pregnancy and maternity (Sargeant and Lewis, 2014). Another form of direct discrimination is associative discrimination. This is where the person concerned does not have the protected characteristic but they are discriminated against through association with a person who has a protected characteristic. This may occur, for example, where a woman has to take time off to care for a disabled child and the employer makes no attempt to discuss the possibility of making reasonable adjustments or help the employee with her responsibilities.

Indirect discrimination occurs when someone is treated unfairly because of some provision, criterion or practice that would particularly disadvantage the particular group that person belongs to, and when the requirement cannot be objectively justified. For example, if you wished to hire someone to drive a truck, and you stipulated that applicants must be six feet tall, could this requirement be justified in terms of the skills and abilities required to do the job? Which groups might such a requirement discriminate against? Fewer women than men, for instance, are six feet tall. This requirement therefore discriminates indirectly against female applicants.

Informal practices can also constitute indirect discrimination. For example, if an informal workplace culture has grown where employees are expected to entertain clients late in the evening in places where alcohol is served, and this is necessary to secure promotion, there are some groups of people who would be less able or willing than others to participate in such activities, for example women with small children and members of religious groups which ban alcohol.

Activity 4.2

Look through the records of cases heard by employment tribunals and you will find examples of direct discrimination, indirect discrimination, victimisation and harassment. To find reports of such cases you can use several sources:

* A number of human resource management journals have a section that gives updates on the law and describes recent cases. For example, in *People Management* and *Personnel Today*.
* There are also numerous cases reported in the *Equal Opportunities Review* and some issues of the *IRS Employment Review*, both publications of XpertHR (**www .xperthr.co.uk**).
* CIPD members have access to descriptions of numerous tribunal cases in the Employment Law at Work section of the CIPD website (**www.cipd.co.uk**).

Did you know?

At the start of employment, there is a short period when the employee does not have any rights against unfair dismissal. This is known as the 'qualifying period'. For employees who started their employment contract before 6 April 2012 the qualifying period is one year's continuous service but for employees who started their employment contract on or after 6 April 2012 the qualifying period is at least two years. This qualifying period does not apply if the complainant feels that the reasons for the unfair dismissal were connected to any of the types of discrimination covered by equality legislation under the Employment Rights Act 1996 and the Equality Act 2010. You can read more about this in the section on the burden of proof later in this chapter.

Harassment is defined as unwanted conduct that violates the dignity of the person with a protected characteristic or creates an intimidating, hostile, degrading, humiliating or offensive environment (Sargeant and Lewis, 2014). The behaviour in question can be verbal or physical. It can include such things as ignoring someone, obscene gestures, pestering, spying, stalking, setting impossible deadlines, personal insults and persistent unwanted criticism (CIPD, 2015).

Victimisation occurs when someone is treated less favourably because that person has, in good faith, made a complaint, or indicated an intention to make a complaint, about discrimination under the Equality Act 2010, or given evidence to support someone making a complaint or made allegations that another person has contravened the act. An example of this might be a woman who has raised a grievance about a less-qualified man being promoted and who is subsequently dismissed unfairly.

Combined discrimination: dual characteristics

The act includes a new provision for a person to complain of discrimination on a combination of two relevant protected characteristics. For instance, an employer may hire white male applicants, black male applicants and white female applicants, but reject black female applicants. Since this employer hires black males there is no particular evidence to suggest that race discrimination has taken place, and since white females are hired there is no particular evidence to suggest that sex discrimination has occurred. But if black females are excluded as a group then they are being subjected to combined discrimination. This form of discrimination could be a combination of any two of the protected characteristics. Two protected characteristics are excluded from combined discrimination provisions: marriage and civil partnership and pregnancy and maternity. Combined discrimination can only be brought in relation to claims of direct discrimination. An individual would not be able to bring a claim of combined discrimination in relation to indirect discrimination, victimisation or harassment.

Simpson (2010) provides some interesting sample scenarios of possible dual discrimination making it clear that a case that may fail on a claim of discrimination based on a single protected characteristic may in contrast succeed if it is based on a combination of two characteristics. One of his examples of a case of combined age and disability discrimination is based on Henry, a 62–year-old factory worker, who, because of repetitive work in the factory, had developed arthritis and, as a result, had higher-than-average levels of absence. After announcing redundancy plans his manager commented that he should retire because he was often absent. Henry was placed in a redundancy pool with two other workers (of similar age) and, as he received the lowest score, was made redundant. Henry could claim discrimination on the basis of age but this may prove difficult because the other two workers in the redundancy pool were of similar age. He may also claim discrimination on the basis of disability but this may prove difficult if the employer could point to an employee of a similar age with a disability who was not made redundant. The combination of age and disability in a dual claim would strengthen Henry's case.

Occupational requirement

There may be a requirement for an employee to be of a particular sex, racial background, religion, sexual orientation or age and so on but this is only likely to happen in exceptional circumstances. These are known as occupational requirements and they represent a requirement to have a particular protected characteristic. This provision applies to all of the protected characteristics. For example, having a specific disability may be designated as an occupational requirement and a charity providing supported employment may give preference to a person with a relevant disability. The application of an occupational requirement must be a proportionate means of achieving a legitimate aim.

Such requirements have traditionally been acceptable in instances where authenticity is required, for example in entertainment, modelling (for instance male or female fashion clothes) or where privacy and decency in the provision of personal services are concerned. An example of an occupational qualification would be to advertise for a female to work in a women's refuge. A further example might be an organisation that offers support and advice on relationships to same sex couples and may wish to recruit gay and lesbian counsellors who may be more able to empathise with their clients.

The presence of an occupational requirement means that not only persons from the specified group are being invited to apply, but also that only such a person will be considered for selection. This is often confused by less well-informed jobseekers with encouragement for members of under-represented groups to apply for vacancies so they can be considered along with all other qualified applicants in the selection process. You can read more about the recruitment of under-represented groups in Chapter 6.

Positive action in recruitment and promotion decisions

There are two sections of the Equality Act 2010 that deal with positive action:

- Section 158 concerns employers being able to take positive action to help a member of an under-represented group in order to help overcome or minimise the disadvantages that members of that group face.
- Section 159 concerns voluntary provisions similar to those contained in Section 158 but these focus on treating a person with a protected characteristic more favourably than another in terms of recruitment or promotion, but only where both people are equally qualified.

The CIPD (2014d) states that, with respect to Section 159, it will be difficult to establish whether or not candidates are really equal, whether groups are really under-represented or disadvantaged and how to deal with a claim from an unsuccessful candidate. Therefore, as Section 159 of the Equality Act 2010 is voluntary some employers may choose to ignore it.

The equality duty of public sector employers

Public authorities include organisations such as local councils, the police and fire service, educational establishments and the NHS. Under the Equality Act 2010 there are two specific duties required of public sector employers:

- To publish equality information, at intervals of no more than one year, to demonstrate compliance with its equality duty related to its employees (only for public authorities employing at least 150 people) and other persons affected by its policies and practices.
- To publish equality objectives at intervals of no greater than four years.

Burden of proof in discrimination cases

A problem with discrimination cases is the ability of the complainant to demonstrate that discrimination has taken place (Sargeant and Lewis, 2014). Once an employment tribunal is satisfied that an applicant has provided *prima facie* evidence of discrimination (that is, it considers that on the balance of probabilities discrimination may have occurred) it is then up to the employer (the respondent in the case) to provide a non-discriminatory explanation.

If we take the recruitment and selection processes as an example in assessing the burden of proof, positive evidence of non-discrimination could include equality policies, non-discriminatory job descriptions and person specifications and evidence that only non-discriminatory questions were used during interviews. Further evidence might include notes made during interviews, the results of non-biased tests, analysis of data collected for monitoring purposes, evidence of how the position was advertised and a description of equality training that is provided to managers and others involved in the selection process.

The government's Equality and Human Rights Commission (**www .equalityhumanrights.com**) provides information about the choices for making a complaint, the procedure to follow to obtain information if a person feels they may have been discriminated against, together with links to organisations, such as ACAS, who publish information on discrimination in the workplace.

Concluding comment on the Equality Act 2010

Although a major goal of the Equality Act 2010 was to streamline and simplify the discrimination legislation, this is, nonetheless, a complex area of law. As with all major pieces of legislation we can expect further amendments to the law in the future. Ultimately no single piece of legislation is complete and adjustments and additions will need to be made to take into account the changing landscape of equality, diversity and discrimination.

Activity 4.3

Check the websites for the Equality and Human Rights Commission (**www .equalityhumanrights.com**) and the Advisory, Conciliation and Arbitration Service (ACAS) (**www.acas.org.uk**) to find out what the most recent developments are with regard to equality legislation.

● Good practice in equal opportunities

To operate within the spirit of the equality legislation, all actions and documents involved in HR processes must be free of any criteria that could be interpreted as being discriminatory within the terms of the Equality Act 2010 legislation. The existence of an up-to-date equality policy is a good indication that an organisation intends to follow good practice with regard to all discrimination issues covered by the law. A good policy establishes a framework that enables current employees to know how they are expected to behave with regard to these issues and that they themselves will be treated fairly. Prospective employees may also be attracted to an organisation that demonstrates its intentions of treating everyone fairly. It must be noted, however, that the mere existence of an equality or equal opportunities policy does not necessarily mean that the risk of unlawful discrimination is reduced (Slater and Murthy, 2015). Communication of the equality policy and training of line managers in implementing it are crucial in ensuring its success.

The equality legislation has practical implications for all aspects of people management, and some of these are dealt with in other chapters. For instance, the role of flexible working was dealt with in Chapter 3 on the employment relationship; equal pay will be addressed in Chapter 9. To illustrate the practical implications of equality here we shall take a look at some examples from the area of recruitment.

Advertisements, job descriptions and person specifications (which are explained more fully in Chapter 6) must not include anything that could be construed as an intention to discriminate on an unlawful basis. Except in the case of a genuine occupational requirement, as described earlier in this chapter, advertisements should not include words that might indicate a preference for hiring females rather than males, or vice versa. For example, it is not lawful for a restaurant to advertise for waitresses as this would imply that the employer is only interested in hiring females. This would represent direct discrimination on the basis of sex. The same applies to the other groups protected by equality legislation.

With the introduction of age discrimination regulations, there was, and continues to be, much discussion about words which might imply a preference for persons from a particular age group. To advertise for 'young people' or 'someone aged 18–30' would quite obviously be unlawful, but practitioners have had to examine the viability of other terms such as 'mature' (which might imply a preference for an older person) or 'energetic' (which might imply that a younger person was being sought). ACAS (2013) states that the terms 'recent graduate' or 'highly experienced' should be avoided unless they are genuine requirements of the job as they may indicate a preference regarding a candidate's age. Whether or not these and similar terms suggest that unlawful age discrimination is intended, the wording of an advertisement is certainly something that employers need to consider with much care and attention.

The existence of a good person specification or competency framework can assist an employer in avoiding inadvertent sex, race or other unlawful discrimination when advertising for a post and undertaking the selection process. The design and use of person specifications

Did you know?

It is generally regarded as unacceptable to request an applicant to attach a photograph to a job application in the UK, whereas this is still common practice in other countries such as France and Germany. Such a requirement would conflict with the spirit of the UK legislation as a photograph can only provide information about sex, racial background and age and not about skills and knowledge. The use of such input can be seen as unfair discrimination.

is discussed more fully in Chapter 6 with specific reference to recruitment. Direct discrimination is rarely overtly expressed but the intention to discriminate can be inferred from various events, and introducing new criteria after the person specification has been agreed and made known is one such event. If a post involves an occupational requirement to have a particular protected characteristic, this should be decided before the post is advertised and made clear to everyone through the person specification and the job advertisement.

The acceptance of diversity and equality in organisations and attempts to create a more inclusive workplace have become even more important in the twenty-first century with the broadening of the equality law and growing recognition of the business case for diversity. With regard to harassment, it is necessary to make it clear to all employees that so-called 'banter' can be regarded as offensive and harmful by some individuals and should be avoided.

In terms of equal pay, the Equality Act 2010 provides for members of one sex to claim equal pay (not only restricted to wages but also including occupational pension schemes, company cars, gym membership, private health care insurance, redundancy pay, sick pay, holiday pay etc.) with a member of the opposite sex who is doing like work, or work of a different nature which can be shown to be similar in terms of the requirements for skill and effort, that is, work of equal value. Equal pay is dealt with in more detail in Chapter 9, which examines payment systems and the evaluation of jobs. The major point to be made here is that it would be unlawful to advertise different pay rates for men and women doing the same work, or to offer employees of one sex disadvantageous terms and conditions. However, a man may be paid at a higher rate than a woman and be objectively justified where there is a 'material factor' other than sex involved (Marson, 2014).

Organisations that wish to promote diversity and equality can introduce a complaints procedure, so that applicants who feel they may have been discriminated against can appeal in the first instance to the organisation concerned. This would normally mean that at least one staff member would be designated as responsible for the promotion of diversity and equality so that applicants felt they were approaching a committed but unbiased person.

Monitoring of diversity and equality and the extent to which it is reflected in an organisation is also regarded as being crucial to the achievement of diversity and equality goals (ACAS, 2014). The purpose of monitoring is to enable the organisation to examine how its diversity and equality policy and action plans are working. Monitoring involves gathering data on potential recruits and new employees and then comparing and analysing this information against other groups of workers in the organisation, jobseekers in the local community and the national labour market (ACAS, 2014). The organisation should monitor by sex, ethnic origin, disability, age, marital status, grade and payment in each unit (McKevitt, 2015). Such monitoring can reveal whether the organisation's recruitment practices are reaching a wide range of candidates and to avoid future possible issues arising from discriminatory practices (McKevitt, 2015).

Rehabilitation of Offenders Act 1974

Under the Rehabilitation of Offenders Act 1974 a conviction becomes 'spent' after a defined period of time, allowing a job applicant with a conviction to be treated,

Did you know?

Sir Richard Branson has commented, 'I believe our society should do more to support positive initiatives to encourage the rehabilitation of prisoners. We should create more chances for people who have been in jail to make a positive contribution to the workforce.' Sir Richard Branson has stated that he would like to encourage more companies to actively recruit ex-offenders. Virgin's experience of recruiting ex-offenders has been positive, he claims, pointing out that the firm has worked successfully with Working Chance, the restorative recruitment charity, who offers recruitment to women ex-offenders.

Another firm that is proactive in recruiting ex-offenders is Timpson, the UK retailer, which has a programme called 'The Academy' that creates job opportunities for people leaving prison. Timpson provides training workshops inside prisons and this has led to over 40 jobs for prison leavers in the past two years. Timpson also offers advice to other retailers on recruiting ex-offenders. Another initiative is to employ ROTL (release on temporary license) offenders who work as apprentices for the firm during the day and return to prison at night.

(*Sources*: **www.virgin.com** and **www.timpson.co.uk**; accessed 29.01.15)

in most cases, the same as someone who didn't have a conviction. With some exceptions, past offenders should not be expected to reveal their offence once the conviction is spent, and should not be denied employment because of this previous offence. An offence that attracts a sentence of life imprisonment or a sentence of more than 48 months' imprisonment is never spent. The time periods over which convictions become spent vary from one year from the date of conviction for a fine to seven years from completion of a sentence of imprisonment, or youth custody for more than 30 months but not more than 48 months.

There is a long list of excluded jobs and professions under the Rehabilitation of Offenders Act 1974. This means that it is lawful for such jobs and professions to ask questions about the candidate's spent convictions and to refuse employment to a person with a spent conviction. Under such circumstances the employer will need to explain to the job applicant that the post falls into an excluded category and spent convictions will need to be disclosed. Excluded categories include jobs in the health care profession, veterinary surgeon, solicitor, chartered accountant, police constable, prison officer, children's home worker and a worker in a fostering agency.

Case study 4.1   Discrimination

Mrs Julia Mgobo applied for a post as an administrative officer with a local authority in the north of England. The advertisement and person specification for the post had listed three years' experience in administration as one of the criteria being sought, and Mrs Mgobo had worked as an administrator for a firm of accountants for four years. The local authority received a number of good applications and the selection panel had difficulty in shortlisting a smaller number of applicants to call for interview. After some deliberation they decided that they would interview those candidates who had experience of administrative duties with a local authority. Mrs Mgobo was not one of the applicants called to interview. She felt that she was well qualified for the post according to the advertisement and the job description and person specification that had been sent to her. Mrs Mgobo felt that she must have been discriminated against unfairly and decided to pursue the matter.

Comment on the equal opportunities implications of this case. Why might Mrs Mgobo feel that she has been the victim of unlawful discrimination? What should the employer, the local authority, do?

Discussion of case study

In times of high unemployment it is common to find large numbers of people applying for vacancies. Some vacancies, irrespective of labour market conditions, attract a large number of applicants. It is difficult to achieve the correct balance between a tightly formulated person specification and one that excludes people unnecessarily. However, introducing criteria after applications have been submitted could be seen as an attempt to exclude people for reasons not connected to the job, for example to exclude women or certain ethnic groups. Depending on who was ultimately hired for this post, Mrs Mbogo could believe that she had been discriminated against because of her sex or ethnic origin or a combination of these.

Let us assume that there was no discriminatory intention on the part of the selection panel and that they were merely trying to shortlist candidates after an unexpectedly large number of applications from well-qualified people. The case points out the importance of developing a good, detailed and, as far as possible, complete person specification and job description.

The local authority should ensure that there is an adequate internal mechanism for dealing with Mrs Mbogo's query. The fact that an employer tries to address any problems of this nature in a sincere fashion would be recognised by the Equality and Human Rights Commission as part of good equal opportunities practice. Local authorities are also subject to the duty to promote equality in terms of race, gender and disability and so on, so this employer should also have the relevant policies in place. The employer should also ensure that training is provided to all employees involved in recruitment and selection to ensure that they understand the importance of each element of the process.

Review questions

You will find brief answers to these review questions on page 463–4.
1. Explain the concept of diversity and equality in the workplace.
2. Outline the business case for a diverse workforce.
3. Comment on how diversity and equality should be managed.
4. Define the protected characteristics listed in the Equality Act 2010.
5. Explain the following terms and give examples: direct discrimination; indirect discrimination; victimisation; harassment.

Improving your employability

Earlier in this chapter we examined the notion of 'banter' with respect to harassment. Banter is defined as 'to speak to or tease lightly or jokingly' (*Collins Dictionary Online*). For a period of a week take note of any 'banter' in your workplace or place of study. Assess this banter in terms of its likely effect on the recipients. Could any of the banter constitute harassment? This knowledge will help you to design or improve a policy on harassment in the workplace and you will be more sensitive to the harm that banter might cause.

HR in the news

How do I increase diversity without alienating people?

By Janina Conboye

I have to implement a recruitment and promotion policy that attracts a broader group of people, including senior women. But how can the company engage its white male employee majority, who could feel threatened by inclusivity targets and moves to attract a broader base of people?

Stephen Frost, UK head of diversity at consultancy KMPG, says: Diversity programmes often fail because they are framed poorly. You need to answer three questions for your key audience, the decision makers. Why are we doing this? What are you proposing? How are we going about it?

Let us start with "why?". The business case for greater diversity is compelling: it counters "groupthink", provides greater cognitive challenge and informs better decisions. However, the lack of action reflects the fact that many people do not fully accept this. Implicit bias is important to understand here. We are all biased. This means you need to be empathetic because you are challenging people's view of their own objectivity.

Moving to "what?". Data enable us to display conceptual views of diversity or gender. For example, if we present the gender statistics at various grades in an organisation, we typically see a pyramid shape – perhaps 50-50 men and women in junior ranks and a big narrowing of women at the top. By introducing proportionality by grade or department, we can challenge bias in a less threatening way. For example, if a third of a particular grade are women, yet the grade above is only 10 per cent, it raises the question: why are we not promoting about 33 per cent women to reflect the actual talent pool available? This is not positive discrimination but an effective and measurable check on naturally occurring bias.

Crucially, the only way we will succeed with greater diversity programmes is to talk about "how?". One way is to increase the decision-making timeframe. Quick decisions exacerbate bias. Instead of a one-year promotion cycle, consider a three-year timeframe with midyear promotions. It gives diversity a better chance. Second, break the silos and make promotions in unison. If a manager is looking at one part of the business, there may only be two or three promotions. Looked at across the organisation, the number could be 10 times as large. And 30 male promotions company-wide stands out as a red flag, more so than two or three in one part of the business, thus making the system a natural check-and-balance tool.

Questions

1. What are the pros and cons of diversity for an organisation?
2. Why is it that some workplaces are not diverse when the labour market is?
3. How can diversity be increased in an organisation without alienating people?

What next?

The journal *Equality, Diversity and Inclusion*, previously published as *Equal Opportunities International*, provides contemporary research from around the world on matters concerning equality, inequality, discrimination, equal opportunities, disadvantage, diversity and inclusion. If you are studying at a university then your institution should provide you with access to the journal via an electronic platform such as Summon. Here are a number of recent articles from this journal that should be of interest to you as they cover many of the aspects of equality, diversity and discrimination covered in this chapter.

Hussein, S., J. Manthorpe and M. Imail (2014) Ethnicity at work: the case of British minority workers in the long-term care sector, *Equality, Diversity and Inclusion: An International Journal*, Vol. 33, No. 2, 177–192.

Jenkins, A. and J. Poulston (2014) Managers' perceptions of older workers in British hotels, *Equality, Diversity and Inclusion: An International Journal*, Vol. 33, No. 1, 54–72.

Rudin, J., S. Ruane, L. Ross, A. Farro and T. Billing (2014) Hostile territory: employers' unwillingness to accommodate transgender employees, *Equality, Diversity and Inclusion: An International Journal*, Vol. 33,No. 8, 721–734.

Smith, L. (2013) Working hard with gender: gendered labour for women in male dominated occupations of manual trades and information technology (IT), *Equality, Diversity and Inclusion: An International Journal*, Vol. 32, No. 6, 592–603.

References

Advisory, Conciliation and Arbitration Service (2013) *Job Adverts: How Not to Discriminate against Applicants*, ACAS (available at www.acas.org.uk; accessed 29.01.15).

Advisory, Conciliation and Arbitration Service (2014) *Delivering Equality and Diversity*, ACAS (available at www.acas.org.uk; accessed 29.01.15).

Allen, R., G. Dawson, K. Wheatley and C. White (2008) Perceived diversity and organizational performance, *Employee Relations*, Vol. 30, No. 1, 20–33.

Biddle, D. (2006) *Adverse Impact and Test Validation: A Practitioner's Guide to Valid and Desirable Employment Testing*, Gower Publishing, Aldershot.

Chartered Institute of Personnel and Development (2012) *Diversity and Inclusion – Fringe or Fundamental? Survey Report*, CIPD (available from www.cipd.co.uk; accessed 21.01.15).

Chartered Institute of Personnel and Development (2014a) *Diversity in the Workplace: An Overview*, CIPD (factsheet available from www.cipd.co.uk; accessed 21.01.15).

Chartered Institute of Personnel and Development (2014b) *Employment Law: Key Differences between Northern Ireland and Great Britain*, CIPD (factsheet available from www.cipd.co.uk; accessed 28.01.15).

Chartered Institute of Personnel and Development (2014c) *Disability and Employment*, CIPD (factsheet available from www.cipd.co.uk; accessed 28.01.15).

Chartered Institute of Personnel and Development (2014d) *DS10: What Is Positive Action and Can Employers Do This?* CIPD (employment law FAQ, available from www.cipd.co.uk; accessed 29.01.15).

Chartered Institute of Personnel and Development (2015) *Harassment and Bullying at Work*, CIPD (factsheet available from www.cipd.co.uk; accessed 28.01.15).

Clements, P. and J. Jones (2010) *The Diversity Training Handbook*, Kogan Page, London.

Daft, R. and D. Marcic (2013) *Management: The New Workplace*, South-Western College Publishing, Cincinnati.

Daniels, K. (2004) *Employment Law for HR and Business Students*, CIPD, London.

Daniels, K. and L. Macdonald (2005) *Equality, Diversity and Discrimination: A Student Text,* CIPD, London.

Deloitte Consulting (2014) *Global Human Capital Trends 2014*, Deloitte University Press, Westlake, Texas.

Derven, M. (2014) Diversity and inclusion by design: best practices from six global companies, *Industrial and Commercial Training*, Vol. 46, No. 2, 84–91.

Incomes Data Services (2010) *IDS HR Study 921: Managing Diversity in the Workplace*, July, IDS, London.

Kandola, R. and J. Fullerton (1998) *Diversity in Action: Managing the Mosaic*, 2nd edition, IPD, London.

McCartney, C. and D. Worman (2010) *Opening Up Talent for Business Success. Integrating Talent Management and Diversity*, CIPD, London.

McKevitt, T. (2015) *Equal Opportunities Policies and Monitoring* (available at www.xperthr.co.uk; accessed 29.01.15).

Nathan, M. (2015) Same difference? Minority ethnic inventors, diversity and innovation in the UK, *Journal of Economic Geography*, Vol. 15, No. 1, 129–168.

Newell, S. (1995) *The Healthy Organization: Fairness, Ethics and Effective Management*, Routledge, London.

Niederle, M., C. Segal and L. Vesterlund (2013) How costly is diversity?: Affirmative action in light of gender differences in competitiveness, *Management Science*, Vol. 59 No. 1, 1–16.

Reynolds, D., I. Rahman and S. Bradetich (2014) Hotel managers' perceptions of the value of diversity training: an empirical investigation, *International Journal of Contemporary Hospitality Management*, Vol. 26, No. 3, 426–446.

Rose, E. (2001) *Employment Relations*, Pearson Education, Harlow.

Sargeant, M. and D. Lewis (2014) *Employment Law*, Pearson Education, London.

Simpson, S. (2010) *Equality Act 2010: 10 Example Dual Discrimination Scenarios* (available at xperthr .co.uk; accessed 14.04.15).

Singal, M. (2014) The business case for diversity management in the hospitality industry, *International Journal of Hospitality Management*, Vol. 40, 10–19.

Slater, H. and K. Murthy (2015) *Equal Opportunities Policy* (available at www.xperthr.co.uk; accessed 29.01.15).

Stevens, M. (2012) Diversity and inclusion 'rising up corporate agenda', 26 November, *People Management* (available at www.cipd.co.uk; accessed 21.01.15).

Thompson, N. (2012) *Anti-discriminatory Practice: Equality, Diversity and Social Justice*, Palgrave Macmillan, Basingstoke.

Tomei, M. (2003) Discrimination and equality at work: a review of the concepts, *International Labour Review*, Vol. 142, No. 4, 401–418.

Trades Union Congress (2013) *Under-representation by Gender and Race in Apprenticeships: Research Summary*, unionlearn, London.

Trades Union Congress and the Confederation of Business Industry (2008) *Talent not Tokenism: The Business Benefits of Workforce Diversity*, CBI, London.

Wolff, C. (2007) Arriva: dramatic results on diversity, *Equal Opportunities Review* (available at www .xperthr.co.uk; accessed 21.01.15).

XpertHR (2013) *Flexible Working Policies and Practice: 2013*, XpertHR survey (available at www .xperthr.co.uk; accessed 25.01.15).

Further study

Books and reports

Advisory, Conciliation and Arbitration Service (2014) *The Equality Act: Guidance for Employers*, ACAS, London.
A useful booklet which provides a concise and readable summary of the act, including types of discrimination, the protected characteristics and examples of discrimination.

Macleod, A., D. Worman, P. Wilton, P. Woodman and P. Hutchings (2010) *Managing an Ageing Workforce: How Employers are Adapting to an Older Labour Market*, CIPD, London.
Presents results from a survey conducted in 2010 and an overview of what some employers are doing to deal with in an increasingly older labour force. The report focuses on key areas, including recruitment, training and development, flexible working practices, redundancy and redeployment, retirement and organisational policies.

Marson, J. (2014) *Beginning Employment Law*, Routledge, London.
This is a concise text that deals with a complicated and vast topic in an accessible manner. The text does not assume any prior knowledge of employment law.

Articles

Guillaume, Y., J. Dawson, V. Priola, C. Sacramento, S. Woods, H. Higson and M. West (2014) Managing diversity in organizations: an integrative model and agenda for future research, *European Journal of Work and Organizational Psychology*, Vol. 23, No. 5, 783–802.
This paper provides a comprehensive and cohesive view of diversity in organisations. A multilevel model of diversity is presented.

Riley, R., H. Metcalf and J. Forth (2013) The business case for equal opportunities, *Industrial Relations Journal*, Vol. 44, No. 3, 216–239.
This research paper analyses data from the Workplace Employment Relations Survey 2004 to establish the benefits and costs associated with equal opportunities policies for organisations.

Shore, L., B. Chung-Herrera, M. Dean, K. Ehrhart, D. Jung, A. Randel and G. Singh (2009) Diversity in organizations: where are we now and where are we going? *Human Resource Management Review*, Vol. 19, No. 2, 117–133.
This paper presents the dimensions of diversity (age, race, gender, sexual orientation, disability and culture) and discusses common themes across these dimensions. An integrative model of diversity is also presented.

Stone, D. and L. Tetrick (2013) Understanding and facilitating age diversity in organizations, *Journal of Managerial Psychology*, Vol. 28(7–8), 725–728.
This represents the editorial to two special issues on age diversity in organisations and, for a complete understanding of the topic, journal articles relating to the two special issues should also be read. An understanding of the issues presented in the special issues will enable organisations to be in a better position to enhance the skills and abilities of older workers.

Internet

Advisory, Conciliation and Arbitration Service   www.acas.org.uk
ACAS offers a range of courses (such as equal pay, disability discrimination, equality, diversity and the Equality Act 2010 and age and the repeal of the Default Retirement Age) in a number of locations throughout the UK.

Business Disability Forum   www.efd.org.uk
This website provides a range of information for employers, including guidelines and factsheets, information on events and awards, blogs and case studies in order to assist businesses to become 'disability smart employers'.

Chartered Institute of Personnel and Development   www.cipd.co.uk
The CIPD website contains a wealth of information on various aspects of diversity and equality. The website provides a number of podcasts dealing with equal pay for women (Podcast 73), the business case for diversity (Podcast 8) and managing an ageing workforce (Podcast 47). There are also factsheets, research reports, blogs and toolkits on diversity and equality.

Equality and Human Rights Commission   www.equalityhumanrights.com
The Equality and Human Rights Commission has been established to deal with all equality issues. The website offers a series of extensive guidance booklets for both employers and individuals on aspects of the Equality Act 2010.

UK Government   www.gov.uk
Documents relating to the Department for Work and Pensions' 'Age Positive' initiative can be found here as well as other equality information relevant to recruitment.

XpertHR   www.xperthr.co.uk
This site provides you with a wealth of information on developments in equality legislation and employment practices. The site includes good practice manuals, law reports, case studies, line manager briefings, policies and documents and survey reports.

5 Human resource strategy and planning

Objectives

When you have studied this chapter you will be able to:

- describe what strategy is, including the different levels of strategy, and how corporate strategy affects HR strategy

- explain the concept of strategy formulation

- explain the need for human resource strategies in organisations

- describe the stages involved in human resource planning

- identify and describe the issues that have an impact on human resource supply and demand forecasts

- use appropriate techniques to produce accurate forecast supply and demand figures for an organisation's human resources

- describe the skills shortages encountered by employers, their causes and possible solutions

- comment on the use of IT systems in relation to an organisation's human resource strategy.

Chapter 1 introduced you to the concept of human resource management (HRM) and established that a key characteristic of the HRM approach is the involvement of the people management function at a strategic level. We will now examine the different levels at which strategy can be formulated and the generic types of strategy that are encountered, and comment on the links between the formulation of business strategy and consideration of human resource issues. It should be remembered, however, that we will be looking at the ideal situation or models of how corporate/business strategy and HR considerations interact. What we describe is not always found in reality. Indeed, the specific circumstances in which a business is operating might call for a different approach. You will find that we sometimes refer to contingency approaches, which means that there is no one right way to manage human resources in an organisation.

After providing an overview of corporate/business and human resource strategies we examine the activities that underpin the development of HR strategies, namely the techniques involved in human resource planning and the factors which have a major impact on planning decisions. This chapter ends with a discussion of the role of IT in supporting strategic human resource management (SHRM) endeavours.

Strategy

Essentially, strategy is about the long-term direction of an organisation (Johnson *et al.*, 2014). However, there are many different definitions of what strategy is and how strategy develops in organisations. Essentially, there are two different approaches to strategic development: the prescriptive and the emergent approach (Lynch, 2012). The prescriptive approach is the 'classical' approach to strategic development where strategic development is linear and rational and the main elements of strategy are determined in advance. The emergent approach is where strategy emerges over time and cannot, therefore, be usefully summarised in a plan. Lynch (2012) comments that the prescriptive approach works perfectly well where growth is continuous, linear and predictable but is much less suited to conditions involving rapid change.

In the 'classical' approach to strategic development, strategy is defined as a plan of action for the future. The three common questions used to give a simple explanation of the strategic process are: Where are we now? Where do we want to be? How do we get there? A strategic plan should have a long-term focus with business plans usually being developed around a three- to five-year time frame. The aim of designing and following a strategic plan is to create competitive advantage, and all efforts in the formulation and implementation processes should be directed towards this. As far as organisations are concerned, strategy can be formulated and implemented at different levels, and there are recognised generic forms of strategy that organisations or subdivisions of organisations might adopt.

Levels of strategy

The levels at which strategy is formulated and implemented are most frequently identified as corporate, business and operational or functional (see, for example, Boxall and Purcell, 2008 and Johnson *et al.*, 2014).

Corporate and business strategies

Corporate strategy is concerned with the overall direction that an organisation will follow. For large corporations this is a question of which lines of business they will choose to be engaged in. These organisations would then develop separate business level strategies for their strategic business units, or divisions, each of which might be engaged in producing very different products or services. Corporate-level issues concern the geographical scope of the organisation, the products and services offered, the methods used to grow the business and how resources are allocated in the organisation (Johnson *et al.*, 2014). Typical business-level issues concern innovation, scale and response to competitors (Johnson *et al.*, 2014).

Operational or functional strategy

Operational strategies concern the delivery of corporate and business strategies in terms of resources, processes and people (Johnson *et al.*, 2014). The functions represented in an organisation depend on the type of business, its size and structure, but may include production, marketing, sales, logistics, procurement, finance, research and development and human resources. Each of these functional areas needs to be following strategic plans that are consistent with the corporate and business plans adopted by their organisations. The strategic plans followed by all these functional departments must be integrated, however, to ensure the success of the organisation; they are interdependent and cannot be formulated without reference to each other. Indeed, it can be stated incontrovertibly that human resources is an integral part of every one of the above-named functions.

The strategy formulation process

Strategy involves gathering and processing information in order to make long-term decisions. There is a need to focus on relevant information, but it is also important to be as comprehensive as possible in order that you do not miss something that could have an impact. Since planning implies forecasting future actions there is always the potential for developments that you may not have foreseen. This means that planning becomes an ongoing process, and that a strategic plan developed for 2015 to 2020 cannot be followed slavishly until 2020 but will probably need to be adjusted on an ongoing basis to account for unforeseen developments.

Pause for thought 5.1   What information would senior managers of an electronics retail business need in order to formulate a strategic plan?

You may have considered a variety of factors and included changes that businesses in general are facing. Your list may include some or all of the following:

- **The product life cycle**: Is the product or service a new one with room for development and an expanding potential market? How frequently do customers replace the product? Is the product mature and not likely to attract many more customers? How likely are customers to look for an alternative to the product or service?
- **Changing consumer tastes**: How are these likely to affect the demand for the product? Are there changes in customer expectations that organisations need to respond to?
- **Expansion of the business into other countries**: Are there opportunities to sell your product or service in other countries? What adaptations to products or services are needed?
- **The economy**: What are the prospects for the UK and world economy? How might changes in the economy affect demand for the product or service?
- **The competition**: What are the threats from competitors and the opportunities to compete? What advantage do we have over our competitors? What do we need to do to ensure we are more successful than our competitors (e.g. offer products and services that cost less or are better in terms of quality)?

- **Technological developments**: How will new technology affect the design of products, work processes and costs?
- **Legislation**: What legislation is being considered and what are the implications for costs, work processes and product standards?

These are just some of the factors that affect business planning and you may be able to identify many more. Information about all of these factors will influence what managers see as opportunities and threats and will therefore affect the strategic choices made and formulation of the strategic plan.

Identifying these issues, and collecting relevant information concerning them, is referred to as environmental scanning, and the acronym PEST or its alternative forms of PESTEL or PESTLE, are commonly used as a reminder of the issues that businesses need to take into consideration when formulating their strategies. The initials in PEST stand for political, economic, social and technological issues whilst the E and L in variations of the basic acronym variously stand for environmental and legal issues (Thompson *et al.*, 2014).

Activity 5.1

For a low-cost passenger airline, such as Southwest Airlines, Ryanair, easyJet, Air Berlin or AirAsia, list the principal political, economic, social, technological, environmental and legal issues currently affecting the firm.

In summary, then, a strategic approach implies a long-term view, encompassing information from all relevant perspectives, and focusing on the ultimate goal of corporate success through achieving and exploiting a position of competitive advantage. Furthermore, a strategic approach requires the integration of activities, processes and people throughout an organisation aligned to the organisation's goals.

Generic types of corporate and business strategy

There are a number of recognised generic types of strategies that companies may choose to follow. These include growth, stability and retrenchment (Millmore *et al.*, 2007). There are a number of ways of pursuing each of these strategies. Growth can be achieved, for example, through the development of new products and services, by acquiring a larger share of the market for existing products and services in domestic or overseas markets, through mergers and acquisitions or through another means of growth such as franchising or management contracts. The strategic directions of growth, stability and retrenchment are normally associated with the life cycle stages of products and markets, and the idea behind the BCG matrix put forward by the Boston Consulting Group in the 1970s is that large corporations would aim to have a balanced portfolio of businesses which have products that are stable and products that are growing (see Lynch, 2012).

The work of the strategy guru Michael Porter (1980) is frequently cited in discussions of business-level strategies. Porter's generic strategies, as cited in Evans (2013), are cost leadership, differentiation and focus. One or a combination of these can be adopted in order to achieve the chosen corporate strategy. In adopting a strategy based on cost, companies will attempt to improve efficiency by reducing staffing, production and other costs. A strategy of differentiation means emphasising the distinctiveness of the firm's products or services, for example by being known for consistently excellent customer service. A focus strategy entails concentrating on a particular segment rather than the whole industry. Innovation as a strategic direction can also provide a major focus (see, for instance, Johnson and Johnson's website at **www.jnj.com**), and Guest *et al.* (1997) make the point that all business strategies need an element of innovation.

Human resource strategies

Human resource strategies arise from the adoption of a strategic approach to managing people which is aligned with the business strategy and which is reflected in a set of HR policy initiatives specifically designed to achieve the organisation's strategic goals. This implies that an appropriate HR strategy, linked to the corporate strategy, provides the 'best fit' between the overall business strategy (also termed corporate strategy) and the HR strategy (discussed in detail by Marchington and Wilkinson, 2005, pp. 106–113). Ideally, however, human resource considerations should inform the corporate strategy and affect what is included in it (CIPD, 2010b). The costs of the HR strategies and the probability of their success should have been a factor in the decision to pursue the particular business strategy in the first place.

HR strategies reflect the philosophy of senior management with regard to the treatment of human resources and address various activities related to their management. The underlying premise of this is that the HR function supports corporate goals by developing and implementing HR practices that engage employees and encourage them to direct their efforts towards the achievement of the organisation's goals (CIPD, 2005). The most tangible aspect of strategic HRM is, therefore, the set of HR policies and processes in existence in an organisation. These would normally address the various aspects of people management such as recruitment, diversity management, development, reward and employee relations. Rather than being able to identify the human resource strategy of an organisation, you will encounter an organisation's recruitment strategy or its diversity strategy or its reward strategy, either explicitly addressed as a strategy or reflected in the organisation's policies and processes. For many organisations, the main focus of their HR strategies is to acquire, develop and maintain an engaged workforce, and this is discussed in Chapters 2, 6 and 8.

Given that the business environment is constantly changing different issues may assume critical strategic importance. One example of this, which is examined later in this chapter (see the discussion of skills shortages) and elsewhere in the book, is the issue of talent management. Because of increased competition for skilled employees in

---

Did you know?

According to an XpertHR survey (Wolff, 2012) on how employers align HR with the business, the key findings were as follows:

1. The HR planning process in organisations is often informal, yet the majority of respondents believe it has had a positive impact on the performance of their organisation.
2. Two thirds of employers without an HR strategy believe that their organisation would perform better if they had one.
3. Among the organisations that have an HR strategy, the majority either link it to – or integrate it with – the main organisational strategy, indicating a sound connection between people management planning and overall goals.
4. Senior HR staff are only involved in two thirds of HR functions involving HR planning.
5. In 82 per cent of businesses, HR line managers are not involved in strategic HR decisions.

(*Source*: Wolff, C. (2012) How employers align HR with the business: 2012 XpertHR survey. *IRS Employment Review*, 30 July)

a wide range of positions many organisations around the world have developed a talent management strategy or talent management processes (Wooldridge, 2006; Ready and Conger, 2007; CIPD, 2010c; Vaiman and Collings, 2013). The need to acquire and/or retain highly competent employees is still important during an economic downturn or recession, as the organisation needs to ensure that it has the necessary human resources when opportunities arise (Murphy, 2009).

It is widely recognised that strategic human resource management (SHRM) is a complex subject. Theoretical interpretations of SHRM are constantly evolving and the definition of SHRM and its relationship to strategy and planning are not absolute but are subject to interpretation, based on an author's understanding of the phenomena under investigation (CIPD, 2013a). The CIPD (2005) has produced a useful toolkit for creating an HR strategy incorporating a nine-step HR strategy development process. The steps are:

1. Decide who is to be involved and how.
2. Define the business strategy.
3. Analyse the context.
4. Identify the business needs.
5. Identify the key HR issues.
6. Develop the strategic framework.
7. Define specific HR strategies.
8. Assess HR capability and resources required.
9. Prepare action plans.

Because there are so many important aspects of an HR strategy, it is essential that these various strategies are coherent and support each other as well as being aligned with the overall business (or corporate) strategy. Other crucial aspects of successful strategic HRM are effective communication and effective change management (CIPD, 2005). In order for an organisation to achieve its goals, its people need to understand what is expected of them and how their efforts contribute to the organisation's success. Also, of necessity, operating in a strategic manner means dealing with change since strategy involves planning for the future and adjusting to a turbulent business environment. The CIPD (2005, p. 3) poses a number of questions to consider before embarking on formulating, developing and implementing an HR strategy. Examples of these questions include: Is this the first time the strategy is formulated or is this an updating of an existing strategy? Will line managers support strategy initiatives and do they have the skills to implement them? How are staff generally likely to react to the strategy? Are the resources available to develop and implement the strategy? These questions help the practitioner to focus on more general aspects of project and change management processes as well as develop the HR strategies per se.

The discussion of strategic HRM and HR strategies so far has emphasised the role of the HR practitioner as a business partner, one of the roles in HR described by Ulrich (CIPD, 2010b). However, in many organisations, HR responsibilities have been devolved to line managers at all levels in an organisation. This is recognised as a basic element of the HRM approach (Storey, 2007). Hutchinson and Purcell (2003) emphasise that front-line managers, defined as line managers with no managerial staff reporting to them, play a crucial role in ensuring that

HR strategies are carried out effectively, and ongoing research into aspects of people management continues to affirm the key role that line managers play. You can find examples of this in the research reports on employee engagement published by the CIPD (2010a) and the government (Macleod and Clarke 2009). Furthermore, the CIPD factsheet (2014c) on the role of line managers in HR states that these managers need to be carefully selected and supported by strong organisational values to clearly show what behaviour is acceptable and what behaviour is not tolerated. Line managers should have the necessary skills to perform HR activities and should reflect on their own behaviour and how this affects workers' motivation and performance (CIPD, 2014c).

Due to the important role that line mangers play in an organisation's HR strategy strategic HR practitioners need to incorporate the view of line managers into the HR strategy planning process, nurture the relationship between the HR function and line managers and ensure that line managers are actively engaged with the HR strategy. Unfortunately, achieving these goals is difficult and the achievement of mutual understanding between HR strategists and line managers has been identified as problematic (Smethurst, 2005). This is obviously another instance where improvements in communication and change management are required.

Human resource planning

Whatever strategy an organisation follows, it is widely recognised that, in today's workplace, an unrelenting and increasing rate of change is unavoidable. The implication of this change is that tomorrow's workplace will not be the same as today's. Employment patterns are continually changing and evolving, as we discussed in more detail in Chapter 3 on the employment relationship. Changing work methods resulting from technological advances, for example, requires a new set of employee skills and for flexibility to acquire these new skills or adapt to new methods of working. This highlights the need for human resource planning which takes a long-term view and works towards preparing an organisation for its future requirements and helps it achieve its strategic objectives. The information acquired through the process of human resource planning will provide an organisation with a foundation for the development of its human resource strategies.

Similar to the need for environmental scanning that was described earlier in this chapter regarding the formulation of a corporate or business strategy, up-to-date information is the key to effective human resource planning. Managers need to be aware of local, regional, national and global trends and be able to integrate this knowledge into their strategic plans. Knowledge of the key issues will enable an organisation to assess the threats and opportunities in

Did you know?

There has been a resurgence of interest in human resource planning in a wide variety of organisations, including public sector organisations, small- and medium-sized enterprises as well as large private sector companies. The CIPD (2010d) believes that workforce planning – having the necessary people resources to deliver the organisation's short- and long-term objectives – should be a core process of HRM. The CIPD (2010d) has compiled a guide to what it calls 'workforce planning'. The guide covers many of the issues addressed in this chapter and so represents excellent further reading for anyone interested in consolidating and deepening their understanding of this area. Six case studies also provide information on the approach adopted by various organisations.

(Source: Baron, A., R. Clarke, P. Turner and S. Pass (2010) Workforce Planning: Right People, Right Time, Right Skills. A guide, Spring, CIPD; available at www.cipd.co.uk; 06.01.15)

their environment and to evaluate their ability to respond with their existing and available resources, including, of course, the organisation's human resources.

The following sections of this chapter examine the stages involved in the human resource planning process, the types of issues and information that need to be considered and techniques for processing that information.

Estimating the demand for human resources

Whatever the corporate/business plans are, they can only be achieved by the effective use of the organisation's human resources. One of the primary stages in the human resource planning process is, therefore, to establish the organisation's future requirements, in terms of the number of people needed and the knowledge and skills of these people, in order for the organisation to meet its corporate goals. We will now examine some examples of corporate goals so that we can envisage what this exercise might entail.

Activity 5.2

For the following two scenarios evaluate what will be required in terms of human resources in order to achieve the goals stated in each case.

1. A UK distributor of children's clothing has announced plans to expand its customer base into Europe. It intends to open a warehouse and distribution depot in Belgium.

2. Two medium-sized UK engineering companies have announced that they will merge their business activities and create a new, larger engineering company. The new firm will increase its market share, make significant cost savings and will be better able to compete with larger engineering firms.

Discussion of Activity 5.2

In order to assess the requirements for human resources in the above scenarios you would have to envisage:

- the tasks that need to be done;
- the skills required to complete these tasks;
- how the tasks could be grouped together to form jobs, taking into consideration the skills requirements;
- how many people would be required to complete the work.

First, then, discrete work tasks need to be identified, followed by the organisation of work tasks into jobs (i.e. a collection of tasks that belong together and could reasonably be carried out by one individual). A qualitative analysis of the skill base required to perform those jobs and achieve the organisation's goals will then need to be undertaken. The records that document tasks and skills in an organisation are the job descriptions (JDs) and person specifications, and the information contained in these documents is collected and organised through the processes of job analysis and job design (discussed more fully in Chapter 6 which deals with recruitment and selection). Alternatively, an organisation may use a competency framework to establish the skills and attributes required to create job profiles (see page 160). The next issue concerns the numbers of people required for each scenario.

In scenario 1 you will have identified the need for staff to manage and operate the new warehousing and distribution depot in Belgium. Staff needed for this operation will include a manager, picking and packing staff, administrative staff and drivers. You may further have considered the need for language skills among some of the staff to communicate with customers, suppliers and retailers throughout Europe and with the home base in the UK. The expansion of business into new European countries might also mean adding new tasks and skill requirements to existing posts in the home country (i.e. UK), or it may mean recruiting a new manager and/or administrative staff who have the necessary language skills and knowledge of marketing and business processes in those countries. At the very least, the expansion of business into new countries implies a need for someone to coordinate the activities with headquarters. You would need additional information about the expected volume of business to be able to calculate how many people will be required for each type of employee.

Scenario 2 requires an examination of where skills and functions are duplicated within the two businesses, which implies that some duties can be merged and not all of the existing posts will be needed (indeed, an objective for undertaking a merger may be to reduce labour costs). Alternatively, because the new, merged organisation will cover a wider range of tasks than either of the separate organisations had, there may be a new requirement for people who can combine skills and manage tasks in both areas. The new, merged organisation may have the resources to take advantage of opportunities and this will affect the number of tasks, jobs and activities. Another consideration is what happens to the two headquarters. It is unusual for a firm to have two headquarters and, therefore, a decision is usually made to consolidate key personnel into one headquarters. This will involve considerable change for some personnel and, depending on the location of the 'new' headquarters, some staff may consider the move, if offered by the employer, to be too disruptive.

Quantitative aspects of estimating demand

Having established what is required in terms of tasks to be performed and skills needed to complete those tasks an analysis is required of how many people are needed for the volume of work.

> **Pause for thought 5.2** Imagine you are a sports and outdoor clothing manufacturer who is going to export men's and women's jackets to Asia. You have estimated that you will require sewing machine operators to produce an additional 8,000 jackets in the first year. What methods could you use to estimate how many people you would need for this task?

It is likely that you have some measure of the productivity of your employees and you can use such knowledge to determine how many jackets can be produced by an employee in a given period of time. If, however, you have no previous measures of how much work is produced by your employees you can engage in work study techniques. This involves determining the most efficient way the particular task can be performed and the time taken to perform the task. You would then calculate how many jackets can be sewn at this rate in one year by one operator and divide your production target of 8,000 by this number to get the number of employees required.

If prior information exists, you can use past production figures and calculate the ratio of operatives to the number of jackets produced by taking the total figure of jackets produced divided by the total number of operatives engaged in this or similar work. You might also apply managerial judgement by basing your calculations on a task that is similar to producing a jacket.

Another historical figure employers might use is the ratio of various categories of personnel to the number of customers or volume of sales. For example, if a distribution company has one administrator for every 15,000 customers and it intends to increase its customer base by 15,000 the historical ratio indicates a need for one additional administrator.

You would, of course, need to take into account the fact that new employees might not be fully productive until fully trained. You might also envisage savings from economies of scale from changing work methods or from technology used. Therefore, even when statistical methods are used to calculate the demand for human resources managerial judgement will also be an important factor that needs to be considered.

Estimating the internal supply of human resources

Organisations need to combine qualitative data based on managerial judgement with quantitative data to assess whether the requisite resources will be available. A properly designed human resource information system will provide information on the number of existing staff in various categories of posts. This represents the internal supply of human resources and may include personal data that may impact on a person's performance and how long they are likely to be employed with the organisation.

There are some simple statistical techniques that enable employers to forecast workforce numbers. The basic figure that most employers calculate is the labour turnover rate. This is sometimes referred to as the wastage rate or the separation rate and it represents the proportion of employees who leave in a given period of time, usually a year or a quarter of a year. This figure is calculated as a percentage by dividing the number of people exiting the workplace by the total complement of staff and multiplying this figure by 100. Should the requirements for staff vary during the time period the total complement can be calculated as an average of the number required at the beginning of the period and the number required at the end. This would give an overall turnover rate for an organisation but it is usually more useful to calculate the rate for specific categories of staff such as administrative staff, IT specialists, sales and marketing staff and operations managers.

For example, if a company requires 80 engineers throughout the year, and 8 of these have left in one year, then the turnover rate is $(8 / 80) \times 100 = 10$ per cent. The average turnover rate experienced over a period of time can be used as a trend to forecast requirements for the future. For instance, if the turnover rate for engineers in our example company has been stable at about 10 per cent over the past three years then this employer knows that it is likely to be necessary to recruit eight engineers next year to maintain the necessary supply of labour. If the demand forecast implies that additional engineers will be needed over the next three years the 10 per cent turnover rate should be factored into the recruitment calculation.

Activity 5.3

At the end of 2015, the employer in question (see above) decides that they will require eight additional engineers in each of the next three years. The new engineers are to be recruited at the beginning of each year. How many engineers will they have to recruit during each year to maintain the workforce?

Discussion of Activity 5.3

These figures are best calculated by tracking the base figure required each year, the increase in personnel required and an adjustment for the expected turnover. As you can see, the engineering company needs not only to recruit the additional eight employees each year, but also to cover the turnover on the new base figure. With a typical labour turnover rate of 10 per cent, in 2015, eight of the original employees may leave and, perhaps, one of the new employees. The figures are presented in Table 5.1.

Another calculation that can be made is known as the stability rate, which is the calculation of the proportion of the workforce employed for a specific time period, usually a year. The figure is calculated as follows: (number of people currently employed with one year or more of service/number of people employed one year ago) × 100.

Activity 5.4

This is an activity that will help you to focus on the information that can be obtained by analysing the same data in different ways. Imagine that you are the HR manager for a logistics firm that provides transport and supply chain management solutions for a range of customers. Your firm has 40 drivers.

1. You are asked to perform a simple calculation for each of three situations.
    (a) In one year 10 of these drivers leave and have to be replaced. Calculate the turnover rate.
    (b) At the end of one year you still have 38 of those drivers with you but you have had to recruit 10 times to keep your staff complement up to 40. Calculate the turnover rate and the stability index.
    (c) In one year 10 drivers leave. Each of them had two to five years of service. You have had to replace each of them and your new recruits are still with you. Calculate the turnover rate and the stability index.
2. What do these turnover and stability index figures tell you?

Discussion of Activity 5.4

In relation to question 1, sections (a), (b) and (c), you should have calculated a turnover figure of 25 per cent for each of these circumstances. The turnover

Table 5.1 Estimated recruitment figures adjusted for labour turnover

	Number of engineers required	Increase over previous year	Projected turnover during year	Number to recruit during year
End of 2015	80	–	–	
2016	88	8	9	17
2017	96	8	10	18
2018	104	8	11	19

Did you know?

An XpertHR 2014 survey of 256 employers regarding labour turnover rates in the UK revealed that, for the previous year, the median voluntary resignation rate was 9.9 per cent. Another way of interpreting the data is that an average of 1 employee in 12 resigned from their job in 2013. An analysis of the survey data reveals big differences in the voluntary resignation rates between different industries, ranging from a median total labour turnover rate of 8.1 per cent for general manufacturing to 46 per cent for hotels, catering and leisure.

(Source: Suff, R. (2014) Labour Turnover Rates: 2014 XpertHR Survey, available at www.xperthr.co.uk; accessed 06.01.15)

figure reveals nothing about the underlying causes of turnover and this is emphasised by the fact that you have the same figure for the three very different circumstances described. The turnover rate on its own becomes meaningful only if you can compare it with rates experienced by your organisation in the past or by other organisations in your industry for similar categories of staff. You can then deduce how you are performing relative to your competitors and if there are problems you need to investigate. This is, however, not a straightforward exercise as employers may include or exclude various categories of people exiting the organisation, such as employees who have been dismissed for misconduct, staff who have been made redundant or workers who have retired from the organisation.

The stability index figures, 95 per cent in scenario (b) and 75 per cent in scenario (c), are much more revealing than the figures for labour turnover. The similarity among all three scenarios in the exercise is that there have been 10 recruitment actions in each case; the stability index, however, reveals that the situations are different and the reasons for the vacancies are different. The higher figure means that the turnover is not occurring among the longer serving employees, indicating that there is a problem with retaining new recruits. The lower figure indicates that the problem lies with the retention of longer serving employees. Each problem requires a different set of actions and this will be very important when you have to formulate human resource management action plans.

Pause for thought 5.3 In the discussion of Activity 5.4, we stated that comparing your labour turnover rates to that experienced by your competitors might assist you in identifying and analysing retention problems. Imagine that such a comparison revealed that labour turnover rates for certain posts in your firm were considerably higher compared to similar firms in the same industry. What might some of the causes and remedies be?

A reflection on the above might have lead you to consider the following causes and remedies of excessive labour turnover, as represented in Table 5.2.

Table 5.2   Labour turnover: causes and remedies

Cause	Remedy
Poor handling of new recruits	Design and implement an induction process
Unfavourable salary/terms and conditions of employment	Revise the reward strategies
High levels of job dissatisfaction	Improve the job design
Low levels of morale	Change the organisational culture Improve employee involvement and engagement practices Introduce employee opinion surveys
Recruits are not equipped for the demands of work	Improve recruitment and selection practices Improve training

There are other factors that have an impact on the turnover rate. Some of these might be reflected in long-term trends and others may cause occasional fluctuations. One such factor is the age composition of the workforce. Retirement may account for a certain percentage of leavers on an ongoing basis but sometimes an organisation has a large number of people due to retire at the same time and this will temporarily increase the turnover rate. This continues to be a consideration even if one pays due attention to the changing regulations with regard to the age at which people retire from work, as discussed in Chapter 4, 'Diversity and equality'. Retirement needs to be taken into consideration in forecasting the supply of human resources and when adjusting the estimates to reflect the effects of labour turnover. To achieve successful strategic planning, the human resource information system (HRIS) should be set up so that it can provide this information.

In addition to information about workforce numbers, the analysis of various aspects of the workforce can highlight a range of problems or issues that require attention. Some of the analyses that could be obtained for both retained workers and people who have exited the organisation are:

- the gender distribution of personnel across the whole workforce or in each category of employee,
- the distribution across the workforce or by employee category of members of specified ethnic minority groups,
- the age profile of the workforce and for each category of employee,
- the length of service for each category of employee.

These analyses of human capital could help managers to establish where new approaches or policies are needed to help the organisation achieve its strategic goals.

A further factor that may have an impact on future internal labour supply is the fact that people often have skills that their employer may not have required them to use in their current post. These could include fluency in a foreign language, knowledge and expertise in using a computer software package, training and coaching skills and interpersonal skills. In order to have a full picture of the skills available from the current workforce the organisation needs to develop a skills inventory with each individual's competencies recorded on their personal record. This will then form part of the organisation's HRIS. The skills inventory should list skills that are available but not being used as well as those skills that are currently being used.

Assessing the external supply of human resources

At the same time as analysing the internal supply of human resources, employers need to be aware of the availability of potential employees from outside the organisation. If the internal supply of employees cannot meet the demand for workers managers must know whether there are problems with the availability of workers from outside the organisation. The CIPD (2014a), in its labour market predictions for 2015, conclude that, in the short term, businesses will attract suitable candidates for vacancies but, at some stage in the future, labour shortages will become more acute and it may be difficult to obtain workers even by offering higher rates of pay.

The labour force is defined as the number of people aged 16 and over who are either in employment or available for work. As such, those members of the labour force who are not currently employed by a particular employer constitute the employer's external labour market. In the UK the youngest age a child can work part-time (with the exception of television, theatre and modelling) is 13 and children can only work full-time when they have reached the minimum school-leaving age (**www.gov.uk, a**). There have been significant changes to the state retirement age in many countries in the past decade. For example, the Default Retirement Age (formerly 65) has been phased out in the UK and, with certain exceptions, an employee can work for as long as he or she wants (**www.gov.uk, b**).

Pause for thought 5.4 There are many factors that have an impact on the size of the labour force in general and the availability of employees from the labour force to any particular employer.

Before you go on to read about these factors, make a list of as many of them as you can think of. You may also wish to consider how employers might deal with any problems you identify.

Size and composition of the labour force

Projections for the UK labour for the years 2006–2020, as reported in *Labour Market Trends* (Madouros, 2006), include the following data:

- Between 2006 and 2020 the labour force is set to increase but the rate of increase will decline over that period. The labour force is projected to consist of 32.1 million economically active people in 2020.
- The labour force is ageing with the age distribution showing a distinct shift towards older age groups by 2020.

- The working age is defined here as 16–64 years old but a growing number of people *above* the age of 64 are expected to continue to be economically active and, as noted earlier, there will be compelling reasons for people to continue in employment as the default retirement age in the UK has been abolished.
- The proportion of younger people in the labour force, defined as those between 16 and 24 years of age, is projected to decline from 6.9 million in 2005 to 6.6 million in 2020, a fall of 4.9 per cent.
- The rising trend of female participation in the labour face is set to continue but at a slower rate.

Changes in the numbers of people in the labour force are caused by a combination of population effects and activity rate effects. The largest population effect is caused by the variation in the fertility rate. The fertility rate can represent the age-specific fertility rate (ASFR), the number of births per 1,000 women of a stated age group, or the total fertility rate (TFR), the average number of children that a group of women would have if they experienced the ASFRs for a particular year throughout their childbearing lives (ONS, 2010). There have been concerns in Europe that falling fertility rates will reduce the population (and therefore the labour force) but recent evidence points to a revival in fertility rates for many European nations (Rand Europe, 2011). However, despite this recent increase in 2012 the fertility rate for EU-28 countries was 1.45 live births. A figure of about 2.1 is needed to keep the population size constant if there is no inward or outward migration (Eurostat, 2014). Two other major demographic changes are likely to have a major impact on the labour force: increased life expectancy and migration (immigration and emigration), and these will now be briefly examined.

On average people are living longer. Life expectancy has increased in almost every country. In the UK, for example, life expectancy at birth for a male has increased from 70.8 years in 1980 to 78.9 years in 2012. For women, the figures were 76.8 years in 1980 to 82.7 years in 2012 (ONS, 2014a). An increased life expectancy has repercussions for the labour market as many more people will be living longer, many of whom will want to continue working. Moreover, as the value of pensions has tended to diminish for many older workers continued employment is an economic necessity. Immigration and emigration will also affect the labour force. For the UK, immigration represents those people who permanently move to the UK whilst emigration represents people who leave the UK to settle permanently in another country. In the year ending June 2014, immigration to the UK was 583,000 people whilst, for the same period, emigration was 323,000 people. The net migration for this period for the UK was therefore 260,000 people (ONS, 2014b). A significant trend in terms of immigration to the UK is the number of people from the so-called A8 countries (Czech Republic, Estonia, Hungary, Latvia, Lithuania, Poland, Slovakia and Slovenia) who have settled in the UK. These countries joined the EU in 2004 and, since this date, many people from these countries have relocated to the UK. For example, in the year ending September 2014, 98,000 Polish citizens registered for a National Insurance number in the UK (ONS, 2014c).

Economic activity rates also affect the size and composition of the labour force. Increasing numbers of young people are studying full-time which, together with the ageing population and low fertility rates, account for the lower numbers of younger people available for work. However, this may be offset by an increase in the numbers of students, many of whom work part-time. The ageing of the labour force is a noticeable phenomenon and there is an expectation that a greater number of older people will wish to extend their working lives, many of them because they enjoy work and some for financial reasons such as poor pension provision. The important issue from the point of view of analysing the external labour market is the extent to which employers are noting these changes and adjusting their recruitment strategies in response. As will be seen later, skills shortages are a continuing challenge for employers, even in times of recession, and if the people available in the labour market belong increasingly to an older age group this may call for different strategies in recruiting them, a different approach to training may be required and older employees may have different requirements with regard to flexible working arrangements.

The numbers of people presenting themselves for work can also be affected by the state of the economy. As an economy grows, employment opportunities increase. During times of recession, fewer jobs are created. In the period September–November 2014 there were 690,000 job vacancies in the UK, an increase of 126,000 from a year earlier (ONS, 2014d). For the period August–October 2014 there were 30.80 million people in work in the UK. Of these, 22.54 million people were working full-time (ONS, 2014d).

The growing proportion of women in the labour force is attributed in part to socio-economic influences such as the greater availability of part-time work, the social acceptability of women in employment and changes to pensions for women. All of the factors discussed in this section have implications for human resource planning, particularly for employers who have a traditional view of who they might employ, for instance in positions thought of as being suitable for school leavers. The changing demographic structure of the external labour market may oblige employers to adopt more open and inclusive approaches to recruitment.

The figures provided by surveys of the national labour force are important in providing a broad indication of factors to be considered in human resource planning. There are, however, some limitations on their usefulness. The statistics represent estimates, projections of the numbers of people expected to be economically active in the future. As such they have to be predicated on some basic assumptions linked with patterns of economic activity observed at the time of analysis. Unexpected events can occur which may have a sizeable impact on the validity of the projected figures. The CIPD's (2013b) factsheet on understanding the economy and labour market provides some insight into the complexity of broader economic factors affecting human resources.

Tight and slack labour markets

As the CIPD (2009b) explains, the interplay of many factors in the economy may result in a tight labour market or one that has more slack in it. Factors that affect labour markets include the demand for goods and services, employers' recruitment intentions and rates of pay and benefits. Also, as we have already indicated, the number of immigrants who choose to seek employment in the UK has an impact on the number of people who are economically active in the country.

The number of people looking for work is affected by the rate of unemployment and the prevalence of redundancies. This does not necessarily mean, however, that meeting the organisation's requirements for human resources is automatically easier in times of high unemployment. Redundant jobseekers may have a range of skills but not necessarily the skills sought by an employer. There is also resistance among some newly redundant people to accept a large immediate drop in earnings. The existence of large numbers of unemployed or newly redundant people, therefore, does not equate directly with a ready supply of human resources.

The demand for workers from other employers will obviously influence the availability of human resources especially where employers seek workers with certain skills, knowledge and experience. This may have a direct impact on recruitment and pay strategies as employers try to attract the best people in direct competition with other companies. For the purposes of human resource planning it will be important to be informed about existing competitors and to assess the likelihood of new competitors setting up business in the area.

If the labour market is tight this means that employers experience difficulties in recruiting and the term 'skills shortages' is used to describe this. A slacker labour market means that there is an abundance of appropriate human resources and employers can fill their vacancies more easily. Skills shortages can arise for a variety of reasons and this term does not necessarily imply that the required skills are actually in shortage. They may not be available to employers for other reasons which we shall explore later.

Skills shortages

The issue of skills shortages fluctuates over time but, at the present time, there are discussions about skills shortages in the UK. Ben Willmott, Head of Public Policy at the CIPD, has stated that with a higher proportion of low-skilled jobs than its competitors, stalling productivity levels and lack of investment in training the UK has real questions to answer about its education and skill system (Willmott, 2014). A 2013 CIPD survey on resourcing and talent planning reported a growing mismatch between the skills organisations need and the skills available in the labour market. In the survey the most common reason given for recruitment difficulties was lack of specialist or technical skills and the survey also reported that few employers considered that schools, colleges and universities were equipping their students with the skills needed by organisations (CIPD, 2013c).

It is vital that organisations take steps to counteract skills shortages as they have a detrimental impact on the effectiveness of the business and its operations. The UK Commission for Employment and Skills (UKCES, 2010) refers to a heavier workload for colleagues as being the most frequently reported negative effect of skills gaps along with higher costs, problems with quality standards and difficulties in introducing new working methods. Skills shortages are detrimental to employees too as HR specialists and line managers might have to neglect important areas such as training and development, coaching and general employee welfare issues (Sloane, 2007) to spend more time on difficult recruitment campaigns. The UKCES (2010, p. 24) reports on a lack of 'technical, practical and job-specific skills' as well as customer handling, problem solving and team working skills.

A report by the UKCES (2014) on skills and performance challenges in the logistics sector revealed that one in seven employers in the sector experienced skills gaps in their workforce with skills gaps being more prevalent in sales, customer service, skilled trades and machine operative positions.

Reasons for skills shortages

As indicated previously, there can be a number of reasons why an employer is experiencing recruitment problems. It might be that there is a lack of specific skills available in the labour market. It may also relate to the failure, perceived or real, of the educational system to prepare young people properly for business life. Recruitment difficulties might be a regional issue connected to the cost of living in different parts of the country. Furthermore, it might be the case that the terms and conditions, pay and benefits offered by a particular employer are less attractive than those offered by a competitor.

The organisation's reputation in general might attract or deter people from applying for a job. Also, the public's perceptions of a job will make some occupations seem more attractive than others. Social work, particularly work involving the care of children, has notoriously suffered in this way for some years. Negative media coverage of social work, highlighted by the deaths of Victoria Climbié in 2000, Baby Peter in 2007 and Keanu Williams in 2011, has affected the morale of people working in child protection services. In October 2013 over a fifth of front-line social worker posts in the UK city of Birmingham were unfilled, equivalent to 106 full-time posts (BBC, 2013). Given such a large number of vacancies, and the negative publicity of social work, it will be a challenge to ensure that sufficient numbers of social workers are recruited and retained.

With so many potential causes for skills shortages it is self-evident that there could be a variety of solutions and an appropriate solution or mix of responses will be necessary to address the problem.

Solutions to skills shortages

Provide training

If employers identify that the required skills are not available one solution is to recruit people who can be trained. Organisations may also look to their own current employees (their internal supply of human resources) for skills they do not have. The CIPD's survey on recruitment, retention and turnover (2009a) indicates that the provision of training is the preferred response to skills shortages, with 74 per cent of respondents providing training for new recruits and 75 per cent training up their current employees. This approach is seen as leading to improved retention of existing staff in which case employers would have less need for recruitment activities in the first place.

Did you know?

In the USA, each year the HR consulting group Manpower Group releases its Talent Shortage Survey, identifying the 10 jobs that are hardest to fill with qualified candidates for that year. In 2014 the top 10 of hard-to-fill jobs were:

1. Skilled trade workers
2. Restaurant and hotel staff
3. Sales representatives
4. Teachers
5. Drivers
6. Accounting and finance staff
7. Labourers
8. IT staff
9. Engineers
10. Nurses.

(*Source: Annual Survey of Talent Shortages*, available at www.manpowergroup.us; accessed 07.01.15)

The CIPD's autumn 2014 *Labour market outlook*, based on a survey of 1,089 employers in the UK, identified the roles that employers are having difficulty filling. IT/software development staff was the role mentioned most, followed by engineers, management/executives, sales and marketing, technicians, nurses and care/social workers.

(*Source*: CIPD, 2014b)

Some organisations have gone to the extent of setting up their own educational establishment and qualifications to ensure a supply of skills at the appropriate level. In 2005 the BBC founded a College of Journalism (CoJo), supported by online learning opportunities, to raise the level of skills and knowledge in its reporters and newsreaders in areas such as writing skills, politics and law. McDonald's Centre of Training Excellence (known as Hamburger University), established in 1961, has had more than 80,000 graduates since its inception and now has campuses in Oak Brook USA, Sydney, Munich, London, Tokyo, São Paulo and Shanghai (**www .aboutmcdonalds.com**).

Recruiting overseas/targeting migrant workers/offshoring

Subject to immigration laws it is possible for employers to turn to other countries and recruit people to come and work in the UK. The CIPD's (2014b) survey reveals that 57 per cent of employers currently employ migrant workers. The survey also indicates that 64 per cent of public employers, 56 per cent of private sector employers and 42 per cent of voluntary sector employers use migrant labour. The main reason offered for employing EU migrant workers by employers in the survey was a lack of applicants from the UK. A number of employers (15 per cent) also mentioned that EU migrant workers had a better work ethic than their UK compatriots (CIPD, 2014b).

Although often undertaken for reasons of costs, skills shortages could also be addressed by relocating jobs to countries such as India, Bangladesh, China or Vietnam where human and other resources are in plentiful supply. Offshoring may also relate to the outsourcing of business activities or activities to a third party overseas. According to a CIPD (2012) survey, 8 per cent of employers intended offshoring UK jobs to other parts of the world in the next 12 months, with the most popular destinations being India (favoured by 67 per cent of the survey respondents), Eastern Europe (20 per cent), Asia, excluding China and India, (15 per cent) and China (13 per cent). The survey also revealed the roles likely to be offshored in the following 12 months. For the firms planning to offshore jobs, the most popular functions identified were IT (38 per cent of respondents), finance and accounts (36 per cent), HR operations (31 per cent) and call centre operations (21 per cent).

Diversity and the labour market

The problem of skills shortages can be addressed by eliminating entrenched stereotypical ideas about who might and might not be suitable for particular types of jobs. In spite of laws providing equality of opportunity in the workplace there are still certain occupations where barriers need to be broken down to facilitate access for particular groups of people. Sometimes it is not just employers that have stereotyped ideas about the suitability of certain people for certain occupations but employees, or prospective employees, themselves.

The Scottish Government (2014) has recognised the existence of occupational segregation in relation to gender

Did you know?

An article in the *Telegraph* in November 2013 commented on statements made by foreign ministers of EU accession countries that immigrants from Eastern Europe add far more to the UK economy than they take out. These immigrants boost the UK economy by contributing more in taxes and spending than is claimed back in social benefits, the ministers claim. But the article also reports on comments by the UK prime minister, David Cameron, who said he wanted to restrict the ability of migrants from poorer EU states to move to richer ones, a statement that angered the European Commission.

(*Source*: Riley-Smith, B. (2013) Eastern European immigrants 'overwhelming benefit UK economy', *Telegraph*, 29 November, available at **www.telegraph.co.uk**; accessed 08.01.15)

where men and women in Scotland are segregated horizontally in different types of jobs and vertically in relation to different grades of jobs. This segregation prevents women and men from reaching their full potential in the labour market and results in a 'pay gap' between women and men with women being concentrated in lower-paid jobs such as caring, catering, cleaning, clerical and cashiering.

Employers can engage in targeted recruitment to encourage applications from groups who do not normally apply for certain jobs. This has been an important issue for police forces across the UK with the chief constable overseeing police recruitment in England and Wales, Alex Marshall, saying that new legislation may be needed to boost the number of black and ethnic minority police officers (*The Guardian*, 2014). Long before age discrimination regulations were in force, B&Q, the DIY and home improvement retailing company, experimented by opening a store in Macclesfield, Cheshire, staffed entirely by the over 50s, an initiative that produced 18 per cent higher profits and six times less staff turnover (Thornton, 2010). However, B&Q also targets younger age groups, specifically people aged 18–24, and the firm recognises the need to have a mix of people working in its stores (Thornton, 2010).

An example of an innovative approach to ease recruitment difficulties through the promotion of diversity comes from British Gas. The company is striving to change the perception of engineering as a career, particularly amongst women and ethnic minority groups. Since 2003, the firm has used a range of recruitment approaches to increase the proportion of female and ethnic minority trainee engineers. The result has been more than doubling of BG's women and ethnic minority engineering workforce (Suff, 2009). Another example of how an organisation is using diversity to increase its pool of candidates is the UK's Secret Intelligence Service, MI6, which has recognised the need to for more black and Asian recruits to help the service cope with changing threats to the country (*Telegraph*, 2008).

In considering the suitability of applicants, from whatever background, it is advisable to reacquaint yourself with the person specification for jobs to confirm that all the requirements listed there for qualifications and experience are really necessary. Indeed, the CIPD (2009a) has reported a marked increase in the numbers of employers willing to consider a broader range of candidate qualities during recruitment rather than focusing on formal qualifications alone.

Employer branding

Being known as an employer that is committed to diversity is very much a part of creating an employer brand. This will help an organisation attract applicants. As an employer of choice this would also entail having good pay and working conditions, ensuring employees have a voice and ensuring that employees are fully engaged. In order to maintain and enhance the employer brand employers must obviously treat employees appropriately and to communicate this, partly through advertising, to attract prospective employees. According to Whitford (2014) employer branding is important in attracting suitable candidates and enabling the employer to market their employment value proposition (EVP), that is, what an organisation stands for, what it requires of its employees and what it has to offer as an employer.

Research conducted by the CIPD (2010d) on employer branding, based on a survey with 44 organisations and in-depth interviews with nine companies, found that all companies agreed that aligning rewards with the employer brand can help the organisation in recruiting, retaining and motivating staff. However, the research also concluded that, for some organisations, the aspiration to align employer brand with reward has only just begun.

Although it is only one of a list of the attributes of employer brand, it is worth highlighting the importance of the work–life balance, which was addressed in more detail in Chapter 3 on the employment relationship. We have discussed workplace diversity here and also in Chapter 4 on diversity and equality, and diversity of necessity brings about a requirement for greater flexibility in working arrangements to respond to the needs of people from different cultures and at differing stages in their lives. If employers wish to obtain the benefits offered by diversity they will have to make reasonable efforts to accommodate their employees' needs and help them to achieve an acceptable balance between their working and their non-working lives.

Comparing demand and supply forecasts

A comparison of your expected demand for human resources and your expected supply of human resources will identify what you need to accomplish in your human resource plans in order to achieve your corporate goals. As already mentioned there may be an indication that the corporate/business plan will need to be adjusted. You can be faced with a number of situations:

- internal supply = demand,
- internal supply > demand,
- internal supply < demand,
- internal plus external supply < demand.

As we have already discussed since there are so many changes affecting organisations, and since this is likely to continue for the foreseeable future, the internal supply of human resources is not likely to equal demand. This is more likely to occur in very stable conditions. If internal supply is greater than demand then the human resource plans will need to focus on reducing the surplus through redeployment, redundancy or through other adjustments to working arrangements. However, during the recession of 2008–2010 it was noticeable that employers opted to retain employees through adjustments to their working hours rather than losing them altogether by making people redundant. This reflects strategic thinking and decision making in terms of a desire to be ready to compete when the economy improves. When internal supply is less than demand an organisation will be involved in recruitment or other methods of acquiring the necessary skills and knowledge, such as outsourcing activities. In the final instance, where internal supply plus external supply is inadequate to meet demand, the solutions we have just described with regard to combating skills shortages can be used, or, perhaps less desirably, organisational goals must be adjusted to reflect the resourcing issues.

Developing and implementing human resource strategies

Chapter 1 described HR activities which can be grouped into four broad areas: resourcing, development, reward and employment relations. It is useful to refer to these categories to identify the areas in which it is necessary to develop human resource strategies and action plans.

Resourcing

If demand exceeds supply the organisation will have to develop plans to increase the size of its workforce. This will invariably involve recruitment activities but there may also be a need for career and succession planning for existing employees, and the organisation may also consider subcontracting work. If internal supply exceeds demand the organisation may have to reduce the size of its workforce but consideration should first be given to redeployment and to providing the training that this might entail.

Development

If skills gaps are present in the workforce then competencies the organisation needs to have in order to effectively compete are not present. Managers should therefore make plans to develop those skills and competencies through training, team and individual development and performance management. The provision of opportunities for career development and progression is identified by the CIPD (2014c) as significantly important in reducing employee turnover and aiding employee retention.

Reward

A review and restructuring of the reward system might enable an organisation to attract and retain an effective workforce. The organisation should examine its pay levels and the attractiveness of its benefits packages and terms and conditions compared with those of its competitors. Action plans also need to address the issue of linking both financial and non-monetary rewards to the achievement of corporate goals.

Employment relations

Employees make a valuable contribution to the organisation's goals, and improvements to employee motivation and commitment can be achieved through developing better employment relations. Areas to consider in relation to employment relations include consultation, communications, employee involvement and engagement and the development of a partnership approach.

The four activities above are discussed in much greater detail in the individual chapters concerning these activities. Employment relations was discussed in Chapter 3 whilst resourcing will be discussed in Chapter 6; development in Chapter 8 and reward in Chapter 9.

Information technology systems and HR

Some comment about HR uses of information technology systems is necessary at this point. We have established the need for a broad range of information to manage HR activities in a strategic manner. The use of IT is seen as being instrumental in the successful delivery of a number of HR strategies once these have been formulated. Long and Ismail (2012) consider that HR specialists need to optimally use information technology. An integrated human resource management system (HRMS) or human resource information system (HRIS), which integrates human resource processes and a firm's information systems (Hoch and Dulebohn, 2013), is a method that enables managers to better use information technology.

There are some indicators that HR may be making a strategic use of IT, but the evidence is not strong. The CIPD (2006), for instance, mainly addresses operational uses of IT, but it does also allude to HR undertaking more strategic work by providing managers with quantifiable data to drive strategy and the important role that HR can play in the formulation of strategy by making explicit the human resources necessary to support strategy.

The CIPD (2006) comes to the conclusion that the technology-driven changes in HR roles 'will undoubtedly lead to a change in the skills needed as their role shifts towards more strategic issues' (p. 12). The CIPD (2014a) still comments, however, that 'HR data is more often collected for administrative rather than evaluation purposes', and that 'HR people do not always have the skills or resources to interpret or explain data to evaluate the contribution of people to business performance'. These statements imply that the HR profession still has some way to go before it is fully effective at the strategic level, and that the potential of IT systems is yet to be fully realised.

An organisation needs to have a strategy in terms of how it, and other stakeholders, uses the Internet and social media and how it can facilitate job-related networking, both internally and externally (Phillips and Phillips, 2014). According to Kirton (2014), the Internet has had six significant impacts on HR: it has created almost limitless channels to engage and attract people; it has created spaces where candidates can develop an online presence; it has helped employers brand their organisation; it has transformed workplace learning; it has helped employers with PAYE (Pay As You Earn) submissions; and it has made remote working possible for the majority. However, not all of these developments are positive, for example employees are now able to rate their employer (via a website such as **ratemyemployer.co.uk**) and such reviews could be damaging to the firm. Therefore, the organisation should consider introducing a policy on the use of social media and social networking sites.

Review Questions

You will find brief answers to these review questions on page 464–5.

1. Explain how business strategy affects HR strategy.
2. Outline the major stages of the human resource planning process, and comment on the key considerations at each stage.

3. Assess the importance of information as a basis for decision making in the human resource planning process.

4. Explain what is meant by the terms 'skills shortages' and 'skills gaps'. Why do they arise and what can employers do about them?

Improving your employability

You have been shortlisted for an assistant HR position at a bus company. In addition to being interviewed, you are required to give a 10 minute presentation, using PowerPoint, on the labour turnover of drivers, establishing what labour turnover is, what the principal causes and effects are and what the company can do to reduce the labour turnover of its drivers. You have been informed that the current labour turnover of the firm's drivers is twice the industry average. The presentation must be exactly 10 minutes.

HR in the news

Shortage of engineers threaten UK growth, employers warn

By Brian Groom, Business and Employment Editor

Six out of 10 engineering employers fear a growing shortage of engineers will threaten their business in the UK, research has found. A study by the Institution of Engineering and Technology underlines concerns that skills shortages could hold back the recovery in parts of the economy.

Manufacturing output remains 8 per cent below its pre-recession peak but companies say the right skills are becoming harder to find. In the IET's survey, 76 per cent of employers reported problems with recruiting senior engineers with five to 10 years' experience, up from 48 per cent in 2011. The difficulty of finding engineering managers, graduates, technicians and apprentices had also increased. "We feel it is holding our company back," said Matt Wilson, chairman of Telecoms Cloud, a Liverpool-based telecom services company with a £4m turnover that has six unfilled vacancies including telephony engineers and software specialists. Mr Wilson said the company was having to turn work down because it could not find enough people, including a prospective contract for a London council that would probably go to a German company. Other work is being outsourced to Malaysia and Vietnam. He said his business partner had suggested moving to San Francisco,

where there would be a better supply of skills, which he did not want to do but might have to consider in future if the situation did not improve.

One route to improving the supply of engineers is to encourage more women to join the profession, but the IET study of 400 employers found that only 6 per cent of the workforce was female, barely changed in the past six years. Despite this, the survey found that 43 per cent of employers were not taking any specific action to improve workplace diversity. "They need to take urgent steps to improve recruitment and retention of women, for example by promoting flexible and part-time working, together with planned routes of progression that can accommodate career breaks," said Nigel Fine, chief executive of the IET.

Britain needs to train 87,000 engineering graduates a year – double the previous rate – until 2020, in part to replace those retiring, according to industry body Engineering UK. The government is trying to tackle the problem by funding more apprenticeships, offering schemes to encourage more young people and women to choose a career in industry and investing in university facilities and teaching. But employers are pressing for further action.

$\rightarrow$

The CBI employers' group wants university fees reduced for some science, technology, engineering and maths (Stem) courses. The International Monetary Fund this week called for immigration controls to be relaxed in areas such as manufacturing to help rebalance the economy. Carol White, head of UK recruitment at WSP, the engineering design consultancy, which will hire 800 staff this year, said recruiting people with engineering skills had become as difficult as before the recession. WSP was managing to get the numbers it needed but had to work harder to achieve that, she said. The company had kept graduate and apprenticeship hiring as high as possible during the recession and was using social media to attract expatriate engineers back from Australia, Canada and the Middle East. Ms White said: "It's everybody's responsibility, whether that be employers, universities, colleges or the government, to start the education process with youngsters and bang the drum about engineering being a really good career route."

The IET survey found that 44 per cent of employers said engineering, IT and technical recruits did not meet their expected levels of skills. Employers were also increasingly dissatisfied with standards of literacy and numeracy among school leavers. More than half of employers believed they should get more involved with schools, colleges and universities to help change the perception of engineering among young people, and 52 per cent expected to employ more apprentices in four to five years' time.

Source: Groom, B. (2014) Shortage of engineers threaten UK growth, employers warn, *Financial Times*, 30th July.
© The Financial Times Limited 2014. All Rights Reserved.

Questions

1. What effects might a shortage of engineers have on the UK economy and UK engineering businesses?
2. Why are there so few female engineers compared to male engineers and what can the engineering sector do to encourage females to take up a career in engineering?
3. How might an engineering firm that has a shortage of engineers attract overseas applicants?
4. How might the engineering sector engage with schools, colleges and universities to influence the skills levels of graduates?

What next?

In this chapter we have looked at the factors that affect the external labour market and the impact this can have on employers in resourcing their strategic plans. The supply of labour can fluctuate from year to year bringing ever-changing opportunities and threats to employers. It is therefore important to keep up to date on developments, and reading of the following publications can assist you in doing this.

Labour Market Statistics bulletin, produced by the Office for National Statistics (ONS), is a monthly online resource for data on such things as employment, unemployment, economic activity and redundancies. The ONS also produces a useful video outlining key data on labour market concepts for the UK and is available on the ONS website (**www.ons.gov.uk**).

Labour Market Outlook, a quarterly review published by the CIPD.

There are a number of other survey reports produced by the CIPD which are useful in assessing the state of the labour market. These include HR outlook survey reports, employee outlook survey reports and specific survey reports such as the 2014 report *Managing an age-diverse workforce: employer and employee views*. Go to the survey report section in the CIPD website to locate these resources.

References

BBC (2013) *Birmingham Struggles to Recruit Social Workers*, 4 October (available at www.bbc.co.uk; accessed 07.01.15).

Boxall, P. and J. Purcell (2008) *Strategy and Human Resource Management*, 2nd edition, Palgrave Macmillan, Basingstoke.

Chartered Institute of Personnel and Development (2005) *HR Strategy: Creating the Framework for Successful People Management*, CIPD (CIPD tool available at www.cipd.co.uk; accessed 05.01.15).

Chartered institute of personnel and development (2006) *HR and Technology: Beyond Delivery*, CIPD (change agenda available at www.cipd.co.uk; accessed 09.01.15).

Chartered Institute of Personnel and Development (2009a) *Recruitment, Retention and Turnover. Annual Survey Report 2009*, CIPD, London.

Chartered Institute of Personnel and Development (2009b) *Understanding the Economy and Labour Market*, CIPD (factsheet available at www.cipd.co.uk; accessed 07.05.10).

Chartered Institute of Personnel and Development (2010a) *Creating an Engaged Workforce*, CIPD (research report available at www.cipd.co.uk; accessed 01.03.10).

Chartered Institute of Personnel and Development (2010b) *HR Business Partnering*, CIPD (factsheet available at www.cipd.co.uk; accessed 03.05.10).

Chartered Institute of Personnel and Development (2010c) *Employer Branding and Total Reward: Research Report*, CIPD (available at www.cipd.co.uk; accessed 08.01.15).

Chartered Institute of Personnel and Development (2010d) *Workforce Planning: Right People, Right Time, Right Skills*, CIPD (research report available at www.cipd.co.uk; accessed 06.01.15).

Chartered Institute of Personnel and Development (2012) *Labour Market Outlook Autumn 2012*, CIPD (available at www.cipd.co.uk; accessed 08.01.15).

Chartered Institute of Personnel and Development (2013a) *Strategic Human Resource Management*, CIPD (factsheet available at www.cipd.co.uk; accessed 05.01.15).

Chartered Institute of Personnel and Development (2013b) *Understanding the Economy and Labour Market*, CIPD (factsheet available at www.cipd.co.uk; accessed 07.01.15).

Chartered Institute of Personnel and Development (2013c) *Resourcing and Talent Planning. Annual Survey Report 2010*, CIPD (available at www.cipd.co.uk; accessed 07.01.15).

Chartered Institute of Personnel and Development (2014a) *Labour Market Predictions for 2015*, CIPD (available at www.cipd.co.uk; accessed 06.01.15).

Chartered Institute of Personnel and Development (2014b) *Labour Market Outlook Autumn 2014*, CIPD (available at www.cipd.co.uk; accessed 07.01.15).

Chartered Institute of Personnel and Development (2014c) *Employee Turnover and Retention*, CIPD (factsheet available at www.cipd.co.uk; accessed 08.01.15).

Eurostat (2014) *Fertility Statistics: European Commission* (available at ec.europa.eu/eurostat, accessed 06.01.15).

Evans, V. (2013) *Key Strategy Tools*, Pearson Education Limited, Harlow.

Guest, D., J. Storey and W. Tate (1997) *Innovation: Opportunity through People. Consultative Document*, June, Institute of Personnel and Development, London.

Hoch, J. and J. Dulebohn (2013) Shared leadership in enterprise resource planning and human resource management system implementation, *Human Resource Management Review*, Vol. 23, No. 1, 114–125.

Hutchinson, S. and J. Purcell (2003) *Bringing Policies to Life: The Vital Role of Front Line Managers in People Management*, CIPD, London.

Johnson, G., R. Whittington, D. Angwin, P. Regner and R. Scholes (2014) *Exploring Strategy*, Pearson Education Limited, Harlow.

Kirton, H (2014) Six ways the Internet has changed HR (available at www.cipd.co.uk; accessed 08.01.15).

Long, C. and W. Ismail (2012) The HR specialist as an agent of change, *Human Resource Management International Digest*, Vol. 20 No. 2, 24–28.

Lynch, R. (2012) *Strategic Management*, Pearson Education Limited, Harlow.

Madouros, V. (2006) Projections of the UK labour force, 2006–2020, *Labour Market Trends*, January, 13–27.

Marchington, M. and A. Wilkinson (2005) *Human Resource Management at Work: People Management and Development*, 3rd edition, CIPD, London.

Macleod, D. and N. Clarke (2009) *Engaging for Success: Enhancing Performance through Employee Engagement*, Crown Copyright, London.

Millmore, M., P. Lewis, M. Saunders, A. Thornhill and T. Morrow (2007) *Strategic Human Resource Management: Contemporary Issues*, Financial Times Prentice Hall, Harlow.

Murphy, N. (2009) Talent management's role in a time of recession, *IRS Employment Review 927* (available at www.xperthr.co.uk; accessed 05.01.15).

Office for National Statistics (2010) *Fertility Summary for 2010* (available at www.ons.gov.uk, accessed 06.01.15).

Office for National Statistics (2014a) *National Life Tables, United Kingdom, 2011–2013* (available at www.ons.gov.uk; accessed 07.01.15).

Office for National Statistics (2014b) *Migration* (available at www.ons.gov.uk; accessed 07.01.15).

Office for National Statistics (2014c) *Migration Statistics Quarterly Report* (available at www.ons.gov.uk; accessed 07.01.15).

Office for National Statistics (2014d) *UK Labour Market, December 2014* (available at www.ons.gov.uk; accessed 07.01.15).

Phillips, J. and P. Phillips (2014) Developing a human capital strategy in today's changing environment: eight forces shaping HC strategy, *Strategic HR Review*, Vol. 13, No. 3, 130–134.

Porter, M.E. (1980) *Competitive Strategy*, Free Press, New York.

Rand Europe (2011) *Europe's Demography: Are Babies Back?* (available at www.rand.org; accessed 06.01.15).

Ready, D.A. and J.A. Conger (2007) Make your company a talent factory, *Harvard Business Review*, June, 68–77.

Sloane, W. (2007) *We Put in an Infrastructure More Efficiently Ourselves*, The Sunday Times, 14 January (available at www.timesonline.co.uk; accessed 07.01.15).

Smethurst, S. (2005) HR roles: the long and winding road, *People Management*, 28 July, 25–29.

Storey, J. (2007) *Human Resource Management: A Critical Text*, 3rd edition, Thomson, London.

Suff, R. (2009) How British Gas is improving the diversity of its engineering workforce, *IRS Employment Review 922* (available at www.xperthr.co.uk; accessed 08.01.15).

Telegraph (2008) *MI6 Launches Ethnic Minority Recruitment Drive*, 20 November (available at www.telegraph.co.uk; accessed 08.01.15).

The Guardian (2014) *Police Recruiting Chief Says Force Needs to Change to Put More Minority Officers on Beat*, 18 January (available at www.theguardian.com, accessed 08.01.15).

The Scottish Government (2014) *Occupational Segregation* (available at www.scotland.gov.uk; accessed 08.01.15).

Thompson, J., J.M. Scott and F. Martin (2014). Strategic Management, Cengage Learning, Andover.

Thornton, J. (2010) *Interview with Liz Bell, HR Director at B&Q* (available at www.hrmagazine.co.uk; accessed 08.01.15).

UK Commission for Employment and Skills (2010) *National Employer Skills Survey for England 2009: Key Findings Report*, UKCES, London.

UK Commission for Employment and Skills (2014) *Understanding Skills and Performance Challenges in the Logistics Sector. Evidence Report 86*, UKCES, London.

Vaiman, V. and D.G. Collings (2013) Talent management: advancing the field, *The International Journal of Human Resource Management*, Vol. 24, No. 9, 1737–1743.

Whitford, A. (2014) *Candidate Attraction. Good Practice Manual* (available at www.xperthr.co.uk; accessed 08.01.15).

Willmott, B. (2014) *Solution to Skills Shortages Rests with Better Management* (available at www.cipd.co.uk; accessed 07.01.15).

Wooldridge, A. (2006) A survey of talent, *The Economist*, 7 October, 3–20. (available at www.aboutmcdonalds.com Hamburger University, accessed 07.01.15).

www.gov.uk (a). Child employment. Accessed 06.01.15.

www.gov.uk (b). Retirement age. Accessed 06.01.15.

www.jnj.com. Accessed 08.01.15.

Further study

Reports

Advisory, Conciliation and Arbitration Service (2014) *Managing Attendance and Employee Turnover*, ACAS (available at www.acas.org.uk; accessed 09.01.15).

This is a detailed and practical guide containing information about how to effectively manage attendance and employee turnover. The appendices contain valuable information regarding how to measure absence, how to measure employee turnover and how to develop an absence policy.

Chartered Institute of Personnel and Development (2007) *Technology in HR: How to Get the Most Out of Technology in People Management*, CIPD, London.
This is a practical and interactive tool that provides useful tips and good practice in the use of a Human Resource Information System (HRIS).

Joseph Rowntree Foundation (2014) *Future of the UK Labour Market*, Joseph Rowntree Foundation, York.
This report focuses on the labour market and poverty in the UK. The full report can be downloaded at **www.jrf.org.uk**, where you will also find other reports of research on social issues concerning employment.

Articles

Flint, D., L.M. Haley, and J.J. McNally (2013) Individual and organizational determinants of turnover intent, *Personnel Review*, Vol. 42, No. 5, 552–572.
This paper applies social exchange theory to predict the effects of procedural and interpersonal justice on turnover intentions.

Joppe, M. (2012) Migrant workers: challenges and opportunities in addressing tourism labour, *Tourism Management*, Vol. 33, No. 3, 662–671.
This article focuses on the potential of migrant workers to help address labour shortages in the tourism industry

Knies, E., P. Boselie, J. Gould-Williams and W. Vandenabeele (2015) Special issue of *International Journal of Human Resource Management*: strategic human resource management and public sector performance, *The International Journal of Human Resource Management*, Vol. 26, No. 3, 421–424.
This 'call for papers' article discusses key debates concerning strategic HRM and invites authors to submit their research to the journal for a forthcoming special issue. The reference list provides some key research texts on strategic HR and the forthcoming special edition should provide an excellent and in-depth overview of strategic HR and public sector performance.

Sivertzen, A., E. Nilsen and A. Olafsen (2013) Employer branding: employer attractiveness and the use of social media, *Journal of Product& Brand Management*, Vol. 22, No. 7, 473–483.
This paper investigates the factors employers need to focus on when developing an employer branding strategy.

Internet

Chartered Institute of Personnel and Development   www.cipd.co.uk
The CIPD site provides a wide range of useful information on HR strategy and uses of technology. The tool on technology in HR, available to members, includes a number of interesting case studies of organisations, including BOC Gases, Norwich Union, BSkyB, the NHS and Cancer Research UK. The site also contains a number of informative podcasts such as Number 94 (2014) concerning the impact of immigration on the UK workforce.

Objectives

When you have read this chapter you will be able to:

- identify the steps in the recruitment and selection process and explain the aims of recruitment and selection, describing how specified policies and procedures contribute to these aims

- understand the role of human resource managers and line managers in the recruitment and selection process

- describe and design support documentation for the recruitment and selection process

- understand the role of competencies and a competency framework

- evaluate and draft recruitment and selection policies and procedures

- identify and evaluate a range of recruitment and selection methods

- recognise typical interviewer errors and explain how to avoid them

- plan and conduct an interview and assess the candidate, recording and justifying your decisions and provide feedback to candidates

- suggest a range of work sample exercises and design them.

Organisations know the crucial part their employees play in achieving and sustaining competitive advantage, and they therefore recognise the need to attract the right people. Although recruitment intentions inevitably declined during the recession in 2008–2009, employment prospects had, by 2014, improved significantly with two thirds of employers planning to hire (CIPD, 2014b). Despite the increase in employment, UK employers report that 40 per cent of vacancies are hard to fill (CIPD, 2014b). Vacancies requiring highly skilled or skilled workers are particularly hard to fill and the three most popular reasons are lack of skills (57 per cent), too few applicants (42 per cent) and a lack of experience (38 per cent) (CIPD, 2014b). All of this data point to the continued need for good practice in recruitment to ensure that organisations attract the most suitable applicants in the most cost-effective way.

Attracting and retaining talent is critical to a firm's success (CIPD, 2013a). Although talent management focuses largely on the development and retention of employees, in order to achieve business strategic goals an organisation has to recruit and select people with appropriate competencies. Thus, recruitment and selection are strategically important, as discussed in Chapter 5. Competition for the best people also means that organisations have to be innovative in their recruitment and selection methods, and examples of some recent innovations will be presented in this chapter.

The processes of recruitment and selection are closely related. Both activities are directed towards obtaining employees with the requisite competencies and attitudes. Recruitment activities establish the groundwork for the selection process by providing the necessary pool of applicants from whom the selectors may choose. However, although recruitment and selection are closely linked, each requires a separate range of skills and expertise. Hence, in practice, these activities may be carried out by different individuals. The recruitment activity, but not usually the selection decision, may even be outsourced to an agency.

Recruitment

The aims of recruitment

Organisations are in constant interaction with their environment, and when an organisation recruits it is in direct contact with the outside world. Other factors that affect recruitment are the legislative framework and the budget. In relation to this and the definition of recruitment given above, the aims of recruitment are:

- to attract a pool of suitable candidates for vacant posts,
- to use a fair process and be able to demonstrate that this process was fair,
- to ensure that all recruitment activities contribute to organisational goals and the desired organisational image,
- to conduct recruitment activities in a cost-effective and efficient manner.

These statements raise a number of questions of how recruitment is undertaken. What is meant by a 'suitable candidate', and who decides if the candidate is suitable? Does the organisation have a process for evaluating the need to fill a post? What is a fair recruitment process and how can fairness be evaluated or demonstrated? What recruitment activities contribute to, or damage, an organisation's image? What are the costs involved in recruitment and how can they be controlled to maximise efficiency? How can recruitment activities be tailored to the organisation's strategic plan?

Most human resource management issues can be analysed in terms of legal, moral and business considerations. Legal considerations concern, for example, the need to comply with anti-discrimination legislation; moral considerations concern the need to avoid unfair discrimination for moral and legal reasons and business considerations relate to the need to ensure that efforts are directed towards the organisation achieving its strategic aims.

To achieve these aims, and because recruitment is likely to involve different people in an organisation, it is important to have a systematic approach so that all steps of the recruitment and selection process are conducted in line with the organisation's human resource strategy and its diversity and equality goals.

In ensuring that the recruitment process achieves these aims in a coordinated manner, the first step is to develop and implement appropriate policies and procedures.

Recruitment policies

A policy is a statement of intent on the part of an organisation. It states the approach everyone is expected to take and the standards they should achieve for the organisation. A recruitment policy enables employees to be involved in the process and to direct their efforts towards achieving the organisation's goals. At the very least a basic recruitment policy should include statements about the organisation's overall goal of recruitment and equality of opportunity.

Organisations may adopt a policy of giving preference to suitably qualified internal applicants over external applicants as a way of demonstrating that they value their employees, wish to retain them and want to provide them with every opportunity to develop. This too would need to be stated explicitly in the organisation's recruitment policy. Such a policy would have implications for the way recruitment procedures are developed and implemented.

An argument that is sometimes raised against internal recruitment policies is that they may exacerbate any existing equality problems. That is, if the organisation, for example, has failed to adequately recruit from a particular ethnic group then it will not improve its equality record by hiring from within the organisation. However, a counter-argument to this is that if current employees obtain new positions a vacancy will presumably be created that must be filled by external candidates. Organisations with good equality policies would be able to address any problems at this stage. In order to enhance the contribution and commitment of their employees organisations should consider adopting a policy on internal recruitment.

Pause for thought 6.1   You are required to produce a recruitment policy for a company which reflects its commitment to equal opportunities whilst giving preference to internal candidates. Before reading the next section, consider what might be included in a recruitment policy for this company.

The following is an example of how such a policy might be worded:

> This company aims to employ the best person for the job without regard to sex, marital status, racial origin, disability, sexual preference, religion, age or any other factor that cannot be reasonably construed as being related to a person's ability to do the job.
>
> The company values the contribution of its employees and will seek, wherever possible, to help employees develop new skills so that they may be considered for promotion. The company will advertise vacancies externally only if there are no suitably qualified internal candidates.

Recruitment procedures

The first step in the recruitment process is to assess the need for additional labour and decide whether or not you have a vacancy to fill. The vacancy may be a new position that has been identified from the strategic plan, or it may have arisen because an employee has resigned, retired or been dismissed. The latter are sometimes referred to as replacement posts whereas the former represent new posts. Another option is to recruit a job-share partner for an established employee who no longer wishes to work full-time.

Filling vacancies which arise because of a new post or because an employee has decided to leave should be part of a careful planning process, assessed in terms of how the action contributes to the organisation's strategic goals. When a person leaves the organisation, HR and line managers should take the opportunity to examine the work done to establish whether it can be covered in a different way. The following questions should be asked:

- Are all the tasks necessary?
- Could some tasks be incorporated into another post?
- Should the job be redesigned to include more interesting and challenging work?
- Could some tasks be completed in a different way, for example by machine, by computer?
- Can the work be done on a part-time, flexitime or job-share basis?
- Is there a permanent need for the post or could it be filled on a temporary basis or contracted out?

The recruitment process, as recommended by the CIPD (2014a), involves a number of stages:

- defining the role,
- attracting applicants,
- managing the application and selection process,
- making the appointment.

Documentation to support the recruitment process

Job descriptions and person specifications/competency profiles

Organisations that fully engage in human resource planning will produce and maintain job descriptions and person specifications/competency profiles as these documents contain important information required for the planning process. The name of the process which is followed to produce these documents is job analysis. However, even if the organisation does not engage fully in human resource planning it is essential that it produces job descriptions and person specifications/ competency profiles for all existing posts as a basic framework for recruitment and selection activities. These documents contain the information required for designing the job advertisement and the criteria used to assess candidates. They can also be used to provide evidence that the process is fair.

Job analysis

Job analysis is the process of gathering together information about an existing job, establishing the activities to be performed, the expected outcomes of tasks and the skills required. A decision needs to be made, as described in the next section, of who will carry out the job analysis most effectively. The collected data are then structured to create job descriptions and person specifications or a job profile related to a competency framework. A similar process can be used to create this documentation for new posts though this would inevitably rely more on the knowledge and judgement of management.

The following aspects of job analysis need to be considered:

- What techniques can be used for gathering the information required?
- Who can best gather and provide the information?
- Who should write the job description and person specification?

What techniques can be used for gathering the information?

There are a number of techniques available for performing job analysis. These include observation, critical incident analysis and the use of questionnaires and interviews.

Observation involves shadowing employees and observing what they actually do. This method can be very time consuming and could stretch over a long period of time, for example where some tasks were performed infrequently. Thus, the technique is most appropriate in the case of routine jobs with a narrow range of repetitive tasks.

In critical incident analysis a number of jobholders and their supervisors describe events that demonstrate successful behaviour on the job and events that demonstrate unsuccessful behaviour. The analyst collects a large number of such events and produces a list of dimensions that represent the job. The advantage of this method is that it focuses on behaviour, that is, what people actually do, but the process is very time consuming and may fail to acknowledge some of the more routine aspects of the job.

A robust method for gathering information would involve the use of written questionnaires and face-to-face interviews. A structured questionnaire can be used to gather initial data from the jobholder, supplemented with information from the line manager. The job analyst can then interview the jobholder and line manager to obtain clarification on the details outlined in the questionnaire. The draft job description could then be submitted to the jobholder and line manager for further comment. A structured questionnaire will provide guidance as to what information is needed.

Pause for thought 6.2   You have been asked to design a form in order to conduct a job analysis. What questions would you ask and why?

To some extent, the questions on a job analysis form might be dictated by the type of company you are working in. For instance, if you work in a bank which is closed in the evening you would not include questions about night shift work, whereas if you worked in an automotive manufacturing plant operating 24 hours a day you would ask questions about shift patterns. Ignoring such differences between organisations there is some basic information that you would want to include in any job analysis. These would include such things as

- a description of the duties to be performed,
- what the jobholder is expected to achieve (the expected outcome of the tasks),
- the most important duties,
- the time spent on each duty,
- how often each duty is performed (daily/weekly/monthly/annually),
- the level of supervision/independence,
- the skills and skill levels needed to perform each task,
- any special conditions related to the performance of these tasks.

The questionnaire and interview should be designed so that information needed for each section of the job description will be obtained. Asking employees and their managers to describe ways in which they think their jobs will change will add information to the job analysis beyond what is already observable about the job.

Many people are happy to talk about their job but some people do not respond well to questioning or they may find it difficult to express their views. The person performing the job analysis needs good interviewing skills in order to extract all the relevant information. Interviewing skills are an essential part of human resource management and you will find more information about relevant techniques and skills development later on in this chapter.

Who can best gather and provide the information?

The post holder is a good source of information about any post. However, the direct line manager will also know the job requirements intimately and will probably have a better overview of how the job fits into the organisation's goals. Gathering information from the post holder and line manager will create a better picture of the post than gathering information from only one of them.

HR specialists too are often able to develop detailed knowledge of the tasks performed in the organisation, and in fact must do so, particularly if they are involved in the human resource planning process. They can therefore bring an even wider perspective to the description of an individual post. To that extent they can also provide input to the job description but their key role as far as job descriptions are concerned is to structure, standardise and maintain them rather than providing content-based information.

Activity 6.1

Before continuing to the next section, list the advantages and disadvantages of involving the post holder and the line manager in the production of job descriptions.

Your list may include the following points:

1. The post-holder
   - knows the job well,
   - may inflate the importance of certain duties in order to enhance their status or self-image,
   - may represent duties they prefer as more important duties,
   - may not have a true knowledge of the level of authority they can exercise,
   - may not have the specialised knowledge and skills needed to gather information and produce job descriptions.
   - may be reluctant to spend the time necessary to develop a good job description.

2. The line manager
   - knows the job reasonably well, but may not know every task,
   - can provide information on how the job fits in with other functions performed in the company,
   - may sometimes be reluctant to state which tasks their subordinates have full authority for,
   - may not have the specialised knowledge and skills needed to gather information and compose job descriptions,
   - may be reluctant to spend the time required to develop a good job description.

Most line managers would not consider the production of job descriptions to be part of their duties and there is no reason to assume that line managers would necessarily have the knowledge and skills needed in order to produce a good job description. The human resource management function would normally provide this service to line management and people with the requisite knowledge and skills would be recruited and selected to perform this duty. It is rare today to see an HR position totally devoted to job analysis but the task could be allocated to a recruitment specialist or an HR generalist, depending on the structure of the HRM division.

Who should write the job description and person specification?

The HR specialist is probably the best person to perform this task because of the writing skills required and the opportunity to become familiar with jobs throughout the organisation. This also means that all job descriptions will be written in a uniform manner thus providing an excellent database of all tasks performed in and throughout the organisation. This will help to facilitate a range of HR tasks such as the human resource planning activities described in Chapter 5. The various uses of job descriptions and person specifications are examined later in this chapter.

How to write a job description

Structure and content

It makes sense to adopt a standard format for all job descriptions (JDs), given that a collection of job descriptions can serve as a database of all tasks performed within an organisation. This means that the same type of information is gathered for each post, and will make it easier to code and enter this information onto a computerised information system. A job description usually contains the job title, the reporting structure, the purpose of the job and the major duties to be performed.

These are the essential elements of a job description but you will find other dimensions included in some job descriptions, for example: working conditions, salary grade, contacts and performance standards. The organisation needs to decide what factors should be included in a job description and this will depend on the nature of the business. The four elements listed above, however, represent the basic information you would expect to find in any job description.

Most JDs contain a short description of the post or, as we have called it, an outline of the purpose of the post. This concerns what the job is all about – what the jobholder contributes to the organisation. A JD should contain the major duties, providing a detailed, itemised list of activities the jobholder undertakes and what they are meant to achieve.

Writing style

When you are writing a job description it is a good idea to use verbs to describe what a person is doing. For instance, the phrase 'responsible for customer complaints' does not indicate what this employee would actually be doing. It is much better to employ a verb and state: 'communicates with customers about their complaints'; 'sorts and distributes letters and emails regarding complaints' and 'replies to letters and emails about complaints'.

Where possible, you should also avoid using the phrase 'assists with', as again this does not give a clear picture of what an individual employee is actually doing. Take, for example, the phrase: 'assists the manager in managing stock/inventory'. It would be much better to state that the person 'purchases appropriate goods, materials and products'; 'keeps accurate records of sales and inventory levels' and 'works closely with other employees to ensure that there are proper stock levels'. Each of these indicates a different activity and a different level of responsibility, and each is more meaningful than 'assists the manager in managing stock/inventory'.

Uses of the job description

Job descriptions can be used for a number of purposes. These will be dealt with more extensively in other chapters but it is useful to consider how job descriptions can be used and the implications for how job descriptions are compiled and written. The major uses of job descriptions are human resource planning, recruitment and selection, day-to-day performance management and long-term performance management/performance appraisal, identification of training needs and job evaluation.

Is it possible to produce one description for all of the purposes mentioned above? Some HR managers may argue that different inputs are needed, for example in the job evaluation process. The question arises of whether a different job description is required for the purposes of job evaluation.

Activity 6.2

1. Design a questionnaire that could be used to obtain the necessary information from an employee to draft a job description. Think of the questions would you need to ask in order to elicit all the relevant information.
2. Test your questionnaire on a willing volunteer and follow up with an interview to fill in the gaps.
3. Analyse this process and make recommendations for improvement.
4. Draft the job description from the information you have gathered.

Person specifications

The person specification outlines the knowledge, skills and qualities a person would need to have in order to be able to do the tasks or achieve the outcomes required on the job description. In producing a person specification you will need to judge what level of skill is necessary and be careful *not* to inflate these requirements, especially with regard to academic qualifications and length of experience. The requirements in a person specification represent the minimum standards required for a person to be able to do the job and there should be an expectation that any person will improve performance while doing a job. The fact that training could be provided should also be considered.

How to write a person specification

There are several models of person specifications available. Those designed by Alec Rodger in 1952 and John Munro Fraser in 1978 are the most widely known. We shall briefly describe the criteria set out in these two models and indicate how you might interpret the models in today's business environment. We will then apply a simplified model to our sample job description.

Rodger developed the seven-point plan which described people in terms of:

- **Physical make-up**: Any particular physical requirements of the job, such as vision (e.g. you would not be able to become a train driver if you had colour blindness).
- **Attainments**: Education and training.
- **General intelligence**: You cannot really make a meaningful statement about intelligence unless you intend to test for it.
- **Special aptitudes**: Verbal, numerical and diagrammatical abilities related to the job.
- **Interests**: Private interests are not good indicators of job performance.
- **Disposition**: Job-related behaviours such as determination.
- **Circumstances**: Only job-related circumstances such as availability to work evening shifts.

The criteria suggested by Fraser are known as the five-fold framework:

- **Impact on others**: Similar to Rodger's physical make-up and disposition.
- **Qualifications and experience**: Education, vocational training and work experience.
- **Innate abilities**: Quickness of comprehension and aptitude for learning.
- **Motivation**: Difficult to apply for recruitment and selection purposes since differing motivational structures can lead to equally good performance. However, the person's career goals, determination in achieving these goals and the success of whether the goals have been achieved may be considered.
- **Emotional adjustment**: Relevant personality factors such as the ability to cope with the stresses of the job and the ability to get on with people.

In essence, the person specification should cover three areas of requirements: knowledge, skills and personal attributes or qualities. In North America these dimensions have long been used to create person specifications where they are referred to as KSAs (Knowledge, Skills and Abilities).

The person specification can be produced by examining each task in the job description and determining what each task requires in terms of knowledge, skills and personal qualities and how these might be acquired.

As stated earlier, you will need to decide on relevant criteria when writing a person specification. You must be able to justify any requirement and be able to explain why it is reasonable, particularly when the specification is to be used in recruitment and selection. You should also take care to avoid meaningless clichés like 'thinking on your feet', when what is really required is the ability to prioritise.

Once you have produced a list of the criteria they must be arranged in a logical and understandable manner. Similar criteria, such as all skills and knowledge involving numeracy, should be grouped. Criteria can then be designated as essential for the post or desirable.

An example of a person specification is given in Table 6.1.

Table 6.1 Example of a person specification

Person specification		
Post: Operations manager		
Attributes	**Essential**	**Desirable**
Knowledge	Degree	Membership of a professional organisation
Skills	Leadership skills including team development	Fluency in a second language (Chinese, French, Spanish or German preferred)
Personal qualities	Good team player	Good presentation skills

Competency frameworks

Competencies are work-related behaviours necessary for successful performance in the workplace. Rather than designing a person specification for each post it may be possible to develop a framework of competencies that can be applied to all jobs performed in a particular organisation. It should be possible to identify a set of core competencies required of all employees with more specialised competencies attached to the job descriptions of specific posts. Given changes to equality legislation the focus in setting requirements during recruitment and selection is shifting firmly towards the use of competencies. The use of competencies means that candidates are assessed on their abilities, not on aspects such as length of work experience or non-essential academic qualifications that may be affected by their sex, ethnicity, age and so on. Requirements for particular qualifications or work experience can take attention away from an evaluation of actual competencies.

Developing a competency framework is complex and the organisation may wish to employ the services of a firm of occupational psychologists to assist in the design and implementation of such a framework. Competency frameworks come in many different guises and the questions that would typically need to be answered in designing a system include the following:

- Should the framework be geared towards particular categories of employee (e.g. managers) or designed for all employees in the organisation?
- What competencies does the organisation need (e.g. communication skills, analytical abilities, ability to work in a team, leadership, and ability to plan work)?
- How many competencies should we include to build a comprehensive but manageable representation of the skills, knowledge and personal qualities required in the organisation?
- Which competencies can be grouped together as clusters?
- How many performance levels should there be for each competency and how will these levels be described?
- How do these competency clusters, individual competencies and levels of competency relate to individual jobs in the organisation?

The Incomes Data Services (IDS, 2012) provides a review of issues companies need to consider when designing and implementing a competency framework, and the CIPD has a useful factsheet on competence and competency frameworks (CIPD, 2013d).

The job description in the recruitment context

The four basic elements of the job description are: the job title, the reporting structure, a statement of the purpose of the post and a description of the major duties. Taken together these elements should provide a job applicant with a good idea of what the job entails.

The job title, such as warehouse manager, assistant marketing manager or midwife, already contains a lot of information about the position. In choosing a job title you should be careful not to inflate the level of the job by inappropriately using terms such as 'executive' or 'director'. You should also avoid any potentially sexist language such as waitress and foreman.

In the sections on reporting structure the information provided should enable the applicant to establish where the job fits into the organisation's structure and if there are any supervisory responsibilities. Any pertinent details about terms and conditions, such as the need to work unsociable hours, should also be included since this will enable candidates to judge whether they are willing to accept such conditions.

The person specification/competency profile in the recruitment context

Having a person specification/competency profile demonstrates the organisation's attempt to introduce some objectivity into what can otherwise be a very subjective process. The employer with a person specification/profile is following a much more methodical, reasoned and transparent process, recording, in written form, decisions made. These written records can be requested by employment tribunals should there be a complaint of unfair treatment, but many employers now share this information with applicants so applicants also know in detail what the employer is looking for in a candidate.

It is important that the requirements for a job are not set unnecessarily high as this may unfairly exclude a person from being considered for a position, possibly constituting indirect discrimination, as certain disadvantaged groups may have more difficulty in acquiring some qualifications or competency levels. Care should also be taken that none of the criteria set might cause unlawful direct discrimination.

As mentioned above, the person specification/competency profile can be sent, with other relevant information, to candidates to give them more information about the requirements for the job. It is considered good practice to send applicants a form showing each requirement and how it will be assessed, for example from information included in the application form, from the interview or from references. Table 6.2 shows an example of this, based on the person specification for an operations manager which was given earlier in this chapter (Table 6.1).

Table 6.2 Assessment of person specification criteria

Post: Operations manager		
Attributes	**Criteria**	**How assessed**
Knowledge	Knowledge of operations Knowledge of the company	Application form, interview Interview
Skills	Experience of operational work Experience of managing employees Ability to interpret financial data	Application form, interview Application form, interview Application form, interview
Personal qualities	Ability to work well with different people Ability to work under pressure	Interview Interview

Recruitment methods

Job advertisements

Once you know you have a vacancy to fill you must decide the best way to let people know about it. The following are some methods for advertising a vacancy:

- on-site noticeboards,
- local or national newspapers,
- professional journals,
- minority group newspapers and magazines,
- recruitment agencies,
- university/college/school careers centres,
- job centres,
- radio/television,
- Internet sites,
- a recruitment fair or exhibition.

Deciding where to place an advertisement

You will need to assess the advertising method in terms of its appropriateness for a particular vacancy. Such considerations will include: the likelihood of finding people with the necessary skills and knowledge; the qualifications and experience you are seeking and which publications people with those qualifications and experience are likely to read; salary level and whether you are likely to be able to attract someone to move to your area for the salary you are offering and the cost of placing an advertisement. Some judgement is required in making these decisions, but try to keep recruitment open and fair.

The cost of advertising is a major consideration. You will probably be more willing to spend more money from your advertising budget on a senior post than on a junior one. However, you may have a relatively junior post that requires skills not readily available in the local area.

Word-of-mouth advertising is often mentioned in textbooks as a possible method of recruitment and it is used to varying degrees in some organisations. However, we do not recommend it because of its potentially discriminatory effects. Organisations that recruit heavily using word of mouth run the risk of reinforcing the composition of their workforce in terms of gender, age and ethnic origin and so on. It is common for employees to recommend people like themselves for a vacancy from among their family and friends. For example, in general, if an organisation's workforce were almost exclusively white Europeans, word-of-mouth recruitment would tend to result in more white Europeans being recruited. A commitment to equal opportunities means that this cycle needs to be broken, and one way of doing this is to advertise in the ethnic press.

Designing recruitment advertisements

The first principle of writing job advertisements is to *give sufficient information about the post so that suitable candidates will apply, but also so that unsuitable candidates will be discouraged from applying.* First consider what the objectives of a job advertisement are, and what techniques might be used to achieve those objectives. The overall aim of the advertisement is to secure sufficient applications from suitably qualified persons with the end result that the employer will find 'the best person for the job'. Employers will want to obtain a reasonable number of applications, but not an overwhelming number.

When writing a job advertisement, consider what will attract good applicants to apply for the position. For example, if salary is a major selling point for your organisation, should the salary be included or excluded? Should it be displayed at the top of the advertisement, in the body of the text or at the end? The following are some suggestions of the factors you may wish to include in a job advertisement:

- the organisation's name and information about the organisation,
- job title and major duties,
- competencies required,
- opportunities and challenges,
- salary and benefits,
- policy statement of important issues such as equal opportunities,
- how to apply.

The organisation's name and information about the organisation

People need to know which organisation they are applying to. Information about the organisation and what it can offer as an employer can be a selling point.

Increasingly, 'employer brand' is being used in recruitment (Marsh, 2012). This involves matching an organisation's recruitment practices to its corporate brand. An example of this is Ernst & Young where the employer brand is the same as the company brand because, as reported by its global head of people, it is a people-based business (Marsh, 2012).

> **Did you know?**
>
> One way of promoting employer brand would be to achieve a listing in the Sunday Times 100 Best Companies to Work For. There are four categories of award: best small companies, best companies, best big companies and best not-for-profit organisations. The top companies/organisations per category in 2014 were: UKRD group (best small company and best company); Iceland Foods (best big company) and SLH Group (best not-for-profit organisation). You can find out more at **http://features.thesundaytimes.co.uk/**

Job title and major duties

The job title should be used in the job description, and the main duties should be summarised for the advertisement to give potential applicants a good idea of what the job entails.

Competencies required

Job advertisements should contain enough detail to enable candidates to identify how suitable they are for the post. The person specification/competency profile will provide a good basis for identifying the abilities you are looking for. This should make an important contribution to the cost-effectiveness and overall success of the process.

Opportunities and challenges

Emphasise the opportunities a job will offer the candidate, for example personal and professional development, overseas travel, customer contact. State the challenges they are likely to face, such as developing an effective team, growing the business or dealing with complex projects.

Salary and benefits

Every organisation will have a record of the salary ranges and benefits that are attached to each job. An organisation might have a particularly attractive package of benefits. It is important to advertise these benefits as they could be the deciding factor on whether a candidate applies for a position. You can read more about salaries and benefits in Chapter 9.

Policy statement of important issues such as equal opportunities

An organisation needs to decide on its policy regarding equal opportunities and managing diversity. Many organisations choose to make a short statement about such issues in a job advertisement. For example, an online job advertisement for a Policy and Planning Manager with the General Medical Council (GMC) in London (advertised July 2014) states that 'The GMC values diversity and has made a public commitment to processes and procedures that are fair, objective, transparent and free from discrimination'.

How to apply

A range of options exist and the most appropriate will depend on the nature of the post, the volume of applications expected or desired and the systems and capabilities of the department receiving the applications. You may require interested applicants to do any of the following:

- complete an online application form,
- call in person,
- attend an open day interview event,
- phone/leave a message on a 24-hour answer machine requesting an application form,
- write a letter applying for the post or apply by email,
- contact a particular person in the organisation,
- request further information,
- email or send a curriculum vitae (CV) with a covering letter,
- email or send a CV with an application form,
- apply by a certain date.

Writing style

The writing style that is appropriate for a job advertisement depends on the position. Traditionally, advertisements were written in a very formal style using phrases like: 'The successful candidate will possess a good university degree and three years of work-related experience'. In more recent years, most advertisements have been written in a less formal and more direct style using 'you' as if the recruiter were speaking directly to the applicant.

Other methods used to attract the reader's attention are the use of questions or bold statements. The following online job advertisement for a Graduate Recruitment Consultant in Manchester (advertised on **totaljobs.com**) demonstrates this.

> Are you a graduate? Do you want to start your career in a fast-paced sales environment with the opportunity to earn uncapped commission? Do you want to have the opportunity to build and develop a career?

Care must be taken when using such methods in a job advertisement as a list of questions at the start of an advert can become tedious. Once you have caught your reader's attention you should proceed swiftly to giving information. You should also avoid using clichés or essentially meaningless phrases. Most employers would like to employ enthusiastic, intelligent, well-motivated and outgoing people. Given that practically no one is likely to admit to not being any of these it seems pointless to include them as criteria in a job advertisement.

Use of colour and graphics

Colour and graphics are often used by organisations to draw attention to their advertisement. A company logo may be part of promoting the employer brand and photographs can convey an impression of an organisation's culture or perhaps its commitment to diversity.

Job advertisements: whose responsibility?

Every organisation needs to decide who should be responsible for producing job advertisements. There are several factors to consider. For instance, has the post changed a great deal? Is the post routine in nature, with straightforward duties? Does an advertisement exist that can be used? A junior member of the HRM department could deal with these questions or the administrative staff in any unit where this activity has been devolved to line management.

If the post is new or has changed a great deal the line manager should be more involved as expertise in writing a job advertisement will be needed. If the post is difficult fill (maybe due to a local skills shortage) you may consider using a recruitment agency. The additional cost of this would need to be weighed against the cost of unsuccessful recruitment campaigns. Some organisations reduce costs by maintaining a list of preferred agencies and negotiating special deals with them. The main reasons why organisations use recruitment agencies are to access skills and knowledge, to improve quality and to reduce costs (CIPD, 2009a).

Online/e-recruitment

For many employers, the Internet is one of the most important ways of recruiting good applicants (Branine, 2008). The term 'e-recruitment' describes the process of recruiting people online (Allden and Harris, 2013). According to Holm (2014), e-recruitment covers a number of digital practices, including:

- advertising posts on Internet sites;
- e-recruitment systems for application submission;
- tracking, screening and candidate management;
- CV databases.

The use of the Internet to advertise posts and deal with recruitment processes is becoming ever more well established, and developments in Web 2.0 technology are allowing for more innovative approaches. Job vacancies are listed by many organisations on their own website, in other cases by recruitment agencies, on job boards such as Monster (**www.monster.co.uk**) and on the online jobs pages of newspapers and journals. In the CIPD's (2013a) annual report on resourcing and talent planning, the most effective methods for attracting candidates were through corporate websites and recruitment agencies. The same report points to the increased use of social media with LinkedIn, Twitter and Facebook being the most commonly used social media sites for recruitment. The widespread use of smartphones has also altered the way organisations recruit. Many people use their smartphones to go online rather than accessing information via a computer. Therefore, firms wishing to attract younger applicants, such as recent graduates, need to make sure that their recruitment information is accessible to smartphone users (Human Resource Management International Digest, 2013). Other technological advances in recruitment processes include using text messages to inform potential applicants of vacancies (Whitford, 2014), candidates' use of video CVs to present themselves (Chynoweth, 2009), the production of podcasts offering careers advice, employee video blogs included in company websites and virtual tours of a company's premises (*The Sunday Times*, 2007).

Reduced costs are regarded as being a benefit from recruiting online, particularly through the organisations' own corporate websites. There are, however, a number of other advantages to online recruitment. One of the major reasons for using the Internet for recruitment is that it provides access to a large pool of applicants, but this is a mixed blessing as it could lead to an increased number of unsuitable applicants (CIPD, 2009a). If organisations wish to make their recruitment process more effective and efficient the design and content of web-based advertising needs careful consideration (Henkes, 2007). The issue of equal opportunities and managing diversity also needs to be addressed. Williams (2009) reports that diversity is enhanced because of the broader reach of online advertising but the CIPD (2009a) cautions that Internet recruitment could act as a barrier to the recruitment of older workers.

Further expected advantages from e-recruitment processes are better-informed candidates, flexibility and ease of use for applicants, improved speed in completing the recruitment and selection processes, enhancement of employer brand for those employers seen to be using modern and innovative techniques, particularly when applicants are driven to an organisation's own website.

Did you know?

When recruiting, social media sites can provide employers with a great deal of information about prospective candidates. Many employers view social media profiles on Facebook, Twitter and LinkedIn. Screening applicants using social media sites can be a quick way of obtaining information, but employers need to consider the possible risks such as discrimination and infringing a person's privacy.

(*Source*: ACAS workplace snippit, August 2012)

Activity 6.3

For any two firms, compare and contrast how the firms use e-recruitment. How could they improve their e-recruitment?

Targeted recruitment

The Equality Act 2010, described in detail in Chapter 4, is essentially designed to protect specified groups from being treated less favourably. A somewhat controversial aspect of this act is contained in Section 159 which allows for positive action in recruitment and promotion. Positive action means that it is possible to recruit or promote a candidate who has a protected characteristic, or suffers a disadvantage because of that characteristic, if the candidate is of equal merit to a candidate not possessing such characteristics. However, positive action does not mean that a less suitable candidate can be selected just because the candidate has a protected characteristic or is disadvantaged because of the characteristic.

Targeted recruitment is somewhat different to positive action and is a method of encouraging previously disadvantaged groups to apply for vacancies. In keeping with the basic intention of equality legislation, any subsequent selection must be based on merit only.

Targeted recruitment can be drawn to potential applicants' attention in job advertisements in a number of different ways including

- a statement that encourages under-represented groups to apply for a post,
- a statement not targeted at any particular specified group but emphasising that diversity is valued and that all candidates will be assessed on merit,
- photographs and text that show people in non-traditional roles, thus emphasising an employer's desire to receive applications from groups that do not traditionally apply for particular posts ,
- an assurance that qualified candidates with a disability will be invited to interview,
- photographs showing a mix of different people.

Employers who use targeted recruitment recognise that good, suitable people are discouraged from applying for certain jobs because of a history or perception of discrimination. A number of such companies were profiled in a seminal *Personnel Management* article by Paddison (1990). The experience of these companies was that targeted recruitment attracts a much greater pool of suitable candidates and not only from the specified groups as there was an overall improvement in the quality of applications. Targeted recruitment, then, makes a statement about an organisation's level of commitment to equality. It may help the organisation to address equality issues per se, but a side effect is that it also attracts applications from better candidates.

Activity 6.4

Review a number of job advertisements from different sources. How good are these advertisements? In making a judgement, consider the following:

- What made you select the advertisement?
- How complete is the information about tasks, skills requirements, salary, etc.?
- Does the advertisement assist the reader in self-selection?
- Are important aspects of organisational culture presented, such as equality and diversity policies?
- How could the advertisement be improved?

You may wish to discuss your findings with others in your class in small groups, and present your findings to the whole class.

Application forms

Having provided candidates with information about your vacancy you must decide on the best way for individuals to present information about themselves. The major choices are:

- application form,
- CV,
- letter of application,
- handwritten/typed submission,
- personal call.

The application form is a bridge between the recruitment and selection process. Once a completed form has been received, it can be used as a basis for the initial selection exercise. Until this occurs, it is part of the recruitment process and its design should be subject to recruitment considerations. A poorly designed form could alienate potential applicants and discourage potentially good candidates from applying.

Many organisations prefer to use their own application form because it can be designed to elicit information specific to the types of work done in your organisation. The information can be ordered so that very important information is seen first. An advantage of application forms over CVs is that the organisation controls the information that is given. In this way the organisation can ensure that the same type of information is obtained from all applicants, the information is relevant to the work on offer and information that could potentially lead to unlawful discrimination is excluded.

Application forms should be designed so that so that they are age neutral. Forms should also address issues such as making arrangements to assist people with disabilities, monitoring for equality and diversity purposes, data protection issues and other legal aspects.

Questions regarding disabilities

According to the IRS (2014c), except in a limited number of cases, it is not permissible to ask questions about the health or disability of a candidate prior to offering the person a job. It is, however, permissible to enquire as to any adjustments needed to be made to facilitate the application process and enable the candidate to perform the work in question. The application form may need to be provided in an alternative format, for example in large print, electronically or as an audio file (IRS, 2014a).

Age neutral application forms

Instead of concentrating on qualifications and experience, the age discrimination regulations renewed the focus on competencies in the recruitment and selection process. These two latter factors continue to be important but employers are being encouraged to focus on a person's capabilities rather than depending, for example, on length of experience. The Employers Forum on Age (**www.efa .org.uk/**) has interesting information on its website about eliminating dates from the application process so that employers focus on competencies rather than making judgements based on information linked to age. Although much of the information on this website is only accessible by those who have paid for a corporate membership, the template and guidance for an age neutral application form is still generally accessible at **www.efa.org.uk/data/files/publications/507/ Getting-Recruitment-Right.pdf** (accessed 04.08.14).

Equality and diversity monitoring

Many application forms contain an equality monitoring section so that employers can evaluate their success in attracting applications from qualified members of designated groups and monitor the processing of these applications at all stages of the selection process. The information on this form should not be used as part of the selection process but only be used to provide feedback to the organisation on its equality processes. It is essential that candidates are informed about why information on equality is being requested and how it will be used. Candidates should also be informed that it is not compulsory to provide this information and that this will not affect their application.

It is better if the monitoring form can be detached from the application form so that it is clear to applicants that the monitoring and selection processes are completely separate. Monitoring forms usually request information about characteristics which are directly addressed in the legislation on discrimination. Monitoring for sexual orientation is likely to be a sensitive issue but collecting data on religion or belief may help the organisation to better understand employees' needs (IRS, 2014b).

Data protection and other legal issues

Employers inevitably collect a lot of personal information about their candidates (and existing employees) so the design and handling of application forms is subject to the Data Protection Act 1998. The principles of data protection are described in more detail in Chapter 3 on the employment relationship, but the principles that obviously apply here are that the information collected should be appropriate for its intended use, it should be used only for the purpose for which it was collected and it should be handled in a secure fashion. Application forms should include a statement that the employer intends to process information provided by the candidate. Applicants should be asked to sign alongside the statement indicating acceptance of the organisation's stated use of their data (IRS, 2014f). A sample data protection statement can be seen on the age neutral application form template on the EFA website and there is also detailed guidance available from the Information Commissioner's Office (**http://ico .org.uk/**).

Employers need to ensure that potential employees have the right to work in the UK, so application forms must request information about eligibility.

Activity 6.5

- Choose an employer and design an application form that could be used for all posts within that organisation.
- Check that your form elicits all relevant information from applicants.
- Consider the design and layout of your application form: is it easy to complete; is it easy for employers to locate relevant information?
- Compare your application form with the sample form given on the website of the Employers Forum on Age at **www.efa.org.uk/data/files/publications/507/Getting-Recruitment-Right.pdf** (accessed 04.08.14).

Equality implications

In order to promote equality employers may wish to assist those with limited language skills in completing application forms. There are many posts where the duties to be performed do not require high levels of skills in reading and writing. Positive measures to ensure that such people are not unfairly excluded from such posts could lead to an organisation acquiring committed employees who might otherwise have been excluded. Employers who are genuinely interested in equality and diversity would also naturally include a statement on their application forms to this effect as part of their employer branding initiatives.

CVs

Although we have focused on the advantages of using an application form there are some advantages to using CVs. If an advertisement required all applicants to submit a CV instead of an application form the organisation would have eliminated the steps, and therefore the cost, of designing, producing and sending out application forms. However, it must be remembered that preparing a CV requires a fairly good standard of writing skills, so it would not be appropriate to require this for all positions. Many advertisements for managerial posts request interested candidates to apply by sending in a CV. Some posts require the candidate to complete an application form with the choice of attaching a CV.

Administrative procedures

The final aspect of the recruitment process needs to consider how applications are going to be handled, in addition to any data protection requirements. You will need to design administrative procedures that deal with accepting applications by phone/walk in/electronically, sending forms/information and acknowledgement of applications received.

In deciding on the appropriate administrative procedures you will need to address questions about what you want to achieve versus the cost. Also, there is a public relations element in every recruitment exercise, as your organisation will have contact with many unsuccessful candidates but who may be potential customers and will certainly tell others how you treated them. You will want

Did you know?

Adidas was one of the first graduate employers to use an iPhone recruitment app to reinvigorate the company's graduate recruitment process. The app includes an RSS feed to live vacancies and the firm is hoping to encourage students to apply for specialist graduate schemes in HR, marketing, communications, finance and IT. The app is part of Adidas' efforts to improve its employer branding.

(*Source*: Stevens, 2011)

to create a good impression with every applicant but this must be balanced by the question of cost. Many organisations use an automated email to inform candidates that their application has been received. Other organisations inform candidates that they will not receive an acknowledgement of receipt of their application form due, for example, to the large number of applications expected.

Selection

A successful recruitment campaign should result in a good number of suitably qualified applications for a vacancy. The next task is to select the most suitable person. Employers must decide who should be involved in this task and provide support in terms of policies, procedures and training.

As with all other aspects of human resource management, organisations can adopt a strategic approach towards selection. Effective selection processes, aligned to the organisation's strategic goals, add value by ensuring the necessary human resources are in place for the achievement of these goals. It is therefore advisable to view selection processes within this wider context.

Aims and objectives of the selection process

The ultimate goal of selection is 'to choose the best person for the job'. Selectors attempt to match candidates to the job requirements predicting how well they will perform if offered the position. Selectors also need to ensure that the candidate fully understands all major aspects of the job so that new recruits are not likely to become disillusioned and leave within a short period of time. The objectives of the selection process are as follows:

1. gather as much relevant information as possible,
2. organise and evaluate the information,
3. assess each candidate

in order to

4. forecast performance on the job and provide information to applicants so that they can decide if they wish to accept an offer of employment.

Selection policies and procedures

Every effort should be made to design a methodical and objective system for selecting employees in order to achieve a fair, non-discriminatory outcome. It is very difficult to totally eliminate personal factors and perceptions but having objective policies and procedures in place will help reduce any potentially harmful effects of individual bias. Having good selection policies and procedures will provide guidance and support to line managers and others involved in the selection process to carry out this duty successfully, confident that they are following best practice.

Like recruitment policies, selection policies are a statement of an organisation's intentions and should normally address such issues as equal opportunities, maybe giving information about targeted groups. A selection policy might read as follows:

> The objective of the selection process is to obtain employees who will be committed and productive members of staff, who will work towards developing their full potential. This organisation will select employees on the basis of merit only. Internal and disabled applicants who have the required knowledge and skills are guaranteed an interview.

Selection procedures should establish the stages and techniques that should be used, who is involved in assessing candidates and the administrative processes to be used.

For each of these issues, a number of factors need to be decided on and relevant guidelines provided. For example, the procedures documentation might indicate that a shortlist must be prepared and interviews conducted for each vacancy; guidelines might be given on who is to prepare the shortlist and conduct the interviews and the methods to be used to accomplish these tasks. Further issues to be addressed in the selection procedures include guidelines on non-discriminatory questioning, the use and appropriateness of testing and how references are used.

According to the CIPD (2013b), the most well-established selection methods include:

- interviews,
- psychological testing,
- assessment centres,
- using references.

The CIPD (2013b) has further identified the interview as the most frequently used selection method among those listed, with competency-based interviews being the most popular form of interview used.

Selection as a strategic activity

In Chapters 1 and 5 we established that employee selection contributes to the achievement of strategic goals and is therefore too important an activity to be conducted on the basis of what is familiar. Depending on the circumstances, organisations may need to engage in a broader range of activities rather than simply shortlisting and interviewing. Sophisticated selection has been identified as part of the best practice associated with the HRM approach (Marchington and Wilkinson, 2005) and thus a necessary part of a strategic approach dedicated to gaining competitive advantage that comes from having a superior workforce. The importance of getting the selection right is the crucial contribution it makes to an organisation's talent management processes. As Ready and Conger (2007, p. 68) state: 'Stop losing out on lucrative business opportunities because you don't have the talent to develop them'. The full range of techniques may not be needed for every vacancy, but the process should be examined and the appropriate action chosen for each contingency.

It should be noted that employers can use considerable flexibility in the design of their selection process. Tests may, for instance, be used early in the process to screen out unsuitable candidates and increase the efficiency of time spent on competency-based interviews.

Shortlisting

Most employers will wish to interview a number of applicants before offering a position. In many instances, a successful recruitment campaign will attract more applicants than it would be possible to interview. The first step is to reduce the applications to a manageable number, a process known as shortlisting. The short-listing of applicants is a selection procedure that may be performed purely on the basis of the written information that applicants have supplied. It may involve acquiring additional information about candidates, for example by conducting a telephone interview.

Screening written applications

When assessing written job applications, it is important to be objective and make notes that refer only to relevant selection criteria. Often candidates provide information that is not requested. For example, candidates might describe their family situation in order to explain a gap in their employment record. Applicants have to give their name so that the organisation can communicate with them. A name, however, can reveal information that is not relevant to the selection process, such as gender and racial origin. In order to reduce bias, the candidates can be referred to by their initials in the selection notes.

As well as avoiding criteria that could lead to unlawful discrimination selectors should take care to avoid using any other criteria that is not strictly related to the candidate's ability to do the job.

Pause for thought 6.3 Can you suggest a methodical approach to shortlisting that would be fair and effective? How would you decide on the 'relevant selection criteria' referred to above?

Some selectors introduce criteria that reflect their own preconceived ideas about people's circumstances and how people are likely to act in those circumstances. Some examples of this are:

- selectors who exclude applicants who do not live locally assuming they will often be late for work,

- selectors who exclude applicants who are currently earning more than the vacancy offers,
- selectors who exclude people who are currently unemployed.

You should carefully consider whether to reject an application simply because the writing is difficult to read. General practitioners notoriously have poor handwriting (although this is a stereotypical image and, as such, should be questioned), yet they hold professional, responsible jobs.

Certain documents should be available to support the recruitment and selection process. The person specification or competency profile, in particular, plays a key role throughout the selection process. Applications should be assessed against the skills and knowledge requirements listed in the person specification and where possible against the personal qualities (although it may be more practical to assess this at the interview stage). Selectors should note where candidates meet the requirements of the person specification/competency profile and where they lack the required skills and knowledge. Each applicant could be scored with a series of signs (+/?/–) or with numerical grades. Table 6.3 demonstrates how this is done.

Pause for thought 6.4   Why do you think one of the skills and personal qualities listed in the person specification in Table 6.3 has been marked with a question mark?

A preliminary evaluation of most of the knowledge and skills of the applicant can be made at the shortlisting stage but, in many cases, it is not possible to judge the applicant's personal qualities based on the information contained in the curriculum vitae or application form. The question marks indicate that no assessment can be made at present but an assessment of these elements will have to be made later in the selection process, for example in an interview.

It is not a good idea for only one person to shortlist candidates. The involvement of two people increases the objectivity of the process and helps to eliminate the effects of individual bias. If possible, at least two people should produce a shortlist from the applications received, and they should do this independently of one another.

Table 6.3   Assessment of CV with reference to person specification for an operations manager

Person specification		
Post: Operations manager		
Attributes	**Essential**	**Desirable**
Knowledge	Degree +	Membership of a professional organisation +
Skills	Leadership skills including team development?	Fluency in a second language (Chinese, French, Spanish or German preferred) –
Personal qualities	Good team player +	Good presentation skills?

After the initial selection the selectors can compare their evaluation of the applicants, discuss any discrepancies and justify the decisions they have made. If the two assessors follow the same objective process, there should be a lot of agreement about suitable candidates. The aim of shortlisting is to rank candidates by means of an objective scoring system using symbols or numbers. The selectors may rate candidates into one of three groups: suitable, possibly suitable or unsuitable. A discussion will then need to be made about the number of candidates selected for interview. Typically, for a single vacancy selectors will invite six suitable candidates for an interview, but this number depends on the circumstances.

Increasingly, technology is being used in the selection process (Stone *et al.*, 2013). Whilst electronic techniques can be useful in eliminating a number of unsuitable candidates (CIPD, 2009b) some candidates may potentially also be rejected simply because they did not use the precise terminology that the IT system is set up to search for (CIPD, 2009a). Therefore, it is important to use this type of shortlisting software with caution.

Job interviews

Is it possible to be a good judge of a person's character and ability based on very short acquaintance? Some managers will tell you that they can tell in a few minutes whether they are going to get on with someone, and whether that person is able to do well in the job. This overconfidence is a major contributing factor to the low validity of interviews as a selection method. The concept of validity will be discussed in more detail later in the chapter, but it is important that a strategically important resource such as employees are not selected or rejected in such a subjective and uninformed manner.

Telephone interviewing

As an initial part of the recruitment and selection process, telephone interviewing has become more popular especially where candidates are from outside the UK, and where a cost-effective method, such as Skype, can be used (CIPD, 2013b). Naturally, for jobs requiring good interpersonal communication skills, such as telephone sales, telephone skills are an essential requirement, and the telephone interview can be used as a legitimate method of testing the skills of applicants (CIPD, 2010a). However, the CIPD cautions that telephone interviews should be monitored to ensure that they are conducted fairly. They should be just as structured and focused as face-to-face interviews and not take the form of a casual chat over the phone.

According to the IRS (2014d), the telephone screening interview can be used prior to the shortlisting process. It is considered good practice to ask candidates the same questions but there should be flexibility in terms of not asking certain questions if the candidate has already provided this information or asking follow-up questions to interesting responses. Telephone screening interviews do not normally exceed 20 minutes.

Did you know?

Telephone interviews are becoming increasingly popular and represent a cost-effective way of communicating with candidates. Employers are using telephone interviews for two main reasons: to screen unsuitable candidates out of the selection process and as an integral part of the selection process. Telephone interviews should not replace face-to-face interviews but instead be used to supplement the main selection process.

(*Source*: IRS, 2014c)

Face-to-face interviews and the concepts of validity and reliability

Almost every employer uses face-to-face interviews as part of the selection process. As stated above, a telephone screening interview may be used (this might be delegated to a recruitment agency or a local job centre) but most employers would be reluctant to offer a candidate a job without having met them in person. The face-to-face interview continues to be the most popular and frequently used method of selection even though numerous research studies have demonstrated that interviews are a poor predictor of future job performance. Poorly conducted interviews can lead to decisions with low predictive validity, which means that they do not test what they are supposed to test, that is, ability to perform a job well. The problem of the low validity of interviews is compounded by evidence about poor interviewer reliability, that is, that two interviewers may arrive at different opinions about the same candidate. Brittain (2012) claims that most job interviews are poorly conducted resulting in data that is not sufficiently robust to make valid judgements about candidates. However, an awareness of interviewer errors is one step towards eliminating them or at least reducing their impact.

Interviewer errors

Interviewer errors arise because of the processes we all use to deal with the world around us. From the myriad of stimuli that surround us we select those to which we will pay attention. This process is known as perceptual selection and what we select is determined by our own experience, motivation and personality. This means that we focus on certain aspects of our environment and ignore others. Our experiences might lead us into focusing on inappropriate stimuli in some circumstances but ignoring information that is appropriate. A number of such perceptual errors have been identified and those most relevant to the selection process are discussed in the next section.

The halo or horns effect

A candidate may make a very strong impression on the interviewers as soon as they enter the room. They may be well dressed, attractive, have a firm handshake and have a very confident manner. Research has shown that if interviewers form an initial good impression of a candidate it positively influences their interpretation of everything else that happens in the interview. As a result, the interviewers will seek more positive information to confirm their initial judgement. Opposite to the halo effect is the horns effect where interviewers develop an initial negative impression of the candidate and seek negative information to confirm their first impressions.

Making snap decisions

It is often stated that interviewers make up their minds about a candidate in the first five minutes and then do not change their views of that person's suitability. In terms of the perceptual process this means that interviewers are responding to a very limited range of stimuli and are not taking the opportunity to elicit a wide range of information.

Hiring people like oneself

There is an innate human tendency to identify with people who are similar to us and share several of our characteristics. These characteristics do not, however, necessarily equate with good job performance. It is probably detrimental for an organisation to have only like-minded employees. It is generally considered a good thing if the organisation has a diverse range of people with different personalities from different backgrounds. If interviewers hire people who are like themselves they are said to be hiring in their own image.

Stereotyping

Allowing a stereotyped image of people to influence selection decisions is a very dangerous perceptual error and could result in some form of unlawful discrimination. Stereotyping occurs when a person is identified as belonging to a group with certain characteristics and then is assumed to have a range of characteristics that are thought to be common to all members of that group. It should be remembered that people sharing the same group identity, for example students, can be very different to each other.

Making assumptions

The halo or horns effect, making snap decisions and stereotyping are all specific forms of assumptions based on limited information, but making assumptions can also be a more generalised fault. There are many instances of where inexpert interviewers, instead of finding out how the interviewee would act, impose their own personal view of how they would act in particular circumstances. One example of this is assuming that women will bear the major responsibility for childcare, or that women are not as likely as men to move their families to take up a new post.

Gathering insufficient or irrelevant information

In order to make an informed decision about a candidate sufficient and relevant information is needed. Again, all the specific perceptual errors discussed in this section could be attributed to gathering insufficient or irrelevant information. Interviewers need to be aware of this as a general fault and make sure they obtain the necessary information to guide decision making.

The contrast effect

This is an effect where an assessment of a candidate is affected by who is interviewed before and after them in an interview. It may be that a satisfactory candidate is interviewed after an unsatisfactory candidate. This may result in the satisfactory candidate being considered 'good', even though this is not the case. Similarly, it is 'difficult to follow a good act', meaning that a good candidate following an outstanding candidate may be rated as satisfactory when, in fact, they merit a better ranking.

Good practice designed to eliminate interviewer errors

The very fact that you are aware of interviewer errors can help you to eliminate them assuming that you wish to do so and you make a conscious effort while you are interviewing. There are also some techniques that you can employ to reduce the effects of interviewer errors.

Gather sufficient information

The interviewer should not decide that a candidate is unsuitable early in the interview and then fail to obtain the necessary information to make a proper decision. Interviewers who persist in gathering information even when a candidate has initially failed to make a good impression are resisting the halo/horns effect, they are making an effort to gather the full range of information and they are giving candidates every opportunity to present themselves fully.

Structured interviews

In order to obtain sufficient information on candidates, it will help if interviews are conducted in a structured manner. Structured interviews involve designing a set of questions to elicit information relevant to the selection decision and providing all candidates with an opportunity to answer this complete set of questions.

Pause for thought 6.5 Before reading the section below answer the following questions: How would you go about producing a relevant set of questions to ask candidates? Should you ask the same set of questions to all candidates or should you customise your questions?

In designing the basic set of questions for a structured interview you should refer to the person specification/competency profile and the job description and write questions related to the tasks, knowledge, skills and personal qualities listed there. The quality of the information you gain in an interview will be influenced by the types of question asked, and this is dealt with later in this chapter.

If you ask all candidates the same questions then you will have a similar profile for each candidate. These profiles can then be used in comparing the candidates. The CIPD (2013b) recommends using structured interviews where

- questions are carefully planned before the interview,
- all candidates are asked the same questions,
- the answers to questions are scored using a rating system,
- the questions focus on the behaviours and attributes needed for the job.

Despite these clear advantages, using such an approach may limit the information collected. Introducing some flexibility into interviews, for example not asking some questions, asking supplementary questions or changing the order of the questions, may be more fruitful. An interview that is neither wholly structured nor unstructured is often referred to as a 'semi-structured interview'.

The structured interview will give you a basic set of information but you may wish to supplement this with individualised information on each candidate focusing on particular details of their knowledge, skills, qualifications, experience and so on. In other words the structured interview will give you certain information but it should not be a straitjacket that restricts you to that information.

Giving all candidates an opportunity to respond to a set of questions can also help to diminish the halo or horns effect and give a nervous candidate time to relax and do better in the interview. Preparing a set of questions in advance also means that interviewers can relax during the interview and concentrate on the candidates' responses rather than be thinking about what to ask next. Good preparation should also reduce the risk of asking a question that may be construed as discriminating illegally.

More than one interviewer

In general, the one-on-one interview is not regarded as best practice for selecting candidates although one advantage, according to IRS (2014d), is that candidates may feel more at ease and, therefore, perform better. The IRS (2011a) identified that 92.9 per cent of employers in their study on selection interviews involve at least two interviewers in face-to-face job interviews. One reason for this is to do with equal opportunities as interviewer errors based on individual perceptions are less likely to occur if more than one person is involved in interviewing.

The staff involved in selection interviews will vary from one organisation to another depending on the size of the organisation, management philosophy and organisational culture. There is an increasing trend to devolve selection responsibilities to line mangers (IRS, 2011b). Line managers are well placed to judge whether candidates have the appropriate knowledge, skills and personal qualities as they know most about the work that needs to be done. Selection interviewing demands particular skills so there is a need for training for line managers and others to be able to carry out this duty successfully.

Since human resource management specialists are often responsible for an organisation's equality programmes they often have an input into the interviewing process even if responsibilities are devolved to line managers. As there is not always an HR presence at the interview itself it is important that line managers are trained in undertaking selection interviews. Employers are liable for discrimination in the recruitment process and, therefore, it is important that good practice is followed (IRS, 2014e).

In deciding who undertakes selection interviews it is not just a straightforward choice between HR specialists and line managers. Consideration can also be given to involving other staff affected by the post, such as co-workers or workers in other departments. Acceptance of the new employee can be increased if others are involved in the selection process but you will need to ensure that everyone involved in interviewing is sufficiently trained.

Although the people involved in interviews may have different backgrounds and interests they should all be working towards the same outcome: to select the best person for the job in a fair and objective manner. Training for interviewers usually includes an understanding of equality law and issues, effective questioning techniques and methods to reduce bias.

Time and location considerations

Given what we have said about the need to gather full information from candidates through careful questioning it is self-evident that sufficient time must be allocated to the interview for this to take place. The amount of time needed will, naturally, depend on the post but it is important that the interview is not rushed as this will compromise the validity. It is also necessary to consider where the interview is to take place. You should check that a suitable room is available and ensure that this room is accessible to all candidates. Conducting job interviews in a room affected by internal or external building work is likely to distract both the candidate and the selectors.

Improving interviewer skills

In addition to the techniques you can use to avoid common interviewer errors there are a range of skills you can develop to ensure your effectiveness as an interviewer. As HRM specialists and line managers should be involved in selection interviews these skills are important to both. The skills needed to be an effective interviewer are:

1. to plan and prepare for the interview,
2. to put candidates at ease,
3. to ensure that body language and tone of voice are neutral,
4. to ask a range of relevant questions,
5. to encourage the candidate to talk,
6. to record the information,
7. to invite and respond to candidates' questions,
8. to close the interview,
9. to evaluate information and reach a decision,
10. to record and justify the decisions.

Planning and preparing for the interview

This stage entails thinking through and planning the whole process especially if you are responsible for coordinating it. You will need to:

1. arrange for the reception of candidates,
2. ensure you have a suitable room where you will not be interrupted,
3. review the application forms so that you are properly informed about the candidates,
4. review the job description and person specification/competency profile so you are properly informed about the requirements of the position,
5. prepare the interview questions,
6. design an assessment scheme in order to evaluate the candidates,
7. ensure everyone knows what role they have in the process.

Putting candidates at ease

Most job applicants feel nervous about interviews and this anxiety may be increased if the candidate is faced by a panel of interviewers or a series of interviews with different people. Some interviewers deliberately subject candidates to stress arguing that they are trying to test the person's ability to handle stress in the job.

A counter-argument to this is that the interview situation is stressful enough so there is no need to induce more stress into the process. As one of the main objectives is undoubtedly to acquire as much information as possible from candidates it is probably better to try to put candidates at ease. It is also worth remembering that for every candidate who eventually joins your organisation there may be five or more for whom the interview is their only contact with the organisation. It is therefore better for an organisation's public image if candidates leave the interview feeling they were treated properly.

Pause for thought 6.6 What would you do to make candidates feel welcome? Would you provide refreshments? Would you ask them about their journey that day?

The techniques that can be used to help put candidates at ease include:

- making introductions and explaining clearly the interview process.
- engaging in small talk about the weather, the traffic etc.
- starting the interview with easy questions that require straightforward description rather than opinion or interpretation, for example: 'What are the major duties in your current job?' rather than 'How do the duties you currently perform make you qualified for this post?'.

Keep body language and tone of voice neutral

Interviewers should encourage applicants to open up and divulge relevant information. However, it is important that they do not overly influence candidates during interviews by necessarily agreeing with candidates or indicating that the candidate is doing well. It is also important not to appear impatient or bored as this will invariably make the candidate more nervous, contributing to the horns effect. Maintaining good, appropriate eye contact with the interviewee, looking interested and not yawning are all components of active listening.

Questioning techniques

Whilst asking the right questions is important, it is also important to listen to what the candidate has to say. It is often difficult to concentrate for prolonged periods of time and recruiters may find themselves involved in a series of interviews stretching over many hours or even a number of days. Interviewers need to become good, active listeners (Rogers and Farson, 1976) to ensure that they maintain their concentration and gather as much information from the interviewee as possible. A further effect of active listening is that the interviewee is constantly reassured of your attention, which makes him or her more comfortable with the process.

In general, active listening refers to the development of listening skills to promote better communication and includes the use of reflective responses to develop and check understanding. It also involves a range of techniques to reassure the other person in conversation that they are being listened to. Reflective responses are used when the interviewer is trying to gain a better understanding of an interviewee, and this can be achieved by the use of silence, non-committal conversational sounds, paraphrasing and asking questions to seek clarification of what an interviewee has said.

Silence and conversational sounds

These techniques are used to encourage the candidate to continue in conversation. Using silence means not jumping in too quickly to fill a pause, thereby allowing the other person to gather their thoughts. Silence must be used judiciously since a prolonged silence could lead to embarrassment and would inhibit communication rather than promoting it. The term 'conversational sounds' refers to those sounds we make to reassure someone who is talking that we are listening. We use phrases often, such as: 'Yes, I see', 'Mmm' and 'Oh, right'. These are often accompanied by a nod of the head, a questioning frown or a smile. It is possible to consciously practice these techniques to ensure that you listen more and talk less.

Paraphrasing, summarising and asking for clarification

Paraphrasing, or restating what a person has said, demonstrates that you are actively listening. Similarly, summarising an interviewee's comments can lead to further clarification as the person confirms or amends your understanding in response. Asking for clarification of a specific point again confirms that you were listening attentively and elicits more information.

Types of question

The three basic forms of question are the closed question, the leading question and the open question. The closed question invites a response of 'yes' or 'no'; the leading question indicates to the interviewee what kind of response is expected and the open question is constructed in such a way that interviewees are encouraged to provide more information about themselves. Given below are some examples of the three types of question, together with a comment on what sort of response might be expected.

Closed questions

- Did you conduct employee appraisals in your last job?
- Do you have experience of delivering training?

Comment

Each of these questions could be answered by a simple response, either 'yes' or 'no' (it is difficult to imagine that the interviewee would respond 'don't know'). If the interviewer is trying to obtain more information, these questions are not particularly useful. Closed questions can, however, be useful for checking the accuracy of information. An example might be: 'Did you handle customer complaints in your last job?'

Pause for thought 6.7	Before you go on to read about other types of question, rephrase the two closed questions in the example above as open questions. How would you construct these questions so that an interviewee is encouraged to speak more freely?

Leading questions

- You do enjoy serving customers, don't you?
- You like solving problems, don't you?

Comment

The phrasing of these questions implies that the interviewer expects an affirmative response. Leading questions are used in job interviews but their usefulness is questionable given that the candidate is almost certain to agree.

Open questions

- What experience do you have of leading teams?
- Tell me about your experience of solving a complex problem.
- What did you like about working in marketing?
- Why did you decide to take up a career in HR management?

Did you know?

Competency-based interview questions assess whether or not the candidate can provide evidence of the requested behaviours. For example, in assessing whether or not a candidate can demonstrate evidence of a competency relating to teamwork, the interviewer could ask the interviewee, 'give me an example of when you worked effectively as part of a team'. Typically, several questions will be developed to help assess one competency. The organisation should score the candidate against each competency, with each competency weighted according to its importance for the job.

(*Source*: IRS, 2014d)

Comment

These questions cannot be answered with a one-word answer. They are not leading questions as there is no assumption of an expected, right answer. Open questions usually start with words like what, why or how. Another way of constructing an open question is to ask the interviewee to 'Tell me more about. . . '.

It should be fairly obvious that the majority of the questions in an interview should be open questions, with relatively few closed questions to check facts. Leading questions should, wherever possible, be avoided as they are not very useful. There are a number of ways of phrasing a question and each will have an effect on the likely response. In choosing which type of question to ask you should consider what the purpose of the question is. What type of information do you wish to elicit from the candidate?

Situational and behavioural questions

It is a fairly straightforward task to obtain information about qualifications and skills by careful questioning, listening and by using a variety of tests. It is more difficult to assess attitudes, interpersonal skills and how these translate into behaviour in the workplace. Situational and behavioural questions can be used for this purpose. Research has long since indicated that the use of these two types of question improves both the reliability and the validity of selection interviews (see, for example, Macan's (2009) research into the employment interview). Some organisations use competency-based questions in their selection interviews. These are essentially behavioural or situational questions based on a competency framework.

Situational and behavioural questions require an analysis of critical incidents in the job. Interviewers can establish the critical incidents required for the post by consulting the job description or the performance appraisal criteria. For the purposes of selection you will need to get candidates to talk about their performance in these areas and the competencies they would call upon (situational) or have demonstrated in the past (behavioural).

Situational interview questions

This type of question involves the interviewee being presented with a situation that represents a typical incident in the job for which he or she is being interviewed. The candidate is then asked to describe what he or she would do in this situation.

The responses to a situational interview question need to be assessed carefully in order to achieve better reliability between interviewers. There should be prior agreement on what constitutes a good, satisfactory or poor answer to the question. A model answer for each question should be designed and points assigned to the response. Each interviewer then grades the actual answers of interviewees accordingly.

Behavioural interview questions

Behavioural questions are similar to situational questions in that interviewees are presented with a situation that represents a typical incident in the job for which they are being interviewed. The interviewees are then asked to recount what they did in a similar situation in a previous job. Candidates may also be asked to recount the circumstances in which they have demonstrated that competency. Although this is a very useful approach, there are disadvantages compared to situational interview questions:

1. Candidates who do not have any previous experience of the specific incidents because, for example they have little or no work experience, will be at a disadvantage. Interviewers will need to decide whether it is the previous experience that is important or the way people would behave in a given situation.
2. It is very challenging to design and rank expected answers as candidates may respond with a wide range of examples. However, it should be possible to identify the range of skills and competencies you would expect candidates to provide in their answers.

Activity 6.6

1. Choose a job advertisement and design one situational and one behavioural question that could be asked in the job interview.
2. Try out your questions on a colleague.
3. How useful are the questions in terms of making a selection decision?

Probing questions

Often interviewers will have to 'dig deeper' and obtain information that the interviewee is not readily providing. By probing we are seeking clarification, determining relevance, checking for accuracy, requesting examples, evaluating opinions and establishing how the person feels.

Questions to be avoided

Despite what we have said about relating interview questions to the job description and person specification for the post, you will still encounter many interviewers who ask questions that do not seem to have been designed in this way. Some very general interview questions have almost become prescribed, such as:

1. What are your strengths?
2. What are your weaknesses?
3. Where do you see yourself in five years' time?
4. Tell me about yourself.

Such questions might obtain relevant information but they are vague, and given the time constraints of the interview it is better for the interviewer to focus more narrowly on essential information.

Be careful about enquiring what a person does outside work as this may be regarded as an infringement of a person's right to respect for their private and family life under the Human Rights Act 1998. According to IRS (2014g), candidates should not be asked for information on their marital status or marriage plans, the age of children or any childcare arrangements, domestic arrangements or family commitments, a partner's occupation or mobility and any actual or potential absence from work because of family reasons.

Discriminatory questions

You should not ask any questions that are discriminatory in terms of the Equality Act 2010. If you conduct structured interviews with a planned set of questions that have been designed on the basis of a properly constructed person specification, you are unlikely to do so.

A procedure that is often recommended to avoid accusations of unfair sex discrimination is to ask the same questions of men and women. This will help eliminate any suspicion of an intention to discriminate against female applicants. It is best practice simply to avoid questions about personal circumstances unless there is some specific aspect of the job, such as the ability to undertake shift work, where personal circumstances are relevant. Even in such a situation candidates can be asked whether shift work will cause them any difficulties rather than the interviewers imposing their own view of problems the applicant will have or whether or not the applicant should undertake such work.

Questions for candidates with little or no work experience

It is best practice to acquire work-related and job-specific information from applicants to make good selection decisions. However, a modified approach may be necessary when dealing with individuals who have no work experience, no recent work experience or little work experience. Typical examples include

- school leavers,
- students graduating from college and university,
- the long-term unemployed.

Pause for thought 6.8   Review what we have said about questioning techniques and consider how you might have to adapt your approach for each of the categories above.

Asking open questions about work experience related to the tasks involved in the vacancy would generally not be very productive with this group of applicants, although many college and university courses offer a traineeship and so, for those who have undertaken a traineeship, questions about work experience would be relevant. For candidates without work experience it should still be possible to ask about relevant transferable skills. Situational questions, rather than behavioural questions, are suitable for people with little work experience. In addition, interviewees who are not accustomed to the working environment might be especially nervous. The interviewer, therefore, might decide to spend more time at the beginning of the interview on putting the applicant at ease.

Encourage candidates to talk

Whoever we are interviewing, it is more important for the candidate to talk than the interviewer. Interview questions are designed as keys to unlock information and a proper formulation of questions should ensure that the candidate does most of the talking. Allowing candidates to talk to obtain the information you need is the objective of the interview.

Sometimes a pause will allow the candidate time to reflect and this can be more effective than jumping in with a new question. For all questions you should decide in advance what you are trying to find out. You can then rephrase and probe if the candidate does not respond with the expected information.

Record the information

You could simply note how the candidate has scored on the criteria you are using to assess applicants, but it is much more helpful to have a fuller record of what the candidate actually said. This usually requires someone taking notes during the interview. It is difficult to ask questions, pay attention to what the candidate is saying, take notes and keep conversation flowing, but interviewers develop this skill with experience. Alternatively, roles/tasks can be assigned to interviewers before commencement of the interview. It is desirable to explain to candidates what you are doing and why a person on the panel is taking notes.

Candidates' questions

It is good practice in an interview to allow candidates an opportunity to ask questions about the post. This usually happens at the end of the interview but it should be remembered that both parties can benefit from the interview being a two-way process and, therefore, candidates should be encouraged to ask questions. It is important that prospective employees are well informed about the job and the organisation so that they can make an informed decision of whether, if offered, to accept the job offer.

As well as responding to candidates' questions in an interview, organisations can use other techniques to inform applicants about the post and the organisation.

Some of these are relevant to the recruitment process, such as supplying job descriptions and organisational literature. Others, such as realistic job previews, usually take place during the selection process. Realistic job previews are discussed fully later in this chapter. Company web pages provide an excellent source of information for candidates.

Close the interview

To close the interview, the interviewer should thank the interviewee for attending and inform them of what happens next. This may, for example, include a second round of interviews for selected candidates, a variety of tests, the time frame for the decision and information about how candidates will be informed about the decision.

Evaluate information

In order to achieve an objective evaluation of the information that has now been gathered a scoring system can be employed, either for the answers to interview questions or for the elements of the person specification. Marks can be allocated to each question and questions can be weighted according to their relative importance. It is possible to stipulate that a candidate must achieve a pass mark on a question of particular significance in order to be considered for the post. For example, candidates for an HR position might be rejected for giving an unacceptable answer on a sex or race discrimination question, no matter how well they performed in the rest of the interview.

Using an agreed method to produce a numerical score for each candidate will allow the interviewers to create a ranked order of candidates. Another system that could be used is to mark the person specification/competency profile for each candidate, for example 1 to indicate the criteria that have been met, and 2 for those that have not.

Record and justify the decision

The methodical approach described in the previous section helps the selection panel to justify why they have selected the chosen candidate and why other candidates have been rejected. The rationale for the decisions reached should be expressed in terms of where candidates did or did not meet the criteria, as stated in the person specification/competency profile.

It is important to keep a written record of these factors for a number of reasons:

- to be able to present evidence of a proper and fair procedure should a candidate decide to pursue a case under any aspect of the equality legislation,
- to be able to provide feedback to candidates who request it,
- to ensure that interviewers follow a rigorous and methodical process.

Increasingly, applicants seek feedback on how they have done in a job interview to make a good impression and improve their chances of securing a future post. As you will read in the following sections there is an obligation to provide information to candidates who have completed psychometric tests, but providing feedback to candidates who have been interviewed may enhance an organisation's reputation and image.

Further selection techniques

Thus far in this chapter we have discussed interviewing techniques in great depth. This is justified because of the popularity of interviewing as a selection method. However, there are some strong arguments for utilising other selection methods and these concern the relatively low validity of the interview as an assessment tool, the importance of the selection process as part of talent management and the achievement of the organisation's strategic goals. Given the impact of selection decisions it may be a good idea to obtain, in addition to the interview, some objective information. Such information may be obtained, for example, from a test that is scored objectively and not subject to individual interpretation.

In choosing any selection method the essential criterion is that it should provide information that is directly related to job performance. This should be the guiding principle both in choosing ready-made tests and in designing tailor-made exercises for a particular workplace.

Did you know?

How does an organisation recruit when it is prevented from being too explicit about the nature of its work? This was one of the challenges facing Government Communication Headquarters (GCHQ), one of the UK's intelligence agencies, in its search for potential employees. GCHQ recruits around 250 people each year. Some 70 per cent of all new recruits are graduates. Based in Cheltenham, Gloucestershire, it has more than 4,000 staff. The agency recruits people from many disciplines, including technologists, linguists, librarians, mathematicians and accountants. These people monitor communications and provide the government with intelligence in the fight against terrorism and serious crime, support military operations and offer information assurance. As a government intelligence agency, GCHQ is bound by guidelines on nationality and security. It has to recruit on a national and local level and must comply with equal opportunities legislation as laid out in employment law and the civil service code of conduct.

The development of a GCHQ logo and the shift to bolder recruitment advertising campaigns are part of a more open approach to recruitment. In 2001, the agency ran a campaign based around James Bond with the strapline: 'Stirred, not shaken'. It attracted national media attention.

(*Source: People Management*, 2013)

● Psychological testing

Psychological testing is a method of acquiring objective information about a range of individual abilities and traits. Psychological testing is sometimes referred to as psychometric testing. Psychological tests have the following characteristics:

- They are developed professionally and checked for reliability and validity.
- They are administered and scored in a standardised manner.
- They test maximum performance and habitual performance.
- They produce scores that can be compared to norms for relevant populations.

The characteristics of psychological tests listed above means that their inclusion in the selection process will add an element of objectivity, increase the predictive validity of selection decisions and measure some factors that cannot be assessed through the application form and interview.

The standardised administration of tests means that all applicants answer the same test questions under the same conditions. Objective scoring means that the scores are not open to individual interpretation as is the case with interview responses. Commercially produced tests are underpinned by a vast amount of research, including evidence of their reliability and validity. If these tests are used properly they will improve the validity of the selection process.

Psychological tests are complex instruments and, as such, they should be used only by people who have had specific training in how to administer and interpret them. Indeed, reputable test providers will only supply commercially developed tests to properly accredited persons who have undertaken appropriate training. The British Psychological Society (BPS) and its members develop, promote and apply psychology in a range of settings, including the workplace. One of the BPS' objectives is to set standards in psychological testing. For more information about the BPS, visit their website at **www.bps.org.uk**. The volume of activity in this area has led to the creation of a special unit within the BPS, the Psychological Testing Centre (PTC). Further information about the centre's work is available at **www.psychtesting.org.uk**. Through the PTC the BPS provides nationally recognised qualifications in test use, and provides independent reviews of psychological tests used in organisational settings.

The CIPD (2013b) factsheet on selection methods, including psychological testing, outlines the considerations of whether or not to use a psychological test. Their recommendations include ascertaining if a psychological test is actually needed, if there are there sufficient resources to undertake effective testing, if the test is relevant to the job and person specification, who will choose, recommend and demonstrate the value of the test, at what stage the test should be incorporated into the decision-making process, the issues concerning equal opportunities, the way in which the results will be used, the policy on confidentiality, the people who have access to the results, storing of the test results, the law regarding the copyrighting of tests and the policy and provisions concerning feedback.

There are many tests to choose from, and test suppliers provide information outlining the sort of information each test will provide and the designated groups each test might be suitable for. Some examples of designated groups for whom tests are available are middle to senior managers, administrative/supervisory employees, skilled operatives and staff who have direct customer contact. Test suppliers should provide evidence that the test is reliable, valid and free of any bias against any particular group of people.

Types of intelligence

Over the years there has been much debate about exactly what intelligence is and how to measure it. There are many different types of intelligence but in relation to work and organisations three types of intelligence are pertinent: practical intelligence (PI), intuitive intelligence (IE) and emotional intelligence (EI) (CIPD, 2010b). Practical intelligence is what might be called 'common sense' and represents the ability of a person to find the best fit between themselves and the environment (CIPD, 2010b). Intuitive intelligence requires intuition based on expertise, understanding and self-awareness (CIPD, 2010b) and emotional intelligence has been defined as 'the ability to perceive and express emotions, understand and reason with emotion, and regulate emotion in self and others' (Nowack, 2012, p. 62). It is important to consider the type of intelligence required for the job and how these types of intelligence could be tested.

Ability tests

Ability tests focus on specific mental abilities and separate scores are produced for the different skills. These tests are examples of tests of maximum performance, meaning that they reflect the best performance an individual is capable of at that point in time in the skill being tested. A distinction is sometimes made between tests of attainment and tests of aptitude, but in reality it is not always easy to distinguish between the two. Attainment tests assess skills and knowledge that have been acquired through experience and learning whilst aptitude tests measure a person's potential to develop ability. Since both types of test examine verbal, arithmetical and diagrammatical skills it is probably more helpful to consider them as ability tests. There are aptitude tests for specific occupations, such as banking, and test batteries that produce a profile of the candidate over a range of abilities.

Interest and motivation tests

The relationship between interests and motivation and successful performance is a complex one. It is therefore not advisable to use these tests in the selection process. Interest tests can be used for career guidance and counselling while motivation tests can be used for enhancing performance for employees by responding to what motivates them.

Personality questionnaires/tests

In terms of measuring personality characteristics, a 'personality questionnaire' does not capture right and wrong answers as would be the case in questions of verbal or arithmetical reasoning. Personality questionnaires are indicators of habitual performance, reflecting stable traits that are likely to be revealed in typical behaviour. Of all the assessments that may be used in the workplace, personality questionnaires are probably the most contentious. In particular, candidates may be critical of their use. For this reason, it is important to explain to applicants how the test is going to be used and provide feedback on the results. Test users should also monitor test results to ensure that tests do not discriminate unfairly.

Personality has been shown to predict job performance and personality questionnaires examine aspects of personality that have been shown through research to correlate with work performance. Murphy and Davidshofer (2001) refer to evidence that some personality characteristics are related to job performance in general, including agreeableness, conscientiousness, openness to experience, extraversion and neuroticism. These traits are known as the 'Big Five'.

Morgeson *et al.* (2007) report three key issues concerning the use of personality tests: they have a very low validity for predicting job performance; their use in selection should be carefully considered and alternatives should be found to self-report personality measures. This leads to a very important point with regard to the use of personality tests: they should never be the sole means of assessing candidates but should always be used as part of a wider process.

Work sample tests

A work sample test is an example of an attainment test. As its name suggests, a work sample test consists of getting a candidate to perform some task or element of a task that forms part of the job. The first consideration is that a work sample test needs to assess abilities that are a major and integral part of the job. A critical incident analysis and selection of a critical task are therefore the first step in designing a work sample test. A second consideration is how the performance of the work sample will be assessed, as this will affect the way the exercise is designed and it may influence the instructions provided to candidates.

Pause for thought 6.9 List the criteria on which you would assess a candidate's performance in providing excellent customer service in a supermarket.

Some work samples, such as IT tests, can be assessed on an objective basis using a mathematical formula, but assessment of activities like providing excellent customer service in a supermarket setting is subjective. It is important to have assessment guidelines to provide some level of standardisation and, consequently, to improve reliability among the assessors. Assessment criteria should obviously be related to what is regarded as excellent customer service. This being the case, the firm's documentation relating to service quality should be a good source of material to be used when designing such a work sample test.

To make the test more acceptable to the candidate, it may be useful to inform candidates how they will be assessed. You should consider incorporating this into the instructions to be given to candidates. For example, the instructions on customer service might be phrased as follows:

> As part of the selection process for this job, you are requested to deal with a customer. The customer will be played by a trained actor and you will interact with this person. Imagine that you are talking to the customer in one of our stores. Your performance will be judged in terms of how you deal with the customer and whether you have the right customer service skills to work for us.

Assessing performance in the work sample exercise

The assessment criteria will already have been established in the process of designing the work sample. What remains is to ensure that all the assessors involved know the assessment criteria, and that there is agreement on what represents acceptable standards of performance. This goal can be facilitated in two ways: the involvement of line managers in the design of the work sample test and in the selection process and the use of a scoring sheet listing the assessment criteria.

Integration of work sample tests into the selection process

Work sample tests can easily be included in a selection process to provide additional information. For example, a written work sample can be requested along with the application form. This is especially useful if you are expecting a large number of applications for a particular post. By asking for a written report along with an application form, you can potentially obtain a vast amount of additional evidence about applicants' capabilities including knowledge, report-writing skills, ability to work under pressure and attitudes gleaned from the report.

If these factors are included in the job specification, this information would greatly assist the employer in shortlisting candidates. The exercise also has the additional advantage of discouraging any applicants who were not seriously interested in the post or not willing to make the effort to complete the assignment.

Activity 6.7

For the following jobs, decide on a job sample test that could be used prior to shortlisting or that could be run within the context of an interview day. Describe the test and explain how it would provide information that could be used to assess a person's suitability for the job.

- Restaurant manager
- University lecturer
- Tour guide.

When you have compiled your own list of three jobs, get together with two other students to compare your lists. Select the best three examples and present these to the rest of the class.

Assessment centres

An assessment centre is a selection method whereby a number of competencies are assessed using a range of approaches for a group of candidates at the same time (Cook, 2009; Hargadon, 2014). Each organisation needs to decide how many or how few assessment methods to use but a range of techniques would have to be used to classify a selection event as an assessment centre.

An assessment centre approach basically means that a number of people are assessed together by a number of assessors using a variety of selection techniques. This results in the collection of a range of information and observations of how individuals interact with other people. In terms of validity, the basic assumption underlying assessment centres is that the behaviours displayed will be carried over into the workplace. Because assessment centres are expensive, Hargadon (2014) recommends using them only for high-value roles such as senior management, specialist staff and graduates.

The use of assessment centres in the selection process is increasing in popularity. According to a CIPD (2013a) survey on resourcing and talent planning, 35 per cent of businesses reported using assessment centres in 2009 but in 2013 this figure had risen to 43 per cent. In their survey of assessment centres in 2011, the IRS (2011c) reported a much higher usage of assessment centres amongst its sample of employers: 67 per cent. The likelihood of an employer using an assessment centre increases according to the size of the organisation. The larger the organisation, the more likely it is to use assessment centres (IRS, 2011c).

In considering whether to use an assessment centre, we should consider this method's advantages and disadvantages. Advantages include the opportunity to evaluate several candidates together, the increased validity of selection decisions and the role an assessment centre can make in facilitating talent management.

The main disadvantages are the relatively high cost associated with assessment centres (these include: the training of a number of assessors; the design of exercises and line manager time devoted to this; arrangements for facilities; the time needed to organise the events and coordinate group activities with individual activities; and the time spent giving feedback) and the potential lack of acceptance by line managers and some candidates.

Work simulations

Work simulations entail candidates performing tasks that would actually be done on the job. These exercises can be performed by individuals, as in the in-tray and role-play exercises described below, or in groups, for example a team trying to build a structure using certain materials. When deciding what type of exercise to use, it should be noted that individual exercises such as role plays require greater assessor input and time, since one assessor will have to be assigned to one individual rather than a group.

In-tray exercises and role plays should be developed by isolating critical tasks, setting the assessment criteria, designing the exercise and assessing it. Thus, they would be developed in the same way as work sample tests. A typical in-tray exercise is to present a candidate for a managerial post with a number of different tasks that a manager would encounter at the beginning of the day. The candidate would then need to prioritise the tasks, respond to emails, write memos, make phone calls, etc. In an IRS survey on selection methods, Murphy (2010) reports that in-tray exercises were used by 56 per cent of employers. A role play could, for example, be used in situations where a manager has to deal with an employee with a high level of sickness absence. In such a situation, the manager would have to interview the employee to ascertain why the sickness absence is so high. The manager would be observed and assessed on how they dealt with the situation.

Group exercises

These may be incorporated into an assessment centre in the form, for example, of a candidate-led discussion group. However, because of the nature of group dynamics, it should be remembered that a candidate may perform well as a leader in one group but not in another (IRS, 2014d). Group exercises may also be integrated into interview days if a number of candidates are called together. As with work sample tests, candidate performance can only be judged fairly if assessors have agreed in advance which competencies and job-related behaviours they are looking for. To ensure that the exercise is productive, the employer should inform all candidates of the skills and behaviours being observed (such as leadership, teamwork, negotiation).

References

Employers ask for references in order to ascertain a candidate's employment history, qualifications, experience and/or an assessment of the candidate's suitability for the post in question (CIPD, 2013b). References are a popular method for assessing candidates but should be requested once a job offer has been made rather than prior to an interview (CIPD, 2013c). An IRS survey in 2013 on using background checks for recruitment reported that 99.5 per cent of employers use references (Suff, 2013). However, it seems that the use of references depends on the sector. The CIPD (2013b) reports that pre-interview references were requested by 38 per cent of organisations in the public sector compared to 21 per cent in the private sector and only 14 per cent for not-for-profit organisations.

In spite of their popularity, references suffer from poor validity. In their analysis of the accuracy of selection methods, Anderson and Shackleton (1994) found that references rated a correlation coefficient of only 0.13 with 0 being equivalent to chance and 1.0 being the equivalent of perfect prediction. This would suggest that great care is needed when using references as part of the selection process.

Pause for thought 6.10   At what stage in the selection process should you obtain a reference for a candidate? Which candidates would you solicit a reference for? Do you need to ask a candidate's permission before you contact a referee?

As there are costs associated in providing references, most employers would only ask for references later on in the selection process. A further argument for obtaining references later on is that candidates on the whole prefer their current employer not to be approached unless there is a serious possibility that they will be offered the post. The disadvantage of this approach is that some time may elapse before a reference is received and this could delay the hiring decision.

In making a job offer, some organisations use all their other assessment techniques and then make the offer subject to receipt of a satisfactory reference. However, in this instance, if a job offer is retracted the candidate will know this was because of an unsatisfactory reference. This may have an impact on the content of references and may lead to an organisation providing purely factual data on an employee such as job title, dates of employment and job duties. This data, whilst having some use, does not help the prospective employer in making an objective decision about a candidate because it does not contain a judgement on the person's effectiveness.

Requesting a reference

Referees are able to respond better if you indicate what information you need. Providing a job description or a brief outline of critical tasks will help the referee identify what you are looking for. You might also consider supplying documents and checklists you will be using to evaluate candidates, such as the person specification or a list of competencies and behaviours.

Some employers provide a questionnaire to help guide the referee and to make the process easier and quicker. This, together with a covering letter explaining your request, may improve the information you receive.

Supplying references

An employer does not usually have to give a reference but when it does it needs to ensure that it is fair and accurate (**www.gov.uk**). In providing a reference to a potential employer, referees owe a duty of care to the receiving organisation. That is, referees would render themselves culpable if they knowingly deceived another organisation and misled it into hiring a person whom they knew to be unsuitable. Perhaps it is because of this legal pressure that most references are positive. Indeed, a 2013 survey on background checks for recruitment by XpertHR revealed that 72 per cent of employers had 'hardly ever' received references containing unfavourable information in the past two years.

The law on discrimination also applies to references. It is unlawful to make discriminatory statements in references, for example with regard to a person's actual or perceived sexual orientation or beliefs as covered in the Equality Act 2010. ACAS (2009a and 2009b) provides some guidance on this with reference to the previous regulations which are now incorporated into the Equality Act 2010.

Criminal record checks

You may remember that the Rehabilitation of Offenders Act was mentioned in Chapter 4. The Rehabilitation of Offenders Act 1974 outlines the concept of offences that are spent and protects offenders from having to reveal these spent offences. There are, however, some offences that are never spent and some positions for which those guilty of particular offences will not be suitable. For example, a person who has been found guilty of assaulting a child would not be considered suitable for a position working with children. Such positions are excluded from the Rehabilitation of Offenders Act, and there are arrangements for organisations to obtain a check of criminal records for individuals applying for these types of posts.

The Disclosure and Barring Service

Formerly the Criminal Records Bureau (CRB), the Disclosure and Barring Service (DBS) is part of the Home Office and it helps employers make safer recruitment decisions and prevents unsuitable people from working with vulnerable groups (**www.gov.uk**). This service covers England and Wales. Scotland has a separate service, Disclosure Scotland, an executive agency of the Scottish Government, and Northern Ireland has Access Northern Ireland, part of the Department of Justice. All three agencies are able to search police records and government departments and issue a certificate relating to the individual's background regarding criminal history.

Under the Safeguarding Vulnerable Groups Act (SVGA) 2006, there is a legal duty on employers to refer any person who has harmed or poses a risk of harm to a child or vulnerable adult, satisfied the harm test or received a caution or conviction for a relevant offence. If a job involves work with vulnerable groups, such as children, you will need to ensure that a DBS/Disclosure Scotland/Access Northern Ireland application form is completed. Each agency charges different rates according to the type of disclosure (document containing criminal history information) required. All three agencies offer a basic, standard and enhanced service.

Securing employment is a major factor in the rehabilitation of ex-offenders. It is therefore socially desirable that every opportunity is made to secure suitable employment for these people. However, there is also a business rationale for employing ex-offenders: the overwhelming evidence is that they are successful and there are very few problems (Worman, 2013). According to the CIPD (2013c), ex-offenders need to be employed in a responsible and balanced way that maintains a duty of care to employees and customers whilst protecting business interests and giving access to the widest pool of talent. It should be remembered that a person who has a criminal record should be treated fairly and not be discriminated against.

Making the final selection

If you are using a variety of selection techniques, you must decide in advance the weighting of each technique to the overall assessment. Some things will be designated as essential prerequisites, and the lack of other things may be balanced by the presence of something else. You will need to decide what to do if there is conflicting evidence, for example if someone performs well in the interview but not in the ability tests or vice versa.

Scoring and ranking

It is necessary to use a methodical approach to evaluating the information you have obtained about all candidates. This will enable you to rank the candidates in order of preference. There are several approaches to this and a number of issues to consider:

- Decide on the cut-off percentage score a candidate must achieve in order to be considered.
- Decide on the criteria that must be met.
- Decide on the criteria that are not essential and can be traded off against other criteria.
- Use ticks and crosses to record the assessment of candidates.
- Decide on the relative weight of each assessment criterion and assign points accordingly to each, amalgamating scores from the various assessment methods.
- Calculate a total score for each candidate.

After all the selection activities have been completed, the selectors should compare their rankings of the candidates and decide who the best candidate is. If there are discrepancies in the ratings, these discrepancies can form the basis of discussion. Where necessary, further information can be obtained to aid decision making.

Providing information to aid self-selection

Applicants for a post also have a decision to make about whether or not they wish to accept the offer of employment. It cannot be assumed that merely applying for a job means the applicant will ultimately want the post. If new employees leave shortly after they have been hired, this cannot be considered to have been a successful selection. Just as employers gather information on which to base their decision, so applicants should gather or be given information in order to decide if they want the job.

An obvious way of giving applicants information is to encourage them to ask questions during the interview. Also, if your interview questions and work sample tests are properly constructed to obtain job-related information from applicants, these questions and tests will have informed the interviewee about many aspects of the organisation and the work to be undertaken. However, applicants may still be unaware of certain aspects of the job, and it is incumbent on the selectors to make sure that applicants know about any key factors that might influence their decision and the likelihood of the applicant remaining with the organisation for a reasonable length of time, should they accept the job offer.

As an employer, should you disclose negative aspects of the job and the organisation? If recruitment and selection were only about getting people to accept employment in your organisation, it would make sense to hide information about the negative aspects of your workplace. Many organisations, however, have realised that there is a greater likelihood of retaining new recruits if they are open and honest about the less positive aspects of their work environment. Providing candidates with such information is known as a realistic job preview. Realistic job previews can take the form of oral information given by interviewers or written documentation provided to candidates.

Realistic job previews can be provided at any stage in the recruitment and selection process, but they are probably most useful at the interview stage when there is an opportunity to discuss and clarify details. Innovative approaches to realistic job previews can be useful such as uploading a video-based case study to the corporate website of a current employee discussing their job, or using web-based experimental testing giving candidates a preview of the role in action (Whitford, 2014).

Other activities that could be undertaken with the specific purpose of giving information to candidates include a tour of the organisation's premises or letting applicants chat unattended with prospective colleagues. Rankin (2008) states that the most effective ways of aiding self-selection are those which provide a job preview, either through a work sample test or a visit to the workplace.

Administrative procedures

Once you have completed the selection process and made a decision about the successful candidate(s), there are a number of things you still need to do. In relation to the successful candidate(s):

1. offer the position to the candidate(s),
2. secure their acceptance of the position,
3. agree the details of the appointment,
4. confirm the details in writing,
5. check essential qualifications,
6. initiate new employee processes.

In relation to the unsuccessful candidate(s):

1. inform them of the outcome,
2. provide feedback if appropriate,
3. prepare adequate records,
4. monitor the process.

Offer the position and agree details of appointment

Many employers prefer to speak directly to the person they hope will be joining their organisation. A popular way of doing this is to telephone the candidate. Some organisations still prefer to make the initial offer in writing, either by letter or email. Important details that need to be agreed at this stage include the start date, the starting salary and details about salary progression.

Confirm details in writing

An oral agreement can be regarded as a contract but most employers and employees feel more secure about the arrangement if it is in writing. Usually the employer will write to the candidate to confirm the appointment and will require written confirmation of acceptance from the candidate. The employer may also send the successful applicant a health-check questionnaire to complete and return. There is also a legal obligation to give a statement of terms and conditions to most employees, as was discussed in Chapter 3.

Check essential documents

If specific qualifications are required for the job, for example a degree certificate, a driving licence or professional certification, then the selected candidate should be required to present the documentation as proof that they do in fact possess the relevant documents.

A further, general requirement that applies to all employees is that they are legally entitled to work in the UK. The Asylum and Immigration Act 1996 (Section 8) reinforced the employer's responsibility for ascertaining that every new employee has the appropriate status. If employers check only those applicants who arouse doubts about their citizenship status, such action could be deemed to be unlawful racial discrimination. To avoid this and at the same time fulfil the requirement to check employees' status, employers need to audit the documentation of all new employees at some stage in the selection process.

According to the UK government website (**www.gov.uk**), an employer can be fined up to £20,000 for employing each illegal worker. Such a worker would include a student whose visa has expired, a student working more hours than they are permitted to or a person who is working in the UK whilst on a visitor's visa (**www.gov.uk**). Therefore, it is important that the employer checks the candidate's documents in order to establish if the person has a right to work in the UK before the person starts employment. In order to check for eligibility, you need to see the candidate's original documents, check that the documents are valid and that the person presenting the documents is the candidate concerned. You will also need to make and keep copies of the documents and record the date you checked the documents (**www.gov.uk**).

Employers may also hire asylum seekers, but only if they have permission to work in the UK. An asylum seeker does not have a subsisting right to work in the UK and may only be lawfully employed if the UK Border Agency has lifted restrictions on the person taking employment (Home Office UK Border Agency, 2010). Failed asylum seekers are not normally allowed to work in the UK. If the asylum seeker is permitted to work they will hold a Home Office issued Application Registration

Card (ARC) which will state 'allowed to work' or 'employment permitted' on both sides of their card (Home Office UK Border Agency, 2010). If you are presented with an ARC which states 'forbidden from taking employment' or 'employment prohibited' on either side then the holder of the card does not have permission to work in the UK. If you employ them, you may be fined for employing an illegal migrant worker, or be charged with a criminal offence of knowingly employing an illegal migrant worker, unless the person can otherwise demonstrate they are entitled to work in the UK (Home Office UK Border Agency, 2010).

Initiate new employee processes

In addition to the appointment letter and check of credentials, a number of administrative details need to be attended to for each employee. These include details on pension arrangements, ascertaining preferences with regard to benefits, personal details such as bank account data for payroll purposes and determining whether the person wishes union dues to be deducted from salary where a check-off system is in place. These administrative details vary according to the workplace but they need to be effectively planned and administered.

Informing the unsuccessful candidates of the outcome

Unsuccessful candidates should be informed as soon as possible of the outcome of the selection process, usually as soon as the preferred candidate has accepted the post. As we have mentioned before, there is a public relations element in the way that recruitment and selection are performed. You will usually reject more people than you hire, and these people could be customers, suppliers or even still potential employees whom you would not wish to alienate. Most candidates who have made it through the final stages are serious about wanting the job and they inevitably will be disappointed that they did not get the job. The rejection message, therefore, needs to be delivered with some sensitivity. If possible, avoid implying that the applicant has failed or is of inferior calibre.

Activity 6.8

Compose a standard letter that could be used for informing applicants that they have not been selected for a post. A model letter is given in Appendix 6.1 for you to compare with your proposed letter.

Feedback to candidates

Employers do not usually take the initiative of offering feedback to rejected candidates unless psychological tests have been used, in which case it is considered to be good practice to do so. However, some candidates request feedback in order to make a good impression with potential employers or feel that honest feedback might help them in their career. If employers undertake an assessment of candidates properly, they should be able to give candidates feedback on their performance, although this needs to be done in a sensitive manner.

Record keeping

You will need to record your justification of why a candidate has been selected or rejected. Preparing a summary statement of the reasons for your decisions, that is, a statement of why the selected candidate was the preferred candidate and why the unsuccessful candidates were rejected, adds rigour to the selection process. It is also necessary to keep such records to be able to provide evidence of good practice where an applicant feels they have been subjected to unlawful discrimination and takes their complaint to an employment tribunal. Before going to an employment tribunal the individual must contact Advisory, Conciliation and Arbitration Service to use their 'Early Conciliation' service. If conciliation doesn't work, the individual is issued with a certificate from ACAS which they use to progress the claim in the employment tribunal. The time limit for submission of tribunal claims is generally within three months of the date of termination of employment, or the complained of act. Some claims, such as those for a redundancy payment, have a six-month time limit. An extra month is allowed for the process of ACAS conciliation plus a further 14 days in some situations (CIPD, 2014c).

Monitor the process

It is necessary to monitor the selection process in order to ensure that selection is being conducted according to the organisation's policies and equality legislation; examine the validity of selection decisions and ensure there is an acceptable level of reliability among assessors and interviewers. A statistical analysis of the candidates who proceed through the various stages of selection will provide information on how successful different groups are throughout the selection process. The groupings could relate to type of candidate (internal versus external), gender, age, disability, ethnicity and so on. Public sector employers are obliged by law to undertake monitoring of their recruitment and selection processes with regard to equality issues covered by the Equality Act 2010. Monitoring by private sector employers is not covered by legislation but is regarded as good practice and may be helpful if a decision is challenged in an employment tribunal.

Another important consideration concerns the relationship between the selection process and the acquisition of high-performing employees. Data obtained from performance appraisals and promotions could be cross-referenced with assessors' ratings of candidates in the various selection exercises to show whether high scores in selection tests correlate to high performance on the job. Such data could also be used to identify the training needs of assessors.

Conclusion

This chapter has discussed a variety of techniques for recruiting and selecting staff. From the discussion it is evident that all techniques have their uses and limitations and, therefore, it is desirable to use a number of techniques. Now that you have reviewed the approaches to recruitment and selection, you must now consider what you can do to help integrate this person into your organisation as quickly and smoothly as possible. You will find a discussion of induction activities in Chapter 8. You should find the Case Study 6.1 a useful exercise in putting together and applying most of what you have learned about selection methods in this chapter.

Review Questions

You will find brief answers to these review questions on page 465–6.

1. Choose three different job advertisements from three different sources (one from an Internet recruitment site, one from a newspaper and one from an employer's corporate website). Comment on the structure, content and wording of the advertisements, evaluate their effectiveness and suggest improvements.
2. Describe the uses of the job description and person specification/competency profile in the recruitment process.
3. What approaches to recruitment can an employer adopt in order to create and project a positive public image?
4. Describe the aims of the selection process and describe a methodical approach that can be used to achieve these aims.
5. Why do employment interviews have such a low validity and what can be done to improve the validity?

Case study 6.1

Sue, the HR manager, and Mark, one of the HR assistants, were both conducting interviews of candidates for the post of sales assistant in a large media organisation. The sales assistant job would entail a high level of customer interaction, meaning that the person would require good customer facing and communication skills. In order to expedite the process, Sue and Mark had decided to interview the candidates separately and then get together to compare the results. Mark was rather inexperienced at interviewing as he was new to HR. However, he liked to approach work in a calm, methodical manner.

Mark particularly liked one of the candidates, Sam Jones. Not only did Mark and Sam like the same music, they were also avid gamers. Although Sam seemed somewhat tense at the beginning of the interview, Mark got Sam to relax by talking about his interests. Mark went on to tell Sam a little about the job, and Sam said he thought it sounded very interesting. Mark also confirmed that Sam, whist not actually having a great deal of experience in sales, did have a lot of experience of dealing with customers.

Mark noted the following points in his assessment of Sam:

- was professional and appropriately dressed,
- was enthusiastic about the job,
- has relevant experience for the job,
- made a good impression,
- will be good at the job.

Mark wasn't very enthused about the other two candidates he'd interviewed that morning. They hadn't seemed as enthusiastic as Sam, weren't as smart in appearance and hadn't been very expansive about their experience in response to open questions about dealing with customers.

→

When they got together to discuss the candidates afterwards, Mark recommended Sam to Sue, but Sue responded by saying: 'He's the person I'd least likely appoint. Despite what he said in his CV, he's got too little sales experience. The other candidates have far more sales experience.'

Questions

1. Identify the errors that may have occurred in this case.
2. Suggest what Sue might do to help Mark to avoid such errors in the future.
3. Assume that the interviews conducted by Sue and Mark, followed by line manager interviews, constituted the entire selection process. Suggest how the process might be improved, giving the rationale for your choice of selection methods and the order in which you would use them.

Improving your employability

If you haven't already done so, write a curriculum vitae (CV). Where you have access to one, consult the university's careers service for guidance of what to include in your CV. Otherwise, consult the following textbook:

McGee, P. (2014). *How to Write a CV That Really Works: A Concise, Clear and Comprehensive Guide to Writing an Effective CV*, How To Books, New York.

Thinking about your career, select a job you would like to apply for. Does your CV match the competencies required? How could you make your CV more 'attractive'? What qualifications and experience could you gain to make yourself more marketable? Imagine that you have applied for this job and have been invited for an interview. Write a list of possible interview questions and answers to these questions.

HR in the news

Smart questions root out CV liars

By Janina Conboye

It's the episode of *The Apprentice* everyone looks forward to, when the remaining candidates face the interviewers, their CVs are scrutinised and the liars are caught red-handed. But how many people lie, or at least embellish, their work experience and skills? According to LinkedIn-based research by Adecco, the UK's largest recruiter, one in 10 people have lied on their LinkedIn profile. Ten per cent have lied about their qualifications and 9 per cent about job titles, while 9 per cent have told the odd fib about their age, 7 per cent about their university and school and 5 per cent about the length of time in a particular job or experience.

For some, the figures are not surprising. "You always get some people fabricating information on their CVs. In a challenging marketplace, people want to get a foot in the door," says Alex Fleming, managing director of Adecco UK. But the key to catching them out is having a good interviewer who can adequately scrutinise the details of a candidate's skills and experience. "An interviewer who has knowledge of the sector that a specific job is for can ask the relevant questions," adds Ms Fleming. This ensures that those fabricating CVs can be weeded out. The key is to find any gaps in a CV and dig into these: if someone has not outlined exactly what they have been doing, dates, length of time in or out of a job and education, then it needs investigating. Adecco uses two interview techniques, one is competency-based and the other Ms Fleming calls strength-based. The first method teases out whether someone really has the relevant skills and the second involves firing short quick questions that make candidates think on their feet. "Liars can't answer so fast," she says.

One person who is surprised by the research is Matthew Pack, chief executive of Holiday Extras, which sells travel add-ons such as airport hotel and parking bookings. But he is confident his company has a thorough process to weed out those who lay claim to certain skills and experience, which, when it comes to the interview, they clearly do not have. He has also come across people who simply copy and paste sample paragraphs from websites on to their CV. "In the interview it becomes apparent that what they've said on their CV clearly isn't them and they've not taken the time to write it," he adds. "Some of our roles also require a test: computer programmers, for example." In the past,

he has had candidates that said they had up to five years experience with programs such as Java or PHP, but in tests, "they just don't cut it". For some, it may seem easy to hide behind a fabricated CV in order to get to speak to someone, but this is likely to become harder as the use of digital tools increases. "Employers are using LinkedIn more and more and the fact it asks for endorsements really helps," says Ms Fleming. "The majority of employers use it in addition to a CV, using the two to get to the bottom of any lies."

But if you still think you might chance it, consider this: you could go to prison. In 2010 Rhiannon Mackay, then 29, was jailed for six months after she lied on her CV to get the job of capital projects administrator with Plymouth Hospitals NHS Trust. She was convicted under the Fraud Act 2006, making her the first woman to go to jail for falsifying a CV.

Questions

1. Why do people tell lies on their CVs?
2. What is the difference between an 'embellishment' and a 'lie'?
3. What interview questions can help to reveal the accuracy of a candidate's CV?
4. How can social media be used to check a candidate's experience and qualifications?
5. From the techniques presented in this chapter, which ones would be useful in establishing if the candidate has the knowledge and skills, as stated in their CV?

What next?

Having mastered the fundamental aspects of recruitment and selection presented in this chapter, you may wish to deepen your understanding of the subject area. The article cited below is an American publication reviewing the major current issues in recruitment and selection. Ployhart describes the key issues concisely, but the advantage of this article is that he identifies a large number of potential research questions. These could be interesting in relation to a possible dissertation topic. Examples of research questions ('what we need to know') include:

1. 'How do organizations best acquire a brand image, present it, and manage it?
2. How can organizations best attract and retain a diverse applicant pool?' (p. 877).
3. 'What are the key implementation issues with Web-based testing?
4. In relation to personality tests, what are managers' perceptions of faking and validity?' (p. 883).

Ployhart, R.E. (2006) Staffing in the 21st century: new challenges and strategic opportunities, *Journal of Management*, Vol. 32, No. 6, 868–897.

References

Advisory, Conciliation and Arbitration Service (2009a) *Religion or Belief and the Workplace: A Guide for Employers and Employees*, ACAS, London.

Advisory, Conciliation and Arbitration Service (2009b) *Sexual Orientation and the Workplace: A Guide for Employers and Employees*, ACAS, London.

Allden, N. and L. Harris (2013) Building a positive candidate experience: towards a networked model of e-recruitment, *Journal of Business Strategy*, Vol. 34, No. 5, 36–47.

Anderson, N. and V. Shackleton (1994) Informed choices, *Personnel Today*, 8 November, 33–34.

Branine, M. (2008) Graduate recruitment and selection in the UK, *Career Development International*, Vol. 13, No. 6, 497–513.

Brittain, S. (2012) Interviewing skills: building a solid structure, *People Management*, 27 March.

Chartered Institute of Personnel and Development (2009a*) E-recruitment*, CIPD (www.cipd.co.uk; accessed 19.04.10).

Chartered Institute of Personnel and Development (2009b) *Selecting Candidates*, CIPD (www.cipd .co.uk; accessed 19.04.10).

Chartered Institute of Personnel and Development (2010a) *Resourcing and Talent Planning: Annual Survey Report 2010*, CIPD (www.cipd.co.uk; accessed 12.07.10).

Chartered Institute of Personnel and Development (2010b) *Using the Head and Heart at Work: A Business Case for Soft Skills*, CIPD (www.cipd.co.uk; accessed 07.08.14).

Chartered Institute of Personnel and Development (2013a) *Resourcing and Talent Planning Annual Survey Report*, CIPD (www.cipd.co.uk; accessed 05.08.14).

Chartered Institute of Personnel and Development (2013b) *Selection Methods*, CIPD (www.cipd .co.uk; accessed 05.08.14).

Chartered Institute of Personnel and Development (2013c) *Pre-Employment Checks: An Employer's Guide*, CIPD (www.cipd.co.uk; accessed 12.08.14).

Chartered Institute of Personnel and Development (2013d) *Factsheet: Competence and Competency Frameworks*, August, CIPD, London.

Chartered Institute of Personnel and Development (2014a) *Factsheet: Recruitment: An Overview*, April, CIPD, London.

Chartered Institute of Personnel and Development (2014b) *Labour Market Outlook, Spring 2014*, CIPD, London.

Chartered Institute of Personnel and Development (2014c) *Employment Tribunals: Factsheet*, CIPD (www.cipd.co.uk; accessed 13.08.14).

Chynoweth, C. (2009) Smile for the CV camera, *The Times: Graduate Career*, 16 September.

Conboye, J. (2014) Smart questions root out CV liars. FT.Com, 19 March.

Cook, M. (2009) *Personnel Selection: Adding Value through People*, 5th edition, Wiley-Blackwell, Chichester.

Employers Forum on Age (n.d.) *Getting Recruitment Right*, EFA (www.efa.org.uk/data/files/publications/507/Getting-Recruitment-Right.pdf; accessed 14.08.14).

Fraser, J.M. (1978) *Employment Interviewing*, 5th edition, Macdonald and Evans, London.

Hargadon, J. (2014) *Assessment centres, IDS Good Practice Manual* (available at www.xperthr.co.uk; accessed 08.08.14).

Henkes, M. (2007) *E-recruitment – Sorting the Wheat from the Chaff*, HR Zone (available at www .hrzone.co.uk; accessed 07.09.10).

Holm, A.B. (2014) Institutional context and e-recruitment practices of Danish organizations, *Employee Relations*, Vol. 36, No. 4, 432–455.

Home Office UK Border Agency (2010) *Guidance for Employers on Preventing Illegal Working: Asylum Seekers and Refugees* (available at webarchive.nationalarchives.gov.uk; accessed 13.08.14).

Human Resource Management International Digest (2013) Recruitment goes virtual: Use web-based technology intelligently for best results in recruitment, *Human Resource Management International Digest*, Vol. 21, No. 3, 19–21.

Incomes Data Services (2012) *Applying Competency Frameworks*, June, IDS, London.

Industrial Relations Services (2011a) Selection interviews survey: effectiveness and training, *IRS Employment Review* (www.xperthr.co.uk; accessed 06.08.14).

Industrial Relations Services (2011b) Improving line managers' capability, *IRS Employment Review* (www.xperthr.co.uk; accessed 06.08.14).

Industrial Relations Services (2011c) Assessment centres 2011 survey: the process and employer practices, *IRS Employment Review* (www.xperthr.co.uk; accessed 12.08.14).

Industrial Relations Services (2014a) Equal opportunities policies and monitoring, *Employment Law Manual* (available at www.xperthr.co.uk; accessed 04.08.14).

Industrial Relations Services (2014b) Job applications, *Employment Law Manual* (available at www .xperthr.co.uk; accessed 04.08.14).

Industrial Relations Services (2014c) Shortlisting job candidates, *IRS Employment Review* (www .xperthr.co.uk; accessed 05.08.14).

Industrial Relations Services (2014d) *Recruitment Selection Techniques. Good Practice Manual* (www .xperthr.co.uk; accessed 06.08.14).

Industrial Relations Services (2014e) *Interviewing Job Candidates: Line Manager Briefing* (www .xperthr.co.uk; accessed 06.08.14).

Industrial Relations Services (2014f) *Attracting Suitable Candidates* (available at www.xperthr.co.uk; accessed 04.08.14).

Industrial Relations Services (2014g) *Recruitment Interviewing. Good Practice Manual* (www .xperthr.co.uk; accessed 06.08.14).

Macan, T. (2009) The employment interview: a review of current studies and directions for future research, *Human Resource Management Review*, Vol. 19, No. 3, 203–218.

Marchington, M. and A. Wilkinson (2005) *Human Resource Management at Work: People Management and Development*, 3rd edition, CIPD, London.

Marsh, V. (2012) *Employers project 'brand' message*, 12 June (available at FT.com; accessed 30.06.14).

Morgeson F.P. *et al.* (2007) Reconsidering the use of personality tests in personnel selection contexts, *Personnel Psychology*, Vol. 60, No. 3, 683–729.

Murphy, K.R. and C.O. Davidshofer (2001) *Psychological Testing: Principles and Applications*, 5th edition, Prentice Hall, Harlow.

Murphy, N. (2010) Effective selection tools: what works for employers, *IRS Employment Review* (www.xperthr.co.uk; accessed 12.08.14).

Nowack, K.M. (2012) *Emotional Intelligence*, American Society for Training and Development, Alexandria.

Paddison, L. (1990) The targeted approach to recruitment, *Personnel Management*, November, 54–58.

People Management (2013) GCHQ: uncovering the secrets of recruitment success, 30 January.

Rankin, N. (2008) How self-selection can improve recruitment and retention, *IRS Employment Review 889* (www.xperthr.co.uk; accessed 12.07.10).

Ready, D.A. and J.A. Conger (2007) Make your company a talent factory, *Harvard Business Review*, June, 68–77.

Rodger, A. (1952) *The Seven Point Plan,* National Institute of Industrial Psychology, Windsor.

Rogers, C.R. and R.E. Farson (1976) *Active Listening*, Industrial Relations Center of the University of Chicago, Chicago.

Stevens, M. (2011) Adidas recruits graduates using iPhone app, *People Management*, 11 February.

Stone, D.L., K.M. Lukaszewski, E.F. Stone-Romero and T.L. Johnson (2013) Factors affecting the effectiveness and acceptance of electronic selection systems, *Human Resource Management Review*, Vol. 23, No. 1, 50–70.

Suff, R. (2013) *Using Background Checks for Recruitment: 2013 XpertHR Survey* (www.xperthr .co.uk; accessed 12.08.14).

The Sunday Times (2007) *Recruiting: How Technology Is Shaping the Future*, 1 July (special supplement distributed with *The Sunday Times*).

Whitford, A. (2014) *Candidate Attraction* (www.xperthr.co.uk; accessed 13.08.14).

Williams, H. (2009) E-recruitment: rethinking recruitment, *Personnel Today* (available at www .personneltoday.com; accessed 10.06.09).

Worman, D. (2013) *Pride and Prejudice in the Workplace: Recruiting Ex-Offenders*, CIPD (www.cipd .co.uk; accessed 13.08.14).

www.gov.uk. *References: Workers' Rights*; accessed 12.08.14.

www.gov.uk. *Penalties for Employing Illegal Workers*; accessed 13.08.14.

www.gov.uk. *Check a Job Applicant's Right to Work Documents*; accessed 13.08.14.

www.gov.uk. *Take Your Employer to an Employment Tribunal*; accessed 13.08.14.

Further study

Books

Amos, J. (2009) *Handling Tough Job Interviews: Be Prepared, Perform Well, Get the Job*, How To Books, Oxford.

This book prepares you for anything that job interviewers, recruitment agencies, headhunters and employers of human resources departments can ask in a job interview. Also deals with assessment centres and psychometric tests.

Lees, J. and M.J. DeLuca (2008) *Job Interviews: Top Answers to Tough Questions: 201 Questions Answered*, McGraw-Hill, London.
This book discusses the latest in competency interviewing techniques and equips you with the ability to do well in any interview situation.

McGee, P. (2014) *How to Write a CV That Really Works: A Concise, Clear and Comprehensive Guide to Writing an Effective CV*, How To Books, New York.
This practical book will show you how to present your skills and knowledge, identify your achievements and communicate these successfully.

Redman, T. and A. Wilkinson (2013). *Contemporary Human Resource Management: Text and Cases*, Pearson, Harlow.
This book provides students with a comprehensive and critical exploration of the key functions and issues in HRM.

Articles

Egan, J. (2010) *Employers' Use of Competencies: XpertHR Survey* (available at www.xperthr.co.uk; accessed 18.08.04).

Suff, R. (2010) Benchmarking competencies: the 2010 IRS survey, *IRS Employment Review* (available at www.xperthr.co.uk; accessed 18.08.14).
Two articles from XpertHR which provide an overview of current uses of competency frameworks.

Fernandez-Araoz, C., B. Groysberg and N. Nohria (2009) The definitive guide to recruiting in good times and bad, *Harvard Business Review*, May, 74–84.
This article argues for a systematic approach to the recruitment and selection of people for senior posts involving seven key steps.

Macdonald, L. (2014) Determining the needs of the job, *Employment Law Reference Manual* (available at www.xperthr.co.uk; accessed 18.08.14).
This article addresses the factors that should be considered when drawing up a job description and employee specification, discrimination as related to the Equality Act 2012 and detailed guidance on how to handle genuine occupational qualifications and requirements

Watson, S. and A. Sutton (2013) Can competencies at selection predict performance and development needs? *The Journal of Management Development*, Vol. 32, No. 9, 1023–1035.
This paper explores the utility of an organisation-wide competency framework, linking competency ratings at selection to later development needs and job performance.

Internet

British Psychological Society   **www.psychtesting.org.uk**
The BPS provides information and services relating to standards in tests and testing for test takers, test users, test developers and members of the public.

Chartered Institute of Personnel and Development   **www.cipd.co.uk**
The CIPD website contains a wealth of information on various aspects of recruitment and selection, equality and diversity and employment law. The annual Resourcing and Talent Planning survey examines organisations' resourcing and talent planning strategies and practices and the key challenges and issues they face.

Department for Work and Pensions   **www.dwp.gov.uk**
Age Positive documents can be found here, as well as other equality information relevant to recruitment and selection.

DHL Careers and Jobs   **www.dhl.co.uk/en/careers/jobs.html**
There are thousands of Internet recruitment agencies. In addition, most employers advertise jobs using their corporate website. For example, DHL is a multinational firm in the transport sector that advertises employment opportunities on its website.

Disclosure and Barring Service www.gov.uk/government/organisations/disclosure-and-barring-service
Provides a range of information regarding checks to establish if a person should be barred from working with vulnerable groups. Similar arrangements are in place for Scotland (Disclosure Scotland) and Northern Ireland (Access Northern Ireland).

Equality and Human Rights Commission www.equalityhumanrights.com
Produces a wide range of information on protected characteristics relevant to recruitment and selection.

GOV.UK www.gov.uk
Offers practical advice for employers on a wide range of topics, including expenses and employee benefits, contracts of employment, dismissing staff and redundancies, payroll, pensions, recruiting and hiring, statutory leave and time off, and trade unions and worker rights.

Jobability www.jobability.org
Jobability is an initiative of Leonard Cheshire Disability supported by Accenture. The aim of Jobability is to use technology to enable people with disabilities to access job and career opportunities.

Monster Board www.monster.co.uk
A worldwide professional employment and job search agency. The site includes graduate jobs, company profiles, employer videos and career advice.

Appendix 1

Company name and logo
Company address
Town
PC1 1XX

Ms I Person
1 The Street
UpTown
PC1 1XX

14 August 2014

Dear Ms Person,

On this occasion, the selection panel has chosen another candidate for the position of human resource assistant. I would like to thank you for the time and effort you put into your application for this post and for your participation in our selection process. The panel was impressed with the calibre of the candidates and had a difficult decision to make.

Please do not hesitate to apply again for any suitable position with (Company Name).

Yours sincerely

S Thomson

Director of Human Resources

Performance management and performance appraisal

Objectives

By the end of this chapter you will be able to:

- state what is meant by the term 'performance management'
- give examples of techniques used in the management of performance at work
- design a simple performance appraisal system
- analyse your own performance and set yourself objectives for the future.

It is always important for managers and supervisors to get the best performance from their workforce in terms of levels of production and quality of output. The performance management process is concerned with getting the best performance from the individual but goes further in that it also aims to get the best performance from the team and from the organisation as a whole. It aims to improve performance in the workplace and should be clearly linked to and integrated with the organisation's strategic objectives in order to help the organisation to achieve these objectives.

Definition of performance management

Armstrong and Baron (2004), in what is now regarded as a classic work on the subject, define performance management as a process which

> contributes to the effective management of individuals and teams in order to achieve high levels of organisational performance. As such, it establishes shared understanding about what is to be achieved and an approach to leading and developing people which will ensure it is achieved.

How organisations actually carry out the performance management process and the methods they use will vary, but ultimately the aim is to motivate everyone in the organisation and ensure that they are all working towards the same strategic objectives.

Performance management as an integrated and strategic process

As you can see from Figure 7.1, performance management is not just one HR technique but a process that can involve many aspects of people management, and each of the topics covered in this book make a contribution towards it. It is, or should be, a continuous process but simply initiating a new performance management scheme or introducing new HR practices or policies as part of the process will not in itself bring about the desired motivation of workers.

Performance management should be a shared process between managers, individuals and teams in which objectives are agreed and jointly reviewed and in which corporate, individual and team objectives are integrated. All should feel ownership of the process and share a complete understanding of the system. Because it should also be strategic in nature it should be clearly linked to broad issues and the establishment of long-term goals.

The main HR tools used in performance management

According to the CIPD (2014a), the main tools typically used in performance management include the following:

- performance appraisal,
- 360 degree feedback,
- learning and talent development,
- objectives and performance standards,
- measurement,
- pay.

Learning and talent development and pay and reward will be discussed fully in later chapters but this chapter will focus on other key aspects of performance management, such as performance appraisal, 360 degree feedback, objectives and performance standards and measurement. In some organisations performance management is linked to an even wider range of HR processes, and in a 2009 CIPD survey 69.6 per cent of the sample felt that performance management should be aligned with at least four other HR processes (CIPD, 2009a).

There was a great deal of variation about which HR processes it should be linked with but there was general agreement among 85 per cent of the sample that learning and development should form a major part of performance management. Other HR processes mentioned included career development, coaching and mentoring. Succession planning and talent management was included by 65 per cent of the participants. Performance management was also in some organisations

Figure 7.1   Performance management: a dynamic approach

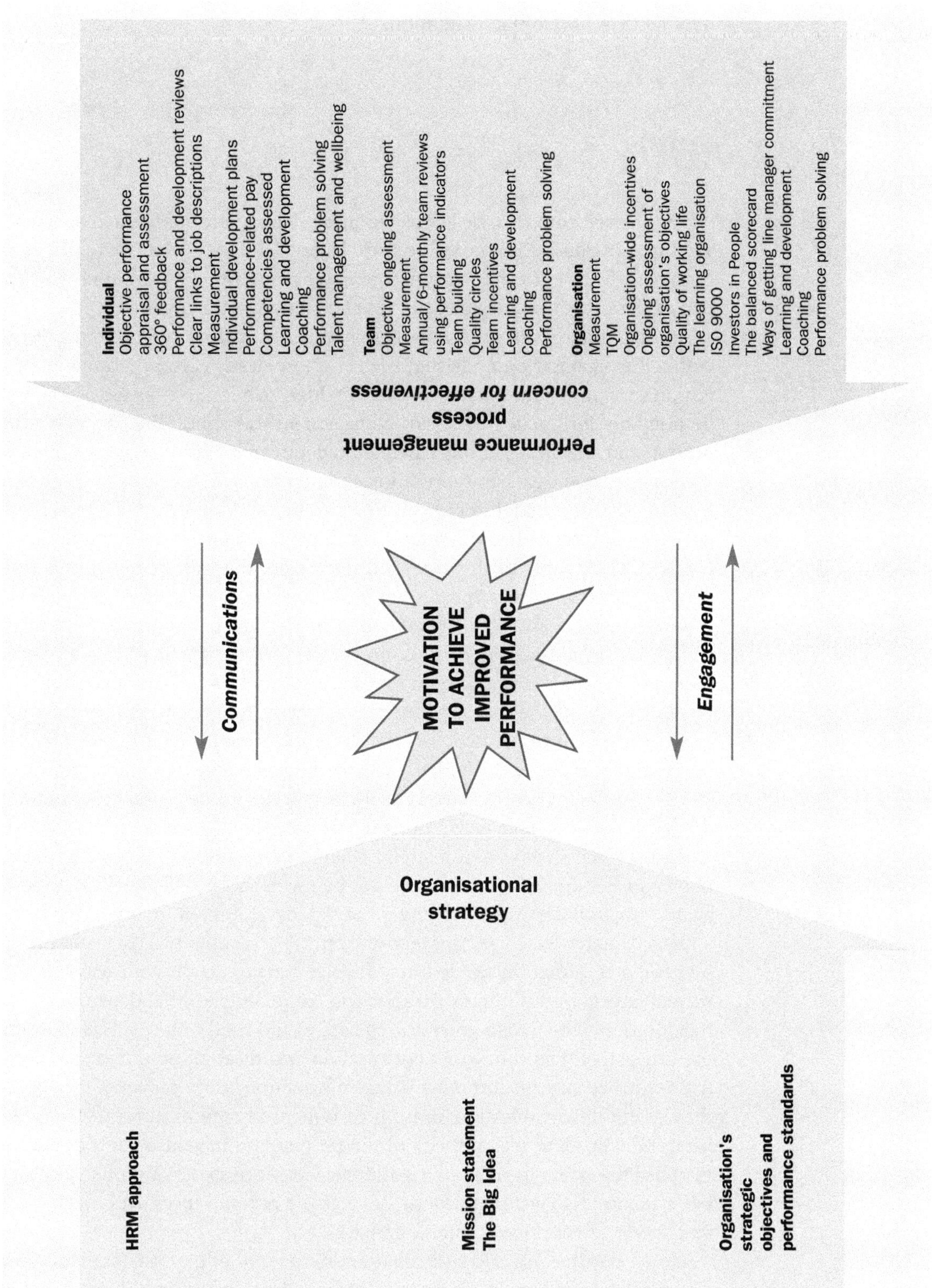

Individual
Objective performance
appraisal and assessment
360° feedback
Performance and development reviews
Clear links to job descriptions
Measurement
Individual development plans
Performance-related pay
Competencies assessed
Learning and development
Coaching
Performance problem solving
Talent management and wellbeing

Team
Objective ongoing assessment
Measurement
Annual/6-monthly team reviews
using performance indicators
Team building
Quality circles
Team incentives
Learning and development
Coaching
Performance problem solving

Organisation
Measurement
TQM
Organisation-wide incentives
Ongoing assessment of
organisation's objectives
Quality of working life
The learning organisation
ISO 9000
Investors in People
The balanced scorecard
Ways of getting line manager commitment
Learning and development
Coaching
Performance problem solving

Performance management
process
concern for effectiveness

Communications

Engagement

MOTIVATION
TO ACHIEVE
IMPROVED
PERFORMANCE

**Organisational
strategy**

HRM approach

**Mission statement
The Big Idea**

**Organisation's
strategic
objectives and
performance standards**

being integrated with HR processes designed to promote wellbeing, engagement and development of potential. The integration of various HR policies is sometimes referred to as horizontal integration.

Models of performance management

As you can see from this the HR techniques used in performance management will vary from organisation to organisation. Figure 7.1 shows what we regard as some of the key features of the performance management process, but the specific mix will depend on the strategic objectives and culture of the organisation.

The organisation's strategic objectives need to be expressed in a way that everyone within the organisation understands, in effect by clearly communicating the organisation's vision for the future, or their Big Idea. While the strategic objectives will be primarily formulated by senior management this should be part of a two-way process and the strategic objectives should be agreed after extensive discussion. Involvement and clear communication should mean that everyone in the workforce feels engaged and that they can contribute to the achievement of the organisation's goals or Big Ideas either individually or as part of a team. The right-hand side of Figure 7.1 lists some of the tools and techniques that can be used as part of the performance management process for individuals, teams and the organisation itself.

While the tools and techniques used in performance management for the individual, the team and the organisation differ slightly, the performance management process itself is very similar for each and can be shown as a cyclical process. Figure 7.2 shows the performance management implementation process in this form. It does not matter whether the focus is on the individual, the team or the organisation as for each the performance management implementation process involves evaluating current levels of performance and assessing them against the desired levels. The aim is to improve performance, add value and contribute to meeting objectives at whatever level. Different techniques will be used in the evaluation and assessment of current levels of performance. Individuals may be assessed against their objectives by using personal development reviews, performance appraisal interviews, or perhaps reports of errors or complaints. For teams or departments the information needed may involve a comparison with team or departmental targets, or a summary of faults and complaints for that department. On an organisation-wide basis a great deal of data would need to be collected to indicate the extent to which the whole organisation was meeting objectives and cumulative feedback may be compiled using information from performance appraisals throughout the organisation, or from customer satisfaction surveys. Organisations need individuals to feel engaged in the process and may also conduct surveys to establish the extent to which the workforce feel motivated by various aspects of the performance management process, such as the pay and incentives or the learning and development opportunities offered.

In each case the aim is to evaluate the current levels of performance and compare this with the assessment of the performance levels required. These will depend on the organisation's objectives, which in turn feed into departmental objectives,

Figure 7.2   The performance management implementation process

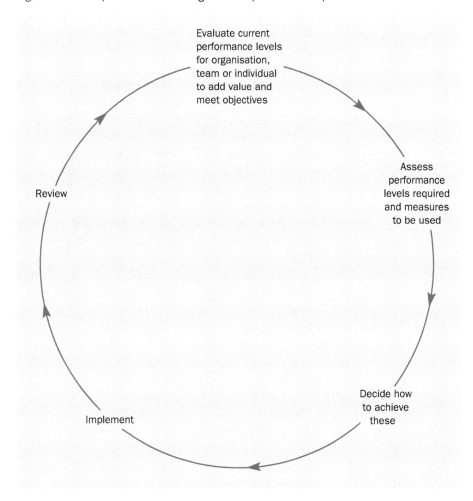

Evaluate current
performance levels
for organisation,
team or individual
to add value and
meet objectives

Assess
performance
levels required
and measures
to be used

Review

Implement

Decide how
to achieve
these

team objectives and individual objectives. In each case it will be necessary to decide whether the aim is to achieve a satisfactory level of performance, whether it is to achieve higher performance levels to add more value to the organisation or whether the objective is to transform performance levels by encouraging and enabling increasingly new or innovative ways of working.

Once a comparison has been made between desired performance levels and existing performance levels, choices have to be made about how these can be achieved for individuals, teams, departments or across the organisation. Some of the techniques listed in Figure 7.1 may be chosen for each category and these then need to be implemented. The process on an organisation-wide basis is likely to take a substantial amount of time.

Whatever techniques are chosen as part of the performance management process, there should be a review to establish whether or not they have succeeded in meeting the objectives set, and this continues into evaluating current performance levels against those required as new objectives are set to meet strategic objectives. There has been a slight shift away from measurement of individual performance to a focus on the individual's contribution to the achievement of the organisation's strategic objectives. Consequently many organisations now also use performance management to encourage engagement and to collect information to establish what improves and drives performance. This should be a continuous process for individuals and teams and it should be integrated into every aspect of running the organisation (CIPD, 2014a).

We can see that performance management is a very important part of achieving high performance in an organisation. In a recent CIPD survey (2014b) 39 per cent of those surveyed regarded the performance management in their organisation as fair but it is disappointing to note that 30 per cent of employees surveyed felt disillusioned and that the performance management process in their organisations was unfair, with this figure rising to 33 per cent of employees in the public sector. There is obviously scope for improvement as these dissatisfied people are clearly not feeling motivated.

As far as the individual is concerned, the performance management process could be viewed as starting at the selection stage as individuals are selected because of their skills, knowledge and competencies in order to make a contribution to the achievement of the strategic objectives. When the individual joins the organisation the induction into that organisation will be a way of communicating the organisation's strategic objectives, perhaps in a simpler form of one Big Idea that encapsulates the objectives. It also reinforces the organisation's culture and values. As they find out more about their job they should also discover how they can make a contribution to the performance of the organisation and the achievement of its strategic objectives. Figure 7.3 shows a model of the performance management process for the individual employee.

The induction should also be used as an opportunity to evaluate the individual's skills, knowledge and competencies using a personal development review and to compare these with the organisation's or team's needs. Even though the person has been selected to carry out a specific job they may lack some of the skills, knowledge or competencies needed to work in that job or team. Plans should be made to meet any gaps between the individual's skills, knowledge and competencies and the organisation's or team's requirements for these. Decisions need to be made about the appropriate ways to fill any gaps between the two and this may involve using formal and informal learning and development methods. Individual goals and objectives will be set and the contribution expected by the individual to team or departmental goals and objectives will also need to be discussed.

In a performance management system there will be regular performance reviews throughout the year and also formal performance appraisal interviews at regular intervals. Each aims to monitor performance and see how individuals or teams are contributing to and meeting their targets or objectives, and they are important in helping to identify learning and development needs. Their aim is to motivate for better performance, but regular reviews could also help to identify poor performance at an early stage. Pay systems are often used to reward excellent performance and if performance seems to be slipping below an acceptable standard then counselling, the absence management system or even the disciplinary system may be used. Even when these processes are used the aim should be to make clear what the required standards are and motivate the individual and team to achieve them.

Many organisations are linking their performance management system to talent management and according to Angela Baron (2009) some of the best practices

Figure 7.3   A model of the performance management process: the individual employee

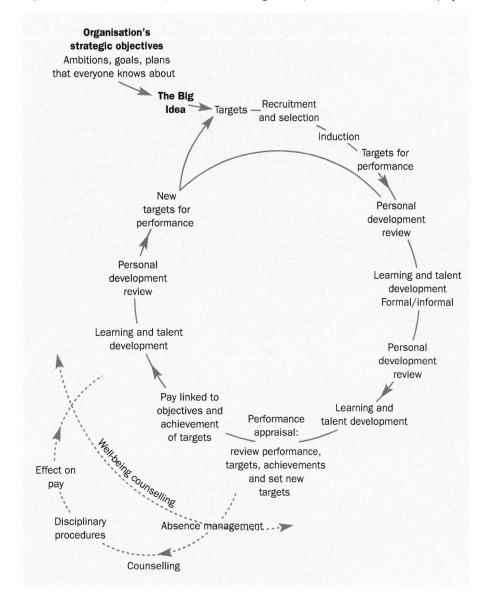

appeared to be 'where performance management was acting as a portal to talent management'. According to the CIPD (2009b), talent management and performance management each have a different focus, with talent management trying to ensure the correct people are in place and that they have the skills necessary to perform well, while performance management aims to ensure that they are aware of not only what needs to be achieved but also how to achieve it.

In the organisations referred to by Baron (2009), the term 'talent management' was used in its widest sense, a view endorsed by the authors of this book, so that everyone and not just the chosen few had access to a review process: each staff member's performance was reviewed and they were each helped to find ways to do their job better.

We have advocated throughout this book the need for policies and procedures so that everyone knows and shares a common understanding of what is supposed to be done and this is clearly a key aspect of performance management. This is a good start, but the way things are done is also important. This is an approach we emphasise throughout this book, as the way organisations manage performance can impact on most other aspects of HR.

Pause for thought 7.1	The term 'performance management' is used in a rather different way in a few organisations when they refer to 'performance managing someone out of an organisation' or putting someone on 'performance management'.
	Have you heard the terms used like this?
	What do you think of this approach to performance management?

Performance management should be about trying to get improvements in performance but, as we showed in Figure 7.3, processes like absence monitoring or disciplinary procedures are likely to form part of a performance management system. However, organisations that use the term 'performance management' as almost a synonym for disciplining someone have not got the right idea about managing performance and motivating people. Performance management should be about motivating individuals, teams and organisations to make a contribution to the organisation's strategic objectives and should have much more focus on incentives and the positive aspects of motivation rather than just focusing on a negative approach to people management as is the case when an organisation thinks that performance management is about 'performance managing someone out of the organisation'. Such a negative approach to performance management is certainly not an approach that we advocate.

The people and performance model

In Chapter 1 we also referred to the research carried out by Professor John Purcell and his team at the School of Management at the University of Bath (Purcell et al., 2003). Their people and performance model also showed the interrelationship of different HR policies. However, while traditional HR policies and procedures were important in this, the other area that they said really made a difference in organisations was 'the way people work together to be productive and flexible enough to meet new challenges'. They found in the organisations they studied that the organisation first had to have strong values and an inclusive culture and, second, have sufficient numbers of skilled line managers to be able to bring the HR policies and practices to life. Both elements fit well with the view of performance management shown in the definition from Armstrong and Baron (2004) that we used earlier.

Purcell and his team found that in the organisations that were most successful at managing performance, everyone did share common values. There was generally what the researchers called 'a Big Idea' that was meaningful to everyone in the organisation (Purcell et al., 2003). This could be about the importance of customers to the organisation or the pursuit of quality, but in all cases it was an idea that everyone could relate to. Whatever it was, they all shared the idea and then managed the performance of people accordingly.

The people and performance model indicates that it is not just the people management policies and practices that create value to an organisation but that they help form part of the process by creating the building blocks that form the basis of achieving increased performance, which Purcell calls ability, motivation and opportunity (AMO) (CIPD, 2007). This assumes that people have the *ability* to learn new skills and will want to work in organisations where their abilities and skills are recognised and can be developed further. *Motivation* assumes that the organisation will be successful in motivating them to use their abilities in a way that is useful to the organisation in achieving its strategic objectives, while *opportunity* makes the assumption that people will use opportunities to do high-quality work and participate in team activities or problem-solving initiatives if the organisation provides them with opportunities to do so. A successful performance management system, perhaps linked to an inclusive talent management system, should certainly help to identify *ability*, *motivate* both individuals and teams and also provide them with *opportunities* to use their skills and abilities.

The role of line managers in performance management

Another important strand in Purcell's effective performance model is line managers. Some traditional appraisal schemes have been accused of being run for the benefit of HR managers or top managers, with many other people in the organisation not really understanding or appreciating what the performance appraisal scheme was trying to achieve. This may have been true of some poorly designed schemes, but is a rather harsh judgement on many excellent appraisal schemes and HR managers and on the contribution they make to their organisations' effectiveness. In order to ensure that performance management does not make the same mistake, there is an increased emphasis on the role of the line manager and on gaining involvement of teams and individuals.

An early definition of performance management taken from Michael Armstrong (1994) is 'a process which is designed to improve organisational, team and individual performance and which is owned and driven by line managers'. It is certainly true that line managers now have increased responsibility for many HR areas in relation to managing their staff, but it is disappointing to note that in some organisations they do not always see the necessity for performance management, or consider that it is not a key aspect of their job.

This reluctance to get involved in performance management may not be entirely the fault of line managers as they may not have been adequately trained, and the relevance of performance management to them and to the organisation's strategic objectives may not have been made clear. In order to make the performance management process as effective as possible it is vital that line managers are trained properly (Cunneen, 2006; Rankin, 2012; CIPD, 2014b). They have to understand the relevance of performance management to the performance of their team and that it can make a difference to meeting their targets and improving their team performance. It should not be perceived by them to be just an exercise completed once a year where they tick boxes to satisfy the whims of the HR department, but as a continuous process involving coaching and feedback which will make a difference to improving performance and developing the talents in their team. If line managers are to use this process to maximum effect to achieve both their team's and the organisation's strategic objectives then top management also have responsibilities to ensure that they clearly demonstrate the importance and relevance of performance management and that they provide adequate resources and training to support this (Cunneen, 2006; CIPD, 2014b).

To achieve this, line managers have a crucial role and must ensure that the people or teams they manage

- know and understand what is expected of them,
- have the skills necessary to deliver on these expectations,
- are supported by the organisation to develop the capacity to meet these expectations,
- are given feedback on performance,
- have the opportunity to discuss and contribute to individual and team aims and objectives (CIPD, 2014a, p. 1).

Performance appraisal

A good system of performance appraisal is important as part of the performance management process, but many organisations that have not yet developed a strategic viewpoint also use performance appraisal on its own. Performance appraisal systems were developed as a tactical approach to developing people before the more strategic idea of performance management had been thought of. Performance management as an approach is widely held to have grown out of performance appraisal, and also to have absorbed some of the newer techniques used in performance appraisal such as emphasis on setting objective standards of performance and competence-based appraisals. However, while most performance management systems do use performance appraisal as a central tactical activity in the good management of employees, there are still many other organisations which use performance appraisal as a standalone activity, so it is important to consider performance appraisal both as a tool in performance management and as a procedure in its own right.

Performance appraisal is one formalised way of giving employees feedback about their performance at work and in most organisations this will happen once or perhaps twice a year. As well as providing feedback, performance appraisal can also help to identify potential or talent and identify training or development needs. It provides a formal opportunity to take an overall view of work content, loads and volume and to look back on what has been achieved during the reporting period and agree objectives for the next. It does not mean that all feedback should be kept until the performance appraisal as regular feedback is important. This clearly shows that the employee does get feedback about past performance, but also indicates that in performance appraisal there is the opportunity to assess or judge various aspects of an employee's past work performance but then also look forward to agree future objectives or workload.

Performance appraisal schemes may be used for a wide range of reasons, some of which may conflict with each other, but the main reasons are likely to include the following:

- to improve current performance,
- to provide feedback,
- to increase motivation and retention,
- to identify potential,
- to identify training needs,

- to aid career development,
- to award salary increases,
- to solve job problems,
- to let individuals know what is expected of them,
- to clarify job objectives,
- to provide information about the effectiveness of the selection process,
- to aid in career planning and development,
- to provide information for human resource planning,
- to provide for rewards,
- to assess competencies.

Randell *et al.* (1984), in a classic work, suggested that for most employers there are three main uses for appraisal reviews: *performance*, *potential* and *reward*. That is to say that organisations want to assess an individual's past performance; they may also want to identify their potential for future roles in the organisation and any development necessary to achieve this and may also want to use the appraisal interview as a means of allocating rewards for good or excellent performance. There could be conflicts between the various approaches. For example, if the organisation uses performance appraisal as a means of allocating rewards then it is likely that individuals will be much less likely to discuss any developmental needs, in case this prevents them from getting a bonus. It is becoming increasingly common in organisations to use reviews of potential and development needs as a part of the talent management process. Many organisations try to get too much from one appraisal scheme and try to use one scheme to fulfil all three purposes. This is unlikely to work, and usually results in the scheme falling into disrepute.

Consequently organisations that use performance appraisal as part of a performance management system will usually conduct the performance appraisal on an annual or biannual basis, but will separate these from the personal development reviews which they will organise at various times throughout the year. In this instance the development reviews would be used to discuss development issues while the performance appraisal might be used as part of the process for identifying reward for excellent work.

360 degree appraisal

In many organisations where performance appraisal is used as a part of the performance management process it is increasingly common to find 360 degree feedback or appraisal being used. This, as the name suggests, puts the appraisee at the centre of the feedback which is gathered from various people with whom the employee comes into regular contact as part of their job. This could include colleagues who work within the same team, the person themself self-appraising, subordinates who work for that person as well as the manager or managers to whom they report. According to the CIPD (2014c) this typically involves 8 to 10 people in the appraisal process. This means that the feedback covers a much wider range of possible behaviours as the person's manager may see a very different set of skills and abilities to someone who works for that person. In most organisations the appraisee is allowed to select a certain number of people to conduct their appraisal. In some organisations the information is even gathered from contacts the person has who are outside the organisation itself, such as customers.

This is a very thorough and time-consuming process, but it has been made considerably easier with the use of information technology to gather the information from the various sources together. There is a need for training for all involved so that the appraisal reports are as objective as possible and that all involved appraise against the same set of objective criteria rather than someone giving a poor appraisal review because of grudges.

Personal development review

As well as the formal performance appraisals, most organisations that use a performance management system also use regular separate personal development reviews (PDRs). In some organisations these are referred to as 'one-to-ones' as they provide an opportunity for the line manager to have a one-to-one discussion at regular intervals with individual members of their teams. These are often used alongside performance appraisals, either as stand-alone tools or as part of the strategic performance management process. Personal development reviews are likely to happen much more frequently than performance appraisals and in some organisations this can be as often as once a week. Cannell (2007) emphasises the constructive nature of personal developmental reviews and the need to use a variety of techniques to encourage the individual to participate fully and do most of the talking.

Regular personal development reviews will result in each individual having an individual development plan designed to give detailed goals and provide for activities to enable that individual to achieve their goals. This should start at induction, although some aspects of the individual development plan may have been identified as early as the selection stage, and then this continues throughout their career. The plan is jointly designed by the manager and the employee, and the manager will provide support and coaching to help the employee to meet their goals. Once again this can form a part of the performance management process.

Objectives or competencies

There are basically two different approaches that can be used by employers when assessing performance. The first is concerned with outputs from the employee: it uses objectives and sets targets for the employee to work towards. The alternative approach is to examine the input that the employee makes to the organisation and determine the level of competence that the employee must achieve in their job.

If the first of these approaches (using objectives) is to work well, then clearly the organisation needs to be clear itself about the strategic direction that it intends to pursue and its objectives, and then it needs to ensure that each team's and individual's objectives contribute to this (vertical integration) while also ensuring that the objectives for both the individual and team are SMART. That is to say that they specific, measurable, achievable, realistic or relevant and time bound (ACAS, 2014).

In organisations where job descriptions based on competence are used, and where staff are used to working towards the achievement of National Vocational Qualifications (NVQs), the second approach is likely to be favoured. If the focus is on the employee's level of competence then people will need to feel valued so they can talk confidently about their work and learn from both successes and failures. The term 'competence' relates to a system of occupational standards with specified levels of achievement, so is job related. Competency or competencies concerns the behaviour that a worker must have or gain in order to be able to contribute to the achievement of high levels of performance, so is about the worker. CIPD (2013) says that although there are distinctions between these terms, nowadays they are used interchangeably.

Employees need to be able to operate in a competent way and to possess behavioural competencies that reinforce their technical skills. Many organisations use competency frameworks and when an organisation adopts this approach then competence will be measured and this gives a useful way of comparing actual levels of competence with required levels. This can obviously provide a useful tool for measurement of performance and consequently for the performance management process and it is not surprising that it has grown in popularity. Whichever approach is used there will still be a need to develop a method of assessing the employee's performance using some form of scale.

Ways of setting standards and measuring performance in performance appraisal

SMART objectives

We have already said that appraisal schemes are most likely to succeed if the criteria to be appraised can be assessed objectively rather than subjectively, and that the appraisal of aspects of a person's personality should be avoided. One way of achieving this is to set clear objectives for the employee to achieve before the next appraisal, and then to focus the discussion at the appraisal interview on the extent to which these objectives have been achieved. An appraisal interview also provides an opportunity to look forward, so the next stage would be to set and agree objectives for the next review period. This should be done by ensuring that the individual's objectives are aligned with the organisation's. For instance if the organisation plans to increase sales by 5 per cent in the next five years then a short-term objective for a sales person might be that in the first year they increase their sales by 2 per cent.

Here the appraisee has an opportunity to write comments, as do the manager and countersigning manager. This type of appraisal can also link with overall organisational objectives, and is often used as part of a performance management system, as we shall show later.

In the previous chapter we discussed the design of job descriptions as a part of recruitment and their other possible uses. In performance appraisal the job description could be used as a starting point with an evaluation of the individual's performance for each task and specific objectives then set for each of the main tasks. This has the advantage that the objectives can be linked very clearly to the individual's job and to the organisation's strategic goals, so that the individual can see exactly what to do to help the organisation meet its objectives, and it enables the person conducting the appraisal to have a standard against which to measure performance. While the use of objectives is the most common form of performance appraisal, one potential disadvantage could be that the focus is on short-term objectives rather than developing some transferable skills that could be of use in the longer term and could possibly discourage flexibility if they are not reviewed as the organisation changes (Rankin, 2012). A sample form for this type of performance appraisal is shown in Figure 7.4.

Figure 7.4   Sample form for performance management using management by objectives

NAME ....   JOB TITLE...

DATE OF APPRAISAL ....   DEPARTMENT/SECTION.....................................

JOB DESCRIPTION (To be agreed with employee)

REVIEW PERIOD........................

1. Objectives agreed for this last review period. (This should include any special tasks, personal training or development.)
2. To what extent have these objectives been achieved?
3. Were there any other major achievements?
4. Were there any obstacles which prevented achievement of agreed objectives?
5. What steps need to be taken to overcome these obstacles?
6. What training, development and education were undertaken during the review period?

NEXT REVIEW PERIOD........................

1. What specific objectives have been agreed for the next review period?
2. What training, development and education should be undertaken during the review period?
3. What follow-up action is needed and by whom?

COMMENTS OF APPRAISER

Signed.. (Appraiser)
Date...

COMMENTS OF APPRAISEE

Signed.......................................(Appraisee)
Date...

COMMENTS OF COUNTERSIGNING MANAGER

Signed.. (Countersigning manager)
Date...

● Rating scales

This is another form of performance appraisal scheme that seeks to encourage objectivity by focusing on aspects of the employee's job and then indicating by graded statements how successfully the employee has fulfilled each of the main duties listed in their job description. The statements are linked to the job description with a statement for each category of the job description, indicating levels of performance or level of competence required in that duty, ranging from excellent to poor. The appraiser discusses the person's performance using these scales during the appraisal interview, and then ticks the statement that they and the appraisee agreed best summed up the appraisee's performance or which matches their level of competence.

Activity 7.1

Read the job description and the main duties listed for this in Figure 7.5. For each of these duties, write a series of statements to indicate the possible degrees of success of someone who is working in this job. It is intended that these statements will form the basic information with which the individual's performance in that job is compared by the appraiser. We have started this for you in Figure 7.6 by suggesting some graded statements for the first row.

Figure 7.5   Job description

JOB DESCRIPTION

Job title:	Receptionist
Reports to:	Office Services Manager
Responsible for:	Assistant receptionists (2)
Main purpose of job:	To ensure the smooth running of the reception area by greeting visitors in a welcoming manner, and by handling all queries, telephone calls, mail and clerical duties appropriately.
Major duties:	Greet walk-in visitors and ascertain purpose of their visit
	Handle or redirect queries as appropriate
	Answer phone queries as above
	Answer all initial queries about receipt of payments using the online payment system
	Open and sort the incoming post by department
	Organise the delivery of the post by the assistant receptionists
	Perform clerical duties as assigned by departments in agreement with the Office Services Manager
	Supervise assistant receptionists and delegate work as appropriate
	Perform other reasonable duties as assigned by the Office Services Manager or other authorised manager

---

Figure 7.6 Job rating

Name of jobholder: ....

Job title: Receptionist

Date of appraisal: ....

Main duties	Appraiser's comments	A (Well ahead of standard performance)	B (More than satisfactory, slightly above job requirements)	C (Less than satisfactory, needs slight improvement)	D (Requires constant supervision)
Greet walk-in visitors and ascertain purpose of their visit. Handle or redirect queries as appropriate		Always quick to greet visitors and ascertain purpose of their visit, dealing with queries extremely rapidly and effectively so visitors are always highly satisfied	Greets visitors, ascertains purpose of visit and deals effectively with queries	Normally greets visitors promptly and ascertains purpose of their visit; sometimes slow to redirect queries	Slow to notice walk-in visitors, does not always greet them promptly and is not always able to deal with queries or redirect them to the appropriate place
Answer phone queries as above					
Answer all initial queries about receipt of payments using the online payments receipts system					
Open and sort incoming post by department. Organise delivery of post by assistant receptionist					
Perform clerical tasks assigned by department in agreement with the Office Services Manager					

Main duties	Appraiser's comments	A (Well ahead of standard performance)	B (More than satisfactory, slightly above job requirements)	C (Less than satisfactory, needs slight improvement)	D (Requires constant supervision)
Supervise assistant receptionists and delegate work as appropriate					
Perform other duties as assigned by the Office Services Manager or other authorized manager					

Comments of appraiser

Signature............................ (Appraiser)

Comments of appraisee

Signature ....(Appraisee)

Comments of countersigning manager

Signature...............................(Manager)

Discussion of Activity 7.1

This gives a simple way of rating the employee's behaviour in the job that is clear and easy to use, as the appraiser simply ticks the box containing the comment that most nearly reflects the actual performance of the employee. It also means that there is a common standard which all appraisers would use when appraising a person doing that job. In this case, examples of four types of behaviour had to be provided for each aspect of the main duties listed in the job description. This was because many appraisers tend to rate employees as average just to avoid upsetting people or to avoid giving too much praise; by not allowing a middle category, they are encouraged to be more decisive. There may still be a tendency to go for the middle two boxes (and for many employees this will be highly appropriate), but appraisers must be encouraged by training to use the full range of categories if and when this is needed.

In this activity you were the only person to choose the descriptions for the criteria to be rated, so there could still be some degree of subjectivity involved, as you may have described the performance of each duty in a different way to other people. It would be more usual to involve a team of people to provide the descriptors for each main duty and to get consensus about the descriptors to be used.

Behaviourally anchored rating scales

If this appraisal system were to be introduced in a large organisation, it would not rely on just one person's ideas of a suitable range of categories. In the first section of the ratings exercise we have used the following terms as descriptors of the first of the major duties listed in the job description:

- Always quick to greet visitors and ascertain purpose of visit, dealing with queries extremely rapidly and effectively so visitors are always highly satisfied
- Greets visitors, ascertains purpose of visit and deals effectively with queries
- Normally greets visitors promptly and ascertains purpose of their visit; sometimes slow to redirect queries
- Slow to notice walk-in visitors, does not always greet them promptly, and is not always able to deal with queries or redirect them to the appropriate place.

These were purely our own subjective choices, and we had not checked whether or not other people would describe this aspect of the job in the same way. You could find other descriptors that may be more effective than these. We may have chosen terms to describe each level of performance that is different from the way in which other people would describe the same task.

One way to try to get round the subjectivity of having just one person writing the descriptions of behaviour is to use a newer technique, known as behaviourally anchored rating scales (BARS). In this case a group of other raters would also be asked to suggest descriptions for a range of behaviours for each aspect of the main duties, so that a wide range of behavioural examples could be collected.

These descriptions are then collated and returned to the sample raters, but this time there is no indication of the scale point for which they were suggested. The sample raters are asked to indicate a scale point from A to D, where A represents excellence and D represents bad work, to which they think each descriptor most aptly relates. The descriptors that are consistently located at the same point of the scale are then used in the final version of the behaviourally anchored scale. This is intended to remove the subjectivity inherent in the simpler rating method and ensure that descriptions used are likely to mean the same thing to most people.

Activity 7.2

What do you see as the main advantages and disadvantages of the system of behaviourally anchored rating scales? Make a list.

Discussion of Activity 7.2

Compare your list of advantages and disadvantages with the following lists.

Advantages

- Objective rating of each of the main duties listed in job description
- Agreement over suitable descriptors for each category of behaviour
- Easy to use
- Useful if lots of people have the same job descriptions so that the amount of time involved in designing the system will be repaid.

Disadvantages

- Time consuming, as it takes a long time to get agreement on descriptors for each job
- Only takes account of existing job performance; does not allow for discussion of future potential.

Behavioural observation scales

These form another method of rating performance in a job. Behavioural observation scales (BOS) are also developed as a result of lengthy procedures, and indicate a number of dimensions of performance with behavioural examples for each scale. Job analysis is used to identify the key determinants of performance and the performance dimensions are once again related to the job description, but in this case the appraiser is asked to indicate a point on a scale by a numerical value.

An example of such a scale in relation to selected aspects of a lecturer's job is given below. The appraisers simply circle the number that they think relates most closely to the usual behaviour of the appraisee.

Activity 7.3

You can try this for yourself by selecting a lecturer you know well and assessing them on this scale. Circle the number that most closely relates to the lecturer's normal behaviour.

1. Provides clearly structured lecture that is easy to follow
   Almost never   5   4   3   2   1   Almost always
2. Provides up-to-date and interesting material in lectures/tutorials
   Almost never   5   4   3   2   1   Almost always
3. Explains to students exactly what is expected of them when they complete written work
   Almost never   5   4   3   2   1   Almost always
4. Is willing to give advice and guidance
   Almost never   5   4   3   2   1   Almost always
5. Gives detailed and helpful feedback concerning written work that students have completed
   Almost never   5   4   3   2   1   Almost always

Discussion of Activity 7.3

We hope that you were fair in your assessment and were not influenced by personality or past grades given to you! In this case you were assessing the lecturer from the position of a student, and you are likely to have a very different view of their work performance to the lecturer's manager or the human resource manager. You may not, however, be able to assess all aspects of the lecturer's job such as their ability to carry out research, or an individual's administrative capabilities, but this exercise is similar to the assessment by a person's subordinates which we mentioned earlier. It has the same type of limitations that we discussed then, but it gives you some idea of the way in which different points of view can be important and shows that if this were combined with appraisal from other perspectives, as in a system such as 360 degree appraisal, it could contribute to developing a full picture of a person's effectiveness and provide valuable feedback.

Pause for thought 7.2

Problems do arise from time to time in performance appraisals. In August 2014 HR managers were asked to email *People Management* magazine with their worst appraisal nightmares. These included a manager whose senior manager had thrown the appraisal form back at her in a fit of rage because she had ranked an employee's time management skills with the highest possible mark and according to him 'nobody gets the top mark on these scales!'

What do you think of this?

(*Source:* HR confessional: appraisal nightmares, *People Management,* August 2014, p. 66)

This shows the need for training for all managers and that there has to be agreement about standards. Even with a clearly structured scale for assessment there can still be a high degree of subjectivity in something which is as easy to measure and record as timekeeping or attendance and clearly the full range of marks on the scale should be used if deserved.

Critical incidents

This involves keeping a record of positive and negative behaviour during a specified period of time. This record of critical incidents is the basis for the appraisal interview, although the appraiser would normally be expected to also give feedback on both positive and negative critical incidents as and when they happened. This method does have some benefits as it does not just rely on annual reporting and has the benefit of giving immediate feedback, but the main disadvantage is that it is also very time consuming.

Narrative report

Using this method the appraiser describes the behaviour of the individual being appraised in their own words in either an essay or report style, as preferred, but without the use of any form for a prompt or for structure. For a narrative report one could start with just a blank sheet of paper as this form of recording is a flexible format which can be adapted to varying circumstances. However, for some appraisers this lack of structure and choice of approach will be too vague and they may have difficulty choosing which aspects of performance to focus on. It also requires the appraiser to have good writing skills and the subjectivity of this format also makes it very difficult to compare levels of performance. There could be accusations of too much subjectivity, particularly if there is any link to pay involved.

The appraisal interview

Interviews have already been discussed in some detail in Chapter 6, and the points made there with regard to selection interviews also apply to appraisal interviews. Preparation, privacy and confidentiality, good questioning technique, avoidance of bias, good records and attention to the style of interview will also be important in the appraisal interview.

Preparation

There is a need, as we explained in Chapter 6, for careful preparation before any interview, and employees should be given adequate notice of the date of the appraisal interview to allow them time to prepare. In the appraisal interview this is also likely to mean that care needs to be taken with the layout of the room, so that the person being appraised will not be intimidated by a formal set-up with barriers such as a big desk, and so that they feel comfortable and at ease. There is also a need to avoid interruptions and to ensure that telephone messages are taken elsewhere and that there are no unnecessary distractions.

If the person has been appraised in the past, then the last appraisal record will need to be read to check what objectives, if any, were agreed for the current appraisal period. The individual's job description will also need to be checked and the training and development records examined to discover what training and development has occurred since the last interview. In some cases, if the person who is to be appraised works for several people, it may also be necessary to obtain information from other managers, or in the case of other types of performance appraisal, from subordinates or peers.

As stated earlier it is also useful for both parties in the appraisal to prepare for the meeting, and both the appraiser and appraisee need to have received training so that they know what to expect in order that they can both skilfully handle what is potentially a difficult interaction. A constructive approach used by many organisations is to give both the appraiser and appraisee a form to complete prior to the appraisal interview. In some organisations these are then exchanged, and this has the advantage of focusing the attention of appraiser and appraisee on common issues. In other organisations these forms are simply used as an *aide-mémoire* for the individuals concerned, but if they are exchanged prior to the interview they can help to clearly identify areas where there is broad agreement so that more time can be allowed to discuss other topics where there are differences of opinion.

Privacy and confidentiality

We have already indicated that the appraisal is an important way of giving feedback to the employee about their work performance. In the past some organisations did not allow the appraisee to see the records of their appraisal, but we feel that this misses a valuable opportunity for providing feedback from which the employee could learn. On the other hand, the appraisal form and interview have to be kept confidential from other people as there will probably be very personal information on the form, and no one who feels that half the department can hear every word of the conversation is likely to feel willing to discuss their performance openly.

Pause for thought 7.3   The issue of privacy seemed to crop up in several of the appraisal nightmares sent to *People Management* by HR managers. What do you think of the following for lack of privacy or confidentiality?

1. An HR manager was waiting to pay for his groceries in a supermarket when a manager from that company approached the till operator and asked her to sign a form. She asked what it was and was told it was her appraisal form. The girl was mortified at her appraisal form being shown in public in front of customers and she was also given no time to read it. In this instance the HR manager who was from another company then tackled the manager for their lack of professionalism.
2. Another HR manager said they had once worked in an organisation where their manager would take poor performers to the stockroom for their appraisal interview and the good ones to a cafe for chocolate cake. Everyone in the department knew whether the appraisal was going to be good or bad depending on the direction in which this manager was heading with the person to be appraised!
3. One HR manager had been running appraisal training in a hotel and had stressed the need for privacy and confidentiality. Later a young female member of staff ran into the trainer's office in tears. Her similarly aged male boss had chosen to conduct her appraisal in a bedroom!

(*Source*: HR confessional: appraisal nightmares, *People Management*, August 2014, p. 66)

Good questioning techniques

The appraisal interview has, as we have already said, much in common with all other types of interviews. Once again the type of questions asked will be important. As this is an opportunity to provide feedback to the employee there will perhaps be slightly more opportunity for the interviewer to do more talking than in some other forms of interview, but this should be treated with caution. It is certainly not the time for the appraiser to do all the talking.

There should be an introductory phase where the interviewer tries to put the person being appraised at ease. It is generally better to follow this with a discussion of the employee's strong points and then try to get information, especially about any areas of perceived weakness, from the employee by asking open questions and teasing out the information. Areas of weakness need to be raised and discussed fully, and open questions are important here. If the interviewer uses closed questions that merely need yes or no answers, they will end up doing most of the talking. Leading questions, which put words in the appraisee's mouth or indicate what the appraiser wants them to say, should also be avoided.

Appraisers should also take great care not to be unduly influenced by a high assessment in one particular area, and should not allow this to cloud their judgement so that they rate all other areas of the employee's performance highly, even though these may not deserve such a high rating.

Pause for thought 7.4.   What is meant by the 'halo effect' and the 'horns effect'? Refer back to Chapter 6 if you are unclear about these effects.

The contingency approach to interviews

While it is fair to say that the style of interview that is generally recommended for appraisal interviewing is a joint problem-solving approach which involves the appraiser and appraisee equally, it is also possible that some other styles of interview may be appropriate in certain circumstances. For example, if the person being appraised is new to the department they may have less to say than someone who has been there longer and so it may be appropriate for the appraiser to do a little more of the talking. If, on the other hand, the person being appraised is very experienced and has worked for the organisation for many years then they may hold many views about their own performance and have clear ideas for improving it. In this case it is possible that the person being appraised might be allowed to do slightly more of the talking. The contingency approach means that the most appropriate style of interview will depend on the circumstances at the time: the approach will be contingent on the circumstances.

The choice of style depends on factors such as the manager's own style, the organisation's culture and the behaviour of the appraisee themselves. In an autocratic organisation where people are not used to having their views considered, there may be a high degree of suspicion if at the time of the appraisal interview the manager suddenly adopts a joint problem-solving approach and actually asks for the views of the employees. This can be a problem for many organisations, because if the organisation normally conducts its affairs in such a way that the employees don't trust the managers to treat them fairly, then it is going to be extremely difficult, if not impossible, for the employees to suddenly start trusting the person who is conducting their appraisal, and to talk in an open and honest way to them. This shows that appraisals should not be used just as an isolated technique to try and motivate the workforce. They need to be an integral part of the way the organisation treats people, and fundamental issues such as the culture of the organisation and its normal style of management also need to be addressed.

The role of the line managers in performance appraisal

We have already emphasised the role of the line manager in performance management and traditionally the people who are most likely to be involved at the tactical level in the appraisal process are the person who is to be appraised and their immediate manager. This has the advantage that the managers or supervisors should know their subordinates and should also know about each subordinate's job and the way in which the subordinate carries out their duties. Managers and their subordinates will see each other every day but may be too busy to discuss performance. The performance appraisal interview provides the time for the individual and the manager to sit down together to discuss the individual's progress. This should enable the manager to feel that they are helping the career of one of the staff, and prove to be a motivating experience for the employee, who has the undivided attention of the manager listening to their views and focusing attention on their development.

There can, however, be some disadvantages in having the employee's immediate manager carry out the appraisal, especially if there is a conflict of personalities or if the manager perceives the employee to be a threat and is therefore unwilling to look for positive aspects of the employee's performance. If the appraisal scheme allows a high degree of subjectivity in comments made by the manager, then there is a danger that more will be learnt about the manager's attitudes to work and managing employees than about the employee's performance. Training in performance appraisal techniques is obviously extremely important here.

While it is always important that the line manager is involved in the process of performance management, there are others who could be involved in performance appraisal, particularly if 360 degree appraisal is used.

Although, as we said earlier, line managers are the most frequent group to be involved in conducting appraisal interviews, they do not always relish this part of

Activity 7.4

The appraisee's immediate supervisor or manager is usually the person most involved in the appraisal process, although in some organisations other people may be involved instead, or in the case of 360 degree appraisal this could be as well as their supervisor or manager. Using Table 7.1, write a list of people who you think might be involved in the appraisal process. For each of them, list the advantages and the disadvantages of their involvement.

Table 7.1　People involved in the performance appraisal process

People who may be involved in the appraisal process	Advantages	Disadvantages

their job or see its importance. A list of the others who could be involved in performance appraisal is given in Table 7.2 at the end of this chapter.

The main problem with line manager involvement according to Gillen (2001) is that some managers see appraisal as a low priority for two reasons. It is necessary to understand their viewpoint on this in order to be able to convince them of the relevance of appraisal to them and to their department. According to Gillen (2001), the first reason why it can be difficult to get managers to conduct performance appraisal interviews is because they prefer to spend their time doing things rather than managing things or managing and leading people. Gillen (2001) says that generally most managers went into their jobs not to manage, but to do things, for example to build things, to teach things or to sell things. They did not specifically go into the job to manage either things or people and often consider that these parts of their job are difficult and mean they spend less time on what they enjoy. They therefore tend to put off doing them because they do not see the immediate relevance, to themselves or to their department, of initiatives such as performance appraisal.

According to Gillen (2001), the second reason is because managers perceive some specific problems related to appraisal. These will vary from organisation to organisation but are likely to result in line managers saying or feeling some of the following:

1. I've got enough to do without also having to fill in forms for Personnel.
2. The appraisal process is 'divorced' from the realities of my 'business cycle'.
3. Appraisal is inherently unfair.
4. Appraisal is amazingly time consuming.
5. Giving staff feedback on their performance during an appraisal interview is uncomfortable. (Gillen, 2001)

Some of these statements are undoubtedly true. As we said, it can be difficult to give staff feedback on their performance and sometimes managers struggle to remember their employee's key achievements, particularly those that occurred some months earlier. Appraisal can seem quite time consuming and may appear to be organised to suit someone else's time schedule.

Some of the other statements are less easy to justify and may result from the line manager's false perception of the situation. If an organisation has established a performance appraisal scheme in the ways we will describe, then it should certainly not be perceived as 'inherently unfair' and managers who feel that the appraisal process is undertaken just to please the personnel or HR department have not had the process properly explained to them.

Whatever the reasons for these negative perceptions of performance appraisal, they do need to be overcome if the scheme is to be successful. Gillen (2001) suggests various ways to erase these misconceptions and to help line managers appreciate the benefits of appraisal. One useful idea he suggests is that line managers should be made aware of the three main elements to their job: doing things, managing things and managing and leading people, and that they should be involved in a discussion about which of these they enjoy most. After a discussion in which he establishes that performance requirements in a job are generally getting harder and that people do not want to work even longer to achieve them, he then draws a parallel with lifting a heavy load using a lever and explains that this becomes easier if one uses a longer lever. He says that for managers, using performance appraisal and working on the managing and leading element of their job is the equivalent of using a longer lever. It is about working smarter and not harder.

Case Study 7.1   Performance appraisal

Joan Bywell is a busy manager in an insurance company, heading the life insurance division. She has worked with the company for six years and has always enjoyed organising the work to reach targets and implementing new ideas to improve sales and streamlining the processing of policies.

The company has now introduced a performance appraisal system so that managers can formally evaluate their staff on a regular basis. Angela Jones, the HR manager, sees this partly as a preliminary step to introducing performance-related pay for administrative staff within the next five years. Angela has devised a form for managers to use to evaluate their staff and she has distributed these to managers with instructions to complete the evaluation within four weeks and return the forms to the HR department, to be held on the employees' personal files.

Joan is reluctant to waste valuable managerial time on this process but she duly fills in the forms for her administrative staff. She decides not to waste more time on endless discussions with her staff, so she gives each employee the completed form and asks them to sign it to confirm they have seen the evaluation and return it to her the next day. She suggests that if they wish to discuss any points, they should make an appointment to speak to her.

George has been with the company for three years. He feels that he works hard and he is hoping he will be considered for a supervisory post when one of the unit supervisors retires next year. George is incensed when he looks at his evaluation and sees that his performance has been graded as 'satisfactory' on a number of criteria such as 'initiative', 'reliability', and 'amount of work completed'. He would have expected a grading of very good or excellent.

George storms into Joan's office and says: 'I know you said we could talk to you if we had any queries about this so-called performance appraisal, but if this is what you think of me, I do not see any point. I think my best plan is to look for a job with a company that will appreciate hard work.'

Joan actually thinks quite highly of George and is perturbed at this turn of events.

Question

Comment on what is wrong with this performance appraisal system and make suggestions for improvement.

Discussion of case study 7.1

This disastrous appraisal nearly ended with the loss of George, a good worker, and is the result of several factors. First, the HR manager Angela Jones has not actually consulted with or involved anyone in the organisation in the design of the appraisal forms or in conducting the appraisal interview and no one has received any training in how to use them. Consequently managers such as Joan are not aware of how important an issue performance appraisal is for motivating her team, identifying talent and improving her team's performance.

Joan is also typical of many of the supervisors described earlier who are very good at the aspects of the job which they see as important, such as achieving targets. However, she does not realise that managing people is an equally important part of her job. If Angela Jones had explained how the performance appraisal process could help Joan achieve her targets and had given her training to this effect then she would have viewed the process in a much more positive light and would have spent time on it.

The performance appraisal form is designed badly so that employees and their supervisors are being asked to rate the individual against criteria which may have nothing to do with their jobs. The amount of work is probably much less important than the quality of the work done and this should be broken down to consider various aspects of the job or to specific objectives or competencies needed. Initiative could be difficult to assess and may not be particularly useful in a job where perhaps there is very limited scope to exercise initiative. Reliability is also a rather vague term as it does not describe the circumstances in which reliability is needed. Angela Jones needs to consult more widely about the criteria that would work on a performance appraisal form and needs to tailor the forms to objectives, job descriptions or competencies required. She then needs to provide training for both managers and subordinates so that everyone is clear about the purpose of the performance appraisal scheme before it is introduced into the organisation. The next section discusses the design of the documentation.

Design of documentation

In most appraisal systems it is necessary to have some type of documentation to record what has been agreed. At its simplest this could just be blank sheets of paper for both the appraiser and appraisee on which they both assess the performance of the appraisee. This provides a means for jotting down ideas and views on performance which can then be used as a basis for discussion at the time of the performance appraisal interview. The disadvantage of this system is that there may be little basis for agreement about the topics to be discussed.

In order to provide for a systematic and consistent approach to performance appraisal, many organisations design an appraisal form. In this case, the manager and the person being appraised both complete a form prior to the appraisal interview. They then exchange forms and at the interview use both the forms as a basis for discussion. This has the advantage of both parties having focused on similar topics and saves time at the interview, as both should have already done quite a bit of preparation for the interview. When designing such a form, there should be clear guidelines explaining what is meant by each section, and the points already discussed in the section on problems must be borne in mind. The criteria to be appraised should not be subjective and should be fair. They should relate to things that employees could improve, and there should be opportunities for the employee to see the appraiser's comments and a section in which to respond to those comments. There should also be a right of appeal. The guidelines should indicate what should then happen to the appraisal forms. Where will they be kept? Who will ensure that action is taken on key points?

Problems

A number of problems may prevent the appraisal schemes from being as effective as they should be as some try to create an appraisal scheme that does not fit with the normal culture of their organisation. These problems include

- the organisation not being clear about the purpose of the appraisal system and consequently trying to use it to fulfil too many different purposes;

- links with pay preventing open discussion of problems or of areas where improvement could be made;
- keeping information secret from the employee;
- the appraiser attacking the appraisee's character;
- being too subjective in judgements;
- using appraisal as part of the disciplinary process.

Lack of clarity

We have already shown that most appraisal schemes fall into one of three categories, that is, they are concerned with performance, potential or reward. An organisation should not attempt to use one appraisal scheme to fulfil all three categories. The particular objectives of an appraisal scheme should be clarified before the scheme is designed in detail, and should have been discussed with employees and other workers, trade unions and managers in order to take account of their views and to gain their commitment to the new appraisal scheme. Everyone should then be clear what the particular scheme is trying to achieve. Any scheme, however good the design, is unlikely to succeed if the managers and the workforce are suspicious of the reasons for its introduction and are opposed to making it work effectively. Performance appraisal schemes also need to be reviewed at regular intervals to ensure that they still meet the objectives of the organisation.

Did you know?

It is often suggested that as many as two thirds of all appraisal schemes are abandoned or altered substantially within two years of their creation. This, to a very large extent, is due to organisations not being aware of, or not paying enough attention to, a range of problems that can be avoided with sufficient forethought and planning, and trying to make one scheme serve too many incompatible purposes.

While there are good reasons why employers should seek to appraise performance potential or give rewards to good employees, problems can also occur if employers try to achieve too much from their performance appraisal scheme. It is difficult, if not impossible, to devise a scheme that will appraise successfully all three areas, and there is a grave danger that the performance appraisal scheme will be rejected if it fails to live up to all that is claimed for it. This can easily happen if the scheme is poorly designed or if the managers show a reluctance to impart critical assessments, or if people are not trained properly in the appraisal process.

Linking appraisal with pay

It is quite common for appraisal-related pay to be part of the performance management process, and if done well this can be effective and of benefit to both employers and employees. It is generally introduced in order to emphasise a clear link between achieving high standards of performance in jobs and increased pay is used to reward those who have performed most effectively. For individuals this is supposed to increase motivation to work harder as well as emphasising ideas of fairness in terms of rewarding who have worked hardest; for organisations it also helps to create a high-performance culture (CIPD, 2014d). More recently some employers have started to use performance-related pay as a means not just of measuring their output or what the individual has achieved but also of measuring their contribution or input (CIPD, 2014d).

However, there are also problems associated with the introduction of performance-related pay. In particular, it is difficult to imagine that a person being appraised is likely to admit to any developmental need, or be willing to accept any help in their performance, if their salary increase depends on a good appraisal. It can also be problematic if the results from the work are not solely under the control of the individual, for example the results achieved by a teacher or medical practitioners do not just depend on their effort but on the students or patients with whom they are working. If carried to an extreme this could result in teachers only wanting to teach the best students or medical practitioners only wanting to treat the patients who are likely to have the best outcomes. It is therefore recommended that employers should in general try to keep reward considerations separate from the other areas of performance review and review whether or not pay linked to performance is appropriate for particular jobs.

In spite of this advice and research evidence which suggests that performance-related pay (PRP) does not always motivate everyone in a workforce, many employers think that the offer of an incentive or reward is the only way to motivate employees to work harder, and this is often their main reason for introducing performance appraisal. The motivational aspects of pay will be discussed in more detail in Chapter 9, but the important point here is that great care needs to be taken if appraisal systems are linked to pay. It will be especially important to ensure that the criteria being appraised are objective and free of unfair bias, and that there are genuine opportunities for all employees to be rewarded for their efforts. Some employees may be motivated by other things such as increased holiday or more flexible benefits, so appraisal-related pay may not motivate them to work harder.

In many organisations financial constraints mean that the number of people who are awarded PRP is severely restricted and there is a serious danger that if the vast majority of the workforce does not feel they have any opportunity to receive a reward, they may feel much more demotivated than they did before the appraisal scheme was introduced. Only the select few who receive the reward will then feel positive about the experience and about the organisation, and even they will not necessarily be motivated to work harder.

When appraisal-related pay is introduced as a part of the performance management system, there will be also be other regular development reviews or performance reviews which provide opportunities for discussion of both good and bad performance. These reviews are normally kept separate from the review at which pay is discussed. Consequently they do not provide such an immediate deterrent to discussion of any weaknesses or aspects of poorer performance since their focus should be on past and future performance and the development needs of the individual. However, although this approach does weaken any direct link between pay and performance and learning, it would be foolish to think that it breaks the connection entirely. Employees may still feel reluctant to fully discuss their development needs unless they feel confident it will not affect their pay, even if that review is held at a different time of year. On the other hand, they may take the view that discussion of areas of their performance in which they have done less well are worthwhile if this means that they gain access to more learning and development opportunities which may ultimately result in them getting more pay or being more employable.

Keeping information secret from the employee

Appraisal involves being both a judge and helper for an individual employee. In order that we can help the individual it is also important that they know about the judgements that have been made about them and that they receive feedback about these. Therefore, if people are to be helped to develop there must be discussion about problem areas, and any judgements made about employees should not be kept secret from them. Obviously the appraisal interview and reports of it do need to be confidential, but not so confidential that they are a secret from the employee concerned.

Subjectivity or attacks on the appraisee's character

If the person doing the appraising feels insecure about their own performance, there could be a tendency to try to ensure that the employee being appraised doesn't become a threat to them by focusing solely on the aspects of the job that have not been handled well and failing to show recognition for jobs that have been done well. In some cases, subjective judgements may be made because there are no clear criteria on which to appraise the employee, and the appraiser may resort to attacking aspects of the person's character that the person cannot do anything about. In the past many appraisal schemes were based on assessing personality traits that were thought to be important to a particular job, but that in fact were very broad categories that could only be judged subjectively. These included personality traits such as enthusiasm, application, intelligence and resourcefulness.

> **Pause for thought 7.5** How would you feel if one of your tutors or managers said that you lacked integrity or that your intelligence was inadequate?

Did you know?

Not all organisations view performance appraisal as essential. Netflix, a highly successful film rental organisation, believes in forgetting about formal appraisals and form filling but instead concentrating on filling the organisation with the best performers, getting them to work in teams and creating an environment in which they can be inspired to be excellent. Instead of appraisals they encourage managers to engage in conversations about performance as an integral part of the daily job.

(Source: Mendoza, 2014)

We imagine that you would not feel very happy with comments about your lack of integrity or poor level of intelligence, and would want to know on what criteria these comments were based.

If appraisal schemes are to be credible to employees, great care must be taken that judgements made are objective and have some basis that can be discussed with the employee. Integrity is likely to mean slightly different things to different people, and judgment of a person's integrity is likely to be fairly subjective. Rather than focusing on subjective topics such as this or on aspects of an individual's personality which they cannot alter, it is better to examine aspects of the job that the person actually does, and make an objective judgement about the person's effectiveness at carrying out each aspect of the job or their success in meeting their objectives.

Appraisers should also concentrate on seeking to help to bring about an improvement in areas of the employee's work where the appraisee can do something to make an improvement. Criticising someone for not being intelligent enough is similar to criticising them for being too short. There is really not much that they can do about it, so it is pointless to judge them on it and impossible to help them to change.

The relationship between appraisal and the disciplinary process

We have already said that appraisal is partly about making judgements about an employee's performance and that areas where performance is not as effective as it should be need to be discussed. However, this does not mean that disciplinary matters should be saved for several months to be dealt with at the appraisal interview. If a disciplinary offence occurs, then it should be dealt with immediately. The appraisal interview should be about seeking to motivate employees, not an opportunity to discipline them; dealing with poor performance should be part of the performance management process.

Information technology and performance management

Increasingly organisations are using information technology as a part of their performance appraisal or performance management system. This is not just about record keeping although some organisations do use their intranet site for this and also to explain procedures and for online training for appraiser and appraisee. Some organisations even complete the initial stages of the performance appraisal system online and both appraisee and appraiser can complete online forms and exchange these prior to meeting for a face-to-face interview where they discuss the contents, focusing particularly on differences in their views of performance. In *People Management* there are increasing numbers of IT systems which claim to help with performance appraisal and Google UK lists over one and a half million online references to providers for 360 degree feedback, so this is clearly an area where IT is providing a great deal of support (Coomber, 2006).

The opportunity to complete performance appraisal questionnaires online is particularly useful when 360 degree appraisal is used. Getting forms completed using pen and paper from several sources is arduous and collecting and collating the information from a range of sources manually can be very time consuming. Using online resources has made the use of 360 degree appraisal much easier and may be partially responsible for the increase in its popularity. Online forms can also benefit from being interactive so that the appraisee can even elect to receive feedback on specific aspects of their competence or performance. According to Coomber (2006), other benefits of online collection of appraisal information include improvements in confidentiality and accuracy. It is also much easier and requires much less administration to collate the information from several appraisers into an easily accessible format using graphs and charts.

Conclusion

Performance management derives from the human resource management approach as a strategic and integrated approach to the management and development of people and it uses many HR techniques. It emphasises the important role of line managers to take responsibility for the management of the performance of the people in their department. With its emphasis on the need for continuous performance review, performance management also relates clearly to the ideas of continuing talent development and learning. It uses the techniques of performance appraisal but prefers to use the more objective types, such as setting objectives.

It does, however, go further than performance appraisal as what is appraised is clearly derived from the strategic plan and both individuals and teams are involved in setting objectives for themselves and in evaluating their success in achieving these objectives.

Line managers play an important part in reviewing the performance of individuals and teams and have responsibility to review progress and development throughout the year, not just at the time of the annual appraisal interview. Both individual and team objectives are clearly derived from the corporate strategic objectives, and everyone is aware that management of performance is the concern of all in the organisation, and not just HR management or the senior management team. Performance management is, above all, a process for sharing an understanding about what needs to be achieved, and then managing and developing people in a way which will facilitate this so that excellent communications, in all directions, are achieved, particularly in global organisations – and employee involvement and engagement are also extremely important.

Improvements in online performance appraisal schemes are helping to increase the use of 360 degree appraisals and can also be particularly useful in international organisations where it may be very time consuming to collect information from participants who work in different parts of the world. Performance appraisal and performance management are important tools that can contribute not only to an organisation's effectiveness, but they can also help to ensure that it becomes a high-performance workplace.

Review Questions

You will find brief answers to these review questions on page 466–9.

1. Discuss the reasons for some line managers' apparent reluctance to get involved in performance management and suggest ways to convince them of the value of this process to them.

2. What are the main advantages and disadvantages of using 360 degree appraisal?

3. Performance appraisals are intended to motivate employees towards greater productivity and improve communication/relations between managers and their team members. Explain why performance appraisals often fail to achieve this goal, and comment on the skills that managers need to make performance appraisal work.

4. Performance management is described by Armstrong and Baron (2004) as a process which 'contributes to the effective management of individuals and teams in order to achieve high levels of organizational performance'.

   (a) Describe the key stages in the performance management implementation process.

   (b) List the different HR techniques that could be used as part of performance management in relation to the organisation, the team and the individual.

5. Describe three different approaches to performance appraisal and comment critically on the benefits to be gained from these systems.

Improving your employability

While this chapter has focused on the skills you need if you are an HR manager with responsibility for the overall performance management in an organisation or a line manager who has to review the performance of their team on a regular basis, you can also see that individuals have an extremely important part to play and responsibilities for their own performance. Developing skills of reflection and increased self-awareness will help you to analyse your own performance at college or university and in the work place. This can also be a useful skill if you apply for a job and as part of the selection process you participate in an assessment centre. You are often asked to reflect on and analyse your own performance as a part of the assessment centre process.

One approach is to use a technique, a SWOT analysis of your own strengths, weaknesses, opportunities and threats.

SWOT analysis of your own strengths, weaknesses, opportunities and strengths

STRENGTHS	WEAKNESSES
OPPORTUNITIES	THREATS

You need to be honest with yourself but if you then choose you could also get someone who you trust to review your strengths weaknesses, opportunities and threats.

Where do you want to be in five years' time? What are your strategic objectives? Write some SMART objectives for yourself.

What small or large steps do you need to take to get to where you want to be?

Are these achievable? Why or why not?

What problems will you have to overcome? What will you do to overcome what you perceive to be threats?

What can you do immediately? In the longer term? How can you turn the threats into opportunities?

What will success feel like?

HR in the news

FT – Unpaid workers need deft handling

By Virginia Marsh

David Cameron's pledge to create a "Big Society" of empowered volunteers and vibrant communities generated some of the positive headlines that helped his Conservative party scrape to victory in 2010.

With the UK again in election mode, the role of its large charitable and voluntary sector in stepping up when the state falls away is set to be debated afresh.

$\rightarrow$

From school governors and youth sports coaches to the well-spoken retirees that staff National Trust properties, the British were a nation of volunteers long before Mr Cameron coined the Big Society. Nearly 30 per cent of UK adults formally offer their services for nothing (through a group, club or organisation) at least once a month, according to the 2013 Citizenship Survey.

Moreover, the roughly 20m volunteers working within the charitable sector dwarf its paid workforce of about 750,000, making effective volunteer recruitment and management critical to many important organisations.

Professionals have been among those to respond to the prime minister's call to arms, but even these well briefed individuals are frequently surprised at the complexities of working with and within an unpaid workforce.

Newcomers Julie Hopes, chief executive of The Conservation Volunteers (see below), and Caroline Davis, a former City lawyer who volunteers at a local hospice, both use the word "shocked".

"You think of how fabulous it is to have people's time," says Ms Hopes. "It is easy to miss all the costs and the infrastructure that is needed."

Ms Davis, who began visiting terminally ill people under a "hospice in the home" programme last year, finds herself amazed at the inefficiencies that arise from box-ticking and bureaucracy, and at how time-poor managers are.

While more people want to contribute time and skills, ways of volunteering and motivations are changing, says Lynne Berry, a former chief executive of the Charity Commission. People are living longer and retiring later.

More people of all ages are travelling, studying and juggling part-time work and caring responsibilities. More of them want to use their professional skills rather than just help out. "Volunteers want more flexibility," says Ms Berry. "Managing volunteers is becoming more skilled," .

Having 20 volunteers each working one two-hour shift a week is considerably more difficult and expensive to manage than hiring one full-time paid staff member: "It is the volunteer manager who has the Rubik's cube and has to work it all out," she says.

But volunteers bring things that money cannot buy: "[They] are incredibly committed and passionate, and give incredible amounts of time to incredibly difficult roles," says Debbie Kerslake, chief executive of Cruse Bereavement Care, the counselling charity.

Their leaders "can't say thank-you too often" and have a duty to ensure volunteers are well supported and trained, she says. Before becoming Cruse counsellors, volunteers are put through 16 three-hour modules, a significant upfront cost.

As at many charities, Cruse's 6,000 or so volunteers deliver front line services, in its case going into people's homes at a time of great distress.

As such, they are central to reputation management. At their best, volunteers are ambassadors connecting organisations to their communities; at their worst they can inflict considerable damage.

"It is paramount they deliver outcomes. You need that clarity of purpose. This can create tensions," says Ms Berry, whose current commitments include chairing a commission on the voluntary sector and ageing.

She adds that a proper description of the volunteer role, how it might change, and clear lines of reporting are good starting points.

A subtle approach is also important, says Helen Timbrell, director of volunteering and community involvement at the National Trust.

The trust works with more than 70,000 volunteers a year. Although it reviews volunteers' performance, it shies away from using the term "appraisal".

"You need to find a tone and language that reflects the gifting relationship," she says. "It is always about mutual benefit."

Another trend is "micro-volunteering". In this case, individuals donate a day or other short periods of time rather than make a continuing commitment, says Kristen Stephenson, volunteer management and good practice manager at the National Council for Voluntary Organisations, the umbrella organisation.

Cruse, for example, has set up "Cruse at Christmas", whereby it recruits volunteers to help vulnerable people during the holiday period.

Many organisations are trying to improve the diversity within their volunteering body, adds Ms Stephenson.

With greater diversity, however, can come greater challenges. Richard Mehmed leads a Brighton-based national community wood recycling network, the aims of which include providing work experience and employment for ex-offenders and others who find it hard to find jobs.

"The volunteers are part of a team. There is the utmost respect but there is also discipline and a hierarchy. Inappropriate behaviour is not tolerated," he says.

The complexities inherent in working with volunteers can help to create good leaders.

Ms Berry believes "third-sector" leaders deserve much more recognition than they get.

"[They've] got to be very sophisticated managers," she maintains. "There is a lot that the corporate world can learn from them."

A bigger plan: Emphasis is on sharpening leadership skills

Like many good things, Kevin Hughes's involvement with The Conservation Volunteers – the environmental charity, whose mission is to preserve and reclaim green spaces for local communities – evolved from a conversation in a pub.

The executive coach had been high on the list of people that Julie Hopes, the new chief executive of the then-troubled charity, wanted to get in touch with again. They had met years earlier when Ms Hopes worked in the City.

Her pitch succeeded and Mr Hughes has run a leadership development "awayday" for TCV and mentors its finance director.

Mr Hughes is one of 10 high-level volunteers that Ms Hopes has mobilised. Others are working on marketing, strategy and retail. Almost all have come from the 46-year-old former insurance executive's personal network.

They are either people she knew herself or "friends of friends of friends", a common way of operating in the cash-strapped but collegial third sector.

Hit by government funding cuts, Ms Hopes has made it a priority to sharpen the leadership skills of her management team.

An early move was to create an executive-level position – director of people and change – to lead human resources. She thought that it was important to use the word "people" to encapsulate TCV's paid and volunteer workforce, which is among the sector's largest and most complex.

TCV works directly with about 115,000 volunteers a year. Many are "part of a bigger plan": they are people referred to TCV by GPs, Mind, the mental health charity, and local authorities. Working with TVC helps the volunteers with health and other problems, such as long-term unemployment.

"There are fewer and fewer 'pure' volunteering groups," she says. "It is a lot more complex when you are dealing with people with health issues."

Volunteering is "a great way to develop leadership skills", she adds.

Source: Marsh, V. (2014) Unpaid workers need deft handling, *Financial Times*, 8th May.
© The Financial Times Limited 2014. All Rights Reserved.

Questions

1. What do you think are the main problems in using performance management when working in an organisation where many of the workers are volunteers?
2. What approach would you use as a way of ensuring good performance which is consistent with the ethos of the organisation among these volunteers?

What next?

If you feel ready to examine this subject in more depth, there have been several research studies that could help you to further your understanding of how organisations achieve improvements in performance.

A study from the research team at the University of Bath examines case study organisations and how they achieve success when times are difficult:

Hutchinson, S., N. Kinnie, J. Purcell, J. Swart and B. Rayton (2003) *Understanding the People Performance Link: Unlocking the Black Box*, CIPD, London.

Some organisations have adopted a very different approach and have abolished some of the traditional HR tools such as performance appraisal. Netflix is one such organisation. Read about its approach in the following article.

→

McCord, P. (2014) How Netflix reinvented HR, *Harvard Business Review*, Jan/Feb, 71–76.

1. In what types of organisation might this be a better approach than traditional performance management?
2. How does this approach compare to that advocated in the previous article?

You can also find a free interactive tool on the ACAS website at **www.acas.co.uk** which can help those of you who work in organisations to assess your organisation's performance against the ACAS model workplace.

References

Advisory, Conciliation and Arbitration Service (2014) *How to Manage Performance*, ACAS (www.acas.org.uk; accessed 08.04.15).

Armstrong, M. (1994) *Performance Management*, Kogan Page, London.

Armstrong, M. and A. Baron (2004) *Managing Performance: Performance Management in Action*, CIPD, London.

Baron, A. (2009) in *Performance Management – Podcast 25*, CIPD.

Cannell, M. (2007) *Performance Management: An Overview*, February, CIPD, London.

Chartered Institute of Personnel and Development (2007) *The People and Performance Link*, May, CIPD, London.

Chartered Institute of Personnel and Development (2009a) *Performance Management in Action: Current Trends and Practice*, CIPD, London.

Chartered Institute of Personnel and Development (2009b) *Performance Management: A Discussion Paper*, CIPD, London.

Chartered Institute of Personnel and Development (2013) *Factsheet: Competence and Competency Frameworks*, CIPD (www.cipd.co.uk; accessed 19.08.14).

Chartered Institute of Personnel and Development (2014a) *Factsheet: Performance Management an Overview*, CIPD (www.cipd.co.uk; accessed 19.08.14).

Chartered Institute of Personnel and Development in partnership with Halogen (2014b) *Employee Outlook*, CIPD (www.cipd.co.uk; accessed 19.08.14).

Chartered Institute of Personnel and Development (2014c) *Factsheet: Feedback – 360 Degree*, CIPD (www.cipd.co.uk; accessed 21.08.14).

Chartered Institute of Personnel and Development (2014d) *Factsheet: Performance-Related Pay*, CIPD (www.cipd.co.uk; accessed 20.08.14).

Coomber, J. (2006) *360 Feedback*, CIPD, London.

Cunneen, P. (2006) How to improve performance management, *People Management*, 12 January, Vol. 12, No. 1, 42–43.

Gillen, T. (2001) *Appraisal: Getting Managers' Buy-in*, CIPD (www.cipd.co.uk; accessed 17.09.07).

Mendoza, M (2014) Breaking better, *Work*, CIPD, Issue 1, 23–24.

Purcell, J., N. Rinnie and S. Hutchinson (2003) Open minded, *People Management*, Vol. 9, No. 10, 31–33.

Randell, G.A., P.M.A. Packard, R.L. Shaw and A.J.P. Slater (1984) *Staff Appraisal*, IPM, London.

Rankin, N (2012) *Performance Management*, XpertHR (www.xperthr.co.uk; accessed 19.08.14).

Further study

Books and reports

Advisory, Conciliation and Arbitration Service (2014) *How to Manage Performance*, ACAS (www.acas.org.uk; accessed 08.04.15).
A clear guide to all aspects of managing performance, including performance management and performance appraisal.

Armstrong, M. and A. Baron (2004) *Managing Performance: Performance Management in Action*, CIPD, London.
This has become a classic text on the subject of performance management.

Articles

Arkin, A. (2007) From soft to strong, *People Management*, 6 September, Vol. 13, No. 18, 30–33.
An overview of how Kimberly-Clark, a multinational corporation, introduced performance management into its companies across the world.

Cunneen, P. (2006) How to improve performance management, *People Management*, 12 January, Vol. 12, No. 1, 42–43.
A short article that makes suggestions about getting the best from a performance management system.

Fielder, R. (2006) How to unlock discretionary behaviour, *People Management*, 12 October, Vol. 12, No. 20, 44–5.
Another brief article that explains how to energise and motivate staff to work at peak performance.

Internet

Advisory, Conciliation and Arbitration Service   **www.acas.org.uk**
ACAS provides a range of information on performance management. For example the 2014 advisory booklet 'How to manage performance'.

Chartered Institute of Personnel and Development   **www.cipd.co.uk**
The CIPD website contains a wealth of information on various aspects of performance appraisal and performance management. The website provides a number of podcasts dealing with managing performance. There are also factsheets, research reports and blogs.

XpertHR   **www.xperthr.co.uk**
This site provides information on developments in performance management practices. The site includes good practice manuals, law reports, case studies, line manager briefings, policies and documents and survey reports.

Table 7.2   People involved in the performance appraisal process

People who may be involved in the appraisal process	Advantages	Disadvantages
The appraisee's manager's immediate manager	Often used as well as the appraisee's manager to check that the manager is being fair. When used as sole appraiser there is the possible advantage of being more objective about employee's work and of not being directly threatened by their success.	Not likely to know the appraisee well and likely to have to obtain information about the individual's performance from their immediate manager.
The HR manager	Often used as a check that the manager is being fair and as a monitor of consistency of approach throughout the organisation. HR managers are sometimes used as sole appraiser for reasons of fairness and consistency and because they are not perceived to be a threat to the manager.	Not likely to know the appraisee well and likely to have to obtain information about the individual's performance from their immediate manager.
Colleagues	This can be especially useful where teamwork is important or in an enterprise with a matrix organisation structure where the individual may report to more than one manager. The main advantage is that colleagues are likely to have a clear idea of how effective the individual is at working with them and the views of several people are likely to provide a balanced perspective.	The colleagues concerned may not know about all aspects of the individual's job. They may be reluctant to express an honest opinion about a colleague, and may be influenced by whether they have a good or poor relationship with that person, or by jealousy or rivalry.

→

Table 7.2   (*Continued*)

People who may be involved in the appraisal process	Advantages	Disadvantages
Subordinates	People who work for the individual who is being appraised will certainly have a different view of that individual's abilities and performance and can therefore provide valuable information about the person's performance.	They may be too frightened to express their real opinion if they feel that their manager might hold this against them at some future date. The person being appraised may be reluctant to accept the views of their subordinates.
Self-appraisal	Often used as part of the appraisal process, as in many systems the appraisers and the appraisee complete forms independently of each other and then use them as the basis of discussion. The individual will have more detailed knowledge of the standard of their own work performance than their manager. Since individuals should be encouraged to take a great deal of responsibility for their own development, this increased self-awareness will be useful.	Some people may find it difficult to analyse their own work performance and may have unrealistic views of how well they have actually done. They may not be willing to admit to weaknesses, although in many cases the opposite is true, and people are more critical of themselves than their manager would be.
360 degree appraisal (not actually a person, but gathers information from all the people mentioned so far)	This form of appraisal gathers information from all the above sources to gain an all-round view of the person's performance. This is extremely thorough and will provide information on different aspects of the individual's performance so that it is possible to compile a total picture of the person's job performance. This may also include those outside the organisation, such as clients or customers who may be able to provide very valuable insights into how an individual is performing.	It can be very time consuming to collect information from so many people, and may not always be cost effective. It is also subject to all the disadvantages listed above. If it uses customers or clients it may prove particularly difficult to organise as customers or clients may not wish to spend time participating in questionnaires and cannot be coerced into doing so. Many employers will also be hesitant to use this approach as they may not wish to give their clients or customers any cause to think that they, or any of their employees, might ever provide a less than perfect service or product.
Assessment centres (not actually a person, so you may not have included assessment centres in this list, but we include them as they form yet another important way of assessing performance)	Individuals undertake a battery of tests to measure: aspects of personality; verbal, numerical and reasoning skills and ability to lead and work in a team. This provides an all-round view of the person's talents and abilities. Particularly useful when assessing future potential and in the appraisal of potential supervisors or managers.	Expensive and time consuming to carry out for all employees.

8

Learning, training and talent development

Objectives

By the end of this chapter you will be able to:

- identify the main ways in which you learn
- explain why learning, training and talent development are important both to individuals and to organisations
- describe a model for achieving strategic learning, training and talent development
- identify when to use a variety of learning and development techniques
- explain what is meant by experiential learning
- demonstrate the importance of induction training.

This chapter will first define what is meant by the terms 'training', 'learning' and 'talent development' before examining how individuals learn. One of the main objectives of this book is to help you to develop employability skills and an understanding of how you and others learn, and an ability to reflect on your own learning is a fundamental part of this. Consequently this chapter will discuss some of the ways in which individuals learn before examining some learning theories which may enable you to understand and reflect more fully on your own and others' learning, as well as helping you to design learning, training or talent development activities. If you are already in employment you are likely to want to improve your performance in your job or learn new skills, perhaps to get a pay increase or promotion, or maybe to move to a better job, so learning to learn is a fundamental skill. Understanding how you learn and becoming a more effective learner can help you to achieve your aims and improve employability.

This book is also, of course, about HR topics and HR-related skills, and the second part of this chapter will focus on issues relevant to organisations and the ways in which specialists working in this area of HR and line managers plan and organise learning, training and development opportunities for individuals, teams and the organisation.

What do we mean by learning and talent development and how does this differ from training?

The term 'training' was originally used to refer to some specified event designed to improve an individual's performance in a specific aspect of their work. Egan (2013) defined this as follows: 'Training is instructor-led, content-based intervention designed to lead to skills or behaviour change'. Training is still important but as the UK moved from a largely manufacturing economy, where it was appropriate to train people to carry out clearly specified tasks and where a top-down instructor-led approach was suitable, to a much more flexible service- and knowledge-based society, good workers became a source of competitive advantage to an organisation and it became more appropriate to focus more on individual learning and encouraging people to learn how to learn. Egan (2013) explains that within an organisation 'Learning is a self-directed, work-based process that leads to increased adaptive potential (as might be provided by coaching or mentoring opportunities for instance)'.

More recently the term 'learning and talent development' (L&TD) has gained in popularity as organisations increasingly recognise that in order to stay competitive they must use, develop and then retain the knowledge and talent of their workers. Their focus has started to switch to L&TD as a means of achieving their organisation's strategic objectives. This should be as a part of human resource planning, discussed in more detail in Chapter 5, as it may be necessary to develop talent from within the organisation so that future roles can be filled as people retire or leave, or to meet demand for new skills and knowledge because of a change of strategic direction.

Stewart and Rigg (2011) identify three main approaches that organisations adopt in relation to talent management. Organisations could use a very wide definition of talent as it can be argued that everyone has talent and potential and that organisations should seek to maximise this. However, in times of scarce resources and limited budgets many organisations will only seek to identify those who will make the biggest difference to the organisation's performance, either because of their perceived high potential or because they are in critical roles within the organisation and they will be given opportunities to be developed. A third group of organisations may use talent as a part of succession planning having identified those required to be developed to take up future roles. Focusing on a narrow band of people who are perceived to have talent, however, can be counterproductive as it may build resentment among other workers and may result in higher labour turnover among these groups.

For individuals, in an increasingly competitive job market, it is also vital that they are aware of the need to develop their own talent to keep a competitive edge. The word 'development' also implies something that is ongoing and that progress is made over time. This fits also with the emphasis nowadays on lifelong learning: as people work longer they need to continue to develop to improve their skills, knowledge or competencies and nurture and develop their talent throughout their lives. Many people would like to see their employer offering more opportunities for development such as training or personal development packages, and employers who do not provide this could fail to attract staff to their organisation or retain existing staff (Brockett, 2010).

The concept of individualised L&TD implies that it occurs in all sorts of situations, not just in the more traditional, formal training opportunities although we hope that learning will occur here too. L&TD includes less formal, more learner-centred approaches to learning such as coaching, mentoring, work shadowing and job swapping, some of which will be discussed later in this chapter. Changes in technology also play a part, enabling individual workers to learn regardless of where they are in the world, whether at home or at work, as long as they have access to a computer or telephone. Developments with interactive forms of Internet use, such as social networking sites, sometimes referred to as Web 2.0, also mean learning from sharing information has become easier.

How do you learn?

In a knowledge-based economy, where there is constant change and where people are regularly required to develop new knowledge and skills, perhaps the most useful skill of all is knowing how you and others learn. You cannot rely on your employer identifying you as a part of its talent management process, so you also need to be proactive and take steps to develop your own learning and skills. If you work in an organisation in a capacity where you need to help develop your team members then an understanding of the key principles involved in designing learning and development programmes is also vital.

In this section a range of learning and development and training techniques will be discussed which may also help you to learn more efficiently as well as prepare you to help others to learn. There is no one foolproof method of learning effectively, but by studying these theories you will gain some insights into how you and others learn.

Did you know?

Henry Ford said, 'Anyone who stops learning is old, whether at 20 or 80. Anyone who keeps learning stays young. The greatest thing in life is to stay young.'

Henry Ford's statement is becoming even more relevant today, not just so that we all stay young but so that as retirement ages increase we can continue to lead productive and enjoyable lives as we continue to update our skills, knowledge and learning, whether for work purposes or for leisure. According to Age Positive (2013, p. 11), a team working on strategies and policies to support people making decisions about working and retirement for the Department of Work and Pensions, 'All staff should be offered the same training regardless of age. It does not make good business sense not to.' Increasingly people are working longer so it would be foolish of an employer to not continue to provide equal training and learning opportunities for all generations of workers.

Factors affecting your learning and development

In view of the change of focus to individual L&TD a good place to start is to consider your own approach to learning, which you can do by completing Activity 8.1.

Activity 8.1

1. Make a list of a range of situations where you feel that you have learnt something.
2. In each case consider what helped you or motivated you to learn.

    - Was there something that started you learning? What was it?
    - Was there something that encouraged or motivated you to keep learning? What was it?

3. How did you ensure that your learning was thorough and that you would remember it in the future? (Reinforcement of your learning)

4. Did you receive any feedback for your learning? If so how did you obtain it?

Discussion of Activity 8.1

People are motivated to start, and indeed to continue to learn, by a variety of things, so you may have listed quite a few things that encouraged you to learn and to continue learning. These could be incentives, encouragement or rewards. Some people may be motivated by the need to do well in an examination or they may perhaps be motivated to learn a new skill because it may provide an improved opportunity for getting a better job or more pay. In other cases the motivation may be the pleasure of learning something new for its own sake or for the respect that other people may feel towards you when you have learnt something impressive. Others may be motivated to learn by a sense of curiosity or by anxiety or fear of failure and your motivation may change at different stages of your life as you continue with lifelong learning.

In order to reinforce your learning you will probably have also developed a range of techniques such as using mnemonics, testing yourself by writing out answers to questions, mind-mapping or practising newly learned skills repeatedly.

Learning theories

Psychologists have always been interested in how people learn and there are far too many theories of learning to discuss them all here. Besides, you will undoubtedly study some of these theories of learning in other subjects such as organisational behaviour. However, it is important to consider some of the common issues that occur in these theories as they may provide insights into how you learn. They may also help us to help others in our organisations to learn so that we create high-performing organisations or nations.

Motivation to learn

Behavioural psychologists such as Pavlov and Skinner referred to the instinctive need or motivation that led to learning as 'the drive'. In animals this was normally provided by a desire for food, but in people the drive or motivation might be to pass an exam or just to achieve the satisfaction derived from mastering something new. This aspect of their work points to the importance of considering people's motivation to learn. If we can find out what makes people want to learn we should then be able to tailor our instruction better and be more likely to create better performance at work. In Activity 8.1 you identified your own motivations to learn, but if you compare them with those of your friends you may find that they are motivated by different factors. Organisations also need to be aware of what will motivate their workers to learn as part of their approach to performance management, and need to ensure that other HR policies, such as that for reward, clearly support their approach.

Behaviourist concepts

Although work with pigeons and dogs may not appear at first sight to be very relevant to your learning or to the learning that occurs within organisations, this work does, in fact, raise many important issues, of which those specialising in learning and development should be aware.

Early in the last century Pavlov (1927) trained dogs to salivate when he rang a bell. He noticed that dogs salivated naturally as a reflex response when food was put in front of them. For his experiment he rang a bell every time the dogs were fed; after a time, the dogs would salivate when the bell was rung, whether there was food or not (Figure 8.1). He deduced that the dogs had learnt to salivate by associating the bell with the food, and came to see the learning process as the development of responses to the new stimuli. He called them conditioned responses, as opposed to the unconditioned or natural responses that came before. His term for the process of learning was 'conditioning'.

Later, Skinner (1953) took the theory further. The limitation of Pavlov's work was that it showed that animals (or people) could learn to apply instinctive responses to new sets of circumstances but it did not show how totally new responses could be learnt. Skinner in fact succeeded in teaching pigeons to play ping-pong by a process that he called operant conditioning. In this process, the pigeons were watched for any patterns of behaviour that might be useful when

Figure 8.1 Conditioned responses: Pavlov's dogs

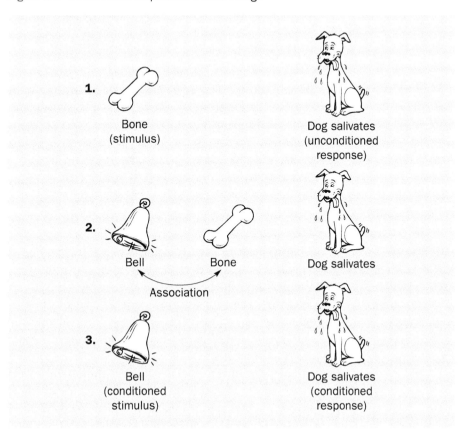

1. Bone (stimulus) — Dog salivates (unconditioned response)

2. Bell Bone — Dog salivates
Association

3. Bell (conditioned stimulus) — Dog salivates (conditioned response)

playing ping-pong, and whenever they performed they were rewarded with food. Not surprisingly, the birds soon learnt to do certain movements, and they retained their learning better if the reward was repeated regularly, a process Skinner called 'reinforcement'. In human learning, Skinner believed, reinforcement mainly took the form of feedback – information telling the learner whether they are getting the task right and if they are not how they can improve.

Skinner believed that all learning took place in this associative manner, and that all complex patterns of behaviour, such as learning ping-pong or learning to speak, could be broken down into small steps that could be taught one by one in a simple fashion. He applied this theory both to training workers and to the education of his own children, and his work is still very influential. It obviously makes sense to break down routine tasks into their component parts, and to provide methodical training to cover them. In addition, his emphasis on the visible or objective side of learning led to the practice of setting learning objectives or statements of what a learner had to achieve in terms of action.

Criticisms of behaviourism

On the other hand, you might be wondering whether Skinner's account of the pigeons' learning process was complete. Did insight play no part in their grasp of the rules of the game? In human learning insight often seems to enable people to cut the corners on the road to knowledge, and experience of behaviouristic attempts to teach complex matters suggests that they can lead to a slow, mechanical set of activities. Many psychologists have challenged Skinner's view, particularly with regard to the learning of complex behaviour such as speech.

Reinforcement and feedback of learning

The behaviourists used reinforcement to indicate a correct behavioural response. The reinforcement could be negative or positive. Rewards such as food for animals or praise for people are positive forms of reinforcement of the desired behaviour, while punishments aim to eliminate incorrect behaviour. Research suggests that positive reinforcement is generally more effective than negative reinforcement in gaining a change in behaviour in the long term, as with negative reinforcement the desired change often occurs only as long as there is the threat of punishment. When this threat is withdrawn then behaviour often reverts to the original behaviour.

How can you use this to improve your skills in learning and development?

Reinforcement of your learning could occur by your reading or viewing something and being tested on this and praised by your tutor for your efforts, or by you completing a self-check exercise and giving yourself a pat on the back if you have done well. This will reinforce correct behaviour or show you that you have the right answers, but won't necessarily give you any detailed understanding of what you have done well or of what you did wrong. For that you also need knowledge of results or feedback.

Knowledge of results or feedback is important if we are to learn effectively. In a training situation this could be by the trainer giving comments on the person's progress, or perhaps by a manager appraising the work of one of their staff as part of the performance management process.

Activity 8.2

The illustration in Figure 8.2 shows what happens when Caroline makes a cup of tea. She often chooses to feed the cats at the same time as putting the kettle on. Thus the kettle and the tin of cat food being opened are linked in the cats' minds. Sometimes she puts the kettle on but she doesn't open a tin of cat food. However, the cats now appear when they hear the sound of the kettle.

Figure 8.2   Caroline's cats

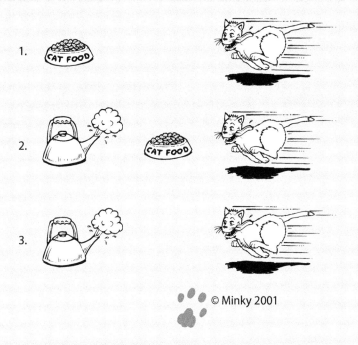

© Minky 2001

1. What is this effect known as?
2. According to Pavlov, how should we label the cat food at point 1 in Figure 8.2?
3. According to Pavlov, what is the link between the kettle and the cat food known as? Label point 2 in Figure 8.2.
4. According to Pavlov, what should the kettle be labelled as at point 3 in Figure 8.2?

Suggested answers will be found on page 469.

When giving constructive feedback one should start with the positive, and focus first on the behaviour that has been done well before giving feedback about behaviour that has been done less well. Feedback about incorrect behaviour, if given skilfully, is extremely important; it doesn't have to be destructive, and it is important to focus on specific aspects of behaviour that can be changed. General statements such as 'that was awful' are much too vague to be helpful in changing behaviour. Unless the person who is giving the feedback also suggests alternative ways of behaving, it would be easy for the person receiving the feedback to feel that they are just being criticised.

Feedback is a very important part of the learning process. The saying 'Practice makes perfect' could well be modified to 'Practice with appropriate feedback makes perfect', since without the feedback the person could just carry on with the same inappropriate behaviour over and over again. The feedback could also be provided by the individual themselves reflecting on what they have learned and how they can improve but this does require the individual to develop skills of reflection and to be self-critical about their learning.

The amount of practice and time you spend learning something is also important. The psychologist K. Anders Ericsson (1993) formulated an idea that 'deep practice' involving 10,000 hours or 10 years of practice was necessary for individuals to gain such an amount of knowledge and understanding that they could become an expert in their field so the decisions they made and problems they solved then appeared effortless and appeared to be intuitive. This idea was discussed and made popular by Malcolm Gladwell in his book *Outliers* (2004). However, Gladwell did also stress the fact that people needed talent too and opportunities to use their talent, but if they were to become an expert a large amount of practice was needed to hone these skills.

It is unlikely in a workplace setting that most people are going to be able to devote such a huge amount of time to learning and improving their skills and knowledge, and one does not normally get the chance at work to keep doing the same thing for such a long time. However, it is still important to spend time practising and refining things learned in order to fully embed learning, even though most of us will not spend 10,000 hours doing so.

Experiential learning

Experiential learning, or learning from experience, is particularly useful for learning and development in the workplace situation. The concept is derived from the work of Kolb *et al.* (1974) in America, and of Honey and Mumford (1992) in Britain. Honey and Mumford's approach to experiential learning can be illustrated by the learning cycle shown in Figure 8.3. Their theory also suggests that different people may have different preferred styles of learning and this is an important factor to consider if we want people to learn effectively.

The learning cycle

Students in college and people learning in the workplace are both likely to meet a range of different learning opportunities. Most full-time students nowadays will also work to support themselves to some extent while studying and will themselves have a range of work experiences from which they can learn. Some of you will be mature students who have already worked for a number of years, some will be part-time students combining study with a career and yet others will be on sandwich course degrees where you have the opportunity of gaining work experience in a placement. Knowing about your own learning preferences may help you to understand and you may become more efficient in learning from these experiences.

Figure 8.3 The learning cycle

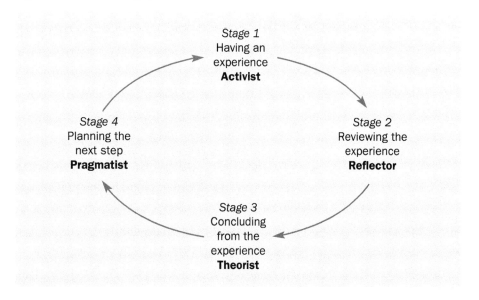

Stage 1: Having an experience

Most people have plenty of experiences from which to learn, but age does not necessarily mean that people have learnt more. Some people do not use the experiences that they have. One way of learning is to let experiences come to you (reactive), and the other is to deliberately seek out new experiences (proactive). Anyone who provides learning development opportunities whether as a specialist or a line manager needs to provide suitable experiences from which people can learn (in the form, for example, of case studies, role plays and other simulations), but learners also need to be proactive and seek for themselves appropriate learning opportunities. The use of suitable, willing individuals as mentors, or the formation of a supportive study group of friends, can assist in this process by:

- helping to identify suitable learning experiences,
- reviewing with individuals what they have actually done and helping to draw out what they have learnt,
- encouraging the individual to be proactive in seeking suitable learning experiences.

Stage 2: Reviewing the experience

If we are to learn from an experience it is important to review what has happened. Unfortunately we are often too busy to do this, and some people never develop the habit of reflection. The individual should be encouraged to:

- think about what actually happened,
- think of other ways in which the situation could have been handled,
- make comparisons with what happened in other similar situations,
- read about the subject,
- compare theory and practice.

Stage 3: Concluding from the experience

There would be little point in reviewing the experiences unless we then drew some conclusions from them. This involves scanning the raw material for lessons to be learned and reaching some conclusions. The individual should be asking:

- What have I learnt from this?
- What could I have done differently?

Stage 4: Planning the next stage

Having reached a conclusion, it is important to try to do things better next time. To do this we need to be able to plan, and this involves translating at least some of the conclusions into a basis for appropriate action next time. The individual should be encouraged to:

- state what they would do next time,
- draw up a plan of action for handling such a situation again.

The four stages in the process of learning using experiences are mutually dependent. The whole process is summarised in the learning cycle (Figure 8.3).

Learning styles

People learn in a variety of ways and over the years may develop certain learning habits which enable them to benefit from certain types of experience more than other types. Honey and Mumford developed a questionnaire so that individuals can establish their preferred learning style. This approach was developed as a result of their work with managers, as they became concerned to discover why one person will learn from a particular experience but another does not appear to learn anything from the same experience. Further details of their approach are given in the Further study section. Most people only use one or two learning styles although these are not fixed and can change over time. Honey and Mumford (1992) say that there are four differing learning styles that clearly link with the four stages of the learning cycle: activists, reflectors, theorists and pragmatists.

Activists

Activists like to get fully involved in whatever is happening, seeking new experiences and enthusing about new ideas and techniques. They tend to be open minded and not sceptical, and are often enthusiastic about novelty. They tend to act first and then consider the consequences later. Their days are filled with activity and they often tackle problems by mind mapping.

Reflectors

Reflectors prefer to stand back and observe experiences from different perspectives. The thorough collection and analysis of data are important to them, so they try to avoid reaching definite conclusions. They would rather take a back seat in meetings and discussions and get the drift of the discussion before making their own points. When they act it is as part of a larger picture which includes the past as well as the present and considers other people's observations and their own.

Theorists

Theorists adapt and integrate observations into complex but logically sound theories. They think problems through in a vertical, step-by-step logical way. They assimilate disparate facts into coherent theories, and tend to be perfectionists who will not rest until things are tidy and fit into a rational scheme. They value rationality and logic.

Pragmatists

Pragmatists are keen to try out new ideas, theories and techniques to see if they work in practice. They positively search for new ideas and take the first opportunities to experiment with applications. They are the type of people who return from a training course full of ideas that they want to try out immediately. They like to get on with things and act quickly and confidently on ideas. They hate long ruminating discussions.

Activity 8.3

1. Read the description of the four learning styles again or go to **www.campaign-for -learning.org.uk/cfl/yourlearning/whatlearner.asp** (accessed 16.06.14). This site provides clear explanations about Honey and Mumford's learning styles and hints on how to make learning more effective for each style of learner. It also provides lots of useful information about ways to learn more effectively.

2. From the descriptions given, which learning style do you think you use most frequently?

3. You could also test whether how you think you learn matches an analysis of your learning style by using Honey and Mumford's online questionnaire at **www.peterhoney .com/index.aspx** (accessed 16.06.14). There is a charge for this which at the time of writing was £11.40. Alternatively you could use a shorter online version which claims to provide similar results in a rough and ready learning styles questionnaire: **www.brainboxx.co.uk/A2_LEARNSTYLES/pages/learningstyles.htm** (accessed 16.06.14)

4. Reflect on your findings. Examine the theory by rereading the description of the styles outlined earlier and on these websites.

Discussion of Activity 8.3

You may have discovered that you are equally at home learning in each of these styles. Two per cent of the population use all four styles. The majority of the population – 70 per cent – tend to prefer using one or two learning styles. You can use your understanding of learning styles in various ways. You might choose to seek opportunities to use the learning styles that you generally use less often, and in this way you may become a more rounded learner who is able to make use of a wider range of learning opportunities.

You might, on the other hand, choose to make use of the learning styles for which you have a preference, so that if learning opportunities are presented to you in ways you don't like, you may look for alternative ways to learn about the topic which are more in line with your learning style preferences.

Other approaches to learning styles and methods

There are many different ways of analysing approaches to learning. We have already mentioned the Honey and Mumford learning styles inventory and that of David Kolb *et al.* (1974).

However, other approaches are used. For example, are you a visual, auditory or kinaesthetic learner? This is sometimes referred to as VAK.

Activity 8.4

You can check whether you are a visual, auditory or kinaesthetic learner at **www.businessballs .com/vaklearningstylestest.htm** (accessed 16.06.14).

If you like to visualise, seeing things in colour and using pictures such as mind maps then you are probably a visual learner. If you prefer to listen to the sounds of things then you are probably an auditory learner, and if you like to move around while learning and link learning with movement you could be a kinaesthetic learner.

Questionnaires such as these are useful tools to help you to understand the ways in which you learn and they are also frequently used in organisations when planning training or learning and development. They do not mean that you will always learn in the same way; however, they can be a device to encourage you to reflect on your own learning and to make choices about using different approaches to learning so can be an aid to learning to learn.

Did you know?

There is evidence to question the validity and reliability of many of these questionnaires. Coffield (2008) analysed 13 of the most widely used questionnaires and found no evidence in the majority that they were either reliable or valid. Despite this, they are widely used, extremely popular and do provide a basis on which to question, analyse and reflect on your approach to learning.

Recent insights into how people learn

More recently, as the technology has improved, clearer images of what goes on within the brain are allowing new insights into the ways people learn. It is no longer only psychologists who are studying learning but further insights are being provided by neuroscience, cognitive science and decision research (CIPD, 2012). There is increasing evidence that our brains can change in structure throughout our lives and that this depends on the use of our skills and experience. So the saying 'use it or lose it' seems appropriate and Henry Ford appears to have been right when he said that one should keep on learning throughout life to stay young as our brains seem to be able to change as we learn. According to the CIPD (2014e) while 'our brains are certainly more "plastic" when we are younger...their connectivity, function and even structure can change dramatically in response to learning throughout our lives'. Studies of London cab drivers and even people who have taken a short course in juggling were found to result in noticeable changes in areas of their brains as a result of learning particular skills.

Research from neuroscientists also show evidence that increased levels of physical activity may help people to learn more effectively. For example in one study after just short two-minute sprints a group of healthy adults showed 'a 20 per cent increase in the speed of recall for words they learned following their intense exercise' compared with others who had been sedentary or had followed more moderate exercise regimes. Students who had 30 minute breaks of aerobic exercise each day also improved their attention spans in class compared with others who participated in shorter periods of exercise (Winter *et al.*, 2007 pp. 597–609).

Though more work needs to be done, insights gained from neuroscience mean that we are starting to understand the potential for learning from other sources such as computer games. Playing this type of game can appear to outsiders to be a complete waste of time but there is evidence to suggest that skills such as an enhanced performance in visual-motor skills and an ability to avoid becoming distracted can be developed. This type of activity can also achieve extremely intense involvement from the participant and this appears to be linked to both the rapid sequence of rewards available and the built-in uncertainty of achieving those rewards. Benefits in visual-motor skills and attention appear to transfer to other areas of learning and many trainers would like to get such intense involvement from and attention to their training materials from participants in their training.

Practical issues relating to individual learning

It is important when learning from experiences for the individual learner to be aware of their preferred learning style. Trainers, L&TD specialists and line managers also need to know about learning styles and be aware of the newer discoveries about learning from the neuroscientists so they can provide a learning experience which will enable each individual to learn effectively.

Recent approaches to learning and development

Mind-mapping techniques

Psychologists say that our minds work using patterns and that several ideas can be developing simultaneously. The brain then goes through a process of integrating ideas, but this doesn't necessarily happen in a linear order.

Tony Buzan (1982) developed the idea of mind maps to allow people to express themselves freely and encourage creativity, without being necessarily governed by the linear form. Many people, when presenting information in the form of a mind map, show a very detailed grasp of the subject which they were not able to demonstrate in a traditional written form. The mind maps (some examples are used as chapter summaries in this book) start with the central subject, which can be presented pictorially. Lines then lead from this to other connected topics. This gives more freedom for ideas to appear without worrying at first about the connections, and it allows for several links to be made between related parts of a topic.

The mind map shown in Figure 8.4 illustrates our view of the key points with which this chapter has been concerned so far. Mind maps encourage creativity, and if they are to be used in a way that helps someone to remember and learn effectively they should be very visual. The central topic should be written clearly, preferably in capital letters, and underlined. A pictorial representation of that topic is also useful, as it encourages easier recall. Lines should be drawn from this key word, and the main areas relating to the subject area should be drawn.

Further diagrams or pictures can make the mind map of the topic memorable. Further lines and words should branch from each of these, and the pattern is then developed. Groups of ideas can be linked by the use of different colours. Links can be made easily, by using arrows or lines, between related topics. Relationships and links with other subjects can also be made and identified at the edges of the mind map.

According to Banks and McGurk (2014, p. 12) one of the most effective ways of learning is to write things down because this means that you are actively engaging

Figure 8.4   Partial mind map of this chapter

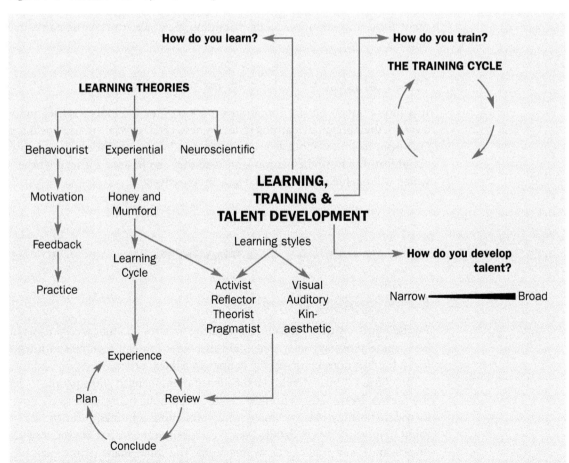

with and reflecting on what you are learning and mind maps are particularly useful for this as they create a different dynamic in our brains which is more effective than just trying to remember information.

Activity 8.5

The mind map in Figure 8.4 is incomplete, since it is being used part way through this chapter. When you have read the rest of this chapter, complete the remainder of the mind map in a way that will make it memorable for you. Draw links with other subjects or topics around the edge of the mind map.

Discussion of Activity 8.5

After reading the whole chapter you may want to include more things that you consider relevant such as e-learning, bite-size learning and blended learning so you can continue to build your mind map and add further topics to make it relevant to you. In order for it to be useful and memorable you should try to make your mind map as visually attractive as possible.

Activity 8.6

Make a list of learning, training or talent development techniques that you think will suit activists, reflectors, theorists and pragmatists. This will help you to get more actively involved in your own learning and will help you to reflect on what you have learned. (Some of the techniques may suit more than one style of learning.)

L&TD techniques to suit people who prefer each of the four learning styles

Activist	Reflector	Theorist	Pragmatist

Discussion of Activity 8.6

Your list is likely to include a variety of different learning techniques. We will consider in turn each of the preferred learning styles.

Activist

The techniques that allow activists to participate fully in the learning experience will be the ones that appeal most to them. These could include: role play, group discussion, project work, case studies, computer-based learning and in-tray exercises. The role play is especially likely to appeal to the activist, as it provides plenty of opportunity for them to become involved in a leading role. Interactive learning on social networking sites may also appeal. Activists are likely to be bored by the lack of involvement required from them in techniques such as lectures, videos or films.

Reflector

Reflectors are likely to appreciate learning techniques where they are presented with information that they can then think about, so lectures, films, videos, information from Internet sites and guided reading are likely to appeal to them. They will probably also appreciate to some extent group discussions and case studies, as long as they do not have to take too active a part and have plenty of time for reflection afterwards. Computer-based training courses, in which they can progress at their own speed and go back to examine again points that they want to look at in more detail, may also prove popular.

Theorist

Theorists welcome opportunities to examine new theories and compare them with other points of view. Lectures and guided reading are likely to appeal most to them as training techniques. They may appreciate the ease with which they can find research articles using Internet searches or online databases. Lectures with a fairly academic content are preferred, so that ideas gained can be compared with other ideas and theories. If the guided reading covers a suitable range of material this could also be useful to a theorist, although if the material is not extensive or theoretical enough for them, they are likely to want to delve further into other areas.

Pragmatist

The pragmatist wants to know how things will really work in practice, so they are likely to find training techniques that are close to reality useful. Case studies, role plays and in-tray exercises will appeal to them if they think that they are realistic and of immediate use to them at work.

Bite-sized learning

Some of you may have experienced bite-sized learning for yourselves. The BBC's revision programmes for GCSE use this approach but also provide a range of bite-sized resources online starting from key stage 1 for infants and going through to GCSEs. Octavius Black (2004), managing director of the Mind Gym, says that:

> People often thought that the more time they spent on learning, the better their knowledge would be. In fact, they could learn equally effectively – if not more so – in short bursts. Research shows that we remember and apply much more knowledge when we learn little and often than when we learn lots in one go.

This fits very well with what we said earlier about remembering information. You are likely to be more successful in remembering information if you are frequently going over what you have learned.

According to Crofts (2004), one of the most common barriers to learning cited by CIPD members is the amount of time it takes, and as workers in the UK and places such as Hong Kong and Japan work increasingly long hours, bite-sized training certainly fits a need. However, trainers are likely to need to develop different skills to deliver material in a fast-paced way, with exercises taking only a few minutes to complete. This view is supported by a survey of line managers conducted in 2010 where ongoing

Did you know?

According to Ben Connell, Google's learning and development specialist, 'There are a wide range of learning opportunities provided internally including "learning on the loo" where impromptu bite-sized lessons are placed on the back of lavatory doors!'

(*Source*: Brockett, 2012)

accessible learning using bite-sized modules on a regular basis and the 'ability to dip into learning' was seen as being one important factor which contributed towards the success of training for busy managers (Wolff, 2010a).

Current trends in training, L&TD in organisations

On-the-job training

In 2014 a survey of members of the Chartered Institute of Personnel and Development asked participants to list their three most-used learning and development methods and their three most effective. This survey showed that on-the-job training was the most frequently used approach to learning and was used by 51 per cent of the respondents. This was also regarded as being the most effective method of learning and development by 53 per cent of the sample (CIPD and Cornerstone 2014, p. 8). This is a fairly cheap method of providing learning and development and has the benefit of being tailored to the needs of the organisation though it does depend on the person providing the training being skilled in training techniques.

There can be problems associated with this approach which was sometimes referred to as 'sitting by Nellie'. A new recruit was often just told to sit and watch and learn from another member of staff and their chances of learning just depended on how good that member of staff was at teaching them and whether or not they were interested in teaching them and had the time to do this. If they were good at it, and a naturally good instructor, then it could work well, but there was always a danger that the trainee would learn faults as well as good practice. This was one of the main disadvantages of using 'on-the-job' training.

This approach does still get used today but hopefully with more attention paid to the person running the training, or providing the learning and talent development opportunities, being trained in this skill themselves. Recently the emphasis in many organisations has returned to on-the-job training with the introduction of National Vocational Qualifications (NVQs). This time, however, the person providing the training and assessment is trained themselves, and there are national standards to work towards, so there should be much greater consistency in approach. NVQs aim to harness the benefits of on-the-job training, in terms of low cost and relevance to the organisation, while ensuring that standards are high and consistent. Using on-the-job training could be beneficial, as the training has been planned, there is a trainer who knows how to train and a qualified person will test whether the individual is competent in that job.

In-house development programmes

The second most popular method of learning and development, in-house development programmes, listed by 46 per cent of CIPD survey participants as one of their top three methods, is also an internal form of training and development. This reflects the fact that organisations want to get effective training without spending a great deal of money. In this survey 39 per cent of participants rated in-house development programmes as one of the three most effective learning and development methods that they used and they also considered it to be the second most effective learning and development method (CIPD and Cornerstone 2014, p. 8).

E-learning

As well as the more traditional approaches to learning, trainers and individual learners now have a choice of using e-learning techniques. In the survey by the CIPD and Cornerstone (2014) this was the third most popular method and 30 per cent of participants claimed to use this, though only 15 per cent of those surveyed regarded it as effective. There is some confusion about what exactly constitutes e-learning but it can include computer-based training and learning, technology-based training and learning and web-based training and learning. The CIPD (2013a) defines electronic learning or e-learning as 'learning that is delivered, enabled or mediated using electronic technology for the explicit purpose of training, learning or development'. It may be integrated alongside traditional learning as a support mechanism, or be used separately as part of a distance learning or open learning course. Some university degrees, post-graduate qualifications and training packages are delivered totally using e-learning methods, resulting in them being easily accessible to people in any part of the world at any time.

One major advantage is that individuals, so long as they have access to the technology, should be able to choose when, where and what they learn and this should increase opportunities for learning. Learning on the move using phones or tablets is also sometimes referred to as m-learning. Support can be provided by chat rooms, discussion groups, webinars and online tutoring with everyone involved able to respond at a time that is convenient. Alternatively, approaches such as virtual classrooms, social networking sites, audio-visual conferencing and two-way live satellite broadcasts provide immediate feedback so learning and development managers and learners can interact with each other almost as quickly as they would in a more traditional classroom situation.

Some organisations such as BT are already embracing the interactivity of social networking and other forms of Web 2.0 technologies as part of their approach to learning, training and talent development (CIPD, 2010). This is in line with the desire of people to learn in more flexible ways and creates new opportunities and ways of learning that could also appeal to those wanting instant access to L&TD.

With the current concern for environmental issues and our carbon footprints it will be interesting to see whether these approaches will become even more popular and replace some of the travel by students and their lecturers.

Did you know?

A MOOC could help you learn! Some universities and other organisations now use MOOCs or massive open online courses as a part of their online learning. Some universities offer platforms where groups can learn simultaneously using multi-media and chat rooms and these can be delivered to anything from a few dozen people to thousands. Professionals in other types of organisation are increasingly using MOOCs as a part of their continuing professional development and these are attractive to participants who want to learn more about a topic, engage with others in online conversations and collaboration and where they do not want to achieve a specific qualification.

(*Source:* Crush 2014a, p. 29)

Did you know?

In a survey of workers in the UK, Germany, France and Spain conducted by CEGOS UK, Britain was found to lead in what were regarded as the more innovative approaches to learning with the use of blended learning, mentoring and social media all being stronger than in other European countries.

(*Source:* Brockett, 2010)

Activity 8.7

How do you feel about e-learning or m-learning as an approach to learning? Is it a method you enjoy or is it an approach you dislike?

What about using social networking or social bookmarking sites as a part of your learning?

Do you do this already by sharing documents using methods such as those listed or by using blogs or tweets? Is it an approach you welcome or dislike?

You will find the symbols on many HR documents that you find for yourself and on many that we have used if you choose to look at the originals for some of our references. Some Internet sites such as those of the CIPD and ACAS also have facilities for people to share information on blogs or by using other resources such as LinkedIn or Facebook. Check for yourself and evaluate the usefulness of these resources for you.

Blended learning

Another type of learning and development that has proved popular is the concept of blended learning. According to Allison Rossett and Felicia Douglas (2004):

> A blend is an integrated strategy for delivering on promises about learning and performance. It involves a planned combination of approaches as varied as coaching by a supervisor, participating in on-line class, self-assessments, and in on-line attendance in workshops and in on-line discussions.

We have already advocated that there should be a mix of learning and talent development methods to suit the needs of the learners, and blended learning involves planning for this in ways to suit the needs of particular groups. A blended learning approach is attractive to organisations as it is claimed that it may help to reduce the costs of delivery while at the same time improving the quality of the learning, though there is little firm evidence to support these ideas (Hofmann, 2008).

In many instances, online learning forms part of the blend and this may cut down the need for time spent on classroom-based learning, but every organisation has to reach its own blend of learning and development ingredients to suit the needs of the organisation and the participants in the learning and development programme. According to Blain (quoted in *Training and Coaching Today*, 2008), 'the effectiveness of any blended mix hinges on agreeing goals and recognising the outcomes that the company, individual and the trainer is looking for – with senior management sponsors forming another crucial element'. Blain further advocates that a blend does not have to include technology-based methods but could use any mix of the methods. In the 2014 survey of learning and development initiatives among CIPD members 15 per cent of those surveyed claimed to use some form of blended learning (CIPD and Cornerstone, 2014).

Other L&TD techniques

Many other techniques could be used and we have summarised the suitability of some in Table 8.1. Complete the second column to identify whether in your opinion the particular type of learning and development activity is led more by the L&TD

Table 8.1   Training and L&TD techniques and their suitability

Training technique	Formal trainer-centred or informal learner-centred approaches	Suitability
Lecture	Formal trainer-centred	This is suitable when a large amount of information needs to be given to a large number of people at the same time. The information can be prepared in advance but a disadvantage is the lack of participation from the audience.
Role play		Here a small group of people have the chance to act as if they were in a real work situation. They have a problem or situation to deal with which would be similar to a situation that they might experience at work. They can practise their responses and receive help and support from the trainer and from the others in the group. This can help in developing awareness of interpersonal skills and can give confidence, as there is an opportunity to practise skills in a protected environment where it does not matter if mistakes are made. There can sometimes be a problem if the role play is not taken seriously or if trainees are too nervous or embarrassed to perform their roles.
Group discussion		This can lead to a free exchange of knowledge, ideas and opinions on a particular subject among the trainees and the trainer with the opportunity to air various viewpoints. It can be useful when there are varying opinions about an issue, or a range of ways in which a situation could be handled. There is a danger that the trainees may wander too far from the subject if it is not handled skilfully by the trainer, and that important points may not be discussed.
Video or film		These can be used to show a real situation and differing ways of handling that situation, or to give information to several people at once. They can show examples of good and bad use of interpersonal skills to a large number of people at once and be used as the basis for a group discussion. They do not demand much involvement from the audience, although the trainer could add to this by use of discussion or questions after each showing.
Project		Normally a task is set by the trainer which will give an individual or group general guidelines to work to, but will also leave a great deal of scope for them to show creativity or initiative. This is a good way of stimulating creativity or initiative but, in order to do so, the project has to be about something that will interest the trainee.
Case study		A case study is a history of some event or situation in which relevant details are supplied for the trainee to get an overall picture of the situation or organisation. Trainees are then asked to diagnose the problems or suggest solutions. A case study provides the opportunity to examine a situation in detail yet be removed from the pressure of the real work situation. This allows for discussion and provides opportunities to exchange ideas and consider different options. Since a case study can limit the number of factors or issues that should be discussed, it may sometimes seem too easy and trainees may not fully appreciate that in the real-life situation there may be other more complex issues to take into account.

Training technique	Formal trainer-centred or informal learner-centred approaches	Suitability
Computer-based training		This allows the trainee to work at their own pace through a series of questions or exercises using a computerised training program. The trainees get immediate feedback from the computer program and can cover a range of work in a short space of time, going back over exercises if necessary and learning at a time that is convenient for them. Trainees may be nervous of the technology or may experience difficulties so it is normally useful to have easy access to help or advice at least via a telephone.
Guided reading		A series of recommended reading is provided on a topic, perhaps graded according to difficulty. The trainee is able to work at their own pace through this. Since the reading has been selected by someone else to highlight points on that subject this can save the trainee time since they know that the materials will be relevant to the subject. It does not encourage the trainee to research further around the subject or seek materials for themselves.
In-tray or in-box exercise		Trainees are given a series of files, memos, letters or emails similar to those that they might have to deal with in a real work situation. They need to decide on the appropriate action to take and the priority for action. This gives an opportunity for trainees to experience the sort of issues that can arise, but it is important that the contents of the in-tray are realistic.
Online discussion groups		
Audio or videoconferencing		
Podcasts		
Using social networking approaches such as blogs, tweets, webinars, information sharing or Second Life		

specialist, the learner or equally by both. Use the blank spaces in the table to assess the suitability of online discussion groups and audio- or videoconferencing and the use of podcasts and social networking sites. Spaces have also been left at the end of Table 8.1 for you to add your own suggestions for different training or learning techniques.

Some of these training or L&TD methods are much more participative than others, and it is a good idea to use a variety of techniques to avoid the learner becoming bored and to give opportunities to practice skills if a skill is being taught. This also means that if you are working with a group of people and utilising a variety of techniques, you are likely to use the preferred learning styles of different individuals at various times. Learning is an active process, and even if it is a list of facts that needs to be learnt, most people learn more effectively when they test themselves, or rewrite information in their own words. This also improves their recall of the information.

These points emphasise the importance of providing some opportunities for the learner to practise what they are learning, and underline the value for you of completing the exercises as you go through this book.

Mentors

Rather than just leaving learning experiences to chance, many organisations use mentors to help individuals to learn. Mentors are traditionally people with experience who can provide advice and guidance to their mentee, though the role varies from organisation to organisation. They are not usually that person's line manager and the relationship works best when the mentee is able to choose their mentor. Mentors need to be prepared to guide and suggest suitable learning experiences for their protégé. They may encourage reflection on learning experiences by asking for reports, and may suggest books to read on the subject. They may also sometimes provide opportunities for the individual to demonstrate what they have learnt by, for example, reviewing a presentation before the learner makes it to the target audience. While their main aim is to encourage individuals to learn, mentors are also likely to learn a great deal themselves by their involvement in this learning experience. In effect, mentors will be encouraging the individual to learn in different ways according to their development needs and to practise using different learning styles and different stages of the learning cycle. Sometimes there can be some overlap with coaching as this is one of the many techniques that a mentor could also use.

Coaching

Coaches also help individuals or groups to perform better, rather like a sports coach, as they try to motivate the individual or team and advise or instruct them on performance. They could be external to an organisation or internal.

According to Sol Davidson (2002), there are three types of coaching: traditional, transitional and transformational:

- Traditional coaching is closely related to training and involves a coach who is an expert in a subject helping to improve the skills and knowledge of an individual or group.
- Transitional coaching is useful where large changes are about to be made in an organisation. Here the coach does not necessarily know all the answers, but will help the group to find successful new ways of working.
- Transformational coaching is targeted at senior management but is aimed at helping the whole organisation move to new ways of working. It could be appropriate when an organisation is faced with a great deal of change.

Did you know?

According to the CIPD and Cornerstone's (2014) survey of L&TD, coaching and mentoring are used by 75 per cent of the organisations in their survey.

● Learning logs

Another way in which individuals may be encouraged to learn from their experiences is by the use of a learning log. A learning log is a way of keeping track of a person's development, with emphasis on unstructured, informal activities. This is likely to involve individuals in describing events that they feel are important for their own development process. They would then need to comment on what they had learnt from the experience and how, if a similar situation were to arise again, they would handle that situation. The idea is that because individuals have to write up their learning experiences, they will be likely to do things better in the future. Learning also ceases to be a haphazard process, as it becomes conscious and increasingly learner-centred and puts them in charge of developing their own talent and abilities. This means that the individual will have used several of the stages of the learning cycle.

Keeping a learning log should encourage activists to be more reflective and encourage reflectors/theorists to take action and to do things after reflecting on them. This could be undertaken with a mentor or as a totally self-directed method of gaining insights into your own learning processes. This method is very subjective but tends to encourage an analytical approach to problems. It can also be helpful to get a problem sorted out on paper, with clear targets for how you would handle a similar situation in the future.

Nowadays the pace of change is rapid and people, who studied 20 years ago, or even a couple of years ago, may find that their skills and knowledge are outdated. In order to update their members, many professional groups have introduced the concept of continuing professional development (CPD) and they often use learning logs as one way of recording the learning that has occurred and for planning for future learning.

Why are learning, training and talent development important for organisations?

This chapter has already discussed some of the ways in which you can assess your own learning. However, training, L&TD can make a huge difference not only to individuals but also to organisations in terms of improving their performance and helping each to achieve their particular objectives. It is also about what organisations and the people in them need to do to ensure that L&TD makes this positive contribution to performance. The chapter will now focus on training and L&TD in organisations.

Learning, training and talent development are key aspects of performance management and can help organisations achieve high performance; they are also a key factor in managing and retaining talent even in times of economic uncertainty. Wolff (2009) found that even during the recent recession most employers still recognised the value of L&TD, even if they had to work within reduced budgets. However, two thirds of those surveyed had actually responded to the recession by increasing their efforts to develop skills and talents within their workforce, while at the same time trying to minimise their costs. The CIPD and Cornerstone survey (2014) found organisations continuing to be affected by economic challenges. In the public sector there had been cutbacks in the last five years, and even in the private sector there was still concern about the economy and employers were trying to be creative and continued to develop and retain talent in a cost-effective way as often they too continued with reduced budgets.

Creating a learning culture

If an organisation is to encourage learning, it must develop a culture which recognises that people learn in different ways and must provide a range of experiences from which they may learn. As the CIPD (2008) points out it is only learners who can do the learning. Therefore, the organisation has to be effective in creating a positive environment in which learning can occur and where it can also transfer successfully to the workplace.

Learning organisations

Sometimes organisations aspire to calling themselves a learning organisation. In some ways the term is confusing, since people actually do the learning, but it is good that people have started to see learning within organisations as being of importance. According to Jones and Hendry (1992), the term at its simplest means an organisation where there are 'a lot of people learning' and according to Pedler *et al.* (1988) it means 'an organisation which facilitates the learning of all its members and continuously transforms itself'. In today's fast-changing world it is necessary for organisations constantly to try to keep ahead of the competition and, in order to achieve this, increasingly many organisations are creating a coaching culture to facilitate in a cost-efficient way the learning of all in their organisation.

Not all organisations have been as proactive about encouraging learning and development as those that aspire to become learning organisations so governments have also developed many initiatives to encourage organisations to promote learning so that the skills of the country improve. The UK Government has had many such initiatives and individuals now have a legal right to request time off for training, though this does not necessarily mean that their request will be granted.

L&TD strategy

As we explained in Chapter 5 it is important that all HR strategies contribute to the achievement of the organisation's strategic objectives; L&TD strategies are no exception to this. The CIPD (2014a) say that each organisation needs to identify its particular strategic direction and ensure that its L&TD strategies align with and contribute to the achievement of the organisation's strategic goals. This is known as vertical alignment. They also need to contribute to the overall performance management in the organisation, to identify learning and training needs (discussed later in this chapter) and establish priorities and pools of talent. All learning, training and talent development policies should also relate to the other HR policies in the organisation and support them and this is known as horizontal alignment.

Did you know?

A survey of 2,200 workers in the UK, Germany, France and Spain conducted by the training provider CEGOS UK, found that workers were highly motivated to learn, to the extent that 76 per cent of those in the survey were willing to train in their own time, while 53 per cent were also willing to pay, at least partially, for the training.

(*Source*: Brockett, 2010)

Designing learning and talent development interventions

It is not enough just to choose the techniques and hope that these will develop into a programme as all training or L&TD interventions should have clear objectives. What do you want the learners to be able to do and what do you want them to know by the end of the course?

Our approach to the design of learning opportunities is derived and adapted from systematic approaches to training and learning such as the systematic training cycle, which is shown in Figure 8.5. Most recent models of the training L&TD process, including our own, have used it as a starting point. There are of course many valid criticisms of the systematic training cycle which relate to the fact that its focus is on training rather than individualised learning, and that it is more suited to a stable work environment rather than a rapidly changing environment in which the focus has shifted from formal training to more informal approaches to learning. It is also claimed that organisations and learners do not always work through all the stages sequentially and that it is also not clearly linked to the strategic objectives of the organisation. We have tried to address some of these criticisms in our own model for L&TD included in Figure 8.6 and each of the stages will now be discussed in more detail.

Assessing learning, training and talent development needs

It is important to assess what learning, training and talent development is needed for organisations, teams or departments and individuals. There needs to be an accurate assessment of business and organisational requirements (CIPD, 2014b). Since the performance of the organisation is only as good as the skills and knowledge

Figure 8.5   The training cycle

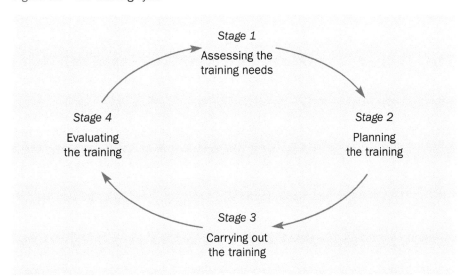

Figure 8.6   Model for learning and talent development

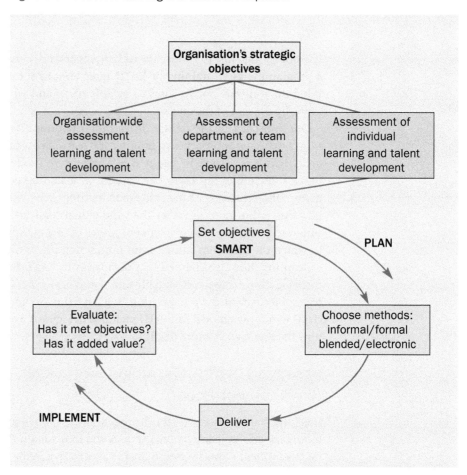

of the individuals and groups in it this should be done in conjunction with the people or groups concerned and be aimed at contributing to the organisation's strategic objectives.

While there is much to be gained from both formal training and less formal learning and development opportunities in terms of improved skills and productivity for the workforce, they are nevertheless costly activities, so it is important to provide learning opportunities of the right type for the people or groups who need them. This may in itself present new challenges as different generations of workers have different expectations and preferences for learning approaches. Increasingly people want freedom and flexibility in their learning and also learning on demand when needed, so organisations need to think carefully about the methods they use, not just because of their cost but to meet the changing needs of individuals.

This stage of the cycle is referred to as assessing training or L&TD needs and this is frequently done for individuals using the performance appraisal process or personal development review. Training and L&TD needs can be assessed in many ways, but one of the easiest ways is to examine the job that has to be done and the knowledge, skills or competencies that the organisation needs, and then to examine the knowledge, skills and competencies of the job holder and assess whether there is any gap between the two. This was discussed in detail in Chapter 7.

This type of assessment can be completed for a whole organisation, a team or department or for an individual. If there is a gap then a training, a L&TD initiative may help the individual, team or indeed the whole organisation to progress to the required standard, but if the gap is caused by some other factor such as poor recruitment then it may be a waste of money to use training or L&TD to try to bridge this gap. However, individuals do not always want the same opportunities as their organisation wants and may try to develop their careers by identifying their own gaps in their skills in comparison with the direction in which they wish to develop. Figure 8.6 shows how the organisation's strategic objectives affect learning and talent development.

Did you know?

The Weinan Education Bureau (China) required new high school teachers to pay a 20,000 yuan deposit (about £1,890) to prevent them moving to other jobs. A human resource official in the bureau stated that a teacher would get this back after working eight years!

(Source: *South China Morning Post*, 2009)

Although no organisation has a limitless budget for training, L&TD some organisations are able to cope better with the differences between individual learners' aspirations than others. Organisations that are flexible in their approach and that budget for a certain amount of money to be spent on each individual's learning, whether or not it contributes directly to the strategic objectives, are likely to benefit from this approach as they are creating a positive feeling about learning which should result in the individual being more positive about the organisation, resulting in turn in them being successful in learning in other ways that will benefit the organisation. Some organisations are willing to fund specific training or L&TD activities but try to ensure retention of the staff by making it a contractual requirement that the employee pays back the cost of the training and talent development initiative if they leave within a certain specified time, such as two years. Some organisations specify a much longer timescale for this, such as the need to stay for five years, and instead of being motivational the employee can feel resentment as they feel tied to the organisation for what, to them, may feel like forever. This can be counterproductive if it causes resentment and is a negative way of using L&TD to improve retention. It would be far better to concentrate on the positive motivational aspects of L&TD that encourage people to want to work in an organisation and to want to stay working there.

Job analysis needs to be undertaken to establish what is involved in the job. Refer back to Chapter 6 to refresh your memory of the ways in which to carry out this process. The usual result of job analysis is a job description, and a training specification can be written from this. In many organisations, where employees are encouraged to work towards NVQs, there will already be a national standard.

L&TD needs can also be assessed by asking the person or people concerned about their learning and development needs, by using questionnaires or by an analysis of mistakes (faults analysis). If there are any gaps where they do not meet the standards then there is a possible need for learning and development to help to close the gaps, and so a need has been identified.

The CIPD (2014b) says that while the analysis has to be thorough it also needs to be possible to respond quickly to a rapidly changing work environment.

They suggest focusing on key business and organisational outcomes using the following three areas which can be remembered using the mnemonic RAM:

- relevance,
- alignment,
- measurement.

Following this pattern all planned training, L&TD opportunities should be assessed to ensure that they are relevant to the needs of the business and to identified future opportunities and challenges. They should be checked to ensure that they align vertically with the organisation's strategic objectives so that they can be shown to contribute to these and also be aligned horizontally so that they are consistent with other HR policies such as pay and reward, so a consistent message is given. Appropriate measures of the success for the learning interventions should also be identified and evaluated, whether that is using a return on investment (ROI), return on expectation (ROE) or improvements in other desired outcomes such as quality, productivity, labour turnover and so on.

Setting objectives

To do this the person organising the L&TD event or process needs to be clear about what the individual, team or organisation needs to know, or be able to do or the competencies they need to have acquired after the learning and development has taken place. It is important to establish clear objectives for the learning or development event since without them there is a danger that the event will become unfocused and will not achieve its objectives. It also provides a basis for one way of evaluating the L&TD by establishing whether or not the objectives of the event have been met. 'SMART' objectives are recommended: the acronym can stand for a variety of things but generally refers to the objectives being specific, measurable, achievable, realistic and timely or time bound.

Planning the learning or development initiative

Once you have decided your objectives for the training, learning or talent development event or intervention, you are then able to plan a programme that uses a variety or blend of techniques in order to achieve this aim in the most effective way.

If the intervention is to be effective it cannot be left to chance and a great deal of planning needs to happen first in terms of basic preparation of materials and administration, such as notification to all participants and organisation of the event itself. You need to ensure that everyone is aware in advance of what will be involved in the learning and development event and its timing and location in plenty of time. Letters should have gone to the learners, the people involved in running the event and the supervisors and managers of those who will be involved so that there is time to arrange cover for their absence from work, if necessary.

Once a learning, training or talent development need has been identified, there are a number of choices to be made about how it should be met. First, should it be carried out in the organisation (in-house) or by an external organisation, such as a college or other training provider? We have already seen how in-house methods were very popular with organisations in the 2014 CIPD and Cornerstone survey but other methods may sometimes be more appropriate, particularly if there are not people in the organisation with the requisite skills to organise and deliver the chosen intervention. Second, the line manager or learning and development specialist needs to consider which techniques should actually be used. Should formal instructor-led traditional training be used or might the need be better met by less formal individualised learning such as e-learning, coaching, mentoring or the use of learning logs or a blend? Once this has been established a specific learning, training and development programme needs to be identified or designed.

Internal or external learning, training and talent development

Activity 8.8

Make up your own list in which you compare the advantages and disadvantages of providing learning, training and talent development in-house with the possible advantages and disadvantages of using an external provider.

In-house learning, training and talent development	
Advantages	Disadvantages

External learning, training and talent development provider	
Advantages	Disadvantages

Discussion of Activity 8.8

Your lists are likely to contain several advantages and disadvantages for both approaches. Among the points you should have considered are the cost and resources available to carry out the initiative. It is likely that in-house training or L&TD will be cheaper and will be tailored perfectly to meet your organisation's needs. However, if the particular need identified is very specialised and is required for only one or two people, or if there is no one with suitable qualifications or experience available to conduct or facilitate the initiative, then it may be better and more cost effective for them to join a course run by an external provider. However, this depends on the organisation's priorities for training or L&TD. This, although it may not be tailored to meet the organisation's specific needs, will have the advantage of providing wider experience and opportunities to find out how other organisations do things.

Learning, training and talent development techniques

Once the decision has been made about where the learning and development activity is to take place, it is also important to decide on which technique will be most appropriate. Will formal trainer-centred approaches work best or will more informal learner-centred approaches be better? How much technology should be used? The method used must be chosen to be appropriate for the particular need that has been identified for that person or group and it must fit with the culture and resources of the organisation.

Delivering the required learning, training or talent development event

Although specialist managers will be trained in learning techniques it is also important that line managers and any other members of staff involved in facilitating or running learning and development events should also be trained appropriately. This is still important if informal learner-centred approaches are being used, since mentors, coaches or group facilitators also need training.

Even if the people involved are trained well they will still find that delivering specific learning events will seem different each time as the process also involves interaction with learners who may have different learning styles as well as differing personalities. Some degree of flexibility is therefore necessary to take account of these differences.

Evaluation

This is an extremely important stage in the L&TD cycle and one that is often neglected by organisations. According to Findlay (2004), it is still true to say that

> many learning and development specialists do not evaluate the outcomes of their work – beyond handing out 'happy sheets' at the end of courses. These provide feedback on whether the learners have enjoyed a course or other learning interventions but do little to measure its impact.

If no evaluation of learning and development is carried out at all then the organisation does not know whether it has been enjoyed or been successful, or even whether the learning and development objectives have been met, so it may have wasted money and resources on events that were not very effective and which did not help the organisation meet its strategic objectives.

Until recently very little had actually changed in the way training or L&TD was evaluated since Donald Kirkpatrick set out the general principles in 1956 in an article 'How to start an objective evaluation of training' (see Findlay, 2004) and, although there have been criticisms of his work, his ideas have lasted well. He basically argued that there should be four levels of evaluation. First, at the end of the learning and development event the participants should be asked for their views on the effectiveness of the learning experience. This could be done by means of a simple questionnaire for the course participants after the event and this will at least give clear views as to whether the people concerned liked the learning or developmental experience, what they felt would be useful and what they felt was less useful. Consequently it should yield a great deal of valuable material, which the manager responsible for the design of the learning event should be able to incorporate usefully in the next course.

According to Kirkpatrick's levels of evaluation, the happy sheets equate to level one evaluation. However, this only establishes what the participants say they feel about the course or learning event and it is also important to establish what they have actually learnt so both knowledge and skills also need to be tested. One very effective way to achieve this is to test these both at the start of the learning event and at the end of it. This achieves Kirkpatrick's level two evaluation as it should show how much the person has learnt during the learning and development event.

If the learning is going to have an effect on the department and on the organisation and contribute to its strategic objectives it is also vital to find out what effect the learning and development event has had when the person actually gets back to work. Sometimes people may do well in a learning situation but when they return to their normal work area they revert to their usual behaviour and they seem to forget or not use the learning that has occurred. From the perspective of their line manager and from the organisation's point of view this is a waste so it is important to find out whether transfer of learning to the work situation has occurred. This can be done by questionnaires or with interviews with participants and their line manager a few weeks later, or by a review of the person's work and the effect that the learning or development opportunity has had on them. Kirkpatrick's level three evaluation aims to test whether the learning that has occurred has successfully transferred to the workplace, and essentially this level of evaluation aims to measure changes in job behaviour.

Kirkpatrick's fourth level of evaluation relates to whether the learning and development activity has made a difference to the bottom line in an organisation. Has it succeeded in making a difference to the organisation or added value? According to Martin Sloman (2004), 'If you focus your training on the organisation's learning requirements, you won't need to get hung up on assessment'. To achieve this level of evaluation it may be necessary to examine organisational statistics to see, for example, whether sales targets have been met or whether levels of customer satisfaction have improved.

According to Ian Thomson (2004), 'Evaluating training is a way of combining the assessment of the impact of training and development, while raising the profile and influence of HR and training functions.' Therefore it is in the interest of these departments to evaluate at all levels, not only to ensure that the learning objectives have been met, but also to demonstrate to the rest of the organisation that they have been successful in adding value to the organisation by making a difference in key strategic areas.

One of the things that have changed since Kirkpatrick's day is the emphasis that is nowadays placed on the reason for the evaluation. If you understand why you are evaluating something it is easier to select an appropriate method of evaluation. It has been suggested that there are four key reasons why learning and development should be evaluated. These are to:

1. **prove the value of the training** to try to find out whether or not it has worked and achieved what it was supposed to achieve,
2. **control the training** to ensure that it is achieving value for money, is fitting with the organisation's priorities and is of a consistent standard
3. **improve the quality of the training** so that standards of administration or of training delivery are improved
4. **reinforce the learning** as a part of the learning process itself (adapted from CIPD, 2014c).

For example some measures of evaluation will be of use to the trainer or person running the intervention, others may be of use to the organisation in seeing a direct impact on the strategic objectives, while yet other forms of evaluation may be of use to the individual who is involved in the learning. Sometimes methods of evaluation can be of use to more than one group.

Various methods that can be used for evaluation of learning and development or training including the following:

- questionnaires completed at the end of a course by course participants,
- interviews of learners asking their opinion of the value of the learning,
- calculation of the return on the investment in training,
- assessments by tests of what the person has learned or is able to do,
- self-review by participants of what they had learned,
- discussion with the learner's immediate superior of the improvement in performance,
- cost analysis of the learning and development.

Activity 8.9

For each of the main purposes listed in Table 8.2 write next to it which forms of evaluation are likely to be most useful and in the third column write for whom that form of evaluation would be particularly useful.

Table 8.2   Forms that evaluation can take and those who would find them useful

The purpose of the evaluation	The main forms that the evaluation could take	The people or groups who would benefit most from the evaluation
1. Prove the value of the training		
2. Improve the quality of the training offered		
3. Evaluate as a contribution to the learning process		
4. Evaluate as a control over the training		

Suggested answers will be found on page 469–72.

Sometimes the measure of evaluation used is a return on investment. This measure shows whether the money spent has been worthwhile. Nowadays we may also refer to a return on expectation. Has the learning, training or development opportunity fulfilled the expectations of all the stakeholders or were some disappointed that it did not fully achieve their objectives?

We have gone through the key principles involved in designing L&TD activities but the choices made will depend on the organisation's strategic objectives, what the specific L&TD is aiming to achieve, the organisation's culture and the resources and skills available. We shall now examine some of the ways these could be undertaken in one specific form of training called induction.

Induction training

Induction training

Many of you will have experienced some form of induction training when you joined a work organisation or perhaps a university or college. Anyone who leaves one organisation and goes to work in another will appreciate that things are done differently in different organisations, and people sometimes suffer a feeling of culture shock if behaviour that had been acceptable in their previous organisation is not viewed in the same way in the new one. This feeling of culture shock is likely to be even greater if the individual has moved from another country to work or to study. The new person picks up clues from the behaviour of others as to what is acceptable and what is not. Supervisors and managers will be seen to praise certain types of behaviour but will frown on others. At its simplest they are learning about the common view within that organisation of 'the way we do things around here' – the organisation culture.

Although employees will learn a great deal in this informal way, it is also a good idea for organisations to try to ensure that they have the opportunity to learn things that will enable them to perform to their best ability. This will mean that the organisation will need to

- assess what it thinks people need to learn in order to, both, do their jobs and contribute effectively to the organisation's strategic objectives;
- plan opportunities to facilitate learning experiences;
- evaluate what has worked well, and what has been less successful.

Wolff (2010b) found that 9 out of 10 participants in the 2010 XpertHR induction survey stated that induction was the most important part of the employee's training but 4 in 10 thought that the induction in their own organisation needed to be redesigned. Disappointingly only half of the organisations actually carried out any evaluation of the induction process, so they would find a redesign difficult since they would not have factual information on which to base their redesign.

Case Study 8.1   Induction

Read the following story about a student, Ros, who hoped to improve her language skills and earn some money for university by working as a waitress in a hotel in France for the summer. She has just started work as a trainee and is telephoning her mother a few days after her arrival.

Read the story and answer the questions at the end of it.

Ros   Hello, Mum. I got here in the end and I've survived the first day, but it has been quite difficult. I'm not sure how long I will stay.

Mum   Oh dear! What has happened? Was the journey OK? Were you met by someone with a car from the hotel, as they had arranged?

Ros   No, the hotel car didn't turn up. I had to get a taxi and it was miles from the airport so it cost a fortune. The human resource manager took me to my accommodation, but no one else seemed to be expecting me. I'm living in an

→

	apartment with about another eight people, but they were just going out when I arrived and no one had told them that I was also going to be joining them in their accommodation. They were really nice but had trouble finding a bed for me and the only spare bed is in the kitchen and it's broken.
Mum	Well, I expect you felt better when you found out what your job was and got your uniform.
Ros	Well, I'm still not sure what is happening. I got up early yesterday morning, because no one had told me when to start work, but when I got to the office I was told that I was not on duty until today so I'm still not sure what hours I'm actually working. I thought I would only be working for 35 hours a week in France, but some of the others told me that this can be averaged over a few weeks, so it may be more.
I haven't got a uniform yet either, as the only one the HR manager had left was extra large, so was much too big for me. He suggested I wore a black skirt and white blouse until they can get a uniform in a small size for me. I spent the day on the beach with some of the other trainees, so at least that was good, but I had to borrow some clothes for work as the airline has lost my luggage.
Mum	Oh dear! Have you reported it? I hope your luggage will turn up soon. You'll feel a lot more positive when you have your own things.
Ros	Yes, I reported it at the airport and it will be sent here when they find it, but I wonder if I'll still be here by then. Everything is different to what I expected.
The HR manager told me that I would be joining the receptionists rather than the waitresses. Then when I turned up for work again this morning, I was placed in the marketing department. Another girl, who had been working there, has been moved to help at another hotel this week, because the Tour de France is going through the town. Consequently that hotel is full, so a lot of the temporary staff have been moved there to help for the week.
Mum	You should get plenty of opportunities to improve your French working in marketing.
Ros	My boss in marketing is really nice and I have been phoning French and English hotels to check on competitors' prices and I'm going to be helping to do a customer satisfaction survey in both French and English. Mind you, they really need a staff satisfaction survey!
Mum	Well, at least the job sounds interesting.
Ros	Yes, my boss says she wants to keep me in the marketing department, as she has plenty of work for me to do, even when the other trainee returns. The HR manager was talking about me helping to clean chalets next week, so I'm still very confused about the job I'll be doing. I want to come home.
Mum	You're bound to feel unsettled for the first few days, but I'm sure you'll feel better when you get a bit more established and when you have your luggage. Have the meals been good? At least you get your board and lodging provided on top of your wage.
Ros	I hope I'll feel better soon, but today I missed meals so I've only had a baguette.
Mum	Oh dear! Why was that? I thought free meals were part of your payment and in France you would expect them to be good, even for the staff.
Ros	The office staff have breaks at a different time to the people working in the restaurant and the hotel, so there was no food left when I arrived. I'll have to buy something later. I thought I was being paid weekly in cash, as it said in the letter that I was sent. The others say we get paid at the end of the month and that I'll need to set up a French bank account for myself as we get paid by cheque. I hope my euros will last until I get paid. It is proving much more difficult than I thought. All the information I was sent has been wrong.

Questions

1. Comment on what happened.
2. What information should Ros have received before she left England?
3. What information could have been made available on the organisation's intranet site?
4. How could Ros' first few days have been made easier?

Activity 8.10

Imagine that you are the learning and development manager at the hotel in France where Ros had her summer job.

Design an induction course for Ros and the other students at this hotel.

- What will be your objectives for the induction programme?
- What would you want Ros to know at the end of the programme?
- What do you want her to be able to do by the end of her induction programme?

Induction

Induction is the process of helping a new employee to settle quickly into their job so that they soon become an efficient and productive employee. It also helps create a favourable image of the organisation in the mind of the new employee, and is therefore also a valuable public relations exercise. Part of the induction process starts at the time of interview, with the information and impression of the organisation that is given at that stage. Any letters or booklets given after this also form an important part of the induction process and information given should help to build the employer brand.

New employees need to learn a great deal of information when they join an organisation. This could be learned informally, but this may take a long time and the employee may learn the wrong things. It will be even more important if the person is working in another country or using a second language and an intervention to help awareness of cross-cultural differences or in language skills may also be needed as part of the induction. New employees are each likely to have their own individual learning needs; establishing what these are during the induction process is important as is starting individual personal development reviews and setting times for individual interviews to review progress regularly.

Some of the induction may be completed online with materials and tests of knowledge provided on the company intranet site. In some organisations social media is used to gain two way interaction and involvement even before the individual joins the organisation. This helps to ensure employee engagement. The use of online resources also means information can be available to future employees, whether they are full or part-time or in international organisations, wherever the person will be working in the world (CIPD, 2014d).

When new employees actually start work, they will also need to get to know people with whom they will be working, become familiar with their surroundings, learn about their new job and learn about the organisation in which they will be working. Although there is a great deal of information to impart to the new employee, not all of it is needed immediately and in fact there is a danger of overloading the individual with information if it is all given at once. If formal induction courses are run for all new starters then these could be spread over parts of several days, imparting first the most urgent information, such as the geography of the building, canteen arrangements and introductions to supervisors and work colleagues. It may be that the formal courses do not even need to start on the first day, especially if recruitment is sporadic. Small groups of employees may be gathered, perhaps once a month, for the formal induction course providing of course that their immediate induction needs, such as information on safety rules, have been adequately covered.

A formal induction course is useful, as several new starters can be given information at the same time. However, the new employees are likely to be starting different jobs in various departments, so that there is still an important role for their line managers to play in their induction, particularly in carrying out personal development reviews and then tailoring individual learning and development initiatives to meet the specific learning and development needs of the individual in that department. A checklist indicating which topics will be covered, when they will be covered and who will cover them is also extremely useful. This can be signed by the employee when they have gone through all the topics and then stored with their training records. It also provides a useful reminder to all of the need to cover these topics.

Table 8.3 gives an indication of the type of things that need to be covered during an induction period. It is useful to indicate who is responsible for dealing with each topic and when it should be covered. A section for the trainee to sign to say that they have completed each topic would also be useful.

Table 8.3   Sample induction checklist

Topic	Person responsible for covering this topic	Day 1	First week	First month
Reception	Human resource manager	*		
Documentation and introduction to manager	Human resource manager	*		
Hours, clocking on, flexitime, lunch breaks, overtime	Human resource manager	*		
Layout of department, outline of function and introduction to staff	Supervisor	*		
Tour of main work areas, staff restaurant, toilets, fire exits	'Buddy' or person delegated by the supervisor to look after and befriend the new starter	*		
Health and safety rules	Supervisor	*		

Topic	Person responsible for covering this topic	Day 1	First week	First month
The organisation – products, services, the organisation's handbook	Learning and development officer or on company intranet			*
Rules and procedures – discipline and grievance	Human resource manager and on company intranet site		*	
Payment, holiday pay and sickness pay	Human resource manager Support materials on intranet system		*	
Communication and consultation	Learning and development officer			*
Training and development	Learning and development officer			*
Performance appraisal and set-up of personal development plan and reviews	Learning and development officer Additional materials on the intranet system			*
Pensions	Learning and development officer Additional materials on the intranet system			*
The trade union and trade union appointed learning representatives	Shop steward			*

Some of the information will need to be given in a written form, perhaps in a handbook, although increasingly nowadays organisations will keep much of this information on their intranet system. Although much of this information may also have been given verbally in the formal induction course, it is useful to have a source of reference for things such as who to notify when you are ill. This might not have seemed particularly relevant to a new starter, and indeed may not be needed for a year or two, by which time it may have been largely forgotten unless there is a loose-leaf handbook to refer to or preferably an intranet site where the information is easily accessible and kept up to date.

Since it is important not to give too much information, as the new starter may feel overwhelmed, it is better to spread the information over a period of time and alternate with periods where the person is introduced to their new job and given a chance to settle in. After all, that is the reason they have joined the organisation. Even though some organisations may already have given information on their intranet site prior to the person actually joining the organisation, there will still be some things which it is necessary to deliver face to face. In some organisations new recruits are asked to arrive later than the rest of the workforce on their first day, so that those who will be involved in their induction can get things organised and deal with any crises that may occur, and then have time to spend on the new recruit.

It is important to get the induction right as if new employees are not happy they are likely to leave. Crush (2014b) says that in some industries such as the hospitality sector as many as 45 per cent of employees leave within three months of starting and 15 per cent go during the first month. If the new employee comes from another country, or if the work is in an international organisation where workers come from many different countries, a good induction is even more important as there is also likely to be a need to deal with cross-cultural issues to encourage greater understanding and increase tolerance of different ways of working. Every organisation will have a slightly different culture and part of the induction involves the new recruit being initiated into this and becoming a part of the organisation. The induction period provides a useful foundation for this and progress could be reviewed during subsequent personal development reviews. It is sometimes said that it takes around 90 days for a person to become really engaged with the organisation and feel a part of it. Some organisations refer to this process as 'on-boarding' and see the induction continuing with a 30, 60 and 90 day on-boarding plan during which there are regular reviews and discussions with the new recruit (CIPD, 2014d).

The roles of learning and development specialists and line managers

Human resource managers, learning, training and talent development specialists and the line managers all have important roles to play to ensure that the organisation develops in a way which facilitates the learning that the organisation wants to occur, and that a suitable environment is created in which continuous improvement and talent development is actively encouraged. They themselves need to understand the learning process and the key stages in the provision of learning and development activities to ensure that this happens.

The move from training to learning and to talent development also means that different roles need to be adopted by line managers, human resource managers and L&TD specialists, and the growth in flexible working and increased use of technology also means the roles will continue to change as people learn in new ways and at different times. As line managers take increasingly more responsibility for training their own teams the L&TD specialists have to become increasingly flexible, often adopting a facilitator role rather than always appearing to be the expert as the traditional trainer might have been. Harrison (2009), in her typology of future-orientated roles, states that there could be several potential new roles which the specialists in learning, training and talent development might need to adopt such as

- professional advisor,
- knowledge architect,
- brand manager,
- commercial lead,
- learning specialist,
- administrator.

Both the professional advisor and knowledge architect would operate at a very high level within the organisation and would probably be business partners operating at board level. The professional advisor would be involved in advising on the strategies for learning, training and development and ensuring alignment with both the strategic objectives of the organisation (vertical alignment) and with the other HR policies and practices (horizontal alignment).

However, if the role of knowledge architect was adopted by the L&TD specialist within an organisation then the focus would instead be on ensuring that the organisation obtained, maintained and developed knowledge essential to achieving the organisation's strategic objectives.

If the role was that of a brand manager then in some organisations it would be more like a marketing role with the learning, training and talent development specialist developing a L&TD brand that underpinned everything done in the organisation. The brand and way the organisation presented itself to others would be closely linked to the provision of a quality of service or product clearly linked to the learning, training and talent development.

However, if the role was one of providing a commercial lead in that organisation then the focus would be on seeking and creating new markets where the organisation could sell its learning or training or its expertise in talent development. In this instance the learning, training and talent development manager would be promoting its services and skills to other organisations and would seek to make money from them.

In Harrison's view there would still be some organisations where it would be more appropriate to have what might be regarded as a more traditional L&TD specialist who was an expert in all aspects of L&TD and who could analyse L&TD needs, design appropriate strategies to meet those needs, plan and run these events and evaluate them afterwards. They would also provide guidance and support to line managers and others.

The last role in her typology of future-orientated roles is that of administrator and this would be suited to an organisation where there was a great deal of administration to complete in order, perhaps, to secure funding and organise learning and development events that were carried out for others.

Harrison (2009) intended her typology of future-orientated roles for L&TD specialists to promote discussion about the way the role was changing and might develop and there are certainly many examples of people who have these types of L&TD roles today. Some large organisations may adopt several different roles. However, although these changes in role are undoubtedly occurring, you will still find job titles such as training manager being used as different organisations will be at different stages in changing the emphasis from training to L&TD.

The specialists in learning, training and talent development are increasingly adopting more strategic roles within organisations. This also means changes for line managers who now need to understand and encourage learning in their own teams or departments and who often have to organise and run an appropriate learning intervention themselves. There is a clear link between the performance of their teams and meeting their targets for the team and department so this is a vital part of their jobs and one for which they should be suitably prepared and trained.

Changes in technology and the ability to access learning whenever or wherever required on smartphones or tablets also mean further changes in the role and that the specialists also need to update their skills. As learning moves away from the classroom the fact that people can access learning independently creates a need for 'content creators' who are able to sort through the huge amount of information to find the most relevant (Clegg, 2014). There could be quite a choice of roles for the L&TD specialists but whatever role is adopted has to be appropriate to the organisation and to the strategic direction it plans to take.

Trade union learning representatives

As part of the shift from training to learning, and in order to promote learning at all levels and within all organisations, the Employment Act 2002 established a new group known as learning representatives. These learning representatives are appointed by trade unions so only occur in unionised organisations and have several statutory rights. These include the right to time off work in certain circumstances in order to

- analyse learning and training needs,
- provide information or advice relating to any learning or training issues,
- organise specific learning or training,
- consult with the employer about learning and training issues,
- participate themselves in training for their role as a learning representative.

The ACAS (2010) *Code of practice 3: time off for trade union duties and activities* gives further details of these rights. Union members also have the right to time off to discuss issues or attend learning activities organised by trade union-appointed learning representatives, although they do not have to be paid for this time.

> **Pause for thought 8.1**   Compare the role of the union learning representative with what you consider to be the role of the training and L&TD specialists within an organisation. To what extent do the roles differ? To what extent do the roles overlap?

Both the trainers and L&TD specialists and the trade union learning representatives promote learning so to that extent their roles do overlap but their focus will be different. The specialists, according to Harrison (2009), will be concerned that learning and development adds value to the organisation and to make the link between learning and development and the organisation's strategic objectives. They will want to operate at a strategic level and may take on roles such as promoting L&TD, managing knowledge, or generating income from L&TD activities; there will still be many other L&TD specialists involved in running specific training, L&TD activities and in training managers, so they are also able to provide these types of training and learning and development experiences.

Learning representatives will also want to promote learning but they operate at a different level as they try to encourage more of the workforce to become involved in learning. As they are a part of the workforce their role is to reach and inform workers – who might not normally get involved in learning and development activities – to do so: to encourage and discuss options with workers who might have been put off by having to discuss their learning needs with management. If lifelong learning is to become a reality then their role should help to kick-start some learning and development activities for all workers.

The learning representatives have a role to play in fostering a positive attitude towards learning and development and increasing motivation to learn. It has also been claimed that large numbers of workers lack basic skills in numeracy and literacy but have successfully hidden this from their employers for many years. In many organisations L&TD specialists are now working with learning representatives to reach groups of workers who have not traditionally participated in learning and development and who may have poor basic skills which could be holding back their career progression, so the roles of the learning and development specialist and the union learning representative are in many ways complementary.

Conclusion

In this chapter we have provided an introduction to learning, training and talent development and particularly to how you learn so that the intention is that you will have started to reflect on your own learning and will have commenced learning to learn. We have shown that people learn in a variety of ways and that specialist L&TD managers and line managers will need to adapt the learning experiences they provide to suit individuals and groups. However, while individuals often use only one or two preferred learning styles these are not fixed but will vary over time and will be affected by the culture within an organisation or indeed a country.

While the concept of the learning organisation may still be aspirational, organisations wishing to improve learning and develop and retain talent do adopt a wide range of approaches including formal and informal methods. There is an emphasis throughout such organisations on all aspects of L&TD and of identifying and agreeing the learning needs with the people concerned. We have emphasised the need for a systematic approach which helps the organisation to achieve its strategic objectives. All programmes also emphasise the difference that L&TD can make to an organisation by adding value to that organisation and as a powerful means of attracting and retaining talent.

Review questions

You will find brief answers to these review questions on page 472.

1. Many organisations do not provide an adequate induction programme for new employees. Comment critically on the benefits to be gained from implementing a good induction programme, and outline what should be contained in that programme.

2. Critically evaluate the relative effectiveness of on-the-job training and off-the-job training.

Improving your employability

Developing skills in managing self and your own learning

In this chapter we encouraged you to analyse your own learning style and identify how you learn. Learning to learn is a vital skill and reflecting on your learning is an important part. You cannot always rely on external sources such as employers, or even your lecturers, to provide you with learning opportunities, so in this exercise you are not only learning how to learn but are also being proactive about your learning and developing skills of self-management.

In order to develop these skills further write your own learning log for a week or month using the following headings.

1. Describe briefly what learning occurred during this period.
2. What learning styles did you use?
3. Were these the same or different from your usual preferred learning style?
4. Have you tried to be proactive about your own learning and to use different styles to your preferred approach?
5. How will you use what you have learned in the future?
6. How will you continue to develop your skills or knowledge further?

HR in the news

Nations fight global war for talent

By Maxine Boersma

Muhammad Hazim left Malaysia for Coventry and the promise of an accountancy career. Now his home nation wants him back.

The fast growing southeast Asian country needs him – and thousands like him – as it seeks to address a "brain drain", or emigration of skilled professionals, that threatens its ability to fulfil its economic and development goals.

Mr Hazim, 21, is in the first year of an accountancy and finance degree at the University of Warwick. His experience in the UK, he says, has been "nothing less than spectacular – from the chance to volunteer to teach maths to primary school children to acting in a play at Warwick Arts Centre". He has even improved his survival skills – "I finally had to learn to cook as I missed Malaysian food so much," he says.

To lure him back, Malaysia is going to great lengths and with good reason. A 2011 World Bank study estimated the Malaysian diaspora had quadrupled in three decades – for every 10 skilled Malaysians, one elects to leave the country – double the world average.

Malaysia is not alone. Last year, the Associated Chambers of Commerce and Industry of India estimated that Indians studying abroad cost the country as much as $17bn a year in lost revenue. The African brain drain is also acute.

The issue is not confined to emerging nations. Between 1996 and 2011, more than 23,000 scientists left Germany. As a result, German scientists constitute the largest group of foreign researchers in places including the US, the Netherlands and Switzerland. In February, Angela Merkel, Germany's chancellor, was warned that she should implement programmes to entice more of them home.

As for the UK, figures last year from the Organisation for Economic Co-operation and Development (OECD) revealed that 1.3m university-educated Britons are now overseas – higher than for any other developed country.

Even the US is not immune to the drift of the highly educated abroad. There is a certain irony in this, as the term "brain drain" is said to have been coined by the UK's Royal Society to describe the movement of technologists and scientists from postwar Europe to North America.

In his 2014 State of the Union address, President Barack Obama outlined plans to address the nation's need for trained professionals.

Despite the fame and drawing power of Silicon Valley, the US is facing a shortage of IT specialists. This has led Microsoft to highlight an emerging skills shortage as one of its biggest problems.

Developments in the cyber security and cloud computing fields have intensified the need for IT experts, but it can take time to give people the right skills.

The US is a popular destination for high tech employees from India and China (Satya Nadella, who was born in India, is now Microsoft chief executive), but US IT executives are concerned that in this case the government is being a hindrance, rather than help.

They argue that visa restrictions are seriously hampering the smooth flow of IT professionals from abroad.

However, more generally governments and recruitment organisations are making great efforts to encourage a "reverse brain drain". Recruiter Careers in Africa, for example, runs events in Lisbon, New York and London to recruit leading talent from the African diaspora across Europe and North America.

South Africa is experiencing a homeward trend. A 2014 report by Adcorp Holdings revealed 359,000 highly skilled South Africans – about 18 per cent of the total pool of managers and professionals – had returned in the past seven years.

A growing number of Indian professionals, too, is returning home, according to a recent Deloitte study. It linked this to the availability of world class amenities and improved research opportunities.

Another possible factor is the Indian government's schemes to encourage engineers and scientists of Indian origin to apply for research positions. These include the Ramalingaswami Re-entry Fellowship.

Sometimes, however, recruitment programmes fail to entice back the right people. Benjamin Zhai, managing director of the offshore China desk at executive search firm Russell Reynolds Associates, says the imperative should be to retain and attract managerial, not just technical, talent.

A "sea turtle" himself – a Chinese mainlander who was raised in China, worked abroad then later returned – he recalls the shortfall of talent in China that led to the "1,000 Talents Recruitment Programme" in 2008. It was successful in the healthcare, automotive and property sectors, yet did not "address the critical shortage of leadership talent", says Mr Zhai.

Mr Hazim, meanwhile, was one of 4,000 UK Malaysian students who attended a careers fair in London this March run by the United Kingdom and Eire (Ireland) Council of Malaysian Students and Graduan, a careers resource for Malaysian graduates. It is supported by TalentCorp, a Malaysian government-established body to help meet the country's talent needs, and the Institute of Chartered Accountants in England and Wales (ICAEW).

For Johan Merican, TalentCorp chief executive, Malaysia has to "take employers to students" to meet its skills requirements.

"You can have an international career in Malaysia – graduates can obtain ICAEW's international chartered accountancy qualification back home," he says. A tax break also allows returning Malaysian experts to pay 15 per cent income tax for five years rather than the top rate of 25 per cent, he says.

Once qualified, Mr Hazim will indeed return home. "First and foremost, I wish to get a job I will enjoy," he says. "My father told me: 'With passion Hazim, one will go far' and I really believe this... I'm looking for a clear career path with ample growth prospects."

Out of Africa: Countries compete to poach Nigerian doctors

The brain drain of doctors from some African countries is so severe that in 2013 Ethiopia's health minister revealed there are more Ethiopian doctors in Chicago than in Ethiopia.

In Nigeria recently, Saudi Arabia tried to recruit doctors by offering on-the-spot interviews conducted by a government delegation.

Ola Fajemirokun is a UK-based Nigerian medical graduate, specialising in obstetrics and gynaecology. He began working in the NHS in 2002, gaining a training post in 2008, and now hopes to become a consultant.

He was attracted to work in the UK, as Nigeria is a Commonwealth country and he was educated in English – Nigeria's academic structure mirrors that of the UK.

Despite the need for doctors in Nigeria, Mr Fajemirokun sees no "pull" to lure doctors home: "There is a huge shortage of medical specialists because of quality of training, remuneration, medical facilities," he says.

→

"My long-term aim is to return home. However, I can only make a meaningful contribution if there is change in healthcare policy, especially funding. Less than 4 per cent of Nigerian GDP goes to health."

Mr Fajemirokun is not alone. An April 2014 study by University College, London found more than 88,000 foreign doctors are registered to work in the UK, including 27,758 from continental Europe.

Now, the NHS is setting up an assessment centre in India where aspiring trainee doctors can be interviewed via video link. This recruitment drive is in response to current shortages in the UK's accident and emergency departments.

Meanwhile, as foreign students arrive, UK-trained medics are heading to Australia in search of a better lifestyle and remuneration.

 Source: Boesrma, M. (2014) Nations fight global war for talent, FT.com, 12th June.
© The Financial Times Limited 2014. All Rights Reserved.

Questions

1. According to this article what are the key features that attract people to work in a different country?
2. What efforts are countries making to reverse the brain drain?
3. In your view what are the ethical considerations when employing talented people from a third-world country?

What next?

1. The Advisory Conciliation and Arbitration Service (ACAS) provides some excellent opportunities for you to experience e-learning on its website at **www.acas.org.uk**. When on this site click on Training and Business Solutions and then on ACAS learning online. You will need to register to access the online training materials but using them is free and you do not have to be in the UK to use this site (accessed 21.06.14).

   ACAS has developed a range of free e-learning resources and you can undertake short e-learning courses and test your understanding of several topics already covered in earlier chapters of this book, such as equality and diversity and performance management. There are also learning resources which relate to later chapters of this book such as discipline and grievance or redundancy and dismissal.
2. Listen to the two podcasts (CIPD, 2013b, 2014e) which examine different aspects of recent research into the ways in which people learn at **www.cipd.co.uk/podcasts.**
3. Find and read articles about neuroscience and learning. What else is new in this area of research?

References

Advisory, Conciliation and Arbitration Service (2010) *Code of Practice 3: Time Off for Trade Union Duties and Activities*, ACAS (www.acas.org.uk; accessed 27.06.14).

Age Positive (2013) *Employing Older Workers: An Employer's Guide to Today's Multigenerational Workforce*, Department for Work and Pensions (www.gov.uk/government/collections/age-positive; accessed 17.06.14).

Banks, A. and J. McGurk (2014) *Fresh Thinking in Learning and Development: Part 2 Cognition, Decisions and Expertise*, CIPD (www.cipd.co.uk; accessed 16.06.14).

Black, O. (2004) The future's bite, *People Management*, Vol. 10, No. 8, 25.

Brockett, J. (2010) *UK is Ahead of European Rivals in Innovative Learning Methods*, PM Online, 18.6.2010 (www.cipd.co.uk/pm/; accessed 03.07.10).

Brockett, J. (2012) HR Reporter: 'frugal Google' shows learning may have a free future, *People Management*, 21 April (www.cipd.co.uk/pm/; accessed 19.06.14).

Buzan, T. (1982) *Use Your Head*, BBC, London.

Chartered Institute of Personnel and Development (2008) *Supporting, Accelerating and Directing Learning: Implications for Trainers*, CIPD (www.cipd.co.uk; accessed 09.04.15).

Chartered Institute of Personnel and Development (2010) *Pushing the Boundaries of Learning and Development: Podcast 42*, CIPD (www.cipd.co.uk; accessed 19.06.14).

Chartered Institute of Personnel and Development (2013a) *Fact Sheet: E-learning*, CIPD (www.cipd .co.uk; accessed 21.06.14).

Chartered Institute of Personnel and Development (2013b) *Neuroscience and Its Impact on People Development* (no number), CIPD, 30 September (www.cipd.co.uk; accessed 21.06.14).

Chartered Institute of Personnel and Development (2014a) *Fact Sheet: Learning and Talent Development Strategy*, CIPD (www.cipd.co.uk; accessed 20.06.14).

Chartered Institute of Personnel and Development (2014b) *Fact Sheet: Identifying Learning and Development Needs*, CIPD (www.cipd.co.uk; accessed 20.06.14).

Chartered Institute of Personnel and Development (2014c) *Evaluating Learning and Development*, CIPD (www.cipd.co.uk; accessed 20.06.14).

Chartered Institute of Personnel and Development (2014d) *Rethinking Staff Inductions: Podcast 89*, CIPD (www.cipd.co.uk; accessed 20.06.14).

Chartered Institute of Personnel and Development (2014e) *What Neuroscience Tells Us about Insights, Intuition and Creativity: Podcast 90*, CIPD, 7 May (www.cipd.co.uk; accessed 19.06.14).

Chartered Institute of Personnel and Development and Cornerstone (2014) *L&TD: Annual Survey Report 2014*, CIPD (www.cipd.co.uk; accessed 20.06.14).

Clegg, A. (2014) If you think learning belongs in the classroom…enjoy the view as your competitors overtake you, *People Management*, August, 10–11.

Coffield, F. (2008) Next time you see a learning style questionnaire, burn it, *Education Guardian*, 25 July.

Crofts, P. (2004) Support key to success, *People Management*, Vol. 10, No. 11, 55.

Crush, P. (2014a) Could a MOOC help you learn smarter? *People Management*, July, 28–29.

Crush, P. (2014b) How to stop your new joiners quitting, *People Management*, August, 40–41.

Davidson, S. (2002) How to choose the right coach, *People Management*, Vol. 8, No. 10, 54–55.

Egan, J. (2013) *Factsheets: Learning Methods*, CIPD (www.cipd.co.uk; accessed 13.06.14).

Ericsson, K.A., R.T. Krampte and C. Tesch-Romer (1993) The role of deliberate practice in the acquisition of expert performance, *Psychological Review*, Vol. 100, 363–406.

Findlay, J. (2004) Evaluation is no white elephant, *People Management*, Vol. 10, No. 6, 50.

Gladwell, M. (2008) *Outliers: The Story of Success*, Penguin, Harlow.

Harrison, R. (2009) *Learning and Development*, 5th edition, CIPD, London.

Hofmann, A. (2008) Developments in blended learning, *Economics and Organisation of Enterprise*, Vol. 1.1, Institute of Organisation and Management in Industry.

Honey, P. and A. Mumford (1992) *The Manual of Learning Styles*, Peter Honey Publications, Oxford.

Howard-Jones, P. and J. McGurk (2014) *Fresh Thinking in Learning and Development: Part 1 of 3, Neuroscience and Learning*, CIPD (www.cipd.co.uk; accessed 16.06.14).

Jones, A.M. and C. Hendry (1992) *The Learning Organisation: A Review of Literature and Practice*, HRD Partnership, London.

Kolb, D., I. Rubin and J. McIntyre (1974) *Organisational Psychology: An Experiential Approach*, 3rd edition, Prentice-Hall, Harlow.

Pavlov, I. (1927) *Conditioned Reflexes*, Oxford University Press, Oxford.

Pedler, M., J. Burgoyne and T. Boydell (1988) *The Learning Company Project*, Training Agency, London.

Rossett, A. and F. Douglas (2004) The house blend, *People Management*, Vol. 10, No. 8, 36.

Skinner, B.F. (1953) *Science and Human Behaviour*, Free Press, New York.

Sloman, M. (2004) Evaluation and evolution, *People Management*, Vol. 10, No. 14, 50.

South China Morning Post (2009) Deposit to force teachers to stay, *South China Morning Post*, 17 December.

Stewart, J. and C. Rigg (2011) *Learning and Talent Development*, CIPD, London.

Thomson, I. (2004) The power and the impact, *People Management*, Vol. 10, No. 8, 15.

Training and Coaching Today (2008) Blended learning: the experts' opinions, Issue 1, September, RBI (www.xperthr.co.uk; accessed 08.08.10).

Winter, B., C. Breitenstein, F. Mooren, K. Voelker, M. Fobker, A. Lechtermann, K. Krueger, A. Fromme, C. Korsukewitz, A. Floel and S. Knecht (2007) High impact running improves learning, *Neurobiology of Learning and Memory*, Vol. 87, 597–609.

Wolff, C. (2009) Managing learning and development in a recession: the 2009 IRS survey, *IRS Employment Review*, 21 September, Issue 929, IRS (www.xperthr.co.uk; accessed 20.06.14).

Wolff, C. (2010a) IRS line manager training survey 2010: how to get results, *IRS Employment Review*, 5 May, IRS (www.xperthr.co.uk; accessed 20.06.14).

Wolff, C. (2010b) XpertHR induction survey 2010: delivery and evaluation, *IRS Employment Review*, 1 November, IRS (www,xperthr.co.uk; accessed 20.06.14).

Further study

Books and reports

Advisory, Conciliation and Arbitration Service (2014) *Recruitment and Induction*, ACAS (www.acas .org.uk; accessed 27.06.14).
A very useful guide to this subject.

Harrison, R. (2009) *Learning and Development*, 5th edition, CIPD, London.
An excellent textbook for those who wish to study the subject of learning and development in more depth.

Stewart, J. and C. Rigg (2011) *Learning and Talent Development*, CIPD, London.
This is another excellent textbook that covers various aspects of learning and development. It aims to provide a thorough guide to the whole subject of L&TD.

Articles

There are many specialist journals covering the subject of training, learning and talent development, including the following:

Coaching at Work
Development and Learning in Organizations
Human Resource Development International
Human Resource Development Quarterly
Talent Development and Excellence
Training and Development
Training Journal

Internet

Apprenticeships and Traineeships (England and Wales)   **www.apprenticeships.org.uk**
This provides advice and information about apprenticeships in England and Wales.

Apprenticeships (Scotland)   **www.apprenticeshipsinscotland.com/**
This provides similar advice and guidance for those interested in apprenticeships in Scotland.

Chartered Institute of Personnel and Development   **www.cipd.co.uk**
There is a wide range of information on this site about all aspects of HRM, including learning, training and talent development.

Department for Education   **https://www.gov.uk/government/organisations/department-for -education**
The department is responsible for education and children's services in England and has information and data about education and support for children and young people.

The Information Network on Education in Europe   **www.eurydice.org**
This site provides information and analysis of European education systems and policies.

Investors in People UK   **www.investorsinpeople.co.uk/**
Investors in People UK (IIP) provide a framework for achieving high performance in organisations and those organisations that meet their standards can gain a form of accreditation. This site provides information about the standards and the ways to achieve a high level of performance by investing in and training people.

learndirect   **www.learndirect.co.uk**
There is a wide range of information on this site about qualifications, apprenticeships and skills for work.

Skills Development Scotland   **www.myworldofwork.co.uk/**
This site provides advice and guidance about learning and training opportunities in Scotland.

The National Academic Recognition Information Centre for UK   **http://ecctis.co.uk/naric/**
There is information here about vocational, academic and professional skills and qualifications from around the world.

Qualifications and Curriculum Authority   **www.qca.org.uk**
This organisation is responsible for the national qualifications framework and this site provides information about the national curriculum with information for all age groups.

Pay and reward systems

Objectives

By the end of this chapter you will be able to:

- explain the main factors that influence the choice of a particular pay and reward system and the advantages and disadvantages of different types of systems

- explain the importance of developing a pay and reward strategy for an organisation

- explain the process of job evaluation and how to use particular job evaluation systems

- identify current issues relating to equal pay in organisations

- identify potential ethical and environmental issues about pay and reward.

We have indicated in previous chapters that human resource management is concerned that people should work as effectively as possible for the organisation, and that one of the ways in which the organisation attempts to achieve this is by using an appropriate system of pay and reward. The system that is adopted must, as stated in Chapter 5, be in line with and support the key elements of the strategic plan and organisations should develop a pay and reward strategy that suits their particular organisation and the mix of generations of staff within it.

Pay and reward is a key element in performance management and is a vital part of an organisation's HR strategies for the attraction and retention of staff. As we have already discussed in earlier chapters, the economic situation and social and demographic changes mean that organisations have to be flexible to respond both to changes in the financial environment and to the expectations of different generations of workers, so the pay and reward system should be reviewed regularly to ensure that it continues to achieve its aims. In the past this has sometimes been an area of HR that was neglected, with some organisations not thinking about the strategic impact of their pay and reward systems

Did you know?

According to Paul Mason 'Wages as a share of UK GDP have fallen by around 10 percentage points since 1973. And now we are in the seventh straight year of falling real wages.' That means that for many there is a temptation to move into the grey economy and to do dodgy things.

(*Source:* Mason, 2014)

or the message they give to employees. The economic situation and scandals over excessive bonuses has helped to focus attention on this area so more HR departments are now starting to think about how to use pay and reward to keep the talent they have, or to attract new talent. In this chapter we shall be examining a variety of payment systems and discussing the philosophies on which they are based as well as the circumstances and the people or groups of workers who may be attracted to and motivated by particular payment systems. People also need to feel that they are paid fairly and that they can live on the amount that they have been paid, so the minimum wage and the living wage are also important. A growing inequality in society can also have profound social repercussions since if people working on low wages are struggling to make ends meet some may be tempted to work in the grey economy.

Definitions

Before we proceed, it will be useful to explain and define some of the words we shall use throughout this chapter. According to the CIPD (2014a), 'historically, the aims of reward were to attract, retain and motivate staff. Salaries were what attracted them to an organisation, benefits kept them there, while bonus and incentive schemes motivated them.' However, it is not always so simple and, as we discussed in Chapters 1 and 8, many young people in Generation Y may also be attracted to an organisation and may stay with it because of the opportunities for learning and talent development that it provides: they may choose to work as volunteers in a not-for-profit organisation because the organisation's values and corporate and social responsibility policy are in line with their own values. Other perhaps slightly older workers may be attracted to an organisation where there are other benefits such as excellent holidays, better pension provision or opportunities for more flexibility in their working week, while those regarded as knowledge workers may want to achieve success in their chosen area and to achieve recognition for their successes. Since all organisations will have different strategic objectives and will employ different mixes of generations of workers and of part-time and full-time workers, it is important to ensure that the pay and reward strategy chosen helps attract, motivate, engage and retain their workers so that they can achieve their strategic objectives.

Several words are commonly used to refer to the payment made to people at work, and these include the terms 'pay', 'reward', 'wages' and 'salaries'. We shall also explain another term used in connection with pay and reward systems, 'job evaluation', before examining some of the different types of pay and reward system that are available for an employer to use. We have chosen to call the chapter Pay and reward so will start with these terms.

'Pay' is the most straightforward term and normally refers to a monetary award for work done, but it can also include monetary payments which do not directly relate to work done such as sickness pay, maternity pay and pension arrangements.

'Reward' is frequently used nowadays to refer to payment systems, especially since many payment systems are strongly motivational to encourage people to work harder and then reward them for their extra effort. The word 'reward' is also useful as it could also apply to either a monetary or non-monetary reward.

We have chosen to use the phrase 'pay and reward' in this chapter since systems of both basic pay and incentivised pay and reward exist today and organisations have to be increasingly flexible in their pay and reward strategies so are likely to use a mixture of approaches. Other terms that are commonly used in pay and reward are discussed next.

'Wages' refers to weekly pay and may be based on an hourly rate of pay, with possible deductions for lateness or absence, and this hourly rate is often the rate that is referred to in negotiations. Wage earners are often still paid in cash and are less likely to have benefits such as luncheon vouchers, company cars or expenses. Organisations paying wages have traditionally expected short-term thinking from their employees, and incentives for wage earners are also usually quick and precise. There has been less job security for wage earners than for salaried employees and that is particularly the case for those on zero hours contracts where the emphasis has often been on a short-term relationship with the employing organisation.

'Salary' refers to monthly pay, and these monthly payments are normally expressed as an annual salary, this being the figure that is normally referred to in negotiations on salary. Those who are salaried normally have their salaries paid directly into a bank or building society and they are also likely to have several fringe benefits, such as company cars, extra payments for additional qualifications or luncheon vouchers. Some salaried workers get immediate incentives added to their incomes, but traditionally the most widely held incentive was supposed to be a much longer-term consideration, that of good prospects. Salaried employees either are in managerial posts or tend to identify very closely with management, and they perceive themselves to be on a lengthy career progression with the peak of their earning power achieved relatively late in life. In addition, until fairly recently they have expected to have long-term job security.

> ### Did you know?
>
> Up to 500,000 people are employed on zero hours contracts with no guaranteed hours so their working weeks and pay vary from week to week.
>
> (*Source:* Marlow and Goodman, 2013)

Nowadays there is also much less job security, and career progression for salaried employees as promotion and even job security cannot be regarded as automatic. Many organisations in which salaried jobs were normally secure have removed whole strata of managers and during the recession may not have been replacing people who left or offering opportunities for promotion. The growing trend towards the acquisition of a flexible workforce with increasing numbers of part-timers and contract workers has also led to a blurring of distinctions between the groups, as have the efforts that HR professionals have made during the recent recession to keep workers but perhaps on altered forms of contracts, working fewer hours than before.

Pay structures

All but the smallest of organisations have to create some form of pay structure in order to provide a logical way to pay and reward people. According to the CIPD (2014b), having a payment structure achieves three main aims:

1. It ensures that the pay structure is clearly aligned with the organisation's strategic objectives and rewards behaviours that support those objectives.
2. It provides for an orderly way for pay increases to occur and for career progression to be made clear.
3. It helps to ensure that the basis for the pay is fair and that it avoids illegality and unfair gender bias.

There are several ways, or indeed combinations of ways, that can be chosen to form the basis of pay structures but when designing these there are choices that the organisation needs to make about the number and width of the pay grades or pay bands within the structure. Many organisations, particularly in the public sector, have harmonised their entire wage and salary systems of payment into a common pay spine (CIPD, 2014b).

Job evaluation

In order to achieve this type of orderly pay system many organisations will use some form of job evaluation. This will be discussed fully later in this chapter. ACAS (2014a) defines job evaluation thus: 'Job evaluation is a method of determining on a systematic basis the relative importance of a number of jobs.' As you can see, job evaluation does not actually determine rates of pay that any individual employee should receive, but it can be used as a systematic basis for determining differences in jobs and subsequently the different pay levels for those jobs. As such it seems to us to be an appropriate topic to discuss in this chapter as many organisations use it as the basis for determining their pay structures.

Did you know?

Douglas McGregor (1960) stated that the way managers perceived work and employees would affect the way in which the employees actually carried out their work. He said that there were two contrasting assumptions that managers made about the behaviour of employees, which he called theory X and theory Y.

Theory X

A manager who adopts the theory X viewpoint would tend to assume that the average worker will dislike work and avoid it if they can, and will only be made to work by a mixture of control and threats. A 'carrot or stick' approach is what is generally seen to be appropriate here. The use of the words 'compensation' and 'reward' would seem to fit this perspective, and to lead to the idea of management needing to provide either control or incentives to motivate the employee to work effectively.

Theory Y

Theory Y assumes that work is a natural and welcome activity which need not be controlled by the manager, as the employee will seek responsibility and will be motivated by the work itself. Managers who hold a theory Y view are not going to be particularly interested in providing control or incentives, and so the words 'reward' and 'compensation' seem less appropriate for them. Instead these managers are more likely to be concerned with having a fair, easy-to-understand payment system and are also more likely to involve workers in its design.

The main influences on payment systems

What the organisation decides to pay staff will depend on many factors, some of which are under the control of the organisation and relate to its strategic plan and some of which are external, such as the economy.

Activity 9.1

We have provided you with a selection of job titles and you have to decide how much to pay these staff. You are to consider who you think ought to be paid the most rather than considering what actually happens in reality.

1. Put the jobs listed below in order of importance, that is with number 1 being the job that you judge should be paid the most.

2. List the factors that will influence how much you will pay these staff.

Waiter or waitress	_____
Nurse	_____
Sales assistant (clothes shop)	_____
Car park attendant	_____
Office cleaner	_____
Accountant	_____
Police officer	_____
Receptionist	_____
Teller (bank)	_____
Warehouse supervisor	_____
University lecturer	_____
Truck driver	_____
Secretary	_____
Traffic warden	_____
Security guard	_____
Safety officer (manufacturing company)	_____
Warehouse picker	_____
Doctor	_____
Human resource manager	_____
Church minister	_____
Fruit picker	_____
Ambulance paramedic	_____
Transport manager	_____
Computer services officer	_____
Lawyer	_____
Undertaker	_____
Professional football player	_____
IT consultant	_____

3. Compare your order with others and try to reach agreement about a list of factors that should be taken into account when you are making these decisions.

Discussion of Activity 9.1

The relative worth of these jobs is likely to vary according to the type of organisation, and your ranking is likely to vary compared with that of your colleagues because you have been highly subjective. You should think about what influenced your choice of each job's worth. Did you have knowledge of some jobs? Did you most value strength, skill, level of responsibility or a caring response, or were you influenced by people you know who do some of these jobs, or by your own career aspirations? There will be many highly subjective influences on your decision.

Did you know?

The 10 best jobs in 2014, in terms of pay, were as follows:
1. Head of company or organisation – average pay before tax £107,703
2. Aircraft pilots – average pay before tax £90,146
3. Marketing and sales directors – average pay before tax £82,963
4. Information technology directors – average pay before tax £80,215
5. Financial institution directors (including heads of banks and building societies) – average pay before tax £78,782
6. Public relations directors – average pay before tax £77,619
7. Financial managers and directors – average pay before tax £75,416
8. Air traffic controllers – average pay before tax £75,416
9. Rail engineers (including aircraft engineers, ship and hovercraft engineers and other transport professionals) – average pay before tax £74,402
10. Company lawyers – average pay before tax £73,425.

(*Source*: Ferguson, 2014)

Many other factors may influence the relative worth of jobs. Your list is likely to include at least some of the following:

- what the organisation can afford to pay,
- what other organisations in the area are paying for similar jobs,
- changes in rates of pay in particular markets,
- legislation and the minimum wage,
- trade union or worker demands,
- government initiatives,
- the scarcity of particular skills,
- the state of the economy,
- the introduction of new technology,
- the relative worth of jobs as rated by a job evaluation exercise,
- the actual performance of the person in the job.

As you can see from this list, an organisation does not have a completely free hand when it decides how to pay someone. In a CIPD survey of reward (2013) the top three factors that affected organisation's pay review were

1. its ability to pay,
2. the rate competitors were paying,
3. movement in market rates.

Many factors influence the decision of how and what to pay, and we shall discuss these more fully in turn.

What the organisation can afford to pay

Obviously, no organisation can afford to put itself out of business by paying more than it can afford, so this has to be one of the first factors that influence how much an organisation will pay. However, the way organisations view pay and reward has a big effect on what they decide to pay and the way they pay. Some organisations tend to see pay and reward as a cost and therefore try to keep down their costs. This is particularly true in organisations where there is no rigorous method for assessing the return on investment of the pay and reward strategies. In 2013 32 per cent of the employers in a survey undertaken by the CIPD said that their pay system was a fixed cost while a further 32 per cent said that their pay system was split 90:10 between fixed and variable costs though most wanted to increase flexibility in the way they rewarded staff, to increase the amount that was paid in variable pay and benefits to their employees and to reduce the amount of their fixed pay (CIPD, 2013).

What other organisations in the area are paying for similar jobs

Most organisations will at least take account of the market rates that other organisations are paying. The organisation may refer to published pay surveys or do its own survey of the local area to establish rates that others are paying for similar jobs.

The CIPD (2010) survey of pay trends found that the four most common methods to establish market rates were to

- use local, national or international pay surveys as appropriate,
- review other people's job advertisements,
- use national research from specialist organisations such as Incomes Data Services (IDS) or Industrial Relations Services (IRS), or
- use job-evaluated pay databases.

If the organisation can afford to, and if it wants to be able to select the best employees, it may choose to pay slightly more than the going rate. This can cause a spiral of wage increases as other employers retaliate by increasing their wages. When labour is scarce or there is demand for people with a particularly scarce skill this is one way in which many employers will behave.

Even when employing people on a small scale, the rate of payment can have quite an effect locally. Sometimes people from London, or perhaps those moving to or buying second homes in countries such as France or Spain, may have an effect on local wages when they employ a local gardener or cleaner and pay much more than the local rate. Those with second homes will probably be able to afford to pay good wages, particularly if they are used to paying for similar services in a more expensive area such as London. When they pay these same rates to local cleaners they obviously attract good staff, but are then accused by other locals of poaching their cleaners and of setting rates that the locals cannot afford to match. In this situation the second home owners get excellent cleaners but may not make many friends.

Changes in rates of pay in particular markets

If the organisation is part of a larger organisation, there may be national or international agreements that will affect what is actually paid, and the human resource manager also needs to assess these rates.

Nowadays as travel to other countries is easier and quicker than in the past, pay rates often have global implications. In recent years poor pay for nurses in Britain, and the subsequent staff shortages, have meant hospitals and NHS trusts increasingly had to search further afield for qualified nurses. Many have carried out recruitment drives which attracted nurses from countries such as the Philippines to Britain.

What is considered poor pay in one country may seem a fortune to an individual coming from a poorer country. Individually they gain an opportunity to travel and broaden their own experience and may even be able to save money to send home to their families. This may in turn create skills shortages for those countries losing people and consequently some governments have requested that Britain does not carry out recruitment drives in their country.

There may be other ethical and legal issues where companies employ large numbers of low-skill migrant workers who come to this country in search of jobs and better pay than that found in their home country. While they are recruited to fill skills gaps and work in jobs which many UK workers are unwilling to do, in some cases they have been exploited. There have been claims that they are

Did you know?

The Gangmasters Licensing Authority (GLA) was set up in April 2005 to end the exploitation of workers in agricultural, horticultural, shellfish-gathering and associated processing and packaging activities.
In April 2006 the GLA began operating a licensing scheme for providers (gangmasters) supplying workers into these industries.

(*Source*: Health and Safety Executive, 2007)

treated badly and are not even paid the legal minimum wage. In 2007 administrators were called into Bomfords, a company which supplied more than 50 per cent of large UK supermarkets with vegetables such as spring onions, beans and peas. According to Felicity Lawrence (2007),

> the company which has a turnover of £150m a year and employs more than 2,000 people at the height of the season – the majority migrants who pick and pack its vegetables – was recruiting its temporary staff through seven agencies. Each of those agencies was found to be breaking the law and had its licence revoked. Some of the Poles employed by one of the agencies were in such fear that the GLA revoked its gangmaster's licence on the spot.

Lawrence (2007) claimed 'Bomford's offered gangmasters an hourly rate for workers that made it all but certain that these gangmasters would be breaking the law'. Subsidies to workers such as working tax credits, and financial incentives to employers to take on apprentices may contribute to keeping wages low and may stop employers paying a proper rate for the job.

The global effects of pay rates are not all in one direction. In the 1960s and 1970s there was talk of a 'brain drain' from Britain and more recently similar problems have arisen as some senior academics and particularly scientists go to America in search of better pay and working conditions and for better research facilities. Multinational organisations also have a range of other issues to consider in relation to achieving equity and fairness in their payment systems and these aspects of international payment will be discussed later in the chapter.

Legislation

All organisations are affected by the law of the country in which they operate, even if they are bringing in migrant workers. In Britain they will also be affected by European Union legislation. The legislation that will have most effect on payment or reward systems is the Equality Act 2010 which harmonised and replaced much of the previous legislation such as the Equal Pay Act 1970, which dealt with differences in pay between men and women, and the other equality legislation that dealt with prohibited forms of discrimination such as race or disability. For example, in the past a person claiming discrimination because they were paid less than someone of a different race would have been dealt with under the Race Relations Act 1976. Since October 2010 all claims for equal pay which related to protected characteristics such as race or disability have been dealt with by the Equality Act 2010 (ACAS, 2014b).

The Employment Rights Act 1996 and the National Minimum Wage Act 1998 are also of importance in setting out rules relating to pay and the minimum wage and these two pieces of legislation will also be discussed in more detail here.

The Equality Act 2010

Equal pay

According to ACAS (2014b), 'the Act retains the framework that was previously in place' and this means that normally when claiming equal pay it will be necessary to compare the pay of one member of staff with someone of the opposite sex who works for that organisation. However, in some organisations the employees doing a particular job may all be of the same sex and the Equality Act made it possible for them to also bring a claim. If a claimant can provide evidence that they would have received better pay from that employer if they were a different sex it may be possible for them to bring a claim (ACAS, 2014b).

It is also illegal to pay different rates to men and women who do different jobs, but whose jobs have been rated the same under a job evaluation scheme. The whole topic of job evaluation and problems of fairness and equality within job evaluation will be discussed later in this chapter.

Equal value

The concept of equal pay for work of equal value had been established by the 1983 Equal Pay Amendment Regulations and continues in the 2010 Equality Act. This means it is also possible for men and women who are doing totally different jobs and who are paid differently to bring a case against their employer if they feel that their job is of the same value to the organisation as the job done by the higher paid group. The legislation is complex, and most who have brought cases have been supported by their trade union or the Equality and Human Rights Commission. Criteria such as the level of qualifications required, the level of effort or skill involved, and the amount of responsibility and decision making involved in each of the jobs are factors that are likely to be taken into account. In a tribunal hearing of this type, the person of the opposite sex with whom the claimant wishes to compare themselves has in the past had to be identified. As we discussed earlier, under the Equality Act 2010 this problem may be overcome to some extent if the claimant can provide evidence that they would have received better pay from that employer if they were a different sex and it may now be possible for them to bring a claim on this basis.

Pause for thought 9.1 Do you think a real comparator should be used in equal pay or equal value cases or should there be the option of using a hypothetical comparator if there is no suitable comparator of the opposite sex within the organisation?

Secrecy

One barrier to achieving equal pay in the past was the fact that employees in some organisations did not know what others were paid and were not allowed to discuss their pay as this had been written into their contracts. The Equality Act 2010 opened up opportunities for discussion as the act makes it unlawful for an employer to prevent or restrict employees from having a discussion about pay that could be related to protected characteristics, though the employer can still insist pay rates are kept confidential from people outside the organisation.

Activity 9.2

Poppy works full-time in a small bookshop. There are four shop assistants, two male and another female who are all employed to work the same hours and do the same job. She suffers from depression and has to sometimes have some time off work when it gets particularly bad. One of her colleagues has dropped her payslip on the floor and when

Poppy picks it up and hands it to her she realises she is being paid less than her. She suspects that she is paid less than all the other three full-time members of staff and asks them all how much they are paid. The manager of the shop is very unhappy when he hears of this and asks Poppy to attend a disciplinary interview in which she is told that this information is confidential.

1. What would be the situation if Poppy found by discussing the rates of pay that the two female members of staff were paid less than the two male members of staff?
2. What is the situation as Poppy definitely is being paid less than the other female member of staff?
3. What are Poppy's rights concerning the issue of discussing the pay of the other staff and relating to the disciplinary action taken against her?

Discussion of Activity 9.2

1. If Poppy discovered that she was being paid less than the two male shop assistants for doing the same job then that would be a straightforward case of direct sex discrimination.
2. If Poppy is paid less than the other female member of staff she may be able to show that this is because of her disability. Disability is one of the protected characteristics referred to in the Equality Act 2010. Poppy can only make an equal pay claim comparing against someone of the opposite sex but she may be able to claim direct discrimination because of her disability. She might be able to bring a claim for combined (dual) discrimination if the men are also paid more than her.
3. When she is disciplined for discussing pay with the other members of staff this is unlawful and she could make a claim for victimisation.

Gender pay reporting

The Equality Act 2010 was intended to broaden the scope of previous legislation and from 2011 public authorities with more than 150 employees have had to produce annual statistics relating to gender pay gaps and also to ethnic minority and disability employment rates (CIPD, 2014c). The aim is to provide a transparent pay system so that gender pay gaps can be easily identified and men and women can easily compare pay.

The act originally envisaged that similar requirements for equal pay audits would be compulsory in the private sector from 2013. This changed, however, and in 2011 the Home Office said that alongside the requirement for the public sector to undertake gender pay reviews there would be a voluntary gender equality analysis. This voluntary reporting of gender equality applies primarily in the private and not-for-profit sectors and is applicable particularly to employers with more than 150 employees. The government hopes that this will help organisations to identify and act on any unfairness based on gender without it becoming necessary to introduce further regulations. This has been expressed as the Think, Act and Report framework.

1. **Think** – employers in the private or not-for-profit sectors should review their workforce and pay and check if they could do more.
2. **Act** – employers should then do something to address any problems or differences to ensure that they are maximising the use of all their talent regardless of gender.
3. **Report** – on achievements – this could involve gathering various statistics so that these could form the basis for action. The data which needs to be collected could vary depending on the organisation but could include measures such as

- the gender composition of whole workforce;
- an analysis of the representation of men and women at different levels in different jobs. This could include an analysis of
  - pay by gender,
  - promotion rates by gender,
  - take-up of flexible working by gender,
  - or measures of numbers of employees returning from maternity leave.

- Pay measures – more statistics about pay need to also be collected and these could include data about some or all of the following:
  - full-time workers gender pay gap,
  - part-time workers gender pay gap,
  - overall pay gap,
  - differences in average basic pay and total average earnings between men and women by grade and job types,
  - differences in the starting salaries of men and women,
  - measuring the reward element for each group at different levels.

- Narrative to contextualise and support measures taken:
  - Here the employer should describe what they have done and whether a pay audit has been completed. This can then be used in a positive way to ensure transparency and to tell both current and future employees, shareholders and customers the organisation's attitude towards gender equality and steps taken to address any imbalances found.
  - Staff satisfaction surveys may also be useful as a way of checking on current state of gender equality and results after changes have been made (ACAS, 2014c).

There are concerns about whether such voluntary gender pay reporting will in itself be sufficient to solve the pay gap between men and women. If implemented it will provide information so comparisons can be made between the pay of men and women in the same organisation, but inequalities start much earlier and may be formed by attitudes in society and the career choices and qualifications chosen at school or university (Cotton, 2009).

The Employment Rights Act 1996

The Employment Rights Act 1996 is a consolidation act which brings together previous legislation relating to

Did you know?

One of the causes for the differences in pay is segregation of jobs:

Three quarters of women work in sectors which are sometimes referred to as the 'five Cs': cleaning, catering, caring, cashiering and clerical jobs.

(*Source:* Welfare, 2006)

A study of gender equality across Europe has estimated that if full gender equality was achieved it would result in an increase in gross domestic product in Europe of between 15 per cent and 45 per cent and in the UK of potentially a 35 per cent increase in gross domestic product. So there is a clear business case for gender equality in the labour market.

(*Source:* Wild, 2010)

employment rights. Under the Employment Rights Act 1996 an employer is not allowed to make deductions from an employee's wages except in the following circumstances:

- When deductions are authorised by law, such as tax or National Insurance contributions or orders such as a court order relating to the provision of maintenance.
- When there is a statement in the employee's written contract which specifies that certain deductions may be made from wages and when the worker has already given consent in writing to the deduction, for example to pay membership fees for a sports or social club or when deductions are agreed for lateness or poor work.
- Accidental overpayment of wages, or of expenses, even though this is likely to be the fault of the employer if this overpayment is due to a mistake of fact and if the employee realising that they have been overpaid does not report this to their employer. However, if this overpayment is due to a misunderstanding or mistake in law, such as a misunderstanding of the Minimum Wage Act, then these overpayments would not be recoverable (Marson, 2014).
- When the employee has been absent from work due to strike or other industrial action it is permissible for the employer to deduct money from the employee's wages.
- In retail organisations, employers may also deduct money from wages to make good any cash deficiency in the till or any shortfall in stock. This deduction should not exceed 10 per cent of the wages due to the employee concerned on a particular day and the deduction must also be made within 12 months from the date that the discrepancy or shortfall in stock was discovered.

The National Minimum Wage Act 1998

The National Minimum Wage Act 1998 established a single national minimum rate with no variation for regions, jobs, size of organisation or industrial sector. Differences in the minimum wage rate will be allowed, however, based on age and this has not changed in spite of the changes to the legislation relating to age. The national minimum wage is supposed to provide a degree of protection for some of the lowest paid groups of workers as it applies not just to full- and part-time employees but also to workers paid by piecework, to homeworkers, agency workers, commission workers and casual workers. So the migrant workers involved in fruit picking who were discussed earlier in the chapter are among those who should be covered by it. However, Professor George Bain, the founding father of the minimum wage, who chaired the low pay commission when it was originally introduced, feels that the minimum wage is no longer achieving its main purpose and must change in order to tackle Britain's low pay problem (Allen, 2014). Although the minimum wage legislation does apply to all employers regardless of their size, the type of business or the region in which they are based, there are still certain groups who are exempt from its provisions. The main groups which do not qualify for the minimum wage are:

- the self-employed,
- volunteers,
- students working as part of their undergraduate or postgraduate degree programme,

Did you know?

It is not always clear what should count in calculations for the minimum wage and investigations by the National Minimum Wage Enforcement team showed nearly 3,000 care staff had not been paid for travel between visits and in 2014 they were due to receive shares of £600,000 in arrears!

(*Source: People Management*, 2014a, p. 17)

- workers on specified training schemes,
- residents of some religious communities,
- prisoners,
- the armed forces.

From 1 October 2014 the adult standard national minimum wage rate for workers aged 21 and over is £6.50 per hour while the rate for workers aged 18–20 inclusive is £5.13 per hour. The youth rate for 16- and 17-year-old workers is £3.79 per hour. There is also an apprentice rate which is £2.73 per hour for those apprentices who are under 19 or who are aged 19 or over but are in the first year of their apprenticeship (Gov.UK, 2014).

These rates are usually updated each year. Employers have to keep records for national minimum wage purposes and employees should have access to these records with a right to complain to an employment tribunal if the employer fails to give them the required access to the records. The penalty to an employer who fails to pay the minimum wage to their workers can range from £5,000 up to £20,000.

Trade union and worker demands

It is important to consider the views of both trade unions and employees in general, and any payment system that an organisation may design needs to be introduced after full discussion and consultation with employees and trade unions. The most effective payment systems will have been selected to meet the needs of both the organisation and the workforce, will have the commitment of all groups and will have been developed, introduced and updated with the participation of employee representatives, whether or not they are members of a trade union. In 2010 the Nationwide Building Society showed how to achieve this and won a CIPD People Management Award for their innovative review of their pay and bonus system which staff helped to design. Nationwide's previous scheme had become outdated and focused too much on volume instead of value, was not very cost effective and did not differentiate sufficiently clearly between high and low performers. Changes needed trade union support as they would form a part of the employees' contracts. Nationwide talked fully with everyone so all generations of workers were consulted, listened to what employees said they wanted and gained full union support. In 2009 Nationwide launched their new total reward package which succeeded in increasing sales performance by 184 per cent of the target in the first quarter and which received excellent feedback from employees. This organisation also clearly had tools in place to measure the return on investment of its reward strategy (*People Management*, 2010a, p. 12).

The living wage

As the cost of living has risen faster than wages there have recently been demands for a so-called living wage as a way to ensure that workers on low salaries, particularly in expensive areas such as London, can afford to live. This goes beyond the minimum wage but is voluntary rather than a legal requirement. The Living Wage Foundation, established in 2011, is a national initiative to encourage employers to pay a living wage. This is based on the basic cost of living and is updated annually. At the time of writing in November 2014 the living wage for London is £9.15 per hour and the national living wage in the rest of the country is £7.85.

Employers who sign up to the living wage gain accreditation and to date over 1,000 employers have done so. In London there are over 2,200 employees working for companies with contracts from the Greater London Authority who are now paid the living wage and according to Boris Johnson (2014), Mayor of London, 'paying the living wage is not just morally right, but makes good business sense too'. Many employers in all parts of the country have claimed benefits as a result of introducing the living wage. These include: enhanced quality of work, less absenteeism, improved recruitment and retention and increased awareness by consumers of their organisation's ethical position.

Government initiatives

The government can have an effect on the supply of labour as it introduces various training initiatives for adults or young people who are facing unemployment. This should have the effect of providing people with relevant skills that employers need, but it also has an effect on wage expectations, since if people are used to receiving a very low training allowance they are likely to feel pleased if they get a job that pays more than this, even if it is still a comparatively low wage.

The scarcity of particular skills

Even in years where there has been high unemployment, there has also been a scarcity in some industries of particular types of skilled workers. This may be due to failure in the past to train people adequately, but it appears that there is often a mismatch between the skills that employers require and the skills that those who are without jobs can offer. In a situation such as this, the relatively small number of people who do have the necessary skills can command high wages or salaries and may move from one organisation to another as different employers try to outbid each other for their scarce skills.

The state of the economy

We have already mentioned that the availability of labour and the scarcity of particular skills will have an effect on the wages paid. Other economic factors such as inflation will also have an effect, as in times of high inflation there will be increasing pressure from workers to increase salaries to keep pace with, or get ahead of, inflation. In the recent economic downturn in 2009 the private sector suffered most, but with government cuts planned across most areas and with more planned for the public sector the situation is likely to be more difficult for workers in that area.

New technology

The relative pay levels of people in different jobs can change over time, for example when new skills have to be learnt with the introduction of new technology, so that a particular group of workers change from being of low skill level to needing a high level

Did you know?

In China there already exists a fully robot-staffed restaurant where the cooking and serving is all provided by robots.

(*Source:* Somerset Webb, 2014)

of technical expertise. This change in skill level is likely to be reflected in a demand for higher wages. However, it is claimed that as many as a third of jobs will be replaced by software, robots or some form of smart machine by 2025 (Somerset Webb, 2014). According to Merryn Somerset Webb (2014) 'this is not just about nasty capitalists trying to avoid paying a living wage: ordering by machine is quicker and better. Robots don't get sick, get pregnant, ask for more money, argue about repetitive tasks'. So technology could bring positive benefits to some in terms of improved wages for those with relevant skills but for others could mean a loss of jobs.

The relative worth of each job as rated by a job evaluation exercise

Job evaluation is a way of rating the value to the organisation of the jobs that people do. It does not in itself decide what pay should be awarded to each job, but it is a systematic way of comparing different jobs so that this can be used as the basis for forming a payment system. The various ways in which job evaluation can be carried out and the different types of scheme will be discussed later in this chapter.

The performance of the individual employee in the job

In many organisations it will also be important to assess the effectiveness of the person doing the job. Whether this happens will depend on the type of payment system used and the organisation's views on collectivism or individualism with regard to payments. Organisations that favour collectivism will want to minimise differences in pay between employees as this may avoid costly or time-wasting disputes, while other organisations will want to pay everyone individual rates as far as possible in order to reward each person for their efforts, and these two perspectives will result in a variety of differing types of payment system.

It is clear that the last two factors are of great importance to payment systems, so we shall now go on to discuss each in detail.

Job evaluation schemes

Very few organisations will pay all the people who work for them exactly the same regardless of the job they do or how well they do that job. Organisations do have to have regard to equality legislation and create a fair and transparent system for pay and reward, so most organisations seek to find ways to compare the worth of different jobs to the organisation, as well as a person's performance in each job. We considered in Chapter 7 the ways in which individual performance may be assessed, but here we shall concentrate on ways of comparing the relative worth of different jobs. If organisations were to base decisions about the relative worth of different jobs on managerial whims, they would be accused, quite rightly, of being unfair. That is why many organisations use a system for assessing the worth of different jobs based on job evaluation.

Job evaluation does not determine the correct payment level for a job, but rather provides a possible ranking of a job relative to other jobs. This has the merit of being systematic and of appearing objective, although in reality there is usually some degree of subjectivity in all job evaluation schemes. There are normally three stages involved when an organisation is deciding how much to pay for each job:

1. Evaluate the jobs in the organisation and get a ranking for them.
2. Decide which jobs are similar in terms of the job evaluation exercise and group them together.
3. Decide what pay to attach to these jobs, partially on the basis of market value.

There are a variety of job evaluation schemes in existence, and discussion of these could occupy a full chapter in its own right. We shall seek to give a brief outline of some of the more commonly used types of job evaluation scheme. They can be divided into non-analytical and analytical schemes, and we shall consider each of these groups in turn.

Non-analytical schemes or analytical schemes

Non-analytical job evaluation schemes compare whole jobs, rather than analysing the components of each job, and assessing them factor by factor. When you completed Activity 9.1 you were doing a very simple form of job evaluation. As you saw then it was very subjective and non-analytical schemes are not sufficiently rigorous or analytical to be able to withstand an equal pay claim so are not to be recommended. Sometimes they appear to be more rigorous than they really are so we shall consider these so that you can find out for yourselves the problems and drawbacks to them. There are three main types of non-analytical scheme:

- whole job ranking,
- paired comparisons,
- job classification.

Analytical schemes break the jobs down and try to compare skills or competencies needed in each job. The main analytical schemes are:

- points rating,
- proprietary schemes.

In order to understand the basics of each of these approaches, you should read the following case study and complete Activities 9.3, 9.4, 9.5 and 9.6.

Case Study 9.1 Job evaluation

The Hookworth Department Store is concerned that its payment system does not accurately reflect the true value of different jobs to the organisation. The management is trying to decide on a form of job evaluation to use as part of a review of the jobs for the whole organisation. They have provided you with three job descriptions to use as a way of identifying the most suitable form of job evaluation to use. You need to consider the job descriptions provided and imagine that you have to evaluate the jobs as part of a job evaluation exercise which will ultimately be used as the basis

→

of the organisation's payment system. You are being asked to evaluate only three jobs, whereas in reality there would be far more jobs than this in a full job evaluation exercise in most organisations.

Read the following three job descriptions and complete Activities 9.3, 9.4 and 9.5. When you have completed these you should be in a good position to decide on an appropriate form of job evaluation to adapt for the whole organisation as requested in Activity 9.6.

Job description A

Job title:	**Office receptionist**
Reports to:	Office services manager
Responsible for:	Assistant receptionists (2)
Purpose of post:	To ensure that visitors to the company are received in a welcoming fashion, answer routine queries and ensure that all other queries are handled expeditiously by the appropriate staff member. To ensure that all telephone queries are handled in the same manner.
	As the first point of contact for the company, the receptionist must maintain high standards of customer care.
Contacts:	All customers and other visitors, to deal with initial and routine queries. All members of staff, to pass on queries as appropriate.

Major duties:

- Greet walk-in visitors and ascertain purpose of their visit. Handle or redirect queries as appropriate.
- Answer phone queries as above.
- Answer all initial queries about receipt of payments using the online payment receipts system.
- Open and sort incoming post by department. Organise delivery of post by assistant receptionists.
- Perform clerical tasks assigned by departments in agreement with the office services manager.
- Supervise assistant receptionists and delegate work as appropriate.
- Perform other duties as assigned by the office services manager or other authorised manager.

Job description B

Job title:	**Human resource assistant**
Reports to:	Human resource manager
Responsible for:	No one
Purpose of post:	To provide a day-to-day advisory service for the managers in the company on matters of human resource management policy and procedures, and to monitor and implement procedures.
Contacts:	Managers from head office and throughout the branches. Employees, to deal with initial and routine queries. Prospective employees, to deal with initial enquiries regarding job vacancies. Outside organisations such as employment agencies, training organisations and newspapers.

Major duties:

- Answer all initial queries about applications for employment.
- Pass all rejected applications to typist for standard rejection letters and check and sign these letters.
- Monitor application for employment forms submitted by line managers on behalf of candidates selected by them.
- Agree salary details, in accordance with company pay scales, with line manager.
- Enter agreed salary, contract, job title and joining details on successful applications and pass to typist for documentation.
- Sign joining documentation on behalf of the company.
- Advise line managers on the interpretation of the organisation's human resource policies and procedures.
- Advise line managers on the interpretation and implementation of the organisation's sickness pay and pension schemes.
- Advise line managers on the interpretation of relevant employment legislation.
- Advise line managers on employees' salary entitlements.
- Ensure that the human resource management records are kept up to date on the computerised information system, and that there is no unauthorised access to these or any manually produced records.
- Provide up-to-date reports or data for use by managers.

Job description C

Job title:	**Sales assistant**
Reports to:	Buyer of china department
Responsible for:	No one
Purpose of post:	To sell china goods and assist customers with their purchases and with any queries or problems that they might have.
Contacts:	All customers and other visitors to make sales of china and deal with routine queries.

Major duties:

- Sell china goods to customers.
- Provide expert advice about the various products on sale.
- Provide a high standard of service and customer care.
- Unpack with care valuable merchandise and pack customers' purchases carefully, including packing them for export.
- Display products attractively to encourage sales and promote certain special offers.
- Perform clerical duties associated with the work of the department, for example completion of orders, forms for returns or breakages.
- Handle accurately and honestly cash and credit transactions.
- Total cash and credit transactions and deliver money to cash control office.

Non-analytical job evaluation schemes

The first two activities ask you to consider the non-analytical approach to job evaluation.

Whole job ranking

Activity 9.3

a Consider each of the three job descriptions given in Case study 9.1 and decide which job you feel is worth most to the organisation, which is the next in value and which is of least value to the organisation. Rank the jobs in order with the job you feel is worth most to the organisation being ranked as number 1.

1. _____

2. _____

3. _____

b What are the advantages and disadvantages of this approach, which is known as whole job ranking?

Discussion of Activity 9.3

This is the simplest form of job evaluation exercise and we have ranked the three jobs in the following order: 1. Human resource assistant 2. Sales assistant in china department; 3. Receptionist. You may have reached a different rank order to us or to other students. This is because this is a very subjective way of ranking the jobs, and the criteria we took into account may be different to those that you have used. There is nothing in this method to indicate what criteria have been chosen. We have asked you to make decisions about only three jobs, and it would be more difficult to use the whole job ranking system in a large organisation where there were many different jobs to rank. In that case, the jobs would probably have to be grouped into categories first for ease of comparison and so that the appropriate criteria were used, for example for clerical jobs, as it could be a problem to identify suitable criteria if the jobs were very dissimilar.

We could make this system slightly more objective by agreeing on the criteria to be considered in advance of the exercise, but even this would not help us to identify the extent of difference in the value of the different jobs to the organisation, so we would still have difficulty deciding how much more to pay the job that was ranked first compared to the job that was ranked second. In reality, job evaluation schemes should not depend on the subjective judgements of just one person. It would be better to involve more people in an exercise such as this and then get a consensus view from this job evaluation panel about the ranking of each job.

Advantages of whole job ranking

- simple
- cheap to operate
- easy to understand

Disadvantages of whole job ranking

- subjective and of no use in defence of an equal pay claim
- no analysis of jobs to explain reason for ranked order
- difficult to use with large number of jobs

Paired comparisons

Activity 9.4

(a) Refer to the three job descriptions given in Case study 9.1, but this time compare pairs of jobs and decide which you feel is worth more to the organisation, so that each job is compared with the other jobs in turn. Use the following points system to work through this exercise.

- If you feel that a job is worth more than the job it is being compared with, give it 2 points.
- If you feel it is worth the same as the job it is compared with, give them both 1 point.
- If you feel it is worth less than the other job, give it zero points.

Enter the values that you give each job in the chart below, and then add the scores for each job. The job with the highest value will be the one that you decide to pay the most, followed by the job with the next highest value and the job with the lowest value.

We'll start by examining Job A, the job of the receptionist, and will compare our view of its value to the organisation with the value of the other two jobs to the organisation. Place all your scores for Job A in the vertical column below the heading Job A so that at the end of the exercise you can add up all the points for this job.

For example, if you think that Job A, the office receptionist's job, is of more value to the organisation than Job B, the human resources assistant's job, then on the chart below you should write '2' in the vertical column below Job A and on the horizontal line next to Job B.

Now compare Job A with Job C and, for example, if you decide that Job A is perhaps of less value to the organisation than Job C, you should write '0' in the next space down in column A, on the horizontal line next to Job C. Then add the total points in this column to gain a total score for Job A. Now complete this exercise for yourself and add up the total score in each column for each of the jobs in turn.

	Job A	Job B	Job C
Job A	No score in this section as Job A cannot be compared with itself		
Job B		No score in this section as Job B cannot be compared with itself	
Job C			No score in this section as Job C cannot be compared with itself
Total scores for each job			

Total points for each job: A = B = C =

1st job _____

2nd job _____

3rd job _____

(b) Did you rank the jobs in the same order as before? What are the advantages and disadvantages of this approach?

Discussion of Activity 9.4

This is also a simple method of job evaluation, but it is slightly more systematic than whole job ranking. It still does not analyse particular jobs in detail and, although the numerical values attached to each job create an impression of objectivity, this is really not the case as again there is nothing to indicate what the criteria used might be. A large number of calculations may need to be made – for an organisation that intends to analyse 50 or more jobs, 1,225 calculations would need to be made. There are, however, computerised systems that work on this basis and solve this particular problem. Once again, an improvement to this approach would be to involve a job evaluation panel, drawn from various sections of the workforce, and then try to get agreement about the rating of various jobs.

Advantages of paired comparisons

- Simple
- easy to understand
- slightly more systematic than whole job ranking
- it is easy to fit new jobs into this system.

Disadvantages of paired comparisons

- Subjective and no defence in an equal pay claim
- no analysis of jobs to explain reason for ranked order
- the need for an enormous number of calculations if it is to be used with a large number of jobs.

Job classification

The exercises you have just completed indicate in a very simple way the main stages and the main problems with two forms of non-analytical job evaluation. The third non-analytical form of job evaluation is known as job classification. It is similar to job ranking but uses a different approach. In this case the number of groups of jobs, or pay grades, is decided first and a general job description is then produced for all the jobs in each of these groups. An individual job that is considered to typify this group of jobs is then used as a benchmark. Each job is compared with the benchmark jobs and the general job description, and placed in an appropriate grade.

Advantages of job classification

- simple to operate
- easy to understand
- it is easy to fit new jobs into job classification structure

Disadvantages of job classification

- difficult to use with a wide range of jobs
- not analytical and so provides no defence in an equal pay claim

Analytical job evaluation schemes

Now consider an approach to job evaluation which is described as analytical by completing Activity 9.5.

Points rating

Activity 9.5

In this approach you will work with a job evaluation committee who have specified that the following criteria should be used in evaluating jobs:

- skill,
- responsibility for people, for example in a job caring for children,
- responsibility for equipment and materials,
- responsibility for other employees,
- mental effort,
- physical effort,
- working conditions.

Rate the three jobs, as described in their job descriptions in Case study 9.1, according to these criteria. You can give up to 10 points for each of these factors for each job:

10 exceptional
7–9 high
4–6 medium
1–3 low
0 negligible

Then add the total scores for Job A, Job B and Job C.

For example, if you feel that a medium level of skill is required by an office receptionist as described in job description A you will give that job between 4 and 6 points in that category. If you feel that Job B, the human resource assistant, shows a high level of responsibility for people, you will give it between 7 and 9 points. Remember that in job evaluation it is the job you are evaluating, not the person, so you do not need to know how effective a person actually is in that job.

Discussion of Activity 9.5

The points rating approach is probably the most commonly used type of job evaluation scheme, and is regarded as analytical because instead of comparing whole jobs, the jobs are broken down into a number of factors such as skills, responsibility, physical requirements, mental requirements and working conditions. Each of the factors is awarded points based on a predetermined scale, and the total points determine the position of that job in the rank order. A weighting is often attached to the particular importance of each attribute to the organisation.

Having completed the earlier exercises on non-analytical job evaluation schemes you should now be able to see the benefits of an analytical approach to job evaluation. However, although this scheme is analytical, there is, as we said earlier, an element of subjectivity in all job evaluation schemes, as subjective decisions are made about which factors will be weighted most highly to show their importance to the organisation. Care should be taken to avoid sex bias in the choice of factors for high weighting. Some older schemes based on this system were

Did you know?

These methods of job evaluation are not just used in the UK. In May 2000 the Hong Kong Equal Opportunities Commission (2003) established a task force to encourage the implementation of equal pay for work of equal value in two pilot areas: the Hong Kong Civil Service and the Hospital Authority. They chose to base their approach to equal value on work done in both the UK and Canada. The factors chosen for this job evaluation exercise were typical of a points rating approach: skill, responsibility, effort and working conditions, although different weightings were given to each factor.

(*Source*: Hong Kong Equal Opportunities Commission, 2003)

biased against women as characteristics such as physical strength, normally associated more with male employees, were given higher weighting than factors such as dexterity, which is more often associated with women.

Points rating schemes are easy to understand and are more objective than the non-analytical schemes. Because they are analytical, they can be used to explain the extent of differences between jobs and hence to justify subsequent differences in pay. They can, however, be time consuming and costly to develop as a panel of people is likely to be involved.

Proprietary schemes

Faced with the time and costs involved in designing and validating their own job evaluation scheme and checking that it is free of unfair bias, many organisations decide to buy a proprietary scheme or employ a consultant to design a scheme specifically for them. A scheme designed specifically for one organisation is obviously a good idea and is likely to have a great deal of credibility with the workforce, but buying a proprietary scheme has the additional advantage of giving access to extensive comparative data on job markets and rates of pay which designers of proprietary schemes also collect. This can provide much more comprehensive data on which to base decisions about payment levels to relate to jobs than any one organisation could collect.

Activity 9.6

Compare your evaluation of the three jobs using this points rating method with your earlier evaluations of the same jobs completed using the whole job ranking method and then the paired comparison method.

Were your rankings of the jobs the same or different in all three cases? Why was this? Which of these methods would you recommend to the senior management at the Hookworth Department Store for use in their full job evaluation for the whole store? Why?

Discussion of Activity 9.6

Having completed activities to establish the ways that two non-analytical approaches to job evaluation work, and Activity 9.5 to see how one analytical scheme, the points rating method, works, you should now be in a position to make a recommendation to the management of the Hookworth Department Store as to the most suitable form of job evaluation for them to use.

Since only the analytical forms of job evaluation would stand up to examination in an equal pay case at an employment tribunal we hope that you have selected the points rating method, or a proprietary scheme based on a system of points rating, to recommend to the management of the Hookworth Department Store.

Different types of payment system

There are, as we have shown, many factors that affect what the organisation pays its workforce, but whatever payment system is chosen will give a different message to the workforce about the issues and values that the organisation feels are important. It is important that the message given is appropriate to support the strategic objectives of the organisation. In this section we shall consider some of the different payment systems that the organisation might choose. There are many variations in systems of payment; some of the more common types will be considered here.

- time rates,
- individual payment by results (piecework),
- group incentives,
- profit sharing,
- performance-related pay or merit rating,
- non-monetary awards,
- cafeteria-style payments or flexible pay,
- total reward.

Time rates

This is the simplest of all payment systems: as the name implies people are paid according to the time they spend at work. This may be based on an hourly rate, a weekly rate or an annual salary. In spite of all the talk of incentive schemes and movement towards a human resource management approach with performance-related pay systems, this is still an extremely popular way for many organisations to pay people. This is largely because it is a simple system that is easy to understand and does not result in a great many disputes. On the other hand, organisations that have moved away from this system of payment have done so because it provides little incentive to improve productivity or efficiency.

As we said earlier, each employer needs to establish what motivates their employees. If it is a really interesting job then the employees may be motivated primarily by the satisfaction gained from the job itself. If the employer wants an organisation where everyone works together then they will want to provide a reasonably competitive level of pay for all employees and won't want to pay bonuses or divide the workforce by performance-related pay systems, so that time rates and harmonisation of terms and conditions of employment are likely to appeal to them. The basic rate paid must be sufficiently high that it is adequate for most people's needs. If the rate of pay falls behind this level then the workforce is likely to be demotivated.

Pause for thought 9.2 What do you think about this philosophy? Does it link with anything you have studied on other modules about motivation theory?

The idea that pay is necessary at a certain level to provide for an employee's basic needs, but that to increase pay beyond this is not likely to result in increased performance at work, links very clearly with the work of another motivation theorist, Frederick Herzberg (1966), whose ideas you may have studied, and with his motivation/hygiene theories. Herzberg said that certain things, such as pay and good conditions at work, which he referred to as hygiene factors, were necessary to prevent employees from becoming dissatisfied with work. He said that these were the sort of things that people moan about, but that when the dissatisfaction had been removed and the pay or working conditions improved, these people would still not be actually motivated to work harder. The motivators, according to Herzberg, were factors such as making the job more interesting or giving the employee more responsibility.

Payments on time rates, as we have said, don't normally vary from week to week and people are paid for going to work, regardless of how hard they actually work when they are there. However, if workers are paid on a zero hours contract then the number of hours worked could vary and hence the pay causes problems for the worker who still has the same bills to pay each week. In the next activity we would like you to consider a particular example of a time rate payment system, where there are some variations in the payments people receive.

Activity 9.7

Imagine that you are a branch manager in a large building society. You are talking to one of your staff, a graduate who is regarded as being bright and a hard worker and who should have an excellent future with the organisation. You ask how things are going and are rather dismayed when she replies, 'OK, but I'm getting a bit disillusioned. I seem to work hard and yet it will take me at least six years to get to the top of the pay scale. Most people around here seem to be at or near to the top of the pay scale already and they seem to take life easy and don't work nearly as hard as I do. I'm thinking seriously about looking for another job.'

1. What is this type of pay scale supposed to achieve for the organisation?
2. What are the advantages and disadvantages of this type of payment system?
3. How does this payment system relate to what you know about motivation theory?

Discussion of Activity 9.7

1. An incremental pay scale is a form of time rate payment system, as people are still paid for the time that they spend at work regardless of the amount of effort they put into their work. In this case, they are also paid an extra amount or increment for each year that they work for the employer. This is supposed to encourage employees to stay with the same employer for a long period of time, and so result in a stable workforce. There is also an implication that people will become more knowledgeable and effective in their job as they work for more years and gain more experience. This is not necessarily true, and although some people do learn from experience and will become more valuable employees the longer they are employed, you may be able to think of people that you know who have done the same job for years and who seem to have stopped learning from experience, and who do not appear to be any more effective in their job than they were on the day they started. Care needs to be taken with this type of payment scheme to ensure that it meets the requirements of the Equality Act 2010.

2. Advantages of incremental payment schemes:

- simple,
- easy to calculate wages,
- rewards experience,
- leads to a stable workforce.

Disadvantages of incremental payment schemes:

- no incentive to work harder,
- slow progress for high fliers,
- needs to be used with great care to avoid accusations of age discrimination,
- no incentive at top of the scale,
- could be open to accusations of age discrimination.

3. This approach tends, like other forms of time rates, to reflect a collectivist view that everyone should be treated the same and that to pay people differently would be divisive. With incremental pay scales such as this, differences that are taken into account are usually about non-contentious things such as length of service. Everyone can see that people are treated fairly and that they will get the same treatment. This approach tends to be favoured in relatively large, impersonal, bureaucratic organisations which place emphasis on determining pay on the jobs rather than the people. This form of payment system will also work best where the pace of change is slow and where there is little scope for individual initiative. An incremental pay system doesn't tend to work well in a fast-moving organisation where it is likely to stifle initiative and innovation.

We shall now examine a group of payment systems that reflect a more individualised approach, where individuals are rewarded for their contribution. We shall consider both individual payment by results and performance-related pay. Though these are very different approaches it is important that whatever approach to incentives is chosen is relevant to the workers, is measurable and fair and open to all. Incentive schemes can inadvertently have the effect of demotivating staff if they are not communicated clearly to all and if the targets are unrealistic or the process lacks clarity so it is not understood. Employees need to know what is expected of them to get the reward, how it will be measured and what the reward for their effort will be (Goss, 2010).

Individual payment by results (piecework)

This approach, based on individualism, reflects the view that since some people work harder than others they should be paid different amounts to reflect the differences in effort that they have made. In this system the amount that people are paid depends on how much they produce, so there are very clear criteria and a strong link between earnings and effort. This system is most common in types of manufacturing environment where it is easy to identify the products that each individual has made, or to identify clearly an individual's contribution to a manufactured product.

The main advantages to the employer of payment by results can be summarised as follows:

- There is a strong incentive to increase effort, as there is a very clear link with earnings.
- If an increased number of tasks are completed in the same amount of time, using the same equipment, the costs per unit of output will be lower.

Like all payment systems there are disadvantages as well as advantages. The main disadvantages are that:

- It can be expensive to install and maintain.
- It can result in many disagreements about standards or levels of production.
- Production may increase at the expense of quality.
- The emphasis on personal performance can cause friction between employees.

This payment system is expensive to install and maintain as there needs to be a fair system for assessing the norm for levels of production so that production over and above this level can be paid. Work study engineers are often employed to find the most efficient method of carrying out a task, and managers and trade union officials may spend a great deal of time timing different stages in the production process. There is an emphasis in the payment by results system on providing an incentive, but also on control and measurement. Even with controls in place there can be problems, as Activity 9.8 shows.

Activity 9.8

Imagine that you are the human resource manager in a knitwear manufacturing company. You are about to negotiate with the trade union on the current round of pay talks.
The sewing machinists are paid on a piecework system but there is a great deal of absenteeism, particularly on Fridays. It seems to you that many workers increase their levels of production on the other days of the week so that they can have Fridays off. The company wants to ensure regular high levels of production on every day of the week in order to meet its full order books.

1. What is the underlying message that a piecework system, such as this one, intends to give to the employees?
2. Why is this system not working as well as the organisation wants?
3. How does the situation within this organisation link with motivation theories?

Discussion of Activity 9.8

1. The underlying message that a piecework system is intended to give is that a person will be rewarded for working hard, and the more they produce, the more they will be paid.
2. The system is not working as well as management had hoped because management have assumed that the workforce is only motivated to work harder for money, and that they will continue to work harder and harder for more and more money. Remember the factors that Herzberg (1966), for example, suggested as motivating factors.
3. This situation relates to the view that people may be motivated by a variety of things. In this case the workers wanted a high level of income, but they also wanted some time to relax and spend that income. Some people may be motivated by the opportunity of earning more money, especially if they are saving for some large expenditure. However, not everyone will attach the same degree of importance to financial rewards all the time, and the organisation needs to find out what its employees will value. The employees here seem to

be sending a message that leisure is something they value, but other people might be motivated by promotion, a company car, increased responsibility or the increased respect of colleagues.

Individual payment by results is not always particularly appropriate, as we have seen in Activity 9.8. This payment system is most appropriate where

- it is possible to measure work,
- it is easy to attribute it to individuals,
- the pace of work is under the employee's control,
- management can provide a steady flow of work for the employee to do,
- the work is not subject to constant changes in method, materials or equipment.

There is a variety of payment by results schemes. These include:

- group incentives,
- individual time saving,
- measured day work.

Group incentives

These are based on the same principles as the individual payment by results system, but are used when the individualistic approach is not wanted by the organisation. For example, in order to try to encourage team working or to take into account support workers who contribute to overall output but whose contribution may be difficult to assess, some organisations introduce a system of group payment by results. The form of incentive or reward chosen should reinforce behaviour that results in effective teamwork and this also needs to fit with the culture and structure of the organisation. For instance in a very hierarchical structure it may be difficult or inappropriate to introduce team bonuses as it is could be hard to foster team spirit if individuals are focusing on their own interests and their own promotion.

The size of the group may vary from small teams or work units to the whole plant or enterprise. All types of reward or incentive can work with teams and the most usual include team pay or bonuses through to non-financial rewards such as recognition or increased responsibility for the team.

Activity 9.9

Make a list of the advantages and disadvantages of plant- and enterprise-wide payment by results schemes.

Discussion of Activity 9.9

You may have suggested some of the following advantages and disadvantages. Advantages:

- Employees see how they contribute to the whole organisation's effectiveness.
- Employees are usually encouraged to find ways to improve performance and productivity.

- Employees become interested in how the organisation is managed.
- It is cheaper to install plant- or enterprise-wide payment by results schemes than individual payment by results schemes.
- There is usually a need to discuss financial information with employee representatives and this can result in an improved understanding of how the organisation is run.

Disadvantages:

- There is a weaker link in employees' minds between the bonus and the level of their effort, so it may not be a strong incentive.
- Schemes can be difficult to understand.
- Bonus payments could be affected by factors such as inflation which the workforce can do nothing about.

Profit sharing

This is a form of payment scheme where the focus is on the group rather than the individual. Employees all receive a bonus and its size depends on the profits made by the organisation that year. Once again there is little direct incentive for individuals to work harder, as it is difficult to see how their contribution actually relates to the profit made, but many profit-sharing schemes encourage employees to get involved with how the scheme is run. Sometimes bonus payments are made in shares rather than cash. This is also intended to give employees an interest in the enterprise, but can result in a risk to both shares and job if the organisation does not do as well in the future. It is difficult to see this as a strong motivational force.

Performance-related pay or merit rating

Performance-related pay, which is sometimes referred to as merit rating, is also a way of linking an individual's pay progression to their level of performance or to a rating of competence. It is once again an individualistic approach which favours rewarding people differently according to level of performance or competence, and it aims to motivate all employees and give clear indications of what the organisation expects from employees. Performance-related pay differs from payment by results as it doesn't relate just to the quantity of a product that is produced, and may apply to workers even where there is no end product to measure.

Initially, performance-related pay was used as a motivational tool primarily for non-manual employees, but in the 1980s it was extended to shop floor workers and has been discussed and used as a tool in some parts of the health service and in education. Increasingly some organisations have become aware of limitations to performance-related pay as it did not always deliver the results expected or may have had unintended consequences as it encouraged employees to focus on their own results rather than working as a team.

Performance-related pay is often regarded as a key feature of performance management, as outlined in Chapter 7, and although some performance management schemes do not operate performance-related pay, most do use it. While the motivational theorists cast doubt on the value of money as a motivator, many managers instinctively feel that money will motivate employees. Some organisations, even if they do not feel that it will have a strong motivational effect, introduce performance-related pay as a way of being fair and rewarding high performers' past performance, and so argue that equity is the rationale for the introduction of such a scheme. The fact that performance is considered at all can also have positive effects in that it helps to create a culture in which performance is valued and recognition of good performance can be a reward in itself. According to Egan (2010b), 60 per cent of private sector workers, but only 36 per cent of public sector workers, would like their pay to reflect their performance, once again showing how important it is for employers to find out what motivates their particular workforce. If a performance-related pay system is to be perceived to be fair it is important to emphasise that performance-related pay needs to be based on what can be seen to be a fair and just system of allocation, with clear, objective criteria being used.

In some organisations wider definitions of performance are now being used and the focus is moving towards assessing an employee's contribution or input to the organisation rather than just their output. This is much broader than measuring their performance simply in terms of what they have achieved. Some of their achievement, or lack of achievement, may be because of external factors outside their control such as a change in the economy, or a competitor going out of business, but their contribution to helping to achieve departmental or organisational objectives is under their control more (Egan, 2010b).

Activity 9.10

Imagine that you work in an organisation where performance-related pay has recently been introduced. You are appraising one of your subordinates, a man in his fifties who has been with the organisation for about 15 years. You have discussed most of the rating criteria, which have all been satisfactory. You say, 'Your work has been good but are there any areas where you feel there could be improvements?' He replies, 'I'm happy in the job but I don't really see much point in working a great deal harder. The mortgage is paid off now, the children have finished their education and if I earn more money I will only have to pay more tax on it. I want to take life a bit easier now and spend more time at home or away in the caravan. I don't always want to be taking work home with me.'

1. What are the advantages and disadvantages of performance-related pay?
2. How does the situation here link with what you know about theories of motivation?
3. Suggest alternative ways of motivating this employee to work to his full potential.

Discussion of Activity 9.10

1. Advantages of performance-related pay:

- Rewards the individual by linking systematic assessment of their performance to their level of pay or to a bonus.
- The factors taken into account may be weighted to reflect their relative importance to the organisation.
- It can be used where an incentive is needed but the actual work rate is difficult to measure.
- It can reward factors not easily taken into account in other payment systems.

Disadvantages of performance-related pay:

- There may be disagreements about the performance factors to be assessed, and if great care is not taken in the choice of the factors there may be claims that they are too subjective or even of sex bias.
- Bonus payments may be too infrequent to provide a direct incentive.

2. This is another example of the view that individuals will be motivated by different things and that we value different things. This would link with Maslow's (1954) hierarchy of needs mentioned in Chapter 10 on health, safety and wellbeing.

3. The situation described reflects the view that there needs to be a range of different forms of incentive so that individuals can choose what will motivate them. In this case the employee might well be motivated if he was offered the opportunity to work for increased holidays.

Performance-related pay can be paid in several ways, and may even involve non-financial rewards. The most commonly used financial rewards are

- salary increases within the normal salary scale,
- salary increases above the maximum point of the normal pay scale,
- where each employee is paid on an individual fixed rate, with good performers getting something above the normal rate,
- lump sum payments that are not included in salary.

Salary increases within the normal salary scale

This is a commonly used form of performance-related pay, and gives a clear message that although there is a fixed scale for the job and everyone's pay depends on performance, exceptional performers can progress through this scale more rapidly than others.

Salary increases above the maximum point of the normal pay scale

This is sometimes used when the organisation wants to maintain its existing incremental pay scales but also wants to reward excellent performance. In this case high performers benefit as everyone else progresses along the normal scale until they reach the maximum, but it is of no benefit to average employees who have reached the top of the scale because of the length of their employment.

Each employee is paid on an individual fixed rate, with good performers getting something above the normal rate

In this case the individual is paid on a particular rate, but there is no automatic annual salary increase. The organisation budgets for a percentage increase each year, but then allocates this money according to assessments of employee performance, with excellent performers receiving most, good performers getting some allocation of award and poor performers receiving nothing at all. This gives a very clear message to all concerned, and may result in those who are assessed as being poor performers leaving the organisation.

Bonus payments that are not included in salary

Bonus payments and cash incentives are forms of payment that are not incorporated into an employee's salary. Incentives are used to influence future employee performance and to encourage the employee to meet predetermined targets. Bonuses can be used in the same way or could be ad hoc one-off rewards given retrospectively for work that has been done well. Both are intended to help attract and retain talented workers, to motivate and ensure they are engaged with the organisation with the intention that this will ultimately lead to an enhancement of the performance of the organisation.

Traditionally bonuses and cash incentives were used as a motivational tool for manual workers to use alongside basic pay or as an addition to a piecework system. More recently it has become normal to use this approach for managers and non-manual workers, and according to the CIPD (2014d) this forms a part of a 'new pay' philosophy in which the guaranteed basic pay forms a small proportion of the overall reward package, with the aim that the bonuses will be linked clearly to improved performance which in turn links very clearly to achieving the organisation's strategic objectives. There is less security of income for managers and therefore more incentive for them to work harder to be successful and this is ongoing as bonuses constantly have to be re-earned during each financial period.

Organisations are also attracted to the idea of bonuses as it means that they have less to pay in terms of some of the add-on costs to salary such as employer's pension contributions. They may also provide a way for differentiating the level of pay between workers with high or low levels of performance and as a way of having some flexibility related to the organisation's overall financial position: bonuses could be set at a higher level if the organisation is in good financial shape but could be reduced or stopped when the financial situation is less favourable.

Bonuses have become very controversial after revelations of the huge sums that city bankers or executives received in bonuses, sometimes even when they did not meet their targets! This has resulted in a huge amount of discussion about bonuses and their usefulness. Many employers, including those in the world of finance, argue that a lump sum payment has more impact than if the same amount were included in normal salary and this is used as a way of attracting people to these organisations and also as a way of retaining them, since they will want to stay until their bonus has been paid. Bonuses do draw attention to the organisation's policy for rewarding excellence, especially if the opportunity is used for a special presentation ceremony, but in many organisations it seems to be expected that there will be a bonus even if targets have not been achieved.

Mathews raises questions about the role of HR in relation to what she calls 'fat-cat failures'. They are the 'group of former MPs, directors and sporting figures who have successfully turned logic on its head by attracting enormous rewards for being no good at their jobs' (Mathews, 2008). When organisations want to attract someone who in their opinion has some rare talent, they often do not consider that the person may not perform as well for them as they have done in their previous role. They tend to be so focused on getting that person to work for them that they create a fantastic package of pay, reward and benefits without giving sufficient thought to what will happen if the individual does not perform at expected level. The use of bonuses has become extremely contentious since remuneration practices were deemed to have played a part in the global banking crisis.

Mathews emphasises the point that HR managers need to have more input into identifying performance criteria and play a role in ensuring exit packages take into account the possibility of failure. The Financial Services Authority also has a new duty to ensure that remuneration policies in banks are consistent with effective risk management and this further emphasises the role that HR managers should play (CIPD, 2014d).

Non-monetary awards

As shown in Activity 9.10, people may be motivated by a range of different factors and may not always be motivated by being paid more money directly in their pay, especially if they lose a great deal in tax. Although we are all pleased to get more money, there is no public recognition of a job well done in that approach. This view is recognised in many organisations, which now seek to provide both monetary and non-monetary awards. Some of the non-financial awards we have selected will also have a monetary value. We have included them as non-monetary awards as the fact of an award being special, in recognition of a job well done or special effort made, may have a motivating effect larger than purely monetary value. Saying 'thank you' is a much overlooked form of non-monetary award in many organisations.

Some organisations are very original with the types of awards of offer. Sky TV achieved a profit of £780 million for the year up to June 2009 and so asked their staff what forms of rewards they would like for an employee reward day. As a result, they organised two, two-day music and entertainment festivals, one in London and one in Edinburgh, for 20,000 staff and their friends and family. Other individual rewards which proved extremely popular were the opportunity to stand on a replica of the empty Trafalgar Square plinth. Dev Ravel, the director of reward at Sky, is quoted as saying, 'Skyfest is designed to be great entertainment and to enhance our employee reward package' (*Rewards and Benefits Today*, 2009).

In spite of the ingenuity used at Sky TV the most commonly used non-financial rewards are:

- commendation,
- overseas travel,
- gifts,
- gift vouchers,
- green/environmental rewards.

Commendation

The opportunity to commend someone for the efforts that they have made can be extremely important as a way of rewarding and motivating them, whether this is done through the normal performance appraisal interview or at a public ceremony at which a letter or certificate of commendation is presented. The latter situation, with the attendant publicity, will serve as a reinforcement of the values that the organisation wishes to encourage and may also motivate others to improve their work performance.

Overseas travel

This type of reward used to be used primarily to reward sales staff for improvements in sales, but in recent years it has become an incentive on offer to many other individuals. Sometimes overseas travel is used as an incentive for team effort, with the whole team being rewarded with a trip abroad.

This type of reward can be in the form of overseas holidays or the opportunity to attend a high-profile training course held at an exotic destination.

Gifts

Other gifts awarded to people who have made significant improvements in their performance include consumer items such as cameras, household luxuries or jewellery. Once again there is the problem of choosing an appropriate range of gifts, as individuals are not likely to be motivated by the opportunity to acquire a new microwave oven, for example, if they already own one.

Gift vouchers

Gift vouchers are perhaps the most flexible form of incentive payment and are also very popular with individuals, as they offer real choice. Many high street stores promote the use of their gift vouchers to organisations that are thinking of establishing this type of scheme.

Green/environmental rewards

This is a new type of award which recognises workers' concerns about environmental issues or about individuals' carbon footprints and which aims to provide rewards which address in a positive way their environmental concerns. Clive Wright (2007) said at a CIPD meeting that the forms these awards could take included the following: 'company discounts for solar panels or wind turbines; home efficiency consultancy as another option in a flexible benefits programme; extra volunteer days for green projects . . . discounts or preferential loans for public transport or access to discounts on recycled products'.

Pause for thought 9.3 What do you feel about green awards as a motivational tool? Which potential green or environmental reward would motivate you to work harder?

Cafeteria-style payments or flexible pay

An even more flexible approach to pay is sometimes referred to as the 'cafeteria approach' or 'flex pay', because employees can choose their own preferred reward or combination of rewards. It gives an opportunity for employers to find a pay package that will suit a diverse range of staff, whether male or female, full-time or part-time, and who come from a wide age range. This can prove attractive for recruiting and retaining labour. In the cafeteria approach the workforce is told what rewards or benefits they can choose from each year. This could mean that they select from gift vouchers, gifts or holidays or they may prefer to choose from other benefits such as improved health care options, health or life insurance, an improved pension scheme, longer holidays or even additional cash. Companies that have introduced flexible schemes such as this have done so not to cut costs but to tailor their benefits to the needs of their workforce, and they have found that younger staff prefer cash or a second car, older staff often prefer to improve their pensions or health cover, while staff with young families may prefer longer holidays.

In order for a flexible system to work there has to be an excellent system established for administration, and improvements in computer technology help here. There must also be an appropriate culture within the organisation and excellent communication with members of the workforce and their representatives. Not all organisations have moved towards a complete menu of options: some have felt that staff might be confused by too much choice and have gone for schemes that offer core benefits to all staff with some additional choice over certain options.

Total reward

Total reward, like that of flexible pay, recognises that pay is not the only motivating force for people but it goes even further to include other aspects of employment in the total reward package. Total reward is a newer concept than flexible pay that some organisations are developing. Total reward schemes normally do offer flexible pay and benefits but also include aspects of work such as career and personal development, flexitime, a challenging job at work, opportunities for individual growth and development and recognition for achievements. Sometimes they even allow for individual preferences for type of office layout, space and equipment as well as for administrative support. Total reward schemes aim to align employers' HR and business strategies with employees' needs in order to ultimately achieve improved performance. According to the CIPD (2014e) the concept of total reward goes much further than standard remuneration and can include any aspects of work that are valued by the employees, so could include an attractive working environment or excellent learning and development opportunities. In return the employer hopes they will gain an extremely engaged workforce performance.

Many organisations are having to rethink their reward strategies as a result of the economic situation and changing demographics such as the ageing workforce. It would be illegal to offer different rewards to people of different ages but it would be possible and desirable to design a total reward package with sufficient choice to appeal to all employees regardless of their age (CIPD, 2014f). All types of organisations are currently having to rethink their reward strategies since there are no longer jobs for life in the old, more traditional style of organisations and newer organisations, who may not have had such good job security anyway, can in some cases no longer afford large financial rewards and stock options. The increasingly diverse workforce also demand different benefits so some organisations are adopting a total reward approach in order to attract and retain workers.

These organisations clearly do understand that pay and reward does contribute to achieving the organisation's strategic objectives. While they are still nervous and keen to minimise costs they are also aware that total reward is a strategy for improving employee engagement and for keeping the talent that they already have in their organisations.

Reward strategy

We have shown some of the influences on the way that pay is determined within an organisation and the messages that each payment system gives to workers. Because the payment system is important for motivating and giving clear messages about what is considered by the organisation to be important, it should be related to the organisation's strategic objectives. This has not always happened and although some organisations are clearly using pay and reward as a strategic tool to attract and retain talent, many other organisations have not yet adopted this approach. Ideally organisations should have a formal, written statement of their reward strategy but even if they do not it is still possible to adopt a strategic approach to reward. In the CIPD's annual reward survey only one third of the organisations surveyed had a written reward strategy (CIPD, 2014g). Even if there is no written reward strategy document it is nevertheless vitally important that the organisation does communicate clearly its message of what its pay and reward strategy is intended to reward in terms of appropriate performance levels, behaviours and values.

Ethical issues

Low paid foreign workers

When considering what to pay people there are many ethical issues to consider in terms of what society values and is willing to pay people in differing jobs and professions. While the law does provide some guidance to employers in terms of equal pay or ensuring the minimum wage is paid there are still some groups such as migrant workers who, as we have seen, are sometimes exploited by unscrupulous employers and who have not even received this minimum level of protection, and other groups such as bankers or senior executives who seem to be able to pay themselves huge bonuses whether or not they have achieved their targets.

While people in the UK continue to expect clothes and food at cheap prices this is often also achieved at the expense of overseas workers who may be working long hours in poor conditions for less than a living wage. According to McVeigh (2007a), 'Charities campaigning for workers' rights accuse retailers of maximizing profits in demanding rock bottom prices from suppliers in the developing world'. As a result of allegations in *The Guardian* newspaper about the exploitation of workers in Bangladesh, MPs called for action to protect overseas workers.

> Lynne Featherstone, who at that time was the Liberal Democrat international spokeswoman, said legislation should guarantee that pay and conditions of overseas workers met international standards: "It's obscene that [UK shoppers] can earn more through their club card points than the people who produce the goods they are buying."
>
> (McVeigh, 2007b)

Some countries are developing rapidly and becoming sufficiently powerful that they can put pressure on foreign firms. For example in China the communist party called on employers to raise salaries and improve the training of workers after some foreign firms, including Honda, Toyota and Hyundai, were hit by strikes. The premier Wen Jiabo was quoted as saying 'that the era of low cost labour in China was coming to an end and that firms should improve skills, boost spending power and provide fair conditions for migrant workers' (*People Management*, 2010b). These are the same types of things that workers in the UK also appreciate.

Pause for thought 9.4 What do you think? Should there be stronger legislation in place to protect overseas workers? Would you be willing to pay more for goods you buy if it meant that overseas workers received a living wage?

Bonus culture

After the global banking crisis there is also the question of whether or not a bonus culture was partly to blame as it drove individuals to operate in ways that achieved their own short-term targets and those of the organisation, for example by selling more mortgages. But this emphasis on a short-term fix may have had an impact on financial stability worldwide as often mortgages or other products were sold to people who would not be able to repay them. According to the Financial Services Authority, quoted by CIPD (2009), 'Although it is difficult to prove a causal link, there is widespread consensus that remuneration packages may have been a contributory factor to the global crisis.'

There are also the ethical questions of whether it is right to pay bonuses at all to people who have not earned them or in organisations that have not made a profit, and also the question of exactly how much difference there should be between the salaries of the workforce and their directors who may receive huge bonuses. Levels of inequality appeared to be growing with the bonus culture and the whole issue of creating what is a fair and equitable system of reward is one that is going to be discussed a great deal in the future.

Pause for thought 9.5 What do you think? Should directors, bankers or top sports people have limits set on their pay?

Should they be rewarded for failure?

In your view how much difference should there be between the pay of directors in an organisation and their workforce?

What would you base their bonus payments on?

Conclusion

We have examined some of the types of payment systems that are available to employers and related them briefly to what they are supposed to achieve for the organisation. No scheme is perfect for all organisations, and all schemes have advantages and disadvantages. Each scheme gives a clear message about the values of the organisation and should be a reflection of its mission statement. The choice of payment scheme will depend on the wishes of the workforce as well as the culture of the organisation and these should be taken into account before any scheme is introduced. The workforce should be involved in discussion, design, implementation and review of whatever payment scheme is introduced. With the increasingly diverse workforce at the start of the twenty-first century, and moves towards a flexible workforce, many organisations have introduced flexible approaches to the pay and benefits that they provide for employees, using their payment systems as one mechanism for achieving their strategic goals, whether these are national or international.

Particular care should be taken to ensure that the basis for the chosen payment system is transparent and understood by the workforce, full consultation with the workforce has occurred and the selected pay system does not lead to unfair discrimination based on gender. This is still as necessary today as it was more than 40 years ago when the Equal Pay Act 1970 was first introduced. All organisations should ensure that they are rewarding and motivating all members of their workforce, regardless of their sex, in a fair way. A modern workforce has to be based on fair reward. The voluntary gender-pay audits which are being conducted by the Equality and Human Rights Commission should help provide data for starting to address the gender pay gap. However, employers should be regularly reviewing their pay systems not only to ensure there is no unfair bias but also to ensure that their pay and reward strategies achieve what they were supposed to achieve, and that they continue to attract, motivate, engage and retain staff and, ultimately, that they contribute to the achievement of the organisation's strategic objectives.

Review Questions

You will find brief answers to these review questions on page 472–3.

1. The minimum wage alters each year. Find out how much the minimum wage actually is at the present time. How much is the rate for adults aged 21 or over? How much is the rate for those aged 18–20?
   What are the rates being paid to those who are on government training schemes such as apprenticeships?

2. Interview managers or employees from three organisations of your choice from different industrial sectors to establish what effect, if any, the introduction of the living wage has or would have on that organisation.

3. Explain the process of job evaluation and comment on how a points rating job evaluation scheme can contribute to perceptions of fairness from the point of view of employees.

4. Fairness in pay is an objective of both employers and employees. Describe briefly the issues that need to be considered with reference to fairness, and evaluate critically the approaches that employers could adopt to achieve fairness.

5. Imagine that you are a consultant employed to select a job evaluation scheme for an organisation that employs 500 employees in a large range of clerical jobs. Write a report to the human resource manager in which you outline the advantages and disadvantages of the various types of job evaluation scheme and recommend what you consider to be a suitable job evaluation scheme for this organisation.

What next?

1. This chapter aimed to introduce you to the topic of payment systems and by this stage you should be able to meet the objectives stated at the beginning. You may now want to go further with the subject and the resources listed in the references and further study sections will help you to do this.

2. Go to **www.cipd.uk/podcasts** and listen to or print the transcript for podcast 93 CEO pay.
    What are the reasons for the increase in CEO's pay?
    Should CEO's pay be a multiple of the average pay of their workforce?
    What are the pros and cons of this approach?

HR in the news

Network rail face equal pay claim from women

By Gill Plimmer

Network Rail is facing the biggest equal pay claim in its history only a week after it was found to have missed punctuality targets and amid protests that bonuses for senior male staff have topped £1m.

The claim against the rail operator involves 30 women, but could cover 3,000 if won, according to the Transport Salaried Staffs Association, which is launching the claim.

It says the women are being paid between £3,000 and £4,000 a year less than their male colleagues for the same job.

Network Rail was fined a record £53m last week for failing to meet punctuality targets, with many thousands of late trains running on its tracks.

The state-backed organisation, which owns and operates Britain's railway infrastructure, was given a target of 92 per cent of trains running on time over the past five years. The Office of Rail Regulation found that from 2009 to this year, it managed only 86.9 per cent.

In London and the southeast, which accounts for the majority of the national network, Network Rail had a target of 93 per cent, but only 89.6 per cent ran on time.

The TSSA union is planning a protest outside Network Rail's annual meeting tomorrow as part of its campaign against executive bonuses.

Directors received about £50,000 each in annual bonuses last year. The awards of 12.5 per cent of salary, about a quarter of the maximum possible, were paid to five directors, two of whom have left the company to run the HS2 high-speed rail project. Three directors also received £300,000 retention bonuses in April.

Lorraine Ward, assistant general secretary at the TSSA, said: "It is simply outrageous that a taxpayer-funded company should reward those at the top with huge amounts while at the same time discriminating against thousands of their own staff who happen to be women."

Network Rail said the organisation was "committed to equal opportunities and fairness and equity in its pay. We are working hard, in partnership with our trade unions, to address any legacy imbalances within our pay structure."

 Source: Plimmer, G. (2014) Network rail face equal pay claim from women, *Financial Times*, 17th July.
© The Financial Times Limited 2014. All Rights Reserved.

Questions

1. Do you think that chief executives should still receive an enormous bonus even if the organisation that they have led has performed badly? List the arguments for and against.

2. To what extent do you think that the bonus culture is increasing the gap between rich and poor?

3. What legislation makes it unlawful for men and women who are doing the same job to be paid differently?

4. This was the situation in July 2014. Try to find out what happened in this equal pay case.

Improving your employability

Employers always say that they want to recruit people with good skills of analysis, problem solving, working with others, communication and business awareness. The following exercise can be completed individually or in teams and may help you to practice some of these skills.

Case study brief

AirgardXL is an organisation based in Huddersfield which designs and manufactures environmental, energy saving and pollution minimising products. The organisation was originally set up by two science graduates from the University of Huddersfield who developed an innovative product while conducting research. The company has been extremely successful and the product lines have expanded, which has meant that the company has gone through a period of rapid growth. It now employs designers and technical installers, and has its own manufacturing company in Huddersfield. It has a team of 10 technical and sales consultants based throughout the UK, office staff and a small HR department.

With the exception of the HR manager, the managers and technical and sales consultants are all male, while the staff working in the offices are all female. The workforce is predominantly white British but there are some Eastern European workers and a small number of British-born Asians.

The nature of the specialist expertise required means that the technical and sales consultants tend to travel a great deal within the UK and sometimes to other European countries and increasingly to the Far East. This has resulted in a degree of work overload for a few of the consultants who have suffered high levels of stress and increased levels of absenteeism.

AirgardXL have no future plans to develop further in the UK but want the current workforce to be more effective. Current political and economic developments have persuaded the company that there are better opportunities for expansion into China, where they have already started to develop a network of contacts, and they have already outsourced some of their manufacturing to a factory in Shenzhen. Their main strategic objective is to expand into this region and to establish their own manufacturing base and distribution centre to supply energy saving and environmental and pollution minimising products to the market in South East Asia. The UK base is still of strategic importance both as the head office and as manufacturing base providing products for the UK and Europe, and the intention is that a Chinese branch will provide a similar service for the South East Asian market.

The Huddersfield HR department is led by a recently appointed head of HR and she has a further two staff working for her as the HR manager and the HR administrator. She herself is supposed to contribute at board level to inform the strategic direction of the organisation and has responsibility for ensuring all HR and HRD policies are aligned with the strategic objectives of the organisation and that they add value to the organisation. However, this role is new and this has not happened in the past. She has only been working for the organisation for a few months and is in the process of reviewing all the HR and HRD policies and procedures.

As a first stage in this process she has recently conducted a staff satisfaction survey and found that there was a great deal of dissatisfaction with the pay and lack of incentives. Staff also feel that the supervisors and other managers tend to have rather a paternalistic approach to their staff, and that there is a command and control style of management which does not encourage the sharing of information or questioning the way that things are done in the organisation, and this includes a total

→

ban on discussion of pay levels. Discontent tends to be highest among the younger, more recent recruits. Many of the specialist technical and sales consultants also indicated that they are thinking of leaving as they say there are very few opportunities for promotion and a lack of opportunities to further develop their knowledge, skills or careers and they are dissatisfied with the pay. They could be difficult to replace. The managers and clerical staff are dissatisfied with their pay also as this is on an incremental scale based on length of service, so for younger staff it will take them some time to reach the top of the scale.

The working week is normally 38 hours and at the present time there is no overtime available for the manufacturing staff, though in the past they have tended to rely on this. The following table has details of the salaries and gender of the workforce.

Job titles	Male workers	Female workers	Salary ranges
Managers	9		£30,000–50,000
		1	£34,000
Designers and technical installers	10		£34,000
Technical sales consultants	10		£20,000–25,000 plus annual bonus of up to £1,000 each, depending on sales for top 2 sales people
Clerical staff		15 (this includes 2 on maternity leave)	£12,000–15,000
Manufacturing staff	70		£14,000–20,000
Caretaker/security	2		£15,000
Cleaners	2 part-time		£6.50 per hour

You have been asked by the head of HR to review the pay in the organisation and to make recommendations as to how she should proceed. She wants to motivate workers to be more effective in the organisation and to retain the talent already within it, and is also concerned about potential age discrimination, gender inequality and potential equal pay or equal value cases arising.

Either review the situation at AirgardXL and

1. write a report for the head of HR about this and make recommendations for improvements

   or

2. make a presentation as if to the head of HR about your findings and recommendations.

   Information sources to help you develop skills of report writing and making presentations are given on page 476.

(The organisation name used in this case study is entirely fictitious.)

References

Advisory, Conciliation and Arbitration Service (2014a) *Advisory Booklet – Job Evaluation: Considerations and Risks*, ACAS (available at www.acas.org.uk; accessed 19.11.14).

Advisory, Conciliation and Arbitration Service (2014b) *The Equality Act 2010 – Guidance for Employers*, ACAS (available at www.acas.org.uk; accessed 20.11.14).

Advisory, Conciliation and Arbitration Service (2014c) *Voluntary Gender Equality Analysis and Reporting: Action for Workplaces in the Private and Voluntary Sectors – Guidance for Employers*, ACAS (available at www.acas.org.uk; accessed 20.11.14).

Allen, K. (2014) Minimum wage system must change says founder, *The Guardian*, 22 February.

Chartered Institute of Personnel and Development (2009) *Bonuses and Cash Incentives*, CIPD (www.cipd.co.uk; accessed 28.08.10).

Chartered Institute of Personnel and Development (2010) *Annual Survey Report 2010: Reward Management*, CIPD (www.cipd.co.uk; accessed 25.08.10).

Chartered Institute of Personnel and Development (2013) *Annual Survey Report 2013: Reward* CIPD (www.cipd.co.uk; accessed 19.11.14).

Chartered Institute of Personnel and Development (2014a) *Reward and Pay: An Overview*, CIPD (www.cipd.co.uk; accessed 19.11.14).

Chartered Institute of Personnel and Development (2014b) *Pay Structures*, CIPD (www.cipd.co.uk; accessed 19.11.14).

Chartered Institute of Personnel and Development (2014c) *EP17: What Is Gender Equality Reporting and Is it Compulsory for Employers to Do This?* Employment law: frequently asked questions, CIPD (www.cipd.co.uk: accessed 20.11.14).

Chartered Institute of Personnel and Development (2014d) *Bonuses and Incentives*, CIPD (www.cipd.co.uk; accessed 22.11.14).

Chartered Institute of Personnel and Development (2014e) *Total Reward*, CIPD (www.cipd.co.uk; accessed 22.11.14).

Chartered Institute of Personnel and Development (2014f) *Research Insight: Managing an Ageing Workforce*, CIPD (www.cipd.co.uk; accessed 26.11.14).

Chartered Institute of Personnel and Development (2014g) *Strategic Reward and Total Reward*, CIPD (www.cipd.co.uk; accessed 28.11.14).

Cotton, C. (2009) *Press Release: Gender Pay Reporting 'No Magic Bullet' to Solve the Pay Gap, Warns CIPD*, CIPD, 27 April (www.cipd.co.uk; accessed 26.8.10).

Egan, J. (2010b) *Factsheet: Performance-Related Pay*, CIPD (www.cipd.co.uk; accessed 25.08.10).

Hong Kong Equal Opportunities Commission (2003) Eliminating discrimination: systems and policy reviews, equal pay for work of equal value, *Equal Opportunities Commission Hong Kong Annual Report 2001–2*, HKEOC www.eoc.org.hk//EOC/GraphicsFolder/Inforcenter/Annual/default.aspx?year=2001; accessed 24.06.04. www.equalityhumanrights.com; accessed 27.08.10.

Ferguson, D. (2014) Where are the highest paid jobs of 2014? *The Guardian*, 28 November.

Goss, F. (2010) How to set up incentive programmes, *People Management*, 12 August, 33.

Gov.UK (2014) *National Minimum Wages Rates*, Gov.UK (www.gov.uk/national-minimum-wage-rates, accessed 21.11.14).

Health and Safety Executive (2007) *The Gangmaster's Licensing Authority*, HSE (www.hse.gov.uk/agriculture; accessed 08.08.07).

Herzberg, F. (1966) *Work and the Nature of Man*, The World Publishing Company, New York.

Johnson, B. (2014) *Employer's Guide to the Living Wage*, Living Wage Foundation (www.livingwage.org.uk/employers, accessed 21.11.14).

Lawrence, F. (2007) The miracle of cheap fresh food depends on illegality, *The Guardian*, 17 July, 28.

Marlow, B. and M. Goodman (2013) The rise of the zero hours contract, *The Sunday Times*, 4 August, 21.

Marson, J. (2014) *Beginning Employment Law*, Routledge, Abingdon.

Maslow, A. (1954) *Motivation and Personality*, Harper and Row, New York.

Mason, P. (2014) Wages have been falling for years and inequality is growing. Are low paid, outraged workers ready to fight back? *The Guardian*, 10 November, 5.

Mathews, V. (2008) Executive pay: fat-cat failures, *Personnel Today*, 2 January (www.xperthr.co.uk; accessed 28.8.10).

McGregor, D. (1960) *The Human Side of Enterprise*, McGraw-Hill, New York.

McVeigh, K. (2007a) Asda, Primark and Tesco are accused over clothing factories, *The Guardian*, 16 July, 1.

McVeigh, K. (2007b) MPs want UK to pay living wage to overseas staff, *The Guardian*, 17 July, 9.

People Management (2010a) The CIPD People Management Awards, 12 August, 12.

People Management (2010b) Pressure's on for foreign firms in China, 1 July, 8.

People Management (2014a) Legal lowdown: minimum wage is not so clear cut, July, 17.

People Management (2014b) Gender pay gap 'narrowest since records began', November (www.cipd.co.uk/pm/; accessed 10.04.15).

Plimmer, G. (2014) Network rail faces equal pay claim from women, *Financial Times*, 17 July.

Rewards and Benefits Today (2009) Sky reward scheme uses arts festival to help celebrate success, Issue 1, 1 September (www.xperthr.co.uk; accessed 25.08.09).

Somerset Webb, M. (2014) Making money in the age of the machine, *Financial Times*, 8 November.

Wild, S. (2010) *Equal Pay Where Next? The Business Case for Equal Pay: How the Business Case for Equal Pay Plays Out in Practice and What Can Be Done to Strengthen it*, May, Equality and Human Rights Commission, London, 2.

Wright, C. (2007) Letter from the chair, *Reward Review*, CIPD, Spring/Summer 2007.

Further study

Books and reports

ACAS Advisory booklets, particularly those on the Equality Act 2010, pay systems, job evaluation and appraisal-related pay are useful sources of information.

There are also several publications about the Equality Act 2010, including a Code of Practice, provided by the Equality and Human Rights Commission.

Internet

The Advisory, Conciliation and Arbitration Service   **www.acas.co.uk**

This site has guidance on various aspects of pay and texts of leaflets that can be downloaded directly or ordered.

UK Government   **www.gov.uk**

Provides up-to-date information about employing people, including the minimum wage.

The Equality and Human Rights Commission   **www.equalityhumanrights.com**

There is a lot of information about all aspects of equality, including equal pay, on this site.

10 Health, safety and wellbeing

Objectives

By the end of this chapter you will be able to:

- explain what is meant by the terms 'safety', 'hazard', 'risk', 'wellbeing' and 'health'

- explain the key points in the main legislation relating to health, safety and wellbeing at work

- explain the reasons for managing employee health, safety and wellbeing

- explain the role of various people and groups in health and safety and wellbeing at work

- describe the Health and Safety Executive's approach to stress management.

In Chapter 1 we traced the history of people management and considered several approaches to what at that time was referred to as 'welfare'. Some people who adopted the 'hard' human resource management approach tried, originally, to distance themselves from welfare approaches, as they felt that these approaches showed a lack of business awareness. However, reducing accidents and improving occupational ill health is extremely important for organisations today, and many are taking an increasing interest in areas such as managing absenteeism. The changing demographics of an ageing workforce combined with what is claimed to be a growing obesity problem in the UK is also likely to result in a new imperative for employers to become more involved in health if they want their organisations to be effective and productive. Paton (2010) quotes from a 2010 survey by BUPA which said that

> government, the NHS, private providers and OH (Occupational Health) providers are all going to have their work cut out in dealing with an ageing, sicker working population, while firms with the healthiest (and therefore least absent) and most engaged workforce will be the ones best placed to thrive in an increasingly competitive global environment.

The ruling from the European Court of Justice that 'obesity can be counted as a disability in certain circumstances' raises issues about potential discrimination for employers who fail to make suitable adjustments for someone with this disability but could cause confusion as not all obese people will be considered to be disabled (Churchard, 2014). This may also force employers to take a greater interest in the health, fitness and waistlines of their workers.

Not everyone takes a negative view. ACAS (2012) indicates that not only can work have a positive impact on people's health but that there is also a reciprocal effect with well-motivated workers having a very positive impact on both the levels of productivity and the effectiveness of the organisation. However, not everyone benefits from the positive effects of work, and a good work–life balance is necessary. This is particularly important if we are to benefit from people working longer as will be necessary with an ageing population and no compulsory retirement age. The growing awareness of a good work–life balance has made people increasingly conscious of the relationship between our mental and physical health and the job we do, so it is no longer sufficient for employers to just comply with legislation.

ACAS (2012) indicates that there is also a need for good relationships between managers and workers, employee involvement, good job design, flexible working and use of occupational health services where appropriate. There is clearly a strong case to be made for organisations to pay more attention to the health, safety and wellbeing of their workforces and to see this as another aspect of their approach to performance management.

Many organisations realise the importance to their success of a healthy and productive workforce and are already seeking to adopt a more proactive approach. As the economy gradually recovers more employers are focusing on aspects of HR where they can get improvements in employee engagement, which will in turn help them retain talent. Strategies to improve safety and improve health are attractive ways to achieve this and should form a part of the organisation's approach to performance management. As we explained in Chapter 7 performance management in some organisations is being integrated with a wider range of HR processes than was traditionally the case and now involves processes designed to promote wellbeing, engagement and development of potential. Clearly issues relating to health, safety and wellbeing can contribute to this and as these approaches are not necessarily costly they may be particularly attractive to organisations trying to keep their budgets under tight control. Investors in People (IIP), which is perhaps better known for its business standard linking training and good HR practices to the strategic objectives of the organisation (discussed in Chapter 1), have also developed a new standard for health and wellbeing. They claim increasing evidence of a direct relationship between developing effective health and wellbeing programmes and increased productivity and that there is an excellent return on investment from these programmes as they result in happy staff who are more engaged, motivated and productive. In spite of this evidence they found that 54 per cent of full-time

Did you know?

The positive effects of work are beneficial not only for employers but employees too and can contribute to their sense of happiness and wellbeing. According to ACAS (2012) 'work can have a positive impact on our health and wellbeing. Healthy and well-motivated employees can have an equally positive impact on the productivity and effectiveness of a business.'

There is also evidence that work can also contribute to our sense of happiness. In the annual happiness survey carried out in Hong Kong in 2009, those who loved their jobs were happiest, followed by those who loved food and cooking, though when analysed by occupation those who were retired were listed as the happiest of all!

(*Source:* Chiu, 2009)

employees worked in organisations where they felt their employer did not care about their health and wellbeing and 48 per cent of them said this meant that they were less motivated in the workplace (IIP, 2014).

In this chapter we shall first examine what the terminology means before discussing some of the key laws relating to safety and the roles of those involved. Later we shall discuss the changing emphasis on health and wellbeing in more detail.

Definitions

Safety

We define safety as absence from danger and avoidance of injury. According to this definition, we should expect employers to do everything in their power to keep employees away from danger and free of injury while at work. This does not sound like a great deal to expect from an employer, but there is often a conflict in the employer's mind between increased production, which may involve some risk taking, and the necessity to keep employees safe and uninjured, which may cost money. Legislation has developed over a number of years to protect workers, and was initially designed to protect those who were weak and particularly vulnerable to exploitation from any employers who, tempted by the lure of increased production, might put their employees at risk of injury. Nowadays, with increasingly flexible patterns of work being available, many employees may work from home or even from their car for all or part of their working week, so employers will also have to consider the health and safety issues arising from this.

Hazard

A hazard is something that could cause harm to someone. Employers who are being proactive about health and safety therefore have to try to identify potential hazards before they actually do cause any harm. Stranks (2010) says that a hazard can be defined as 'the result of a departure from the normal situation, which has the potential to cause death, injury, damage or loss'.

Risk

The term 'risk' relates to the chances of the hazard actually resulting in harm being done to someone. Once the employer has identified a potential hazard then they have to estimate the chances or risk of someone being harmed by it.

We shall discuss the idea of risk assessment later in this chapter. The emphasis, in health and safety today, is on the prevention of accidents if possible by eliminating potential hazards and by predicting the level of risk in various situations. It is not, of course, always possible to eliminate all hazards or minimise all risks in a workplace, but employers are expected to predict potentially dangerous situations and then do something about them to ensure they become less dangerous. The emphasis in modern health and safety is to encourage those who own, manage or work in organisations to take responsibility for health and safety in them. For this to happen, both the workforce and safety representatives also need to be involved, risks need to be assessed and action needs to be taken to reduce these where possible. This is, however, currently a subject of debate as some feel that the UK has become too risk averse to the extent that this stifles initiative, and this will be discussed later in the chapter.

Wellbeing

According to Michaelson *et al.* (2009)

> personal wellbeing describes people's experiences of their positive and negative emotions, satisfaction, vitality, resilience, self-esteem and sense of purpose and meaning. Social wellbeing is made up of two components, supportive relationships and trust and belonging, both of which are critical elements of overall wellbeing.

The forerunners of HR managers were concerned with employee welfare and much of the legislation about health and safety also uses the term 'welfare'. We have chosen to use the term 'wellbeing' instead of 'welfare' as nowadays welfare has a slightly negative connotation and suggests some degree of dependency. Wellbeing clearly includes dealing with what might be regarded as welfare issues but looks at all aspects of a person's wellbeing and does not focus just on the negative aspects. It also has a more positive feel as the individual also has responsibilities for their own wellbeing so should be working in partnership with others on this.

According to Tehrani *et al.* (2007) people have mental and physical needs for social support, safety, health and also need to feel that they are not overwhelmed by events and can cope with life. These are all aspects of wellbeing and as a large part of our lives are spent at work it is natural to expect employers to play a part in employees' wellbeing. In the past many employers merely reacted to issues about health and safety and welfare without appreciating the benefits that adopting a more proactive approach could bring them. Many still operate in this way. However, more progressive employers are adopting a more proactive approach to health, safety and wellbeing to prevent problems arising in the first place.

Did you know?

In 2004 a senior pilot was forced to resign and two senior cabin crew were dismissed by Ryanair after the two off-duty crew members travelled on a full plane from Gerona to Dublin. Since there were no seats available for them, they sat in the rear toilets of the plane for both take-off and landing. The captain had allowed them to do this even though it contravened aviation regulations and was obviously potentially hazardous.

(*Source*: Seenan, 2004)

Health

Here the concern is for good health. We define good health as being physically and mentally well with body and mind in excellent working order. This goes further than safety in that the employer is no longer just expected not to do anything to injure his or her employees, but should seek to promote activities that encourage the good health of the employees. We shall return to a discussion of health promotion activities later in this chapter.

Safety

According to the Health and Safety Executive's *Health and safety statistics* (HSE, 2014a) the provisional figures for 2013–2014 show there were 133 workers fatally injured at work during this period, which is 19 per cent lower than the average for the previous five years. At the time of writing the latest figures available for accidents for 2013–2014 showed that falls, slips and trips accounted for 35 per cent of all injuries and resulted in 29 per cent of the employee injuries that had required absences of seven or more days. It was estimated that injuries and ill health cost £14.2 billion and 28.2 million working days were lost because of workplace injuries or work-related illness (HSE, 2014a).

Activity 10.1

Sometimes employers are reluctant to spend money on safety improvements as they don't feel this is justified. There are, however, costs associated with accidents. What are the possible costs to an individual employer of accidents at work?

Discussion of Activity 10.1

Obviously, depending on the severity of the injury, there are costs to the injured person in terms of pain and suffering, and possible loss of earnings. There are also costs to the employer, and your list is likely to include at least some of the following:

- cost of lost time and production due to absence caused by injury,
- cost of lost time and production due to dealing with the injury,
- cost of replacement worker or of training the replacement,
- cost of replacing broken machinery or unsafe machinery or equipment,
- cost of compensation to injured employee,
- higher insurance premiums if the organisation's accident record is not good,
- cost involved in carrying out a full investigation into the causes of the accident,
- cost of paying fines or even facing imprisonment if the employer was to blame for the accident,
- cost of poor morale within the workforce,
- cost of people not being willing to work for the organisation because of its poor reputation for safety.

You may have found some other costs involved in accidents as well. Employers should be aware of the hidden costs of accidents; if they carried out a cost-benefit analysis they would probably be amazed at how much accidents were costing them and be more prepared to spend money on accident prevention. In their studies of accidents, the Health and Safety Executive (1995) identified one organisation where the costs of accidents amounted to as much as 37 per cent of profits. This organisation did not have a particularly bad record on health and safety, nor had it suffered any major disasters, fatalities or prosecutions.

We believe that health, safety and wellbeing are important areas of concern for all HRM practitioners, since it is in the organisation's interest to pursue any initiatives that will provide benefits and services which the employees will want and value but that will also fit with the strategic needs of the organisation by enhancing levels of employee performance.

Legislation

The early development of legislation to protect employees at work was closely linked to the historical development of people management. More enlightened employers were concerned to improve working conditions for their employees and appointed industrial welfare workers to help with this. Less enlightened employers were compelled to pay some attention to the protection of selected groups of employees, and as early as 1840 legislation designed to limit the hours that children worked was passed. In more recent times several new acts have been passed and regulations issued to protect employees.

The Health and Safety at Work Act 1974

In Great Britain the foundation for the system of regulating health and safety at work was introduced by the Health and Safety at Work Act (HASAWA) 1974. Although this was a long time ago, HASAWA is still very important today and forms the foundation for much of the later legislation. According to Hackitt (2010a) one of the fundamental principles underpinning the Health and Safety at Work Act that still applies today is that 'those who create risk are best placed to manage it'. This means that those who create risks have duties to protect both workers and the public from their actions so that those who are the main risk creators are also the main duty holders in law. The main duty holders are likely to be employers and the self-employed but could also include employees, designers, manufacturers, importers, suppliers and those in charge of premises. In this chapter we shall focus principally on the duty holders who are employers and employees.

Before HASAWA, the legislation that could be used to protect employees at work was patchy and applied to vulnerable groups such as women or children, or to particular industries where there were thought to be high risks. Before 1974 the vast majority of the working population was not actually protected by any health or safety legislation. The Health and Safety at Work Act 1974 set up some new bodies such as the Health and Safety Commission (HSC), the Health and Safety Executive (HSE) and reinforced the power of others such as local authorities. In 2008 HSC and HSE merged to form one single body called the Health and Safety Executive (HSE) and this is now the organisation responsible for the promotion of health and safety at work in Great Britain (Hackitt, 2010a). It does work closely with local authorities and the roles of the Health and Safety Executive and the local authorities will be discussed later in the chapter.

HASAWA was the first piece of legislation designed to protect everyone at work, and also to protect others who were not at work, such as customers or even passers-by. It is estimated that it brought an extra three million people under the scope of protective safety legislation for the first time.

The main aim of the act was to provide a comprehensive system of law which would raise standards of safety and health for all persons at work and also protect members of the public who might be affected by their actions.

More than 40 years after the Health and Safety at Work Act 1974 became law it still forms the foundation of health and safety legislation in the UK, so it is important to understand some of the fundamental principles that underpin this important piece of legislation.

Activity 10.2

Both employers and employees have responsibilities under HASAWA. List what you would expect to be the duties of employers and employees with regard to health and safety.

Duties of employers	Duties of employees

Compare your lists with the duties summarised from the Health and Safety at Work Act 1974 below.

Discussion of Activity 10.2

Your list probably included some indication that employers were to take responsibility for having a safe workplace with safe equipment that would not injure anyone, and you also probably thought that employees too should take care not to harm anyone at work. There are no specific rules about lighting or temperature in the way that there are in some other acts. Instead the act is trying to involve people and make everyone take some responsibility for their actions. This approach is therefore moving towards a human resource management approach, and health and safety is not just in the domain of the human resource specialist but is shared with others. Sometimes the human resource specialist does have some aspects of health and safety included in their job description, and they may, for example, be expected to chair the safety committee if there is one.

The responsibilities of employers under the Health and Safety at Work Act

Employers have a basic duty of care to their employees to ensure their health, safety and welfare. As well as this rather general duty, they have five other duties. These are:

- to ensure that the workplace itself is safe; that equipment has been maintained correctly and work is safely organised;
- that accidents do not occur because of incorrect handling, storage or transportation within the workplace;

- that there is training, supervision and information relating to health and safety;
- that the workplace itself is maintained adequately and that there are safe ways to get into and out of the buildings;
- that provisions for wellbeing are adequate.

All of these duties are expressed in quite general terms and there is nothing in the act to specify, for example, how much training or information should be given. The words 'so far as is reasonably practicable' are used frequently within HASAWA. The exact meaning of this phrase will be discussed later in this chapter. The employer also has a further specific duty to produce a safety policy statement and we shall also discuss later in the chapter what this involves.

As we said earlier, HASAWA was designed to gain involvement in health and safety from as many sources as possible, so the responsibility was not just one way. Employees also have responsibilities.

The responsibilities of employees under the Health and Safety at Work Act

As you might expect, there are fewer responsibilities for the employees than for the employers. They have three main areas of responsibility under HASAWA in relation to health and safety. These are:

- to take responsibility for their own health and safety, and for any health and safety problems which might be caused to colleagues by their actions or in some cases their failure to act;
- not to recklessly interfere with or misuse any machinery, equipment or processes;
- to cooperate with employers about health and safety initiatives.

Although they may not seem very onerous responsibilities, they are important since employees who do not follow these guidelines could be disciplined or even face prosecution themselves if an accident occurred for which they were responsible. They should cooperate about health and safety issues, such as wearing protective clothing, if the employer provides it. Since they must take responsibility for their own health and safety and that of others, they must also not do anything to interfere with safety guards, as this could result in injuries to themselves or to other people.

> **Pause for thought 10.1** The phrase 'so far as is reasonably practicable' is used several times in HASAWA. What factors do you think should be considered in determining whether or not something is 'reasonably practicable'?

This phrase means that circumstances, risks and cost need to be considered when an employer is endeavouring to make the workplace safe for employees. It would be very difficult to make anywhere completely safe and eliminate all accidents. Accidents are by definition something that you cannot predict; nevertheless, many situations do occur where it is possible to predict that someone could be injured if improvements are not made, and employers should try to anticipate the likelihood of these types of accident and take steps to prevent them from occurring. 'Reasonably practicable' means that a calculation must be made in which the risk is compared with the sacrifices, cost and level of effort needed to avert that risk.

If there is a very slim chance that a comparatively minor accident might occur, but this chance could be eliminated by spending thousands of pounds on new equipment and also by disrupting the workforce, it might not be considered to be reasonably practicable to do so. If, however, the risk was of a serious injury or possibly death, then it would be reasonable to take every step and spend any amount of money to eliminate this risk. The term 'so far as is reasonably practicable' therefore means that the employer should do as much as they can to try to eliminate risks but that they need to review the balance between the risk and the amount of effort required to eliminate that risk.

Other health and safety legislation

Control of Substances Hazardous to Health Regulations 1988

This is another far-reaching piece of legislation comprising 19 regulations and four approved codes of practice which came into effect on 1 October 1989 and which have subsequently been revised and amended.

Control of Substances Hazardous to Health Regulations (COSHH) 1988 is designed to protect anyone who works with substances that could be hazardous to health. The regulations apply to all workplaces and include all substances with the exception of asbestos, lead, materials that produce ionising radiations and substances underground, which all have their own separate legislation. The legislation basically applies to any other substances that can cause harm by being inhaled, swallowed, coming into contact with the skin or being injected or introduced into the body, so they do cover a very wide range of substances.

COSHH regulations require all employers to carry out an assessment of risks to their employees from substances that are identified in the workplace as being potentially hazardous to either their employees or others who might be affected. Any risks that are identified must then be controlled. This emphasis on assessing risk and then doing something about it is a very different approach to that of HASAWA.

While it would be easy to assume that these regulations would not have much effect on ordinary workplaces, this is not in fact the case, as many of the substances identified as potentially hazardous will be found in any workplace – such as cleaning products – so in reality all workplaces are affected. The main areas that employers should focus on are:

- assessing the risk of substances used and identifying the required precautions;
- introducing appropriate measures to control or better still to avoid the risk;
- ensuring the correct use of the control measures, and that equipment is regularly maintained;
- monitoring health of employees where there is a known identifiable risk;
- involving workers in development of control measures to ensure their suitability in the workplace and informing and training them about risks that may arise from their work, and of the necessary precautions to take.

The Framework Directive

The European Union Framework Directive had broad objectives which were implemented in EU member states by 31 December 1992. This established in general terms the European Commission's approach to health and safety. The main objectives of the directive were to introduce measures to encourage improvements in safety and health of workers at work. In order to do this it contains general principles concerning the prevention of occupational risks, the protection of health and safety, the elimination of risk and accident factors, as well as informing, consultation and providing balanced participation in accordance with national laws.

The Management of Health and Safety at Work Regulations 1999

The British response to the EU directive was made in the Management of Health and Safety at Work Regulations (MHSWR) 1999. The HASAWA covered some parts of the directive but there were also new things that employers needed to do, such as carrying out certain detailed procedures, assessing risks, implementing certain safety measures and communicating with staff on health and safety. These regulations are accompanied by an Approved Code of Practice published by the Health and Safety Executive and are of particular significance as, according to Stranks (2010), 'all post 1992 regulations must be read in conjunction with the duties laid down in these with particular reference to risk assessment'. This is therefore a very important piece of legislation which has the following key features.

It states that employers shall:

- carry out assessment of health and safety risks to both employees and the public (this may be done in writing or on computer),
- monitor and review protective and preventive measures,
- appoint a competent person or persons to be responsible for protective and preventive measures,
- establish emergency procedures,
- give comprehensible and relevant information and training to employees (the training can be provided by a suitable training provider other than the employer),
- cooperate with any other employers who may share the same work site.

Also, employees shall:

- use equipment in the way in which they have been trained to use it,
- report any dangerous situations or any problem areas that they spot in the arrangements that the employer has made for health and safety.

These regulations are intended for use in cases of criminal action against an employer, and may not be used in any civil cases as evidence of negligence.

Pause for thought 10.2 To what extent do you feel that the Management of Health and Safety at Work Regulations 1999 differ from the HASAWA 1974?

These regulations are more forceful than HASAWA and specify that employers 'shall' do certain things, whereas HASAWA only expected employers to carry out its provisions 'so far as is reasonably practicable' to do so.

They also mean that employers have a legal duty to predict what could go wrong, before it actually happens, and to take preventive action to avoid it happening. They must record the preventive action that they have taken. This is referred to as risk assessment and is the same principle as under COSHH, but it is now applied more widely. Employers have to be proactive and actively manage activities aimed at protecting the health and safety of their employees. This is more in line than previous legislative measures with the human resource approach of being proactive and actively managing human resources.

Reporting of Injuries, Diseases and Dangerous Occurrences Regulations 2013

Reporting of Injuries, Diseases and Dangerous Occurrences Regulations (RIDDOR) 2013 requires employers to report certain work-related accidents, diseases and dangerous occurrences to the enforcing authorities so that they can identify risks and investigate serious accidents. According to HSE (2014e) not all accidents at work require a RIDDOR report and the key issues to consider when deciding include:

- the way the work was organised, carried out or supervised;
- whether or not machinery, plant or specific substances or equipment were being used for work;
- the condition of the premises at the time of the accident.

If none of the above features is present then according to HSE (2014e) it will be unlikely that the accident needs to be reported. The following briefly describes some of the circumstances in which reporting should occur:

- The death of a worker or non-worker must all be reported to the enforcing authorities immediately if this arises from a work-related accident or physical violence to a worker.
- If an employee or self-employed person working on the employer's premises suffers an accident or injury which requires them to be absent from work, or unable to do their normal duties, for at least seven days not including the day of the accident, then a completed accident form must be sent to the enforcing authorities.

There is also a requirement that certain serious specified injuries that have occurred as a result of an accident at work should also be reported. These include the following:

- fractures, other than to fingers, thumbs or toes;
- amputation of limbs;
- loss of or permanent reduction in sight;
- crush injuries that have resulted in internal organ damage;
- unconsciousness as a result of an injury to the head or asphyxia;
- serious burns to over 10 per cent of body;

- separation of skin from head which requires hospital treatment;
- injuries in an enclosed space that result in hypothermia, illness due to heat or that cause the person to need to be resuscitated or kept in hospital for more than 24 hours (HSE, 2014e).

Some work-related diseases, such as occupational dermatitis, any occupational cancer or occupational asthma have also to be reported on a disease report form to the enforcing authority. Carpal tunnel syndrome, tenosynovitis of hand or forearm or even severe cramp in hand or forearm are also notifiable if they have been caused by or made worse by the work the person has done, as are any diseases that have resulted in occupational exposure to some form of biological agent.

There may be instances where something occurs which does not actually result in a reportable injury but which could have done. For example, the collapse of a lift, equipment or machinery coming into contact with an overhead power line, or an explosion or fire, which result in work having to stop for more than 24 hours are all likely to constitute dangerous occurrences, even if no one is actually injured. Any dangerous occurrence can be reported online but fatal and specified injuries have to be reported immediately by telephone to the enforcing authorities, even if this is outside normal working hours. Records should also be kept of any incidents covered by RIDDOR, and accidents and incidents not covered by RIDDOR but which have resulted in absence from work for three or more days should be recorded in the organisation's accident book. (Details of where to find more information are given in Further study at the end of the chapter.)

The Working Time Regulations 1998

We discussed the Working Time Regulations 1998 briefly in Chapter 3, but have also included them here since the hours people work can have a big impact on their health, wellbeing and safety in the workplace, though other factors such as liking their job and the amount of support they get from colleagues can mitigate against some of these negative effects (Ayling, 2014a).

It has often been claimed that the UK is the 'long hours capital' of Europe and that working such long hours adversely affects workers' health. In some organisations there is a culture of 'presenteeism', where people are expected to arrive early for work and leave late, forgoing home and social life. While some workers thrive in a long hours' culture and live to work, such a culture is likely to hide a great deal of inefficiency and result in increased levels of stress and ill health for many other workers. These regulations attempt to control the hours worked and control the way the hours are organised. They also establish minimum holiday levels for employees in the UK, although it is frequently claimed that a large number of UK employees actually fail to take all the holiday they are entitled to, either because they are too busy or are too frightened to be away from work for their whole holiday entitlement, or that if they do take the holidays they still respond to work emails while on holiday.

Although the 48-hour working week means workers in the UK still work much longer hours than their counterparts in France, it is nevertheless considerably better than

Did you know?

Death from overwork is so common in Japan that they even have a special word for it, *Karoshi*. The first documented case of Karoshi occurred in Japan in 1969 but there have been many cases since. In Japan the spouses of those who have died from Karoshi have won claims for compensation from the companies concerned and each year between 20 and 60 claims for compensation are brought. This is still probably a gross underestimate of the real number of cases of Karoshi in Japan.

(*Source*: Nishiyama and Johnson, 1997)

the expectation in countries such as Japan. In Japan it has been documented that many workers regularly work for over 100 hours per week, for many weeks, or even years, at a time and that this frequently leads, not surprisingly, to ill health or even death. Since we work increasingly in a global economy, where people are constantly accessible via mobile phones or email, these long-hour work practices have spread to the USA and the UK.

Statutory holiday entitlement is currently 28 days of paid holiday which is applied pro-rata for part-timers and which can include 8 days for public holidays. This right applies to all workers and not just employees (Ayling, 2014a). (The distinction between workers and employees was discussed in Chapter 3.) Having rights to holiday is not of much use if workers do not take them and employers should take steps to make sure that workers use their holiday entitlement. They should discourage a culture of presenteeism and regard this as good management practice and as a way of contributing to the prevention of ill health.

Legislation about smoking

It is claimed that smoking is still the largest preventable cause of early death and disease and this remains true even after legislation was introduced to discourage it (Iley, 2014). Four related pieces of legislation were introduced in Scotland, Wales, Northern Ireland and England prohibiting smoking in public places, including workplaces, and similar legislation has been introduced throughout the rest of Europe. These related pieces of legislation are designed to protect workers who may previously have been affected by passive smoking and also to promote positive health improvements by encouraging smokers to stop.

Whilst the ban on smoking at work seems to have been effective in encouraging some smokers to quit and also in preventing work colleagues having to suffer from passive smoking indoors, it has produced other problems such as pollution around doorways and entrances to buildings, and many workplaces have banned smoking within a certain distance of their buildings. E-cigarettes are supposed to help those trying to quit smoking and are likely to be safer for smokers than cigarettes themselves but raise other problems because as they are as yet unlicensed and their safety, quality and effectiveness cannot be guaranteed. Employers should be health aware and should try to help those trying to quit smoking, but current advice is for employers to treat electronic cigarettes in the same way as cigarettes and ban them from the workplace: they contain toxins which could harm others as well as the smokers themselves, may create a false sense of safety which could encourage young people to try them and the presence of people smoking e-cigarettes in a workplace will not present a good image to customers or clients (Iley, 2014).

The Corporate Manslaughter and Corporate Homicide Act 2007

The Corporate Manslaughter and Corporate Homicide Act 2007 made corporate manslaughter a criminal offence from April 2008. This increased the interest in health, safety and wellbeing as companies found guilty could face an unlimited fine if they are found to have caused death through gross negligence or failures in their safety systems. People working for some organisations such as Crown bodies,

Did you know?

At the time of writing the largest fine to result from a conviction under the Corporate Manslaughter and Corporate Homicide Act 2007 was £480,000 plus £84,000 in costs. This case involved Lion Steel Equipment Limited, an organisation with more than 100 employees and a turnover of £10,000,000. The prosecution was brought using both the Corporate Manslaughter and Corporate Homicide Act and Sections 2 and 33 of the Health and Safety at Work Act 1974 and was as a result of a terrible accident which resulted in an employee dying after falling through a factory roof in May 2008.

(*Source*: Mew, 2014)

previously exempt from prosecution, are now covered by this legislation. The offence of corporate manslaughter cannot be committed by individuals and it is only the organisation which is prosecuted for this, though individuals can still be charged with gross negligence. Directors and senior staff may be able to insure against claims for gross negligence. While this legislation is to be welcomed, Richard Jones (2007) argues that it does not go far enough and that there are still too many exemptions. He goes on to say that 'HR needs to actively engage workers in helping keep workplaces safe, and should regularly consult them on health and safety issues'. Safety should certainly be of concern to all managers including HR managers and line managers.

Most of the legislation discussed here, with the exception of the anti-smoking legislation, has focused primarily on safety although clearly health and wellbeing are also closely linked to this.

The people and organisations involved in health, safety and wellbeing

We have already discussed at length the roles of employers and employees but there are other health, safety and welfare roles currently undertaken by the Health and Safety Executive and local authorities. What do these organisations actually do? How are they organised?

The Health and Safety Executive

The HSE is the single national independent regulatory body responsible for promoting better health and safety at work within Great Britain (Wintersgill, 2014). It celebrates its fortieth anniversary in 2015 and as an independent body reflects the interests of employers, workers and local authorities though the Department of Work and Pensions (DWP) has overall responsibility for it. The potential size of the board of the HSE is no more than 11 members plus the chairperson and it is responsible for all aspects of running of the HSE as well as its strategic direction. Its mission is 'The prevention of death, injury and ill-health in Great Britain's workplaces' (HSE, 2014b).

It consists of policy advisers, inspectors and experts in medicine, science and technology. They are responsible for making provision for enforcing the legislation, for dealing with daily administration and conducting research and for identifying any new risks or hazards that emerge with changes to technology or work practices. They are also responsible for preparing, after due consultation with stakeholders, draft regulations for the approval of the Secretary of State for Work and Pensions as well as issuing Approved Codes of Practice which provide guidance for employers. Employers do not have to follow exactly a code of practice but a failure to provide safety features at least as good as those outlined in the relevant code of practice could be used in evidence against an employer if an accident occurs and results in a case being brought against them.

In June 2009 HSE launched a new strategy, *The health and safety of Great Britain: be part of the solution* (Hackitt, 2010a), and one of its key features is that it sets out to involve all stakeholders in health and safety. Hackitt (2010b) emphasises the fact that while HSE and their local authority partners lead and coordinate health and safety, the success of the strategy relies on everyone playing a part and not just leaving it to these groups. This is particularly important as the UK economic situation improves as traditionally any improvement to the economy has also resulted in an increase in work-related accidents and ill health.

Alongside local authorities HSE is also an independent regulator for health and safety and their main role is to assist others in preventing work-related accidents and ill health. Its inspectors can achieve this by conducting workplace inspections and by other more proactive measures such as getting stakeholders involved and providing guidance by providing information and advice.

Local authorities

Local authorities (LAs) also have responsibility for enforcement of health and safety in more than one million workplaces. Under HASAWA, the Secretary of State for Work and Pensions can make regulations for local authorities to take on responsibility for certain activities and to ensure that there is no duplication of effort between them and the Health and Safety Executive. The local authority inspectors, normally known as environmental health officers, are responsible for health and safety mainly in the services sector, while the HSE tends to concentrate on the more hazard-prone industries. There is a liaison committee which ensures consistency of approach between the HSE and local authorities. The HSE publishes a wide range of material each year explaining its role and the practical implications of legislation. The Health and Safety Executive can provide guidance, approved codes of practice and regulations.

The Gangmasters Licensing Authority

Not all workers are lucky enough to work in well-organised and regulated workplaces even in the UK. The death of 18 Chinese cockle pickers in Morecambe Bay, Lancashire, in 2004 drew attention to the world of unscrupulous operators who employ migrant workers, sometimes illegally, to work in low-skilled jobs. The Gangmasters Licensing Authority (GLA) was formed to license genuine

Did you know?

Sainsbury's is partnering with the Gangmasters Licencing Authority and is working with them to train their workers to try to recognise and identify exploitation of workers in the global supply chain. According to Judith Batchelor, director of Sainsbury's brand, 'Modern slavery within global supply chains is a serious issue and it is a priority of ours to work with our suppliers to address it.'

(*Source*: PM Editorial, 2014)

workforce organisers and providers of migrant workers and has the power to revoke licences where poor practice has occurred. Initially legislation targeted the agricultural sector where gangmasters and migrant workers primarily worked. There is a continuing need to raise awareness and many of the exploited workers have been found to be working long hours on much less than the minimum wage, in appalling working conditions and producing products that later sell at a much higher price in UK supermarkets.

In October 2013 the GLA's Supplier/Retailer Protocol was launched by the Home Secretary, Theresa May. This involves major suppliers and retailers sharing information with the authorities about possible exploitation or wrongdoing within the agriculture, horticulture, shellfish gathering and all associated processing and packaging (PM Editorial, 2014).

The world of work has changed dramatically and there is now a much more diverse workforce working in increasingly flexible ways. New health and safety issues arise as people work from home, or while on the move and the risks to their health and safety also need to be assessed. There are also fewer large employers and more small ones.

The enforcing authorities

We shall now discuss how the current inspection of workplaces and investigation of accidents is shared between HSE inspectors and local authority enforcement officers. Since April 2013 only businesses that operate in high risk areas such as construction, or those with a poor safety record or who have had a safety incident will be subject to regular health and safety inspections. This has removed many organisations from regular inspections.

The HSE inspectors cover work conducted primarily in factories, building sites, mines, fairgrounds, quarries, railways, chemical plants, offshore and nuclear installations, schools and hospitals. The local authority enforcement officers cover over one million premises in retailing, some warehouses, most offices, hotels, catering, consumer services, sports and leisure activities and places of worship, but with the changes since 2013 many of these low-risk organisations such as offices, shops, pubs and clubs will no longer get inspected regularly.

However, both HSE and local authority inspectors do have similar powers of enforcement when they feel an intervention is needed. These include a right to:

- enter employers' premises;
- carry out inspections/investigations;
- take equipment or materials on to premises;
- take measurements, photographs or recordings;
- carry out tests on articles or substances;
- examine books and documents;
- issue improvement notices;
- issue prohibition notices;
- issue a Crown notice.

The last three points are very important and we shall consider each in turn. However, sometimes when an enforcing inspector finds a breach of the law which is relatively minor, they may feel that improvement notices and prohibition notices are not appropriate.

Informal methods

In the case of a minor breach in legislation the inspector may choose to use informal methods and may simply give the employer or contractor advice about what they should do to comply with the law, and explain the reasons.

Improvement notices

If the inspector feels that an organisation is contravening one of the relevant provisions of legislation then they can issue an improvement notice which will specify that improvements must be made within a specified time limit to bring the equipment or process up to the required standard of safety.

Prohibition and deferred prohibition notices

If when the inspector visits they feel that there is serious danger or risk of injury to employees, they can issue a prohibition notice which will stop work activity immediately until the risk has been dealt with. In some circumstances a deferred prohibition order may be issued: this would occur, for example, if it would be difficult to stop a process in mid-cycle or if there was no immediate risk of injury.

Crown notices

This is a type of notice which HSE can issue to a Crown organisation such as a government department or the Prison Service. It would be issued under the same sort of circumstances that would merit a prohibition notice or improvement notice for other organisations.

Fees for intervention

In October 2012 a cost recovery scheme came into effect whereby the HSE is able to recover reasonable costs that the HSE inspectors have incurred from an employer who they feel has committed a material breach of health and safety law. The inspector must first issue a written notification to the employer in the form of one of the following: a notification of contravention, an improvement notice, prohibition notice or a prosecution (Wintersgill, 2014). During the first year of operation more than 21,000 invoices were issued and the total costs recovered amounted to £8.7million (HSE, 2014b).

Enforcement policy

The Health and Safety Commission's *Enforcement policy statement* (2009a) states the approach which both the Health and Safety Executive and local authorities should take in relation to law enforcement. The overall aims of the HSC are to protect the health, safety and wellbeing of people at work and to safeguard others such as members of the public who may be exposed to risk from the workplace or activity.

Normally in England and Wales most prosecutions would go to a magistrates' court but more serious cases are referred to the Crown Courts. Under the Scottish judicial system the majority of cases go to a sheriff court or before a jury. Organisations and individuals can face prosecution, and prison sentences and unlimited fines can also be given by the Crown Courts.

Any accidents at work that result in death are treated as manslaughter. The police are involved in these cases and have overall responsibility for them. However, there had been general dissatisfaction that the system was not tough enough and that employers were on occasions shirking their responsibilities with regard to health and safety and frequently escaping prosecution even when an employee had died as a result of the company's actions or inactions. The Corporate Manslaughter and Corporate Homicide Act 2007, mentioned earlier, is intended to create a criminal offence of corporate manslaughter for the first time. 'It will certainly lead to greater scrutiny by the courts of the way in which companies organise themselves internally in terms of health and safety' (Baker, 2007). This should make it easier to examine the conduct of senior managers, and a company can be found guilty of corporate manslaughter if it can be proved that the way they managed and organised their activities led to a death and that this amounted to a gross breach of its duty of care to the employee.

The HSE's (2009a) *Enforcement policy statement* gives guidance to those involved with the enforcement of health and safety issues and sets out the principles of enforcement for firm but fair enforcement of health and safety law. This policy statement stresses five main things:

1. **The principle of proportionality**. This means that the severity of the action taken should be in proportion to the level of risk and the seriousness of the breach of law.
2. **Targeting**. The people/organisations who cause the most serious risks or who have failed to control hazards in the workplace adequately should be the ones to be targeted by the inspectors.
3. **Consistency**. For people to have faith in the system and the inspectors they need to feel that they will be treated in a consistently fair way. This does not mean identical treatment for duty holders but involves taking a similar approach when the circumstances seem similar and consequently achieving similar ends.
4. **Transparency**. Every action taken should be clear, with explanations given for any action that is taken so that duty holders know what is expected from them in relation to health, safety and wellbeing.
5. **Accountability**. The enforcing authorities must be held accountable for their actions and so must have policies and standards to be assessed against. They also need to have clear ways for people to make comments or complaints and for dealing with these (HSE, 2009a).

Prosecution

If the case is very serious then the inspector may also need to initiate a prosecution. Any decision about whether or not to prosecute will be taken after considering the HSE's Enforcement Policy Statement.

Consultation with safety representatives and other employees

As we said earlier, there is a duty for employers to consult with and involve both employees and safety representatives in the workplace about safety matters. In October 1978 the Safety Representatives and Safety Committees Regulations 1977 as amended came into effect. These regulations form part of the Health and Safety at Work Act, and within a year over 100,000 safety representatives were in post. The regulations provide that any recognised trade union can appoint safety representatives, and they recommend that in general the people who are appointed should have worked for that employer for at least two years so that they have a reasonable range of experience from which to draw. In some trade unions the shop stewards take on the role of safety representatives, while in others the safety representative is a separate post. The people to fill these positions are, however, selected by the trade union, not by the management. Organisations where there are no recognised trade unions can still appoint safety representatives, and they are normally elected by the workforce. As more employers start to appreciate that there are benefits for the business and a clear return on investment to be gained from focusing attention on health, safety and wellbeing, this role could become even more important.

The safety representative's main function is to represent the employee in consultation with the employer on issues relating to health and safety in the workplace, and they can investigate hazards or potential hazards as well as carrying out inspections of the workplace. They are entitled to paid time off to perform their duties and for training to enable them to carry out their duties effectively, and they may also require some facilities such as the use of a telephone, a filing cabinet and a room to conduct interviews. If two or more safety representatives make a written request to management for a safety committee to be established, then the employer is legally obliged to do so.

The Management of Health and Safety at Work Regulations 1992, as amended in 1999, adds to the Safety Representatives and Safety Committees Regulations 1977 and specify that every employer shall consult safety representatives in good time with regard to

- the introduction of any measure at the workplace which may substantially affect health or safety of the workforce,
- arrangements for appointing or nominating a 'competent person' who is able to assist the employer to carry out risk assessment exercises and help them in carrying out duties in relation to health and safety,
- the health and safety information that the employer is supposed to provide to employees,
- the planning and organisation of health and safety training,
- the health and safety consequences of the introduction of new technology at work.

There are, as you can see, a wide range of duties performed by safety representatives. Safety representatives usually receive excellent training from trade unions for this demanding role and those who take on these roles can also choose to take the training further and use it as part of a professional qualification in health and safety.

The Health and Safety (Consultation with employees) Regulations 1996 (as amended) added a duty to consult more widely with other employees if there are no safety representatives in the organisation, perhaps because no union is represented or if there are some employees who are not members of a union. For small businesses consultation with an individual may be sufficient (HSE, 2014d).

Safety officer or safety adviser

None of the legislation actually specifies the need for a safety officer but, as the law has grown in complexity many organisations have felt that it is necessary to appoint a person to specialise in this area of work. This is a management appointment and must not be confused with the trade union/employee-appointed safety representative. Safety officers are sometimes appointed to advise senior management without being part of any other department and report directly to the board, but in many organisations they form part of the human resource management department. Smaller organisations may not wish to appoint a full-time safety officer and may instead call on the expertise provided by independent consultants to act as safety advisers. It is important that anyone appointed as safety officer or safety adviser has the status and level of competence to provide authoritative advice to management and the workforce on aspects of health and safety.

A competent person

This has a specific meaning in terms of health and safety as the Framework Directive (Article 7) says that employers must designate 'a competent person' who has practical and theoretical knowledge of particular equipment and who is able to identify any problems that may occur with it. The provision of this directive is reflected in Regulation 6 of the Management of Health and Safety at Work Regulations 1992 and clearly refers to a management nominee, although not necessarily to the safety officer but to someone who because of their knowledge and experience of particular machinery, plant or equipment is able to identify problems or defects in it. That person needs to be competent not just to do the job but to carry out risk assessment for health and safety for employees and the public, and must monitor and review protective and preventive measures. A safety officer may fulfil this role but is not likely to be the only designated competent person, as they are unlikely to have the required level of knowledge or experience for all machinery.

Safety committees

Safety committees have to be established, as we said earlier, if two or more safety representatives request the organisation to do so, but many organisations do not wait for this request and it is good practice to set up a safety committee in any case. The main objective of a safety committee is to promote cooperation between employers and employees in instigating, developing and carrying out measures to ensure the health and safety at work of employees. In organisations seeking to improve health, safety and wellbeing this provides a useful way of gaining increased employee engagement. Safety committees are likely to provide some or all of the following functions:

- study figures and trends for accidents and notifiable diseases,
- examine safety audit reports,
- consider reports and factual information provided by inspectors,
- consider the reports of safety representatives,
- assist in development of safety rules and safe systems of work,
- monitor the effectiveness of safety training in the workplace,
- monitor the effectiveness of the safety and health communication in the workplace,
- encourage publicity for health and safety programmes in the workplace,
- provide a link with the appropriate inspectorates.

Safety committees can be a very effective way of increasing involvement with and knowledge of health, safety and wellbeing issues.

Membership of the health and safety committee

The membership of the committee should be agreed between management and the employees. The committee should normally include equal numbers of people from management and the workforce and should have representation from different areas of the workforce and different grades of management. People such as the organisation's doctor, nurse or safety officer should also be invited to attend as *ex officio* members. It is a good idea for the person who chairs the committee to have sufficient status within the organisation that they can authorise money to be spent on necessary aspects of health and safety without having to refer all such decisions to higher authority. A senior member of the management team would fulfil this role well, although in many organisations the chair of the safety committee may also alternate between management and the workforce.

Health and safety arrangements

Safety policy statement

You will remember that under HASAWA one of the duties of an employer is to provide a safety policy statement to show each person's responsibilities, and the arrangements they have made to carry out the policy. The safety policy applies to all organisations that employ more than five employees. This is supposed to be a document that can be used to show in a practical way how the arrangements for health and safety are to be carried out in the workplace, and it should be designed to have a genuine effect on health and safety working practices. This means that it should be clearly written and should be easily available to any employee, and a copy should preferably be given to each employee. It does not mean that it is a secret document, as some organisations in our experience seem to think, kept locked in a filing cabinet well away from the gaze of employees. In order to encourage awareness of health and safety and produce an effective safety policy document, it is also advisable that a range of people, including workforce representatives, should be involved in its design and that key decision makers have been involved fully in these discussions. In some organisations a person will be chosen to champion the policy, and targets for improvements in specific areas of health and safety may also be set. Arrangements should also be made to review the health and safety policy regularly, at least annually, since what is important is whether the policy is having an effect on health and safety in the workplace, rather than how well written it is. There are four steps recommended by HSE which are Plan, Do, Check and Act. Clearly having a safety policy in place with plans for ways to implement this falls into the first category of planning but then organisations need to follow through with the further stages and a safety policy helps form the basis of these stages too.

The HSE has examples of policies for health and safety and risk assessment on their website (**www.hse.gov.uk**) and while individual organisations are recommended to design their own policies to suit their organisations the model health and safety policy provided by the HSE is useful. Key features are:

- the name of the organisation,
- the name of the senior manager or senior employee who has overall responsibility for health and safety,
- the name of the member of staff with general day-to-day responsibility for ensuring the policy is acted upon.

The model policy then arranges issues in columns under three headings and would be a useful starting point. These are:

- Statement of general policy.
- Responsibility of (named person/job title) for health and safety.
- Actions/arrangements made for health and safety? (What are you going to do?)

There should be space for the employer's signature and date and information about location of displayed Health and Safety Law poster(s), the location of the first aid box or boxes and the location of the accident book.

Statement of general policy

The first column of the safety policy should show management's approach to health and safety and should indicate what the management plans to do in relation to different aspects of health and safety, such as the prevention of accidents or work-related ill health, dealing with emergencies, training for health and safety and ways for engaging with the workforce about health and safety. It should also show how they maintain safe and healthy working conditions, maintain their plant and equipment and store safely various substances.

Responsibility for health and safety

The second column should indicate which named person is actually responsible for each of the specific tasks. The safety policy is basically concerned with people, their duties and their accountability. It could also include a management chart showing the chain of command in respect of health and safety, with a clear statement that the ultimate responsibility for health and safety rests with the board or chief executive or equivalent. The safety policy document should carry at the end the signature of the person with the ultimate responsibility for health and safety at work. There should be a clearly defined role for the safety adviser, if such a position exists, and clear explanation of their relationship to senior management and line management. This part of the document should also indicate the role of those appointed as 'competent persons' to assist the employer in implementing the safety policy.

The action/practical arrangements (what the organisation is going to do)

The third column should establish systems and procedures and the practical arrangements for their implementation. It should also show the system for monitoring safety and for publishing results. The section of the safety policy covering arrangements should be a practical section that is regularly reviewed and updated.

Some of the topics that could be included under the arrangements for managing health and safety under the sections are listed below.

- Any specific health and safety risks that arise from the organisation's work activities
- Arrangements for consultation with employees
- Arrangements to ensure that plant and equipment are safe to use
- Arrangements for organising the safe handling and use of substances
- Systems for the provision of information, instruction and supervision
- Ways of ensuring competency for tasks and training
- Methods for dealing with accidents, first aid and work-related ill health
- Methods to be used for monitoring all aspects of health and safety
- The arrangements that have been made for emergency procedures such as for fire and evacuation
- Details of any specific key areas of risk for jobs in that organisation.

The second stage of the HSE's approach to managing health and safety in the workplace is to Do and this section on action and practical arrangements clearly indicates what an employer plans to do in different circumstances.

Specific health and safety risks arising from the organisation's work activities

This means that the arrangements for carrying out risk assessments, the results of the risk assessments and the actions taken will all need to be shown, although the findings and resulting actions will need to be shown in a separate document. The HSE's template for a health and safety policy also shows a template for conducting risk assessments and HSE (2014f) suggests both should be prepared at the same time. Risk assessments will be discussed in more detail later in the chapter.

The third stage of the HSE's approach to managing health and safety in the workplace is to Check and conducting risk assessments and monitoring specific risks fits within this category.

People need to be aware of their responsibilities as, if something goes wrong and a serious accident occurs, the relevant enforcement officers will want to know who was responsible. These enforcement officers would carry out a full investigation and would also want to examine the safety policy document. If a supervisor did not know that they were responsible for checking that a protective guard was in place, then the employer would have to be able to prove that they had informed the supervisor of their responsibilities and had also trained them adequately in the fulfilment of these responsibilities. Many tasks will of course be delegated to different levels of management, and employees do, as we have seen, have some responsibility for their own actions. Senior management cannot, however, abdicate their ultimate responsibility for overall safety within the organisation, and must try to ensure the health and safety of their employees and others affected by their employees' actions. Those who carry the ultimate responsibility for this, such as the board of directors, could face prosecution and possibly a large fine or even a spell in prison for individual directors if their organisation is found to be at fault. Similarly, others with specific responsibilities such as safety officers, human resource managers, line managers or training officers could be charged and convicted of an offence.

First consider the following case study and identify the health, safety and wellbeing issues that you think occur here then complete Activity 10.3.

Case Study 10.1   Health and safety

The Sheffley Company employs nearly 330 employees and specialises in the production of steel castings. The organisation has a director, Mr Jones, whose great-grandfather founded the business. There is a new production manager, Mr Tandy; an import and export manager, Ms Jeffries; and an administration manager, Mrs Groves. Mr Tandy has eight line managers reporting to him, who have a total of 280 employees working for them. Mrs Groves has a payroll manager, a canteen manager and a personnel officer reporting to her and Ms Jeffries runs the purchasing, goods inward and goods outward departments, and the warehouse and export sections.

The work involved in the production of steel castings is hazardous and the company has not had a good record with regard to health and safety. It is not only in the production areas that there have been problems – the offices also have suffered rather a large number of accidents which have required employees to have more than three days off work to recover. The office staff are expected to regularly work long hours and work whatever hours are necessary to complete the job. Several are absent with serious long-term illnesses including the payroll manager and of course this puts additional pressure on those who remain. Mrs Groves is beginning to show signs of the strain from doing her own job and that of the absent payroll officer and is suffering from regular headaches and feelings of anxiety.

The new production manager decides that something must be done about the record on health, safety and wellbeing. He decides a punitive approach will work best and in the weekly meeting with the production supervisors he informs them that from next week any employee who does not wear the protective equipment provided will be dismissed. The safety equipment comprises safety boots, safety goggles and overalls.

During the lead-up to the introduction of the safety equipment, notices are put up to explain the disciplinary penalty for non-compliance with the regulation, but information about the use and location of some of the equipment is not provided. Neither the safety representatives nor the safety committee have the opportunity to inspect the new protective equipment or to advise employees on its suitability.

The employees prove to be reluctant to wear the protective goggles which, they complain, pinch their skin and impair their vision. The production manager realises that the enforcement of safety is going to be problematic and at the next week's meeting informs the supervisors that they do not have to be too rigid in their enforcement of the rules.

Two serious accidents occur just a month later in the production area and a further serious accident occurs in the offices. In the first incident molten metal splashes on to the foot of an employee causing serious burns. In a separate accident a few days later an employee slips, splashing molten metal close to his eyes. Luckily his sight is saved, but he suffers severe burns and scarring. The accident record in the offices is also unsatisfactory, and one employee is injured when chemicals used in the photocopier spill on her leg, causing a severe itchy rash to develop. She has been having problems at home but has felt she must keep working although her mind has not been on her work all the time. Other employees in the wages office complain of backaches and headaches which they say are caused by poor lighting, uncomfortable chairs and badly adjusted screens on their visual display units.

You should be able to identify some of the many issues raised here about health, safety and the wellbeing of the employees, such as the exact nature of the employer and employee responsibilities. The employer in this case, and indeed anyone involved in this area of work, also needs to comply with legislation, so, based on your reading of the chapter so far, you should also be able to identify the key legislation infringed by both the employer and the employees.

Activity 10.3

Design a safety policy statement for Sheffley Company. Remember that this should be a practical document that can be used by people in the organisation. Use the sections and main headings that we have given earlier (see pages 357–9).

Risk assessment

The idea of assessing and controlling risks was introduced to Britain with the Control of Substances Hazardous to Health Regulations 1988 when employers had to assess the risk of harm to people from certain substances being used at work. The 1992 Code of Practice for the Management of Health and Safety at Work subsequently made it a legal duty for employers to assess and record health and safety risks, and to appoint a 'competent person', that is a person who has been suitably trained and who is allowed adequate time and facilities to perform this role and assist in this and other safety tasks.

Every organisation has to carry out its own risk assessment, and strategies for this should be devised by management after consultation with all interested groups in the workforce. If the organisation is small, with less than five employees, then the risk assessment does not have to be written down but it should still be completed and it would be good practice to record it. The process is supposed to be about creating sensible measures to control risks at work, rather than being just a paper-based exercise.

According to the HSE (2014f) there are five main steps involved in assessing risks and hazards in the workplace:

1. Identify the hazards.
2. Decide who might be harmed and how.
3. Evaluate the risks and decide on precautions.
4. Record your significant findings and implement them.
5. Regularly review your assessment and update if necessary.

Assessments do not have to be carried out by health and safety experts and small organisations may choose to undertake the initial assessment of risk by themselves; alternatively, they may prefer to employ a consultant.

Steps 1 and 2: Identify the hazards and decide who may be harmed by them

Most organisations should be able to carry out the first two steps quite easily and identify sources of risk and then identify those who may be harmed by the risks. Many of the risks will probably be well known already such as the risk of slipping in areas where the floor may sometimes be wet, but sometimes even obvious hazards such as this are ignored. Identifying hazards involves looking and talking to people in the area being assessed and examining past records or accidents. It also involves identifying which groups of workers, contractors or visitors are likely to suffer harm and the type of injury that they are likely to suffer.

Step 3: Evaluate the risks and decide on precautions

Once you have identified the hazards and those likely to be affected by them then you must do something about them. Remember under the Health and Safety at Work Act 1974 you have to do everything that is 'reasonably practicable' to protect people from harm.

Pause for thought 10.3 If the floor is sometimes wet due to cleaning or spillages, what could you do as a precaution?

It is best to try to get rid of the risk if it is possible but if not then ways to minimise the risk should be tried. What could you do to prevent accidents in the case of a wet floor that was slippery in your college/university or workplace?

Your answers should be in the following order if possible. Complete them in the grid below.

Order for trying to control risks	Your response to each of these where there is a wet and slippery floor
1. Try to find a way of doing the job that carries less risk	
2. Ensure people don't come into contact with the hazard	
3. Minimise exposure to the hazard	
4. Issue personal protective clothing	
5. Provide adequate facilities to deal properly with people who have suffered in some way because they come into contact with the problem	
6. Involve and consult workers	

Step 4: Record your significant findings and implement them

Small organisations with five employees or fewer do not have to record their findings but it would be good practice to do so anyway. Workers need to know what is happening as far as minimising risks is concerned and it also helps to involve them more in health and safety. According to the HSE (2014f) employers need to show that

- a proper check was made;
- you asked who might be affected;
- you dealt with all significant hazards, taking into account the number of people who could be involved;
- the precautions are reasonable, and the remaining risk low;
- you involved your staff or their representatives in the process.

Although it would be excellent if you could tackle all hazards immediately this will probably not be practicable so you need to plan an order of priority. Which are the most dangerous hazards? Which are quick and easy to solve? Are there any temporary solutions that could be used while a longer-term solution is being organised? How will you monitor your solutions are working? Who is due to take action on each point and by when?

Step 5: Review your risk assessment and update if necessary

All workplaces are subject to constant change so something that works well at first may, due to changing circumstances or work patterns, no longer be so effective. Therefore the risk assessment needs to be monitored on a regular basis. For some organisations where there is a great deal of change this may involve reviewing risk assessments on a monthly or perhaps even weekly basis, while for other organisations an annual review may be more appropriate unless some unexpected change makes it more urgent to review risks.

Pause for thought 10.4 Do you think there is too much emphasis on risk assessment, or not enough?

In 2010 Gareth Malone, the choirmaster, had a TV series called *Extraordinary School for Boys* in which he attempted to improve the literacy skills of boys by getting them to do more adventurous and often more dangerous things. Blogging teachers responded to the programme by saying it was unrealistic as they would have to complete mountains of paperwork and face tons of red tape in conducting risk assessments to submit to local authorities before any such activities would be possible (Millard, 2010).

What do you think? Should there be more opportunities for adventure combined with less risk assessment in schools?

Should it be more difficult for parents of a child injured in an accident at a school to sue?

Wellbeing

One of the earliest roles for HR specialists included that of the welfare officer (Fowler, 1994). The focus of this role was on the wellbeing of employees and it sometimes meant taking a paternalistic viewpoint, that is, adopting a moral stance and telling people what was best for them. The modern HR function has changed and become more complex, adopting a more strategic and integrated approach to human resource management, a theme taken up in a number of chapters. Individual wellbeing, however, is still a factor which has an obvious impact on employees' ability to function at high levels and add value to their organisation. Employees who cannot concentrate at work or who may even stay away from work because of physical or psychological health problems obviously cannot contribute to their full potential, which has a negative impact on the goal of high-performance working.

ACAS (2012) states that there are six indicators of a healthy workplace though these are merely guideline principles and it is not anticipated that every organisation will work in exactly the same way as their chosen methods and approached to wellbeing will depend on their size, type of organisation and cost. However, the ACAS indicators do provide a useful starting point to assess the health of an organisation and are as follows:

- line managers trained in good interpersonal or people skills and who have the confidence and ability to use these skills;
- a feeling by the employees and other workers that they are valued and their work appreciated;
- an attendance culture has been created by the managers and there are return to work interviews conducted by them;
- good job design and flexible approaches to work;
- managers have received training so that they are able to manage common health problems;
- managers use health services such as occupational health in appropriate ways to deal with absence and assist people back to work.

The Health and Safety Executive has also in recent years emphasised the need for all employers to adopt a more proactive approach to wellbeing and has stressed the benefits to be gained from this. Organisations are increasingly operating in new ways, resulting in more flexibility in the way the work is done. The HSE's approach is based on their strategy, *The health and safety of Great Britain: be part of the solution* (Hackitt, 2010a), which aims to increase involvement and which defines goals for HSE and for all other stakeholders in health and safety (HSE, 2014b). The HSE has been consulting with and involving employers to demonstrate the business case for improved health and safety measures and the need to involve everyone.

The role of the employer in employee wellbeing

One area of debate on the subject of wellbeing is whether this is a personal and private matter. We have already said that there is a business case for employer involvement in the health and safety of their workforce but should an employer also have a right to enquire into other aspects of the wellbeing of employees that involve their private lives? If so how far should this go?

Pause for thought 10.5 Before you read on, take a few minutes to think about your position on this issue. Make a list of arguments for saying that employers should be concerned about the personal wellbeing of their employees, and a list of reasons why they should not.

If an employee's personal problems result in falling standards at work, or even in an event that could be construed as misconduct, this could result in formal disciplinary action. On the whole, managers prefer to handle such issues in an informal manner to preserve good working relationships, and regard formal discipline as an action to be taken if the informal approach fails. This approach is encouraged by the ACAS guidelines on discipline (2014). You will find a fuller discussion of this in Chapter 12. It should suffice to make the point here that the proper use of counselling may obviate the need to embark on formal disciplinary action. According to Welfare (2014) two thirds of employers in a survey conducted by XpertHR now use some form of employee assistance programme (EAP) and a further one in five are thinking of introducing one. Most are actually funded by the employer and are provided on their behalf by external suppliers. Typically about 10 per cent of the workforce use the EAP in any year but the popularity of EAPs has increased with employers after a legal case in 2002, when it was argued that just having an EAP provided sufficient defence for an employer against stress compensation claims (Incomes Data Services, 2002). This was subsequently modified in a 2007 case so that it is not now possible just to rely on this as a defence in stress management cases. Typically the EAP service provided involves help with counselling, often by providing access to telephone helplines and to specialist advisers. Since corporate manslaughter is now a criminal offence employers should certainly be diligent in their responsibilities regarding any health, safety or wellbeing issues that could result in death, and should of course take their responsibilities for all health, safety and wellbeing issues equally seriously.

Finally, we can justify an employer's interest in the wellbeing of employees with reference to the basic need to develop good working relationships, on the part of individual employees, individual managers, and from a corporate point of view. Abraham Maslow (1954) was one of the first writers to describe motivation in terms of human needs, and these concepts have often been applied to the workplace. One of the needs that Maslow identified is the social need for relationships, and indeed the importance of relationships has been reinforced by the inclusion of this factor in the HSE's list of aspects of stress management. A number of surveys on motivation have identified the importance of good relationships at work, and specifically the relationship between supervisor and subordinate. It is not inappropriate to care about the people we work with. Much has also been written about corporate image, and many employers wish to be recognised as 'good employers', especially since corporate image can affect an organisation's ability to attract and retain good employees and can therefore have a major impact on the success of the organisation.

The reasons for employers to be involved with employees' problems can be summarised as follows:

- to address problems with productivity, standards of work, attendance and turnover;
- to meet legal obligations to ensure the health, safety and wellbeing of employees;

- to avoid the development of disciplinary problems;
- to maintain good employee relations;
- to improve performance as a part of the performance management process.

Types of problem and their sources

There can be an infinite range of personal problems faced by workers which could affect their work. Many will arise from sources outside the organisation, such as family breakdown, alcoholism, drug abuse, care duties or bereavement, while others might be the result of bullying, working conditions, excessive workload or some form of discrimination in the workplace. The HR department needs to be clear about each of these issues and have policies and procedures in place to deal with issues such as alcoholism or drug abuse and should certainly also have effective policies to prevent unfair discrimination or bullying within work. It is not within the scope of this textbook to deal with all these specific issues but one area which has caused a lot of concern recently is the area of stress, which we shall focus on next. As you saw in the case of *Walker* v. *Northumberland County Council*, there can be serious repercussions for both the employee and the organisation if an employer fails to deal with stress in an appropriate way.

Stress and stress management

Stress is one major area of concern and can be regarded as an umbrella term for a range of problems. Stress is manifested when people are dealing with so many pressures that their normal behaviour patterns become affected. Hans Selye (1956, 1975), a noted writer on stress, used the terms 'eustress' and 'distress' to explain that stress is not always a negative concept. Sometimes people are stimulated by having to deal with a number of issues; this can be exciting and motivating. When it becomes too much and one cannot cope and at the same time continue to behave within the range of one's normal behaviour patterns, this is what Selye refers to as distress. This is what we normally mean when we refer to stress these days (Le Fevre *et al.*, 2003).

What are the causes of stress? There are a wide range of factors that cause stress both in personal relationships and in work relationships (see Figure 10.1); these factors are referred to as stressors. Holmes and Rahe (1967) identified a number of life events as being sources of stress. Ranked at number one as a source of stress was the death of one's spouse, and other factors identified included divorce, taking on a high mortgage and taking a holiday.

It is also recognised that circumstances at work such as poor relationships, especially with one's manager or supervisor, and overwork or underemployment can contribute to stress. The case of John Walker mentioned earlier is an example of too high a workload combined with the demanding nature of the work contributing to stress.

The first symptoms of stress are likely to be shown by uncharacteristic changes in behaviour or performance and these might alert you to the fact that a colleague is under pressure. If not dealt with, the end result can be physical or mental illness leading to mental breakdown.

Did you know?

According to the Health and Safety Executive:

- The total number of cases of work-related stress, depression or anxiety was 487,000 and this formed 39 per cent of the total of 1,241,000 cases of work-related illnesses.
- 11.3 million working days were lost because of stress in 2013–2014.

(*Source*: HSE, 2014g)

Figure 10.1   Some causes of stress

The Health and Safety Executive has played a major role in the development of guidelines for employers on various aspects of stress management. The duty of care addressed in the Health and Safety at Work Act 1974 applies to employees' physical and mental wellbeing, and since these can be affected by stress caused by workplace factors the duty of care constitutes an obvious legal obligation to pay attention to stress management. The Management of Health and Safety at Work Regulations 1999 also imposes a duty on employers to conduct a risk audit on potential hazards in the workplace, which also applies in this area as the effects of stress can be regarded as a hazard.

These standards encourage managers, employees, other workers and their representatives to work together to identify potential causes of stress in the workplace and then to take action to improve the situation. The stress management standards are not legally enforceable on organisations, but the HSE may use them as evidence that an organisation is not fulfilling its duty with regard to stress management.

The standards address six areas of work that should be audited. These are laid out with a brief description of what each entails in Table 10.1. The basic idea is to ascertain what percentages of staff feel that they are able to cope with any work situations in these six areas. According to the International Stress Management Association (2004), 'The target is for all organisations to match the performance of the top 20 per cent of employers that are successfully minimising work-related stress'. Organisations must also be able to show that they have systems in place locally to respond to any individual concerns and should be carrying out risk assessments for stress. As Quinn (2004) points out, the identification of stress factors through such an audit makes the eventuality of stress foreseeable so employers would be obligated to take some action in such an instance.

Table 10.1   HSE stress management standards

Area of work	The standard	Desirable outcomes that organisations should be working towards
Demands This is about demands caused by the workload, work pattern or the work environment.	Employees should be able to indicate that they can cope with the demands of their job. There should also be systems in place to help deal with any concerns of individuals.	The organisation should ensure hours of work are reasonable and that demands made on the workers are not excessive, and that their abilities and skills are matched appropriately to their job. There should be a matching of people's skills to their jobs. There should be systems set up to address concerns that workers may have so that these can be resolved.
Control This is about how much influence an individual has over their job.	Employees should be able to indicate that they get a say in the way they do their work. There should also be systems in place to respond to individual concerns.	Individuals should have control over their pace of work wherever possible. They should get opportunities and be encouraged to use their skills and initiative in their work. They should be encouraged to develop new skills so they can undertake new or more challenging work. The employees should also have a say about when breaks should be taken and be consulted about their work patterns and breaks.
Support This concerns the support mechanisms, or lack of them, from colleagues, line managers and others such as HR staff. It is also about levels of employee awareness of support.	Employees should be able to indicate that they receive adequate support and information from colleagues and superiors. There should also be evidence of systems in place to adequately address employee concerns.	There should be policies and procedures in place to adequately support staff and there should also be systems in place to enable and encourage managers to support staff. Since support is also sometimes provided by colleagues there should be systems in place to encourage employees to support others. Employees should know about available support and also how to access resources necessary to do their job. They should also get regular and constructive feedback.
Relationships This is about encouraging positive behaviour so that conflict is avoided and about creating ways to deal with unacceptable behaviour.	Employees should be able to indicate that they are not subjected to unacceptable behaviour at work such as bullying or harassment and that there are systems in place to deal with these issues.	The organisation should promote positive behaviour to ensure fairness and avoid conflict and encourage employees to share information about their work. The organisation should have policies in place to prevent or resolve unacceptable behaviour and employees should be encouraged to report unacceptable behaviour.
Role This concerns the extent to which people understand their role and whether the organisation ensures the individual does not have conflicting roles.	Employees should be able to indicate that they understand their role and responsibilities and there should be systems in place to address individual concerns.	The organisation should provide information about employees' roles and should try to ensure as far as possible that the different requirements it places on employees are compatible and clear and that the individual understands them. If they have concerns about role conflict or about their role then they should be able to raise them.

→

Area of work	The standard	Desirable outcomes that organisations should be working towards
Change How much change are employees expected to cope with, and how well prepared are they when they do have to deal with change? Are the arrangements for information sharing and consultation adequate?	Employees should be able to show that the organisation engages with them frequently when undergoing organisational change and that there are systems in place to respond to any concerns they may have.	The organisation should be consulting adequately and providing opportunities for individuals to contribute to and influence the changes. This information needs to be timely and sufficient for employees to understand the reasons for the changes and the likely impact on their jobs. Employees also need to be aware of the timetable for changes and have suitable access to support during the change period.

(*Source*: Adapted from HSE, 2009b)

Pause for thought 10.6 Consider any organisation in which you have worked. To what extent to you think that organisation has considered each of the stress management standards?

What is your evidence for this?

How does this compare with the views of others in your class about organisations in which they have worked? Did job roles seem clear and unambiguous? Were you made aware of structures to support you?

As you can see from these standards, there are a great many implications for HR departments to ensure that they have not only policies in place but also that they have designed jobs well to ensure there is no role incompatibility or work overload, that individuals understand their roles through induction and subsequent training and that there are support systems in place for those who may be experiencing problems. Management also need training to ensure they respond in an appropriate way to those suffering from stress. This means that they need to recognise that just increasing workloads and hoping that the person can cope is not a satisfactory way to manage but that there is a need for proper analyses of the job and the workload, and to match these to the person's capabilities.

Organisational policy and procedures

Policy statements and procedures provide guidelines for all employees. They let managers know how to handle problems, and inform everyone about the help, assistance and support they can expect to receive, including the areas covered by the stress management standards. There is a dual role for policies as far as situations requiring counselling are concerned. First, there is a need for policies relating directly to the provision of counselling and, second, an organisation should have policies dealing with workplace behaviour or events that have been identified as causing distress.

In a *Guardian* Careers Section article, Professor Cary Cooper was quoted as saying that bullying probably accounted for a third to a half of all stress-related illness (Venning, 1995). Policies on bullying and sexual/racial harassment can help to eliminate these unwanted behaviours and promote a less stressful working environment. Many organisations such as banks and retail outlets, where staff handle cash and at the same time have direct contact with the public, have recognised that specialised counselling is necessary to deal with the trauma their employees can suffer after an episode involving violence or a threat of violence. This is true when they have either been directly threatened or witnessed an incident. Employers will obviously have to decide which issues are most important for their organisations, and this may involve surveying employees to discover which issues are of concern to them, and which solutions the employees would most like to take advantage of. The package of wellbeing policies, procedures and benefits an employer offers to employees is often referred to as an 'employee assistance programme'.

Policies should also address the following issues:

- who will be involved in providing counselling and what are the parameters of their roles,
- what type of services will be offered,
- issues of confidentiality.

Health promotion

So far, we have focused primarily on approaches to safety and wellbeing in response to legal requirements and as a way for employers to ensure that they motivate their workers. Recent legislation encourages employers to be proactive about safety and to carry out risk assessments and then take action to reduce or eliminate risks identified. The introduction of the 'fit note' to replace the 'sick note' has changed the focus to one where employees do not have to be 100 per cent fit to return to work but could be fit to do some work. According to Woollen (2010) the previous situation was very restrictive with GPs only having two choices, with the patient either being fit for work or not. The government's intention appears to be to get employers and employees talking to each other after taking advice from the GP and that the employee could return to do some work before being fully fit. The 'fit note' also aims to make it easier to have a quicker return to work. Since this is often based on an estimate by the GP of the length of time needed for a particular illness many days which could have been worked productively may have been lost. ACAS (n.d.) also feels that since work can be good for health it is better to get people back to work as soon as possible, and since 2012 GPs can issue a computer-generated fit note. With a 'fit note' a GP can now indicate that a person 'may be fit for work', though this can be work in general rather than their specific job. If they choose to say this then they can suggest at least one of the following options:

- phased return to work,
- amended duties,

The Fit for Work Service was launched in January 2015. This is a voluntary scheme intended to further minimise sickness absence and improve the way it is managed. This is a state-funded health and work assessment and advisory centre which will provide occupational health services, particularly for small- and medium-size organisations. Telephone advice will be provided for employers, employees and GPs. GPs can also refer patients, with their consent, to the occupational health service after four weeks absence from work, or if the GP has not done this after the four weeks' absence then the employer can initiate the referral.

(*Source*: Gers, 2014)

- flexible working,
- workplace adaptations.

Clearly if any of these options are chosen then there should be a discussion with the worker before they return to work to discuss an appropriate way to manage their return (Ayling, 2014b).

Many good employers not only promote measures for improvements in safety and wellbeing but also encourage developments to ensure good health among their workforces.

The high cost of absenteeism is a strong financial reason for both individual organisations and the government to take measures to promote and improve health. According to Griffiths (2009) the current UK recommendation is for moderately intense levels of physical activity for at least 30 minutes every day and the introduction of opportunities for exercise to the workplace could help to alleviate stress, musculoskeletal problems and some common mental health problems. Many people will lapse their membership of gyms after a short period of time because of other pressures in their lives, so suggestions to incorporate exercise into work where people may be already spending between 40 and 85 hours a week could be useful. One innovative solution trialled with nurses and office workers was the introduction of a walking workstation and though this might not be attractive to everyone, users reported improvements in energy and relief from back pain (Griffiths, 2009).

Many employers already provide some preventative measures such as health screening services and membership of private health insurance schemes for their managers, and some are extending this provision to the workforce as a whole. Increasingly, organisations are actively trying to promote a healthier lifestyle among their employees. Employee support programmes, counselling services and employee assistance programmes are the most common wellbeing programmes offered (CIPD, 2014). In their 2014 survey the CIPD found that 70 per cent of the organisations offer some sort of wellbeing programme which included one or more of the following:

- help for smokers to quit, with support/self-help groups and psychologists giving advice and support;
- a healthy diet, with a wider choice of health foods on the menu at work;
- supply of free fruit at work;
- membership of a health club or purchase of multi-gym exercise equipment for employees to use to get fitter and as a way of tackling obesity;
- pedometers;
- in-house gym;
- on-site massage;
- online assessments of health or lifestyle screening with advice available for lifestyle changes;
- stress management programmes;
- policies and education programmes on HIV/Aids;
- policies and education on substance abuse.

In organisations where such programmes have been made available to all the workforce on a long-term basis, there have been benefits to employees' health with weight reduction and improvements in blood cholesterol and blood pressure levels, and also improvements in absenteeism rates. It is claimed that the cost of the introduction of this type of programme is more than offset by the savings from lower rates of absenteeism though not all organisations actually fully evaluate their investment in wellbeing. Those that do conduct a thorough evaluation of their wellbeing spend seem to find it to have been money well spent and usually go further by actually increasing the amount they spend on wellbeing during the next year (CIPD, 2014).

Absence management

While prevention is always better than cure one of the areas that many HR departments are also becoming increasingly interested in, and which can be used in a complementary way to a wellness programme, is absence management. Westminster City Council 'introduced improved absence management procedures which have reduced its absence rate by more than two days per person per annum and saved it £800,000 annually' (Inland Revenue Service, 2007). They achieved this by using a mixture of approaches such as the introduction of an employee assistance programme and a new absence management programme which involved return to work interviews, and earlier and more positive use of the occupational health department and trigger points. This meant that

once an employee had more than seven cumulative days' sickness absence in any rolling [365 day] period, then an enhanced sickness management procedure kicks in. And if sickness absence exceeds 20 days in any one episode, then long-term sickness management procedure applies. Further, when more than eight days of sickness have been recorded over the rolling 365-day period the employee's manager will refer the employee to the council's in-house occupational health service.

Failure to take steps to reduce risks in the workplace is likely in the future to lead to higher insurance payments for organisations as insurance companies start to link premiums to the way that organisations manage risks of accidents and ill health. Smokers generally suffer worse health than non-smokers and the charity Action on Smoking and Health (ASH) claims that 34 million working days are lost in Britain each year just because of smoking. Some employers are becoming more proactive about their employees' health and are introducing measures such as bonuses to encourage smokers to quit. These can, however, prove controversial as non-smokers may then also want to benefit from bonuses.

Conclusion

We said at the beginning of this chapter that it is not enough for employers just to be concerned about preventing accidents in order to comply with legislation, although that in itself is a good start. We have shown in this chapter that there has been a change of approach from mere compliance with minimum legal requirements in the legislation prior to HASAWA to the encouragement of increased involvement of all, and nowadays to seeing a business case as well. In difficult economic circumstances many organisations find their profit margins are extremely tight, and improving health, safety and wellbeing is one way to give their organisation a cost-effective competitive edge.

This approach to health and safety links with the overall business objectives of maximising efficiency and effectiveness by improving morale and reducing costs, and also allows for some scope for individuality and flexibility in how this is to be achieved. It is the approach to health and safety that we would advocate, and it is a very different approach to the purely legalistic one of just being concerned with not breaking the law. This approach to health and safety involves the following features:

- The need to create a culture in which health, safety and wellbeing are seen to be important to the organisation. The safety policy statement will contribute to this if it is effectively written, known about and acted upon. The legal requirements must be complied with and risk assessments carried out, as well as gathering information about health and safety and carrying out a cost-benefit analysis. If there is to be a culture of health and safety awareness, there also needs to be campaigns and publicity, and involvement of top management, individuals and teams. There needs to be regular communications and discussion of health and safety and the contribution that improvements will make to the organisation's overall effectiveness, so that all members of the organisation realise that health and safety are important to the way it operates.
- Commitment from the top to the achievement of progressively higher standards as expressed in the mission statement and safety policy. Top management must not only sign the policy documents but also set a good example in relation to health and safety, and emphasise that it is an area of importance to them and to the future of the organisation by showing their interest and by setting up new systems and monitoring the effectiveness of these systems. They need to follow through on all stages of the HSE's recommendations for managing health, safety and welfare in the workplace so that they Plan, Do, Check and then Act on their findings.
- Commitment throughout the organisation, with all parties clear about their own responsibilities for health and safety, the targets they have to meet and the contribution these make to the organisation's objectives. This should be considered as an aspect of performance management, as individuals and teams would be encouraged to take responsibility for their own actions and to agree and work towards targets when making improvements.

- Managers demonstrate by their example their commitment to the importance of a safer and healthier work environment. They should also find ways to motivate everyone to make a contribution to health and safety improvements. Prizes and awards to individuals and teams can have an important effect.
- Policies and procedures designed to take account of the importance of a safer and healthier environment. There should also be effective systems to monitor their effectiveness.
- Policies to be backed by adequate resources for equipment and training. Provision of good health and safety costs money but the cost of not providing these can be higher, as any cost-benefit analysis is likely to prove.
- The setting of realistic and attainable targets for everyone in the organisation.
- Encouragement of all to take responsibility for their own actions and involvement of all in health and safety.

Our approach seems to be in line with both ACAS and Investors in People in stressing the importance of good management to health, safety and wellbeing. IIP (2014) ⬉ ll look after your business'. E   Investors in people (2014)   ing a supportive culture and en: ved to be an important aspect (organisation's strategic objectiv   nd provide an excellent return c

Review questions

You will fir

1. Interv   ge of
    organ   ealth and safety
    and th   ir particular
    organi   and safety
    differ   ers, safety
    officer   designated to be a 'competent
    person'. Are these roles the same in different types of organisation? How
    do they compare with what we said earlier in the chapter about these roles?
    Is health and safety perceived to be an important part of performance
    management?
2. Obtain a copy of the safety policy for either your college or your workplace.
    a. Use this to identify the roles of various people in the organisation in relation to
        health and safety.
    b. Use the safety policy to assess whether health and safety are linked to the
        organisation's strategic objectives.
3. Design a checklist for carrying out a safety inspection in the workplace.
    Use your checklist to actually carry out an inspection of a designated area
    either at work or in your college. Write a report about your findings for the
    safety officer.
4. Write a short report in which you assess the impact of one piece of health and
    safety legislation in an organisation of your choice. (Sources of guidance for
    report writing are given on page 476.)

HR in the news

Workforce health on a par with profits and dividends

By Paul Betts

Europe's economies are still stuttering and hopes of recovery have never looked so fragile. This is putting the old continent's companies under even more pressure after a dire couple of years. But companies are their employees, and many of these men and women remain under great pressure, with the shadow of unemployment hanging over many households.

Corporate restructurings are still a daily feature of corporate life, as are factory closures. And the pressure for cost cuts to maintain profitability is unlikely to disappear soon.

This relentless demand for performance can have devastating effects on workforces, as was so tragically the case at France Telecom, which has experienced a rash of suicides during the past 18 months. Suicides have also taken place in other restructuring companies.

In France Renault, Peugeot and EDF have all reported such tragic incidents.

Of course, it is always difficult to say with any certainty that an individual has taken his or her life because of unbearable pressure at work.

Nonetheless, the European Union has already recognised that stress at work could be a problem, and Europe's social partners are discussing an agreement on the issue.

In France, the government has asked companies of more than 1,000 workers to negotiate an anti-stress policy with unions to be adopted by each enterprise. They were given the deadline of the beginning of this month to launch discussions.

This week, a government-appointed commission headed by veteran industrialist Henri Lachmann, chairman of Schneider Electric, delivered a long-awaited report on wellbeing and efficiency at work.

It makes a series of enlightened suggestions, such as the need for business and engineering schools to include social responsibility in the workplace in their curriculums.

It suggests that management training in handling social issues should be compulsory in every company.

But most interesting is the recommendation that social performance should be made a key factor in setting the remuneration of managers.

Danone whose head of human resources sat on the Lachmann commission, already does this. But few others do.

The report also underlines the fact that the health and wellbeing of the workforce is first and foremost the responsibility of managers, and cannot be outsourced to external advisers as many French companies appear to be doing.

The question now is how to define social performance. The French report suggests the issue needs to be treated extremely seriously. It suggests the issue is so serious that the board of a company and not just its top management must make it a priority, as much so as delivering profits and dividends to its shareholders.

Questions

1. To what extent do you think the organisations mentioned here would benefit from using the Health and Safety Executive's stress management standards as a part of their stress policies?

2. In your opinion do you think that measures of social performance should be considered when deciding managers' pay? If so what measures should be used?

3. Do you think that measures of health, safety and wellbeing should be included as a part of the balanced scorecard approach in organisations?

4. To what extent do you think measures of a country's wellbeing should be included when comparing the performance of countries? Should there be something like the balanced scorecard, discussed in Chapter 1, as a measure of countries' success and prosperity with measures such as a happiness index or metrics about wellbeing being used alongside economic measures?

What next?

Research conducted by Aberdeen University on 13 offshore oil installations applies the balanced scorecard to occupational health. The article also discusses the results of interviews with UK and Norwegian managers on health and safety performance indicators and the reasons for including occupational health and safety as one measure of performance within the balanced scorecard. What do you think about the idea that measures of occupational health should be included in an assessment of an organisation's performance?

Mearns, K. and J.I. Havold (2003) Occupational health and safety and the balanced scorecard, *The TQM Magazine*, Vol. 15, No. 6, 408–423.

References

Advisory, Conciliation and Arbitration Service (n.d.) *Statement of Fitness for Work or 'Fit Note'*, ACAS (available at www.acas.co.uk; accessed 09.01.15).

Advisory, Conciliation and Arbitration Service (2012) *Health, Work and Wellbeing*, ACAS, 5 (available at www.acas.org.uk; accessed 13.04.15).

Advisory, Conciliation and Arbitration Service (2014) *Discipline and Grievances at Work; The ACAS Guide*, ACAS (available at www.acas.org.uk; accessed 13.04.15).

Ayling, L. (2014a) *CIPD Factsheet: Working Hours and Time Off*, CIPD (available at www.cipd.co.uk; accessed 03.01.15).

Ayling, L. (2014b) *CIPD Factsheet: Absence Measurement and Management*, CIPD (available at www.cipd.co.uk; accessed 12.01.15).

Baker, J. (2007) Net closes on corporate killing, *People Management*, Vol. 13, No. 5, 8 March, 22.

Cacanas, Z. (2004) Where kicking butts is just what's wanted: employers are looking at new ways to help their staff to quit, *The Guardian*, 24 July, 21.

Chartered Institute of Personnel and Development (2014) *Annual Survey Report 2014: Absence Management*, CIPD (available at www.cipd.co.uk; accessed 12.01.15).

Chiu, A. (2009) Food, job best foundations for success in pursuit of happiness, *South China Morning Post*, 8 December.

Churchard (2014) ECJ rules that obesity can constitute a disability, *People Management*, 18 December.

Fowler, A. (1994) Personnel's model army, *Personnel Management*, September, 34–35.

Gers, D. (2014) Will Fit for Work be fit for purpose? *People Management*, December.

Griffiths, L. (2009) Addressing obesity in the workplace, *Occupational Health*, RBI, Issue 1, 1 February (available at www.xperthr.co.uk; accessed 06.09.10).

Hackitt, J. (2010a) Foreword. *The Health and Safety of Britain: Be Part of the Solution*, HSE (available at www.hse.gov.uk; accessed 06.01.2015).

Hackitt, J. (2010b) *Foreword. The Health and Safety Business Plan 2010–11*, HSE (available at www.hse.gov.uk; accessed 08.09.10).

Health and Safety Executive (1995) *Be Safe: Save Money. The Costs of Accidents: A Guide for Small Firms*, HSE Books, 4.

Health and Safety Executive (2009a) *HSE Enforcement Policy Statement – Updated,* HSE (available at www.hse.gov.uk; accessed 31.12.14).

Health and Safety Executive (2009b) *How to Tackle Work-Related Stress. A Guide for Employers on Making the Management Standards Work*, HSE (available at www.hse.gov.uk; accessed 06.01.15).

Health and Safety Executive (2010) *2010 Myths*, HSE (available at www.hse.gov.uk; accessed 30.12.14).

Health and Safety Executive (2014a) *Health and Safety Statistics*, HSE (available at www.hse.gov.uk; accessed 30.12. 14).

Health and Safety Executive (2014b) *The Health and Safety Executive Annual Report 2013–14*, HSE (available at www.hse.gov.uk; accessed 30.12.14).

Health and Safety Executive (2014c) *Busting the Health and Safety Myths*, HSE (available at www.hse.gov.uk; accessed 30.12.14).

Health and Safety Executive (2014d) *Consulting Workers on Health and Safety. Safety Representatives and Safety Committees Regulations 1977 (As Amended) and Health and Safety (Consultation with Employees) Regulations 1996 (As Amended) Approved Codes of Practice and Guidance*. HSE (available at www.hse.gov.uk; accessed 03.01.15).

Health and Safety Executive (2014e) *Reporting Accidents and Injuries at Work: A Brief Guide to the Reporting of Injuries, Diseases and Dangerous Occurrences Regulations 2013* (RIDDOR), HSE (available at www.hse.gov.uk; accessed 03.01.15).

Health and Safety Executive (2014f) *Risk Assessment: A Brief Guide to Controlling Risks in the Workplace*, HSE (available at www.hse.gov.uk; accessed 06.01.15).

Health and Safety Executive (2014g) *Stress-Related and Psychological Disorders in Great Britain 2014*, HSE (available at www.hse.gov.uk; accessed 06.01.15).

Holmes, T.H. and R.H. Rahe (1967) The social readjustment rating scale, *Journal of Psychosomatic Research*, August, 216.

Iley, S. (2014) *E-cigarettes in the workplace*, CIPD in partnership with AXA HeatlthCare (available at www.cipd.co.uk; accessed 14.01.15).

Incomes Data Services (2002) *IDS Studies Plus: Employee Assistance Programmes*, IDS, London.

Inland Revenue Service Employment Review (2007) *Westminster City Council's Successful Absence Management Procedure*, IRS 877, 16July, London.

International Stress Management Association UK (2004) *Working Together to Reduce Stress at Work*, International Stress Management Association UK, Caldicot, Monmouthshire.

Investors in People (2014) *Get in Shape,* IIP (available at www.investorsinpeople.co.uk; accessed 04.01.15).

Jones, R. (2007) Manslaughter Act doesn't go far enough, *Personnel Today*, 6 March.

Le Fevre, M., J. Matheny and G.S. Kolt (2003) Eustress, distress, and interpretation in occupational stress, *Journal of Managerial Psychology*, Vol. 18, No. 7, 726–744.

Maslow, A. (1954) *Motivation and Personality,* 2nd edition, Harper& Row, New York.

McKevitt, T. (2014) *Disability Discrimination*, XpertHR (available at www.xperthr.co.uk; accessed 12.01.2015)

Mew, C. (2014) *CIPD Factsheet: Corporate Manslaughter and Corporate Homicide Act 2007,* CIPD (available at www.cipd.co.uk; accessed 04.01.15).

Michaelson, J., S. Abdallah, N. Steur, S. Thompson and N. Marks (2009) *National Accounts of Wellbeing,* The New Economics Foundation (www.neweconomics.org/publications/national-accounts-well-being; accessed 16.9.10).

Midgley, S. (1997) Pressure points, *People Management*, 10 July, 36–39.

Millard, R. (2010) Gareth Malone's lesson in how to teach boys, *The Sunday Times*, 12 September, 16.

Nishiyama, K. and J. Johnson (1997) *Karoshi – Death from Overwork: Occupational Health Consequences of the Japanese Production Management*, 6th Draft for *International Journal of Health Services*, 4 February (available at www.workhealth.org/whatsnew/lpkarosh.html; accessed 17.09.10).

Paton, N. (2010) Future challenges in workplace health, *Occupational Health*, 1 August (available at www.xperthr.co.uk; accessed 06.09.10).

PM Editorial (2014) Supermarket trains staff to spot hidden exploitation in the supply chain, *People Management*, 16 December.

Quinn, J. (2004) Dodging the draft, *People Management*, 30 June, 17.

Selye, H. (1956) *The Stress of Life*, McGraw-Hill, New York.

Selye, H. (1975) *Stress without Distress*, Hodder and Stoughton, London.

Seenan, G. (2004) No frills – and no travelling toilet class, *The Guardian*, 24 July.

Stranks, J. (2010) *The Health and Safety Handbook: A Practical Guide to Health and Safety Law, Management Policies and Procedures*, Kogan Page, London.

Tehrani, N., S. Humpage, B. Wilmott and I. Haslam (2007) *Change Agenda: What's Happening with Well-being at Work?* CIPD, London, 3.

Venning, N. (1995) Taking the bull by the horns, *The Guardian* Careers Section, 15 April, 2–3.

Welfare, S. (2014) *XpertHR Assistance Programmes Survey 2014*, XpertHR (available at www.xperthr.co.uk; accessed 13.04.15).

Wintersgill, R. (2014) *Health and Safety Bodies and Inspectors*, XpertHR (available at www.xperthr.co.uk: accessed 30.12.14).

Woollen, R. (2010) The fit note – friend or foe, *Managing People*, 1 April.

Further study

Books and reports

Advisory, Conciliation and Arbitration Service (2010) *Health, Work and Wellbeing*, ACAS (available at www.acas.org.uk; accessed 13.04.15).
This booklet focuses on measures that employers can take to help promote good health in their workforce and also discusses the importance of work for keeping people healthy.

Stranks, J. (2010) *Health and Safety at Work: An Essential Guide for Managers*, revised 9th edition, Kogan Page, London.
This is available in book or e-book form and, as the title implies, it provides a wealth of clear practical guidance for managers.

Articles

HSE publications exist on a wide range of topics, too numerous to include here, from general books to detailed explanations of legislation. Many of its leaflets are also available on the web page listed below.

Internet

The Health and Safety Executive   **www.hse.gov.uk**
There are many booklets and advice and guidance pages which are free to download.

RIDDOR   **www.riddor.gov.uk/riddor**
The site gives information about RIDDOR and has forms which can be downloaded to report accidents and dangerous occurrences, or these can now be reported directly online.

XpertHR   **www.xperthr.co.uk**
An excellent source of articles from various publications.

International human resource management

Objectives

After you have studied this chapter, you will be able to:

- understand the context within which international business takes place

- explain the terms used for companies which operate on an international basis such as 'international', 'multinational' and 'global enterprise'

- understand different philosophical orientations to internationalisation: ethnocentric, polycentric, regiocentric or geocentric

- assess the influence of national culture on the workplace

- understand the key issues concerning international assignments

- evaluate the competencies needed for a career in international human resource management.

- Understand key international issues concerning: learning, training and talent development; high-performance working systems; work–life balance and diversity and equality.

Introduction

Most of the contents of this textbook focus on human resource issues as seen from a UK perspective. The growth of business conducted on an international basis, however, means that many UK-based businesses have had to consider the implications of doing business overseas for the management of people. This applies to the whole range of HRM activities and programmes such as recruitment and selection, performance management, learning, training and development, pay and reward packages, employment terms and conditions and the management of employment relations in general.

The growing importance of global business

At the start of the twenty-first century, it is a given that business operates on a global basis, and this trend is only likely to expand in the coming years. The globalisation of business is the result of increasing competitive pressures worldwide, and it has been facilitated by the development of free trade areas, advances in technology and communications and ease of travel. Companies often pursue growth strategies by external means using cross-national mergers, acquisitions and joint ventures. Companies are seeking new markets for their goods and services, looking beyond their domestic boundaries. The sale of goods and services internationally requires the establishment of an international infrastructure. Overseas distribution networks need to be developed and manufacturing plants may also be established. Companies pursuing a low-cost strategy may decide to transfer their manufacturing plants to countries where labour is less expensive. But globalisation is not only about domestic firms pursuing business opportunities overseas. It also means that foreign firms seek to invest in domestic markets. Governments encourage inward investment to support employment and increase the tax base and international trade agreements break down the barriers to conducting business in a number of locations around the world. In sum, there are a multitude of factors that contribute to the globalisation of business activity, and there is every indication that it is here to stay and become even more of an issue in our lives.

Did you know?

According to the International Monetary Fund (IMF), China is the world's largest economy. For the first time in more than 140 years the USA is not the world's largest economy. The Chinese economy is now worth $17.6 trillion compared to $17.4 trillion for the USA economy. However, the IMF calculated these figures using purchasing power parity (PPP) which compares how much you can buy for your money in different countries. As money goes further in China than it does in the USA, the figure for China is adjusted upwards. Without the PPP adjustment the Chinese economy is worth $10.3 trillion less than the US economy.

(*Source*: Carter, B. (2014) Is *China's economy really the largest in the world*? BBC New Magazine (available at **www.bbc.co.uk**; accessed 01.02.15)

From the description of the ways in which global business might develop, it is evident that in considering any particular company there are a number of different options. For instance, if we take the UK as a focal point the business structure could involve any of the following: a UK-owned company selling its products and services to customers in a number of countries; a foreign-owned enterprise with branches overseas, including branches in the UK; a UK-owned company manufacturing its products in a number of countries; UK nationals working overseas on a regular, short-term or long-term basis and foreign nationals working in the UK. Terms that are frequently used in describing this variety of situations include 'international businesses', 'multinational corporations', 'global enterprises' and 'transnational corporations'. In relation to these businesses' employees, terms such as: 'parent/home country national', 'host country national' and 'third country national' are commonly used. Perlmutter and Heenan (1974) also developed a much-cited set of terms in relation to international business: 'ethnocentrism', 'polycentrism', 'regiocentrism' and 'geocentrism'. All of these terms will now be examined.

International, multinational, global or transnational?

International business is defined as 'the study of transactions taking place for the purpose of satisfying the needs of individuals and organizations' (Rugman and Collinson, 2012, p. 7).

Ghoshal and Bartlett (1998) conducted research on a number of companies operating in various ways on an international basis. They designated companies as international, multinational or global. Multinational enterprises (MNEs) have foreign direct investments (Daniels *et al.*, 2013) with some authors stating that the firm has to have a certain number of foreign direct investments before it is classified an MNE. For example, Shim *et al.* (2013) state that a multinational corporation is a firm that operates in two or more counties. Multinational companies or enterprises, according to Ghoshal and Bartlett (1998), have fairly independent operations in a number of countries where they are permitted to establish their own approach, usually responding to local requirements in terms of, for example, customer needs. International firms are somewhere between multinational and global companies. The international company demonstrates a strong attachment to headquarter country policies and decision making, but attempts to adapt these to local conditions and requirements in the various overseas locations. Globalised companies are highly centralised in their decision making, but they take a global perspective. In deciding on their strategy, they look for what will work on a worldwide basis. Globalised companies have become borderless (Sirkeci, 2013), although all businesses have a headquarters in a specific country, often referred to as their 'home' country.

Ghoshal and Bartlett then introduce the concept of the transnational company, which they describe not as an existing type of company but rather as an ideal towards which companies need to strive in order to survive in an evermore complex and competitive environment. The transnational company combines the strengths found separately in international, multinational and global companies. The transnational company needs to recognise instances when centralised or decentralised decision making is necessary and swiftly adopt the necessary approach. It must be able to distinguish when a global solution is feasible and when to develop localised products, services and strategies. In other words, the transnational company utilises the competencies and strategies of the three other types of company and reacts flexibly as circumstances change.

In sum, Ghoshal and Bartlett assign quite distinct meanings to the terms 'international', 'multinational', 'global' and 'transnational' business but there are other views on these terms and their uses. Some writers have presented the first three types as a progression that companies may follow as they become more global (Brake, 1999). These three terms can, however, be used much more loosely. As Aggarwal *et al.* (2011, p. 557) point out, 'the terms multinational company (MNC), multinational enterprise and transnational corporation are widely and often interchangeably used by international business (IB) commentators and scholars'.

Pause for thought 11.1 In relation to human resource management practices, what are the key differences between domestic and multinational firms?

When we turn to a discussion of the HRM implications in such organisations, writers often refer interchangeably to global perspectives, international issues and so on or allude to the differing needs raised by the different situations we discussed earlier, rather than by the typology of organisations (Sparrow, 1999). In addressing the human characteristics needed for their ideal transnational organisation, Ghoshal and Bartlett (1998) review many aspects of HRM covered elsewhere in this text, reinforcing a point that we make more strongly later in this chapter, that HRM on an international basis is basically HRM in general but with an added level of complexity. These aspects of complexity are flexibility, commitment, diversity and a unitarist approach.

Definitions of international human resource management

There is no consensus as to what international human resource management (IHRM) covers (Scullion, 2005). Certainly, IHRM is related to a firm's response to the internationalisation of business. According to Crawley *et al.* (2013, p. 5), IHRM is about 'understanding, researching, applying and revising all human resource activities in their internal and external contexts as they impact the processes of managing human resources in organisations throughout the global environment to enhance the experience of multiple stakeholders'.

IHRM shares many similarities with domestic HRM in that the core functions of recruitment, selection, employee learning and development, diversity and equality and remuneration are present in both. However, IHRM operates on a larger scale, has more complex strategic considerations, more complex coordination and control demands, as well as some additional HR functions (Sparrow *et al.*, 2004). In an international context, the firm needs to recruit, select, develop and retain a workforce that can help it compete globally (Briscoe *et al.*, 2012).

An XpertHR survey (Welfare, 2014) on the international HR practices of 90 organisations that employ people in more than one country revealed that although 74.4 per cent of organisations had an international business strategy or plan only 45.6 per cent had a specific international HR strategy. Of the organisations in the survey, currently 84.4 per cent had staff employed on international assignments. This figure was even higher for firms with 1,000 or more employees (91.7 per cent). Employers were also asked which aspects of international HR were the most challenging for them. The top three answers were recruiting and retaining the right people (17.8 per cent), getting international assignment packages right (16.7 per cent) and keeping up to date with employment law and compliance regulations (10 per cent).

Ethnocentric, polycentric, regiocentric or geocentric?

As companies grow and develop their operations in more countries, they will be faced with decisions about whom to hire in the various locations and at various levels within the business, most particularly in top-level positions but also in other managerial positions. The philosophy underpinning these decisions may alter over time in response to change and business developments, but Perlmutter and Heenan (1974) have provided a typology of early attitudes which may persist to varying degrees in organisations today. These attitudes are called ethnocentrism, polycentrism, regiocentrism and geocentrism. The terms 'ethnocentric', 'polycentric' and 'geocentric' (though not regiocentric) are also used by other authors such as Peng and Meyer (2011).

Ethnocentrism reflects a sense of superiority about a person's home country and ethnocentric people believe that their approach is better, whatever the culture involved (Ahlstrom and Bruton, 2010). An ethnocentric approach means that senior, and perhaps other managerial positions in overseas locations will be filled by nationals from the parent country. The assumption underlying such decisions is that the knowledge and expertise needed to make decisions at that level reside only in the parent country. The parent company may also wish to impose its organisational culture on overseas branches. An ethnocentric approach will result in centralised systems, high levels of authority from the company's headquarters and communication in the form of commands, orders and advice (Nickson, 2013).

A polycentric approach places emphasis on the norms and practices of the host country where the firm operates (Peng and Meyer, 2011). A multinational enterprise that utilises such an approach will treat each international subsidiary as a separate national entity (Ahlstrom and Bruton, 2010). Polycentrism implies that people from the host country would be chosen to occupy managerial as well as operational positions. A regiocentric approach means that a company seeks to exploit opportunities at the regional (for example, the EU) level (Yip and Hult, 2012). Regiocentrism means that the best person for any job at any level would be selected from within a wider geographical region. Geocentric organisations try to distance themselves from any one national culture (Plakhotnik et al., 2014) and such organisations will select personnel from anywhere in the world.

Each of these approaches will have an impact on the way people in different locations around the world are managed on a day-to-day basis, but ethnocentrism in particular might have an inhibiting effect in terms of developing diversity in the workforce. Although the contingency approach to analysing aspects of business life has been emphasised elsewhere in this textbook, that is, a belief that usually no one interpretation can be universally applied to business situations, Perlmutter and Heenan (1974) identify ethnocentrism as being problematic in general and something to be avoided. A polycentric approach also does not encourage the benefits of diversity as the emphasis is on local knowledge, expertise and culture. Regiocentric and geocentric approaches encourage greater workforce diversity, but this then needs to be effectively managed in order to gain the maximum benefits. Management of diversity would involve intercultural awareness, which is discussed in greater detail in the following sections.

From the preceding description of the number and variety of combinations an international employee might encounter, it is obvious that increasing globalisation inevitably means that managers and employees will one way or another work with people from other national cultures, be it foreign nationals in the parent home country, or a parent country national on a business assignment overseas. While not wishing to forget the dangers of racial stereotyping, there nevertheless exists research evidence of national cultural characteristics which mean that people from different

Did you know?

International HRM involves combining and coordinating HRM practices in response to the challenges of internationalising in the firm's home country, host country or third country. In terms of staffing, there are three types of employees:

Parent-country nationals – These are employees who are citizens of the country where the firm's headquarters is based.

Host-country nationals – These are employees who are citizens of the country where the firm's subsidiary is located.

Third country nationals – These are employees who are citizens of a country other than the country where the firm is headquartered or where the firm's subsidiary is located.

(*Source*: Rofcanin, Y., H. Imer and M. Zingoni (2014). Global trends in international human resource management, in M. Ozbilgin, D. Groutsis and W. Harvey (eds), *International Human Resource Management*, Cambridge University Press USA, New York.

nations will react to given situations in different ways. The next section will examine research on national cultural characteristics and their effects on businesses. This information can be useful when interacting with people from different cultures.

Cross-cultural working

One of the best known models used to demonstrate cultural differences amongst people from different nations emanates from the work of the Dutch social psychologist, Geert Hofstede (1980, 1997). Hofstede classified nations according to their score on a number of dimensions of culture and these have an effect on how people from the particular nation would behave in work and other situations. In their 2010 book *Cultures and Organizations: Software of the Mind* by Hofstede *et al.* (2010), the authors conceptualise six dimensions of culture, these being: power distance, individualism versus collectivism, masculinity–femininity, uncertainty avoidance, long term versus short term and indulgence versus restraint. A description of these dimensions can be found in Table 11.1.

Table 11.1   Hofstede *et al.*'s (2010) dimensions of culture

Dimension	Definition
Power distance	'The extent to which the less powerful members of institutions and organizations within a country expect and accept that power is distributed unequally' (p. 61).
Individualism versus collectivism	'Individualism pertains to societies in which the ties between individuals are loose: everyone is expected to look after him or herself and his or her immediate family' (p. 92). Collectivism 'pertains to societies in which people from birth onward are integrated into strong, cohesive in-groups' (p. 92).
Masculinity–femininity	A masculine society is where 'emotional gender roles are clearly distinct: men are supposed to be assertive, tough and focused on material success, whereas women are supposed to be more modest, tender and concerned with the quality of life' (p. 140). A feminine society is where 'emotional gender roles overlap: both men and women are supposed to be modest, tender and concerned with the quality of life' (p. 140).
Uncertainty avoidance	'The extent to which the members of a culture feel threatened by ambiguous or unknown situations' (p. 191).
Long term versus short term	A long-term orientation stands for 'the fostering of virtues oriented toward future rewards, in particular perseverance and thrift' (p. 239). Short-term orientation stands for 'the fostering of virtues related to the past and present, in particular respect for tradition, preservation of "face" and fulfilling social obligations' (p. 239).
Indulgence versus restraint	'Indulgence stands for a tendency to allow relatively free gratification of basic and natural human desires related to enjoying life and having fun. Restraint reflects a conviction that such gratification needs to be curbed and regulated by strict social norms' (p. 281).

The Hofstede Centre (**geert-hofstede.com**) provides further information into national culture and research conducted by Geert Hofstede and others. A Cultural Tools Country Comparison allows the user to obtain data on up to three countries related to the six dimensions discussed in Table 11.1.

Hofstede's work highlights various issues which may affect work relationships. At the very least, an awareness of cultural differences as potential sources of misunderstanding or conflict provides a basis from which to work towards more effective relationships. For instance, western approaches towards performance management rely on managers and subordinates being very open with each other in analysing plans for the future. Upward and 360 degree appraisal require constructive criticism of managers by their subordinates. A person from a high power distance country would probably experience extreme discomfort if asked to do this.

In a multicultural society like that in the UK, you are likely to encounter elements of different national cultures even in the domestic workplace. The benefits of managing diversity have already been mentioned in Chapter 4, but in the international context this becomes even more crucial.

Pause for thought 11.2 Having read about national differences relating to culture, how would you assess the UK, China and India in terms of Hofstede's six dimensions? Having thought about this, go to the Hofstede Centre's website (**geert-hofstede.com**) and undertake a Cultural Tools Country Comparison for the three countries. What do the results mean in terms of managing people?

Human resource management issues

Any company operating internationally is faced with the decision of whether to have global or local HR policies, procedures and practices in areas such as recruitment and selection, reward strategy, learning, training and development and other people management areas. In this section we shall review the concept of the international assignment, and then provide an overview of issues that might arise in the areas of recruitment and selection, learning, training and development and reward management related to the international assignment. We shall then comment on the implications of this for the role of the human resource specialist.

The international assignment

It is usually senior or middle managers and technical experts who spend periods of time overseas, but other personnel may be involved, especially in project work. International assignments vary in nature but the CIPD (2013a) has identified three types:

- a business trip of less than 31 days duration for a single trip,
- a short-term assignment of more than 31 days but less than 12 months,
- a long-term assignment of two years or more.

The term 'expatriate' is frequently used when discussing international assignments. Peng and Meyer (2011, p. 8) define an expatriate assignment as 'a temporary job abroad with a multinational company'. Ahlstrom and Bruton (2010) state that an expatriate is an individual from one country who works and resides in another country, yet there is no notion of time frame in this definition. Initially, expatriates were differentiated into two distinct groups: those sponsored by companies and those taking the initiative outside the corporate context, although the boundaries between these groups have become increasingly blurred (Doherty et al., 2013).

There is much discussion and debate about what an expatriate is. However, it is certainly the case that expatriates are expensive but they do play a crucial role in many organisations (Brewster et al., 2014). Each level of posting brings with it different requirements of the employee and calls for a different level of support from the parent organisation.

Recruitment and selection

Two major questions that arise in recruiting and selecting personnel for overseas assignments are as follows:

- What are the key competencies related to success in overseas assignments?
- What recruitment and selection methods can the employer use to identify whether a candidate has the necessary competencies to undertake a successful international assignment?

Pause for thought 11.3 Before moving on to the next section, list the competencies needed for succeeding in a 12-month international assignment to Brazil. How would you determine if a candidate has the necessary competencies to successfully undertake such an assignment? What selection methods would you use to determine the suitability of the candidate?

Much research on the first of these questions has focused on whether there is a distinctive 'international' competence. A high level of technical competence will invariably be required as the person on international assignment may be away from the usual organisational or domestic professional support system for some time. In relation to the second question, Howse (2015) has identified a number of questions that an employer should attempt to answer when recruiting and selecting an international assignee. These are:

- Does the employee have the right professional and technical skills?
- Where is the employee's home country?
- What international experience does the employee have?
- Can the employee speak the language of the host country?
- What contribution is the employee likely to make to the international assignment?
- Will the employee be able to adapt to the new environment?
- Does the employee have the required communication and team-working skills?
- What effect will the international assignment have on the employee's career?

A number of recruitment methods may be used to attract candidates for international assignments. These include internal promotion, headhunting, cross-national advertising, international graduate programmes and local recruitment (CIPD, 2013a). There are three commonly used selection methods for assessing the suitability of candidates for an international assignment. These include interviews, assessment centres and psychological testing (CIPD, 2013b).

Potočnik *et al.* (2014) propose a holistic four-stage process model for recruiting and selecting international employees. In stage 1 the competencies of the HR managers who will be responsible for the international recruitment and selection will be determined. In stage 2 international recruitment takes place of parent-country nationals (PCNs), host-country nationals (HCNs) and third country nationals (TCNs). In stage 3 international selection will take place, taking into account the person's capacity for cultural adjustment, family situation, linguistic ability, international experience, personality traits, knowledge, skills and competencies and the person–organisation fit. In stage 4 the international recruitment and selection process is evaluated to determine the extent to which it was successful.

Management development

As globalisation has become increasingly significant, so career progression increasingly depends on the ability and willingness of individuals to work overseas. International assignments have in themselves come to be regarded as a method of providing career development opportunities to ambitious employees (Fenby, 2000; Crowley-Henry, 2012). While spending time working overseas, the parent/home country national can increase their knowledge of worldwide business operations, develop greater intercultural sensitivity, perhaps learn a foreign language and 'see the world'.

Companies are also looking more and more to develop and utilise the talents of host country nationals (Mahajan and Silva, 2012). This could be made part of the remit of the parent country national on overseas assignment, but there is also the possibility of developing host country nationals by offering them assignments in parent country locations. These employees, called 'inpatriates', may help the firm to fill skills shortages at headquarters or help to develop a global mindset for such employees (Peng and Meyer, 2011). Harvey *et al.* (2000) highlight an innovative approach towards developing not only managers but global business in general by bringing host and third country nationals into the home country organisation, both to facilitate their contribution to strategic planning and for their own development.

Reward management

Although international assignments can be seen as development opportunities and therefore rewarding in themselves, they can also be challenging in terms of isolation from familiar surroundings and support systems and have additional costs related to housing, health care, transportation and other items. Employees should be compensated for the additional effort, resilience and talent they bring to overseas postings and for the dedication and sacrifice they, and their family, bring to the job (Shaffer *et al.*, 2013).

In determining the reward package for international assignments, there are two main approaches: the home-based and host-based (Menhennet, 2015). With the home-based approach, the employee's home-based reward package is enhanced through assignment-related allowances whereas with the host-based approach the reward package is based on the international assignment location (Menhennet, 2015).

Dealing with compensation for international assignments is not easy and the HR manager needs to balance the need to control costs with the need to deliver an attractive reward package to the individual. McEvoy and Buller (2013) interviewed international human resource managers in seven large American multinational corporations and these managers frequently cited compensation and benefit issues as among the most difficult of challenges they face.

The international HRM specialist

The HR specialist, like any other international manager, needs a solid foundation in all of the core aspects of HRM that the company would require in the domestic environment. That foundation of technical competence is the basic requirement of the international HRM specialist, and the complexity of operating in a multinational arena would then entail some additional competencies, such as knowledge of employment legislation and tax systems. In addition to technical competencies, the international HRM specialist will also need to have generic competencies such as maintaining excellent global knowledge, ensuring global effectiveness in strategic business units and implementing practices to ensure cultural sensitivity.

Knowledge requirements

HRM is significantly affected by formal and informal rules at home and overseas, especially with regards to employment law and practice (Peng and Meyer, 2011). Indeed, every country has its own regulations, rules and laws dealing with employment relations and these will affect how a firm manages its people internationally. Even though the European Union has harmonised many rules, regulations and legislation relating to matters of employment (see Chapter 3), there are many differences amongst the member states in terms of legislation and employment relations structures, and this will no doubt continue. For example, collective bargaining coverage in the UK is lower than in many other European countries, whilst union membership as a share of the workforce is significantly higher in the UK than it is in Germany or France (CIPD, 2015). Another example of differences concerns employee rights. In France, for instance, employers and employees are not allowed to agree to private arbitration of an employment dispute (Howse and Kendrick, 2015).

Again, it should be emphasised that the point being made here is the extent to which there are differences even among European Union countries, where a high level of uniformity might be expected. This highlights the need to be alert to laws and regulations in other countries and regions of the world, and the complexity that this entails.

Communication abilities

Although English is considered as the international language of business, for many people English will not be

> **Did you know?**
>
> A 2011 report by the CIPD on HRM and talent management in 17 countries in three regions (Europe, the Middle East and the Asia Pacific region) concluded that: 'Each country across the world carries the impact of the economic, political, social and technological environment and its own cultural values and norms in different ways. It is therefore wrong to presume that the same human resource management policies and practices will be equally appropriate and effective in each. It is essential that companies and HR managers working globally should take account of the key talent challenges in each country and the environment in which they have to operate when designing HRM and talent management systems and practices' (p. 44).

their mother tongue. Therefore, people will have different levels of proficiency. Within the European Union there are 24 official languages and to gain adequate proficiency in these languages is a daunting, if not impossible, task. Learning a few phrases in a particular language to be able to greet a foreign visitor or host, however, might be regarded at least as a basic courtesy. Sensitivity to potential problems when communicating in English and the ability to adapt one's use of language in communicating with a non-native speaker are regarded as a basic intercultural competence.

In developing intercultural competence, Forster (2000) emphasises the value of intercultural briefings supported by induction in the new workplace, mentoring and a long handover period, and notes the potential contribution of these processes to the success of foreign postings. Research by Kaufmann *et al.* (2014) in tailoring cross-cultural competence training concluded that individuals need to have high levels of emotional intelligence (EI), good communication styles and specific character traits in order to have intercultural competence.

Administration of international assignments

There are many ways in which the international human resource (IHR) specialist might function. For instance, an IHR manager might be involved in visiting branches or units overseas to establish systems or to deal with issues that have arisen. In this instance, the HR manager is likely to be seen as representative of the company, and the importance of general business awareness becomes enhanced. A larger number of HR practitioners are, however, more likely to become involved in organising arrangements for other international managers on an assignment overseas, and it is to this that we now wish to turn our attention.

The IHR specialist will be involved in various ways with recruitment and selection, reward, and development of employees on international assignments. This involvement may include the development of policy on HR functions, the provision of advice and guidance to line management or operational involvement in processes such as training and development. In addition, IHR specialists often become involved in managing the more personal arrangements necessary for a successful international assignment.

Careful selection of people with the necessary skills and personal qualities is the first step in ensuring the success of an international assignment, but the personal factors that also require attention include finding suitable accommodation, assessing the impact on the employee's family, such as their partner's career, and education if the person has any children. Research by Gupta *et al.* (2012) on the role of the spouse in expatriate failure found that, in the instances where the expatriate returned to the home country without completing the international assignment, it was the spouse's inability to cope with the foreign culture that provoked such decisions.

> **Pause for thought 11.4** What problems might an expatriate and their family face when they return from an international assignment? What could the firm do to help the employee and their family adjust to life back in the home country?

Did you know?

The cost of an international assignment will be affected by the cost of living in the country, or city, where the expatriate is based. Each year Mercer, the global consulting firm, produces a survey of the cost of living in different cities. The 2014 cost of living rankings revealed that the 10 most expensive cities for expatriates are:

1. Luanda (Angola)
2. N'Djamena (Chad)
3. Hong Kong
4. Singapore
5. Zurich (Switzerland)
6. Geneva (Switzerland)
7. Tokyo (Japan)
8. Bern (Switzerland)
9. Moscow (Russia)
10. Shanghai (China)

Data from the survey helps multinationals and governments determine compensation packages for employees on an international assignment. The survey measures the cost of over 200 items such as housing, food, transportation, clothing, entertainment and household goods.

(*Source*: Mercer's 2014 Cost of Living City Rankings, available at **www.lmercer.com**; accessed 05.02.15)

Issues concerning repatriation, the process of returning an expatriate from an international assignment, will have to be addressed if employers wish to retain excellent employees or persuade them in the first place to accept an international assignment. Peng and Meyer (2011) identify two principal challenges concerning repatriation: professional re-entry and private life. In relation to the first, the individual may be anxious about their career, be concerned about work adjustment and fear loss of status and pay. In terms of private life, friends and family may have moved on and the individual's spouse and children may find it difficult to adjust to a more mundane life back at home. Peng and Meyer (2011) also state that the returning expatriate may suffer from 'reverse culture shock' because the home country has changed, the company has changed or the expatriate themself has changed.

Repatriation is a complex issue to address but many organisations do not have policies and procedures for the return of expatriate employees (Yeaton and Hall, 2008). It is imperative that companies develop appropriate repatriation policies as returning expatriates are likely to leave an organisation if they perceive that there are insufficient mechanisms and practices to 'reward, utilize and circulate their newly acquired knowledge and skills' (Nery-Kjerfve and McLean, 2012, p. 626).

Ethics

Social responsibility is an issue for companies even if they only operate within a domestic environment. Engaging in international business, however, as with the other functional areas we have discussed, adds levels of complexity to this area.

The International Labour Organization (ILO) aims to promote rights at work, encourage decent employment opportunities, enhance social protection and strengthen dialogue on work-related issues (**www.ilo.org**). Similarly, the United Nations (2011) has developed guiding principles on business and human rights which sets out a plan for implementing the United Nations' 'Protect, Respect and Remedy' Framework. Despite international initiatives, as well as local initiatives, at the start of the twenty-first century, there continues to be issues concerning the abuse of people in workplaces around the world. Examples include the use of child labour in Sub-Saharan Africa, low-paid garment workers in Bangladesh and the intimidation of union workers in the Philippines. Multinational corporations which use labour from such places, under such conditions, may find themselves in a difficult situation vis-à-vis their customers, shareholders as well as other stakeholder groups.

A second ethical question concerns the safety of employees on international assignments. There are always parts of the world where wars are being waged or terrorists are active. There are also places where disease is prevalent and health care is very limited. In such cases, the issue of the employer's responsibility for the welfare of employees becomes crucial. A recent case involving employee safety concerns the plight of a British businessman who was kidnapped in Nigeria whilst on his way back from a nightclub in a business district of Lagos, a city where the kidnapping of foreigners is rare, unlike Nigeria's oil-producing south-east (*The Telegraph*, 2013).

International companies need to consider what their responsibilities are in sending employees to potentially dangerous places and to develop relevant policies and procedures, communications and training systems. The consultancy firm KPMG, for example, uses the risk assessment company Control Risks and an international security organisation, International SOS, to monitor dangers and provide briefings for staff, helping KPMG to decide whether travel to the country should take place and, if it does, what precautions the firm should take to ensure the security of its staff (Personnel Today, 2010). In assessing the potential risk associated with sending an employee abroad, it is important to consult up-to-date information from the UK Government (advice on visiting 225 countries and territories is available at **www.gov.uk**).

Having examined issues concerning international assignments, the concluding section to this chapter will discuss key issues in international HRM in relation to learning, training and talent development; high-performance working systems; work–life balance and diversity and quality. It is not possible to provide a comprehensive discussion of these issues in an introductory text, or to examine in detail these issues for a large number of countries and organisations. The intention is to provide you with a flavour of key issues regarding international HRM from around the world.

International perspectives on learning, training and talent development

Whilst there may be differences in styles of learning, according to Sloman (2007) the issues faced by learning, training and talent development professionals are almost universal. In the CIPD's (2011) survey of international learning and talent development covering the UK, USA and India, it was shown that in-house development programmes were seen to be the most effective method in all three countries. Coaching by line managers was viewed as the most effective intervention by more than half of UK practitioners but was ranked lower for US and Indian practitioners. On-the-job training was the third most effective measure in UK and Indian responses.

The CIPD's (2012) international survey on learning, talent and innovation in Asia found that almost three quarters of organisations in the sample were engaged in talent activities, with a higher proportion in China and South Korea and less in Singapore and Malaysia. More than half of the respondents from the Asia region felt that their organisation's talent management activities were effective, but the key challenges identified by respondents were a lack of people resources and high staff turnover.

Howse and Ash (2015) argue that multinational organisations should develop a global approach to training and development, implementing a standardised approach across all or some of the countries in which the firm employs staff. Also, Howse and Ash state that it may be helpful if the organisation provides employees with training on cultural differences between the countries where it is based, to ensure that staff in different countries can communicate well and work effectively together.

International perspectives on high–performance working systems

The large volume of information on engagement and related topics such as commitment and high-performance working indicates that these issues are high on the business and research agenda around the world.

Beltrán-Martín *et al.* (2008) examine the relationship between high-performance work systems (HPWS) and the expected outcome of improved performance in a survey of 226 Spanish firms. Their research focuses on the role of worker flexibility in this relationship, that is, the workers' capacity to develop and apply new skills, knowledge and behaviours in response to changing demands. The authors conclude that HPWS do lead to improved performance because approaches such as development and performance management allow workers to develop greater flexibility in their working methods.

An examination of HPW in subsidiaries of multinational firms in Turkey by Demirbag *et al.* (2014) revealed that the use of HPWS has a significant and positive impact on the effectiveness of employees. However, the effect of HPWS on employee skills and development, as well as the financial performance of the organisation, was much less clear. The findings highlight the extent to which HPWS need to be adapted to the specific institutional context. The issue of HPWS in relation to organisational change in a German technology firm was examined by Mihail *et al.* (2013). The study found evidence that the HPWS implemented by the firm had a positive impact on key organisational outcomes, such as productivity and revenue growth.

International perspectives on work–life balance

In recent years, there has been substantial interest among researchers in the topic of work–life balance (WLB), especially with regard to Europe, Australia, New Zealand, the USA and Canada. This has even culminated in two special editions dedicated to this subject: *Asia Pacific Journal of Human Resources*, 2008, volume 46, issue 3 and *Human Relations*, 2010, volume 63, issue 1. A review article by Bardoel *et al.* (2008)

identified the major themes of research on WLB in Australia and New Zealand to be organisational work–life policies, focusing on policies set up to improve WLB; work hours and workload, highlighting the tendency toward a long hours' culture; and wellbeing, stress and burnout.

Kossek *et al.* (2010) provide an overview of the developing interest in WLB in the USA since the 1970s, and argue that WLB policies, though well established, are still not regarded as a core aspect of people management. Thus they may still be regarded primarily as accommodating workers' needs rather than as a strategic management tool with inherent business benefits. Those taking advantage of flexible working arrangements may be regarded as less committed to work than others. The authors also compare the USA with the situation in Europe where, they argue, there is more legislated support for WLB practices, but even here, it is observed that such practices still need to be better integrated into the mainstream approach to people management.

Further articles in the *Human Relations* special issue also discuss the theme of conflicting views on where the benefits of WLB policies really lie, focusing on the USA and the EU (including the UK). Adopting the interesting approach of examining employer representations of their WLB policies on their corporate websites, Mescher *et al.* (2010) examined British, American, Dutch, Australian and global websites, and their overall conclusion was that though WLB was ostensibly supported there were implicit indications that such arrangements were really a privilege and readers were discouraged from thinking that they were an entitlement for all.

In comparing and contrasting western and eastern perspectives on WLB, Chandra (2012) found that in Asian countries gender socialisation played a major role in the perception of WLB. While American multinationals focused on flexible working practices, Indian companies focused more on employee welfare programmes. A further conclusion from the research was that western countries have fewer working hours and more generous parental leave than countries in Asia.

International perspectives on diversity and equality

One of the main concerns for international organisations with regard to equality is the different labour laws that exist in different countries. International HR specialists need to be familiar with the legislation in force in countries where the firm currently has or intends to have employees and ensure that the firm abides by the appropriate regulations. The international HR manager also needs to consider the firm's commitment to diversity initiatives and decide how far these can be implemented in overseas locations, taking into account the cultural differences. In terms of selecting employees for overseas assignments, Brewster *et al.* (2007) highlight the issue of the levels of participation of women in foreign assignments, and state that it is necessary to improve on the current situation if the benefits of diversity are to be obtained.

Research from Australia and New Zealand indicate that gender equality continues to be a problem in those countries in spite of equality legislation and the adoption of sex equality programmes by employers. Knox (2008), for example, examined gender equality in the Australian luxury hotel sector and found that the segregation of women into lower paid and lower quality work continues. Knox's research identifies inconsistencies in the commitment of line management to equal opportunity measures across all aspects of hotel work as a major contributing factor to this. Furthermore, gender stereotyping was prevalent among applicants and customers; for instance, the fact that few women apply for portering roles, and some customers refused the services of a female porter. Knox concludes that only a minority of managers were seen to be advancing the employment opportunities for women.

In the context of persistent labour supply and retention problems, Poulston and Jenkins (2013) examined age discrimination in New Zealand, also focusing on the hotel sector. Stereotypical views of hotel employers in this study replicated those identified in prior studies around difficulties with technology, training and flexibility. The significant negative stereotyping of older workers in New Zealand's hotel industry is supported in this study, and surprisingly little correlation was found between the known attributes of older workers and employers' stereotypical views. Poulston and Jenkins recommend hotel employers move away from the paradigmatic view of youth as the main labour source and towards appointing on the basis of skills and attributes.

Posthuma and Campion (2009) present a meta-analysis of 117 American research articles and books on age stereotypes in the workplace, demonstrating that the ageing workforce is indeed an issue in the USA. They recommend seven ways to enhance good practice with respect to older workers: be aware of the law on age discrimination, avoid erroneous decisions, use job-related information, use effective organisational practices, such as training and development, target high-risk settings, use older workers as a source of competitive advantage and add cognitively complex tasks for older workers.

Equal treatment in the workplace with regard to sexual orientation is currently an issue in many countries. In addition to ethical issues regarding the fair treatment of lesbian, gay, bisexual and transgender (LGBT) workers, discrimination against LGBT employees is costly in financial terms, both for employers and employees. Whilst equality legislation exists to protect LGBT people from discrimination in the workplace in many countries, in others millions of LGBT people continue to live in places that outlaw same-sex relationships and prosecute people for being gay. In five countries and in parts of two others, homosexuality is still punishable by death, while a further 70 countries imprison citizens because of their sexual orientation (**www.bbc.co.uk**, 2014). Under such circumstances, equal opportunity for LGBT people is but a dream.

Whilst much has been written about equal opportunities for disabled people in the UK (for example, Berthoud, 2008; Jones and Wass, 2013) and the USA (for example, Lindsey *et al.*, 2013; von Schrader *et al.*, 2014), it is interesting to consider how disabled people are treated in other parts of the world. Nyombi and Kibandama (2014) examine the case of access to employment for people with disabilities in Uganda. The authors point out that, since 2000, the Ugandan government has implemented a number of policies aimed at combating discrimination against disabled people in the workplace but, despite these initiatives, disabled people continue to face many barriers to accessing employment. A South American account of disability and employment is presented by Joly and Venturiello (2013) who examine the situation in Argentina and state that 'as long as persons with disabilities continue to be defined as unable to perform productive work, they will remain condemned to poverty, begging, dependency and a life without projects to fulfill' (p. 325).

An interesting perspective on discrimination in employment because of a person's ethnicity is presented in Widner and Chicoine's (2011) research into employment discrimination against Arab Americans. The authors assigned, on a random basis, a typical white-sounding name or a typical Arab-sounding name to two similar, fictitious CVs. Widner and Chicoine found that, having sent CVs to 265 jobs over a 15-month period, Arab male applicants needed to send two CVs for every one sent by white male applicants in order to be invited for an interview, suggesting that there was discrimination against the applicant because of his race/ethnicity. A study of ethnic minority professionals (of Turkish or Moroccan descent) in Flanders (Belgium) by van Laer and Janssens (2011) revealed that these professionals had experienced subtle discrimination. The authors argue that subtle workplace discrimination can be understood as 'micro-expressions of macro-level power dynamics that operate in ambiguous ways and are based on processes of subtle power' (p. 1219).

The International Labour Organization conducts research on equality issues in employment on a global basis. In their 2011 report, they found that discrimination in the workplace continues to be multifaceted and persistent with a major area of concern being access to jobs. The report also states that discrimination has become more varied and discrimination based on multiple grounds is becoming the norm. In this report, the ILO proposes four areas of action:

- promotion of the ILO conventions on equality and non-discrimination;
- sharing knowledge on eliminating discrimination in employment;
- developing ILO's capacity to implement the fundamental right of non-discrimination at work;
- strengthening of international partnerships with organisations dealing with equality.

Whilst the ILO recognises that much has been achieved with regards to workplace equality, they state that 'having laws and institutions to prevent discrimination at work and offer remedies is not enough; keeping them functioning effectively is a challenge, especially in troubled times' (ILO, 2011, p. x). The ILO report was compiled during a period of global economic recession when workplace equality initiatives were sometimes given less priority. It is to be hoped that a better economic outlook for the global economy will help strengthen anti-discrimination in employment.

Conclusion

After examining various aspects of international business the general conclusion we have reached is that the major requirement of any employees involved in international engagements is that they have solid expertise in their technical field, but the complexities introduced by operating internationally or globally, as opposed to purely domestically, necessitate additional knowledge relating to the particular country or countries involved, plus additional competencies in such areas as cultural awareness and intercultural communication. Since business is becoming increasingly global, international assignments are becoming increasingly popular. The international HR manager needs a range of knowledge, competencies, knowledge and skills in being able to manage international assignments. We have addressed these in this chapter.

Review questions

You will find brief answers to these review questions on page 474.

1. What are the characteristics of domestic, international, multinational and global firms?
2. What do the following terms mean: ethnocentric, polycentric, regiocentric and geocentric?
3. What are the different dimensions of culture (according to Hofstede *et al.*) and how might an understanding of these enable a manager or employee to better understand national culture?
4. What are the key issues associated with managing an international assignment?

Improving your employability

You are in your final year of a business management degree and you are applying for graduate positions. You have seen an international graduate scheme advertised by a global catering firm and, having read the job description and person specification, you are contemplating what information to include in your application. During your degree, you spent almost a year in China on placement in a hotel, working in the restaurant, reception, conferencing, housekeeping, marketing and the human resources department. Whilst you could not claim to be fluent in Mandarin, you did improve your proficiency in the language. As part of your degree, you have studied intercultural communication, international HRM and international marketing and Chinese (Mandarin). What competencies might you have that you could include in your application?

HR in the news

Expat life sets challenge for families with special needs

By Alicia Clegg

When Clare Allum's employer offered a transfer from London to Shanghai, her immediate reaction was to call her husband and say: "Let's go."

A human resources professional at EY, the auditor and consultant, Ms Allum felt her family needed a pick-me-up after learning that their five-year-old son Hugh had developmental problems and hearing loss.

A new beginning, she reasoned, would force them to look forwards.

Then reality kicked in. Finding an international school for their daughter was straightforward; but none of them was equipped for Hugh's needs. The move to Shanghai seemed to be a non-starter. But then her boss came up with a solution: if they based themselves in Hong Kong, where educational provision is somewhat wider, she could take the transfer and Hugh could go to school.

The revised offer was accepted. Now a sociable 13-year-old, Hugh plays Special Olympics golf and is as adept with chopsticks as he is with sign language.

Moving to a country where the healthcare and education systems are unfamiliar, where you perhaps do not speak the language and lack the encouragement of old friends, is daunting enough.

However, when a health condition or learning disability – such as dyslexia or autism – is added to the normal anxieties of parenting, the stakes are higher.

"We got on a midweek flight to Hong Kong with a real sense of hope," says Ms Allum, "but also the question: 'what if this doesn't work?'"

While there is a limit to how far employers can tweak relocation policies, there are basic adjustments that repay the effort and small extra expense, such as allowing families with unusual needs longer to explore local services during "look-and-see" visits.

Family problems are often blamed when overseas assignments come unstuck – accounting for almost a quarter of early returns, according to US-based Brookfield Global Relocation Services. For families already facing challenges, failure rates may be higher still.

Alison Bricknell, an expat spouse from South Africa, says that with hindsight she and her husband – who works for a western multinational with interests in the Asia Pacific region – should have researched the schools in Shanghai more thoroughly before committing to a move. As it was, they jumped at the chance to place their son, who has attention deficit hyperactivity disorder (ADHD), and their daughter in a school regarded locally as the go-to academy. When their son struggled, however, they were asked to remove him. Now, Ms Bricknell is considering taking the children home, while her husband completes his assignment.

Julia Burks, director of Shine Academy, a school in Shanghai that was set up by parents of children with unmet needs, says such experiences are not unusual. International schools, especially in Asia, are "very results-oriented" and relocation agencies often assume that westerners want the most prestigious establishment – regardless of a child's particular needs.

To minimise problems, she advises parents to be candid about their offspring's difficulties. "If you know your child's dyslexia might deny them a place, it's tempting to keep quiet . . . but if your child struggles, or is asked to leave, they lose."

Before agreeing a move, says Veronique Zancarini, secretary of the Autism Association for Overseas Families in the Netherlands, it is important to establish what local services cost, what medical insurance covers and what the employer will contribute. In the US and Britain a state-educated child with special needs will probably have had free access to educational therapists. However, international schools – often the only anglophone option - charge hefty fees and many require parents of children with special needs to hire one-to-one classroom assistants, known as "shadows", at further expense.

"When parents say: 'We get this, this and this, where can I get it here?' My answer is half the stuff you won't get, unless you pay for it," says Ms Zancarini.

Having a fallback is a sensible precaution when a child's wellbeing is at stake. Before moving from Britain to Beijing with two children, both with mild allergies, Katey Logan and her husband agreed with his employer that if either child's condition worsened they could relocate to Singapore. On a school trip, their son suffered a peanut exposure that tipped him into full-blown anaphylaxis. Mealtimes became a nightmare as the presence of counterfeit brands in China meant that even foods guaranteed nut-free were untrustworthy.

The family requested an emergency move. Swapping locations, Ms Logan says, has meant that her husband travels more; but it has allowed him to complete his assignment, kept the family together and bought her some peace of mind. "Having a Plan B meant we had somewhere to run."

Ms Allum advises working parents in her situation to be open about family dilemmas. Colleagues are usually supportive if they know you have a problem, and large employers sometimes have people in their employ who can advise informally on how to overcome red tape – which is what EY did when the Allums wanted a non-Hong Kong national to support Hugh at school. "Without their tips on how to negotiate with the Hong Kong authorities, I don't think we would have got a visa."

Expat families that thrive, whatever their challenges, Ms Burks observes, tend to be those that take matters into their own hands. For example, Ms Allum got involved in shaping special needs provision at her son's school and has joined its governing body.

Through the school, her family has met other families, which has helped socially. "Before we moved, I hadn't realised just how much we relied on old friends who knew our situation and loved us in spite of it."

Likewise, Joy Tong, founder of All Special Kids, a parental support organisation in Switzerland, advises newcomers to join groups begun by other parents, or, if none exist, start one - as she did. "Knowing you're not alone is invaluable."

With Hugh now a teenager, the Allums face another dilemma. Ms Allum would readily return to Britain, as she feels her son is fast outgrowing the special needs provision available locally. However, neither Hugh, nor his sister, wants to leave Hong Kong which they now regard as home.

"Doing what we've done isn't the easiest way to live," she says, "But life has been a lot more exciting than had we stayed in the UK."

Source: Clegg, A. (2013) Expat life sets challenge for families with special needs, FT.com, 2nd December.
© The Financial Times Limited 2013. All Rights Reserved.

Questions

1. What do employees who have family with special needs have to consider when accepting an international assignment?
2. How might an employer assist a family with special needs when relocating their family overseas for an international assignment?
3. What challenges do expatriates and their family face when they return to the home country?
4. What can the employer do to ensure the successful return of the expatriate and what responsibilities does the employer have for the successful repatriation of the expatriate's family?

What next?

What are the key challenges facing international human resource management in an increasingly globalised environment? This is a question posed by Brian Hurn in his 2014 paper. According to Hurn, international HRM has to cope with the following key challenges:

- increased international labour mobility,
- different labour,
- different markets,
- building and sustaining multinational teams,
- resourcing international operations in a competitive market,
- developing career patterns and training requirements to ensure the development of a cadre of international managers,
- designing pre-departure and repatriation courses.

Hurn, B. (2014). The challenges facing international HRM in an increasingly globalised environment, *Industrial and Commercial Training*, Vol. 46, No. 7, 371–378.

In his 2011 research paper, Horwitz discusses future HRM challenges for multinational firms in eastern and central Europe. The nature of transitional economies and HRM in post-Socialist societies presents a range of international HR issues. These relate to the effects of the previous institutional environment and centrally dictated political economies that still influence the type of HRM practices adopted. Horwitz considers the challenges of retention and talent management, remuneration, diversity and cross-cultural management in such economies.

When considering the HR challenges facing multinational firms in the twenty-first century it is useful to consider the issues driving change. However, whilst some of these are global in nature, there are factors that are country or region specific. Fortunately, there is a growing literature on HRM in specific countries. However, there remains a dearth of information on HR practices in some countries.

References

Aggarwal, R., J. Berrill, E. Hutson, E and C. Kearney (2011) What is a multinational corporation?: Classifying the degree of firm-level multinationality, *International Business Review*, Vol. 20, No. 5, 557–577.

Ahlstrom, D. and G. Bruton (2010) *International Management*, South-Western Cengage Learning, London.

Bardoel, E.,H. De Cieri and C. Santos (2008) A review of work-life research in Australia and New Zealand, *Asia Pacific Journal of Human Resources*, Vol. 46, No. 3, 316–333.

Beltrán-Martín, I., V. Roca-Puig A. Escrig-Tena and J.C. Bou-Llusar (2008) Human resource flexibility as a mediating variable between high performance work systems and performance, *Journal of Management*, Vol. 34, No. 5, 1009–1044.

Berthoud, R. (2008) Disability employment penalties in Britain, *Work, Employment & Society*, Vol. 22, No. 1, 129–148.

Brake, T. (1999) The HR manager as global business partner, in P. Joynt and B. Morton (eds), *The Global HR Manager*, Institute of Personnel and Development, London.

Briscoe, D., R. Schuler and I. Tarique (2012) *International Human Resource Management: Policies and Practices for Multinational Enterprises*, Routledge, Oxford.

Brewster, C., P. Sparrow and G. Vernon (2007) *International Human Resource Management*, CIPD, London.

Brewster, C., J. Bonache, J. Cerdin and V. Suutari (2014) Exploring expatriate outcomes, *International Journal of Human Resource Management*, Vol. 25, No. 14, 1921–1937.

Chandra, V. (2012) Work-life balance: eastern and western perspectives, *The International Journal of Human Resource Management*, Vol. 23, No. 5, 1040–1056.

Chartered Institute of Personnel and Development (2011) *International L&TD Comparison Survey 2011*, CIPD (available at www.cipd.co.uk; accessed 12.02.15).

Chartered Institute of Personnel and Development (2012) *Learning, Talent and Innovation in Asia*, CIPD (available at www.cipd.co.uk; accessed 12.02.15).

Chartered Institute of Personnel and Development (2013a) *International Mobility*, CIPD (factsheet available at www.cipd.co.uk; accessed 04.02.15).

Chartered Institute of Personnel and Development (2013b) *International Resourcing and Recruitment*, CIPD (factsheet available at www.cipd.co.uk; accessed 04.02.15).

Chartered Institute of Personnel and Development (2015) *Employment Regulation and the Labour Market*, CIPD (policy report, available at www.cipd.co.uk; accessed 04.02.15).

Crawley, E., S. Swailes and D. Walsh (2013) *Introduction to International Human Resource Management*, Oxford University Press, Oxford.

Crowley-Henry, M. (2012) Re-conceptualizing the career development of self initiated expatriates: rivers not ladders, *The Journal of Management Development*, Vol. 31, No. 2, 130–141.

Daniels, J., L. Radebaugh and D. Sullivan (2013) *International Business: Environments and Operations*, Pearson, London.

Demirbag, M., D.G. Collings, E. Tatoglu, K. Mellahi and G. Wood (2014) High-performance work systems and organizational performance in emerging economies: Evidence from MNEs in Turkey, *Management International Review*, Vol. 54, No. 3, 325–359.

Doherty, N., J. Richardson, and K. Thorn (2013) Self-initiated expatriation and self-initiated expatriates, *Career Development International*, Vol. 18, No. 1, 97–112.

Fenby, J. (2000) Make that foreign posting your ticket to the boardroom, *Management Today*, July, 8–10.

Forster, N. (2000) Expatriates and the impact of cross-cultural training, *Human Resource Management Journal*, Vol. 10, No. 3, 63–78.

Ghoshal, S. and C. Bartlett (1998) *Managing across Borders: The Transnational Solution*, 2nd edition, Random House, London.

Gupta, R., P. Banerjee, P., and J. Gaur (2012) Exploring the role of the spouse in expatriate failure: a grounded theory-based investigation of expatriate' spouse adjustment issues from India, *The International Journal of Human Resource Management*, Vol. 23, No. 17, 3559–3577.

Harvey, M., C. Speier and M. Novicevic (2000) Strategic global human resource management: the role of inpatriate managers, *Human Resource Management Review*, Vol. 10, No. 2, 153–175.

Hofstede, G. (1997) *Cultures and Organisations: Software of the Mind*, McGraw-Hill, New York.

Hofstede, G. (1980) *Culture's Consequences: International Differences in Work Related Values*, McGraw-Hill, New York.

Hofstede, G., Hofstede, G.J. and Minkov, M. (2010) *Cultures and Organizations: Software of the Mind: Intercultural Cooperation and Its Importance for Survival*, McGraw Hill, New York.

Horwitz, F.M. (2011) Future HRM challenges for multinational firms in eastern and central Europe, *Human Resource Management Journal*, Vol. 21, No. 4, 432–443.

Howse, M. (2015) *Making a Success of Long-Term International Assignments* (available at www .xperthr.co.uk; accessed 04.02.15).

Howse, M. and S. Ash (2015) *Guide for Global Employers: Training and Development* (available at www.xperthr.co.uk; accessed 12.02.15).

Howse, M. and C. Kendrick (2015) *Guide for Global Employers: Employee Rights* (available at www .xperthr.co.uk; accessed 05.02.15).

International Labour Organization (2011) *Equality at Work: The Continuing Challenge*, ILO, Geneva.

Joly, E. and M. Venturiello (2013) Persons with disabilities: entitled to beg, not to work. The Argentine case, *Critical Sociology*, Vol. 39, No. 3, 325–347.

Jones, M. and V. Wass (2013) Understanding changing disability-related employment gaps in Britain: 1998 – 2011, *Work, Employment & Society*, Vol. 27, No. 6, 982–1003.

Kaufmann, H., M. Englezou and A. García-Gallego (2014) Tailoring cross-cultural competence training, *Thunderbird International Business Review*, Vol. 56, No. 1, 27–42.

Knox, A. (2008) Gender desegregation and equal employment opportunity in Australian luxury hotels: are we there yet? *Asia Pacific Journal of Human Resources*, Vol. 46, No. 2, 153–172.

Kossek, E., S. Lewis and L.B. Hammer (2010) Work-life initiatives and organizational change: overcoming mixed messages to move from the margin to the mainstream, *Human Relations*, Vol. 63, No. 1, 3–19.

Lindsey, A., E. King, T. McCausland, K. Jones and E. Dunleavy (2013) What we know and don't: eradicating employment discrimination 50 years after the Civil Rights Act, *Industrial and Organizational Psychology*, Vol. 6, No. 4, 391–413.

Mahajan, A. and S. Silva (2012) Unmet role expectations of expatriates, host-country national support, and expatriate adjustment, *International Journal of Cross Cultural Management*, Vol. 12, No. 3, 349–360.

McEvoy, G. and P. Buller (2013) Research for practice: the management of expatriates, *Thunderbird International Business Review*, Vol. 55, No. 2, 213–226.

Menhennet, A. (2015) *Managing Reward for International Assignments* (available at www.xperthr .co.uk; accessed 05.02.15).

Mescher, S., Y. Benschop and H. Doorewaard (2010) Representations of work-life balance support, *Human Relations*, Vol. 63, No. 1, 21–39.

Mihail, D., M. Links and S. Sarvanidis (2013) High performance work systems in corporate turnaround: a German case study, *Journal of Organizational Change Management*, Vol. 26, No. 1, 190–216.

Nery-Kjerfve, T. and G.N. McLean (2012) Repatriation of expatriate employees, knowledge transfer, and organizational learning: what do we know? *European Journal of Training and Development*, Vol. 36, No. 6, 614–629.

Nickson, D. (2013) *Human Resource Management for the Hospitality and Tourism Industries*, Routledge, London.

Nyombi, C. and A. Kibandama (2014) Access to employment for persons with disabilities in Uganda, *Labor Law Journal*, Vol. 65, No. 4, 248–258.

Peng, M. and K. Meyer (2011) *International Business*, South-Western Cengage Learning, London.

Perlmutter, H. and D. Heenan (1974) How multinational should your top managers be? *Harvard Business Review*, November–December, 121–131.

Personnel Today (2010) Managing Expats in Dangerous Areas: What Employers Need to Know, 29 June (available at www.personneltoday.com; accessed 08.02.15).

Plakhotnik, M., T. Rocco, J. Collins and H. Landorf (2014) Connection, value, and growth: how employees with different national identities experience a geocentric organizational culture of a global corporation, *Human Resource Development International*, 1–19.

Posthuma, R. and M. Campion (2009) Age stereotypes in the workplace: common stereotypes, moderators, and future research directions, *Journal of Management*, Vol. 35, No. 1), 158–188.

Potočnik, K., M, Navarro, B. Dereli and B. Tacer (2014) Recruitment and selection in the international context, in Ozbilgin, D. Groutsis and W. Harvey (eds), *International Human Resource Management*, Cambridge University Press USA, New York.

Poulston, J. and A. Jenkins (2013) The persistent paradigm: older worker stereotypes in the New Zealand hotel industry, *Journal of Human Resources in Hospitality& Tourism*, Vol. 12, No. 1, 1–25.

PwC (2013) *Doing Business and Investing in China* (available at www.pwc.com; accessed 12.02.15).

Rugman, A. and S. Collinson (2012) *International Business*, Pearson Education, London.

Scullion, H. (2005) International HRM: an introduction, in H. Sullion and M. Linehan (eds) *International Human Resource Management: A Critical Text*, Palgrave Macmillan, Basingstoke.

Shaffer, M., B. Singh and Y. Chen (2013) Expatriate pay satisfaction: the role of organizational inequities, assignment stressors and perceived assignment value, *The International Journal of Human Resource* Management, Vol. 24, No. 15, 2968–2984.

Shim, J., J. Siegel and M. Levine (2013) *The Dictionary of International Business Terms,* Routledge, Hoboken.

Sirkeci, I. (2013) *Transnational Marketing and Transnational Consumers*, Springer, Dordrecht.

Sloman, M. (2007) World standard, *People Management*, 22 March, Vol. 13, No. 6, 38–40.

Sparrow, P. (1999) Abroad minded, *People Management*, 20 May, 40–44.

Sparrow, P., C. Brewster and H. Harris (2004) *Globalizing Human Resource Management,* Routledge, London.

The Telegraph (2013) British businessman kidnapped in Nigeria, 27 March (available at www.telegraph.co.uk; accessed 05.02.15).

United Nations (2011) *Implementing the United Nations 'Project, Respect and Remedy' Framework*, United Nations, New York (available at www.ohchr.org; accessed 05.02.15).

Van Laer, K. and M. Janssens (2011) Ethnic minority professionals' experiences with subtle discrimination in the workplace, *Human Relations*, Vol. 64, No. 9, 1203–1227.

von Schrader, S., V. Malzer and S. Bruyère (2014) Perspectives on disability disclosure: the importance of employer practices and workplace climate, *Employee Responsibilities and Rights Journal*, Vol. 26, No. 4, 237–255.

Welfare, S. (2014) *XpertHR International HR Management Survey* (available at www.xperthr.co.uk; accessed 11.02.15).

Widner, D. and S. Chicoine (2011) It's all in the name: employment discrimination against Arab Americans, *Sociological Forum*, Vol. 26, No. 4, 806–823.

www.bbc.co.uk. *Where Is It Illegal to Be Gay?* 10 February 2014. Accessed 11.02.15.

www.gov.uk. *Foreign Travel Advice*. Accessed 08.02.15.

www.ilo.org. About the ILO. Accessed 05.02.15.

Yeaton, K. and N. Hall (2008) Expatriates: reducing failure rates, *Journal of Corporate Accounting & Finance*, Vol. 19 No. 3, 75–78.

Yip, G. and G. Hult (2012) *Total Global Strategy*, Pearson, London.

Further study — Books and reports

Brewster, C. (2011) *International Human Resource Management*. Chartered Institute of Personnel and Development, London.
This book presents a comprehensive discussion of comparative and international HRM. It includes teaching notes, case studies, teaching/learning questions and a bibliography to each chapter.

Bridger, E. (2014) *Employee Engagement*, Kogan Page, London.
A textbook grounded in engagement theory and providing an understanding of psychology combined with practical tools, techniques and diagnostics. The book also contains case studies on British Gas, Capital One, ASDA, Ministry of Justice, Mace and RSA.

Edwards, T. and Rees, C. (2011) *International Human Resource Management: Globalization, National Systems and Multinational Companies*. Financial Times Prentice Hall, Harlow.
This text provides an integrated and analytical approach to human resource management through an overview of the broad debates within the political economy and a discussion of the key areas of international HRM policy and practice.

International Labour Organization (2011) *Equality at Work: The Continuing Challenge*, ILO, Geneva.
This is the third global report on discrimination in employment produced by the ILO and contains detailed information regarding the work of the ILO, trends in workplace equality, different forms of discrimination and the ILO's response.

Kramar, R., and Syed, J. (2012) *Human Resource Management in a Global Context: A Critical Approach*. Palgrave Macmillan, Basingstoke.
Using international examples and case studies, this text covers the basic principles of HRM, whilst exposing students to real world issues facing managers on a daily basis.

Articles

Cole, N. and K. Nesbeth (2014) Why do international assignments fail?: Expatriate families speak, *International Studies of Management & Organization*, Vol. 44, No. 3, 66–79.
This study examines the causes of failure of an international assignment by examining why families prematurely returned before an assignment was completed. The authors obtained completed questionnaires from 64 expatriate families and an analysis of the data revealed that the most common reason for the failure of the international assignment, as far as the families were concerned, was insufficient organisational support during the assignment.

Lertxundi, A. and J. Landeta (2012) The dilemma facing multinational enterprises: transfer or adaptation of their human resource management systems, *The International Journal of Human Resource Management*, Vol. 23, No. 9, 1788–1807.
This study, based on firms in the Basque Country and Spain, analyses the readiness of multinational firms to export their HR systems to their overseas subsidiaries. The study concludes that the quality of HR systems at the firm's headquarters had a significant influence when deciding whether to export it to overseas subsidiaries.

Muratbekova-Touron, M. (2008) From an ethnocentric to a geocentric approach to IHRM, *Cross Cultural Management: An International Journal*, Vol. 15, No. 4, 335–352.
This paper investigates the case of a French multinational company which has undergone radical restructuring through internationalisation and assesses how organisational change has affected the firm's approach towards international human resource management. The results show that an ethnocentric model of staffing becomes inefficient when a firm grows its international operations.

Story, J., J. Barbuto, F. Luthans and J. Bovaird (2014) Meeting the challenges of effective international HRM: analysis of the antecedents of global mindset. *Human Resource Management*, Vol. 53, No. 1, 131–155.
This paper examines the construct of a global mindset which is deemed a characteristic necessary for working globally. A quantitative analysis of 136 global leaders in this research revealed that a person's ability to speak foreign languages, experience abroad and having a complex role were positively correlated to having a global mindset.

Internet

Chartered Institute of Personnel and Development   **www.cipd.co.uk**
The CIPD provides information on a range of issues associated with international HRM, including factsheets, survey reports, research reports and blogs.

UK Government   **www.gov.uk**
The UK Government's portal contains foreign travel advice to 225 countries and territories worldwide. Although the information is not specifically designed for expatriates on international assignments, information relating to safety and security, terrorism, local laws and customs, entry requirements, health and natural disasters will be useful.

XpertHR   **www.xperthr.co.uk**
Provides a good coverage of information on international HRM issues, including employment law manuals, good practices manuals, law reports, surveys, and is particularly useful for international HRM and international manuals.

Objectives

By the end of this chapter you will be able to:

- understand the meaning of the terms 'discipline' and 'grievance'
- understand the role of human resource managers and line managers in discipline and grievance handling
- explain the importance of the ACAS *Code of practice* on disciplinary and grievance procedures (2009)
- describe the main features of a disciplinary procedure and of a grievance procedure
- design a simple disciplinary and grievance procedure.

I n any organisation, however good the management and however highly motivated the workforce, there will be occasions when problems or difficulties occur between management and employees. In order that employees are able to work to their optimum performance and that these problems do not turn into even bigger issues, suitable ways of dealing with them need to be devised before they occur. If the problem has arisen from something that management has done, this may result in the employee concerned having a grievance. If, however, it is a problem arising from the behaviour or attitude of an employee then disciplinary action may be called for.

Human resource managers are concerned to get the best out of people, and although the human resource approach tends towards a dislike of rules and procedures, in favour of a more individualised approach there are times when this is not possible because of the need to comply with legislation or codes of practice. This is the case where discipline and grievance are concerned. While discipline and grievances are individual issues it would be unfair to treat each case in a totally different way and to do so might result in a claim for unfair dismissal against the organisation, or dissatisfaction among the workforce. Human resource managers need to consider these issues and design suitable procedures in order to enhance both the performance management process within the organisation and to enable employees to contribute fully to the strategic objectives of the organisation.

The role of the human resource manager and the line manager

Discipline and grievances are sensitive issues requiring skilful handling, and in many organisations they have traditionally been an area that has been left to human resource managers. This has been partly due to the fact that the human resource managers were likely to be trained in skilful handling of sensitive inter-personal issues, but also many managers and supervisors were often unwilling to tackle something that might result in their unpopularity and cause difficulties in maintaining a suitable relationship with someone they had to work with on a daily basis. This attitude has changed considerably in recent years as more and more of the human resource function has been devolved to line management; line managers in many organisations are nowadays expected to handle any discipline or grievance situations that arise in their section, at least in the early stages. Human resource managers still have several important roles to play, however,

- in devising the procedures,
- in providing specialist advice,
- in ensuring that everyone is aware of the procedures and acts consistently,
- in ensuring that line managers are suitably trained,
- in monitoring the effectiveness of the procedures.

Discipline: introduction and definitions

The *Shorter Oxford English Dictionary* defines 'discipline' in the following ways: 'To subject to discipline; in earlier use, to educate or train; later, to bring under control'. The term 'discipline', as we can see from this definition, can be used in various ways. It can refer to self-discipline, where an individual, as a result of practice and training, works in an ordered, self-controlled way, or is trained by others to work in a certain way, or it can be used to refer to the need to discipline someone by pointing out to them the error of their ways or by punishing them for mistakes that they have made. Human resource managers are concerned to motivate people to ensure they reach their maximum potential, and the adoption of a punitive approach is unlikely to facilitate much motivation.

Students dealing with case studies about disciplinary situations often tend to respond initially by enjoying the power to punish and often want to dismiss the alleged offenders. Sometimes new, inexperienced managers may adopt the same approach. In reality this approach is likely to prove counterproductive, as valuable staff who have been costly to recruit and train would be lost, and the motivation of everyone concerned would be low. Handling a disciplinary situation in an unfair way may result in the employee being dismissed, but this might also result in a case for unfair dismissal being brought against the organisation. This could be expensive if the organisation lost, and in any case would be expensive in terms of

- the time needed to prepare for the tribunal,
- the time lost,

- disruption caused as witnesses are called,
- the bad publicity for the organisation itself,
- employee retention,
- the poor employee relations likely to ensue because of unfair handling of a disciplinary situation.

In order to try to minimise these problems and to encourage employers to handle disciplinary offences in a fair and reasonable manner, the Advisory, Conciliation and Arbitration Service (ACAS) has published codes of practice since 1977 and their latest, *Code of practice 1: disciplinary and grievance procedures*, came into effect on 6 April 2009.

Disciplinary procedures and practices

The ACAS *Code of practice* on disciplinary and grievance procedures

This aims to help all who may be concerned with this topic by providing practical advice about handling disciplinary and grievance procedures. A code of practice has an interesting status in law. An employer cannot have an unfair dismissal case brought against it in an employment tribunal just because it has not carried out a procedure as stated in the code of practice, but it would ignore the code of practice at its peril, as failure to comply with it is likely to be used as part of the evidence against it in an unfair dismissal case. It is also possible for the employment tribunal to increase or decrease an award by up to 25 per cent if either one of the parties has not taken account of this code and consequently there is a strong financial incentive to get things right.

In the code, ACAS clearly states that although disciplinary rules are likely to be mainly designed by management, other groups such as trade unions, line managers, workers and employees should also have a part to play in formulating them. ACAS emphasises the fact that the main reason for having disciplinary rules is to promote fairness and set standards of conduct, and to provide a fair and consistent method of dealing with alleged offences. According to ACAS, one of the main reasons for having procedures is to ensure there are orderly employment relations so that everyone knows what is expected of them. If the rules have been designed solely by management without the involvement of other interested parties employees and workers may be more cynical about management's motives and individuals may feel that when they are disciplined it is because of victimisation or because their supervisor dislikes them. In order for the disciplinary procedure to be credible to employees and other workers, it is clearly in management's interests to involve them in its design. Good employers will certainly appreciate this need.

Other employers, however, may merely be motivated in their provision of a disciplinary procedure by the need to comply with the legislation. The Employment Rights Act 1996 requires employers to provide employees with a copy of their disciplinary procedure within two months of the commencement of their employment or provide access for the workers to an accessible document which gives appropriate information. This could be done in their letter of engagement, in their contract or with the written statement of terms and conditions of employment. Following strict procedures may be more difficult for smaller employers, but at the very least ACAS (2014) recommends that the disciplinary procedure should be displayed in a prominent place such as on a notice board. Employment tribunals will take into account the size of the organisation and the administrative resources that are available to the organisation when they consider cases. It is good practice to go through the procedure with all new employees and ensure that they understand it. It is vital that all employers, regardless of their size, do follow the minimum statutory dismissal and discipline procedures.

These factors should prove sufficient to motivate the employer to provide a disciplinary procedure but, if not, in the last resort some employers may be motivated by the fact that they may need evidence that they have acted fairly and followed a fair procedure in the event of an alleged unfair dismissal claim before an employment tribunal. For whatever reason, it is obviously important to adopt a clear disciplinary procedure so that both the employer and the workforce know what standards of conduct are expected and what may happen if these standards are not achieved.

Pause for thought 12.1 Consider for a moment the word 'worker' and the word 'employee'. What is the difference between the two?

'Worker' applies to all workers whether they are employed on a contract of employment or not. As such it is a much broader term than 'employee' since it could also apply to workers who were employed by an agency or who worked as volunteers in a charity. In the ACAS *Code of practice 1: disciplinary and grievance procedures* (2009) both these words are used. Some of the provisions in this *Code of practice* refer just to employees while others, in particular the right to be accompanied at disciplinary and grievance hearings, have a wider meaning and apply to all workers.

The importance of fairness in a disciplinary procedure

The ACAS *Code of practice* (2009) emphasises that it is important to have a fair procedure. According to ACAS (2009), in order to be fair a good disciplinary procedure should allow for the following features:

- issues should be resolved promptly,
- they should be handled consistently,
- thorough investigations should be conducted,
- employees should be informed of the facts of the case against them and should have opportunities to state their side of the case,
- they should have the right to be accompanied at any formal meeting about discipline or grievances,
- there should be clear rights of appeal.

As an employment tribunal clearly has to take these factors into account and since employers could find any awards made against them increased by 25 per cent it is clearly important that they incorporate these points into any disciplinary procedure that they design and that they pay attention to complying with these points when disciplining any individual. Issues such as bullying, whistle-blowing or harassment might need to form part of a separate procedure. ACAS (2014) also recommends that independent third parties could be used as mediators at each stage of the proceedings in either cases of discipline or grievance.

ACAS gives further good practice advice about how to handle disciplinary situations in their booklet *Discipline and grievances at work: the ACAS guide* (ACAS, 2014). This provides practical guidance and is important in helping to clarify what is meant and also suggesting ways to achieve it. It explains some of the features of a disciplinary procedure and these are discussed next. However, it is important to note that though this provides an excellent guide to good practice employment, tribunals do not have to take into account what is said in the guide in the way that they must for the actual *Code of practice* itself.

Features of a disciplinary procedure

ACAS (2014) lists the following as being good features which should be contained in a disciplinary procedure. According to ACAS, good disciplinary procedures should

- be in writing;
- be non-discriminatory;
- provide for matters to be dealt with speedily;
- allow for information to be kept confidential;
- tell employees what disciplinary actions might be taken;
- say what levels of management have the authority to take the various forms of disciplinary action;
- require employees to be informed of complaints against them, and of supporting evidence, before a disciplinary hearing;
- give employees a chance to state their case before management reaches a decision
- provide employees with the right to be accompanied;
- provide that no employee is dismissed for a first breach of discipline, except for gross misconduct;
- require management to investigate fully before any disciplinary action is taken;
- ensure that employees are given an explanation for any sanction and allow employees to appeal against a decision;
- apply to all employees, irrespective of their length of service, status or say if there are different rules for different groups. (ACAS, 2014)

It may seem obvious that rules should be in writing, that any disciplinary cases should be kept confidential, and that disciplinary issues should be dealt with quickly. If they are not written down people will remember the rules differently, and varying approaches to discipline will occur. This becomes an even greater problem if there is a long time lapse before an investigation occurs as witnesses can forget what has actually occurred. Many organisations nowadays will put disciplinary rules on their intranet sites as well as in their organisational handbooks, and will often give guidance about time limits for investigations.

The rules should not discriminate against or disadvantage any specific group. Since the management must ensure that these rules are available to everyone, the rules may also need to be translated into other languages where English is not the first language of some of the workers.

The disciplinary rules should also be explained orally for new workers during the induction period. This will be of help to those with a disability such as a visual impairment, who may also require a large print, Braille or an audio-tape version of the procedure, but will also ensure any workers who are unable to read will know of the rules and will avoid the risk of their experiencing inadvertent discrimination. Employees may otherwise be uncertain as to what they may and may not do.

Clarity is also important for supervisors and managers so it is necessary that the rules specify who can take disciplinary action. If this does not happen supervisors and managers may adopt different approaches to discipline between different departments, with some supervisors unsure of what action they have the power to take.

Although there is a need for consistency in order to be non-discriminatory, in some rare cases it may be legitimate to have different rules for different departments. Employees do need to be aware of the rules that apply to them and what the disciplinary action is likely to involve, and their managers also need to be fully aware of these rules. A catering department is likely to have additional rules about hygiene that are not likely to be as relevant to a transport department. So the rules should specify to whom they apply.

It is necessary that employees know what misdemeanours are regarded as serious by management. In order to be fair the worker should be informed of the case against them and should be able to see the evidence against them before the disciplinary hearing. They must have an opportunity to state their case prior to any decision being made and have the right for a trade union official or a friend to accompany them.

Workers can make genuine mistakes, and as we have already shown it is extremely expensive to recruit and train staff, so as we have said earlier retention is an important area for organisations to consider. On these grounds alone it pays to be fair to workers and to avoid dismissing them wherever possible. In order to give workers a fair chance it is important not to dismiss anyone for a first breach of discipline, unless it is a case of gross misconduct. This ensures that the individual has a chance to learn from his or her mistake.

Management may also occasionally make mistakes, and the worker may not have committed a disciplinary offence at all. To prevent someone being disciplined for something they did not do, it is important to ensure that no disciplinary action is taken before a full investigation into the alleged offence has been carried out.

If workers are to learn from their mistakes then they need to be very clear about what they did wrong, how to do it right and also to have a clear explanation of any sanctions imposed. It is still possible that, in spite of all these precautions, occasionally management may make a mistake in disciplining a person. In order to remedy this and to ensure that people don't feel that they are being disciplined just because their supervisor doesn't like them it is important to have an appeal procedure that is made known to them.

It is also vital to follow the requirements of natural justice so employees should be given the chance to talk with someone who has not been, and will not be, involved at all in this issue. They should then be informed of allegations and the evidence against them prior to any meeting. Opportunities for them to challenge the allegations before decisions are reached should also be ensured and, as already mentioned, there should be a right of appeal. Moreover, these rules should apply to all employees regardless of length of employment or position in the hierarchy.

Did you know?

In China an online game called Happy Farm involved participants in cultivating vegetables but some took a shortcut by stealing vegetables from others. Such was the craze for this game that many employees spent time at work playing this game and subsequently some faced disciplinary action from their bosses, though sometimes their bosses ended up joining in. Maggie Zhang, a secretary in Shenzhen is quoted in the *South China Morning Post* as saying 'My Hong Kong boss warned me several times to stop playing. But…he ended up joining the game and is always stealing my vegetables'.

However, not all employers were so sympathetic and '19 government officials in Hunan province were given a verbal warning after being caught stealing vegetables during working hours'.

(*Source:* He, 2009)

Disciplinary offences

It would be impossible to fully itemise the range of behaviour that might result in disciplinary action. Nowadays many employers find a great deal of their time is spent dealing with disciplinary cases involving the misuse of social networking sites or email abuse. This could involve workers accessing these sites or using their personal email at times when they are not supposed to, but also frequently involves staff posting inappropriate comments relating to work or the organisation on these sites.

Other common offences are issues about absenteeism, timekeeping or poor performance at work. There may also be concern about a range of issues including failure to obey organisation rules, such as rules about health and safety, theft, sexism, racism, problems arising from fighting or threatening behaviour and alcohol or drug abuse. Most employers divide offences into two categories depending on the seriousness with which they are viewed within that organisation. They list issues that they regard as disciplinary offences, and then itemise as gross misconduct further offences that they consider to be more serious. These offences may be handled in different ways, depending on the seriousness with which the organisation views them.

Pause for thought 12.2 Consider any organisation that you know reasonably well, perhaps one where you have worked yourself.

1. What disciplinary rules did the organisation have?
2. How were these disciplinary rules made known to you?
3. What were considered to be disciplinary offences?
4. Were there any offences that were regarded as particularly serious in this organisation and that constituted gross misconduct? List these.
5. Compare your list with the list made by someone who has experience in a different organisation. Can you find reasons for the differences and similarities?

It is probable that there were disciplinary rules in most organisations and that these were made known to you by you being given or shown a copy of them as part of your induction to your new job. Most organisations will have a list of offences that might constitute gross misconduct. When you compare your list with that of a friend who has worked in a different organisation, you will probably have listed many of the same offences as ones that constituted gross misconduct. Theft, dishonesty and verbal or physical abuse are likely to be regarded as serious in most organisations. It is also probable that there will then be some variation in your lists as to what else constitutes an offence, depending on the attitudes in that particular organisation and the nature of the work done there.

Organisations involved in food preparation may be particularly concerned with hygiene, and may list offences concerning lack of personal hygiene as ones

Did you know?

Inappropriate non-work-related use of mobile phones has become a common problem in all types of work situation. Even the Conservative MP Nigel Mills was recorded playing the game Candy Crush on his phone while attending a Work and Pensions Select Committee meeting. He responded to criticisms by saying that he had participated fully in the meeting on pension reform which he considered to be on a very important subject, but that it had been a long meeting and in one or two parts of the meeting he was not concentrating as hard and had played one or two games.

(*Source*: PM editorial, 2014)

that could constitute gross misconduct. Organisations such as banks or building societies, where there is a need for a high degree of security, may be very concerned with email abuse and have extremely strict rules about what is acceptable for workers to both send and receive. Other organisations, such as universities, may be much more concerned with freedom of information so may have very different rules. Offences also change with time, fashion and new technology. Many organisations now have specific policies regarding both email and appropriate use of the Internet at work and some have also had to introduce policies to control the use of mobile phones at work.

Pause for thought 12.3 Tim Hancock has worked for your organisation for nearly a year. He has in general been a good employee, but you have noticed that recently he has started to arrive about 10 minutes late for work each morning. You are his supervisor. Describe the action you would take.

The way in which you, as Tim's supervisor, choose to deal with this situation depends on a number of factors. First, there is your own attitude to this issue, but more importantly there is also the attitude of the organisation to issues of poor time-keeping to consider. You may have personal views about this but you need to act in a way that is consistent with those of the organisation. Personally you may not feel too concerned about this issue as long as the work gets done, or you may take the view that it is a form of dishonesty when an employee steals time from an employer. In some organisations this may not be viewed as a problem at all. Employees may have the opportunity to create their own flexitime system without management worrying unduly about this. However, the views of the organisation will be expressed in its disciplinary procedure, and it is likely that poor timekeeping will be an area of concern. If that is the case, you, as Tim's manager, have to do something about Tim's lateness. It is not as yet a particularly serious offence, but it has the potential to become more serious if left unchecked. There may of course be a perfectly good reason why Tim has suddenly started to arrive slightly late for work. The first thing that needs to be done is for you to have a chat with Tim about it and try to find out the reason for this change in behaviour. This can be informal. It gives Tim the opportunity to explain, and also lets him know that you are aware of his lateness and are concerned about it. If he has a good reason then you will have to consider your reaction. If there is illness at home, this is likely to be a temporary situation and you may reach an arrangement with Tim about his time of arrival for a limited period of time which can be reviewed at a later date. If the problem is related to a change in a public transport timetable you may have to consider whether you can be flexible or not.

Pause for thought 12.4 Jasmine has worked for your organisation for nearly five years. Her work has always been good, but recently you have received many complaints from customers about the goods that they have ordered being late or not being received at all. You check through the records and find that all these delays can be traced back to orders that Jasmine has dealt with. You are Jasmine's manager. How will you deal with this situation?

As Jasmine's manager you will have to take some action about her poor quality of work since it is causing problems to customers and there have been complaints. However, you know that Jasmine has always been a good worker so you need to talk to her about the problem and try to find out what the cause is. Once again, you need to have an informal chat with her to find out the cause of the problem and then decide on the action to take. You may find that there is a perfectly good reason, such as a problem relating to home life, for the change in the standard of her work. If this is the case then a counselling interview is likely to be most appropriate. If, however, there doesn't appear to be a clear reason, an informal discussion which lets Jasmine know of your concerns and reaches agreement about expected improvements should suffice.

The disciplinary procedure

This will be set out in writing and needs to fulfil the criteria already discussed as essential features of a disciplinary procedure. The most important areas to be included in the procedure relate to the ways in which disciplinary issues should be handled and recorded, and you will have seen in the discussions of the previous exercises that informal chats were one of the first procedures that the manager should consider. The types of action that could be used are listed below and will be discussed next:

1. informal actions
2. formal actions
3. informing the worker of the result
4. the appeals procedure
5. the nature of gross misconduct
6. records.

1 Informal action

Informal action is normally the most appropriate way of dealing with alleged minor misconduct or unsatisfactory performance. This may just involve the supervisor or manager having a quiet word with the individual and can be a quick and easy way of sorting out a problem. This type of informal action was exactly what we recommended in both the situations in the 'Pause for thought' exercises 12.3 and 12.4 which you examined earlier in this chapter. However, if this doesn't work, or if the alleged offence is regarded as being rather more serious in nature then it is time for the employer to show his or her dissatisfaction and to take some formal action.

Pause for thought 12.5 Consider once again Pause for thought 12.3. If after the informal chat or chats there was still no improvement in Tim's timekeeping, his manager would be likely to start the formal disciplinary process.

2 Formal action

Investigation

Once the informal action has been taken, if the misconduct reoccurs or the unsatisfactory performance fails to improve, it may be necessary for the employer to try a more formalised approach. The organisation needs to carry out a full investigation and this could take the form of a fact-finding meeting before this is decided upon. This should be conducted by a management representative as a thorough investigation is important.

While workers have rights to be accompanied at disciplinary meetings, Cole (2007) says that we should 'Remember the right to be accompanied does not apply to a genuine investigatory/fact-finding meeting'. Therefore, it should be made clear exactly what the nature of the meeting is going to be and it should not be allowed to drift into a disciplinary hearing as at that stage the worker would have other rights such as the right to be accompanied. The investigatory meetings and potential disciplinary meetings should be kept separate. On this subject Cole (2007) says, 'Halt an investigatory meeting if it looks like turning into a disciplinary meeting and start formal disciplinary procedures.'

If after conducting a thorough investigation in the fact-finding meeting and if it appears that there may have been misconduct then the next stages should involve a letter, a meeting and possibly an appeal. The actual procedure may vary depending on whether the potential disciplinary action involves misconduct or lack of capability, but both will be similar.

Letter

After a thorough investigation has been conducted the first stage in the formal process is to inform the employee of the alleged misconduct in writing to ensure that the individual realises that there actually still is a problem. This letter should explain the nature of the alleged misconduct and the reasons that this not acceptable within the organisation. The letter must also inform the individual of the basis of the complaint against them and should also invite them to a meeting and inform them of their right to be accompanied at this meeting. Copies of documents such as witness statements that will be used at that meeting should be given to them.

Meeting

Setting up the meeting

The date, time and place of the meeting should, if possible, be agreed with the individual concerned and should also be timed to allow them sufficient time to prepare adequately for this meeting. The meeting should be held somewhere private where there will not be any interruptions.

At this meeting the employer should first explain the complaint and go through the evidence. Then the individual should go through his or her case and answer any allegations that have been made against them. They can also ask questions, call witnesses, present evidence and raise any points about witness information.

If there is a problem in holding this meeting at the agreed time due to a legitimate reason, for example employee illness or unavailability of their chosen companion on that date, then the employer can arrange another date. This should normally be within five working days but this can be extended by mutual agreement. However, if the individual simply fails to attend the meeting, without giving any good reason, then the employer could hold the meeting and even reach a decision in their absence.

3 Inform the worker of the results

After the meeting a decision should be made about whether disciplinary action is justified

(a) If it is decided that disciplinary action is not justified, or if no further action needs to be taken, the employer must notify the individual in writing of this fact so they no longer worry.

(b) If, however, disciplinary action is decided upon then the employer has to decide the form of the action, taking into account the individual's explanations, their past employment record, and any actions that have been taken in similar cases in the past and whether the proposed disciplinary action is reasonable in the circumstances. The employee must then be notified of the decision.

Types of formal action that could be taken

Slightly different forms of action may be appropriate for cases of misconduct or for those involving unsatisfactory performance, but basically after conducting a full investigation the steps are as follows.

The first forms of formal action in a case of alleged *misconduct* could include the following:

- A *first written warning* stating the nature of the misconduct and stating what change in behaviour is required
- The individual being told that this is part of a formal disciplinary process and the consequences if they fail to change their behaviour
- The likely consequences arising, such as a final written warning which could ultimately lead to their dismissal or some other sanction, but that this would only happen after they had been given the chance to present their case at another formally convened meeting
- A record of the warning being kept on the person's personnel file, but time limits should also be specified and after the set period of time (e.g. six months) it should no longer be relevant for disciplinary purposes and should be disregarded and removed from the file.

The first forms of formal action in a case of alleged unsatisfactory performance may be slightly different but could include *a first written improvement note* being given to any individual who is performing in an unsatisfactory way which states:

- the nature of the performance problem;
- the required improvement;
- the timescale within which the improvement should occur;
- a review date ;
- the support, such as training, that the employer will provide to help the individual to reach the required level of performance;
- notification that failure to improve, if this is what has been decided upon, could result in a final written warning and ultimately dismissal;
- the record should be kept for a specified period of time (e.g. six months) and the person's performance monitored during that period.

Final written warnings

When the requisite improvement in either performance or behaviour has not been made within the stated timescale, or if the alleged offence is sufficiently serious, the employee should normally be issued with a written warning. Once again, before this stage of the process they should be given the opportunity to present their case at a meeting.

Any final written warning that is issued should once again make the following clear to the individual:

- the grounds for the complaint,
- that failure to make the required improvement within a specified time (e.g. 12 months) may result in dismissal or another penalty,
- that there is a right of appeal.

Final written warnings should be disregarded once the specified time limit has elapsed if the required improvement has been made. ACAS provides an excellent set of sample letters to be used in various circumstances. These can be accessed at **www.acas.org.uk.**

Dismissal or other penalty

The subject of dismissal will be considered in more detail in the next chapter. However, we shall mention it briefly here as it is sometimes the final stage in the disciplinary process. Any decision to dismiss must be taken by a manager who has the necessary authority. The employee must be told as soon as possible of the decision to dismiss them, the reasons for the dismissal, the date on which their employment contract will end and their notice period and right of appeal.

Some organisations may choose to use alternative forms of sanction against the individual rather than dismissal. These could include demotion to another job, loss of seniority or pay or a disciplinary transfer. These types of sanction may only be used if the employee's contract specifies these as alternatives or if agreement is reached with the individual concerned to allow them to be used.

4 The appeals procedure

The last section of the formal disciplinary procedure should indicate what the employee should do if he or she is not happy with the action taken against him or her. There should be a clear appeals procedure with time limits for the submission of appeals stated. There should be the opportunity for a meeting to discuss the appeal and the person once again has the right to choose to be accompanied at this meeting. The appeal should be heard by a senior manager who has not been involved in the original disciplinary meeting. Again the employer must inform the employee about the final appeal decision. Even in a small organisation it is good practice for a different manger, who has not been involved in the case, to hear the appeal.

5 The nature of gross misconduct

As we said earlier, organisations will have different ideas as to what constitutes gross misconduct. The employee should be given some indication of this also in the disciplinary procedure. It is impossible to design a list that covers all possibilities, but the organisation should list some of them. For example, the procedure may say that the following constitute gross misconduct and if any employee, after a full investigation, is found guilty of any of these offences he or she will be dismissed, even for a first offence:

- theft;
- deliberate damage to the organisation's property;
- fraud;
- incapacity to work because of the influence of illegal drugs or alcohol;
- physical assault or bullying;
- bringing the organisation into serious disrepute;
- deliberately accessing Internet sites which contain obscene, pornographic or offensive materials;
- unlawful discrimination such as sexual or racial harassment;
- a serious breach of confidence;
- serious infringement of health and safety rules.

These are examples of offences that normally constitute gross misconduct, but it is not an exhaustive list and other serious offences may also constitute gross misconduct and merit dismissal.

It is also a good idea to state the organisation's position on criminal offences committed outside employment. There should be a statement in the disciplinary procedure indicating that a criminal offence which occurs outside employment may be considered as gross misconduct and may result in dismissal. The word 'may' should be stressed here as this is not an automatic reason for dismissal. The main considerations should be the nature of the offence and the type of work that the employee normally does and whether the offence makes the employee unsuitable for his or her job.

In these cases, the employee concerned will normally be suspended from work on full pay while a full investigation is being carried out. Suspension on full pay does not imply any guilt.

Records

It is extremely important that accurate records of the proceedings are kept. According to the CIPD (2014),

> All records should be kept meticulously, as this will be vital should a case be pursued at an employment tribunal. The type of records that should be kept by employers are minutes of meetings, emails, attendance notes, notes of telephone calls, copies of correspondence etc.

While it is important to keep accurate records should the case become one of alleged unfair dismissal, it is also important at all stages of the disciplinary process to have an accurate record of what has happened so that the organisation is aware of the stage in the proceedings which has been reached.

All warning letters should also state that the warning will be recorded on the employee's file for a set period of time. The period of time will vary between organisations.

It may perhaps be 6 months for a written warning and 12 months for a final written warning. Once that period of time has elapsed, if the worker's conduct or performance has improved to the employer's satisfaction, the letter and note of the offence should be removed from that person's record. If they later commit the same or a different breach of disciplinary procedure then the procedure must be started again. So if the employee who has been given a warning for an infringement concerning timekeeping then commits a different infringement, for example by carrying out poor quality work, the employer should not go to the next stage of the disciplinary procedure but should start with an informal talk and issue a separate warning if that proves necessary. However, if there is an improvement in performance or conduct during the specified time but a relapse after this and this becomes a pattern or shows evidence that the employee is abusing the system, then further longer warnings might need to be issued.

If the employer ignored the fact that the warning was out of date or was about a different type of disciplinary offence, then it could hardly expect to win its case if it eventually dismissed the worker and they later decided to go to an employment tribunal to claim unfair dismissal. Such actions would be regarded as procedurally incorrect.

If records of warnings were kept on a worker's file indefinitely, then this could prejudice the person reading the file at a later date against this employee. The employee may well have changed over the years and so an unfair impression of this person would be given. The employee has the right, under the Data Protection Act 1998, to check records to ensure that erroneous or out-of-date information is not being held and possibly used against them.

Cases that may pose particular problems

The ACAS *Code of practice* (2009) also advises that certain situations may require special consideration. They list as particularly difficult cases:

- trade union officials,
- criminal charges or convictions outside employment.

The ACAS guide (2014) adds to these another situation that may require special consideration:

- employees to whom the full procedure is not immediately available.

The mini-case studies in Activities 12.1 and 12.2 serve to illustrate some of these areas of concern. How would you handle each of these cases?

Activity 12.1

Jane has been employed by your organisation for 10 years. She works as the assistant manager in the wages office and has always been an excellent worker. You hear, on the grapevine, that she has been accused of stealing £100 from the funds of the local youth club, where she acts as treasurer.
   Imagine that you are the manager of the wages office. What will you do when:

1. you first hear the rumours?
2. she is subsequently convicted but given a conditional discharge for this offence?

Discussion of Activity 12.1

1. This is perhaps one of the most difficult situations for a manager to deal with. If the offence had happened at work it would have been a clear case of theft from work and, after going through an investigation and the disciplinary procedure, may have been considered gross misconduct with the possibility of dismissal. As it is, should the manager consider this to be a disciplinary issue or not? ACAS (2014) says that being charged with a criminal offence, and even being convicted of one, does not necessarily warrant disciplinary action being taken. Even if the employee is convicted of the offence and is absent from work because they are being remanded in custody, there is no automatic reason for disciplinary action or dismissal.

   Initially when you, the manager, hear of the alleged theft from youth club funds you will need to establish the facts of the case as best you can. You are likely to need to talk to Jane as part of this process. The main question that you as an employer must decide is whether the matter is sufficiently serious to warrant starting the disciplinary procedure. The main consideration should be whether the offence, or the alleged offence, makes the employee unsuitable for the type of work they are currently doing. You then have three options:

   (a) You could do nothing if you are satisfied with Jane's explanation and decide that the matter is not sufficiently serious to be taken further within the disciplinary procedure.

   (b) You might consider suspending her on full pay pending the result of the court case. This would remove her from the situation at work where there would be gossip and rumours, and would also ensure that if anything went missing from work she would not be automatically accused. In many ways this is an attractive option, but the manager would need to be aware that the organisation may be paying Jane for several months before her case is heard.

   (c) You could consider moving her to another section where she would not deal with cash handling, although of course many wages offices do not necessarily deal with money anyway. This would have the same advantages as in (b), but she would be earning her wages. She still might be accused, however, every time anything went missing. You may of course not have any other suitable post to which she could transfer, and depending on her contract you may need her agreement to the transfer.

2. When she is found guilty, then there are once again a variety of appropriate responses. The main guidance is given in the ACAS *Code of practice* (2009), which states that offences which occur away from the workplace should not be treated as automatic reasons for dismissal. It goes on to say that the most important factor will be whether the nature of the offence makes the employee unsuitable for their particular job. The *Code of practice* on disciplinary and grievance procedures would still need to be followed. She should be written to and called to an interview with representation if she requires it. A decision then needs to be made. The right of appeal should also be explained.

   In the case of Jane, it would be possible to say that since she was found guilty of theft, this would affect people's view of her in a position of trust and so she may be dismissed for gross misconduct. Most disciplinary procedures follow ACAS's guidelines and include a section which states that offences which occur outside work may constitute gross misconduct. Dismissal should not be automatic, however. Other options are available and it depends on the circumstances.

This case study, concerning potential disciplinary offences that occur away from the place of work, helps to illustrate one of the more difficult cases that may arise and shows how useful it is to refer to the ACAS *Code of practice* (2009) for guidance in this area.

Activity 12.2

Paul has worked for Shepley Computers for four years, and for the past six months has worked on the night shift. He has a blemish-free record and is a highly regarded member of the workforce. One hot night in summer he leaves work after signing in at nine o'clock and goes to the pub. He returns to work under the influence of alcohol and his supervisor, who has noticed his absence, tells him that he is suspended and must go home immediately. Paul becomes abusive and threatens to punch his supervisor. He takes his supervisor by the shoulders and shakes him while all the time threatening to punch him. His supervisor tells him that he is dismissed and should collect all his money and documents at the end of the week.

1. Do you feel that Paul's supervisor acted correctly in this case?
2. If not, how would you have handled this situation?

Discussion of Activity 12.2

1. Offences that occur when a manager with sufficient authority to take action, or the HR department, are not available to give advice, as in this case, need particular attention. Paul's supervisor would not be likely to have the human resource manager to turn to for advice when a potential disciplinary situation such as this suddenly occurs, so he needs to be well trained to know how to handle this type of situation. He needs to be very clear in his own mind exactly what powers are available to him. In this case the supervisor initially acted well in suspending the employee. Paul was drunk and abusive and was behaving in a threatening manner towards him. Suspension with pay is a useful technique when there needs to be an opportunity to calm the situation or when time is needed to complete an investigation into whether or not an offence has occurred. He then acted rather rashly in telling Paul that he had been dismissed. No one should be dismissed unless a proper investigation has been carried out. Taking away someone's livelihood is a serious matter which could result in an employment tribunal case for unfair dismissal being brought against the organisation. Even though some of Paul's actions, such as being drunk at work and acting in an abusive and threatening manner, could clearly be classified as gross misconduct, there still needs to be a full investigation with an opportunity for Paul and his superior to state their cases and for union representation before a disciplinary decision is reached, so clearly Paul's supervisor has not acted in a correct manner.

2. In this situation the statutory discipline, dismissal and grievance procedure was not followed, so your answer about how you would have handled the situation should have followed this:

(a) Suspend Paul on pay.

(b) Investigate.

(c) Write a letter to inform Paul of the concerns and give him the opportunity to be represented by a colleague or trades union official.

(d) Hold a meeting with Paul and his representative.

(e) Make a decision and advise Paul of his right to appeal.

Absence control

Absences are often another area of particular concern to employers. Here what is important is to find out exactly what the reasons are for the absence. In many organisations an absence control procedure is used and this may result in the disciplinary procedure being used less frequently. Absence control systems usually require the employee to telephone the supervisor on the first day of absence, and the supervisor will go through a checklist of points with him or her. If the supervisor is not available there will be a second or a third designated person with whom the absent person will have to speak. An interview will be held with the supervisor or other designated person when the absentee returns to work.

There will also be a system of visits for people who are absent on a long-term basis to ensure that the organisation stays up to date with their current situation and knows when to expect them to return to work. Supervisors and managers will be aware of the level of absenteeism in their sections and will encourage good attendance.

The aim of an absence control procedure is to minimise the need for the use of the disciplinary procedure, by creating a culture in which everyone is aware of the importance of good attendance and of their value to the organisation. The danger is that some employees may feel pressurised into returning to work before they are really fit, and this may prove to be counterproductive, resulting in their needing more time off later to recover fully.

If there is not a good reason for the absence then this is likely to be an issue considered to be misconduct. If a person has a record of short-term absences without suitable explanations or adequate medical evidence, then they can be dealt with under the organisation's normal disciplinary procedure. There is usually a specified level of absence, for example 10 days in three months, after which more formal controls will be introduced, leading to counselling or disciplinary action as appropriate.

Disciplinary procedures and ill health

If employees are away on a long-term absence due to a genuine illness then the situation needs to be dealt with in an entirely different way. You cannot warn someone that there must be an improvement in their attendance if you know that this is impossible because of the nature of their illness. Instead, regular contact needs to be maintained with such employees to establish the likelihood of their return, and medical evidence needs to be sought. A company doctor's advice may be needed. In the end it may be that the person is unable to return to work in the foreseeable future, and it may be necessary to consider whether there are any other suitable jobs that they may be able to undertake, or whether their employment needs to be terminated. Other factors, such as whether they have exhausted the organisation's sickness pay scheme, the age of the person, whether the illness is as a result of a disability as defined by the Equality Act 2010, and whether they could take early retirement under the organisation's pension scheme, will need to be considered here in order to find the best solution for both the employee and the organisation. There is also likely to be a need for employee counselling and advice, and this process, if handled with the sensitivity it deserves, is likely to be extremely lengthy.

Disciplinary hearings

The actual disciplinary hearing is similar in many ways to the interviews discussed in Chapter 6. The manager who is conducting the hearing will need to prepare thoroughly, have the relevant information to hand and arrange for a quiet room with no disturbances and with an appropriate layout in which to hold the hearing. The disciplinary hearing should be conducted in a systematic and fair way in order to ensure that all the relevant information is considered. The manager chairing it should explain clearly the purpose, who is present and why they are there, and the sequence.

Although there are many similarities between disciplinary hearings and interviews, and one would expect them to be conducted in a similar way, there are some specific legal definitions that apply to disciplinary hearings. It is important to consider these as there is a legal right for workers to be accompanied at a disciplinary hearing and this is not something that would normally apply at most other hearings, with the exception of the grievance hearing which will be discussed later in this chapter.

Disciplinary hearings are defined as all meetings where either disciplinary action or some other action could be taken against a worker. This includes any meeting that might result in actions such as a warning, final written warning, suspension without pay, demotion or dismissal being taken against the worker. It also applies to meetings to confirm warnings or other disciplinary action and to appeal hearings, even if they are held after the worker has left the employment concerned.

The right to be accompanied at a disciplinary interview

The Employment Relations Act 1999 gave workers the right to request a companion to accompany them at disciplinary or grievance hearings. This can be a fellow worker or a trade union official or even, in certain circumstances, a workplace trade union representative, provided they have been certified as having been trained to do this or having experience to perform this role by their trade union. The companion can address the hearing and advise workers, but is not supposed to answer questions on behalf of the worker. It is in order for a worker to request an alternative date for a hearing if the companion of their choice is unavailable on the designated date for the hearing.

The ACAS *Code of practice* (2009) and the ACAS guide (2014) give practical guidance about workers being accompanied at disciplinary hearings. They explain that as well as the rights to be accompanied already mentioned, some workers may have other additional rights to be accompanied by different people specified in their contracts of employment. Employers should also consider sympathetically any specific needs raised by disabled workers or by a disabled companion.

Trade unions are supposed to ensure that there are suitable training and refresher courses for all their officials, so that they can confidently take on the role of companion if requested. However, ACAS explains that although workers can request a trade union official or a fellow worker to accompany them at any disciplinary hearing, the person selected for this role does not have to agree to do this and should not be pressurised to take on the role if they do not want to do it.

Before the hearing the worker should inform the employer of the name of their companion so that the companion can also be involved in discussions about choosing a convenient date and time for the hearing. The companion may carry out the following roles:

- state the worker's case for them,
- summarise the worker's case,
- respond on behalf of the worker to any views expressed at the hearing.

However, the role of the companion will depend on what the worker wants them to do and the worker may choose not to allow them to do some of these things.

If an employer fails to comply with a reasonable request for a worker to be accompanied at a disciplinary hearing the worker may complain about this to an employment tribunal. If the worker's companion cannot attend the hearing on a specific date and the employer fails to rearrange a hearing to take account of this then this can also be the cause for a complaint to an employment tribunal.

Grievance: introduction and definitions

ACAS (2009) defines grievances as 'concerns, problems or complaints that employees raise with their managers'. We shall use the term 'grievance' in this way as a form of dissatisfaction about which the employee feels sufficiently strongly that he or she formally raises the issue with his or her management representative or shop steward. Sometimes it can be difficult for an employer to differentiate between what may appear to be minor concerns and grumbles, and grievances. However, any communication which contains a problem or complaint that the employees raise with their employer has the potential to be a grievance and should be treated as one. If there is any doubt about whether the issue is a true grievance then the employer is advised to ask the employee or worker directly. Since grievances can be raised in many different ways including letters, emails, memos, resignation letters or more formally by a worker's solicitor and since some of these may just appear to be expressing a general dissatisfaction, case law shows that it is wise for the employer to make this check.

The ACAS *Code of practice* (2009) provides guidance on grievance handling. Grievances may arise for a multitude of reasons. An employee may become dissatisfied with their hours of work or working conditions, they may feel a supervisor shows unfair favouritism to others, or may feel dissatisfaction about pay or sexual harassment. Some grievances may appear trivial and others, such as alleged sexual harassment, may be very serious, but to the employee concerned they will all have been serious enough to raise formally. A survey of 147 organisations by the IRS Employment Review (2007) found that among this sample 'the most common cause of grievances were breakdowns in relationships between colleagues or between employees and their line managers'.

Anyone in an organisation could have a grievance, even a member of management. Some grievances may become a collective issue, with negotiations between management and a trade union arising over an issue such as a collective grievance about pay or working conditions. This chapter will focus solely on grievance as an individual issue.

Grievance procedures and practices

Reasons for having a grievance procedure

Employees need to know how they can raise a grievance and seek redressal for any grievance that they might have. They need to feel confident that their grievance will be treated in a fair way and that they will get to know the result of raising this grievance within a short period of time. It is also important to settle the grievance quickly, to prevent it becoming a larger grievance that involves more people and takes longer to resolve.

If there were no procedure for raising and resolving grievances, it would be likely that employees would grumble to colleagues, and not only their work but the work of the department would be liable to suffer as a result. Therefore the main aim of the grievance procedure is to settle disputes fairly and as near to the source of grievance as possible. If there were a grievance over an issue such as safety or harassment, failure to provide a mechanism to deal with the grievance could result in serious repercussions, with perhaps accidents or a sexual or racial harassment case occurring. A grievance procedure in effect provides a safety mechanism to prevent issues from getting out of control. It also ensures that management has a channel to hear about issues that may be worrying their staff.

Discipline versus grievance

Disciplinary action is, as we have seen, normally initiated by management to express dissatisfaction with, and bring about changes in, employee behaviour; grievance, on the other hand, is normally initiated by employees for similar reasons, but in respect of management's, or perhaps co-workers', behaviour. There is a need for fairness and justice in both procedures although they are initiated by different parties. Because of this it is sometimes claimed that they are the opposites of each other, and should be viewed as complementary processes in industrial justice.

Pause for thought 12.6 Consider what you have just learned about grievance and discipline. In what ways do you consider discipline and grievance to be opposites? Are there any facts which make you think that they are not truly opposites?

As we have shown, discipline and grievance are both concerned with fairness and justice. They differ in that the people who initiate the action in each case differ. The management initiates disciplinary action against employees, and employees initiate grievances mainly against their supervisors and managers. In this way they may be considered to be opposite faces of industrial justice. However, this disregards the balance of power in these cases. To consider them to be true opposites would entail the assumption that when an employee initiates a grievance they have the same amount of power as management, which is clearly not the case. An employee who has a grievance will not be able to insist that action is taken against the person who has caused the grievance, and will have to rely on management's willingness to take action.

The informal grievance procedure

Many managers prefer to resolve grievances in an informal way and according to ACAS (2014) most grievances should be settled in this way. This is particularly appropriate in organisations which have a clear open policy for communication and consultation where it is regarded as perfectly normal for problems and concerns to be raised and settled. However, a small number of complaints will not be resolved informally, and for these it is necessary to have a grievance procedure.

The findings from the 2013 XpertHR survey are consistent with the findings from the 2007 IRS Employment Review mentioned earlier in the chapter, with breakdowns in workplace relationships still forming the bulk of the grievances. Some organisations may choose to have separate policies for bullying or harassment.

We have already outlined the reasons for having a formal grievance procedure, and in the next section will consider the form that the grievance procedure should take and the main points to be considered when designing a grievance procedure, before considering the way in which the grievance interview should be handled.

Did you know?

In a survey by XpertHR of 166 employers during a 24-month period up to May 2013, the three most common causes of grievances were:
1. grievances about a relationship with a manager,
2. grievances about a relationship with a colleague,
3. an allegation of bullying or harassment.

(*Source*: Suff, 2013)

The formal grievance procedure

Sometimes it proves to be impossible to settle grievances in an informal manner, so in order that both workers and managers are clear about how to handle grievances and to ensure grievances are resolved quickly and fairly, a grievance procedure should be designed and issued to all employees and other workers. It is a good idea, once again, to involve various groups in the design of a procedure to suit a particular organisation and to ensure that everyone in the organisation understands the rules, where they can be located and how to use them.

The key features in the formal grievance procedure

ACAS (2009) indicates that grievances should be resolved informally if possible, but if that is not possible then the grievance should be raised formally without unreasonable delay to a manager who is not the subject of the grievance.

After the grievance has been dealt with and a meeting held there is a right of appeal, which should be to a more senior manager, or if this is not possible to a different manager who has not previously been involved in the grievance. In most organisations it should be possible to achieve at least this two-stage procedure. However, where there is only one stage, for instance in an extremely small organisation, perhaps where there is only a single owner/manager, it is particularly important that the person dealing with the grievance deals with the grievance in as impartial a way as possible. In larger organisations ACAS (2014) says a further appeal to a higher level of management, such as a director, may be appropriate. We do not feel that there is any advantage in having more than three levels in the procedure, even if there are more levels in the management hierarchy. We would suggest that three main levels should prove adequate for most organisations.

Outlined below are the possible main stages in the formal grievance procedure.

Stage 1

Inform the employer in writing of the grievance

The worker should raise the grievance in writing with the immediate supervisor who will reply within a specified time, for example five working days. If the grievance is about the supervisor, there needs to be an option to bypass this stage and to raise the grievance with a manager at the next highest level.

Hold a meeting

Once the formal grievance has been raised there should then be a meeting at which the grievance is discussed and then the manager should set out their decision with reasons. The manager should of course take time to prepare adequately for this meeting but should still respond quickly and arrange for the meeting within a reasonable time frame, such as five working days. The manager may need to check earlier records to establish whether any similar grievances have been raised and there may need to be special arrangements made in some circumstances. If English is not the first language of the person raising the grievance, it may be necessary to provide an interpreter. Alternatively, if the person raising the grievance, or their companion, is disabled it may be necessary to make some reasonable adjustments to the room layout.

The manager is in control of this meeting and should ensure that it is conducted in a calm, fair and orderly manner with normal courtesies such as introductions being adhered to, if this is necessary. Many of the features of a grievance meeting are the same as for other types of interview, though ACAS (2009) advises that this type of meeting does differ from a disciplinary interview as it is more likely to result in an amicable solution.

There is a need for a quiet, private room arranged to facilitate ease of communication. The employee or their companion is likely to do most of the talking, since they are raising the grievance. There may be a need to call witnesses, and after hearing all the evidence from both sides the manager should adjourn before reaching a decision. The manager must ensure a fair hearing and that everyone concerned is aware of the purpose of the meeting, who is to be called as witnesses, the time limits within which a decision will be reached and the way in which the decision will be announced to the employee or worker concerned. ACAS (2009) also suggests that consideration should be given to having someone not directly involved in the case to taking notes and acting as a witness to the proceedings. The manager will also need to finish by summing up the key points and may need to adjourn the meeting before reaching a decision.

If there is not a swift and fair resolution of grievances, the grievances may tend to build up and the work of the section is likely to suffer. At worst this could ultimately result in a high labour turnover or a high level of absenteeism as people remove themselves from a situation where they feel unhappy, or it might escalate into an industrial dispute.

Some organisations may, in addition to these procedures, decide to have a whistle-blowing procedure. This will then provide additional protection for workers who raise grievances about issues that involve some form of wrongdoing within the organisation, for example workplace hazards or fraud.

Ensure the worker is informed of their right to be accompanied

The worker has, depending on the nature of the grievance, a statutory right to be accompanied at a grievance hearing and the manager should make them aware of this right. The statutory right applies if the grievance relates to something that concerns the performance of 'the duty of the employer in relation to a worker'. For example, this could apply in relation to a grievance raised about equal pay, because the employer has a clear duty to provide equal pay to all workers. Ultimately it will be the employment tribunals that will decide in which case the worker should have been given the right to be accompanied at the grievance hearing, so it would be good practice to allow any worker raising a grievance to be accompanied, if they request it.

Decide on appropriate action

The manager has to decide what action is appropriate in the circumstances of the case and they should ensure that the worker knows the time frame in which a decision will be reached and of their right of appeal if they are not happy with the decision.

Stage 2

Appeal

If it has not been resolved, the individual should request in writing for an interview with a more senior manager. This manager should then arrange to hear the grievance within a specified time period, for example within five working days. The worker should once again be informed of their statutory right to be accompanied and a date set for them to present their case at a meeting. The manager should make a decision about the grievance within a specified time period and the worker should be informed of this. If there is likely to be a delay in reaching a decision then the worker should also be given a clear reason for this and told when they can expect a decision.

Stage 3

As stated earlier, in a larger organisation there may be a further stage to the grievance procedure. If it has not been resolved at stage 2, the individual should raise the grievance with the general manager or director or the next most senior person. Once again, the worker should be told of their statutory rights to be accompanied at a hearing at which they present their case. As in the earlier stages, an indication about the time it will take to reach a decision should be given to the worker, as should explanations about any unavoidable delay.

Time limits

You will have noted that fairly strict time limits were specified in the section on stages in the procedure. If there is no satisfactory response to the grievance within a specified time limit, then the employee should be able to raise the grievance with the supervisor's immediate management. There should be a clear time limit for each stage of the grievance procedure, as without this there is a danger that, although a manager or supervisor may have good intentions to deal with a grievance, it will nevertheless be overlooked.

Representation

At each stage in the formal grievance procedure the worker should be informed of their statutory right to be accompanied by a companion who is another employee or who is a trade union representative. This right, once again, applies to all workers and not just employees, so agency workers, homeworkers, the self-employed or those doing voluntary work could all raise grievances and have the right to be accompanied. As we said earlier in this chapter, the right applies specifically when there is a requirement to attend a grievance hearing which relates to legal or contractual commitments such as grievances relating to grading or promotion, if they arise out of a contract. Some other grievances may not relate to contractual or legal matters but it may be safer for employers to allow workers to be accompanied rather than finding themselves testing the interpretation of the law at an employment tribunal.

Exceptional circumstances and special considerations

In exceptional circumstances it may not be practicable to raise the grievance with the immediate manager. This may be because the grievance is caused by the manager or because the manager will not be available, perhaps because of illness, to deal with the grievance with the urgency that it deserves. In those exceptional circumstances the grievance may be taken to the next level of supervision.

Some organisations may also want to establish special additional procedures to deal with specific types of grievances relating, for example, to discrimination, harassment or bullying and may design policies specific to these issues. The organisation may feel the need to have separate procedures as these are all very difficult areas that may need extra-sensitive handling.

Records

Records of grievances raised and the responses made to them should be kept. They should, in accordance with the Data Protection Act 1998, be kept confidential but certain information or data should normally be available to the individual concerned on request.

Shazia, as the shop steward, is entitled to reasonable time off to carry out her trade union duties, so she is in order to request time off. However, as we said earlier, a grievance should be settled as near to the source of the problem as possible. You need to remind Shazia, who as a shop steward should certainly be aware of this, that if she has a grievance herself, or if she is acting on behalf of one of your department, then you are the person with whom the grievance should first be raised. You should point out that if you cannot deal with this satisfactorily within the specified time period then of course she may then raise the grievance, in line with the grievance procedure, with the general manager.

Although there is a need for grievances to be settled as near to the source of grievance as possible, this becomes difficult if the grievance is about the manager or supervisor concerned, so if the grievance is about you as the supervisor, Shazia may be unwilling to discuss it with you. Nevertheless, if it is about you, you will need to know about it sooner or later, so at least you should try to ascertain the nature of the grievance before allowing it to go further.

Mediation

ACAS (2014) recommends mediation at any stage in both discipline and grievance procedures and some organisations' disciplinary and grievance procedures formally include this as a stage in both processes. It is likely to work best in a grievance situation involving relationships where there is perhaps a less formal environment, and neutrality from a third party would enable both sides to explore issues in a calm way. Mediation involves someone who has not been involved in the disciplinary or grievance issue, an independent third party, helping the two parties to the dispute to reach a voluntary agreement. Mediators are not supposed to make judgements or say what should happen but help the parties to reach agreement. Mediators could be employees who have received training and who have been accredited by external bodies as mediators, or external mediator providers to the organisation could be used.

Lind (2009) stated that mediation is not an actual part of the legal process but that mediators can be useful as 'completely neutral, they help identify areas of common interest, but the parties reach their own solutions'. Both parties have to agree to mediation and any solution is binding on both parties. Since tribunals have discretionary powers to increase or decrease awards by up to 25 per cent for either party failing to follow the ACAS *Code of practice*, it could increase the role of mediation as it is one way to show that all steps have been tried when attempting to resolve differences in either a disciplinary or grievance situation. However, although it was intended that the use of mediators would help resolve workplace conflicts at an early stage and mean that formal procedures were used less frequently, a recent study has found that it has not worked in the way intended and employers rarely use mediation in the early stages for a dispute (Mitchell, 2014).

Conclusion

We have shown in this chapter the meaning and the importance of grievance and disciplinary procedures to the organisation, and the increasing role that mediation can play in each of these. Both specialist human resource managers and line managers have an extremely important role to play in the design of procedures that are fair to all; it is also important that cases of grievance or discipline are dealt with in accordance with the organisation's procedures. Knowledge and understanding of the ACAS *Code of practice 1* (2009), and *Discipline and grievances at work: the ACAS guide* (2014) are both valuable aids to help ensure that fair procedures are designed and that disciplinary and grievance interviews are handled well. Good procedures and clear policies for dealing with both discipline and grievance issues should result in fewer of this type of problem for the organisation. Any issues that do arise are dealt with in a fair way that everyone understands. Organisations should at the design stage involve representatives from different levels and types of work to ensure policies and procedures really do meet the requirements of both the organisation and the workers. The chosen form of their policies and procedures should also be guided by advice in the ACAS *Code of practice* (2009) and include the statutory right to be accompanied for workers at both discipline and grievance hearings. Organisations must also be clear about whether they are interpreting the right to be accompanied in its strict legal sense at specific types of discipline or grievance hearings, or whether they are extending this right to workers in any discipline or grievance situation. In the next chapter, we examine the consequences of getting a disciplinary case wrong, unfair dismissal and redundancy and changes to the employment tribunal system.

The mind maps shown in Figures 12.1 and 12.2 summarise the key points covered in this chapter. When you have examined these, test your understanding of the chapter with the review questions.

Review questions

You will find brief answers to these review questions on page 476.

1. Interview both a line manager and an HR manager and try to establish what roles they play in relation to grievance and discipline handling in the workplace. How do your findings compare with what we have said in this chapter?

2. Obtain a copy of an organisation's discipline and grievance procedure and compare it with how we have described these processes. Identify and comment on the similarities and differences.

3. Obtain a copy of the ACAS *Code of practice 1: disciplinary and grievance procedures* (2009). Use this, and our suggestions in this chapter, to rewrite or modify either of the procedures you used for question 2, if you find that this is necessary.

Figure 12.1   Mind map: discipline

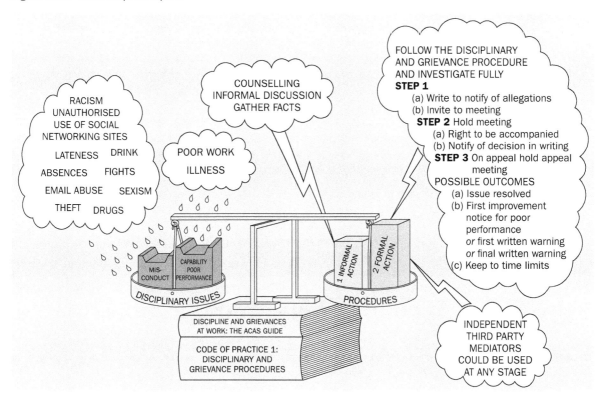

Figure 12.2   Mind map: grievance

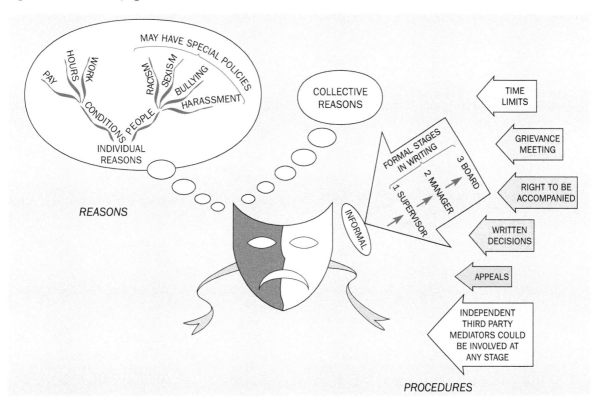

Improving your employability

Good communication skills are very important and the ability to write a business report is one aspect of good communication. In the following exercise, you will need to do some research but will also need to express your findings in a report format that would be appropriate for a business. There are many online sources for report writing but you can also find guidance from your tutor on preferred style. Further information sources are given on page 476.

Imagine that you have joined an organisation which has expanded recently and now has 100 employees. This organisation started as a small undertaking with only 18 employees and has never had a formal grievance procedure. Write a report for the general manager outlining why it is important to have a formal grievance procedure and suggesting what the procedure should contain.

HR in the news

Executive Appointments – Your questions answered – 'How can we control misuse of group email systems?'

By Gill Plimmer

We recently implemented an email system that allows staff to send large group emails at the touch of a button. However, not everyone has grown used to the pitfalls – which became apparent when a sarcastic comment from an employee about next year's modest pay rises was sent to everyone in the firm.

We don't want to appear heavy handed when the atmosphere is gloomy. But what should we do? *Ben Williams, barrister at Kings Chambers says*:

Although this was probably nothing more than a throwaway comment, you need to ensure it doesn't fester and become serious. But unless you have a clear policy for dealing with this type of thing, I would discourage the use of formal disciplinary processes. Instead, an informal word of discouragement should be enough – especially as your email system is new.

For the future, however, there are steps you can take to make sure both you and your staff understand the repercussions of a repeat blunder.

First, set clear boundaries for employees so that problems like this do not undermine trust, confidence or morale at work. The best way to do this is by adopting a policy on the acceptable use of workplace emails.

This could cover private and work-related correspondence, whether sent from a computer or mobile device. The policy would include a clear statement of an employee's accountability in respect of workplace communications; examples of what is unacceptable; a clear indication that a breach of the policy could result in disciplinary sanction; and an indication as to why, how and when emails will be monitored by you.

Second, you might want to adopt robust monitoring procedures, although this would need to be proportionate.

Any new policies or procedures need to be communicated to all staff and managers so that they understand why you are doing it.

Furthermore, employees should feel able to bring concerns to you in a proper way, and should be discouraged from doing so through global emails or social media. *Emma Dickinson, solicitor at Whitehead Monckton, says*:

It might be appropriate to take disciplinary action, but you should first confirm whether the employee's comment was a "relevant pay disclosure".

A comment counts as a "relevant pay disclosure" if it contains information about pay and was intended to find out whether, or to what extent, there is a connection between pay and the employee having (or not having) a protected characteristic (ie, in respect of age, disability, gender reassignment, marriage or civil partnership, pregnancy and maternity, race, religion or belief, sex or sexual orientation).

If an employee has sought to reveal their pay, or received information on these terms, you should avoid taking disciplinary action against them as this might enable them to pursue a claim for victimisation. You will also be unable to enforce any contractual 'pay secrecy' clause that attempts to prevent an employee from revealing what they earn.

If the comment was not a relevant pay disclosure and does not have any discrimination element, you could investigate and discipline the employee as usual.

When doing so, ensure that a reasonable disciplinary procedure is followed that complies with the Acas Code of Practice on Disciplinary and Grievance procedures, as well as any other relevant policies.

It can also be helpful to send a message to all employees explaining the economic reasons behind the need to implement modest pay rises and, if relevant, noting that any policy has been applied consistently.

You could also review your online policies and procedures by, for example, confirming who employees can talk to in confidence about their pay, offering to provide refresher training in the new email systems to all employees; and removing or restricting the use of the group email button.

Source: Plimmer, G. (2014) Executive appointments – Your questions answered - 'How can we control misuse of group email system?', *Financial Times*, 13th February.
© The Financial Times Limited 2014. All Rights Reserved.

Questions

1. Do you think that this incident in which a worker inadvertently criticised the organisation's future pay award in a mass email to all employees should be treated as a disciplinary offence?

2. How should this be dealt with by the organisation?

3. How useful are social networking sites for sharing work-related information?

4. Write a policy document for the organisation in which you clarify the rules about the use of emails.

What next?

Find some good examples of disciplinary and grievance letters and forms by going to the ACAS website (**www.acas.co.uk**).

You can also view a video showing how mediation might work on the ACAS website (**www.acas.co.uk**).

Still on the ACAS website, test your knowledge and understanding of discipline and grievance issues by taking its online course. This is designed for managers but if you have studied this chapter and answered the questions as you have gone through it you should have a good basis for developing your knowledge and understanding further by using these online materials (**www.acas.co.uk**).

References

Advisory, Conciliation and Arbitration Service (2009) *Code of Practice 1: Disciplinary and Grievance Procedures*, ACAS, The Stationery Office, London.

Advisory, Conciliation and Arbitration Service (2014) *Discipline and Grievances at Work: The ACAS Guide*, ACAS (available at www.acas.org.uk; accessed 13.04.15).

Chartered Institute of Personnel and Development (2014) *Fact Sheet: Discipline and Grievance at Work*, CIPD (available at www.cipd.co.uk; accessed 15.01.15).

Cole, K. (2007) Look beneath the labels, *People Management*, 25 January.

He, H. (2009) Stealing cyber veggies thrives in a lonely world, *South China Morning Post*, 12 December.

IRS Employment Review (2007) Survey: dispute resolution, disciplinaries and grievances 2007, *IRS 879*, 20 August.

Lind, M. (2009) Where does mediation fit into dispute resolution? *People Management*, 23 April.

Mitchell, L. (2014) Mediation under-used in early stages of dispute, finds research, *People Management*, 20 November.

PM editorial (2014) Candy Crush MP highlights routing distraction of mobiles, *People Management*, 9 December.

Suff, R. (2013) *Discipline and Grievance: 2013 XpertHR Survey*, XpertHR (available at www.xperthr.co.uk; accessed 15.01.15).

Further study

Books and reports

Advisory, Conciliation and Arbitration Service (2014*) Discipline and Grievances at Work: The ACAS Guide*, ACAS (available at www.acas.org.uk; accessed 13.04.15)..
This gives practical guidance about the *ACAS Code of Practice 1: Disciplinary and Grievance Procedures.*

Internet

The Advisory, Conciliation and Arbitration Service **www.acas.org.uk**
Another source of information for ACAS publications, some of which are published in full on this site.

Department for Business, Innovation and Skills **https://www.gov.uk/government /organisations/department-for-business-innovation-skills**
Many useful publications, discussion documents and some pieces of legislation can be found on this site.

TUC   **www.tuc.org.uk**
This gives the TUC's views on many current issues and new legislation.

Dismissal, redundancy and outplacement

Objectives

By the end of this chapter you will be able to:

- explain what is meant by the term 'fair dismissal'
- explain what is meant by 'redundancy'
- define the term 'outplacement'
- describe the services that an outplacement consultancy may provide.

In Chapter 12 we explained that there may be occasions when not everything in the relationship between employer and worker goes smoothly: the employee or worker may be dissatisfied with the employer and raise a grievance, or the employer may have to use a disciplinary procedure against an individual who is proving to be unsatisfactory. Human resource managers want to get the best from the people they employ: people are, as we have shown, very expensive to recruit and train and HRM specialists will not wish to waste these resources. However, there will be occasions when it becomes inevitable that the organisation will have to end the employment of one or more employees, and line managers as well as human resource specialists will need to know something about this process.

This chapter will examine ways in which employment may be ended fairly. We shall then consider one particular type of dismissal – redundancy – and examine ways in which the effects of redundancy may be lessened by the provision of an outplacement service. Sadly redundancy is usually inevitable in an economic downturn and in both the private and the public sector there have been job cuts resulting in redundancies. At the time of writing, in spite of a claimed upturn in the UK economy, there continue to be redundancies so this topic continues to be of great importance.

The chapter presents general guidance only, and is intended to provide not a complete or authoritative guide to employment law, but rather an appreciation of the general principles with which students of HRM should be familiar and which they may use to guide them in dealing with people who are dismissed from an organisation.

It is important for a number of reasons that any dismissal should be fair. The workforce will be better able to trust and work effectively for a management that operates fair procedures and the reputation of the organisation in general will also benefit from this.

Fairness is both a moral and a legal issue, and sometimes organisations that have tried very hard to be fair in their procedures and practices will still be found in the eyes of the law to have acted unfairly. This may be because individual managers or supervisors have made errors in the way they handled an issue, or failed to document their actions adequately, or because of some legal technicality. HRM practitioners, therefore, need to be aware of the importance of legislation and must endeavour to have systems, procedures and training in place so that everyone involved in the dismissal process acts in a fair way. They also need to know where to find detailed guidance, as they cannot know in minute detail every aspect of the law: there are many specialist texts that can help with this. Although the HRM practitioner needs to be sufficiently aware of legislation and the need for fair procedures to be able to deal with issues that arise on a day-to-day basis, it may be that, faced with an unusual problem, they will also need the advice of the organisation's solicitor.

Legislation changes constantly which means that you should be aware of general principles with regard to dismissal but you should always be prepared to check for the most recent legislation and the most recent interpretation of it, and not just rely on notes that you made years earlier. Textbooks become out of date, and you should always look for the most recent edition to guide you, although even this may not be enough to take account of the latest changes in law. We have also listed some useful sources of information at the end of the chapter.

People leave organisations for a host of reasons, and of course not all who leave are dismissed. Resignations and retirements do not normally cause any legal problems to the organisation, but employers need to take great care in the case of dismissals that they abide by the law and ensure not only that they dismiss for a potentially fair reason but that the way they handle the dismissal and the whole dismissal process is also fair. As we said in Chapter 12, this means that employers who are dismissing someone must also take into account the ACAS *Code of practice* on disciplinary and grievance procedures.

Organisations, particularly those which employ people abroad, need also to ensure that they are fully aware of the legislation which applies within the countries in which they operate.

Dismissal

Usually both employers and employees understand when a dismissal has occurred as it results in a person's employment being ended. That person may have to work their notice period, or the employer may prefer to pay them for this time but terminate their employment immediately. This is often referred to as payment in lieu of notice. In circumstances where the dismissal has occurred because of the employee's gross misconduct, the employee is not entitled to any notice or payment in lieu of notice. There are, however, other circumstances in which dismissal may occur which may be less well known, such as the non-renewal of a fixed-term contract or constructive dismissal. We shall consider each of these in turn.

Fixed–term contract

This sounds straightforward enough, and occurs when there is a fixed-term contract for a particular period of employment. If the contract is not renewed this technically counts as a dismissal although it is normally expected by both the employer and the employee. Sometimes in the past, organisations insisted that individuals whom they employed on fixed-term contracts gave up their rights to claim unfair dismissal by making them sign a waiver clause at the start of their employment. Waiver clauses in fixed-term contracts were abolished under the Employment Relations Act 1999 so an individual can no longer be made to sign away their right to claim for unfair dismissal.

Constructive dismissal

The second definition given here is a little more complicated, and is known as constructive dismissal. It is often hard to prove that the dismissal was unfair, as the person has normally resigned and may have given some other reason for leaving. For a case to succeed, the employer normally has to have done something so seriously wrong that the employee was justified in feeling that he or she could no longer work in that workplace, as the employer's action would be regarded as a significant breach of the employment contract. The person claiming constructive dismissal must also have raised the grievance formally in writing and tried to get satisfaction from the grievance procedure before handing in their notice. Possible examples could be if an employer bullied the employee so that their life was a total misery, to the extent that the person felt obliged to leave. Alternatively if an employer had changed an employee's contract in a major way which meant that the employee felt that they could no longer work at that organisation then this might give the person grounds to claim constructive dismissal (Marson, 2014). In these types of cases the employer would not have followed the statutory discipline, dismissal and grievance procedure since they did not actually dismiss the employee. However, the employee must have followed the statutory grievance procedure before presenting a claim for constructive unfair dismissal and they must act quickly so there is no assumption of agreement to the situation. Normally they will have resigned from the organisation and GOV.UK (2014a) recommends them leaving immediately as otherwise the employer may try to claim that by staying the person is accepting the situation. Marson (2014) says that if they do continue working for the same employer for a short time while looking for another job they must make it clear to the employer immediately that they are 'working under protest' as this might help preserve the right to bring a claim for constructive dismissal at a later date.

Pause for thought 13.1 We said earlier that dismissal should be for a potentially fair reason and that a fair dismissal procedure should also be followed. What do you consider to be potentially fair reasons for dismissal?

Potentially fair reasons for dismissal

You have probably listed offences such as theft, poor attendance, assault, fraud, being under the influence of drugs or alcohol, sexual harassment or racial harassment, or perhaps a serious breach of a safety rule. If you refer back to Chapter 12, you will see that these are all examples of misconduct or of gross misconduct, although poor attendance, if it is due to ill health, may be an example of lack of capability which is also a potentially valid reason.

There are three other potentially valid reasons for dismissal besides misconduct and lack of capability, and each of these covers a wide range of situations. For a dismissal to be fair, an employer must first be able to prove it was for one of these reasons:

- the conduct of the employee,
- the lack of capability or lack of qualification of the employee,
- a statutory requirement,
- some other substantial reason,
- redundancy.

The need to act reasonably

Do you think that if an employee is guilty, for example, of misconduct or proves incapable of doing the job, this means that if the employer dismisses them it will automatically be fair? In Chapter 12 we said that it was important for an organisation to have a fair disciplinary procedure modelled on the ACAS (2009) *Code of practice 1: disciplinary and grievance procedures*. It is important, if an organisation is considering dismissing someone, that it not only has potentially fair grounds for dismissing them (i.e. it is dismissing them for one of the reasons listed earlier), but it also acts fairly in the way that it carries out this dismissal. The organisation needs to have a fair procedure for handling dismissals and should have followed its own procedure in a fair way. This also means, as we have already said, that the employer must have complied with their own disciplinary and grievance procedures. This is what we mean by the condition that the dismissal also has to be actually fair. An employer should strive to be fair but may still face a claim for unfair dismissal, as dismissed employees may have a different perception of whether their treatment was fair.

Employment tribunals examine dismissal cases from two points of view. One is whether employers have acted reasonably in treating the grounds as sufficient reason to justify dismissal. The other is that they must satisfy the tribunal that they acted reasonably in the dismissal procedure. If an employee brings a claim for unfair dismissal, the tribunal will have to make a judgement about what happened after considering evidence from both parties; consequently it is important for employers to follow their own procedure and have clear records and documentary evidence.

Activity 13.1

Susan has been employed by your organisation for three years as a clerical assistant. During the past year there have been many problems with poor attendance and timekeeping. Susan's manager has tried to establish whether there is a problem underlying this poor attendance and timekeeping, but has found no clear explanation.

Susan has been counselled about this situation and has gone through the disciplinary procedure. She was written to and invited to attend two disciplinary interviews to discuss her poor attendance and timekeeping and she has been issued in the presence of her trade union representative with a written warning after the first meeting and a final written warning after the second meeting. The organisation has followed its own disciplinary procedure. The final written warning was issued only three weeks ago, and yet since then Susan has already had one day absent from work and has been late twice. She has not provided any good explanation for this, but simply says that she overslept and then did not feel like coming to work.

Do you think that the employer has potentially fair reasons for dismissing Susan? Give reasons for your answer. Which category of dismissal would this fall into?

If the employer does decide to dismiss Susan, do you think that it is being fair in the way that it is handling this dismissal?

Discussion of Activity 13.1

From the evidence given, this case looks to be a potentially fair dismissal on the grounds of misconduct, as Susan does appear to have behaved badly and the employer does appear to have a valid reason for dismissal. In this case, the management appears to have a disciplinary procedure which they followed and seem, from the evidence given here, to have acted reasonably and fairly. They could perhaps have tried to do more to help with further offers of counselling or training but since Susan has not been willing to discuss reasons for her lateness and repeated absence this would have been difficult. A case such as this would probably not go to an employment tribunal, but there may be other circumstances not given here that might lead Susan to feel her dismissal was unfair and to pursue a tribunal case.

Conduct

Conduct is the most common reason for dismissal and results in the most claims of unfair dismissal at employment tribunals. Both serious acts of misconduct, such as gross misconduct, and more minor but frequently repeated acts of misconduct, result in dismissals that fall into this category. In Activity 13.1 Susan's dismissal was for a series of minor but repeated lapses in her conduct.

Capability

Lack of capability could arise for several reasons. Capability issues normally fall into one of the following three categories:

- qualifications – which could relate to any degree, diploma or other academic, technical or professional qualification relevant to the position held by the employee;
- incompetence or poor performance – occurs where, usually through no fault of their own, the employee is simply incapable of delivering work to the required

standard (Obviously great care must be taken to ensure that the incompetence is not related to a disability.);

- illness – for example, where an employee's illness makes it impossible for them to perform their duties.

The first of these categories is reasonably straightforward and would cover situations where the employee did not have the qualifications that they claimed to possess. Lack of qualification is a potentially fair reason for dismissal. Although good selection procedures should mean that people who do not have the desired qualifications are not employed, there are many well-publicised examples of people who have lied about their qualifications and who have worked for an organisation for a number of years before being found out and dismissed. There have even been cases of doctors who have practised for many years without people realising that they did not have any medical qualification. In a case such as this, there would be a potentially fair reason for dismissal.

In the second situation, the employee simply may not be able to do the job, however hard they try. Some people may prove to be incapable of doing the job required because they lack the required level of skill or ability. This could be a reflection on the organisation's selection techniques or training, but if training and opportunities to improve have been given it may be necessary to dismiss the person if they still prove to be incapable.

Problems relating to absenteeism, particularly relating to long-term illness, can be more difficult. We discussed some of the problems in the last chapter, and clearly not all absenteeism would fall into the category of misconduct as Susan's behaviour did. Many absentees are genuinely ill but the organisation, as we said in Chapter 12, may reluctantly, having exhausted all its procedures and having provided support, counselling or offered training for another job, have to consider whether or not to dismiss. This needs to be handled in a totally different way to a misconduct dismissal, and such a dismissal would be on the grounds of the person not being capable of doing the job. The employer needs to show that it believed in the employee's lack of capability and had made reasonable enquiries about these.

Particular attention, however, should be paid to the requirements of the Equality Act 2010, before making any decision to dismiss on ill-health grounds. If many of the absences are directly attributable to a disability the employer may have to discount these from their calculations when considering whether or not the employee's attendance record is satisfactory. This was the case in *Cox* v. *The Post Office* (IT/1301162/97) where it was decided that the Post Office should have discounted Cox's absences due to asthma, since this is classed as a disability, from the figures for his attendance which they had used to justify his dismissal.

It is also important to note that if the illness itself leads to a disability the employer should first try to establish whether reasonable adjustments could be made to enable them to keep their job before considering dismissal. According to Gill Sage, an employment law specialist, 'No decision to terminate an employee's contract on the grounds of ill-health or to subject someone to any other

Did you know?

An Indian Civil servant was finally dismissed after going on leave for 24 years and never returning to his desk! A.K Verma was an assistant executive engineer who had defied his bosses' orders to return to work after his requests for additional leave were turned down. In 1992 an enquiry had found him guilty of 'wilful absence from duty' but it was to take a further 22 years and the intervention of a cabinet minister to finally get him dismissed!

(*Source: The Guardian*, 2015)

detriment should now be taken solely on the basis of absence from the workplace' (Sage, 1998, p. 23).

A statutory requirement

This is a rarer reason for dismissal, which deals with the situation where the employer would be breaking the law if it continued to employ that person. Possible examples of this would be employing a person who did not have a work permit, or employing a person who was legally too young to work full-time in that particular work environment, the results of police checks on people working with children or vulnerable adults, or possibly employing a driver who had lost their licence and was disqualified from driving.

Some other substantial reason

This category is to cover eventualities not listed already, where there is a genuinely fair reason for dismissal that does not fit neatly into any of the listed categories. One example of this is where the contract is only temporary and is not renewed. Legally the person has been dismissed. They have not been dismissed because of their misconduct or because of lack of capability or lack of qualification, or even because of some legal requirement, so this form of dismissal would fall into the category of some other substantial reason.

Redundancy

Many employers dislike discussing redundancies and invent other names for this type of dismissal. They refer to it as 'downsizing' or 'delayering', or even as being 'forced to let someone go'. It is certainly a very unpleasant form of dismissal for all concerned, as the person involved is not normally being dismissed because of anything that they have done wrong but as a result of the organisation's need to streamline its operations or cut back in some areas because of an unforeseen crisis, or perhaps through poor human resource planning. Many organisations are striving to be increasingly flexible in their deployment of people and often employ temporary or agency staff, with the result that redundancy affects more and more people in an increasingly wide range of jobs as these organisations move from traditional employment patterns to new ones.

Redundancy can occur because of three main circumstances:

- the whole business closes,
- part of the business or a particular workplace closes,
- there is less need for a particular type of work, which results in some employees being surplus to requirements.

We shall return to the topic of redundancy later in this chapter but in the case of City Link Limited it appears that there was a reduction initially in the number of people needed to do a particular job and later that the whole organisation had to close, though clearly their timing in informing people was less than ideal!

Did you know?

The parcel carrier City Link Limited fell into administration on Christmas Eve 2014 and many of City Link's workforce learned of the company's fate on Christmas Day. On New Year's Eve 2,356 people were made redundant. There were also 1,000 self-employed drivers and contractors who were not eligible for any redundancy payment though some drivers who had Christmas gifts for children in their vans carried on working so as not to disappoint any children, even though they themselves were not getting paid.

(*Source*: Farrell, S. (2015) City Link: further 230 redundancies add to tide of human misery, *The Guardian*, 7 January)

Who can bring a case for unfair dismissal

It is obviously important that all dismissals should be fair, but the law normally provides the opportunity for only some employees (those who have two years of service) to bring a case claiming unfair dismissal before an employment tribunal, though for some forms of dismissal categorised as automatically unfair there is no service requirement at all; this will be discussed later. If you remember our discussion of diversity and equality in Chapter 4, you will recall that there was no mention of a qualification period for cases such as sex discrimination, racial discrimination or discrimination on grounds of disability or any other protected characteristic. This is because many cases of discrimination occur before people are actually employed at all. However, for most cases of unfair dismissal to be brought before a tribunal, employees do have to have been employed for a certain length of time although the actual length of employment required has varied over the years. This means that some unscrupulous employers may be tempted to treat people who do not have sufficient length of service with them in an unfair way, as they know that a case for unfair dismissal cannot be brought against them. Clearly this is not good practice and employers should treat all workers in a fair way.

Did you know?

The number of claims for unfair dismissal and other complaints against employers fell by 55% after employment tribunal fees were introduced. Employees now have to pay £250 to launch a claim for unfair dismissal and a further £950 for a hearing at an employment tribunal.

(*Source*: Bowcott, 2013)

How to bring a case for unfair dismissal

Any employee with the required two years of service who feels that they were dismissed unfairly can complete an application for their case to be decided by an employment tribunal, but there are several stages which might prove to be barriers that they need to complete first. The employment tribunal system had originally been intended to provide a speedy and cheap means of getting justice, but over the years the number of cases had grown so it could be very time consuming and costly. Some employers claimed it was unfair to them as they had to spend time and money fighting a case brought against them even if it was totally unsubstantiated with little or no chance of success (Marson, 2014).

The employment tribunal system has subsequently been overhauled by government and procedures introduced which should minimise the number of cases heard, and in particular reduce the number of frivolous unsubstantiated cases. A fee has also been introduced for claimants wishing to pursue a claim in an employment tribunal and this is supposed to ensure that those using this system also contribute to its running costs, but also aims to encourage claimants to use alternative forms of dispute resolution before turning to the tribunal system. While this should save time and money, it may also have the effect of putting off genuine cases.

A prospective claimant now has various checks and stages to complete before submitting a claim to an employment tribunal. According to Ayling (2014c) the prospective claimant must:

- check they are within the relevant time limit,
- ensure they have followed their employer's procedures,

Did you know?

The trade union UNISON brought a legal challenge in the High Court on the grounds that the introduction of fees breached 'the principle of effectiveness' under EU law by making it difficult or impossible for workers to exercise their rights. In the first instance they used hypothetical claimants as examples and their case was dismissed though the High Court indicated that the case had been brought too soon and that there was a need to examine the cases of real claimants.

Despite this initial setback UNISON is determined to pursue this further.

(Source: Pinsent Masons, 2014)

- check that they have followed the ACAS (2009) *Code of practice* on discipline and grievance procedures,
- if they have been dismissed ensure that they have used their employer's appeal procedure,
- check whether there are other forms of dispute resolution available to them such as mediation,
- spend up to one month, with a two-week extension possible in certain circumstances, pursuing ACAS conciliation and then produce a certificate for the tribunal from ACAS that shows that it was not possible to achieve a settlement.

For acceptance of unfair dismissal cases, and most other types of case, there is usually a time limit of three months from the date the employment ended. Employment tribunals do not usually accept cases outside the relevant time limit, but this does depend on the reason for the delay and in some exceptional circumstances late cases may still be considered. Tribunals will not consider claims unless they are assured that the organisation's grievance procedure has been exhausted, any appeals against the dismissal decision have been made and the ACAS conciliation has been completed.

The forms themselves are easy to obtain and available from Jobcentres, law centres or Citizens Advice Bureaux, or the process can be started by applying online at **www.justice.gov.uk/tribunals/employment**. The claimant has to include the fee with their ET1 form. Their application form is then logged and allocated a case number by the tribunal office and a copy is sent to the respondent within five days of the tribunal receiving the application. (The respondent is the person the case is brought against. In most cases it will be the employer.) The respondent will be sent a response form (ET3) which they are asked to complete, indicating whether they agree with or are resisting the claim against them. They must complete this form within 28 days in order to be allowed to answer the claim against them. Copies of both forms are also sent to ACAS, the Advisory, Conciliation and Arbitration Service.

Pause for thought 13.2 Do you think that people claiming that they have been unfairly dismissed by their employer should pay fees in order to bring their claim to an employment tribunal?

Employment tribunals

The tribunal itself normally comprises three people: the chair, who has to be legally qualified and have worked as either a solicitor or a barrister for at least seven years, and two wing members. One of the wing members will be chosen from a list of names submitted by employers' organisations and the other will be chosen from a similar list submitted by workers' organisations. All are there because of their knowledge and experience, in their different ways, of employment issues and work-related problems and their aim is to ensure a fair hearing for all concerned. They will probably ask questions to clarify any points they are unsure of during the course of the tribunal hearing.

Activity 13.2

Find out from **www.acas.org.uk** how many cases of alleged unfair dismissal have been brought during the last year.

1. How many of these cases have been heard at employment tribunals?
2. What was the success rate in each category?

Automatically fair reasons for dismissal

There are a very small number of situations in which dismissal is likely to be viewed as automatically fair. These include situations where the reason or main reason for the dismissal involved the employee

- in problems of national security,
- taking part in an unofficial strike or some other type of unofficial action (this does not apply in all circumstances),
- taking part in an official strike or some other form of official action and where all the relevant employees who participated in the same action were also dismissed and not re-employed during the next three months.

National security is obviously a serious concern, so someone who endangered national security, perhaps by selling secrets, would obviously come into this category. Taking part in unofficial strikes and even official strikes can also be a very risky undertaking for the employee, even though these actions do not seem to be in quite the same category as endangering national security.

Automatically unfair reasons for dismissal

Some reasons for dismissal are likely to be automatically unfair, and in these cases an employment tribunal does not need to go through the process of establishing whether there was a fair reason for the dismissal before it assesses whether or not the employer acted reasonably. These include dismissal related to discrimination on grounds of sex, race, disability or a spent conviction as these areas, which were originally covered by the Sex Discrimination Act 1975, the Race Relations Act 1976, the Disability Discrimination Act 1995 or the Rehabilitation of Offenders Act 1974, have been superseded by the Equality Act 2010. In all of these there is no requirement for a length of service qualification for bringing a claim before an employment tribunal. Similarly, it is also automatically unfair to use any of these as the basis for selection for redundancy.

Some other examples of automatically unfair dismissal are given next but this is not an exhaustive list:

- dismissal due to trade union membership or activity;
- dismissal on maternity- or pregnancy-related grounds;
- dismissal for taking, or proposing to take, some action on health and safety grounds;
- dismissal for having sought in good faith to exercise a statutory employment right;
- dismissal of the employee because they tried to make the employer pay them the minimum wage.

In cases where there are automatically unfair reasons for dismissal, the employment tribunal does not have to go through the two-stage process of first establishing that there was a fair reason for the dismissal, then investigating whether the employer acted reasonably. In these cases, the employment tribunal has to find the dismissal fair or unfair solely with regard to the reasonableness of the actions of the employer and the reason for the dismissal.

Trade union-related dismissals

It is an automatically unfair reason for dismissal if the dismissal is for trade union membership or activities. This will apply whether the employee is dismissed because of expressing their intention to join a trade union or not to join a trade union, or for their actual membership or non-membership of a trade union. It also applies if someone is dismissed just because of their trade union activities, such as handing out leaflets or going to a trade union meeting.

Dismissal on maternity- or pregnancy-related grounds

The law relating to pregnancy is complex but it obviously does not make very good business sense to dismiss someone in whom an organisation has invested time and training just because she is pregnant. This is another automatically unfair reason for dismissal. An unfair dismissal of this type could also prove to be potentially very expensive for an employer as many claims of this type are also brought under sex discrimination legislation and there is no upper limit set on the amount of compensation that the woman could claim.

Dismissal on health and safety grounds

Once again the dismissal will be automatically unfair if the employer dismisses the employee or selects them for redundancy because they tried to bring health and safety issues to the attention of the employer. It would also be an automatically unfair dismissal if it was because the employee carried out or even just tried to carry out designated duties relating to health and safety or prevention of accidents at work, or because of their activities as a safety representative or on a safety committee.

Dismissal for wishing to exercise a statutory employment right

The dismissal will be automatically unfair if it occurs as a result of the employee bringing proceedings against the employer or alleging that an employer has infringed a statutory employment right such as a right to a minimum period of notice or the right of a trade union official for paid time off to carry out duties.

Dismissal of the employee because they tried to make the employer pay the minimum wage

In this instance the employee may have been trying to ensure that the employer pays the minimum wage to themself or to other employees. If they have not been paid the minimum wage it is against the law, and if the employee who raises this issue is dismissed because they have raised it, then it will be an automatically unfair dismissal.

Wrongful dismissal

Wrongful dismissal is based on contract law and relates to instances when the employer has broken the contract. One of the most common examples of breach of contract is when the employee is dismissed without notice in circumstances where this is clearly not deserved because of any wrongdoing on the part of the employee, or where the employee is dismissed but with the incorrect period of notice. Unlike claims of unfair dismissal, there is no qualifying length of service required for eligibility to bring a case of wrongful dismissal. According to Ayling (2014a), 'the most common example of a wrongful dismissal is failure to give the employee the correct length of contractual notice or statutory notice'.

Compensation for unfair dismissal

If a former employee wins their case for unfair dismissal at an employment tribunal the compensation awarded may take several forms.

Reinstatement

In this case the employment tribunal says that the employer must give the former employee their old job back on exactly the same terms and conditions as before and pay compensation for any loss of wages while not employed. Failure on the part of the employer to comply with this order is likely to result in additional financial awards, known as an additional or special award, being made to the employee.

Re-engagement

This means that the employment tribunal states that the employer must re-employ their former employee but it may be in a different job or on different terms and conditions of employment. For example, it may not be possible to give them back their old job as the vacancy may already have been filled by a new employee.

Compensation

This means financial compensation and is divided into the basic award and the compensatory award. The basic award is calculated in the same way as the statutory redundancy payment which is discussed later in this chapter. It is calculated by taking into account the age, number of years in that employer's service and amount of the average weekly wage. In 2014 the weekly wage included in the calculation is subject to a weekly maximum of £464 and the maximum basic award that can be awarded is £13,920. There is guidance about the various awards at GOV.UK (2014a) and there are various sites that publish easy tables for calculating these figures but these amounts are index-linked and change most years in February. One site that gives opportunities to check potential awards in various situations is **www .jobrights.co.uk**.

In some circumstances there may be deductions taken from the amount awarded by the employment tribunal – for example if the employment tribunal feels that the employee partially contributed to their own dismissal or if the employer offered to reinstate the employee and they refused unreasonably.

A compensatory award may also be made and this is to take account of factors such as loss of earnings, loss of pension rights or loss of benefits, such as company car or house. The maximum compensatory award from 6 April 2014 was the lower of the following: £76,574 or an employee's gross weekly pay multiplied by 52. There are unlimited awards made, as mentioned earlier, in cases of dismissal related to sex, race or disability discrimination. An additional award may also be made if the dismissal was for trade unionism.

Redundancy

We discussed earlier the fact that redundancy can be a potentially fair reason for dismissal. However, great care must be taken in the selection of those who are to be made redundant, and a large number of employment tribunal cases are brought each year where employees feel that they have been unfairly selected for redundancy.

Any organisation should first choose to take various steps to try to preclude or minimise the need for redundancies. Good human resource planning should help to minimise this need, but however effective the human resource planning, there may still be a need for redundancies because of other problems, such as the unexpected loss of a large order or the failure of the business of a large debtor. Clearly in the current economic situation this is an important issue which needs to be handled correctly.

Consultation

Consultation is a very important stage in redundancies, both for legal reasons and in order to maintain morale. Morale is always likely to be low when there is a threat of redundancy, but rumour and uncertainty are only likely to make it worse. The purpose of consulting is to minimise the need for redundancies if possible.

In April 2013 the time periods required for consultation were reduced. Since then if 20–99 employees are to be made redundant within a period of 90 days, consultation should start at least 30 days before the first dismissal. If 100 or more employees are to be made redundant within a period of 90 days, this consultation should start at least 45 days before the first dismissal is to occur.

The European Collective Redundancies Directive 2013 changed the way in which the calculation of the numbers potentially involved in the proposed redundancy would work. Although it still says that this is based on the numbers to be made redundant at one establishment, the definition on what constitutes an establishment is broad and could include all of the proposed redundancies by that employer regardless of the separate sites at which the people work (Marson, 2014).

In practice, in Britain, consultation frequently occurs at the same time as the notification of redundancies so that the redundant employees are often already working their notice when the consultation is supposed to be taking place. This has the effect of making it rather more difficult to achieve much by consultation in terms of avoiding dismissals or reducing the numbers since those to be made redundant have already been selected.

Groups to be consulted in collective redundancies

There is no formal requirement for consultation if the redundancy applies to fewer than 20 employees though clearly it would be good practice to consult widely. The dismissal is unrelated to the quality of work of the individual concerned as it could be due to the need for fewer employees to do a particular task or because of reorganisation or reallocation of work. The employer should follow these steps if proposing to make 20 or more employees redundant at one establishment within 90 days:

- Depending on the actual numbers involved notify the Secretary for State for Business, Innovation and Skills at least 30 or 45 days in advance of the first dismissal.
- Consult with any recognised trade union representatives or other elected employee representatives.
- Consult about ways to avoid or minimise the need for redundancies.
- Begin the consultation in good time and at least 30 or 45 days prior to the first redundancies, depending on the numbers of proposed redundancies. There should be no dismissal until the consultation has finished and the 30 or 45 day period has elapsed.
- Provide written information about the planned redundancies and allow time for the appropriate representatives to consider these and their implications for the workforce (ACAS, 2014).

The employer should respond to requests for more information.

- They should give formal staff termination notices to all staff affected by the redundancies with details of their leaving date.
- Issue redundancy notices when the consultation period is finished.

The information needed for consultation

The employee representatives will need sufficient information from the employer about its proposals to be able to participate fully in a meaningful way in the consultations. Certain information must be given to them in writing. This must be handed individually to each of them, sent by post to an address they have given the employer or, in the case of consultation with a trade union, sent to its head office. The consultation must be undertaken with a view to reaching agreement with the appropriate representatives and should include the following:

- the actual numbers and job categories likely to be affected,
- the reasons for the redundancies,
- the proposed criteria for selection,
- the procedures and timescales during which the redundancies will occur,
- the basis for the calculation of compensation if it is different from the statutory minimum (Ayling, 2014b).

If the trade union representatives, employees' representatives or the employees themselves feel that consultation has been inadequate, they can apply to an employment tribunal which can make a protective award of up to 90 days' pay for each employee in cases where at least 20 employees were to be made redundant (ACAS, 2014). Employers can, in their defence, claim that there were special circumstances which made it impossible to comply with the legislation, and in many cases the consultation seems to amount to announcing the redundancies.

Steps to preclude the need for redundancies

While good employers should always be looking to the future and planning their manpower needs to suit their strategic objectives, there can also be changing economic circumstances caused by situations such as global events that are outside the employer's control and not easy to predict. Employers do need to be flexible and so have to develop a range of strategies to avoid or limit redundancies.

Even before the Information and Consultation Directive 2002 came into effect, organisations in the UK were supposed to consult in order to prevent or minimise the need for redundancies. It is foolish to contemplate making good employees redundant if a simpler solution is feasible, so a calm, objective review of the situation is called for and a consideration of all possible alternatives. While this sounds reasonable there have been many occasions in the UK where consultation has only started after the redundancy period has been announced so although it is possible that dismissals may still be avoided, it seems less likely. Some bad employers also prefer to face the financial penalties rather than go through the process in the way in which it was intended.

The steps which can be taken to avoid redundancies will depend to some extent on the timescale available. Some employers are keen to look after their employees and to part company with them on as good terms as possible. Employers are supposed to consider alternatives to compulsory redundancy and, according to Ayling (2014b),

> Organisations should always try to avoid redundancies. Ways of doing this include:
>
> - natural wastage
> - recruitment freeze
> - stopping or reducing overtime
> - offer early retirement to volunteers (subject to age discrimination issues)
> - retraining or redeployment
> - offering existing employees sabbaticals and secondments
> - pay freezes
> - short-time working
> - pay cuts in return for taking time off work
> - alternatives to redundancy (ATR) schemes in which employees do not work for the employer for a specified period, and are free to seek new work whilst receiving an ATR allowance.

The methods chosen will depend on the particular circumstances within the organisation. Natural wastage may work well if two organisations are combining and if there is sufficient time to allow for natural wastage to occur, but is unlikely to be the best solution if the organisation needs to reduce staff immediately and most solutions also carry some costs to the organisation. Some of the options aimed at reducing the need for redundancy might not be possible for all employers as they could involve breaking their employees' contracts, so care must be taken to discuss and consult widely before seeking to implement some of these steps.

Many organisations do already engage in meaningful negotiation with their employees and do take steps to minimise the need for redundancies. Some go much further and provide outplacement services and these will be discussed later.

Selection for redundancy

If the consultations or measures chosen as a result of them fail to work, the employer needs to decide how to select and implement the redundancies. Ideally there should be an agreed procedure for handling redundancies but if not, then criteria which are fair need to be chosen and the pool of workers from among whom the redundancies are to occur also needs to be identified.

Selection criteria for redundancy

Employers need to choose criteria for selection carefully.

Case Study 13.1   Redundancy

Read the following case study and answer the questions that follow.

The Spartan Insurance Company has decided that it is overstaffed and that it must cut back on its office staff. The departmental manager for administration recommends that the post room and print room, which between them employ seven staff, should be amalgamated into one section. This will eliminate the need for three members of staff.

The post room is run by Mr Arshad Mohammed, who is aged 34, is extremely efficient and has been with the organisation for three years. There are three other members of staff in this section – Mrs Sarah Sergeant, Ms Sandra Smythe and Mr Terry Gibbs. Mrs Sarah Sergeant, a widow aged 55, has worked for Spartan Insurance for 20 years. She has always been an extremely reliable employee, but since the death of her husband 18 months ago she has suffered greatly from ill health and has had a series of illnesses linked to depression.

Ms Sandra Smythe is a fairly recent recruit to the organisation. She is aged 25 and has been employed for six months. She has settled into the job well and is very efficient in everything she has to do, but is the first to admit that she still has a great deal to learn.

The most junior member of staff in this section is Terry Gibbs. He is only 20 and joined Spartan Insurance Company straight from school. He has been employed by the company for two years and seemed to have a few problems making the transition from school to work; Mr Mohammed has spoken to him informally once or twice about his attitude to work. More recently Mr Mohammed has had to warn him about his timekeeping, and he received a written warning about this. The written warning is still current and does not expire for a further month, but Terry has taken this warning extremely seriously and there has been a noticeable improvement in both his attitude and his timekeeping.

The print room has three staff – Mr George Brownlow, Mrs Rashida Ali and Ms Sally Wilson. Mr Brownlow, aged 44, is the supervisor of this section but in reality he does not actually perform any supervisory duties. Neither is he qualified to service any of the machines. He spends most of his time grumbling about the company and telling the other staff to get on with their work. He has been employed by the organisation for 10 years and it is generally thought that he was moved to his present job where he would be out of everyone's way, because of his generally uncooperative nature. It is believed that this situation was allowed to develop because he was a close personal friend of a former branch manager. This manager has long since left the organisation but Mr Brownlow is always clever enough not to do anything to warrant dismissal, and has not even received any warnings about his work. He is also a prominent local councillor and spends quite a bit of time attending council meetings.

Luckily for Mr Brownlow there are two very efficient employees who cover for his inefficiency and who do most of the work. Mrs Ali is 35 and has worked for Spartan Insurance for four years. She knows almost everything that there is to know about the machines and in effect runs the section. Sally Wilson is also extremely efficient; she is 17 years old and has been employed for a year, having started last summer straight from school.

Questions

1. What criteria would you propose for selection for redundancy here?
2. Which employees would you select for redundancy?

Discussion of Case Study 13.1

You might have chosen criteria based on length of employment or factors such as level of competence or attendance and timekeeping.

If you chose to use the last in first out (LIFO) principle then you would make the following people redundant: Ms Sandra Smythe (employed for six months), Mr Terry Gibbs (employed for two years) and Ms Sally Wilson (employed for one year). LIFO has traditionally been the preferred choice by trade unions and it seems at first sight to be an objective method of selection, with those who have the shortest length of employment with the organisation being chosen for redundancy. This method also has the advantage of being easy to use and understand as well as being less costly in terms of redundancy pay. It may, however, as in this case, mean that those who are selected for redundancy are those who, although they have the shortest length of service, may be keen, enthusiastic employees who will have much to offer the organisation in the future. This might result in a stagnating, ageing workforce who lack the skills and versatility required for future business success. From an employer's point of view, it is not a very satisfactory way of selecting redundant employees. Care also needs to be taken with this approach to avoid accusations of age discrimination as it is quite likely in many organisations that the last to join may also be the youngest. However, last in first out can still be used as a selection method but only if it is used as a part of a range of criteria – and even then it should be used with caution.

If you chose criteria such as timekeeping and level of efficiency you are likely to have proposed the selection of Mr Brownlow, Mr Terry Gibbs and Mrs Sergeant.

Employers often choose to use other criteria so that they can retain efficient employees while making redundant others who may not have given such good service, even though they have been employed for a much longer period of time. Caution also has to be exercised in this case to ensure that the criteria chosen are objective and fair. Just saying that someone has, for example, 'a poor attitude to work' is not likely to prove adequate grounds for selection for redundancy, as this is rather vague and subjective. More objective criteria need to be used, and the ability to do this depends on whether the organisation has effective records of employee capability and competence. You would need to break job performance down into several areas such as level of skill, knowledge, experience, flexibility, productivity, appraisal records. If you selected Mr Brownlow for redundancy, you would need to have clear evidence about levels of efficiency and output. If, on the other hand, you chose Terry Gibbs for redundancy because of his poor attendance record, you would have to ensure that there are clear records for absence and that the pattern of absenteeism does not appear high because of an uncharacteristic level of ill health just prior to the redundancy period. Criteria such as disciplinary warnings also need careful checks to ensure that they are still 'live'.

Some criteria may also make the redundancies potentially unlawful if, for example, they apply disproportionately to one sex, one ethnic group, one age group or to employees with disabilities. Whatever the selection criteria used, employers should take care to ensure that the criteria are neither directly nor indirectly discriminatory. Selection of part-time rather than full-time employees may, for instance, constitute indirect sex discrimination if the majority of part-time employees are women and the majority of full-time employees are men.

According to Ayling (2014b), where there is a choice between employees selection must be based on objective criteria which may include some of the following:

- length of service, but only if it is one element in a range of criteria;
- attendance records;
- skills, competencies and qualifications;
- disciplinary records;
- work experience;
- performance records.

Employment tribunals generally look favourably on selection procedures based on a points system. However, the fairness may be suspect if only one person has made the selection and care should also be taken to avoid factors which may be discriminatory as even 'selecting part-timers in preference to full-timers could be discriminatory if a high proportion of women are affected' (Ayling, 2014b).

Special envoys or tellers

One of the worst jobs that any manager has to do is to tell one or more of their employees that they could be made redundant. In a survey conducted by Ashman (2012a) people spoke of the emotional impact of being the bearer of bad news as being 'traumatic', 'nerve wracking', 'dreadful', 'stressful' or 'hideous', they developed coping strategies such as emotional hardening or cognitive dissonance and support may be needed to help some managers deal with this role.

This job could be the responsibility of the employee's manager or may be done by the HR manager; according to Ashman (2012a) this person becomes an envoy as the role is one of messenger or diplomat. The person who conducts this task has to have skills of sensitivity, discretion, resilience and be able to mediate if necessary as this role is critical in the success of the whole downsizing process. The whole process involves three elements, strategy, procedure and psychology (Ashman, 2012a). The potential bad news has to be communicated in a clear and accurate manner, and while the strategic objectives of the organisation need to be achieved by making some staff redundant this has to be done in a fair way following the correct procedures and also taking account of the emotional impact it will have on not only those directly affected but also on the survivors.

Rights of redundant employees

Consultation with individual employees

Employers should also consult with each individual employee who is to be affected by the redundancies, even if there has also been consultation with the unions or with employee representatives. This consultation should:

- explain why the redundancies are needed,
- explain why the particular employee has been selected,
- show any relevant documentation,
- explain why no suitable alternative work is currently available,
- explain any requirements during the notice period such as whether normal working or part-time working is required, whether payment will be made in lieu of notice, and explain what time off is allowed to seek alternative work or for training.

Suitable alternative employment

The employer should offer a suitable alternative job if there is one, rather than making the employee redundant. If the employee's job title is broad, there may be sufficient flexibility to make an offer easily. If this is not the case, the employer should not automatically assume that any alternative employment that involved less pay or status would necessarily be unsuitable to the employee; it should still be discussed. The employees should, however, be given sufficient information about any alternative job so that they can realistically reach a decision, and they should also be offered the chance of a trial period. This should be of four weeks' duration, and will give both the employer and the employee the chance to assess the job's suitability. It should start as the old contract finishes. If a longer trial period is required because of the need for retraining, this should be agreed in writing before the date of commencement of the trial period. If either party finds the new job to be unsuitable during this period then the redundancy situation will still apply, and the redundant employee will still be entitled to his or her redundancy pay.

If the offer of suitable alternative employment is refused by the employee, then the employer has the option of withholding redundancy pay. Any claim to an employment tribunal will have to assess the suitability of the offer and the reasonableness of the refusal.

Right to time off for job searching or retraining

Employees who have worked for two years for the employer and are about to be made redundant have a statutory entitlement to a reasonable amount of time off from work to look for other jobs or to retrain in order to be able to improve their employment prospects. Any employee who is not allowed a reasonable amount of time off for these purposes can make a complaint to an employment tribunal.

Redundancy pay

Employers are expected to compensate any employee who has been made redundant, and who has worked for them for at least two years in continuous employment by paying them an amount of redundancy pay. The actual amount that the employee may be entitled to if they are redundant is calculated according to age, length of service and weekly pay. There is an upper earnings limit for the amount of weekly pay that may be included in this calculation, and this amount alters each year. Currently the limit on the weekly rate is £464 (GOV. UK, 2014b). Redundancy pay is tax free and does not affect the right to unemployment benefit. Furthermore, the amount that the employee receives is not affected even if she or he starts another job immediately. Although redundancy pay has been exempt from the Equality Act 2010, there have been some alterations to the upper and lower limits. The calculation of redundancy is based on the actual age of the employee at the date of dismissal, and takes account of each year of service in the appropriate age band as follows:

- for each complete year of employment in which the employee was below the of age of 22, half a week's pay,
- for each complete year of employment in which the employee was aged 22 or over but was below the age of 41, one week's pay,
- for each complete year of employment in which the employee was aged 41 or over, one and a half weeks' pay.

More favourable redundancy schemes

You will have noticed that the statutory levels for redundancy pay are not very high, especially if the person concerned is young, or has not been employed by the employer for very long. This seems to contradict the huge amounts of redundancy pay that some people are rumoured to receive. This is because some employers have decided to make a more generous provision than is required by law. They may do this in some of the following ways:

- calculating entitlements based on actual pay rather than applying the upper earnings limit;
- reducing the length of qualifying period necessary to receive redundancy pay from, for example, two years to one;
- adding amounts to the statutory scheme;
- making a more generous calculation such as two or three weeks' pay for each year of service.

Outplacement

Employers may also be concerned to help their employees in other ways through this difficult period, and may provide an outplacement service. This is the international name given to the process that many employers use to assist redundant employees. Outplacement can be defined as the process whereby the employer actively helps the employee to come to terms with the redundancy and assists them in the process of finding a new job or developing a new career. It is a type of aftercare service for employees who are facing redundancy, though it is by no means standard practice for all employers to provide such a service. It has been defined by Jones (1994) as 'the provision of support to candidates during the transitional phase between involuntary/voluntary job loss and resettlement'. This is a useful definition as, although much of outplacement is concerned with job search skills and the finding of a new job or career, there are other avenues to explore such as further training or part-time or voluntary work, or perhaps self-employment. This definition also states that support is provided to the candidate, and this makes it clear that the responsibility for the resettlement process still rests with the candidates themselves but that help and active support will be given by the outplacement provider.

While the emphasis is on helping the individual during a difficult period the fact that the employer provides an outplacement service also gives a very strong message to those who are still employed that they are working for a caring employer even though times may be hard. This is important as managing to keep morale high among the remaining employees can be a very difficult issue during a redundancy period, but the survival of the organisation depends on the morale and motivation of the survivors (Ayling, 2014b).

While outplacement is generally provided by or for employers not all organisations provide this service and on occasions individuals whose organisation has not provided this facility may buy this provision for themselves. Research conducted by the National Careers Service in 2010 found that 'nearly one in three jobseekers said HR handled their redundancy poorly'. This survey had involved more than 1,000 job seekers and it revealed a 'deep dissatisfaction with HR' (Higginbottom, 2010). Clearly in many cases workers facing redundancy perceive a need for more help from HR and for some form of outplacement service.

Pause for thought 13.3 What do you think are the main benefits to the employer of providing an outplacement service? Make a list before you read on.

The benefits of providing an outplacement service

There are many human resource managers who, when faced with making employees redundant, do realise that it is important for the organisation to handle this difficult process as smoothly as possible, both for the sake of the individuals concerned and for the morale of the remaining employees, and in order to maintain or even enhance the good reputation of the organisation. In particular, the benefits to the organisation are likely to include:

- improved morale for remaining employees,
- key staff are more likely to remain with the organisation if they see that other employees are treated well even in a redundancy situation,
- good public relations with the local community will be less likely to be affected by the redundancies if they have been handled well,
- there may be fewer problems with objections from trade unions if a good outplacement service is provided.

Individuals vary in the effect that redundancy has on them. For a few people it may provide a welcome opportunity to change direction in their careers, while others who have worked for a long time for an organisation may find redundancy a very traumatic experience with which they need help.

The outplacement process normally consists of provision of the following services:

- Counselling about the feelings brought about by the redundancy itself. This may also sometimes involve counselling the partner of the person who has been made redundant.
- Counselling about career or other options.
- Provision of facilities for conducting a job search.
- Provision of facilities for writing letters of application or curriculum vitae.
- Help with writing curriculum vitae and applications for jobs.
- Psychological tests to assist in career choice.
- Opportunities for practising interview skills.
- Possible direct contact with prospective employers.
- There may be provision of facilities in which interviews can be conducted.

According to Wise (2009) it is also good practice for employers to continue to provide support even after the date of termination of employment and she suggests 'maintaining contact with redundant employees via email, letter or telephone, to communicate any suitable re-employment or networking opportunities and to encourage redundant employees to continue meeting with each other or retained staff for social support and information sharing'. This means that the employer should commit to a long-term form of assistance for their former employees.

An outplacement service can be provided either 'in-house', by the human resource department, or by external consultants.

Activity 13.3

List the advantages and the disadvantages of the provision of an in-house outplacement service and compare these with the advantages and disadvantages of external provision of an outplacement service.

Provision of in-house placement services

Advantages	Disadvantages

Provision of external placement services

Advantages	Disadvantages

Discussion of Activity 13.3

Your list probably indicates that provision of an internal outplacement service is likely to be cheaper than using a consultancy. Since many redundancies occur as part of a cost-cutting exercise, employers will be loath to spend additional money and cost may be a major concern. However, an organisation may not have sufficient facilities or levels of expertise to provide the standard of service that is required. Not only that, but it may be difficult, or even impossible, for redundant employees who have recently been told of their redundancy by their line manager or by the human resource manager to be helped by counselling from the same manager or any other manager within the organisation. Even identifying managers or others with suitable expertise may be a problem.

On the other hand, there may also be problems in finding a suitable consultancy with a high degree of expertise in this area. Anyone can establish themselves in business as an outplacement consultant, and they do not necessarily have to have any qualifications. This has been a cause for concern in recent years, with some people being charged high fees for an inadequate service. However, according to a PM Editorial (2007) there are additional benefits to employing an external outplacement service as this leaves those who are in charge of the redundancies free to focus on the future needs of the business and also helps show the remaining employees that they are working for a supportive organisation. It also provides someone who they do not know and who should be unbiased to help the redundant individual assess their options. All providers of whatever type of service should let the client know in advance, in writing, about the fees and terms of payment before the signing of any contract. They should also provide a written breakdown detailing exactly the service they will provide.

Survivor syndrome

While it is important to ensure excellent communication and to provide an outplacement service for those to be made redundant, it is also of importance to pay attention to the feelings of those who have not been made redundant and to ensure that they do not suffer too great a lack of motivation.

Survivor syndrome refers generally to people who have suffered from witnessing traumatic events but has also come to be used in relation to those who have survived redundancy. While organisations plan for the reduction in staff, they do not always take into account how the feelings of those who survived may affect their productivity at work. The organisation will be concerned with retention of other staff and will want employees to be highly motivated, but according to Murphy (2009) 'the survivor syndrome can sabotage some of the effects of a downsizing operation'.

According to Murphy (2009) the most common symptoms of survivor syndrome include 'lower morale and commitment, breakdown of trust in management, increased stress and reduced motivation'. In this survey these four symptoms of survivor syndrome were also the four that exerted the most effect on employers. This survey found that it was important to communicate with all members of staff, not just those facing immediate threat of redundancy.

> According to employers that have emphasised the use of communication, the most effective means of doing so are: first holding general staff meetings (according to 39% of employers) and, second, ensuring that line managers provide briefings for their teams (34%). (Murphy, 2009)

This shows once again the importance of good communication and emphasises again the role of line managers as being crucial to maintaining morale and helping with retention of staff in such a difficult time.

Conclusion

A discussion of dismissal and redundancy may seem a rather depressing topic but they are not always inevitable stages if earlier advice for good human resource practices and procedures is followed.

We have gone through the employment process in an almost chronological order and examined the approaches of human resource practitioners to finding and selecting people by the use of human resource planning. We have also examined the employment relationship and how people should then be treated while they are working for the organisation, whether as employees or in some other capacity, how they should be trained and developed, and how they should be motivated and rewarded to achieve a high-performance organisation. We considered ways in which some problems may be prevented or, failing prevention, how they should be handled and we discussed this in relation to counselling and welfare, employee involvement, health and safety, and discipline and grievance handling. We have included dismissal and redundancy since it is likely that even with the best planning there will be occasional dismissals, as people operate from different standpoints and have different points of view, and will therefore not always act in the way in which the organisation hopes that they will act.

Dismissal and redundancy can be avoided to some extent by adopting the good HRM techniques and programmes described in the rest of the text. Problems associated with redundancy and dismissal, both for employers and for employees, will also be minimised by proper handling and by excellent communication to all employees as described in this chapter.

Just like any other area of HRM, this area is also subject to change, so one needs to be constantly vigilant.

All who are involved in the management of people, whether they call themselves HRM managers, personnel managers or line managers, must be aware of the need for strategic planning and clear links between everyone's work and the aims of the business, even though most of you will not initially have the opportunity to operate at a strategic level.

All who are involved in human resource management also need to be aware of the law and although this may be dealt with in more detail in other specialist modules in your course, we have felt it necessary to include brief summaries of relevant legislation in appropriate chapters for those of you who do not have the opportunity to study employment law modules. As you will have discovered by now, the law is always changing and varies from one country to another, so it is very important to ensure that you know how to find information about the current state of legislation.

Review questions

You will find brief answers to these review questions on page 474–5.

1. Discuss the measures that should be taken to ensure that workers who have been selected for redundancy and those who have not remain motivated at work.
2. Outline the circumstances that are considered to constitute fair dismissal and comment on the extent to which an organisation should be expected to avoid dismissing employees.

Improving your employability

Although there are tables, computers and smartphones which are able to do the calculations for redundancy pay, it is still important to have an understanding of the basic maths to appreciate whether or not the figures they produce are roughly correct. This exercise gives you an opportunity to understand how the redundancy calculation is done.

Consider once again Case study 13.1 and the additional information below about the rates of pay of the individuals concerned. In order to simplify the calculation, imagine that each of the people concerned has worked for a whole number of years for the organisation.

> Mr Brownlow: £500 per week
> Mr Mohammed: £480 per week
> Mrs Sergeant: £400 per week
> Ms Smythe: £350 per week
> Mr Gibbs: £300 per week
> Mrs Ali: £350 per week
> Ms Wilson: £300 per week

How much redundancy pay would each employee be entitled to?
A discussion of this exercise will be provided on pages 475–6.

HR in the news

The 'hello there memo' that meant goodbye staff

By Lucy Kellaway

Barely 10 days old, Stephen Elop's "Hello there" memo has already become a classic example of how not to fire people. It is a 1,110-word document stiff with "appropriate financial envelopes", "ramp-downs" and "ecosystems" which, towards the end, casually mentions that thousands of Microsoft jobs are to go. Rather than dish out the bad news directly, the executive vice-president takes refuge behind a curious subjunctive: "We plan that this would result in an estimated reduction of 12,500 . . . employees."

Yet to focus on Mr Elop's tin ear misses something. This memo deserves to become a set text for all executives interested in communication. It adds value by showcasing the delivery of business piffle that is perfectly aligned with current high-end management guff. It is a case study in how not to write, how not to think, and how not to lead a business.

The only trouble with the text is that it is almost impossible to read. It took me several attempts to get to the end, but having now made it, I feel I ought to perform the public service of passing on eight golden rules that occurred to me while slogging my way through.

Rule 1. Never be chatty unless you are a chatty sort of person. "Hello there," is fine from a grandparent trying to jolly along a five-year-old. It is less good spoken by a corporate leader to his ranks, especially when the jocularity begins and ends there.

Rule 2. Using clear words is nearly always a good idea – except when you don't have anything clear to say. The memo begins: "Microsoft's strategy is focused on productivity and our desire to help people 'do more'." This is attractively simple (if you ignore the baffling inverted commas), but is less attractively stupid. Do more what? There are things I'd like to do more of, like sleep, and other things I'd like to do less of, like nagging my children.

Rule 3. The word "align" serves as a warning that the sentence in which it appears is a dud. Mr Elop performs no fewer than six acts of alignment in this memo, each more heroic than the last. In none of them is it clear exactly what he is lining up, nor why it matters that such things should be in a line at all.

"To align with Microsoft's strategy, we plan to focus our efforts," he starts with unhelpful circularity. He assures us that there will be a lot more aligning: "We will focus on delivering great breakthrough products in alignment with major milestones ahead," thus craftily slipping in five other weasel words. In rising order of obnoxiousness, these are: focus, major, milestone, breakthrough and delivering.

But it is only with Mr Elop's final act of alignment that we see the point of it. "As difficult as some of our changes are today, this direction deliberately aligns our work with the cross company efforts that Satya has described in his recent emails."

In other words, don't blame him. Blame the CEO, Satya Nadella, or, better still, blame the need for arranging things in lines.

Rule 4. When things are cheap or expensive, say so. Don't bang on about the "affordable smartphone space" and "high-end" devices. This fools no one, and alienates practically everyone.

Rule 5. Avoid the word "experience". Not only is it the most fashionable of all management buzz words, it is misleading. An experience is something that leaves an impression on you; everyday activities ought to do no such thing, or we would all be exhausted within minutes of waking up. Using your phone, except perhaps when it's brand new, should not be an experience. I do not want the "device experiences" or even less the "digital life experiences", that Mr Elop is trying to "showcase" to his customers.

Rule 6. The more often an executive uses the word "strategy", the more you fear he lacks a good one. To use it once is just about acceptable. To use it seven times, as Mr Elop does, is very worrying indeed.

Rule 7. Never use a trinity of abstract nouns. It shows you know what you are saying is inadequate.

"Collectively," the memo ends, "the clarity, focus and alignment across the company, and the opportunity to deliver the results of that work into the hands of people, will allow us to increase our success in the future. Regards, Stephen."

It won't, Stephen. Collectively, a trinity of almost identical, empty mass nouns and the opportunity to deliver something that is not specified is not going to increase anything. Except possibly the dismay, disdain and distrust of the people who work for you.

And just as a bonus, here is rule number eight. Don't end a memo with "regards".

Questions

1. To what extent do you agree with the criticisms of Stephen Elop's memo to his staff?
2. What would you say in a formal memo to staff advising them of possible redundancies?
3. How would someone adopting the 'special envoy role' advocated by Ashman (2012a) earlier in the chapter be likely to handle this situation?
4. Go to the ACAS website at **www.acas.org.uk** and view the video 'Breaking bad news at work – the role of the redundancy envoy'.
5. After watching the video what advice would you give to an employer such as Stephen Elop when they are announcing redundancies.

What next?

1. Go to **www.acas.org.uk** and view another short video about the role that ACAS conciliation officers play prior to a case going to an employment tribunal.
2. Read the research paper by Ashman, D. (2012b).
   Visit an employment tribunal to hear a case of alleged unfair dismissal. Assess the merits of each side's case and decide whether or not you think the participants in the case followed the statutory disciplinary dismissal and grievance procedures. A list of employment tribunals and further guidance about bringing cases to employment tribunals can be found at: **www.justice.gov.uk/tribunals/employment**

References

Advisory, Conciliation and Arbitration Service (2009) *Code of Practice 1: Disciplinary and Grievance Procedures*, ACAS, The Stationery Office, London.

Advisory, Conciliation and Arbitration Service (2014) Advisory booklet, *Handling Large-Scale (Collective) Redundancies*, ACAS (available at www.acas.org.uk; accessed 28.01.15).

Ashman, D. (2012a) A new role emerges in downsizing: special envoys, *People Management*, July (available at www.cipd.co.uk; accessed 28.01.15).

Ashman, D. (2012b) *Research paper. Downsizing Envoys: A Public/Private Sector Comparison*, ACAS (www.acas.co.uk/researchpapers; accessed 28.01.15).

Ayling, L. (2014a) *Factsheet: Dismissal*, CIPD (available at www.cipd.co.uk; accessed 16.01.15).

Ayling, L. (2014b) *Factsheet: Redundancy*, CIPD (available at www.cipd.co.uk; accessed 16.01.15).

Ayling, L. (2014c) *Factsheet: Employment Tribunals*, CIPD (available at www.cipd.co.uk; accessed 17.01.15).

Bowcott, O. (2013) Employment tribunal claims fell by more than half after introduction of fees, *The Guardian*, 23 December.

Farrell, S. (2015) Citi Link: further 230 redundancies add to tide of human misery, *The Guardian*, 7 January.

GOV.UK (2014a) *Dismissal: Your Rights*, Crown Copyright (www.gov.uk/dismissal; accessed 17.01.15).

GOV.UK (2014b) *Making Staff Redundant*, Crown Copyright (www.gov.uk/staff-redundant; accessed 17.01.15).

Higginbottom, K. (2010) 'HR handles redundancy badly', say a third of job seekers, *People Management*, 12 March (available at www.peoplemanagement.co.uk; accessed 27.01.15).

HR Zone online (2010) *Lessons to Be Learned from Facebook Sacking*, 25 March (www.hrzone.co.uk/topic/managing-people/lessons-be-learned-facebook-sacking/101835; accessed 04.04.10).

Jones, A. (1994) *Delivering In-House Outplacement*. A Practical Guide for Trainers, Managers and Personnel Specialists, McGraw-Hill, New York.

Marson, J. (2014) *Beginning Employment Law*, Routledge, Abingdon.

Murphy, N. (2009) Survey: managing the survivor syndrome during and after redundancies, *IRS Employment Review*, Issue 921, 26 May, IRS (available at www.xperthr.co.uk; accessed 07.04.10).

Pinsent Masons (2014) UNISON's Employment Tribunal Fees Challenge Dismissed, but Impact of New Regime Not Yet Apparent, Says High Court, Pinsent Masons (available at www.out-law.com; accessed 27.01.15).

PM Editorial (2007) How to… manage outplacement, *People Management Magazine Online*, 9 August. (www.cipd.co.uk/pm/peoplemanagement/b/weblog/archive/2013; accessed 18.01.15).

Sage, G. (1998) Health warning, *People Management*, 16 April, Vol. 4, No. 8, 23.

The Guardian (2015) Indian worker sacked after going on leave for 24 years, *The Guardian*, 9 January (available at www.theguardian.com; accessed 30.01.15).

Wise, A. (2009) Good practice: Assisting redundant employees, *XpertHR*, 15 October (available at www.xperthr.co.uk; accessed 07.04.10).

Further study

Books and reports

Advisory, Conciliation and Arbitration Service (2014) Advisory booklet, *Handling Large-Scale (Collective) Redundancies*, ACAS (available at www.acas.org.uk; accessed 28.01.15).
An excellent, clear guide to good practice in relation to redundancies that involve more than 20 employees at one time from an organisation.

Advisory, Conciliation and Arbitration Service (n.d.) *Handling Small Scale Redundancies*, ACAS (available at www.acas.org.uk; accessed 28.01.15).
This covers the stages that employers should go through if they are considering making less than 20 employees redundant at one time.

Ashman, D. (2012b) *Research Paper. Downsizing Envoys: A Public/Private Sector Comparison*, ACAS (www.acas.co.uk/researchpapers; accessed 28.01.15).
This research focuses on the roles of envoys, the people who break the bad news about redundancies to others. It compares these roles in public and private organisations.

Marson, J. (2014) *Beginning Employment Law*, Routledge, Abingdon.
This provides a good introduction to the topic of employment law and Chapters 7, 8 and 9 are particularly relevant to topics of wrongful dismissal, unfair and constructive dismissal and redundancy and discuss much of the case law relating to termination of employment.

Articles

Ayling, L. (2014) *Redundancy Fact Sheet*, CIPD (available at www.cipd.co.uk; accessed 16.01.15).
This provides a useful summary of the key issues affecting redundancy.

Chiumento, R. (2003) How to support the survivors of redundancy, *People Management*, Vol. 9, No. 3, 48–49.
This discusses what to do to help motivate those who have not been made redundant.

Other sources

ACAS telephone advice service.
There are ACAS offices in most large towns and you should be able to find them in the telephone book.

Internet

Advisory, Conciliation and Arbitration Service   www.acas.org.uk
A very useful source of information relating to dismissal and redundancy in Britain.

GOV.UK   www.gov.uk
Useful information for employers relating to redundancy, dismissal, employment tribunals and other HR topics.

Employment tribunals   www.justice.gov.uk/tribunals/employment
A useful site for everything to do with tribunals including the forms that have to be completed and the fees that have to be paid.

Trades Union Congress (TUC)   www.tuc.org.uk
Lots of information from the perspective of the unions and employees relating to redundancy and dismissal. This also has a useful section for students.

Answers

We have provided a skeleton guide to issues you might address in answering review questions. In an exam or for an assignment you would be expected to develop the ideas more fully to show your understanding of the topic. You can also enhance your response by making references to further reading.

Chapter 1 Introducing human resource management

Answers to review questions

It is not possible to provide model answers to the review questions for Chapter 1 because you will all have arrived at very individual answers to the activities suggested.

Chapter 2 High-performance working: employee engagement through involvement and participation

Answers to review questions

1 Unitarists believe that all members of an organisation share the same interests, accept the organisation's goals and direct all their efforts towards the achievement of these goals. Pluralists, on the other hand, believe that in any organisation there will be a range of interests among the members. Outline the concepts of participation and involvement; state how they differ from each other; identify each concept correctly as a unitary or pluralist idea.

2 Define commitment as an attitude; explain how this attitude might help to motivate workers to become more productive. Explain that engagement is identified when employees in fact do deliver the sought-after discretionary effort. Link the involvement initiatives you have described with motivation concepts; for example quality circles provide employees with feelings of responsibility and achievement because they see they can contribute their ideas. This in turn should contribute to the development of a high-performance workplace.

3 The main categories of employee involvement are sharing information, consultation, financial participation, commitment to quality, developing the individual, health and wellbeing and beyond the workplace. The practices associated with each of these categories are outlined in Table 2.1.

4 Employee engagement is a combination of commitment to the organisation and to the organisation's values, and a willingness to help colleagues. You should have identified elements such as employment security, and information for employees and consultation with them to ensure an adequate channel for employee voice. Employee engagement requires effective leadership. Therefore, managers need appropriate skills to ensure employees are engaged.

Chapter 3 The employment relationship

Answers to review questions

1 The term 'employment relationship' refers to the relationship between the employer and the employee, although this relationship may be mediated by a third party such as a trade union. The employment relationship is governed by a complex arrangement of individual and collective agreements, implicit and explicit understandings and rights and obligations enshrined in legal statutes. It is also affected by other influences such as culture and the balance of power.

2 The distinction between 'worker' and 'employee' status can be difficult to identify. However, it is important to distinguish workers from employees as the two categories have different statutory rights. Whether a person is employed or self-employed depends on the terms and conditions of work. Ultimately only an employment tribunal can pass a definitive judgement on the status of the person concerned.

3 A contract of employment is a legally binding contract between an employer and an employee. Some terms may be assumed and are therefore not stated explicitly. A contract of employment should contain the statement of particulars of employment, notice of termination of employment, employee rights to time off work, guaranteed payments, the written statement of reasons for dismissal, maternity and other parental rights, the rights of part-time staff, working hours and protection of employee data.

4 There has been much discussion and debate about zero hours contracts. These contracts represent an agreement to employ a person as and when required and there is no commitment to a minimum number of working hours. The person is only paid for the hours that they actually work. There are advantages and disadvantages of this type of employment contract. For example, if you are looking to work a limited number of hours per week and you are flexible about when you work then a zero hours contract could be advantageous. However, if you are wishing to work full-time but have been offered a zero hours contract then this is likely to be disadvantageous. At the time of writing this book these contracts are legal but this may not continue to be the case.

Chapter 4 Diversity and equality

Answers to review questions

1 One way of understanding the two terms is to reflect that, logically, compliance with the equality laws will inevitably lead to a diverse workforce. Diversity is about celebrating the differences between people, and using these to enhance creativity, problem solving, productivity and responsiveness to customer needs. Equality is about equal work opportunities and not discriminating against a person because of their gender, race, disability, age, sexual orientation or other protected characteristics.

2 There are many business arguments for diversity. One of these is that the organisation is better able to the meet the needs of its customers. A workforce which reflects the diversity of an organisation's customers should be better placed to understand and better respond to its customers' needs and wishes. Combined with this, organisations can expect to achieve greater creativity and access to a wider range of ideas from a diverse workforce. A well-managed diverse group of people should experience greater job satisfaction and appreciate their employer for their commitment to equality. Being known as an employer who promotes diversity and equality should enhance the employer brand.

3 In order for diversity management to be successful, senior management need to have a commitment to diversity and to develop clear diversity goals. These need to be communicated to line managers. Line managers need to be trained in understanding what the organisation aims to achieve from diversity, and how people can be managed so that they can achieve their full potential. Organisations need to communicate to all employees what is expected of them in terms of diversity and equality.

4 The characteristics which are protected under the Equality Act 2010 are age, disability, gender reassignment, marriage and civil partnership, pregnancy and maternity, race, religion or belief, sex and sexual orientation.

5 Direct discrimination occurs when someone is treated less favourably for a reason directly to do with their sex, race or racial origin, etc. Indirect discrimination occurs when someone is treated unfairly because of some provision, criterion or practice that would disproportionately exclude the particular group that person belongs to, and when the requirement cannot be objectively justified. Victimisation occurs when someone is treated less favourably because that person has made a complaint or indicated an intention to make a complaint about discrimination. Harassment is defined as unwanted conduct that intimidates or humiliates an individual, affecting their dignity or creating a hostile work environment.

Chapter 5 Human resource strategy and planning

Answers to review questions

1 Corporate strategy is concerned with the overall direction that an organisation will follow. The levels at which strategy is formulated and implemented are most frequently identified as corporate, business and operational or functional. Human resource strategies arise from the adoption of a strategic approach to managing people which is aligned with the business strategy. An appropriate HR strategy, linked to the corporate strategy, provides the 'best fit' between the overall business strategy (also termed corporate strategy) and the HR strategy.

2 The human resource planning process takes a long-term view and works towards preparing an organisation for its future requirements and helps it achieve its strategic objectives. The information acquired through the process of human resource planning will provide an organisation with a foundation for the development of its human resource strategies. The key considerations at each stage are discussed in the human resource planning section.

3 Up-to-date information is the key to effective human resource planning. Managers need to be aware of local, regional, national and global trends and be able to integrate this knowledge into their strategic plans. Knowledge of the key issues will enable an organisation to assess the threats and opportunities in their environment, and to evaluate their ability to respond with their existing and available resources.

4   A skills shortage is where an employer is unable to find people with the 'right' skills for a job. In other words, the employer is experiencing recruitment difficulties. A skills gap is where employees lack full proficiency in certain skills. It is vital that organisations take steps to counteract skills shortages and skills gaps as they have a detrimental impact on the effectiveness of the business and its operations. Skills shortages and skills gaps arise for a number of reasons such as lack of skills in the labour market, actual or perceived shortcomings in the educational system or poor pay and conditions of employment offered by the employer. Solutions to skills shortages and skills gaps include providing training, recruiting staff from overseas, recruiting from disadvantaged groups and improving the employer brand.

Chapter 6 Recruitment and selection

Answers to review questions

1   Once you know you have a vacancy to fill, you must decide the best way to let people know about it. Popular methods for advertising job vacancies include Internet recruitment sites, advertisements in newspapers and magazines and the organisation's website (sometimes there will be a dedicated 'careers' or 'jobs' section). Whichever method is used to advertise, the job advertisement should include the organisation's name, information about the organisation, job title and major duties, competencies required, opportunities and challenges, salary and benefits, policy statement of important issues such as equal opportunities and information about how to apply. Is the advertisement logically structured? What style of communication is used (formal or informal, for example)? How can the job advertisement be improved?

2   A job description is a written statement about the contents of a job, based on a job analysis. The four basic elements of the job description are: the job title, the reporting structure, a statement of the purpose of the post and a description of the major duties. Taken together, these elements should provide a job applicant with a good idea of what the job entails. Job analysis is the process of gathering together information about an existing job, establishing the activities to be performed, the expected outcomes of tasks, and the skills required. The person specification outlines the knowledge, skills and qualities a person would need to have in order to be able to do the tasks or achieve the outcomes required on the job description. Competencies are work-related behaviours necessary for successful performance in the workplace.

3   There is a public relations element in every recruitment exercise, as your organisation will have contact with many unsuccessful candidates, but who may be potential customers and will certainly tell others how you treated them. You will want to create a good impression with every applicant, but this must be balanced by the question of cost. To create a positive image amongst the public, the employer needs to treat all applicants fairly and equitably and communicate in an effective manner.

4   A successful recruitment campaign should result in a good number of suitably qualified applications for a vacancy. The next task is to select the most suitable person. The most well-established selection methods include interviews, psychological testing, assessment centres and using references. Each of these has advantages and disadvantages. The section on selection discussed what specific actions the organisation can undertake to improve the validity and reliability of these methods.

5 The face-to-face interview continues to be the most popular and frequently used method of selection, even though numerous research studies have demonstrated that interviews suffer from low validity. In order to improve the validity of interviews the organisation needs to gather sufficient information about the applicant, the interview needs to be structured, more than one interviewer should be used and sufficient time needs to be allocated to the interview. Employment interviews run a particular risk of being low in validity if they are approached in an unstructured fashion. In these circumstances, interviewers are more likely to fall prey to perceptual errors than if they were conducting a structured interview. Perceptual errors include the halo effect, the contrast effect, hiring in one's own image and quite simply not gathering sufficient and relevant data. These perceptual errors can be avoided simply by being aware of them and making a conscious effort to resist them. If a structured interview is conducted using a set of questions which is designed to elicit full information related to the person specification/competency framework, and an attempt is made to assess all candidates objectively against these criteria, then the validity of the interview process should also increase.

Chapter 7 Performance management and performance appraisal

Answers to review questions

1 Line managers may be reluctant to get involved with performance management as they may not perceive this to be a part of their job, or feel that they are too busy and there is insufficient time or they may not have been adequately trained. They would be wrong in this since achieving engagement and high performance in their team or department should be of vital importance to them.

They may just regard it as something that HR wants and think they should be doing it. Line managers would have to see the benefits of performance management and its relevance to them and their jobs and that it could help them achieve their targets. They also need to be made aware that it is their responsibility to manage their own team. It would need to be explained to them that potential benefits of performance appraisal should be to motivate employees and improve relations; to provide a better understanding of, and agreement on, goals; to give opportunities for praise/positive feedback; to encourage agreement on training needs/use of appraisal for staff development; and for improved communication. Performance management should therefore help individuals and their team to contribute to the organisation's goals.

Another possible reason for line managers' reluctance to get involved with performance management could be due to them feeling that they do not have the requisite skills and knowledge themselves so it is important that HR managers ensure that the line managers are adequately trained and that support is provided for them. Line managers need to be trained in relevant skills such as coaching, giving feedback and counselling.

2 There are many benefits to using a 360 degree form of appraisal as it is extremely thorough and information is collected about the individual from a number of contacts of the person being appraised. This may include their subordinates, their colleagues and their managers. This ensures that their performance is analysed from a variety of viewpoints rather than just from the perspective of the manager. In most organisations the appraisee is able to choose who will provide the feedback about their performance and in some organisations they can nominate up to 30 people.

360 degree appraisal is useful as in many organisations nowadays each individual will have a number of roles which they may perform to different levels of satisfaction. This form of appraisal should provide good clear information for development purposes in all aspects of the individual's roles. With the use of computers it is now possible to collect a wide range of information quite quickly.

There can also be disadvantages if those giving feedback have not been trained adequately or if they do not give fair comments because of dislike or jealousy of that person. In a system that draws on responses from many people, there is a greater risk of this occurring if training of the appraisers is inadequate.

It can also be cumbersome to collect so much information and could be very daunting for the individual concerned to have such a thorough analysis of their performance, particularly if there are several areas in which they appear to be underperforming.

3   There could be many reasons why a performance appraisal scheme fails.

These could include a lack of clarity about the reason for the performance appraisal and a lack of training for those conducting the appraisal and for those being appraised. Appraisal systems could become dated and no longer reflect adequately the strategic objectives of the organisation.

Answers should also address the use of appraisal systems for different purposes: appraising for developmental reasons and appraising to make decisions about pay may conflict. In some organisations there is also a lack of involvement from the employees in the performance appraisal system.

The skills needed

Lack of managerial skill and training in areas such as an ability to give critical feedback in a positive way could prevent this working as well as it should. This could be in relation to lack of planning and preparation, poor interpersonal skills such as interview skills, poor communication skills, inability to build and develop teams as well as giving feedback to individuals and teams, etc. Sometimes the processes themselves can be counterproductive if the targets are unreasonable and have not been agreed or are poorly defined. There is a need for managerial training and commitment to the system.

4   (a)   Evaluate current performance levels for the organisation, the team and for the individual.

(i)   Decide what levels of performance are required in order to contribute effectively to the organisation's strategic objectives and what measures will be used to evaluate them.

(ii)   Assess what performance levels are required in the future for each of these groups.

(iii)   If there is a gap between expected and actual current levels of performance, then decide on the best approaches to achieve these and any rewards to give if they are achieved.

(iv)   Implement these methods.

(v)   Review whether or not the required performance has been achieved.

(vi)   Then evaluate performance again and agree objectives for the next period of time.

(b)   The following techniques could be useful

(i) For the organisation

There needs to be a clear idea of the performance level required and the performance that is actually being achieved. Measures such as levels of productivity, absence, quality and complaints, which are measures about aspects of performance for the whole organisation, are needed.

There also need to be ongoing assessments of the whole organisation's performance so these types of metrics need to be collected and analysed. The use of the balanced scorecard approach to measuring performance could also prove useful in this. Excellent communication is needed so everyone knows what is expected of them.

Approaches to help to fill any gap in performance between desired level of performance and actual level of performance, as shown by the organisation-wide metrics, are needed and these could also help improve employee engagement. These could include:

- coaching,
- mentoring,
- line manager involvement,
- learning and talent development initiatives, etc.

(ii) For the team

There needs to be a clear expectation of the performance level required by the teams and the performance that is actually being achieved. Excellent communication is needed so everyone knows what is expected of them.

There need to be objective ongoing regular assessments of the performance of teams.

This involves agreeing measures of performance and using techniques to fill any gaps between actual performance and expected performance and to improve team engagement with the organisation. These could include:

- team reviews,
- team incentives,
- coaching,
- learning and talent development initiatives.

(iii) For the individual

There need to be clear, objective measurements of the performance level required and the performance that is actually being achieved by the individual. Excellent communication is needed so everyone knows what is expected of them.

There is a need for an objective performance appraisal and assessment using techniques such as:

- 360 degree feedback,
- clear objectives,
- clear measures for performance.

If a gap is established between existing performance and desired performance then there could be formal or informal training used to help fill gap, if appropriate, and to ensure employee engagement with the organisation. Coaching or mentoring, e-learning or more traditional training could be used as appropriate.

It would also be important to hold regular one-to-one performance development reviews so performance is regularly discussed and not just left to an annual performance appraisal interview.

5   You should identify and describe three different approaches to performance appraisal, for example individual appraisal conducted by the manager/supervisor, peer appraisal or 360-degree appraisal.

The general benefits relate to improved performance, engagement, motivation, communication and relationships. The actual nature of these benefits will need to be discussed in relation to the specific approach used but in all cases there is a focus on involvement and engagement of the individual, team or organisation in the assessment of their performance.

Other general benefits include the opportunity to focus on future developments and to achieve organisational goals.

Since you have been asked to comment critically on the benefits of these systems of performance appraisal you can also mention some of the pitfalls, such as problems if there is a lack of clarity in the purpose of the appraisal, for example reward or development. You could also mention skills needed in giving feedback and discuss these in relation to the approaches used, for example in peer appraisal or 360 degree appraisal, would everyone involved have the required levels of skills and not be influenced by any personal vendettas they might want to settle?

There is also, regardless of the approach chosen, a need to encourage ownership and participation so whatever approach is chosen should fit with the organisation's strategic objectives and culture and should be clearly communicated.

Chapter 8 Learning, training and talent development

Answers to Activity 8.2

1   This effect is known as a *conditioned response*.

2   The cat food is the *stimulus* for Caroline's cats to make an appearance.

3   *Association*. The cats have started to associate the sound of the kettle with the cat food being put out.

4   In time the sound of the kettle becomes the *conditioned stimulus*, and the cats' response to it becomes the *conditioned response*.

Answers to Activity 8.9

Forms that evaluation can take and those who would find them most useful

The purpose of the evaluation	The main forms that the evaluation could take	The people or groups who would benefit most from the evaluation
1 Prove the value of the training	1 Calculation of the return on investment. This involves being able to fully cost the learning and development (L&D) event and fully cost the returns gained from it.	1 The L&D specialists and the management of the organisation would know whether money had been well spent. It can prove difficult in some organisations to measure the costs of the L&D event and the financial benefits directly gained.
	2 Measures of value that have been added. This could show the extent to which the L&D initiative has made a difference to the strategic objectives of the organisation. It could involve measures to show the difference in levels of performance quality or knowledge before and after the training.	2 The L&D specialists and the management of the organisation would know whether the L&D activities had made a difference to the achievement of the strategic objectives of the organisation.

The purpose of the evaluation	The main forms that the evaluation could take	The people or groups who would benefit most from the evaluation
	3 Questionnaires asking course participants how valuable the training was to them.	3 (i) Those providing the training would get valuable feedback about whether they had met participants' expectations and objectives or not. 3 (ii) The participants themselves would benefit by the chance to reflect on what they had learned.
	4 Interviews with course participants and their managers asking how valuable the learning and development had been.	4 (i) Those providing the learning or development initiative would get valuable feedback about whether they had met participants' expectations or not. 4 (ii) The participants themselves would benefit by the chance to reflect on what they had learned. 4 (iii) Line managers would become involved and would have to review what those in their team had learned and this may well encourage them to ensure that their staff used the L&D opportunities they had participated in.
2 Improve the quality of the training offered	1 Completion of a questionnaire by learners immediately after the learning event.	1 If the questionnaire asks questions relating to the quality of the L&D activity this can be useful to the person or group who provided the event.
	2 Test before the L&D event and immediately after it.	2 Once again this can be useful to the person or group who provided the L&D event.
	3 Test or review of performance of individual in the workplace several weeks after the learning event.	3 (i) Useful to the person or group who provided the L&D event. 3 (ii) Useful to the person or group who provided the L&D event in deciding whether there are any quality issues relating to the quality of the L&D in terms of how easy it is to transfer to the workplace.
	4 Interview with individual immediately after the learning event.	4 An interview about the quality of the event with an individual course participant could be useful to the person or group who ran the event and also to their manager or whoever was providing the funding for the event. It would provide them with the individual's opinions of the quality of the event.
	5 Discussion with the line manager some weeks after the learning event.	5 This would help involve the line manager and get their views about the quality of the L&D event. Since it is a common complaint by HR specialists that it is difficult to get line manager involvement this could be useful to them.

The purpose of the evaluation	The main forms that the evaluation could take	The people or groups who would benefit most from the evaluation
	6 Focus groups.	6 Results of focus group discussions would be useful to management and those running the L&D events. This form of evaluation may relate to learning and development in general and may be part of an organisational review, or may just relate to the evaluation of a specific area of L&D such as training for customer service provision.
3 Evaluate as a contribution to the learning process	1 Completion of an individual learning log or diary.	1 (i) Self-review by individual participants encourages them to be reflective about their learning. 1 (ii) If this is submitted to the L&D specialist it also provides useful feedback for them on what went well and what was less effective.
	2 Discussion by group participants.	2 (i) This helps learners to reflect on their own learning but by engaging in dialogic learning they may also appreciate other aspects of the L&D that they had not consciously realised they had learned. 2 (ii) If this is organised by the L&D specialist it also provides useful feedback for them on what went well and what was less effective and helps them to identify areas where future development may be needed.
	3 Creation of a visual record by group participants.	3 (i) This helps learners to reflect on their own learning and may appeal especially to those who like visual learning. If this is done in a group it also helps the group engage in dialogic learning and again they may also appreciate other aspects of the L&D that they had not consciously realised they had learned. 3 (ii) If this is organised by the L&D specialist it also provides useful feedback for them on what went well and what was less effective and helps them to identify areas where future development may be needed.
	4 Tests before and after the learning event.	4 Tests can also help the learners to see what progress they have made.

The purpose of the evaluation	The main forms that the evaluation could take	The people or groups who would benefit most from the evaluation
4 Evaluate as a control over the training	1 Questionnaires (sometimes referred to as happy sheets) at the end of the learning event.	1 (i) These are useful for those providing the L&D event so that they know what has worked well and what has not. 1 (ii) If external providers are being used these also provide useful feedback for the L&D department about whether to use these external providers again or not.
	2 Tests before and after the learning event.	2 (i) These measure whether learning has occurred but can also be useful for those providing the L&D event so that they know whether or not they have been successful in encouraging L&D to occur. 2 (ii) If external providers are being used these also provide useful feedback for the L&D department about whether to use these external providers again or not as the success or not of the L&D can be measured.
	3 Test or review of performance of individual in the workplace several weeks after the learning event.	3 This would help to establish whether transfer of learning to the place of work had occurred.
	4 Discussion with individual immediately after the learning event.	4 This would help to establish whether transfer of learning had occurred to the place of work.
	5 Discussion with the line manager some weeks after the learning event.	5 This would help to establish whether transfer of learning had occurred to the place of work and would have the additional benefit of involving the line manager.

Answers to review questions

1   Answers should include comments on the cost involved in designing and running an induction programme, but should generally identify the benefits of easing a new employee into the workforce and how this is likely to result in a speedier route to full productivity, less labour turnover and fewer bad work habits being acquired. There should then be an outline of a suitable induction programme spread over some time.

2   Answers should define each concept and list the pros and cons of each, for example learning-by-doing in a realistic environment versus cost of errors and distractions. You should explain which technique you feel is the more successful overall.

Chapter 9 Pay and reward systems

Answers to review questions

1 and 2 provide you with the opportunity to practice research skills and seek relevant, up-to-date information for yourself and so it is impossible to provide guideline answers here.

Use the website of GOV.UK at **www.gov.uk** to find the latest information about the minimum wage and the living wage. The *Pay and Benefits* magazine published by the Office for National Statistics at **www.payandbenefitsmagazine.co.uk** also contains useful information about various aspects of pay and benefits. Publications such as *People Management* or *Personnel Today* may also prove useful, as should quality newspapers.

3   Your answer should define job evaluation as a method of deciding on the value of a job and address the need for a methodical approach. The points rating method and its main benefits should then be outlined. Benefits of the points rating approach to job evaluation include the fact that all jobs are rated using the same method and that these must be perceived to be fair. It is comparatively simple to use and understand and is analytical in nature.

The second part of your answer should examine perceptions of fairness. Involvement of representatives of the workforce in the design and implementation of job evaluations is likely to improve employees' perceptions of whether or not the system is fair. The points rating method is an analytical approach to job evaluation and so does break each job into parts rather than analysing the whole job. This is generally regarded as being more objective and hence fairer than non-analytical schemes. It is also more likely that this system could be justified in a tribunal if an equal pay/value claim was brought against the organisation.

4   Your answer will describe issues such as internal and external relativities and differentials. You will also include and take account of the issues raised by legislation such as the Equality Act 2010. Systems of job evaluation which try to ensure that fair systems of pay are in place need to be discussed. Those based on analytical methods of job evaluation are likely to result in fairer systems and it will be easier to prove the fairness, if necessary. Involvement of representatives of the workforce in the design and implementation of job evaluation is likely to improve employees' perceptions of whether or not the system is fair.

Better answers will also comment on issues such as performance-related pay and how this may affect perceptions of fairness. Issues relating to gender pay reporting should also be fully discussed.

5   Your answer should be in report form as if you are a consultant employed to advise this organisation. You need to describe various forms of both the analytical and non-analytical types of job evaluation and outline the advantages and disadvantages of each. You should then decide on a scheme that you feel is most suitable for this organisation and make recommendations about its use. You are more likely to recommend an analytical form of job evaluation such as the points rating system. This would have benefits of being easy to justify but may be time-consuming to introduce. However, since we are making recommendations for a fairly small organisation, cost is also likely be an issue here and this form of analytical job evaluation will probably be cheaper to install than any designed or provided by a firm of consultants. Better answers would also refer to the need for fairness in whatever scheme is introduced and the need to involve members of the workforce in decisions about which scheme should be chosen. Reference should also be made to the need to take into account legislation, for example the Equality Act 2010, and also the issues of gender pay reporting raised in that act.

Chapter 10 Health, safety and wellbeing

Answers to review questions

It is once again impossible to give ideal answers to the review questions here as your answers will depend on who you talk to or the organisations you analyse.

Chapter 11 International human resource managment

Answers to review questions

1 Companies can be domestic, international, multinational or global in nature. Domestic firms are very much focused on the home market but may have limited involvement in overseas markets. International companies demonstrate a strong attachment to headquarter country policies and decision making, but attempt to adapt these to local conditions and requirements in the various overseas locations. A multinational is a firm that operates in two or more countries and has fairly independent operations in these countries where they are permitted to establish their own approach. Global companies are highly centralised in their decision making, but they take a global perspective.

2 Ethnocentrism reflects a sense of superiority about a person's home country and ethnocentrics believe that their approach is better, whatever the culture involved. A polycentric approach places emphasis on the norms and practices of the host country where the firm operates, whilst a regiocentric approach means that a company seeks to exploit opportunities at the regional level. Geocentric organisations try to distance themselves from any one national culture and are more global in orientation.

3 There are six dimensions of culture, these being: power distance, individualism versus collectivism, masculinity–femininity, uncertainty avoidance, long term versus short term and indulgence versus restraint. At the very least, an awareness of cultural differences as potential sources of misunderstanding or conflict provides a basis from which to work towards more effective relationships.

4 International assignments vary in nature according to the length of the assignment, who is involved and the type of work to be undertaken. The key issues associated with managing an international assignment are: recruitment and selection, management development, reward management and the effective administration of the international assignment, including repatriation. The term 'expatriate' is frequently used when discussing international assignments. An expatriate is an individual from one country who works and resides in another country for a certain amount of time.

Chapter 12 Discipline and grievance

Answers to review questions

It is impossible to give model answers for questions 1–3 as these require you to conduct your own research, so you may all have different findings.

Chapter 13 Dismissal, redundancy and outplacement

Answers to review questions

1 You should discuss outplacement activities for those who are to be made redundant and activities relating to overcoming the survivor syndrome for those who have not been selected but who still may feel demotivated.

Typical outplacement activities would include the following

- Counselling about the feelings brought about by the redundancy itself. This may sometimes involve also counselling the partner of the person who has been made redundant.
- Counselling about career or other options.

- Provision of facilities for conducting a job search.
- Provision of facilities for writing letters of application or curriculum vitae.
- Help with writing curriculum vitae and applications for jobs.
- Psychological tests to assist in career choice.
- Opportunities for practising interview skills.
- Possible direct contact with prospective employers.
- There may be provision of facilities in which interviews can be conducted.

It is also good practice for employers to continue to provide support even after the date of termination of employment.

Typical activities to overcome survivor syndrome and motivate those not selected for redundancy would include the following:

- The provision of an outplacement service for those facing redundancy does much to reassure the survivors, so is important for them too.
- Excellent communication is really important and meetings should be held with all staff to explain what is happening.
- Excellent communication from line managers is also really important if the survivors are to be motivated during these difficult times.

2 You should outline the grounds for potentially fair dismissal as: misconduct, lack of capability, redundancy, statutory bar or some other substantial reason. Better answers are likely to give examples of these types of potentially fair reasons for dismissal.

You should also explain that the process followed for dismissal is as important as the reason for the dismissal and that the employer must act reasonably. This means that they must carry out a full investigation and follow the ACAS *Code of practice*. Better answers are also likely to mention that some forms of dismissal are considered to be automatically unfair and for these there is only a one-stage process undertaken by the employment tribunals. You should outline some of the automatically unfair reasons for dismissal and indicate why these are designated as such.

You should express some considered opinion about the extent to which you feel that employers should try to avoid dismissals of employees. This is likely to include

- commenting about managers taking early action to avoid the development of problems;
- the use of counselling skills by managers; the use of HRM planning to help avoid the need for redundancies;
- planned retirements and following 'the duty to consider' a request to work beyond normal retirement; the training and development of employees if skills need change;
- a proper recruitment and selection process to help minimise numbers of dismissals. Following good HRM policies and procedures should help to minimise the costs involved. Sometimes, however, it is still necessary to dismiss and then it must be for a fair reason and must be handled reasonably in accordance with the ACAS *Code of practice*.

Discussion of Improving your employability exercise

Mr Brownlow has worked for the organisation for 10 years and is aged 44. He has worked for three complete years since age 41, so is entitled to $7 \times 1\frac{1}{2}$ weeks' pay $= 4\frac{1}{2}$ weeks' pay for that period of time. He has also worked for seven years between ages 22 and 40, so is entitled to 7×1 weeks' pay. Therefore Mr Brownlow would be entitled to $11\frac{1}{2}$ weeks' redundancy pay if he were selected for redundancy. His weekly earnings are above the maximum allowed in this calculation, so he would actually be entitled to $11\frac{1}{2} \times £464 = £5,336$.

Mr Mohammed has worked for the organisation for only three years and he is aged 34. He would therefore be entitled to 3×1 week's pay. His weekly pay is £480 which is also above the limit of the maximum entitlement so he would get receive $3 \times £464.00 = £1392$.

Mrs Sergeant has worked for the organisation for 20 years and is aged 55. She has worked 14 years since the age of 41 and would be entitled to $14 \times 1\frac{1}{2}$ weeks' pay = 21 weeks' pay. She worked for a further six years before she was 41 and would be entitled to 6 x 1 week's pay = 6 weeks' pay. The total number of weeks of redundancy pay she is due is therefore 27. Her weekly wage is £400 which is below the maximum entitlement. She would be entitled to $27 \times £400 = £10,800$.

Mr Gibbs is aged 20 and has worked for the organisation for two years. Since he is still under 22 he will only be entitled to $2 \times \frac{1}{2}$ week's redundancy pay = 1 week's redundancy pay. His weekly wage is £300 and so he would be entitled only to £300 in redundancy pay.

Mrs Ali has worked for the organisation for four years. She is 35 years old and her weekly wage is £350. She would therefore be entitled to redundancy pay of $4 \times £350 = £1,400$

Sally Wilson and Sandra Smythe would not be entitled to any redundancy pay as they have not worked for the required qualification period of two years.

Tables are provided by GOV.UK which can be used to make this calculation of redundancy pay easier. This can be found at **www.gov.uk**.

Further sources of information for report writing and presentation skills

Some of the review questions and exercises to help improve your employability require you to write reports or make presentations. Your tutor will be able to provide guidance on preferred styles to use but the following books are also good sources of information for developing these skills.

Burns, T. and S. Sinfield (2012) *Essential Study Skills: The Complete Guide to Success at University*, Sage, London.

Cameron, S. (2013) *The Business Student's Handbook: Skills for Study and Employment*, Pearson Prentice Hall, Harlow.

Cottrell, S. (2013) *The Study Skills Handbook*, Palgrave Macmillan, Basingstoke, Hants.

Trought, F. (2012) *Brilliant Employability Skills*, Pearson Education, Harlow.

Author index

Subject index

Quick guide to employment legislation and related documents